BOLD WARNIE

BOLD WARNIE

SHANE WARNE

and Australia's Rise to Cricket Dominance

Roland Perry

RANDOM HOUSE
AUSTRALIA

Published by
Random House Australia Pty Ltd
20 Alfred Street, Milsons Point NSW 2061
Australia
http://www.randomhouse.com.au

Sydney New York Toronto
London Auckland Johannesburg
and agencies throughout the world

First published in 1999

National Library of Australa
Cataloguing-in-Publication data

Perry, Roland, 1946–.
Bold Warnie.

ISBN 0 091 84001 5.

1. Warne, Shane. 2. Cricket players – Australia – Biography. 3. Cricket players – Australia. 4. Cricket – Australia. I. Title.

796.358092

Internal design by Siobhán O'Connor
Typeset in 11/14 pt Garamond Light
Printed in Australia by Griffin Press Pty Ltd, Adelaide, a division of PMP Communications

Dedication

To Loraine Byrnes and Thos Hodgson—two sober, intrepid Test cricket autograph hunters, whose ambition in life is to have S. K. Warne's signature below.

Contents

Preface

The initial inspiration for a book on Shane Warne was his impact in England in 1993, when he bowled Mike Gatting with *That Ball* and set the tone for a crushing win by Allan Border's team in the Ashes. Since then, Warne has gone on to be the biggest wicket-taking spinner in history in a period when Australia under Mark Taylor has become the top Test side in the world.

His fast-track to pre-eminence in cricket, match-winning performances and involvement in some of the biggest controversies in cricket prompted a comprehensive look at his life and exceptional record. Hence *Bold Warnie*, which covers every Test and one-day international he played in until the end of the 1998–99 Ashes series in Australia.

Warne's struggles in developing his skills and battles for fitness drew out a player of rare drive and character. This book should be an inspiration to all sports aspirants, young and old. Like the great Don Bradman, Warne had the determination to rise above disappointments and setbacks that, at times, threatened his career. Again, like Bradman, he became a master in his field.

• • •

My thanks and appreciation go to Deborah Callaghan, who also supported the publication of *The Don*, editor Roger Milliss and Random House's publisher Jane Palfreyman.

Roland Perry
FEBRUARY 1999

PROLOGUE
That Ball

SHANE WARNE, nicknamed 'Hollywood' because of his blond hair and matching flair, began rolling his arms like a butterfly swimmer, then stretching as Allan Border glanced over at him. Moments earlier, after seventy-four minutes of England's first innings of the opening Test of the 1993 Ashes series at Old Trafford, Merv Hughes had Mike Atherton caught behind. This brought the pugnacious Mike Gatting to the wicket to join his skipper Graham Gooch, who looked in command. His team had started well with one for 71 following Australia's mediocre innings of 289.

Warne felt a nervous tingle. Border, the on-field general, concentrated so much on the game plan that he rarely made eye contact, unless it meant a bowling change. Craig McDermott, who had not looked penetrating, finished an over. Border motioned to Warne.

'Warnie, you're on next over,' the captain mouthed. Warne took a deep breath as he moved to his position behind square leg. Hughes steamed in for another over and the leg-spinner felt a slight clamminess in the fingers. This was it. He was about to bowl in an Ashes Test for the first time. Border wasn't going to protect him by waiting until the quicks might have broken into the middle order. He was throwing Warne into the front line early to take on two of the best players of spin in cricket.

Gooch took a four and a two off Hughes and the over ended. Gatting would be facing Warne. The gritty Englishman, with his gladiator forearms and nose flattened like the front metal of a Roman helmet, had won a place back in the Test team after bludgeoning bowlers in the counties in the first month of the season. He had led England to its last Ashes victory over Australia in 1986–87. Now 'the Gatt' was back to continue where he left off, as the Aussie tormentor. He and Gooch had a prearranged plan to destroy Warne. Hick had carted Warne all over the riverside field in the opening tour game under the Norman cathedral at Worcestershire. That was not a Test, but the intent was the same. Belt him into submission.

Warne rolled his arm over to Hughes, who roared a few words of encouragement, more like a football coach than a cricketer. 'Carn, Hollywood, you can do it!' But Hollywood was not thinking about glittering success. He just wanted to get the ball on the pitch on a good length. Border set the field and looked across to see if Warne approved. He scanned the placings, nodded, rubbed his right palm on the grass and began flipping the ball in the air. Gatting settled in, substantial *derrière* jutting back and face forward, all grim determination. It was that challenging look that caused Warne to focus.

'Pitch it on leg stump and spin it hard' was the thought on his pumped-up mind. One last look around the field, a supportive grunt from Hughes, and in. It was a faster swagger to the wicket than normal. Warne dropped his shoulder, trying not to overpitch a full toss. The ball curled with a left-to-right drift and landed well outside the leg stump in the beginnings of a rough. Gatting lunged forward to block it. The ball darted like a cobra past his copybook positioning of bat and pads. It clipped the off stump, sending the bail high as keeper Healy leapt in the air with it. The ball had snapped 45 to 53 centimetres. Yet it was the dip and curve that had left the Englishman standing frozen like a statue. He heard the death rattle, but didn't believe it.

Healy rushed the length of the pitch to embrace Warne. Gatting stood there, looking at the umpires, first at the bowler's end, then at square leg. The look asked, *Had Healy knocked the stumps? The ball couldn't have done that, could it?* Neither umpire reacted. There was no raising of the finger for a confirmation of what everyone on the field apart from the batsman knew. He had been clean bowled.

Gatting finally moved, more of a bewildered straggle than a march, back to the pavilion. Only the English manager, Keith Fletcher, dared go near his charge, as he was undoing his pads. Gatting was not angry, just stunned.

'What happened?' Fletcher proffered. 'It seemed to spin a yard!'

'I don't know,' Gatting responded, 'it must have.'

'Your front pad was ...'

'I had it covered.'

'It must have hit the rough.'

'It turned all right.'

'It *must've* spun at least a yard.'

Fletcher added some words of comfort and let Gatting settle down alone in the dressing room.

On the field, Warne's nerves settled down as Robin Smith took block, though perhaps with little reason. If Gatting could club you to death, Smith could massacre. He had already done this in a one-dayer, hammering Australian's finest for a record 167 not out. He was fresh and ready to continue that in the Test. Yet there was a problem, perhaps just a tactical one, but a problem nevertheless. Warne had not played in the one-dayer. Smith had not faced a ball from him since 1990 when the leg-spinner was a novice at the Australian Cricket Academy.

Smith blocked the first and crunched a straight drive for four off Warne's second. The English crowd roared their approval. This was more like it. Gooch played out another over at the other end and then Smith faced the spinner again. Smith groped at another ball, which hit the deck more or less in the same spot as *That Ball* to Gatting. It, too, spun sharply. Instead of cannoning into the stumps, it took the outside edge of the bat and carried to Taylor at slip.

Warne liked this delivery as much as the one that got Gatting and all the glory.

After play that night, the England players came into the Australian dressing room for a drink.

'Bloody hell, Warnie,' Gatting said. 'What happened?'

Warne was stuck for words, even a little embarrassed.

'Sorry, mate,' Warne said. 'Bad luck.'

The media wanted to know all about *That Ball.* Fletcher tried to explain:

'It turned 3 feet comfortably. "Gatt" couldn't believe it, nor could anyone else.'

The quote was recorded in all the papers along with analysis that concentrated on Warne's skill and sudden success. The English team, reading the comments the next morning at breakfast and watching the interminable replays of *That Ball* on the news, was psychologically damaged.

Richie Benaud on BBC TV remarked: 'It's one of the best balls I've ever seen in Test cricket, and I've seen some.' By Sunday two days later, Robin Marler in the *Sunday Times* took it a notch further, calling the delivery 'the ball of the century'. Not to be outdone, Richard Williams in the *Independent on Sunday* announced it as 'the best ball ever seen in cricket history'.

The tabloids went even further over the top. Warne himself, when quizzed about it, said, 'I got a bit lucky with Gatting,' and a score of scribes scribbled the immortal words.

Such hype meant that England players would find it hard facing Warne for the rest of the six-Test series.

Warne established himself with *That Ball* in 1993 as the best spinner in the world, a position he has maintained for the rest of the 1990s. Where did he acquire his freakish skills, confidence and cool character so perfect for cricket crises? For answers we must go back to Melbourne's somnolent seaside suburb of Black Rock, where the raw young spinner emerged in the late 1980s against the trend of the times.

1

Bayside Beginnings

The Pedigree

When she was twelve years old, Shane Warne's future mother, Brigitte, lived on a farm at Apollo Bay, on the Southern Ocean, southwest of Melbourne. She had a long walk of about a mile over rugged hills to the school bus stop. Brigitte soon took to running it, timing the effort to just make the bus, and one day decided to time herself.

Her wristwatch told her she came in under or about four minutes. This was in 1957 and, if the distance was actually a mile, such a time would have put her amongst the best *male* milers in the world, right up there with John Landy, Herb Elliott and Roger Bannister running on the flat. Obviously, the run must have been much shorter than a mile, or she had made a mistake with her time.

Over the years, this story has taken on a life of its own, but there can be no doubt that, at just 162 centimetres and about 50 kilograms, Brigitte was a strong, fast distance runner for her age, and she was a good all-round sportsperson, enjoying basketball and tennis.

The aspirations of this vibrant German immigrant, who arrived in Australia in 1949 with her parents, aged three-and-a-half, were cut short when, at fourteen years of age, she developed glandular fever. It weakened her for some years and destroyed her chance to see how good she really could be in the sporting arena.

In 1965, Brigitte, in her early twenties, was working in the payroll office at H. G. Palmer, the Melbourne electrical group, when she met and fell in love with tall, handsome and fit Keith Warne, also in his early twenties. Their relationship was based in part around a love of sport, especially tennis, and the outdoors. They married in 1966 and for a time lived with Keith's parents in Ferntree Gully, where Shane was born on 13 September 1969.

The Warnes, including a second son, Jason, moved to Hampton and then Black Rock in 1975. The emphasis on a family sporting life continued. Shane's love for, and skill with, all ball sports was apparent early. He inherited his parents' body strength, skills and temperament, all vital characteristics for a top-class sportsman. Shane always had a solid physique, muscular limbs and thick wrists which were extraordinarily strong and supple, and were to play an important part in the emergence of his bowling talent. He developed into a powerful lad, a more than useful attribute given that physical strength and fitness are important in modern cricket.

When Shane was a toddler, Keith introduced him to as many sports as possible. 'I remember putting a tennis racket in his hand when he was two or three,' he said. 'Even then he was attentive when I showed him how to swing it.'

He and Brigitte wanted their boys—Shane and his younger brother, Jason—to play sport, but were never too far in front of them. They just encouraged them, stood back, watched and guided. 'The kids were good listeners,' Keith remembers. 'They were natural sports, quick to learn.'

The Coach

Shane Warne, just eleven, was the only lad who wanted Ron Cantlon, the under-13s coach at East Sandringham, to show him how to bowl a leg break, coming out of the hand with a flick of the wrist and fingers. It and its variations are by far the hardest deliveries in the game, demanding great coordination and skill.

Cantlon, a capable leggie himself before injuring his shoulder at football, showed him the difficult grip. The little blond kid, with fingers hardly long enough to hold a ball, ran up and had a go. The ball slipped out and careered into the net. The second attempt hit the pitch and bounced three times. Soon the youngster was landing them properly, making them spin and experiencing that special feeling of being able to deliver something *different.* All the others were running in with cocked wrists imitating Dennis Lillee, every kid's hero at the time.

'Shane was doing it, too,' Cantlon recalls, 'but I would ask him to bowl spinners and he did. He was a great pleaser. He showed a lot of talent—with the bat primarily in the early days. In fact, he was good at all sports. I used to play tennis doubles with him and his parents and he was quite capable of holding up a corner.'

Shane was often reluctant to bowl spin. It wasn't fashionable. Cantlon helped to cajole him into it by saying that 'in ten years they will be combing the country for a leggie'. There would be so few left then. More importantly, there would be a need to try something different and innovative to beat the speed of the West Indies.

'Just keep at it,' the coach told the youngster, especially in matches where he was most inhibited about plying his skills. He would be belted around the ground, which he detested. 'It's part of leg-spin bowling,' Cantlon explained. 'You're going to get hit.'

He needed some convincing and was still anxious to bowl medium-pacers. The coach managed to impart to him that taking a caning every so often was part of the business of being a spinner. You had to wear it and come back for more, often needing to 'buy' a wicket with loose deliveries and by giving the batsman 'sucker' hits.

From eight to twelve years of age, Warne played cricket during the week for his school, Sandringham Primary, while turning out for East Sandringham juniors on Saturday afternoons. He was developing an insatiable appetite for the game. At the age of twelve, he had developed confidence in bowling leg-spinners, his batting was accomplished for his age and his leadership qualities had come to the fore. Warne captained the junior team to a premiership.

Warne, according to Cantlon, had all the right qualities to become a successful spinner, as well as a readiness to learn and to listen. As he began to take wickets, he was always grateful for the advice and encouragement he received from his first coach.

'He was the nicest, most humble kid I ever coached or taught in twenty years,' Cantlon said. 'He was eager to listen, eager to learn and eager to please. That's the term I use most about Shane, the one overriding recollection of him. He was also particularly loyal.'

Cantlon didn't detect anything out of the ordinary that would necessarily stamp him as a top-class cricketer, but he had a dedication to the craft and a willingness to improve. The coach also emphasised the support the boy received from his parents. They were not pushy, but always helpful. Shane's father Keith, for instance, took up cricket for the first time at the age of forty and played in the lower grades at Sandringham just so he could assist his sons.

Cantlon remembered the way in which Shane responded as a twelve-year-old when he scored three successive ducks—at that age, or any age for that matter, a shattering experience.

'He was disappointed but didn't sulk,' he said. 'He asked questions of himself, confronted his poor form and then went out and made a hundred. His first ever.'

For all the promise the youthful Warne showed as a batsman, however, it was as a slow bowler that he was to make his mark.

The Leggie's Art

The type of bowling which Shane Warne concentrated on is based on the leg break, the delivery that is rolled anti-clockwise from the right hand, causing the ball to spin on its axis in the same way through the air. When it hits the pitch, it continues to spin from right to left as the bowler views the right-hand batsman—that is, it spins across the batsman.

The amount of sideways movement on hitting the ground is generated by the quickness of the flick of the wrist and fingers on release. Sometimes the ball will 'drift' off the line delivered in the air after leaving the hand. A delivery may also have 'dip'. This comes from the bowler's capacity to flick the ball higher and cause the ball to drop more quickly than expected by the batsman, who may be deceived into playing at it prematurely.

Cantlon also taught Warne to bowl the three other main deliveries in the wrist-spinner's arsenal—the wrong 'un, the top-spinner and the flipper.

The wrong 'un spins—clockwise—from left to right (the opposite way to the leg break, hence 'the wrong one'), again with a flick of wrist and fingers. In this case, the back of the wrist faces down the pitch and the ball is spun out the back of the hand. The top-spinner has top- or over-spin imparted to it, so that it does not move sideways after pitching. It comes straight through with more forward bounce. Like the conventional leg-spinner, the wrong 'un and the top-spinner are released from *over* the wrist.

The fourth kind of ball, the flipper, is delivered from *under* the wrist. It is so tough on the wrist, bones of the hand and fingers that it is banned from cricket training manuals for children. The ball is squeezed or flipped from the front of the hand. Because it comes from under the wrist its trajectory must be flat. It appears to skid on to the batsman because of under- or back-spin. Victims usually either fall lbw or bowled.

The degree of difficulty in bowling the flipper is such that only extremely capable players need bother with it. Not even Warne, arguably its greatest exponent, is always confident or accurate with it.

A fifth type of delivery which Warne was to develop is what he calls the 'zooter'. The bowler cuts his fingers underneath the ball and pushes it out of the front of his hand, from the palm, which causes the ball to be held back as he lets it go. The seam is straight up. The ball either floats or 'skids' through the air, and may swing a little. It comes through at a slower pace than Warne's other deliveries and tends to die once it hits the pitch. The zooter does not spin.

All other balls in the leg-spinner's repertoire are variations of these five kinds of deliveries. Over the years, Warne experimented with them. His capacity to vary each of the five types of delivery in the amount of spin, speed, drift, dip, skid and bounce imparted made him less predictable and more difficult for the batsman to 'read' out of his hand or off the pitch.

By the time he left school in Melbourne's southeastern suburbs, he was starting to become familiar with the leg-spinner and the top-spinner—although, even then, he had a long way to go.

The Neighbourhood

In the late nineteenth century, the famous Heidelberg School of Australian painters, including Arthur Streeton, Tom Roberts and Charles McCubbin, used to put up their easels at spots round Melbourne's bayside area of Hampton, Black Rock and Beaumaris. They were inspired by the craggy, cliff-top views over Port Phillip Bay. It was an idyllic setting to paint and then relax in the evening over a convivial bottle of wine. In the succeeding decades, pubs sprang up throughout the area, attracting patrons to drink on their spacious balconies while taking in the exceptional view, just as the painters did then and still do now.

The pubs—such as the Red Bluff, the Beaumaris and the Commodore—have become the cultural centre for the young of the area, where on any night they gather to listen to bands, dominated in the 1980s by heavy metal, but with the occasional Queen, Beatles and Jimi Hendrix imitators, and, in the 1990s, dance music and rap.

Alcohol is the main socialising factor. Dope is available on the streets, but hard drugs are rare. There is little violence in this essentially middle-class, outer-suburban setting. It is different from inner-Melbourne suburbs such as Carlton, St Kilda and Fitzroy, with their cafés and bookshops, and terrace houses with small courtyards.

By contrast, the bayside area has a sporting, non-intellectual air, where the beaches are unpolluted and inviting, even in winter, for walks and play. There are golf clubs such as Royal Melbourne and Sandringham, and several yacht clubs, where thumping powerboats are as much in evidence as sleek sloops. There are numerous sports fields and parks interspersed among the houses with their big front gardens and back yards, carefully pruned and manicured.

It's in this environment that Shane Warne mainly grew up—in Black Rock, opposite the beach. Shane went to the local primary school, and early on established himself as a young jock—top at sport and uninterested in study. He was remembered by fellow students as a group leader, a kid always ready for the cheeky remark to the teachers, to whom he didn't always endear himself in the classroom.

'He was such a top dog he could get away with things,' a friend from those days recalled, 'but he was never in real trouble. He knew the limits and just wanted to get a laugh. He loved being the centre of attention. If taking the piss out of teachers helped, he would do it.'

Warne entered Hampton High in 1982, a relaxed, coeducational school, and the next year, so his friends claimed, he was the first to bleach his hair and wear a 'spike' haircut, a mild version of the punk look, which was taken up by several of the boys. He started wearing an earring in his late teens. Yet all this was the norm. Teenagers would do anything to look as if they were in the 'in crowd'.

'He was a "womaniser",' a former fellow Hampton High student recalled, 'but, to be fair to him, a lot of the girls chased him. But he was also a man's man type, because of his sporting interests.'

He liked the beach and gathered with friends at Half Moon Bay near his home, where a mini-culture of its own developed in the summer months. If you were more than thirty, it wasn't the place to be. Young people of both sexes virtually ordered their parents not to come closer than the pier.

Warne stayed at Hampton High for three years, until 1984. Then, the following year, he transferred to Mentone Grammar, where he completed his secondary education, making his mark again more on the sporting field than in the exam room.

Grammar Boy

The pitch was wet, a real school oval 'sticky'. The coach of Mentone Grammar School's First XI that day, John Mason, stressed the importance of team captain Shane Warne winning the toss. They had to get the opposition in first. Shane grinned, nodded and went out to meet the umpires. He had disarmed them with his charm and joviality even before he tossed. Warne invited his opposite number to call and he did: heads. The coin fell and lodged in the soft turf at an angle of about 60 degrees, clearly coming up heads. Warne, the cheeky opportunist, leapt forward and reached for the coin.

'Better do that again,' he said, picking it up and again asking the other captain to call. He said 'heads' again. It came down tails. Warne sent the others in and Mentone won.

'He was a chancer like that,' Mason said, remembering the boy's three years from 1985 to 1987 at the bayside grammar school. Young Shane had come from Hampton High on a sporting scholarship, something the school preferred hushed up rather than trumpeted. Mentone was one of the newer grammar schools, trying to emulate some of the older conservative private schools, such as Geelong and Melbourne Grammar. One way was to improve the standard of games.

The fact that there was a strong sports structure at Mentone was important in Warne's development, following up his early coaching from Cantlon. Warne's main coach there was Barrie Irons, who, like Mason, came from South Africa, where he had coached a young Robin Smith. Smith went on to play for

England and in the Ashes teams which fought Australia in 1989 and 1993. Ironically, the battle between Warne, the aggressive young spinner, and Smith, the hammering bat with the massive forearms, was to be one of the great highlights of the 1993 Ashes battle.

'Shane was also a very good First XI captain,' Mason said. The coach had seen them come and go in schools both in his native South Africa and in Australia. 'He was a good strategist, always thinking, always trying something, and always on the attack. He never missed a chance to try something different to dislodge the opposition. Temperamentally, he was ebullient, aggressive, confident and unorthodox. Shane really seemed to thrive in precarious match circumstances.'

In 1986, playing against Yarra Valley, Mentone had crashed to six for 15 when Warne came to the wicket. He smashed 90 before being run out and his team recovered to 140. In reply, Yarra Valley commenced well, reaching 78 before losing a wicket. Warne then took six for 16 in sixteen overs. This performance more than any other landed him the captaincy of the AGS (Associated Grammar Schools) First XI, the highest position he could achieve as a schoolboy.

'He was himself a strike bowler, even though he was a spinner,' Mason said. 'The schools played limited-over games—sixty-five—and he used to go on as first change. We'd also have him bowl at the end when the other side was going for runs, because he was so competitive and confident. He liked bowling in tandem with Wayne Fuller, a talented left-arm orthodox spinner. As captain, he was able to generate confidence and unanimity in the team.'

Even then, he had a fair armoury.

'I've read somewhere when he first made the Australian side that he had only recently begun using a wrong 'un,' Mason noted. 'This is not true. He always had one. He would use it every so often, and it had a biggish break on it. I used to umpire some of his games. I remember his first game. He took about five wickets and three of them were with wrong 'uns. It was rare for a schoolboy to have such a good one. He always had remarkable control, too.'

Warne didn't do anything special at practice like Benaud, who used to bowl at a handkerchief on a good length. Nor did he practise with a stump and a golf ball against a brick wall like Bradman. He simply worked hard in the nets.

'He was always jovial at practice, but he was a rigorous trainer,' Mason remembered. 'His length and control were natural to him; consistent with his outstanding skills. He could also bat well. Perhaps he was a bit suspect against speed, but he batted well under pressure.'

Warne may have had the wrong 'un, but in those school days the *mighty* leg breaks and the sizzling flippers were not in evidence.

In the winter off-season, Warne played Aussie Rules, and very well. He enjoyed the physical contact, the team play, the thrills and spills. He was a strong mark and an accurate enough kick. He was not fast, but his lack of 'leg speed' was compensated for by his athleticism. He loved kicking goals. On a school visit to Tasmania, he kicked sixteen, and set his sights on being a top Aussie Rules footballer, perhaps even more than being a top cricketer, although as his father pointed out, when it was summer he wanted to play for Australia.

In winter, it was Hawthorn, or later the St Kilda 'footy' club, the only big league organisation east of central Melbourne. It had a massive following in Melbourne's bayside and south-eastern suburbs.

Young Warne, like tens of thousands of others in his age bracket, wanted to play for the 'Hawks' or the 'Saints'. He and Jason, two years his junior, dreamt of starring in the big time. Their heroes, Peter Knights and Dermott Brereton of Hawthorn, and Trevor Barker of St Kilda, were high-flying, blond and athletic. If the two boys weren't watching them, they were in the park or on the beach opposite their home kicking a ball and pretending to be them. Shane adopted Brereton's jersey number—23—as his own lucky number.

Warne was not academically inclined, with no particular ambition outside sport. He showed some form in commerce and scraped a pass in the HSC, the final school exam, at the end of 1987. Teachers found him 'humorous', 'cheerful' and 'affable'. They all noted that he 'got his studies done', although he had no zest for class work. His congenial disposition enabled him to maintain a good relationship with the teaching staff and fellow students. His former schoolmates particularly remember his unconventional eating habits. Spaghetti on toast was his favourite meal and he loved fast food, toasted cheese sandwiches, baked beans, McDonald's burgers and milk shakes. Warne scorned vegetables, while his only meat came from hamburgers in a diet that has remained much the same throughout his cricketing career.

Warne liked to be liked. Apart from on the cricket field, he had a taste of leadership as a house captain. He was regarded as a dutiful student, not the larrikin the UK media wanted him to be years later. However, he *was* one of the boys. He led the way with pranks as he had right through his school life, but his sporting skills gave him status at Mentone.

The prestige helped him respond to typical grammar school discipline. It's something that without his achievements on the sporting field he may have found anathema, especially considering the relaxed mixed-sex high school he had come from and the hedonistic bayside life he was enjoying out of school. He would have preferred the girls closer than across the road in their own enclosure. Young Shane was never sure about the rigidity and discipline needed for achievement at studies. But Mentone served him well, and he it. Certainly his name as an ex-pupil has been excellent public relations for the school. Everything they invested in him has paid off. Many a Mentonian in recent years has boasted, and will for years to come: 'Shane Warne is an old boy.'

Warne continued his connection with the school by returning to coach in the junior school and play against the First XI, even when he was first becoming a 'name'.

Saintly Prospects

While still at school in September 1986, Warne, just seventeen, joined several schoolmates at the sub-district Brighton team, a club that boasted five Test cricketers—John Blackham, Albert Trott, Harry Trott, Lisle Nagel and Jack Iverson. Colin McDonald also played there after his Test career. A senior captain, Mike Tamblyn, told Warne to forget about wrist-spinning and concentrate on his batting.

'You haven't got it, son [as a wrist-spinner],' were Tamblyn's immortal words. This misjudgment will go down in Australian cricket history alongside the Test and state selectors in Sydney who, exactly sixty years earlier, watched Don Bradman, aged eighteen, in the nets and rejected him.

Tamblyn's advice saw Warne for a time even experimenting with medium pace and off-spin in the eight games (five in the seconds and three in the firsts) he played for Brighton during the 1986–87 season. He took nine wickets in the seconds and just three in the firsts. It was the kind of start that saw countless hopeful schoolboys give the game away. But Warne hit some 30s and 40s, and enjoyed his batting and the camaraderie.

The next season, 1987–88, Warne decided, with two other young Brighton players (Ravi Krishnan and Peter Bray) to try St Kilda, a district club from which state players could be drawn. At first, he was considered by everyone there as a hard-hitting batsman. At eighteen years old, he was not viewed by anyone as a bowler, and there was little respect for his batting when he wanted to play all the shots with no discrimination, whether in the nets or in the middle. 'He would smash the ball around for a quick 20 and get out,' his team-mate Krishnan noted.

Warne, overweight and hirsute, seemed like so much talent wasted and going nowhere. Consequently, at an age when aspirants for first-class selection (at state and Test level) were eager to be noticed, Shane Warne was languishing, apparently without much hope, in the St Kilda Fourths. He even took off mid-season for a month's break in Europe, soon after he had finished at Mentone Grammar at the end of 1987.

Yet Krishnan and others noticed something in the nets and, very occasionally, in a match during the rare moments when he rolled his arm over during that first season at St Kilda. This fun-loving, friendly guy coud rip a leg break that was unplayable.

Football Folly

Laziness also seemed to pervade Warne's second football season with the Saints in 1988. Perhaps it was simply the stage most adolescents face when they leave school and can't find a job that suits. Warne, always bouyant, nevertheless appeared to those close to him to be a little directionless. Despite the bold, outgoing exterior, he wasn't sure if he had a future at anything. He dreamt of being a star footballer, or even a cricketer, but the reality was that the competition was tough and skilled in both fields of sport.

Warne felt he was marking time in both games. His cricket was in a rut. He had played five games of football with the under-19s in 1987. Now he seemed destined to see out another season in the under-19 side, or thirds. Then, mid-season, an injury to a senior player saw him receive a phone call on a Thursday night from the coach of the reserves—the grade above the under-19s. Warne was in the side in the coveted full forward position.

Warne had the flu and was about to announce he wouldn't play with the under-19s that week when he received the call. He decided he had to play. This was the first time he had received promotion to the second team in either sport at St Kilda. He felt at the time that it was the biggest opportunity of his sporting life, so he rugged up and returned to bed until Saturday morning.

He still felt flat, but was determined to play. The reserve game was against Carlton at St Kilda's home ground at Moorabbin. After a week of rain, the ground was muddy and damp, and Warne missed a couple of shots at goal that normally wouldn't have eluded him. It wasn't a day for big scores or for forwards. His main opponent was a rugged-looking, powerfully muscled back named Milham Hanna. Hanna had a shaved head and looked like a refugee from a Mad Max movie. If Warne had had to choose the player on whom he should least like to play first-up at this level, it would probably have been the brilliant, straight-ahead Hanna. He was only in the reserves because Carlton had such a strong senior list. Hanna would have walked into most league club firsts. At Carlton, they often had a long period of apprenticeship for future stars, and this one was being nurtured in the reserves. Hanna proceeded to thrash the ailing Warne, who seemed rooted in the mud by comparison to this agile, fast-moving opponent, who out-marked and out-bustled him.

Warne's coach was infuriated that Shane wouldn't 'chase'—go after an opponent when he was clear with the ball. This was considered a major weakness in Aussie Rules then. (Now it's a cardinal sin.) But Warne's illness was affecting him.

After half-time, he was taken off the field and didn't return until the last quarter, when he performed reasonably, but by then St Kilda had been beaten. Warne had been marked down as not capable of making the step up. The image of his struggle against Hanna would live in selectors' minds. He was back in the under-19s the next week.

Things not said after that game were far more telling than those uttered.

The Improver

Warne buried his disappointment about his failure to make the higher grade at football, saw out the football season in the under-19s and, in September, turned his mind to the cricket season of 1988–89. There was more urgency now in his application.

At nineteen, he was at the crossroads as far as his cricket career was concerned. He reckoned he had two more seasons of district cricket. After that, he would be twenty-one and, if he were still in the lower ranks of the local game, that would be it. He could concentrate on Aussie Rules and the beach.

He was often between jobs after he left school and could give more time to practice. Team-mates noticed that Warne was first into the nets and bowling more than any other player at the club. He worked with more diligence than ever before at line and length, and spinning the ball hard.

The effort paid off in a game for the thirds against Ringwood at the Ross Gregory Oval when he took five for 49. This and the record for the thirds of twenty-four wickets at 14.66 earned him selection in the seconds and Warne was more than gratified to have jumped two levels in the season. The seconds felt like the big time. The games were played in the more impressive arenas and the wickets were covered. Suddenly, Warne was inspired.

Instead of being a park cricketer with no future, he could sniff a chance to go higher. Still a teenager, he could dream dreams about playing for Australia—one day, somehow. He was focused on not letting his chance in the higher grade slip, as he felt he had six months earlier in the forgettable football match in the mud at Moorabbin.

In Warne's first game with the seconds, he was used judiciously by his skipper, Stephen Maddocks, who told him not to worry if he bowled a few long hops and over-pitchers. When Warne became tired, Maddocks removed him before he was belted. The end result was a spirit-lifting return of five for 67.

'It was the best I ever felt and bowled [until that time],' Warne recalled. 'I could see that while some of the guys [the opposition batsmen] were good, I could get through with the right delivery, especially if I ripped it. It gave me a boost.'

The Discard

Warne's rise in the cricket ranks from also-ran to potential district player gave him the inspiration to put in a strong pre-season before the 1989 football season in the hope that he could regain a place in the St Kilda Football Club reserves. He applied himself to losing his podgy appearance and shed the kilos until he was down to a rock-hard 82 kilograms, his best sporting weight ever.

It was a critical time. Warne was nineteen and at an age when decisions were usually made about an Aussie Rules future. He was determined—more than he had ever been. This was the moment which would lead on to dreams realised or cold reality. In early practice, he found good form. In Shane's own mind, he felt sure that he was doing enough to make the final lists for the season.

The selection committee sat down in February and began to sift through the list of eighty or so possibles, which would have to be reduced in number to fifty-five. The image in a few minds was that game against Carlton.

Warne arrived home from work one night to a letter from the club. He eagerly tore it open, thinking it would be notification of his selection. The idea that he might be discarded hadn't even entered his head. Yet there it was, the most dismal and depressing communication he'd had in his life:

> *[We] regret to inform you that your services are no longer required. The St Kilda Committee wishes you well in your football future...*

Warne was stunned. No one had given him a hint at training. Not a word. And now it was over. His dreams from childhood had been shattered. He wondered at first whether he could step in at the big league anywhere else. His heart—and loyalty (a big feature of Warne's make-up)—was invested in making it with the club that wore red, white and black. In any case, who would take on a reject from another club? Certainly not in late February.

Someone suggested he have a run with the Zebras—the Sandringham club up the road—who were in the second-ranking Victorian league, the VFA. But young Warne wanted the big time or nothing. Success at that level was so much ingrained in his psyche that he couldn't imagine playing at a lesser standard, much as he loved the game. Within days of receiving the letter, Warne had made a decision to give football away.

At the dinner table at home, his father offered wise counsel. If he were ever going to make it in cricket, perhaps the St Kilda dismissal would be a blessing in disguise. Then a friend from the St Kilda Seconds named Rick Gough, aged twenty-five, rang and suggested they go to England for the Aussie winter and play cricket. Gough had played in Bristol four years previously and knew what to expect. He could now concentrate on his game in the winter months. Hadn't Allan Border drifted across for a cricketing adventure when he was about the same age as Warne was then?

The more Warne thought about it, the more it excited him. Why not take off? He didn't care for any of the jobs he had tried in the past eighteen months such as making signet rings in a jewellery factory (too precise, boring and solitary); manning a cash register at Myer (not the sort of working responsibility he liked); delivering beds for Forty Winks (a lot of laughs, but few opportunities for advancement); and pizzas for Pizza Hut (more laughs, but even fewer opportunities). He had nothing to lose. Besides, Border was taking a team to the UK to fight for the Ashes, and he could see a bit of that.

Warne and Gough wrote a few letters to English clubs, but heard nothing back. They were advised to turn up and knock on doors. By March, they had worked out a plan to get to England with a little assistance from the airline KLM. St Kilda club stalwart John Edwards, a former state player, also guided them. After a string of rejections they ended up with the Imperial Club at the Western League in Bristol, the same competition that had attracted Viv Richards and Allan Border in the early and mid-1970s. Not a bad recommendation for a couple of hopefuls.

They tried out in the nets. Warne's capacity to turn it, and his upright skills with the bat, won over the club. He would be a winner. A small shock was the fact that amateur meant just that, but the club was very keen to acquire their services, so a deal was struck. The lads received free accommodation and a car. They were offered jobs as ground staff, which sounded fair enough to both of them. They became odd-job men during the working week, painting anything that looked drab, rolling the pitch, setting up the nets, looking after the equipment.

'It was OK,' Warne told reporters later. 'We got a few quid. Enough to get by. The life was good, although I missed home.'

He was still not over being discarded by St Kilda and would ring home to get the scores, especially to see how Tony Lockett was going. He was the Saints' full forward at the time and one of Warne's heroes.

The ground-staff work was undemanding, but it helped Warne pick up wickets. He began to have a fair idea of how the home pitch was going to perform. He was finding the wickets in the region conducive to his breaks. Warne was managing sharper turn than in Australia.

He realised that the opposition usually was not even up to sub-district standard in Melbourne, although every now and again he would come across another promising young cricketer who would handle him well. But he would take up the challenge and work hard to get him. He played fifteen games and picked up 900 runs, while taking an outstanding 90 wickets at a good average. His best score was 139 and he took nine for 54 in one innings. Someone at the club had heard that another bowler in an equally obscure competition had taken a few more for the season, but it had been a long time since anyone at the Imperial had done so well.

Off the field things were happening, too. The lads hadn't counted on the 'Neighbours' factor. By 1989, the TV show had taken England by storm. Kylie Minogue and Jason Donovan were household names. The whole of Britain would stop to watch the early-evening show as it soared to new heights of soapie banality and dominated the ratings. The simple sanitised drama, with its emphasis on sun and hints of sin had captured the popular imagination.

Everywhere that the lads went, they were asked about Kylie and Jason. Warne quickly realised that the girls saw him as some sort of manifestation of what they'd been watching on the tube. Here the handsome young man was in living technicolour. He didn't seem to have a worry in the world, happy and outgoing in a way the locals found quaint but charming.

They were living in a country where there was plenty of reason for frowning. The weather was usually grey, the economy was running into a recession and there was unprecedented unemployment.

A hectoring prime minister was out of touch with ordinary people and the young were finding it hard to imagine any kind of future. Here were a couple of Aussie guys with refreshing naivety and positive natures.

There was a downside. Warne was out of the eye of his fit father and health-conscious mother, who would have said something about his weight and diet. He didn't have to be super-fit for Imperial club's standard of cricket, and he was not alone in being overweight.

In short, he still lacked self-discipline. He needed motivation. He and Gough were inspired by the success of Border's Ashes team, who thumped the opposition four–nil. He was interested in the reaction of the English, for, although like everyone they hated losing, they were also impressed by Border's team's performance and were gracious about it.

Every day, the tabloids made a noise about 'Big Merv' or the 'smiling assassin', Terry Alderman, who was on his way to a forty-wicket haul. Warne especially watched the performance of leg-spinner Trevor Hohns, whom Border was using judiciously. In one Test, the Australian captain brought him on to tackle English captain David Gower. Hohns dismissed the graceful left-hander with a superb flipper.

For weeks after that, Warne worked on his own and reckoned he had a crude one. He also felt, but never stated, that he could be a better spinner than Hohns. The Warne flipper was in need of refinement, yet he began to snare the odd wicket with it.

It was then that Warne set himself a new goal. He would work hard on his cricket and aim at Sheffield Shield selection.

In the meantime, Warne ballooned. He and Gough haunted the local pubs through the long summer nights, avoided the warm British beer, which they never liked, and asked for Fosters and XXXX. It was available in modern Britain. At some point in the night the lads would hunt for food. Often they would end the evening consuming beer, greasy fish and fatty chips. The swelling didn't stop until Warne hit 100 kilograms, the heaviest he had ever been and 18 kilograms over his football-playing trimness. Warne didn't care that much, because the English were not health-conscious. It was a different culture. They smoked in restaurants, and liked fatty breakfasts, lunches and dinners. For a few months, he was one of them.

They threw a party at the end of the trip, and Warne and Gough starred in an unscripted video, based on 'Neighbours'. Gough later described the 2½-hour tape as 'disgraceful'. Warne made sure it was destroyed.

In August 1989, the lads flew home and Keith Warne went out to Melbourne airport to meet his son. He saw him at the baggage carousel and was stunned.

That can't be Shane, he thought. But it was, and about 25 per cent more.

2

St Kilda to Zimbabwe

Fat Chance

Warne endured plenty of jibes over his bloated condition on his return to the St Kilda club about the time of his twentieth birthday in mid-September, in time for the start of the 1989–90 season. Yet he didn't seem to care. It was his own, perhaps unconscious, protest against being delisted by St Kilda's football club. All that effort to get super-fit seemed a waste of time, especially as he had been passed over for players that he and other astute judges at St Kilda felt were less skilled and dedicated than he had been. It was going to take something monumental to see him again sacrifice those wonderful French fries at McDonald's. The sacking still hurt, even though he hadn't been near the club during the football season.

Yet Warne's strong character, well hidden under layers of self-indulgence, remained. His cricket had improved and he expected to be selected for the firsts. Despite the wet conditions early that spring, he toiled in the nets and felt sure his improvement would be noticed. The squad had gathered in the rooms after practice on a Thursday night. Selection chairman Geoff Tamblyn read out the names, with the most influential selector, club captain Shaun Graf, looking on. Tamblyn began with the firsts, in alphabetical order. He reached 'Walker' and Shane waited for his name.

'Wingreen,' Tamblyn said. 'Twelfth man, Handscomb.'

Warne sighed. It would have to be the 'twos' again.

Tamblyn read through the seconds list. He got down to naming 'Womersley,' and that was it. There was still no 'Warne'.

Shane was shattered as the thirds was read out. He was in that side and had been relegated after his five games in the seconds the previous season. The teams hived off to meet in different rooms. Warne seemed to hang in the room. He was incredulous.

Graf noticed and approached him.

'Sorry, mate,' he said. 'We just didn't have room for a leggie in the twos.'

Warne wanted to blurt out that he had had an impressive season in England, for it appeared that Graf didn't even know about it. But he held his tongue and accepted the blow which brought back memories of the shock and sadness he had felt when the footy club dumped him.

In fact, Graf had an inkling of Warne's success in the winter. The relegation to the thirds had been based more on discipline than form. Graf wanted him to focus more on his game and to lose weight. He had seen him reduce at the beginning of the year for football and wanted to see him get fitter for cricket.

It was a bleak time. Warne didn't feel wanted at St Kilda and the rain was relentless, ruining the chance for many hopefuls at the commencement of the season. Rick Gough, himself back in the seconds, made a point of talking up Warne's success in England.

The season began three weeks late, on 21 October. Graf and other selectors watched Warne at practice and listened. They looked through the overweight, scruffy, bottle-blond image on show, redrafted the teams and placed him in the seconds. This meant Warne avoided the temptation to join his old school friends at East Sandringham, who were, in the main, happy social cricketers.

It seemed that the whims of Melbourne's fickle weather were a major turning point in Warne's career, rather than any spell of particularly blinding bowling. He had gained a well-deserved return to his position in the seconds without delivering a single competitive delivery.

Real Chance

Warne didn't take a bag of wickets in his first few district seconds games, but this wasn't as important as his new-found consistency. His line and length were good on unhelpful pitches. He was also flighting the ball better and no opposition batsmen in those early games of 1989–90 could belt him. Warne now had a reliable leg break and top-spinner. There was no flipper in sight, however, and he lacked confidence in his wrong 'un. Yet the long hops and full tosses were fewer and he was sending down four or five good deliveries an over.

No one in the St Kilda nets could master him and most who faced him left practice concerned about their form. Some wondered if they were slipping in their technique against spin. But all recognised that Warne had improved. That England season had done it. In addition, Warne had not been afraid to ask even the most yeoman of spinners for tips. He was learning all the time.

Despite his appearance, Warne worked as hard as anyone at his fitness. St Kilda, under Graf's directives, was into physical conditioning—not previously a feature of club cricket. It was becoming fashionable (although still not entrenched) in first-class cricket, as state and Test teams strove to obtain the edge on competition.

In the last Saturday game before Christmas 1989, Warne's form and diligence received due reward and he was promoted to the firsts when the Saints' leading leggie, Jamie Handscomb, injured his hand. Warne's initial game was against Northcote and he delivered just one over. In his second match against Waverley-Dandenong, Graf gave him his big chance late in the innings. Warne was nervous, but the deliveries were on the spot from his first over. He began to beat the bat. He let go some big leg breaks, passing the bat easily and, if anything, by too much. Fieldsmen were hardly exaggerating their whistles of astonishment as Warne began to let them rip. For the first time in his career, he was in some sort of control of capable opposition. No one seemed to pick his top-spinner. This ball, which came straight through, brought cautious prods from the batsmen. Spitting leg breaks then did the damage.

Shaun Prescott, who was about to bat for Victoria, was good enough to get the edge to one that flew to Graf at slip for Warne's initial district firsts wicket. The St Kilda team embraced and encouraged him. His team-mates were as excited as he was. Some of them had never seen a leg-spinner bowl like this, let alone precipitate doubt in the minds of those who faced him. Leggies of quality had been squeezed out of the game after more than a decade of speed dominance.

A few overs later, Waverley-Dandenong's Ian Harvey (then a wicketkeeper-batsman, now a state all-rounder) was caught when he mistimed a drive off Warne. Waverley-Dandenong's captain, Rodney Hogg, a former Test paceman, came in. Warne bowled three big-turning breaks past his probing bat.

Hogg shook his head. He turned to Graf at slip and remarked: 'This bloke should be in the Test side, turning 'em like that!' Hogg commented later that Warne was already a better bowler than Peter Sleep, who was then the Test leggie.

It was too early for such a promotion, but Warne was lifted by his figures of three for 31 off 13.1 overs. (Much later, he reflected with satisfaction that his first three victims at this level were three first-class cricketers, with Hogg a Test player, albeit a bunny.) Despite this promising start, Warne was relegated to the seconds for a one-day game after Christmas. He regained his place in the senior team at the beginning of 1990. St Kilda made the final against Richmond, which batted first and reached 215. Warne bowled twelve tight overs without taking a wicket. St Kilda lost early wickets, but skipper Graf dug in for a fine knock. He was 85 not out, and the score nine for 197, when last-man-in Warne strode to the wicket.

Graf ordered him not to flash outside the off stump, and to let him (Graf) get the runs. Warne, ever the team player, obeyed orders against every instinct as Richmond's fine opening speedsters, Paul Reiffel and David Saker, threw everything at him. He played straight in defence and let go a half-dozen tempting lifters outside off stump. Graf reached a fine century. With the score on 212, however, the skipper nicked one to the keeper down the leg side and Richmond was the winner by 3 runs.

While disappointed to have come so close in the biggest game of the season, Warne was thrilled to have participated and experienced the tightness of a district final in front of a substantial crowd. It was another factor in his steep cricket learning curve.

At the Academy

The year 1990 was to provide the tyro with many more thrills. In February, former Test captain Bill Lawry, the Victorian Cricket Association's new manager, was the driving force behind expanding the state squad. The catch-cry across the nation was 'We need spinners', especially in countering the speed of the West Indies attack, which had nullified all opposition. Anyone in Australia who was thought by good judges to be capable of tweaking the ball well was scrutinised. Warne was invited to join the state squad.

In April, he was asked to join the government-funded Australian Institute of Sport's Cricket Academy based in Adelaide, a nursery for young talent. He was to train and practise full-time throughout the winter months of 1990. By mid-year, former part-time leggie and Victorian state batsman Jack Potter was teaching him how to deliver a flipper and Test leggie Terry Jenner was giving sound, all-round advice about the special art.

The cricket coaches at the academy in Warne's time, apart from Potter and Peter Spence, were former South Australian Shield players Barry Causby and Andrew Sincock. They had the sometimes unenviable task of keeping the players keen during intense training, when all they wanted to do was to play cricket. The coaches were confronted with the bubbly, brash young Warne.

'I always look for life in the eyes,' Sincock said of his first encounter, ' and he had real pale green sparklers. He was *alive.* He had bleached hair and the physical presence of a man confident in himself and pleased to meet you.'

Warne struck up a good relationship with Sincock and Jenner, but didn't quite see eye to eye with Causby. They all found he liked to show them what he had learned along the way, but he sometimes had a way of putting people off-side'. One of the coaches noted he was a 'high risk-taker'. He would be late to training and tired. When the routines became hard, Warne would 'conk out'. He was living life to the full and often spending his nights at local nightclubs, accompanied by the young West Australian Damien Martyn, who also liked partying. Warne became famous for some of the antics he would get up to at the clubs. According to one club manager, he was 'quite outstanding' at events such as pyjama parties. Warne would turn up at training fatigued.

'What Shane wanted to do,' Sincock recalled, 'was make the ball spin violently, get the batters out, then get in and slog the opposition all round the park. We had to explain to him that in order to reach the top, he would have to do more than this. One could do this by not riding him.'

Sincock saw Warne as a gregarious young man, whom most people liked. He drew others to him.

'He always had a laugh,' the coach said. 'When training was tough, there was always something funny that would happen. He was effervescent and bold. He took that attitude that he would slog you out of the attack or make you look a real fool when you batted to him.' Sincock made him captain in some matches and thought he was 'terrific'. The team followed him.

'He worked with me on a team plan and stuck with it,' Sincock remembered. 'He was progressive. He had to bowl and captain, which can be difficult. He managed himself very well. Shane was an entrepreneurial leader. He took risks and was confident in his strategies.'

Sincock thought he showed so much leadership ability that he could one day captain Australia, but described his fielding as only 'OK'.

'He was quite nimble over the first few metres,' Sincock said, 'but he was not beyond that. We worked very hard on his agility.'

Warne didn't go for the hard, repetitive 100-metre sprints. To a degree, Sincock concurred. The longest run a player would have to make in cricket would be about 70 metres. As a coach, he was not convinced that running long distances put strength in people's legs.

'He never could understand then why the AIS was so keen on swimming,' Sincock remembered. 'It's an aerobic activity that doesn't put stress on the body. It's also a coordination activity.'

The coaches found it difficult to make Warne fit into the mould. He was never going to let himself be shaped too much by others, no matter how professional or plausible the ideas being presented to him might be. This went some way towards the eventual run-in he had with Barry Causby. They had different views of life and there was a clash of personalities. Strong words were exchanged.

Warne didn't help his cause on a training program in Darwin. While larking about near a hotel pool, he offended three female Asian students from the Northern Territory University with a crass, yet mock-sexual remark and gesture. They complained to the university vice-chancellor, who contacted Brendan Flynn, the institute manager in Adelaide.

Flynn flew to Darwin in a rush to head off a local police investigation. After smoothing things over with the women, the university and the police, he ordered Warne and two other young cricketers, who had been amused by the incident before it blew up, to take a bus ride home 'to think about' the misdemeanour.

Caribbean Clout

Warne's tribulations over discipline were temporarily forgotten when he was selected in August 1990 for a five-week tour of the West Indies with an Australian 'youth' side captained by Jamie Cox. The team included Michael Bevan, Shane George, Darren Berry, Chris Mack, Brendon Julian, Damien Fleming, Craig White and David Castle.

Warne was soon the most popular player in the squad and kept the others entertained with his clowning, which took everyone's mind off the tough travelling, sometimes poor accommodation and unprepossessing food on offer. He bleached his hair white for the trip and loved being the centre of attention in every activity from pool-side dancing to charming the local women. Warne's eating habits kept team-mates agog, especially when he entered McDonald's. It was a revelation to fitness fanatics such as Bevan and Fleming.

He maintained his likeable, extrovert nature on the field, but applied himself to performing well. Warne played in the three Youth Tests. Despite taking just six wickets, his efforts were described as good by the team management in its report back to the ACB. He often extracted turn on the variable Windies pitches, but was a little wayward.

Yet he was forgiven. Everyone realised Warne was trying out different deliveries he had learned at the Cricket Academy, such as the flipper and the wrong 'un, which he had never previously applied himself to in competition. He was also experimenting with a more angular run-up and going round the wicket in an attempt to 'corner' batsmen who were tied down by spin.

All this came together just once, not in the Tests, but in a first-class game against the Leeward Islands on St Kitts. His control and rhythm were excellent and he went around the wicket more than ever before in a game. The result was self-doubt for every batsman to whom he bowled in the first innings and particularly in the second, when he created his first big cricket 'crisis' for an opposition at the first-class level. His figures of three for 32 and seven for 45 did not do justice to the demoralisation and demolition of the Leeward team.

This fine return of ten wickets made him the leading tour wicket-taker with twenty-three at 19.43 in seven of the eight matches. More importantly, his destructive capacity at St Kitts would live in the minds of watchers such as team manager Brian Taber and coach Steve Bernard. They felt it was only a matter of time before Warne harnessed such power more consistently. Their reports to the ACB reflected this.

Meanwhile, Warne continued his after-hours antics, especially with the West Indies Youth Test players, and it was no surprise when they voted him the most popular player in the Australian team. A video of the tour by Bernard gave clues to their selection.

Up and Down the Escalator

The fast force-feed of cricket experience continued immediately after Warne returned from the Caribbean. He slipped into the Adelaide grade team Glenelg, which was happy to have his services, especially after his performances in the West Indies. In September, it was a case of master versus pupil when Glenelg played East Torrens, which had a new captain–coach, Andrew Sincock. The former medium-quick bowled to Warne, who whacked the ball straight back over his head.

'He ran down the pitch laughing,' Sincock, then forty, recalled. 'I then moved one past him and he acknowledged it. Then I got a couple into his pads. He remained not out for about 14. When we batted, Shane got a few wickets, but he was tired when I came in. Then the real Shane came to the fore. He reached the top of his mark, looked at me, opened his eyes and mouth real wide, and poked his tongue out. He then ran in with his eyes skyward and tongue out. That was one of his tricks. Then each ball he ran in with a new crazy expression. It made me determined not to let him dismiss me. The point is, he is a real fun character.'

Glenelg also found him a match-winner. The club was keen to retain his services as he three times picked up five wickets in an innings.

In October, Warne played two one-day games for the Cricket Academy against the touring England Ashes team led by Allan Lamb, who stood in for the injured Graham Gooch. The rain-affected games were on fast tracks at St Peter's College and the academy took a hiding in both games. Warne top-scored with 11 in both matches, and took a hammering from the batsmen, especially the muscular Robin Smith, who heaved him for six and several boundaries.

Yet he persevered, bowling mainly leg breaks on an unresponsive wicket. Smith stood and delivered without jumping down the track at the leggie. Finally, Warne found the edge and had Smith caught behind. It was his first international wicket of Test quality.

'Apart from Steve Cotrell [a speedster from Victoria], he was our most attacking bowler,' Sincock said. 'We even talked about opening the bowling with him. He bowled well against the England bats.'

Off the field, Warne continued to buck against some directives at academy training, such as running up and down sand dunes on a Sunday morning. But it was more those giving directions that upset him.

In November, there was a meeting between Causby, Sincock, Flynn and Warne, in which his attitude was discussed. As an AIS manager, Flynn had to dress him down. The pool-side 'prank' in Darwin was raised when Warne thought it had been buried forever.

His anger showed throughout the meeting. Soon after this, he was left out of a tour to Sri Lanka. That was it. Warne resigned before he was thrown out of the academy. He drove back to Melbourne, leaving Glenelg miffed that he had not even consulted the club.

'Shane was in the wrong,' Sincock reflected, 'but it was sad. He had something special.'

Selector Pressure

Unfazed by his bitter end at the Cricket Academy, Warne walked straight into the Victorian Second XI. He knew that many people were now willing to push him through the cricket ranks, and he showed himself to be an opportunist concerning the media. During his debut in the seconds against Western Australia in December—in which he took a modest one for 60 and three for 78, and scored a match-saving 36 not out—Warne told journalists he wanted to play for Victoria, but would switch to South Australia if it wanted him. This put pressure on the Victorian selectors and team leaders, who had mixed feelings about promoting him so quickly. Some were out of step with national selectors, who wanted to develop spinners.

Warne joined mates for beers and pies in the outer at the MCG to watch the 1990 Boxing Day Test against England, which was demolished by left-arm speedster Bruce Reid, who took thirteen wickets. Warne appeared just like thousands of other sun-revellers in Bay 13. Yet despite ample padding and a happy-go-lucky manner, he was burning with ambition to make the two final steps to state and then Test cricket.

Whereas his dreams of running out for the St Kilda football team firsts had now evaporated, he considered himself a real chance to represent his country at cricket. Watching Reid and the excitement of his intelligent speed bowling was pure inspiration for Warne. He wanted to be winning a Test out there on his 'home' ground, the vast MCG stadium, in front of a huge crowd.

In January 1991, he played another game for the Victorian seconds against South Australia in Adelaide. On a batting paradise and in a heatwave, Warne took four for 161 and one for 19. It was a sterling effort, but the figures were not those to compel spin-resistant Victorian selectors to elevate him to first-class cricket. Yet despite his not capturing a big bag of wickets, everything else was falling into place. Spinners selected for the Victorian side ahead of him—Paul Jackson, Peter McIntyre and David Emerson— were not taking wickets.

In February, Merv Hughes and Dean Jones took off for a Test series against the West Indies, leaving two places free in the state side. The selectors chose Warne for a match against Western Australia at the Junction Oval, St Kilda, and he squeezed out left-arm orthodox spinner Jackson. Barely eighteen months earlier, Warne had been viewed as a club thirds player. Now he was a state cricketer, due to his own determination and skills.

He had played just twenty-two club games—fourteen with St Kilda and eight with Glenelg—before the big break. In the previous season (1989–90), he had taken nine wickets in eleven matches at 28.66 runs each, with a best effort of three for 31. In 1990–91, he took just eleven wickets at 25.00 in six matches for St Kilda, with a best return of three for 25. He fared better for Glenelg, with twenty-six wickets at 20.73 in eight matches, with best figures of six for 75. Observers wondered if these figures collectively were enough to justify his fast-track elevation.

Into the Shield

Warne had little sleep before his first state game in front of several thousand spectators at the Junction Oval. He smoked nervously in the dressing room before marching out onto the field on the first morning. He was even more on edge out in the middle when thrown the ball by skipper Simon O'Donnell. Former Test opening bat Graeme Wood was powering along with fellow opener Mark Lavender.

Warne had trouble gripping the ball as he stepped up for his first-ever delivery in first-class cricket. It was loose. Lavender smacked it away for four. The second ball was a long hop and was dealt with similarly. His next four deliveries yielded another 2 runs only, meaning he had surrendered 10 runs in his first over. His second cost another 10 as Wood, a left-hander, swatted him with the spin onto the on side.

O'Donnell had an encouraging chat with him before he began his third over and Warne slipped into a groove in another sixteen overs during Western Australia's six for 418 declared. He only conceded 41 more runs—at less than 3 an over. He beat the bat a few times and was unlucky not to have the hard-hitting Tom Moody caught. O'Donnell also dropped a sitter from him. Overall, however, it was an anxious, inauspicious debut.

He bowled a tidy, tight second innings, despite Moody hitting him for a straight six, taking one for 41 off sixteen overs, which was almost the economy rate of his first-innings effort, except for those two opening overs. But the bottom line of one for 102 off thirty-three overs for the match was not enough for selectors, who could not make up their minds on which bowlers they should settle. Collectively, they were indifferent to spin, mainly because Paul Reiffel had fired for the season, taking fifty-one wickets, and was well supported by Damien Fleming, Tony Dodemaide and James Sutherland.

Warne was dumped for the next state game (making way for Jackson again) and once more took the escalator down to the district seconds in a two-day game against University. He made 42 runs and took one for 43 before the St Kilda firsts welcomed him back for the last three matches of the 1990–91 season.

The extent of Warne's hunger to succeed was demonstrated as he flew off with several other Australian professional cricketers, including the in-form Reiffel, for the 1991 season in England, in the Lancashire League. At twenty-one, Warne had to become a professional. He had little choice unless he went back to part-time jobs, for which he had no appetite.

Warne had a poor start and was run out for only a few in the first game. In the second game, Rudi Bryson, a speedster from South Africa, bowled him first ball. However, he settled down and had a successful summer, taking seventy-three wickets at 15.42. Waverley-Dandenong captain–coach Brendan McArdle, also acting as a professional, spent time with Warne in the league and was impressed by what he saw of him, not least his sense of humour. McArdle felt that this would help him through the tough times, and that he wouldn't 'seize up'.

'He's more of an individual than an eccentric like Greg Matthews,' McArdle noted. 'He has a soft, gentle side to his personality like Mike Whitney, although Warne is flashier. Shane wants to be liked. He loves the team camaraderie in the game. He's a good club man and loves the cricket community.'

McArdle thought he was the best Victorian prospect since Jim Higgs.

While playing in the Lancashire League, Warne and Reiffel learned they had been selected in an Australian 'A' team to tour Zimbabwe in September, alongside Test players such as Mark Taylor, Steve Waugh and Tom Moody.

African Interlude

Warne was moving up in the standard of cricket company he was keeping, even though he was the least accomplished of all selected. He was pitted against Peter McIntyre, another Victorian leggie, with whom he was expected to fight it out for a state and, perhaps later, a Test spot.

Taylor was on trial as skipper, being groomed for the day Allan Border stepped down or was pushed out. He and Steve Waugh had the job of reporting on the younger charges. In two first-class games against the Zimbabwean national team, Warne took eleven wickets at 18.82, culminating with a career-best and match-winning seven for 49. McIntyre also did well and the national selectors were pleased with their choices. Waugh was impressed with Warne.

The leg-spinner was frustrated at times by batsmen in Zimbabwe padding the ball away. He was advised to be patient and 'work' the batsman out.

'But I'm impatient and aggressive,' Warne told the press, 'and I say to myself, "Well, stuff you, mate, I'm going to get you out." I'll do anything to get a wicket, even use the Derryn Hinch ball.'

He was referring to the catchphrase of the TV presenter's former program, 'Expect the unexpected.' He used the high full-toss tactic, which was regarded as unsporting in Zimbabwe and raised eyebrows amongst the local cricket purists.

'I usually give mid-wicket and square leg the nod to move back a bit and zing it straight at the batsman's head,' he said. 'It would often surprise him into a mishit.'

His exuberance was in need of a little maturation.

On the team's return from Zimbabwe, Steve Waugh acted as an intermediary in an attempt to lure Warne north to Sydney to play for Bankstown, Waugh's club. On 1 October 1991, the NSW Cricket Association—on the verge of a new Shield season—sought permission from the Victorian Cricket Association to interview the 22-year-old leggie.

Warne was more than tempted to go. There was a big chance for him in Sydney because New South Wales's regular spinner of the past two seasons, Adrian Tucker, had chosen to remain in England to further his business career. Then there was the famous Sydney wicket, the most conducive to spin in the country.

Another factor was competition in Victoria. According to national selector John Benaud, who managed the team in Zimbabwe, there was very little between McIntyre and Warne. In addition, the state had left-arm orthodox spinner Paul Jackson, who was regarded highly. Benaud hoped the Victorian selectors would play both Warne and McIntyre in its 1991–92 Shield season, but he knew this would be an unlikely luxury on the spinner-indifferent MCG.

Victoria had fared badly in pre-season juggling of players with Jamie Siddons, scorer of 1000 runs for the state in 1990–91, becoming captain of South Australia. Fast bowler Martin McCague went home to Perth. The VCA stepped in and said it would block any moves to entice Warne to leave Victoria. It put the spinner in a delicate but good negotiating position. It was nice to be in demand, especially before you had established a position in the state side.

The VCA moved swiftly, invoking an Australian Cricket Board rule which tied players who had been at the Cricket

Academy to their home states for twelve months. Technically, Warne had to stay in Victoria at least through 1991–92. The NSWCA thought about appealing against this at an ACB meeting on 11 October, but dropped the idea.

Warne, for the moment, was still a Victorian. It put the state selectors on notice. They had to give him a chance in 1991–92, or risk losing him the next season.

3

Room at the Top?

Hawke's Good Eye

In early December 1991, Shane Warne learnt he had been selected by the Prime Minister, Mr Bob Hawke, to play in his XI against India in a one-day game in Canberra. A few days later he was told he had been chosen to play in an Australian XI against the West Indies, who were in the country for a one-day series. This meant he had two show-case matches in which to impress the national selectors. He had been fortunate. He had done little to maintain his place in the Victorian state side, let alone play for his country. Warne was yet even to take a five-wicket haul for his district club. His luck revolved around the prophetic words of his first coach, Ron Cantlon, who in 1981 encouraged the eleven-year-old to bowl leg-spinners by saying that 'in ten years time, they will be combing the country for a leggie'.

Cantlon couldn't have been more prescient. It was a decade on, and captain Allan Border and the national selectors were looking for anyone of quality who could deliver. Border, in particular, had noticed that country after country was producing batsmen who could put on the padding and show form and courage against speed, but who had little or no idea how to handle spin, except in India and Pakistan. There were several off-spinners around, but they were often 'change' or part-time bowlers, who were never going to be match-winners, or more pertinently, series winners. Traditionally, too, there had been few 'offies' who could win a match, because they were not huge breakers of the ball. Only the great Jim Laker and Lance Gibbs had been consistent match-winners. Laker was often given assistance in the days when wickets were left uncovered, leaving them vulnerable to the weather.

Border, himself a left-arm orthodox 'offie', knew that the consistent winners had to come from the ranks of leg-spinners, the bigger ball-breakers, and in Australia in those days they were rare. The selectors had managed to unearth one for the Ashes tours of 1985 (Bob Holland) and 1989 (Trevor Hohns), but they had both retired from first-class cricket. Now Border was anxious about the forthcoming series against the West Indies in 1992–93.

He had always felt that a class leg-spinner, one who could perform well not just in Sydney, but on all Australian wickets, was a necessary weapon if he were ever to lead a side that could down the West Indies. Border had seen a chink in their armour against slow bowling and wanted to exploit it, and not just in Sydney, where he himself had won a match against them with eleven wickets. Yet spinners, much more than quicks, had to be nursed and protected. Time was short.

Warne had the inside running, if he could make the most of these two chances. He now had a fair degree of experience behind him—in grade cricket with St Kilda, in English League cricket and at the AIS's Cricket Academy, as well as a taste of Sheffield Shield. The national selectors had sent him on tours to the West Indies and Zimbabwe. He had accumulated any amount of advice from a range of former Aussie talent, including Kerry O'Keefe, Richie Benaud, George Tribe, Jim Higgs, who helped him with his flipper, and Terry Jenner, who showed how he might impart more spin to his leg break and turn to his wrong 'un. Ian Chappell had batted to him in the nets and given him advice from the striker's point of view. But what Warne needed now was more than good advice.

He was coming on so quickly that he could be in Test cricket before he had even proved himself at district level. He would have benefited from a full-time coach, but this was the antithesis of the approach of some former cricketers. Ian Chappell, for instance, had long preached that there was no need for a coach of the Australian team like Bob Simpson. His argument was that if a player reached Test level, he had already mastered his craft, whether keeping, fielding, batting or bowling.

Chappell was virtually saying that a young player with raw talent, who might make the Test side, needed no further help and had learnt all there was to learn. It would be interesting to ask players who had spent a decade or so at Test level if this was the case. They would undoubtedly say that they had developed and learnt plenty, whether they were a Don Bradman or a Max Walker.

Warne's rapid rise made it even more important for constant, intelligent coaching to be available. Simpson was an excellent choice, because he had been a great bat. He was a useful leg-spinner and one of the finest slips fielders ever. But even one all-round coach was not enough, if Australia wanted to be at the top.

There is some comparison with the increasing trend towards specialist coaches in Rugby League and Australian Rules. Essendon's premiership win in the AFL in 1993 was a classic example of where all big-time sport was going, if national and club teams were serious about being the best. As well having an experienced senior overall coach in Kevin Sheedy, in 1993, they added skills coaches in all areas of the game, plus fitness advisers and dietitians for each player. As a result, Essendon surprised the football world by winning a flag two years sooner than the most optimistic prediction. Under the old system, the young players would have had to work out their problems for themselves and would never have developed so fast.

There would be no difference in cricket, especially in highly specialised areas such as leg-spinning, but the cricket world was slower to respond. So Warne was more or less left to make his own way. He was thrilled but concerned at the speed of his rise. He would consult all and sundry for help and he was grateful for it.

Writing in the *Cricketer* magazine in May 1992, Warne said he would never forget an impromptu net session bowling to Victorian state coach Les Stillman, who was having no trouble playing him. The coach told him to get his arm up a bit and slow down his delivery a little.

'Instead of taking my normal run-up,' Warne wrote, 'I stayed at the crease, took one step and bowled. Les was immediately in two minds.'

He started walking in, building momentum, 'remembering to keep my head still'. He made sure he 'powered' through the crease, as Jimmy Higgs had always told him to do. Warne bowled slower and with more loop.

In the same article, Warne named three coaches who had given him similar but not identical advice: Stillman, Jenner and Higgs.

Even his original under-13s coach, Ron Cantlon, was asked for help during a district game. 'I was embarrassed and shocked,' Cantlon recalled. 'Shane was asking for help from me, and he was already a state player.'

Meanwhile, the Australian selectors had hinted strongly to the Victorian selectors that they wanted to develop a leg-spinner quickly. Yet the Victorians were less forthcoming in 'fast-tracking' the young Warne. It was frustrating for the national selectors. Jim Higgs particularly—and probably with some bias because he was both a former Test leggie and a Victorian—had faith in Warne. He felt that Test selection for him was a matter of 'when' and not 'if'. By late 1991, it had reached the stage where he was trying to persuade the Victorians that it would be helpful to the national team if Warne was given a consistent chance in the state side.

The local state selectors, however, had exclusive say in who represented Victoria. They saw different players helping them win the Shield. Consequently, Warne was in and out of the state side at a time when the national selectors wanted him to get a steady first-class diet. The conflict was not resolved but by-passed with Warne's selection in these two high-profile games against the Indians and then the West Indies.

The Prime Minister's XI match had been revived as a fixture after Hawke came to office in 1983. On the previous eight occasions, the XI had beaten the touring teams three times. Hawke would consult the national selectors, but the team was essentially his. The game was a unique way of giving up-and-coming talent a chance to show their wares. The prime minister had a good eye for cricketing skills, having played district grade in Perth as a wicketkeeper–batsman, and just below first-class level in England (twelfth man for Oxford University).

Via the PM's XI, he had given many young players a big opportunity to perform. David Boon, for instance, in the mid-1980s managed a good score for the PM's XI, which had lifted him to national notice. Even though the game was more festive than fierce, Hawke's connection with it guaranteed far more media attention than any other matches apart from Tests or one-day internationals.

Apart from Warne, Hawke chose Border, Greg Blewett, Matthew Hayden, Jamie Siddons, Michael Bevan, Damien Martyn, Tim Zoehrer, Greg Rowell, Damien Fleming and Brad Gilbert. The game was played at Canberra's Manuka oval.

The prime minister was in good form signing autographs, chatting with players and appearing to have a good time, despite the fact that he knew Paul Keating was gathering the numbers in an attempt to depose him in a few days time.

Hawke tossed the coin; Border won and batted. The XI scored seven for 244 in its allotted fifty overs and Blewett (65), Bevan (60) and Martyn (50 not out) acquitted themselves well. But a dashing hundred was needed to make the selectors really sit up. Warne only batted in the last over and scored 2 not out. He received a good chance with the ball, Border giving him the maximum number of ten overs.

The Indians went after him, but never quite managed to hit him out of the attack. The captain took the opportunity to have a close look at him, noticing in particular that when he was hit for four, he didn't go to water with a long hop or a full toss next ball. The young man kept coming in aggressively. Border noted he showed the usual match tension, but that he was not overawed. The captain was impressed by his control and the odd ball that was unplayable. He was raw, but the potential was obvious.

He took Pravin Amre's wicket, caught by Tim Zoehrer behind the stumps for 0. Honours in the bowling went to fast-medium Queenslander Greg Rowell, who took six for 27 off ten overs. India fell apart in the carnival atmosphere and managed just 169 all out, with Vengsarkar (44), Prabhakar (34) and the dashing young Sachin Tendulkar (34) showing some fight. Soon after the match, Keating managed to topple Hawke and become prime minister.

The new leader had no interest in cricket, preferring French clocks to sport, but the PM XI's fixture was kept. It was one tradition started by Menzies and reinstituted by Hawke that Keating didn't mind patronising.

Breakthrough at Bellerive

Warne's effort had been satisfactory, but not enough to get the nod for selection at the next level. He had one chance left for the season, the three-day match between an Australian XI and the West Indies, starting in Hobart on 22 December. Both Higgs and Simpson would be in attendance.

This gave the clash an added sense of urgency for several young hopefuls in the Aussie camp. The team from the Caribbean had a different image without Gordon Greenidge and Viv Richards, and with Richie Richardson as captain. It was not doing well on the field in the one-dayers, losing three in one December week. Yet it was bristling with talent and liable to hit form at any moment.

The Australian XI batted first and had a host of contributors. Of the promising newcomers, opener Wayne Phillips (51), Tom

Moody (70), Michael Bevan (58) and Stuart Law (68) prevailed. Again, no one managed to score a thumping big hundred, which would have made the selectors' job in the short or medium term a lot easier. Certainly, 50s, 60s or 70s never seemed to stick in the memory like a century. The Australians amassed nine for 461 declared.

The West Indies batsmen had trouble with Bruce Reid, who was in fine form. Ian Healy, captaining the side, stuck to his speed brigade of Reid, Paul Reiffel and Chris Matthews, with Steve Waugh helping out with his medium-pacers. It wasn't until the brilliant young Brian Lara looked like making a big hundred that he brought on Warne.

An absorbing battle then ensued. Lara had been billed as the best bat to come out of the West Indies since Richards. His footwork, range of shots and style backed this up. He was at home against even Reid, having been brought up on a diet of express bowling in the Caribbean. However, the vagaries of top leg-spinning were another matter. While he was not at sea against Warne, he was unsure and defensive. After tying him up for a couple of overs, Warne had Lara caught for 83. Healy brought him back at the end of the innings and he wrapped up the tail, ending with three for 14 off just 5.1 overs—about as good as could be expected from limited opportunities. Healy enforced the follow-on and Reiffel carried on where Reid and Warne had finished off in the first innings. The Victorian swinger put back the openers by the time the tourists were 33.

When Matthews disposed of Lara for just 10, it seemed that Warne might have nothing to do. Healy brought him on to bowl at Carl Hooper, who was the only West Indian batting comfortably against the quicks. Warne soon had him out caught while attempting to smash him out of the park. As a reward, Healy kept the spinner on at one end for the rest of the innings. He finished again with best figures—four for 42 off 15.2 overs.

His match results on paper were a formidable 20.3 overs, seven maidens, seven for 56, but flattering considering he had picked up several tail-enders having a heave-ho. But all those involved in selecting the Australian side sat up and took note. Now Warne was a true contender. He had figures to back up his talents and the selectors' judgment of them. Before the Hobart game, it would have been difficult justifying the leggie's selection at Test level on faith and opinion. His capabilities were now a matter of statistical fact.

The West Indies were due for a full tour the following season. Anyone who could deal with them with either bat or ball was going to receive scrutiny. A certain logic began to flow out of the selectors' discussions. If Warne was to have a chance of playing against the West Indies, he had to be blooded in Tests soon. But when was 'soon'? Against Sri Lanka in the three-Test series in August? Probably. Against India in the current series? 'Maybe' was the consensus.

It was too late for the Second Test beginning on Boxing Day. What about the Third Test beginning on 2 January 1992? The selectors—Lawrie Sawle from Western Australia, John Benaud from New South Wales, Higgs and Australian coach Bob Simpson—decided to have a good hard think about it. A lot would depend on how the Second Test unfolded. If Australia won, it would be two–nil up and then there was a chance for experimentation. If off-spinner Peter Taylor turned in an outstanding game, it would rule out dropping him. However, if he stumbled ...

Ordinary Guy with Beer and Pie

Warne spent a couple of days at the Melbourne Boxing Day Test in 1991, aware that he was an even-money chance to play in the Sydney Test that followed a few days later. He stood in the members' pavilion—a beer in one hand and a pie in the other—with a few of his cricket mates, including Dean Waugh, Dean Jones, Brendan McArdle and Warren Whiteside.

Bob Simpson, the Australian team coach, and its manager, Ian McDonald, walked past. Warne greeted them.

'You look set for the day, Shane,' McDonald said. Warne

grinned and agreed that he was. The image of a weighty (95 kilograms) young man devouring fatty food with no known nutritional value would stay with Simpson.

The Melbourne Boxing Day Test was dominated by Bruce Reid, as the corresponding one against England had been twelve months earlier. Then he took thirteen wickets. This time he took twelve. Twenty-five wickets in two consecutive Tests on one ground had to be some sort of record. In some roundabout fashion, Reid's magnificent bowling—with its bounce and swing both ways—and the support of Craig McDermott, who took five wickets, curtailed Peter Taylor's chances and boosted those of Warne, who watched much of the game from the Members' Stand.

A year earlier, he had stood in the outer sipping beer with some mates cheering Reid and company against England. Now he was on the fringe of Test selection himself. What a difference twelve short months could make. Dreams were about to turn into reality as Taylor, a fine one-dayer, but always unconvincing in Tests, was given just seventeen overs. He took one for 60, allowing the selectors a justification for swapping him for Warne.

India batted first and were rolled in a little more than a day for 263. Australia followed up with 349, without anyone scoring a hundred. Geoff Marsh hit 86 in a sluggish day, and Dean Jones 59 in quick time. Healy made an impressive 60. Merv Hughes gave the disappointing MCG crowd something to cheer about apart from the Mexican wave with a swashbuckling 36. India caved in during its second dig and was out for 213. Australia wrapped up the game losing just two for 128 on the fourth day.

The selectors had their usual phone hook-up and didn't take long to decide that Warne should be in the twelve for Sydney. Peter Taylor was dropped and it would be either Warne or Michael Whitney to carry the drinks, if Merv Hughes passed a fitness test for a doubtful hamstring.

Ian McDonald rang Warne that evening to tell him he had been selected. He was asked to come to the ACB offices near the MCG the next morning. Then he was to go for a fitting for a baggy green cap. Warne rang round his close friends and invited them to his parents' home to celebrate that evening. He had too much to drink and was hung-over and queasy when his father dropped him off at the ACB.

Warne asked the board to stall the media because he was feeling ill. He threw up in the toilet, but somehow recovered enough for the media sound bites. The next day he flew to Sydney to join the rest of the team at their hotel, the Parkroyal in The Rocks, including some he'd never met before, such as Geoff Marsh and Mike Whitney.

That night was New Year's Eve and Warne appreciated Marsh and David Boon taking him onto the roof of the hotel to watch the Harbour fireworks display. They drank a few beers and Warne went to bed feeling relaxed and not unloved.

On New Year's Day, he took part in team practice at the SCG nets. There was even time later for a round of golf with Border, the usual way for most of the Australians to relax before Tests. Warne was anxious with cameras clicking all around him. He had an 11 on the first hole, and 60 for the front nine. When the photographers had left with their shots of the new national selection, he settled down and collected a 48 on the back half.

That evening there was a team meeting. Border and Simpson spoke about improving the team's batting. Warne was a little surprised at the 'quiet', 'unmotivated' gathering, which had less zip than in the dressing sheds of his St Kilda district team before a game.

On talking it over with Merv Hughes, he realised there was a basic underlying theory. When a player reached the top in cricket, if he wasn't motivated enough personally and didn't know what he should do out in the middle, then there was nothing that could be done. At least, that was the accepted philosophy. While Warne hadn't expected a passionate harangue Aussie Rules–style, he thought there would be *something*.

Warne had to pinch himself. He had reached the pinnacle of the sport, but didn't quite believe he should be there.

That night the team went to Doyle's, the seafood restaurant on the Harbour. Their table faced the city skyline and the Harbour Bridge, which seemed buttressed between Milsons Point and office blocks opposite. It was a spectacular setting, with the reflection from boat lights sparkling on the water. It should have relaxed everyone. But a few with perennial jitters looked as if they would prefer to be elsewhere. Warne, in particular, was on edge. He went to bed that way and had trouble sleeping.

On the first day of the Test, 2 January 1992, a nervous Warne followed Marsh around to adjust to the routine, while masses of fans circulated around them. It was a far cry from state games where the crowds were so sparse. The Sydney Test was a big event in the city's sporting calendar and every player was under scrutiny. Warne, for the first time, was experiencing what it was like to be a prominent sports star. Whether he would be a one-Test wonder was another matter.

Earning the Baggy Green

That morning, Hughes, the warhorse from Werribee, who learned how to 'carry' an injury in his Aussie Rules footy days, convinced the selectors he could make it through five days. It was down to the home-town, very popular Mike Whitney or the 'flashy'—as one local scribe described him—new blond, who was unknown to Sydneysiders. After an early-morning wicket inspection and consultation between Border and Simpson, Warne was informed he would play.

Earlier he had turned up at the dressing room, not knowing where he should sit. He was soon feeling, if not relaxed, then at ease, thanks in particular to Hughes, who clowned around as usual, putting early-morning headlocks on a few of the boys, just to warm them up.

Warne chose a place on a bench and put his gear on it.

'Hey, Hollywood,' Hughes said, deadpan. 'You going to stay in that spot?'

'Yeah, why?'

'It used to be Steve Waugh's possie.'

'So?'

'Well, he was dropped, wasn't he? Do you want to climb into his grave so early?'

Everyone laughed, including Warne.

Indian captain Mohammad Azharuddin won the toss and surprisingly sent Australia into bat. The tourists included four pacemen and one spinner, Ravi Shastri. Border decided to drop himself down to number six, promoting Mark Waugh to number four.

Newcomer Bannerjee took three wickets with swing, while Boon batted up to his usual standard and Mark Taylor grafted 59. Mark Waugh failed at second drop, scoring just five. In a disastrous bit of drama for Australia, Boon hit a firm chance back to Shastri. He muffed it, the ball flew to mid-on, and Jones, who had called for the run, was run out. He was finding new and creative ways of being dismissed. In Melbourne, there was evidence he should have been out 'handled the ball', a rare method of dismissal, but he got the benefit of the doubt.

Later, Kapil Dev appeared to have Boon lbw, but umpire Steve Randell ruled in the batsman's favour. The decision caused some rancour amongst the Indians, who felt hard done by in Melbourne. Boon was 89 not out, and Australia was a healthy, if sluggish, four for 234.

That night, the team gathered at the Parkroyal for a Northern Territory food feast, put on by the Territory government. Warne found himself munching into camel steaks, buffalo, kangaroo and crocodile. They all ended up enjoying the offering. Warne went to bed early, this time managing to sleep.

The next morning, the Indians carried on their ill-feeling. When Boon reached his century, only a few of them applauded.

Australian wickets tumbled in the morning, and Warne grew nervous as his time to bat came closer. During discussions with Simpson and a couple of the players, the subject of leg-spinners and their problems came up. Someone again mentioned the sad case of John Watkins, who was so nervous he could barely hit the pitch in his only Test on the Sydney ground, against Pakistan in January 1973. Warne grinned ruefully and inwardly expressed a prayer that it would not happen to him.

He had been on edge waiting to go in, yet he felt more comfortable about batting than bowling. His place in the side was not dependent on his skills with the willow. But still, he wanted to impress with the bat. He understood he had to develop before he could be called an all-rounder at this level. It was one of his aims. Warne had been working hard in the nets on his shots and his defensive technique. The eighth wicket—Craig McDermott—fell at 269 and Shane felt that nervous surge.

At five minutes past midday on 3 January, a chubby Warne walked out onto an arena for his country for the first time at Test level. A few remarks about his condition greeted him from slim New South Wales supporters resentful of his selection over Whitney. He had lost little weight from those fish-and-chips days on his first trip to the UK in 1989. But the overall reception for the newcomer was friendly enough.

Boon engineered most of the strike for a while and the spinner wondered if he was ever going to score. It took him twenty-seven minutes, but with quiet encouragement from Boon, who had himself gone into a shell at the other end, Warne accumulated 20 in seventy-one minutes after facing sixty-seven balls. Kapil Dev then snared him caught behind. It was a good debut with the bat and lifted his confidence a bit. There were many times when he had scratched around at sub-district level and done worse.

Reid, a true batting rabbit, was soon out and Australia was dismissed for a mediocre 313, Boon unconquered on 129. Without question, the little Tasmanian had established himself as Australia's best and most consistent batsmen—against all comers.

Warne came back onto the field feeling more keyed up than he ever had running out for the Saints as a footballer, despite the lack of motivation in the dressing room.

'Hey, Warnie,' Border yelled. 'Make sure you don't do a Johnny Watkins on us.'

The debutant grinned. The remark, typical of the chippie, up-front humour in the team, relaxed him just a fraction. When the Indian innings began, his hands started sweating—a spinner's nightmare. It made the ball hard to grip. Whenever he touched the ball, he became aware of his damp palms, more so than ever before. Maybe this was Watkins's problem twenty seasons earlier, he thought. Warne was comforted by the knowledge that there was a buffer of three star quicks between him and his first overs in a Test. He might get ten or so overs. Then again, on current form, the others could roll the Indians for 150, and he wouldn't bowl at all.

The Indians lost Sidhu for 0, caught with panache low-down and left-handed in slips by Mark Waugh off McDermott. Soon after, the injury-prone Reid pulled the intercostal muscle between two lower ribs on his right side. He bowled the last two deliveries of his fourth over at slow-medium pace. The lean and lanky Western Australian walked sadly from the field. It left Border with a vastly different bowling equation.

The wicket was sluggish, tending to keep low and unhelpful to the three main bowlers left, McDermott, Hughes and the novice Warne. Mark Waugh could always be used. Border himself might have a trundle. With the three strikers to call on, Border would have used Warne judiciously, but there was less flexibility now.

The captain threw Warne the ball after fewer than twenty overs. With Reid in full flight, it might have been at forty or not at all, given the way he had been performing, and the way McDermott had begun in this game.

Warne was more tense than he had ever been, but somehow, mechanically, he managed to run in and deliver. The Indians, used to fine spin as much as speed, were unfazed, yet cautious. He wasn't like a spinner from the subcontinent. This tubby figure was feeling the pressure of his initial effort, yet he still stepped up aggressively and kept coming in hard whether his previous ball had been despatched beyond fielders or not. Occasionally, just every so often, he tweaked it like somebody on a real turner in Calcutta.

In his first spell, he could have taken a wicket on four occasions, as Shastri, himself a spinner, and the experienced Manjrekar pushed at the tight, probing deliveries. They began to grip and turn. Wisely, the Indians didn't attempt to blast him out of the park. Warne was bowling too well not to have picked up an early wicket. Instead, they stroked, nudged and padded him out of the attack. Sanjay Manjrekar fell to Hughes again caught by Waugh at slip. India was two for 103 at stumps on Friday evening.

That night the team attended speedster Geoff Lawson's testimonial dinner, but slipped away early to prepare for day three. Rain and bad light disrupted play. Only thirty-five overs were bowled and India crawled along at 2 an over to reach two for 178. Warne continued to bowl steadily, but missed an opportunity for a straightforward return catch from Shastri on 66, which would have given him one for 30. He was disappointed. By the end of the day, he had sent down eighteen overs for not much more than 2 an over. This was a creditable performance. The longer the game went, the more his nerves began to subside.

Warne relaxed with the others during the many rain breaks and became preoccupied with video games that Boon and Reid had been given for Christmas. Then he watched the races on Sky Channel with Dean Jones, who, sensing that his luck had to change, had a bet and won.

On Sunday, day four, and Australia's third successive day in the field, McDermott broke through to dismiss Vengsarkar for 54 at 197. Then the hapless captain Azharuddin came in, cracked a cover drive for four and then nicked McDermott to Waugh—who had now caught all four wickets. India was four for 201 and reeling.

In strode the sensational teenager Sachin Tendulkar. He played like an attacking veteran and his aggression lifted

Shastri. Together they put on a 196-run partnership in even time. Shastri went after Warne, who received his first belting at senior level. The low, slow wicket, which felt like home to the Indians, allowed them to play a range of shots.

Warne watched as Shastri lifted him over the outfield and Tendulkar stroked him through the gaps and cut him. His furrowed brow became a permanent etch of bewilderment as he bravely sent down over after over. He tried not to look as the century of runs came up against his name on the scoreboard.

His figures had been ruined by the rampant pair, who thrived under the conditions. However, he could take solace from the fact that he wasn't alone, as Waugh, Border and McDermott also took stick.

Australia lost control for the first time in three Tests as Shastri compiled 205, the highest score by an Indian in Tests against Australia. He batted just short of ten hours. He was dropped four times before he lofted a ball off Warne to deep cover, where Jones ran in from the fence and took a safe catch. A wicket was a wicket. The spinner was delighted. It had taken him 40.4 overs, but he had one on the board.

Rain held up play and kept the crowd down as Tendulkar, unconquered with a century, led the players off the ground with India seven for 445. Hughes and McDermott looked weary, having hurled down about eighty overs between them. There was still the prospect of Tendulkar flaying them on a fourth day. He had hardly lifted a ball in playing all the strokes. The young Indian was now the talk of Australian sport.

By contrast, Warne faced the slings and arrows of armchair and bar-room selectors. They claimed that the leggie should never have been given a chance to get so far so quickly. Spinners matured at twenty-nine or thirty, didn't they? And what was this guy Warne's record anyway, apart from a bag against a weakened Windies, who couldn't play spin? The critics were expressing their opinions across the nation, and young Warne wasn't even a medium-sized poppy.

His parents and Ron Cantlon, his first coach, went out to dinner with him that night. They were impressed by his usual upbeat, bright demeanour.

'He was pretty impressive,' Cantlon recalled. 'I was in awe of what he was going through, yet Shane was no different. Sure, he spoke about his nerves. But he was showing a temperament well beyond his years. He had performed well under the circumstances—first game, low, slow wicket, the best batsmen of spin at Test level.'

They chatted about his bad luck and went through all the mental replays Warne would rather forget, except for his capable batting and that first wicket of Shastri.

Monday, the fifth and final day of the game began well for Australia and the last three wickets fell for 38, leaving the Indians on 483, with the magnificent Tendulkar on 148 not out, including 14 fours. He had faced 213 balls in a stay of five hours.

Australia had no chance of victory. It appeared that India would not have time to win, unless Australia's bats collapsed, an unlikely event considering their first-innings form. But, as is the norm in cricket, the unlikely occurred, and four—Marsh, Boon, Waugh and Jones—were sent back for 85. Taylor, who had defended with a struggle for three hours, was out for 35, fifteen minutes before tea. Five for 106, and in some trouble.

Healy joined Border, who was going to have to play one of his back-to-the-wall innings, for which he was a legend in every cricket nation. The keeper scratched around before and after tea playing his unnatural game and gathered 7 off twenty-eight balls. He finally top-edged a catch at fourteen minutes after the tea interval. Australia was six for 114 and sinking.

In came Hughes, looking ungainly yet ready as ever to help out with the bat when Australia most needed it. He put his head down with the captain and stayed at the crease for a 76-minute, 50-run partnership, departing for 21 after succumbing to Tendulkar's part-time 'spinning' at 5.31 p.m. with Australia at seven for 164, still 6 runs in arrears, but afloat. McDermott came and went to a doubtful bat-pad catch.

Warne was experiencing his baptism of fire. This had not been a game where he had been shielded by his captain or hidden in the background as Australia coasted to any easy win. It was 'welcome to the real world' of Test cricket—in the deep end, sink or swim. Now he had to help save a nail-biter, with no less than Australia's cricket saviour of the past decade and more at the other end. Warne was effectively last man in. Bruce Reid was unlikely to bat. Even if he did, his injured side or not, he wouldn't last long.

Warne had no idea what he should do. He wandered to the wicket, his brain on automatic. AB would tell him what do, he thought. *AB will protect me*.

Border could see the new man was almost unhinged.

'This a fucking Test match,' he called to him. 'Come on. Dig in. Don't get out.'

Warne took block. Kapil Dev, who was bowling with Manoj Prabhakar, crowded fielders around him. Warne pushed forward, blocking out the over.

Border hammered a four, which gave him his fifty and took Australia into the lead. With ten minutes to change innings, Warne and Border only had to last a few overs to 5.50 p.m. to ensure a draw. Warne faced seven balls in as many minutes and remained on 1 not out, with Border unbeaten on 53. The captain, at his best in the tough going, had done it again.

At the post-match press conference, Border spoke of Australia's luck in sneaking out of it with a draw, and of Reid's injury upsetting bowling strategies. The batting did not click at all, he noted, and added that all the bowlers struggled on the flatter wicket.

'I was forced to bring on Shane Warne sooner than I would have liked,' Border remarked. He added that he didn't think it was a bad baptism for him. Old leggie Bill O'Reilly—the man Bradman regarded as the finest bowler he ever faced—agreed.

'Warne's short amble to the bowling crease is set for a little cleaning up as he devises his own methods of keeping the ball in line with middle and off stumps,' he wrote in the *Age* and

Sydney Morning Herald, '... yet he does spin the ball, and his leg breaks turn enough to keep any batsman on a sharp lookout.

'In the few overs I saw him bowl, he made no attempt to introduce a wrong 'un, and that impresses me ... His grip, arm and hand action all suggest that somewhere in his private locker he does have a wrong 'un wisely kept under lock and key for the present ... His main problems are now length and direction ...'

O'Reilly offered some advice on field settings, saying that the most important positions stretched along a straight line from short leg to the long-on boundary.

O'Reilly concluded: 'I am prepared to accept him with open arms to the important spin society.'

Second Chance

Warne was chosen in the Victorian side for a Shield game against Tasmania in Hobart, which he looked to as an opportunity to impress the national selectors and maintain his place in the Test XI. He scored 10 and helped wrap up the Tasmanian tail in the first innings with two for 26 off fourteen overs, including seven maidens. His bowling was tight. Victorian captain Simon O'Donnell gave him a longer run in Tasmania's second effort. This time he took one for 66 from twenty-two overs with six maidens. It was a good work-out without being spectacular, demonstrating his length and control.

It was enough for him to hold his place in the twelve for Adelaide starting on 25 January, with Paul Reiffel coming in to replace Reid, but missing out on the final line-up to Whitney. Warne was thrilled at getting a second chance. Azharuddin won the toss and amazed everyone by again sending Australia in to bat. He must have known something that nobody else did.

The home side collapsed for 145, with Marsh and Mark Waugh again both failing at the top of the order. Jones batted well, top-scoring with 41, and the only other player to top twenty was

Hughes, who frustrated the Indians for more than two hours in making 26. Warne looked capable in lasting forty-six minutes, before being stumped for 7 off the left-arm spinner Raju.

India lost Srikanth (17) to McDermott and Manjrekar (2) to Hughes, and was two for 45 at stumps. The next morning McDermott at his best ripped through India's middle order and reduced them to six for 70 before Kapil Dev (56) and Prabhakar (33) fought back and were responsible for helping the tail wag to 225—a lead of 80. McDermott ended with five for 76. Hughes picked up a three for 55 and Whitney two for 68. Warne was given the run he would have expected from Border in Sydney but for Reid's breakdown. He bowled seven overs for 18 runs without taking a wicket.

In Australia's second innings Marsh (5) and Waugh (0) missed out once more, as did Jones (0). Taylor hit 100 and Boon 135 as Australia climbed into a recovery position. It was made stronger by Border (91 not out), Healy (41), Hughes (23), McDermott (21) and Whitney (12), who figured in a gutsy last-wicket stand of 42 with Border, taking Australia's score to 451. Warne made his first Test duck, and was looking at a lean second appearance unless he had some fortune in India's second dig.

He ran into a fighting Indian performance dominated by Azharuddin (106) and Prabhakar (64). Only McDermott's continued brilliance (five for 92), and Hughes's persistence (three for 66) held them up. The Indians ran out of steam 38 short of Australia's total, at 333, when Warne took a catch falling to his left at extra cover from Srinath off McDermott. It gave the speedster ten wickets for the match. Warne took none for 60 off sixteen overs, with one maiden. He was astray at times, but did not disgrace himself.

There was a subdued atmosphere in the Australian dressing room after vice-captain Marsh and Mark Waugh were informed on the morning of the last day that they had been dropped for the Fifth Test. The news humbled Warne, who wondered how many more chances he would be given.

Border was bitter. He failed to take the field on the morning of the fifth day. Instead, he rang Lawrie Sawle and told him what his feelings were. He had built a team based on skill, determination and loyalty. Marsh, with his gritty and courageous opening efforts, had been integral to the team's make-up, as well as being an inspiring, selfless deputy—someone whom everyone respected and admired. Now he was gone. Border was going to miss his strengths, support and his mateship, on and off the field.

The captain was so incensed that he remained in Adelaide 'on business' instead of flying out with the team. Despite the win, team morale was low. It was another aspect of Test cricket that Warne had never expected.

Three and Out

Warne was not surprised to be twelfth man for the Fifth Test in Perth. It was traditionally a better bowling strip for quicks. In came Paul Reiffel. Wayne Phillips and Tom Moody replaced Marsh and Waugh.

Before the game Border told the media he was disappointed to have lost his 'right-hand man' in Marsh. He seemed to be testing his authority and enormous popularity with the media and public against that of the selectors. He could not challenge the selectors' decision, although he could consult them and give his views. Occasionally Border had said, 'I'd like X,' but he kept his distance and accepted the teams presented. Loyalty, a key Border characteristic, had caused him to step over the line. It was a factor about which Warne was going to learn a great deal.

Regardless of his feelings, Border had the professionalism and temperament to be able to put aside problems and concentrate on the job at hand. This was to show India necessary respect by attempting to make it a four–nil victory for Australia by grinding the tourists into the turf at Perth.

Border won the toss and batted. After Phillips and Taylor both failed, Boon and Border restored the situation. The latter was out for 59 with Australia 138 for three. Boon then went on to reach his third hundred in successive Tests—his thirteenth overall and his sixth against India—and help steer Australia to a comfortable 346. India replied with 272.

Tendulkar batted beautifully once more, scoring 114 off 161 balls, supported by Srikanth (34), Manjrekar (31) and More (43). Whitney bowled with control to take four for 68, backing up Hughes (four for 82) and McDermott (two for 47). Warne took some consolation from the fact that only two overs of spin—by Moody, who was hit for 15—were bowled by Australia. Even if Warne had played, the quicks were proving too good for India and he would not have been given much of a run.

In Australia's second innings, Phillips and Taylor again went cheaply, while Boon scored 38, a failure for him. Moody and Jones then came together at 113, with Moody going on to make a dashing century and Jones a more restrained 150 not out to enable Border to declare at six for 367.

India was none for 55 at the end of the fourth day and needed to make 130 a session to win. Azharuddin was determined to go for it in a bid for glory. But Whitney ripped through the line-up to take seven for 27. He managed menacing cut off the seam, as did Reiffel, who picked up two for 34. Again, spinners were ignored, so Warne had lost little, except his place in the XI. Still, he had few rivals in Australian first-class cricket. Peter Taylor had been tried and discarded. There was just Greg Matthews who was having a bumper Shield season with bat and ball, putting him at least into contention for a trip to the subcontinent for Tests against Sri Lanka, on wickets that would suit him.

Warne's figures for the series read sixty-eight overs, nine maidens, 228 runs and just one wicket. The Victorian selectors weren't impressed. They dumped him to twelfth man for the last Shield game of the season, reinforcing his insecurities. It was time for hard work before the next Test series way off in August. Warne had to show faith in himself and maintain that of a few believers, such as Jim Higgs and Simpson at the selection table, and Border at player level.

Warne was keen to play in a minor English League in the winter. Border and Simpson, who had much experience of the genre, were against this as a preparation for the Sri Lanka Tests, and beyond that the big series in Australia against the West Indies in 1992–93.

Warne was told that he should concentrate on becoming super-fit at the Cricket Academy in Adelaide. Ever since those Bristol days three years ago, he had hovered around 95 kilograms. He could have got away with it in any era but the current one, when fitness under the Simpson–Border regime was more important than before.

Australia had become competitive in recent years in part by outstanding fielding, even when big scores were being made against them. If a player were really fit, he could bowl longer, more vigorously and better. The same applied to batting, where the extra run could be taken if the player were strong enough. They added up and Australia was augmenting its Test and one-day scores by going for the extra runs, especially with people like Jones, the Waughs and Healy batting. Also, in conditions of extreme heat and humidity, a player in proper shape would be able to cope much better. Often a batsman lost his wicket from fatigue alone. On the fielding side, extra-fit individuals could swing a match by a high leap or diving save.

Warne got the message. 'I knew I had to do a lot of work,' he told Trevor Grant of the Melbourne *Herald-Sun*. 'Sometimes it looked like a mountainous task, but I realised that if I didn't do it I could get left behind.'

It wasn't as if Warne was unused to getting fit. He knew about training and diet from his football days. Now he had the greatest incentive of all—playing Test cricket. Every day he ran 8 kilometres and began watching his junk food and alcohol intake. As well as working out in Trevor Barker's King Club gym in Cheltenham, he swam and played golf and tennis.

His father remembers him at a sporting club function with

the usual jugs of beer on the table. But in front of Warne there were just jugs of water and a very dry argument. He was showing more discipline than ever before and had lost some weight, though not enough. He was given a lift—and more incentive—in April 1992 when he made the list to tour Sri Lanka, along with off-spinning all-rounder Greg Matthews.

Warne, on an ACB contract, was sent to Adelaide to discuss a fitness program with Richard Done, Rod Marsh's assistant at the Cricket Academy. He was told to come back for a three-month regimen to get super-fit for the tour of Sri Lanka in August.

There was the technicality of whether or not Warne should be readmitted to the academy after his walk-out/expulsion in 1990. Under the circumstances of his senior tour selection, the question became a formality provided there was no repeat of his past behaviour. He was, after all, at that stage the first and only Cricket Academy scholarship winner to play Test cricket. Terry Jenner lectured him about his lifestyle and told him it would be wise to quit partying. The flamboyant young man was not about to contradict anyone or flout the regulations this time around. This was his big chance to atone for his misdemeanours and demonstrate he had what it took for success.

Jenner reminded him that he was privileged to make Test level so fast. He himself had had a long wait at Shield level before getting to the top.

Warne joined the May 1992 intake of fifteen, which included several other highly regarded first-class players—Ricky Ponting, Glenn McGrath, Justin Langer, Mark Atkinson, Ashley Hammond and Darren Webber. Warne became a popular figure, leading the way in circuit training. His attitude had changed since 1990.

Warne's weight had to come down and the method was to combine sensible diet with suitable exercise. He had to apply himself to extra circuit work, which entailed treadmill, running and step-up machine exercises. There were also specific drills for endurance, flexibility and strength, as well as technical work under individual coaches such as Jenner.

Emphasis was placed on the cricketer's needs—speed, agility and power. Most exertion in cricket takes place in short, sharp bursts. On top of this were spells in the gym for muscle tone, and in the pool for upper body strength. The water was good for the shoulder muscles, which bowlers need to keep supple and strong.

After consultation with the Institute of Sport's dietitian, who came from Canberra to consult with him, Warne began a strict diet of sugarless cereal in the morning, fruit and salad during the day, and pasta at night—the latter providing carbohydrate for energy expended during training. Alcohol was forbidden. Warne instead began consuming 3 litres of water a day.

For someone who loved sport, but disliked training, it was arduous. Yet it was exciting to be part of the academy when at night he might find himself discussing the mysteries of spin with some of the greatest conjurers and magicians Australia had produced. These included Terry Jenner, Bruce Yardley, Ashley Mallett and Kerry O'Keefe, not to forget Rod Marsh and Ian Chappell, who knew the complexities from different angles.

Each morning, he would weigh himself first thing. He lost a couple of kilograms in the first weeks and then met progressive 'blocks' to his weight loss as his body adjusted to the change. Over May and June, he began to see the result of his labour. He noticed muscle he hadn't greeted for some time. In keeping with his new image, he had his long hair cut.

Warne celebrated on fruit juice and more water when he hit 90 kilograms, and began to lose surplus flesh around his face. He liked what he saw in the mirror, which became another incentive to keep going. By the end of July, he had dropped at least 14 kilograms to his football-playing weight of 82 kilograms, and felt terrific. At the end of the training program, Rod Marsh, the academy's head coach, rewarded him with a party at his house.

When he boarded the plane for Colombo in August, Warne was satisfied he had given himself every chance of slipping back into the Test XI.

4

A Step forward in Sri Lanka

Burying the Hatchet

Sri Lanka, the so-called 'tear drop of India', had had terrorist trouble in the decade leading up to the Australian team's tour beginning in August 1992. The civil strife was hottest in the north and east where the government was fighting Tamil separatists. In the south, there were problems with the JVP, an extreme nationalist group, not unlike Cambodia's brutal Khmer Rouge. Jeff Crowe's New Zealanders had been the previous team to brave the trip.

Their tour was cut short in April 1987 when a terrorist bomb ripped apart a Colombo bus station, killing more than a hundred people and injuring twice that many. After a team vote, New Zealand decided to abandon its tour, much to the chagrin of the captain, Crowe, who realised that pulling out would reflect badly on Sir Lanka and put its cricket development back years.

In 1989, Australia cancelled a planned tour on advice from the Department of Foreign Affairs, which feared the team could be a target, especially for the JVP. It had a policy of grabbing headlines with its bombing. Three years on, Sri Lanka was deemed 'safe'.

Border and others were keen to atone for their collective failure on their last subcontinental tour in Pakistan in 1988. In the acrimonious First Test there, which Australia lost by an innings, the team threatened to return home because of 'biased' umpiring and a doctored wicket.

'In Pakistan, we let things get to us a bit and it distracted from the way we played,' a contrite Border noted at a press conference on arrival in Colombo. 'We let ourselves down.'

That tour was a low point in Border's career and recent Australian cricket. Channel Nine's '60 Minutes' program sent reporter Mike Munro to Pakistan for a hatchet job. The resulting segment in the high-rating national Sunday-night slot did its best to portray the team as a bunch of whingeing losers. Five years on, the captain wanted no repeats.

The Australian Cricket Board saw an opportunity to give the team a combative run up to a Test series against the world's top side, the West Indies. The tour would also be useful in blooding young talent, and experimentation.

The axe had fallen on Bruce Reid, not to be risked on a back-wrenching tour; Geoff Marsh; Peter Taylor; Steve Waugh; and, remarkably, Merv Hughes. Hughes had become the nation's most consistent bowler, taking 19, 34, 15, 19 and, most recently, 22 wickets—against India at 23 runs a wicket in the previous Australian summer—in his past five series. The prime reason given for his exclusion was a minor hernia operation. As Hughes had declared himself available for the tour, it was rumoured that he had been disciplined by a very trim group of selectors for not keeping his weight down.

His ample paunch and 'wild-man' image had caused Hughes to be underestimated. Yet his bowling statistics rather than his waist measurements were telling an impressive story. He was almost surreptitiously becoming one of the greatest Australian speedsters of all time. The run, the pot belly, the clown's moustache and ocker demeanour had fooled the public and the opposition for some time. Merv was becoming the finest match-winner since Dennis Lillee, especially with his capacity to come back for a second spell with an old ball and take a vital wicket or two.

Damien Martyn, aged twenty, a dashing right-hand bat from Perth, was the new boy and youngest in the squad. He had leapt over several others in the growing Australian batting talent pool, including Darren Lehmann, Michael Bevan, Matthew Hayden, Jamie Siddons and the injured Michael Slater. All of these players deserved a good shot at Test standard, having shown potential at the competitive first-class level. Not since the 1950s had Australia seen such a glut of talent with the willow.

Hayden, a big, strong left-handed opener, had scored 1028 runs at 54.11 in 1991–92. Lehmann had come in with 846 at 56.40, with Martyn on 822 at 51.38. Such similar figures made ranking impossible. The selectors had to look at less quantifiable yet more definitive factors such as courage, patience and temperament.

The upright, technically correct Martyn looked like a shorter Greg Chappell. He had an additional touch of brilliance and insouciance, which made him appear advanced for his years. Martyn seemed a fraction more accomplished than the others at this point. He had not been hurt by playing under Bob Simpson's coaching at Leicestershire during 1991, when he scored an unbeaten half-century against the West Indies, who were then touring England. The lad handled the pace with apparent ease. This performance made an impression on Simpson, who was looking ahead to the ultimate test of a further series against the bruising speed of the Caribbean bowlers.

Two seasons previously, Martyn had missed a trip to Sri Lanka with the AIS Cricket Academy because he was about to make his first-class debut with Western Australia. The only other player from the academy not to go on that 1990 tour was Shane Warne, who was being disciplined. Now they were both in Sri Lanka with high hopes and nervous expectations.

Net Profit

Greg Matthews faced Warne in the practice nets and three time hoisted him high in the outfield without difficulty.

'You're giving 'em too much air,' Matthews said. 'Push 'em through a bit. These wickets don't bite. There's no point tossing them so high.' Later, when Dean Jones was batting, Matthews bowled at him with Warne, and demonstrated what he meant with his low-trajectory off-spin.

With this advice from Matthews, who had taken the young Victorian under his wing, Warne began to beat the bat. In the days before the First Test, his bowling in the nets steadily improved and the tour selection committee was gaining confidence in him.

Neverthless, he was left out of the one-dayers. But Border, as usual, supported him for a Test spot. This was despite Warne having been dropped from the Victorian state side at the end of the 1991–92 season, and the fact that he hadn't played a first-class game for six months.

'I think he's got to play,' Border told the media. 'With the wicket starting to turn [on day four or five], Shane could be a bit more of a handful than one of the medium-pacers.' He added with some prescience: 'The idea is that he could be really handy as the tour progresses if he gets into some sort of form. Going into a Test match without having bowled [in a tour match] might be a big ask. But the view is that he could be a bit of a trump card as the game progresses.'

It was a critical moment for Warne in terms of selection strategy. He had taken only one wicket in two Test appearances, yet had bowled better than the figures suggested. If the selectors were serious about using a wrist-spinner against the West Indies, logic dictated that this was the moment to help him establish his form and confidence.

The tour committee showed the courage of their reasoning, if not their convictions. Warne was selected. In a way, it was an act of faith. He had shown his commitment by shedding weight like a regular at a health farm, and had come up looking like an athlete. Simpson and Border would return the compliment and give him a chance. Warne was elated, but began to worry about his performance. He believed in his own skills, but, as yet, had next to nought to show for them at the top level.

Border won the toss at the Sinhalese Sports Ground and batted first on the greenest wicket he had seen for some time on the subcontinent. Moody, who had earned his place after that last Test against India, was experimented with as an opener and looked uncomfortable against the military-medium Sri Lankans. He was soon out lbw for one. Boon and Taylor consolidated and took the score to 84, when Boon departed. Then a rot set in and seven players were out in a procession back to the pavilion.

Warne joined Healy at eight for 162 and gave his best batting display yet under pressure, scoring 24, his highest Test score. Whitney, a true number eleven, showed his usual grit and managed 13, also his best Test score. Healy ran out of support and remained 66 not out while Australia struggled to an ordinary 256. On such a wicket and against an unformidable attack, 400 would have been respectable. It was not an auspicious start to the series.

McDermott and Whitney expended energy in a vain attempt to extract a hint of life from the false greenery. It was left to the subtle movement of Mark Waugh to remove Hathurusinghe with a ball outside off stump, which he nudged to the diving Taylor at second slip. Waugh induced the same shot from the patient and composed Mahanama. The steady Matthews removed the dangerous de Silva—who had flayed the Aussie attack during the one-dayers—for 6, when he shuffled across the crease to a ball which spun nicely into his pads.

At three for 137, the roly-poly Ranatunga joined Gurusinha and the two left-handers nudged and pushed until shortly after tea. Border brought Warne on. It was his second spell, having sent down four overs before lunch. In one, the slight Mahanama had put him away for three confidence-sapping fours in succession—a full toss flicked through mid-wicket and two short balls slashed through point. But that was hours ago and in the back of the bowler's mind. Warne now joined Matthews in tandem.

Ranatunga pushed back the first ball. Warne decided on a little loop with his second, but gave it too much and it ended up lobbing gently. The batsmen cross-batted it over long-off. It sailed on and on for six.

Warne grimaced and hurried in to bowl another faster ball on a goodish length. Ranatunga smashed it straight to cover. No run. Warne, wanting to put that six behind him, rolled in. But the resultant slow spin into the left-hander allowed a pugnacious cover drive, which climbed high out of the ground.

Warne stood with his hands on hips, stunned and not knowing where to look. The little crowd's siesta was over. Matthews said something, Jones called encouragement and Border clapped his hands, as if to say, 'It's nothing.' Matthews kept the batsmen quiet in the next over. The haughty Ranatunga was set for a feast against Warne, slogging with the spin through mid-wicket for four, and then belting him over mid-on for another boundary.

Four dot balls influenced Border to give Warne a third over. Ranatunga said 'Thank you' and smashed the hapless leggie over backward square leg for 6 more. Next, just to show he had refinement, he late-cut him with finesse for 3, taking his personal tally in just three overs against Warne to 29.

Australia was reeling. It was reminiscent of a hammering Craig McDermott had taken in the recent one-dayers. Border spent the following over from Matthews pondering whether to pull Warne out of the firing line, but tossed the ball to him for a fourth dose. Ranatunga grinned at everyone, as Matthews ran up to Warne and told him to repeat what he had been doing in the nets. The Australian fielders shouted encouragement. Warne dived in, spearing the ball too flat. Ranatunga swung and missed. He prodded uncertainly at ball three, ignored the fourth, slashed at the fifth for no run and blocked the last.

The Australians applauded the bowler as if he had taken two wickets instead of delivering a competent maiden. It was a show of solidarity for him. They feared the shock of the attack could crush his spirit.

Matthews was also plundered. The third ball of Warne's fifth over was misjudged in flight by Gurusinha, who smashed at it and lifted it half a metre. The bowler flung out his right hand, but failed it hold it. So near, yet so far. Had he held it, he would have been ecstatic. Instead, he shuffled back to his position behind square at the end of his over wringing a stinging hand.

Matthews contained Ranatunga and Warne bowled number six of the spell. So far he had flung down a couple of flippers to no effect, but as yet had not delivered a wrong 'un. Sensing he had nothing to lose because Border would soon replace him, he decided to try one on the unhelpful wicket. It was right for length, but came back a fraction too far for an lbw. However, it beat the belligerent Ranatunga, who had not picked it. Warne showed all the anguish of the unlucky bowler, staring down the wicket. Ranatunga just grinned, untroubled by his ignorance of the leggie's armoury.

After six overs for 41 runs, Warne was replaced by McDermott. The new ball was due, but Border elected to stay with the old so as to keep Matthews running at one end. The off-spinner was performing too well to be taken off and looked the most likely to take wickets. He finished with one for 55 off twenty-one overs, with five maidens, in a good day's work. Sri Lanka, however, was looking comfortable on three for 265 at stumps on day two, 9 runs ahead and with plenty of batting to come.

Day three meant no respite until Sri Lanka had piled on 367. Ranatunga, on 127, overbalanced trying to lunge at a Matthews full toss and succeeded in top-edging the ball to short fine leg where Warne took a good catch falling forward. It was small consolation for Warne, and indeed the Australian team.

The indefatigable Matthews struck again next ball by bowling Ataputtu for 0, and this brought the tiny Sri Lankan keeper, Romesh Kaluwitharane, to the crease. He had kept poorly in this, his first Test. Now he was facing a hungry Matthews, who rushed in, only to see the ball padded away. Kaluwitharane then proceeded to demolish Warne, smashing six boundaries from his first eight scoring shots. Although the leggie took a hammering, he wasn't alone as the batsman plundered 26 fours in a score of 132 off just 158 balls—an impressive strike rate of 83 per hundred.

Only McDermott could beat him and did so repeatedly with a series of leg cutters. The pocket-sized Sri Lankan responded by driving the fast bowler over mid-off, carving him through the covers and hoicking him through mid-wicket. The crowd built to 5000 as word spread through Colombo that something extraordinary was happening as a new hero worked his magic with supple wrist work. Kaluwitharane brought up three figures with a vicious pull for four through mid-wicket off Mark Waugh. Ten or so well-wishers ran on to the ground, some shoving money in the young man's pockets. Sri Lanka closed at eight for 547, its highest Test score ever—a lead of 291.

Again, Matthews was the container, finishing with a yeoman-like three for 93 off thirty-eight overs, with eleven maidens. Warne's figures were none for 107 from twenty-two overs, with two maidens. He had now bowled in five Test innings for just one wicket. His self-confidence tank was running on empty. All he had left was Border's faith in him.

The Long Haul Back

Australia began the long haul back, losing Moody for 13 after seventy-six minutes of bogged-down batting, an unusual condition for the lanky West Australian, who had built a reputation in English county cricket for rapid scoring. Opening had thwarted his desire to stand and deliver to second-rank trundlers. Now he had to curtail his instincts in order to give the team a start, which meant slow scoring. He lost concentration, had a swish and was bowled.

This brought Boon, the rock of Australia, to the crease to settle down to a three-hour stay. Then, at 107, Australia lost the determined Taylor for 43 and Jones came in. He was another Australian down on self-esteem after a poor season against India. But he was out to show that if a tyro such as

Kaluwitharane could do it, so could he. Usually Jones built an innings on sharp ones and twos, with the occasional three and four. This innings was the reverse, as he drove and cut his way to nine boundaries before running himself out at 57 after facing eighty-two balls.

It was great promise cut short, yet he had contributed. Border pointed out before the innings started that if everyone made 50, or two of them topped a century, then they were in with a rough show. Five hundred was the target and with four for 233 on the board, it looked achievable.

While waiting to bat, Border chatted with Warne, who was down. 'I really don't know whether I'm good enough,' the spinner said. 'One wicket for more than 300.'

Border at first didn't respond. He just squinted at the game.

'I really sweated to get right for this,' Warne complained. 'I didn't have a drink for four months. And for what?'

Border turned and looked at him. He knew what it was like to be humiliated as a batsman, a bowler and as a member of beaten teams, but, unlike Warne, he also knew the feeling of climbing back to the top.

'Mate,' he said. 'I'm a big believer in guys who keep trying, keep putting in, keep working hard. If you keep hanging in there, one day it will click for you.'

A wicket fell and Border was on his way out to bat. He lasted a little over half an hour and was out for 15, with the score at 269. In what was most likely a striking example for Warne at the time, Border was wearing his long run without a century bravely, despite comments from sections of the media who were playing up the three-figure drought. Mark Waugh then drove his way to an effortless 56, followed by Healy with 12. Australia was seven for 361 and struggling with a lead of just 70, not nearly enough on this wicket. Matthews then put in a three-hour stint for 64, ably supported by McDermott, who collected 40 runs from forty-eight balls. Eight for 417 and 126 ahead. The effort had been commendable, but Australia still looked beaten.

After the pep talk from Border, Warne began his innings with more determination. However, he looked like running out of partners as Matthews departed at 431, bringing last-man-in Whitney to the crease. Somehow, 'the Whit' wafted and prodded for fifty-one minutes, making 10 not out, while Warne batted with the composure born of a player who was facing his problems with some resolve.

He made 35. The score of 471 left Australia 180 ahead. Not enough, the neutral pundits said with a shake of their heads. Maybe just enough, Border told his charges, adding his usual logical corollary, 'if we perform at our best in the field'.

Sri Lanka's openers, Mahanama and Hathurusinghe, started as if they were going to knock off the required runs by themselves. The target of 181 had to be reached in fifty-eight overs, which meant a fraction more than 3 an over. This was obtainable if the batsmen grafted with pushes and prods. Instead, they had reached 76 off eleven overs when Border introduced Matthews to put a brake on proceedings as much as anything. Sri Lanka now had forty-seven overs to score 105 for victory and had reduced the rate from 3 to 2 runs an over. No batsman needed to raise his weapon in anger and the home team would be make it with ease.

Matthews appeared to have other ideas. He snaffled Mahanama by forcing him to push forward and Boon took a reflex catch at silly mid-off. But there were still nine wickets to go. In the next over, however, the Australians felt they had a sniff of a chance when Moody swooped on the ball at mid-off and ran out Hathurusinghe.

Aravinda de Silva had evidently decided he could remove the deficit himself. He lived dangerously for three-quarters of an hour, while Gurusinha dropped anchor. De Silva brought gasps from the crowd and groans from Matthews as he swotted and missed a lot, but managed to swipe 7 fours on his way to a whirlwind 37 from just thirty-two deliveries.

It would have been considered a grand effort in a one-day game, but this was a Test. With every swish, hit or miss,

Australia's hopes were kept alive. De Silva seemed intent on showing McDermott who was boss. He hooked the fast bowler for four, then gave him the charge to hit him over mid-on. The ball miscued high in the air for Border to dash 30 metres and take the catch. Three for 127.

Ranatunga rolled to the wicket, chatty and smiling. He was cocky. Winning was a formality. In McDermott's next over he moved into a correct yet casual drive straight to Border, who swallowed it. The little first-innings hero waddled off with a duck. His grin had gone and so had Sri Lanka's composure. Yet there was no need for panic with 49 to win and plenty of wickets and overs in hand.

Matthews continued with renewed enthusiasm, ripping through the middle order and into the tail. He took three wickets in five overs from the scoreboard end, from which he had bowled unchanged since tea.

Success at Last

The score was now seven for 147. Sri Lanka was 23 runs short of victory, with more than enough overs in hand. Border now made one of the most important decisions of his cricketing life and certainly his Test captaincy, as he signalled to Warne with a wag of his head and tossed the ball to him. With a handful of runs to play with and still three wickets to claim, it was a critical moment for both of them. If Border's personal calculations about the young Victorian were wrong, this move would banish him from the Test arena for some time, if not for ever.

There was another consideration at stake. If Warne was destroyed and Sri Lanka won, it could signal the end of Border's Test career. There were some in the media already baying for it. Despite maintaining his 50-plus average, he was no longer insulated from criticism by regular Test centuries. His form had dropped him back to the ranks of mortals. He was gambling once again on his uncanny sense of knowing the right man to show strength under pressure and lift for the occasion. He had long ago marked Warne this way. Now he would see.

Warne and Border took a long time settling the field and so unsettling the batsmen. Gurusinha had a serious mid-pitch discussion within incoming batsman Wickremasinghe. Warne looked round the field, tossed the ball from hand to hand, took a breath and then bowled.

His first delivery was right on the spot and spun past a groping bat. Warne rolled his shoulders, glared down the pitch and grabbed the throw back from Healy, who led the applause for the effort. Warne wheeled in again, plonked the ball on the same spot and caused a cautious one-bounce snick to slip. The bowler looked eager now, sensing something.

The third ball was pitched wide enough to entice a drive. It hit the leading edge and shot away towards cover, where the fleet-footed Mark Waugh covered ground and made a tough catch look regulation.

At eight for 147, the game had swung the visitors' way for the first time in five days play. Gurusinha, the anchor, saw the desperation of the moment and cracked a boundary off Matthews. Yet somehow the Sri Lankans miscalculated and left new-man Anurasiri on 1 facing Warne, who had put every ball on the spot so far. The bowler again pushed an orthodox break a fraction wide, tempting the batsman, who took the bait and attempted a cover drive. He popped the ball up on the off side to Mark Waugh, who darted back from silly point to take another catch.

The packed house had gone silent in despair. They had come excited about a Sri Lankan victory. Now this seemed a forlorn hope. Warne waited at his mark as the last man, Ranjith Madurasinghe, came to the crease with another 25 still needed. Somehow, he managed to see out the rest of Warne's over, giving Gurusinha the strike.

Gurusinha took 2 fours off Matthews, lifting the score to 164 and the hopes of a nation high. But Matthews then sent down four good balls and bottled Gurisinha up. Again, the number eleven had to face Warne. For the first time at this level, the leg-spinner looked dangerous with every ball. Madurasinghe obligingly lobbed the first ball of his third over to Matthews, who gleefully took the catch. The Aussies were jubilant, if not staggered, by their unlikely victory.

Warne had sent down thirteen deliveries for three wickets without conceding a run. His final figures were three for 11 off 5.1 overs, with three maidens. At last he had something to savour, and it was sweet. After the game, Border summed up his decision to offer Warne the chance.

'It was a gamble and it paid off,' he said. 'You've put the whole lot on the red and it comes up.'

It was the leg-spinner's first taste of success at the highest level. Those last three wickets had been a decisive factor in Australia's 16-run victory. It confirmed Border's faith in him as a spinner with the potential to be a regular member of the Test team.

Matthews was named Man of the Match. His seven-wicket haul was his best since bagging ten in Madras in 1986, and he was the adhesive for the middle and lower orders in both innings. He had played a huge part throughout the game in a top all-round performance. Instead of boasting to the press after the game, he spoke of 'the brotherhood of Australian slow bowlers'.

'We took half the wickets in the game,' he noted. 'It shows there is a place in Australian cricket for two slow bowlers in the side. Shane and I have talked about it. We're not in competition. I am a genuine all-rounder and he's going to develop into a genuine all-rounder.'

Speaking of Warne's acceptance of Border's offer to bowl at the end, Matthews added:

'He could have just crawled into a hole and died. But he won us a Test match. And he didn't win it by darting them in. He won it by giving them a rip and tossing them up. We had a talk about it [before the last day] and he had some doubts. But he put his hand up when it mattered most.'

Warne then spoke of his true feelings about his gruelling effort to make the grade, including his shedding of those 14 kilograms.

'How did you feel when you were hammered in the first innings?' a reporter asked.

'Yeah, well I thought about all that beer and junk food I had put aside,' he said with a rueful grin. 'I wondered what all the hard work had been about and I asked myself a few questions like, "Are you good enough to play this cricket?"'

The answer to that now was not 'no', but a definite 'maybe'. Border had the last word and trotted out a useful cliché, which he had been employing occasionally since he led the Australians to an Ashes victory in 1989: 'It's good to get the monkey off your back.' In 1989, it was winning the Ashes in Headingley eight years after Botham had embarrassed the Aussies there. In 1992, it was winning one on the subcontinent.

'It's a five-day game and we just went the whole distance,' Border remarked. 'It's a huge kick for everyone. We didn't play really good cricket, but we came out winners. That's what makes a good team. That's what the West Indies have done time and time again.'

The team celebrated into the early hours. Warne, fatigued, yet a lot happier with life, slept well for the first time while on tour.

Tame Draw and Captain's Comeback

Warne must have thought the great god of cricket was conspiring against him when he injured a heel and couldn't play in the Second Test at Colombo's Khettarama Stadium. Just when he had run into form he was sidelined. He looked on as Australia failed again with the bat for a miserable 247. Again only Jones with a lively 77 and Matthews a stubborn 55 offered respectability.

Sri Lanka wasn't up to a repeat of their first innings in the previous Test and they folded to nine declared for 258.

McDermott bowled at his best taking four for 53, while Dodemaide with two, Whitney, Moody and the always reluctant-to-bowl Border shared the remaining five.

In the second Australian knock, Moody at last got runs (54), but it was left to Jones riding his luck and the reliable Matthews (51) to lift the team tally. Jones survived a stumping chance at 0, a dropped catch at slip at 41, and a missed catch at 69. When Jones was on 98 in the second-last over before lunch, rain began to fall. Jones tickled the ball round the corner and Healy called him through for a quick single. Keeper Kaluwitharane grabbed the ball and tried to hit the unmanned stumps at the non-striker's end. The ever-alert Healy called Jones through for his third Test century against Sri Lanka and his eleventh in all. Sri Lanka had 286 to make to win, but they never considered it seriously. The Test petered out to a tame draw with Sri Lanka left on two for 136, such a contrast to the previous finish.

Warne regained his place at Whitney's expense in the line-up for the Third Test, still with personal doubts. He had been disappointed not to play in the Second Test, yet the injury had given him time to reflect, perhaps too much, on his capabilities.

He had, after all, only knocked over 9, 10, Jack, in the First Test, and this was after Matthews had set up victory with a piercing performance when he dissected the Sri Lankan middle order. Were all the congratulations he received more out of relief than acknowledgment of a top effort, he wondered. He still had a lot to prove to himself.

The Third and final Test began with a mess of problems in the batting department. Moody had yet to convince anyone he was an opener. Mark Taylor was struggling, Mark Waugh had scored one fifty and two ducks, Border was out of sorts, and even Boon was down on form. Jones and Matthews had carried the team, but only the latter could afford to rest on his laurels. Many regarded Jones's place as precarious after his dismal form against India. In terms of Warne's career, Border's form was crucial. If he were to drop away and retire or be pushed out, one of the leggie's main props would be kicked away. Border, an under-performed but capable Test spinner himself, knew the value of the art and in nurturing talent. Spinners needed assistance and protection far more than the pace bowlers, who were rarely belted out of the game.

Where the pace man could reply to an attack with a throat ball, the spinner was far more vulnerable. No spinner in history has ever physically intimidated an opponent. He is left with the variety of delivery and mind games for retaliation. The old boxing adage of 'It's not how you win, but how you get off the deck when knocked down' applies far more to the spinner than the pace bowler. Enticing a batsman to use his feet or stand and attack is part of the spinner's web.

Border himself knew well what it was like to be smashed out of an attack by heavy hitters such as Botham and Richards, and what it did for a man's confidence for months and even years. If he—Border—was pushed out to the land of legends, Warne might not have the help on the field or at the selection table. Although this was not uppermost in his mind, the leggie was rooting for his captain in this Test.

Australia began disastrously with Moody going for 0, Taylor for 19, Boon 18, Jones 11, and Waugh getting a third duck for the series. The score was four for 58, with Border and Matthews, two gritty left-handers, at the wicket. One was established as a great bat; the other a much underrated performer, whose career had been held back by events off the field and personality clashes rather than his efforts on it. They put together a fine partnership of 127 in 144 minutes before Matthews was run out for 57 by a smart throw by Mahanama at point, which hit the wicket at the bowler's end.

During the fightback, no one in the 4000 at the Tyronne Fernando Stadium on the outskirts of Colombo applauded harder than Warne. These two had given him enormous support and he was delighted and inspired by their systematic reconstruction of a near-ruined innings. Healy, another cricketer building a reputation as a fighter, joined Border and continued on from where Matthews had been forced to leave off.

Border, playing with controlled aggression, had sailed to 96 at the drinks break in the final session. The first ball after the break was a generous full toss from left-arm spinner Don Anurasiri. Border used his feet and crashed it through the covers with sweet timing. Long before it reached the boundary Warne and the rest of the team in the dressing room were standing, cheering and applauding. Again, there was some relief in this exuberant show of appreciation. No one who ever led Australia had shown more dedication than this man. His return to form was a boost for every one.

At 106, Border played a rash shot and was bowled through the gate by Ramanayake. He cursed under his breath on the walk back. He had wanted a big hundred, for the team and for himself. It was century number twenty-four, placing him equal with Greg Chappell as the second Australian behind Bradman's twenty-nine. During the innings, Border also equalled Sunil Gavaskar's achievement of passing 50 seventy-nine times in Tests. The former Indian great's record of thirty-four Test centuries in 125 Tests would remain unchallenged, but Border was closing on Gavaskar's 10 122 runs. He had 9697, with Australia due to play twenty-three Tests in the next eighteen months.

Despite the four-year wait since a century in Pakistan, Border had made 21 fifties and had averaged 45 in the interim, which also saw him declare on himself in the 90s. Through it all he had maintained an overall Test average of more than 50. This latest milestone ensured Border's captaincy through the summer against the West Indies. Later the captain, deadpan, told journalists that 'it was good to get that monkey off my back'. The media wondered how much of a zoo was still clinging to Border's sturdy shoulders.

Healy carried on to 71, Warne made only 7, but the tail wagged a bit and the next morning Australia reached 337. Not a substantial score, but unexpected after at once stage being four for 58.

Rain affected the rest of the game, as Sri Lanka battled to nine for 274 declared. Mahanama (50), de Silva (58), Ranatunga

(48) and Tillekeratne (82) batted well, but could not carry on to a big score, which would have challenged the visitors. McDermott, as ever, put in a tough, fitness-stretching stint in the sweat-bowl, taking four for 89, and was backed up by the steady Dodemaide with four for 65. It was not, however, a strip for slowies. Matthews (one for 64) and Warne (none for 40) were left to support/containment roles.

Australia lost four for 9 in its second dig in one of the worst Test starts ever. Taylor (3), Moody (2), Boon (0) and Waugh (0, his fourth successive quack) were unpadded inside twenty-two minutes.

Jones struggled for eighty-one minutes for 21, but was out at 60. Border was joined by Matthews and they repeated their first-innings revival by taking the score to 132 before the captain departed for a powerful 78 off 140 balls. Healy combined with Matthews for a 129-run partnership, hauling their side away from danger as Australia reached eight for 271. Matthews fell for 96 and the game drifted to another draw, before Warne could have some batting practice.

Australia went home with a one–nil winning score line, but in reality had a multitude of problems to sort out before taking on the West Indies in a few months time. The batting order had to be redesigned. McDermott was the solitary bowler certain to line up against Richie Richardson and co. Only Border, Taylor, Boon, Healy, McDermott and probably Matthews, because of his outstanding tour, could be sure of stripping for the First Test in Brisbane on 27 November. This meant that half the team places were up for grabs.

The scramble for inclusion began even before the weary warriors had returned from Sri Lanka. Despite his two Tests and breakthrough in the wicket-taking department, Warne's position was shaky. The selectors at home would take into account the bottom line—averages—when they sat down to discuss the new team.

The spinner's figures on paper didn't look healthy—four for 386 at an average of 96.50 per wicket. He had so far sent down

637 balls in Test cricket. He was picking up a batsman every 160 balls, or 26.4 overs. It was hardly enough to engender confidence in the armchair selectors, who were unlikely to rush to make decisions in his favour. The ray of hope was captain Border, who would keep the faith as far as he could.

The question was whether Warne would have support in those notorious phone hook-ups to decide who would face the might of the West Indies.

5

Windies Warned

Three-Way Splits

'This is the most open side for years,' Border said at the conclusion of the Sri Lanka tour and so fired the starter's gun for eighty or ninety first-class players to scramble to make Shield and Test selection. In batting, Taylor, Border and Boon were 'safe', leaving three places to be filled by Steve Waugh, Mark Waugh, Jones and Martyn. An outsider such as Michael Bevan would have to do something spectacular to slip in. Yet there would be opportunities in two Shield games and a possible two further matches against the Windies before the First Test. That meant from four to eight innings to perform.

The same applied to the bowling department, although this seemed less open than the batting. McDermott, Hughes and Reid picked themselves if in form and fit. This left just one spot for a fourth quick, or a spinner. On previous form, Reiffel would have to be considered. But for variety, the selectors would lean to a spinner. Three had a chance: Matthews, Warne and May.

Border's words gave hints about his preferences. After Sri Lanka he hoped that Matthews could carry his form into a home series and not be 'psyched out' by the West Indies. It was a revealing remark. Reading between the lines indicated that he had his doubts about Matthews handling the Windies' heavy hitters, who had blasted him on Australia's last tour of the Caribbean. The spinner had done well in Colombo, but this was a vastly different competition.

He extended the hint when talking to Trent Bouts of the *Herald-Sun*: 'If he [Matthews] starts the season off well, he could have a real say in how the series goes.' This was another way of saying that Matthews could not rest on his Sri Lankan efforts. He did not have a hold on a spot. As if to emphasise his inner feelings, he added:

'I always think he has been in awe of the West Indies. There's almost too much respect.'

While Border thought this way, the selectors had their own individual views, although just one of them, Simpson, had seen Matthews on both tours of the West Indies and Sri Lanka. While the captain's comments raised eyebrows, they were buried with the arrival of the Windies. They had held the Sir Frank Worrell Trophy since 1978, and were bringing six pacemen to defend it. They had no specialist spinner. This seemed to confirm Australian thinking that there was just a chance that they might be uncomfortable against a sharp-turning spinner. But he would have to be courageous and good. They would make mincemeat out of anything less.

Three power quicks—Ambrose, Patterson and Benjamin—destroyed Western Australia in the opening game, although both Langer and Martyn showed fearless form and managed 40s. Julian and Angel had five-wicket hauls and Reid came through a game, a matter of some relief to selectors. No one had reached his heights. Could his fragile frame carry him through a full season?

In the state games, none of the spinners was outstanding. In a face-off between Matthews and Warne in Sydney early in November, when New South Wales met Victoria, both showed more form with the bat than the ball, although Warne picked up three impressive scalps—Bevan, Mark Taylor and Mark Waugh. The Victorian bats did him a service by taking 116 off Matthews as they compiled 547, with Wayne Phillips (205) reminding the selectors that he had something special in his temperament, despite his first Test failures.

Matthews could only secure one more wicket two weeks later against Western Australia in Perth. Again, he did better with the bat, yet this was irrelevant. He would not be chosen for his batting.

Tim May, in an early game for South Australia against Queensland, showed that he, too, was having trouble warming up. He collected one for 106. A few weeks later, he caused a flutter with a five-wicket haul against Tasmania, but he had left his run a little late to squeeze out Matthews or Warne.

Warne didn't do anything special in a game against Queensland at St Kilda, picking up Warren Barsby and Matthew Hayden in two different innings. But his control was good and he was inexpensive. On 14 November, chances of selection swung Warne's way when he was chosen for his second Australian XI game against the West Indies in Hobart. His last effort there had lifted him into the Test side and he was hoping for a repeat performance.

Matters didn't go according to plan. The visitors attacked all the bowlers. In his first spell with the ball just before lunch, Warne went for 15 off two overs. Captain Healy read the riot act to the bowlers, telling them that this was not the way to start a season against the West Indies.

After lunch, Warne started off in tandem with Hughes, and the Australians performed better in the field. Warne dropped onto a length. He studied the opposition as he went, taking four good wickets along the way—Phil Simmons, Carl Hooper, Gus Logie and Jimmy Adams. He had a heavy stint of forty-four overs and noticed a few weaknesses in the opposition, which he would try to exploit at the next opportunity, hopefully in a Test. In the Windies' second dig, he was carted a bit, although he bagged Richie Richardson before the captain got going.

Warne was feeling far more confident about his Test chances than a year earlier, when he had also done well, despite the competition. Clearly, the Tests against India, his hard training in the winter at the Cricket Academy, his efforts in Sri Lanka and his continued toil into the new season were paying off.

Among the Aussie bats, Steve Waugh hit an impressive double of 95 and 100 not out, which was sure to win him a place in the Test side. Martyn and Hayden also did well but only Martyn would have a chance of selection. It was too congested at the top of the order for the big Queensland left-hand opener just yet.

In the phone hook-up to select the side for Brisbane, debate centred on Matthews or Warne for the last place in the twelve. John Benaud felt Brisbane would be the wrong place to give Warne his first combat against the world's top side.

'The boundaries are too short,' he said. 'If they start hitting him, it be could a disaster.'

Jim Higgs argued that this was part of the spinner's lot. The size of the ground should not be used as an excuse. Other selectors felt Warne had not quite done enough to pip Matthews. Higgs was outvoted. Matthews was given the nod for the twelve, and Warne missed out. In his heart, he had not expected to get in ahead of Matthews, although many people had excited him by saying he would make it. When his name didn't come up, he was disappointed, yet quickly over it. Having been dropped for the second time, he had the challenge now to get back into the side.

The lucky ones coming in were Reid, Hughes, Martyn and Steve Waugh for Jones, Dodemaide, Moody and Warne. Jones was made twelfth man in a decision which shocked the cricket world, giving the stylish Martyn his first chance. However, no one begrudged him his place. He was sparkling and looked to have a special aptitude for the big time, even before he stepped into it. In the selection phone conferences, Simpson and the West Australian Sawle were particularly keen to blood him.

Martyn let no one down in scoring 36 in the toughest possible initiation against Ambrose and Bishop, but Australia's 293 showed they had progressed little since the Caribbean tour in terms of coping with the awkward pace. Yet the West Indies, apart from Keith Arthurton (157 not out), Brian Lara (58), and Hooper (48), fared little better in accumulating 371 against the efforts of Reid (five for 112) and Hughes (two for 58).

The match was marked by acrimony, brought on by exuberant fielders questioning umpiring decisions and an unpleasant incident involving the brilliant Lara. He vehemently disputed being given out stumped by Healy off Matthews. Fortunately, Richardson was in charge in the dressing room to cool feelings and told his players to concentrate on getting even. Ambrose (five for 66) took him at his word and bowled at his best in Australia's second dig. It was left to Boon to show superb resolution in scoring 111 in a half-hour short of a day—his fourteenth hundred, moving him up level with Ian Chappell—as Australia struggled to 308, leaving the West Indies 231 to win.

McDermott bowled like a man possessed to pick up three quick, early wickets—Haynes (1), Lara (0) and Arthurton (0)—while Reid disposed of Simmons (1), placing the Windies at four for 9.

Border felt they had a chance to secure a surprise first-up win. But after trying to restore his team's fortunes with attack, Richardson knuckled down to fight for a draw. When McDermott removed the wicketkeeper David Williams for 0 and it was six for 96, the task seemed hopeless, but Matthew's incapacity to spin the ball on the last day and wrap up the middle order and tail was Border's greatest disappointment. He had the Caribbean killers on their knees and couldn't deliver the *coup de grâce.* Richardson lasted well into the last hour for 66 and the tail hung on, with Bishop lasting 107 minutes for an unconquered 16.

After the game, Border, still smarting from the electricity of the afternoon, was flowing over with what-might-have-beens. He remarked that 'a spinner such as Shane Warne' could have been invaluable, especially on that last tight afternoon. He thought Australia 'won on points'.

The knock-out capacity was what he wanted.

December to Remember

Border's endorsement of Warne lifted his spirits and hopes as he entered a Shield game against Western Australia at the Junction Oval, St Kilda, early in December 1992. Western Australia had a strong batting line-up, but Warne, showing healthy disrespect for the bristling talent, took five for 49, his best Shield bowling. His bag included Marsh, Langer, Zoehrer, Jo Angel—who could bat—and just one bunny, Bruce Reid.

Warne's confidence was high when Victoria went in chase of WA's 212 and he made a brisk 69—including 5 fours and a mighty six over mid-wicket. The knock excited his St Kilda club-mates and supporters in the respectable little crowd in attendance. Warne partnered Dodemaide in a dashing 103-run stand in just eighty-seven minutes against a strong attack of Reid, Alderman, Angel, Zoehrer (himself a good leggie when he removed his keeper's pads) and Julian, who also bagged five.

The momentum for Warne's recall began to manifest itself in the media, with a range of papers speculating about his chances for the Second Test starting on Boxing Day at the MCG. Some began scrutinising his skills and technique.

'Warne's chief fault, I believe,' wrote Peter Roebuck in Fairfax papers after the Western Australia game, 'lies not so much in a lack of variety or length, as in his direction. He attacks leg stump far more than Mushtaq [the brilliant Pakistani], and accordingly is often hit through or over mid-on, as he has been already this season by Mark Waugh and Richie Richardson.

'If he is to locate the famed blind spot, whose merits were so vociferously advocated by the late and great Bill O'Reilly, it would be well to begin searching around middle and leg stump. Mushtaq's extra spin and hidden googly allows him to direct his attentions wide of off stump. Warne spins less and must bowl straighter, but without allowing batsmen to sweep, or pull or on-drive without fear.'

Roebuck added wryly: 'Even in this drenching summer, he [Warne] has taken wickets. Lord knows how many he would get in a dry country—England, for instance.'

Warne duly replaced Jones in the twelve for Melbourne. He was tipped to get the final nod in front of Matthews. As it happened, he did.

December 1992 proved a big month in the 23-year-old Warne's life in other respects. Apart from being selected for his first Test in front of a home crowd on the MCG, he had his first 'date' with Simone Callahan. He had met Simone, a female mirror-image of himself—attractive, blonde, well-built and bubbly—earlier in the year at a celebrity golf event, where she was a promotions model. He asked for her phone number, but she never heard from him because he lost it.

However, as they were moving in the same trendy nightclub and bar circles—Warne was now drifting from Bayside to South Melbourne, South Yarra, Prahran and the city—they bumped into each other again. Simone played a little hard to get, but Warne was keen. This time he remembered the number, and rang and asked her to lunch. She accepted and their first rendezvous occurred just before the MCG Test. Warne suggested she might like to watch him perform. Simone joined the Melbourne crowd at the MCG hoping to see an upset Australian win against the strong but still vulnerable West Indians.

Instead, it was Australia that looked vulnerable. Before a crowd of 50 000 on the opening day, the home side was soon a shaky four for 115, with Taylor (13), Steve Waugh (38), Boon (46) and Martyn (7) back in the pavilion. Walsh and Ambrose were building a dangerous rhythm, and Australia's hopes rested with its last recognised pair of Border and Mark Waugh. Together they saw out 152 minutes to stumps, Waugh on 63, and Border 51. Australia was four for 227, and still a long way from safe ground.

The Windies had a team meeting before the second day. Ambrose was asked to give it everything, which he did, and more. He tore in with that loping, rhythmic run and generated terrific pace on an unresponsive pitch, causing the tiny keeper Williams to hop about as he made the ball steeple at times and deviate sharply.

Only players of Border's and Waugh's class could withstand bowling of this quality, and they took the partnership on to 204 before Ambrose removed Waugh, caught behind by Williams for 112. It was a sedate effort by Waugh, taking him 328 minutes and including nine fours, yet it was just what the captain and the country ordered. Five for 319 was a recovery, but Border wanted more.

When he reached a century, the appreciative, patient crowd rose to applaud. Making a big one against the Windies was the ultimate achievement for a batsman of the modern era. This was his twenty-fifth hundred in Test cricket. Border wanted to go on with a big score, but he never looked on top. Bishop dislodged him at 110, again caught behind by Williams. Border's run aggregate stood at 9975. He was poised to become only the second player in history to make more than 10 000 in Test cricket.

Healy managed to challenge for sixty-five minutes and 24 runs, but was out not long after his captain at 366. That left a longish tail. McDermott had a charmed life for 17, and Hughes managed an uncharacteristic 9 not out in fifty-seven minutes. Warne (1) and Whitney (0) offered little resistance. Australia had grafted 395.

With Reid out injured, a slimline Hughes took the new ball, and with McDermott returned the torrid favours to the West Indies with powerful, hostile bowling. Hughes bowled Desmond Haynes for 7 in his first over and soon after had Phil Simmons snapped up by Boon at short leg for 6. The West Indies looked unsteady at two for 28. In strode Richardson. He started well with a mighty six over square leg in front of the scoreboard off McDermott.

Hughes, however, was not to be trifled with as he bowled at the peak of his form. He had both batsmen playing and missing, until he delivered the near-perfect ball to Richardson. It cut away off the pitch, took the outside edge and was smartly caught by Healy. Lara and Arthurton saw out the day with their team on three for 62.

Warne received his chance against these two the next morning and bowled well, conceding less than 3 an over, which was a feat against these stroke-makers. He looked capable, and soon lost his early nerves, dropping onto an unpunishable line and length. Border liked what he saw and decided to give Warne plenty of work. In all he sent down 114 balls, 111 to left-handers, to whom leggies would prefer not to bowl.

Warne had been working hard on his flipper. He sent down about twelve of them, which mostly ended up as quick, low full tosses. But the surprise element prevented the batsmen taking advantage of them.

It was McDermott's turn to split the opposition apart. He collected four for 66 to take the honours ahead of Hughes (three for 51), Whitney (one for 27) and Steve Waugh (one for 14). Warne ended up with one for 65, picking up Ambrose. A wicket was a wicket, and Warne was grateful. The West Indies was all out for 233, leaving it 162 behind and putting Australia in a good position to win.

It started poorly in its second dig, however, losing Boon for 11. Warne volunteered to be night watchman. He hung on with Taylor to finish the day at one for 26. Next morning, he stayed at the crease for another half-hour until his score was 5 and the innings tally was 40. Warne then spooned a catch to Arthurton off Ambrose and was on his way. Steve Waugh followed a few balls later for Australia to be three for 41.

Mark Waugh looked as determined to stay put as in the first knock until, after an hour of uncharacteristic defence, he flicked one off his pads to Adams off Walsh and was on his way for 16. The score was four for 73, 235 ahead.

The scratchy Taylor, a shadow of the confident opener of previous years, was unfortunate enough to receive a 'shooter' from Bishop after sticking it out for more than four hours for just 42. It wasn't Border's day either, after his great first-innings effort, as he was bowled by Bishop for 4. But the lead was up over 250 and Border figured that 300 was enough to win, provided the bowlers could deliver.

Martyn then came good with a superb innings of 67 not out in a 202-minute stay at the wicket. At the other end, Healy mishit a hook and was caught and bowled by Walsh for 8. Hughes thrilled his home crowd of 20 000 with a lusty six and a four in his 15, McDermott came and went, then Whitney stayed with Martyn for a handy last-wicket partnership of 29. Australia had reached 196, giving it a lead of 358.

The Windies had a tough task—103 overs to score 359, or 3.5 an over, which was very rare in Test cricket. But if Simmons, Richardson, Lara, Haynes and Arthurton hit their straps, anything could happen. They were all capable of fast scoring. A good start would give them confidence.

Hughes denied them. He removed Haynes with a leg cutter which reared like a brumby, forcing the batsman to edge it to Healy. Richardson and Simmons stayed intact until stumps, with the Windies one for 32, leaving them with 327 for victory in a ninety-over day, or just under 3.6 an over. The task was far from impossible, although the odds on past records had to be with the Australians.

In the dressing room just before the game began on the last day, Healy noticed that Warne was looking a bit apprehensive.

'What's on your mind?' the keeper asked him.

'Aw, nothing,' Warne replied, hang-dog. 'It's just that I'm worried I'll get belted.'

'Mate,' Healy replied. 'You can't go out there with that attitude.'

'I know ...'

'Forget the negative thoughts. You'll be fine once you get going. Start thinking positive now. Be confident.'

Healy's words rang true. His positive attitude had the right effect. For the first time at Test level, Warne went onto the field feeling relaxed and confident.

A good thing, too, for right from the start the Windies gave notice that they were going to win or go down fighting. Richardson and Simmons proceeded to hammer the bowling at a run a minute. Border had to meet the challenge. He made several bowling and fielding changes to no avail. There was nothing for it but to bring on his trump card.

On came Warne, earlier than desirable in such circumstances. He bowled tightly, but without penetration. He was turning them, however, causing the batsmen to shuffle, shoulder arms uncomfortably, flash and often miss.

For the next fifty minutes Richardson watched Warne, occasionally stepping hard into him. But the Windies captain was not quite going all out yet. There would be a moment, perhaps when Warne became tired, when he would obliterate him. He was going to show that he and his team had no great respect for the leggie, whom they regarded as overrated. The best way would be to belt him out of the Australian attack, perhaps forever.

Warne rolled down eight overs, and had none for approaching 30. When he began his ninth, he wondered how long it would be before Border took him out of the firing line. Warne had slipped in a wrong 'un and a top-spinner, among his stock big-breaking leggies. But there was a shot in his locker he had not yet fired, mainly because he had not managed to make one work in the first innings or in the nets.

Flipper Time

The flipper was the most fickle, daring delivery in Warne's armoury. It appeared to be bowled like a leg break, but right at the moment of delivery the bowler would bring his hand down, almost clicking his thumb and middle finger together and the ball would go flying out from below wrist level, imparted with back-spin. In effect, it would spin backwards so that when it hit the pitch it would skid fast, low and straight, leaving the batsman vulnerable to being bowled or caught plumb in front.

Warne now decided to try one on Richie Richardson. The game was drifting away from Australia. The Windies were one for 143. They now had 216 to make with two sessions to go and had kept the rate at more or less 3.5 an over. There were nine wickets left. At the beginning of play, the tourists' chances were being touted by bookmakers at between five and ten to one. A West Indian victory was now an even-money bet.

Warne had now bowled eight overs and was getting worried at having sent down forty-eight balls without a wicket. It was definitely time for the flipper. He tossed up three deliveries breaking away to Richardson's off, who swiped at one a little wide and missed. He connected with another and away it went for four through cover to bring up his 50.

Warne tinkered with the cover field, letting the batsman think that he, the bowler, was expecting to be hit there again. The Windies skipper twirled his Bradman bat. He was enjoying this, warming to the task. At that moment, he could sense victory. Simmons was looking good at the other end. Despite a bit of turn and the odd one that kept low, Richardson felt comfortable. He crashed the fourth ball—another stock leggie—but Steve Waugh swooped on it. No run. Down went Richardson, waiting for the spinner to wheel around and come in.

Warne delivered the flipper. In that fraction of a second the batsman had to decide what was coming, Richardson noticed something different. He was excellent at reading a ball from the bowler's hand and body language. He played safe and pushed forward. The ball pitched short and skidded low. It sped between bat and pad, cannoning into the stumps. Healy leapt high. The team descended on Warne.

He had done it. He had set Richardson up perfectly with four leg breaks and then bowled the stunned Windies skipper for 50.

In came the dashing Lara, his promise as yet unfulfilled in three innings. Border had Whitney on at the other end working well in tandem with Warne. The scoring rate slipped as the new partnership adjusted and notched just 5 in the next fifteen minutes. Nothing to panic about from the batting camp while a new consolidation took place.

Then Lara clipped Whitney to leg—but forgot about the watchful Boon, who snaffled a catch close to the wicket. The

Windies were three for 148. The scales had tipped Australia's way for the first time since Hughes had disposed of Haynes late the previous day.

Arthurton came to the crease, went the charge against Warne and raced to 13 in as many balls. He was intent on the team plan to destroy the spinner. He charged again, Warne flighted the ball past him, Healy collected the ball with alacrity and stumped him. Warne had two for 41 off 12.4 overs. The Windies were four down and 194 short of victory.

Hooper joined Simmons, who had slipped back a notch or two, changing from accelerator to anchor. Hooper prodded. He was a spinner and prided himself on rarely surrendering to his own kind. He was as good as his skipper at picking the ball as it left the hand.

Warne bowled a bad long hop and Hooper ignored it. The next ball was a leg break that bounced, gripped and turned a fraction more than expected. Seeing it as off-line, Hooper thought he would collect a four with a heave over mid-on, but miscued and Whitney took a neat catch at wide mid-wicket. Warne had three for 44 off 14.3 overs and the Windies were five for 177.

Adams joined Simmons, who reached a well-deserved century, including 2 sixes. He took block again, indicating he was there for the duration. But Warne, his spirits soaring, was now in full_flight. Simmons began to fiddle, and looked in trouble against the turning ball. Border moved the field in. He had runs to play with again, and the Windies were defending.

Simmons became tentative and pushed forward at Warne, catching the leading edge of the bat. Boon took the catch. Simmons had made a fine, fighting 110. His team was six for 198.

Warne's figures were now remarkable, at four for 49 off 18.1 overs. In fifty-six balls, he had removed four top bats for just 16 runs. He was alight and fulfilling the promise and faith shown in him by many along the short track to the top.

The diminutive Williams was at the wicket. Border brought back McDermott from the Members' end for the kill, fresh and determined. Adams was beaten by a fast one, which he edged low to Taylor at first slip. The Australian fielders were missing nothing. The Windies were seven for 206 and facing defeat. Then Williams drove Warne to Mark Waugh at short cover and made it eight for 206.

Warne had five for 49 off 21.4 overs. He was now not conceding runs, but simply taking wickets. Bishop and Ambrose put up token resistance for twenty minutes or so until Warne unleashed a big-breaking leggie that rolled across in front of the stretching Bishop. He did well to edge it and Taylor did the rest at slip. Nine for 219. Warne had six for 52 off 23.1 overs.

In came Walsh, dragging his bat. Warne was bowling from the outer or southern end. He bowled a regulation break, which Walsh heaved into. Hughes, hovering behind Warne, took a safe catch and dashed in to souvenir a stump.

Man of the Match—and the Media

The Windies were all out for 219, beaten by 139 runs, but more accurately slaughtered by Shane Warne, with seven for 52 off 23.2 overs. The boy from Black Rock had become the Man of the Match. His figures were the best by an Australian legspinner at the MCG since Bill O'Reilly had taken five for 51 against Gubby Allen's Englishmen of 1936–37.

The jubilant Aussies trooped off the field to cheers from the 16 000-strong crowd. Richie Richardson shook each player's hand as they ran up the race. In the media post-mortem, however, he was somewhat less generous, preferring to play down Warne's effort by suggesting it had been a fluke.

'He got seven wickets and bowled well,' the Windies skipper said. 'But I don't think he is a threat really.'

The media sat in stunned silence. The Windies had just been demolished and had lost a Test. Here was the skipper, Viv Richards–style, dismissing reality. Perhaps it was bravado. Maybe he didn't want to praise the opposition for fear of worrying his men. 'I don't think that any of our batsmen are afraid of him,' he added.

Warne in a way backed this up by saying later: 'I still don't feel comfortable at this level. I still have my doubts, although this must give you confidence.'

It took Border to put the matter in perspective. The press began to speculate about the rest of the series and Australia's chances of taking the world crown. Border dismissed this all as premature and noted that the Windies had 'a bad habit of coming back and proving everyone wrong'.

About Warne, he said, with some degree of understatement: 'His performance was very satisfying.'

When a reporter asked if he thought about coming on himself, however, especially when Richardson and Simmons were in full flight, he was more expansive.

'Yeah, I gave it some thought,' he said. 'Then a wicket would fall. This happened three or four times and then there was no need. Shane was doing the job. He's come up trumps. It's hard for him because there are so many expectations for a bloke who is only twenty-three. I was very pleased for him. His time was right today and he showed a lot of guts. He's worked a lot on his technique. He has lost more than 10 kilograms, which is not easy for a good-time lad, and he has sought advice from a lot of people. His approach has been positive and with more cricket under his belt he can only improve.'

Border also spoke of his qualities as a risk-taker.

'He's just one of those guys, who, if you aren't going anywhere, is prepared to try anything. If you suggest a short leg, he'll say "Beaut" and give it a go. He's always thinking positively.'

Warne was already finding it hard to cope with the limelight. That evening, he, Damien Martyn and Mark Waugh went to South Yarra's Saloon Bar, with its gaudy cowboy decor, all set for a night of partying. Warne was handed a free drinks card—a sign of celebrity status—while a couple of hundred young drinkers ogled. It was heady stuff, for until very recently he had been one of them.

The revellers returned unscathed to the team hotel at around 1 a.m. This would give them at least seven hours sleep before departing on the 10 a.m. flight to Sydney.

Warne was woken at 6 a.m. by a call from a radio reporter, and the phone kept ringing until he caught the plane. In Sydney, there was a big contingent of media waiting, particularly TV. They all wanted to capture the hero of the Melbourne Test.

On the one hand, Warne loved the attention. On the other, he felt uncomfortable, remembering the old adage of 'Rooster today, tomorrow a feather-duster'. As he had said at the press conference after the match, he might have achieved on the MCG, but he still felt out of his depth in Test company. Only a sustained effort over the rest of the series would allay his personal fears. This uncertainty didn't stop his partying. Yet it did stop him becoming carried away. He didn't want to be a one-shot wonder who rose and then sank without trace. It tempered his responses to the insatiable demands of the TV news media.

By midday, he had complained to team manager, Ian McDonald, who called a halt to the circus. Shane Warne had a job to do, starting with training and practice that afternoon at the Sydney ground. The 'not available for interview' sign went up.

Nevertheless, a star was born.

Lara's Brilliant Theme

Border won the toss in the Sydney Test a few days later for the third successive time and chose to bat in front of 30 000 fans. Australia began well with Boon and Taylor taking the score to 42, before Taylor departed for 20 caught by new keeper Junior Murray. In came Steve Waugh. He would have to score well in this one or be dropped. Waugh's response was a nice round hundred, made in good time and with the right mix of aggression and defence. It was arguably the best Aussie innings of the series so far.

Boon departed at 160, having scored 76, which took him to 9 short of 5000 in sixty-nine Tests. His dismissal brought the Waughs together for a near-century link-up before Mark ran himself out.

Australia was three for 254. At 261, Ambrose removed Martyn for 0 with the second new ball, then Steve Waugh at 270. Border and Matthews lived to fight the next day, when Australia resumed at five for 286.

These two put their heads down to capitalise on the fine start and added 155, before Border was out for 74. Along the way, the skipper just happened to pass 10 000, but not without drama, as he sat on 9999 for nine minutes. His departure brought Healy to the crease, with the Australians well on top and the Windies attack wilting. Matthews went for a determined 79, Hughes swished his way happily to 17 and Warne hit 14 runs before holing out to the mid-wicket fence. Healy remained on 36 not out and Australia's 503 ensured they could not be beaten.

When the Windies began batting, McDermott induced Simmons into pushing at a superb leg cutter, which left the tourists one for 24. The next morning Haynes played on to Matthews and was out for 22, making the West Indies two for 31.

In came left-hander Lara, the 23-year-old new Wizard from Trinidad. He and Richardson then produced the most scintillating batting of the series. Lara blazed a century from just 125 balls. Every bowler on day three suffered except Warne, who sent down fourteen overs for 39 runs, conceding less than 3 runs an over. He was shown more respect after Melbourne, as Lara stepped into his shots with a full-bat flourish, which reminded onlookers of Kanhai and Sobers in the 1960–61 series.

At the close, Richardson was 94 not out and Lara 121.

On day four, Richardson continued in the shadow of one of the finest all-time innings as Lara stroked on, finding the gaps with monotonous regularity. At 321 and after a partnership of 293, Richardson was out hooking Hughes to Warne, for 109. It was his fifteenth Test century, but he was overshadowed during his five-and-a-half-hour stay at the wicket.

'It was breathtaking,' he remarked later. 'It was difficult to play and be a spectator at the same time.' Richardson could hardly recall a shot in his own innings, so dominant was his younger partner.

Lara was 176 not out when Richardson departed. The junior partner had outscored the skipper by 71 in their partnership, quite a feat considering Richardson was one of the best and hardest hitting bats of the past twenty years.

Lara went on to 277 before Martyn picked up and threw to Healy who made a good 'take' to run out the Trinidadian champion. He had batted for 474 minutes at an extraordinary 70 per cent strike rate, which would be regarded as good in a one-dayer. Lara hit 38 fours. He planned to be 300 at stumps and then go on and break Sobers's record of 365 not out. It was probably his. Youthful fitness and domination of the attack would have seen him through. It took a run-out to remove him.

Ironically, it was the first time Lara had reached three figures in a Test and placed him fourth behind Sobers (365 not out), Australia's Simpson (311) and England's Foster (287 not out) in terms of maiden century scores. It was also the fourth highest in West Indian history, following Sobers's 365, Lawrence Rowe's 302 and Viv Richards's 291. It was the highest Test score in Australia since Bob Cowper's 307 against England at the MCG in 1965–66.

The Windies went on into day five, scoring 606 and taking no prisoners in their onslaught. Hooper was bowled by Warne along the way for 20 and Adams showed class in making 77 not out. Warne kept his bowling tight and conceded 116 runs for one wicket off forty-one overs, with six maidens.

Sydney was not proving a happy hunting ground for him. A year earlier, he had taken one for 150 against India, which left him with two for 266 on a wicket long considered the best in Australia for spinners. He would be keen on reducing that average in future years. Hughes returned three for 76 off just sixteen overs and everyone else had figures they would prefer to forget.

Australia batted the game out to a tame draw at 117 for none, Boon boosting his already fine average with 63 not out and Taylor (46 not out) gaining some much needed confidence after a lean trot. In all, 1226 runs were scored for just twenty wickets on a most un–Sydney-like wicket.

A draw meant the score line was still one–nil in Australia's favour. The pressure was on the tourists to win one of the remaining two games after a three-week break for the inevitable round of one-day romps.

May's Day—Almost

Warne wasn't wanted for the one-dayers and went to Adelaide with the squad for the Fourth Test beginning on 23 January 1993 wondering if he would have another chance in after only an average effort at Sydney. However, his performance in Melbourne a month earlier ensured another opportunity on a wicket that considered wisdom suggested would help spin more than Sydney. Warne was sorry to see Matthews out of the twelve. 'Mo' had been a support to him in Sri Lanka. Tim May, who hadn't played a Test for four years, was given a spot on his home ground. Damien Martyn was poked in the eye at practice and this gave 22-year-old Justin Langer, from Western Australia, his first Test.

The Windies had to go for the 'kill', a word used advisedly with them. They dropped Adams, despite his good batting in Sydney, and went for four pacemen as they had in Brisbane. In came Kenny Benjamin for his second Test and first against Australia.

The West Indians won the toss and opened as if they were going for 350-plus on the opening day. Haynes and Simmons belted McDermott and Hughes and stormed to 84. Then Steve Waugh came on and had Simmons caught spooning to Hughes at mid-off for 46. Hughes was boosted by the catch and the chance to nab Richardson before he was set. He had destroyed Australia in the last series between the two teams in the

Caribbean in the corresponding Test. Border was more than keen to see the back of him. Hughes didn't let the skipper down. He bowled a couple of steeplers then speared in a fast ball. Richardson, doing a calypso shuffle across the crease, was trapped dead in front.

Border brought on May, the thinking man's off-spinner. Border had played against him often in Shield cricket and had a healthy respect for his talent, especially on his own track at Adelaide. He could tweak it a lot there.

Haynes had dropped anchor, content to let Lara drive the innings. He was determined to make one of his huge scores. Haynes had missed out in the three Tests so far, and now he was in the 40s he would not let go. May looped a harmless-looking delivery down leg side and Haynes thought he could see his fifty. He misjudged the loop and was well out of his ground when Healy stumped him. The Windies were three for 129.

In came Arthurton, who seemed to have lost his supreme confidence of the First Test. After a bit of fiddling, and a few nice drives, he had a wild slash at May and was caught by Steve Waugh at cover. Then Hughes had Hooper fending one to Healy for a regulation catch. Five for 134 and tottering. Yet there was still the magnificent Lara, who raced to 52 in seventy-six balls.

Warne began to wonder if Australia was in for another day of leather-chasing, as in Sydney. He watched Border for a sign that he might be on. Instead, McDermott got the nod and made amends for an awful morning by squaring Lara up and causing him to nick one to the keeper. The Windies were six for 184. Australia was still on top. Rain intervened and the visitors went in at six for 205.

The next morning, Hughes finished off the tail and ended with a fine five for 64. May took two, the Waughs one each and McDermott one. Only Warne with a handful of overs missed out. The Windies had managed a one-dayer score of 252, and now it was Australia's turn.

On another interrupted day, Taylor was out for 1 and Langer and Boon not out for 0 and 1, respectively, at the close. No

Australian number three had ever had a harder baptism than young Langer, who had to face a ruthless Ambrose, a fast and efficient Bishop, the aggressive Benjamin and the wily Walsh. It was the best attack in the world and they were all in form.

Next day, Ambrose gave Boon a bullet ball, which smashed into his elbow and retired him injured for treatment. The giant bowler then dismissed Mark Waugh. Langer showed fight, but was no real match for these four and Benjamin had him caught behind for 20.

Border now joined Steve Waugh, who was having a torrid time from all the speedsters and was hit several times. Ambrose dismissed the uncomfortable Border (19) with a beauty leaving him off the pitch and then Healy (0), both caught in the slips by Hooper. For good measure, he also disposed of the bruised Steve Waugh, caught behind for 42. Hughes then chipped in with an equally courageous 43, including one gem of a hook for six off Bishop. No one else offered much resistance, except for the redoubtable Boon, who came back to bat on to be 39 not out in Australia's 213.

It was a one-dayer score and the team was suffering from the long lay-off to play in the 'pyjama' competition. There wasn't the resilience shown in the earlier games by the Aussie bats and they had lost their momentum. It now seemed a matter of which side would lose most from the one-day intervention.

As if to make the point, the Windies slumped to five for 65 in their second effort, with McDermott blasting his way through the opposition by sending back Haynes and Simmons, and then Arthurton for a pair. Hughes chimed in to dismiss Lara, but Richardson, as ever, decided to counterattack. He looked capable of putting his team on top.

Border brought on May and Warne in tandem to accept the challenge once Hughes and McDermott were spent. May had Hooper caught by Hughes. Richardson smashed Warne in his first few overs, but he couldn't quell his aggressive, try-anything spinning. He speared one down past the charging Richardson, who was stumped by Healy. Unfortunately, it was his only wicket, but it was as good as two, for Richardson, at 72, looked set for a big hundred.

No one expected it to be May's day, even though it was his thirty-first birthday. His 'bad' knee was playing up and he had to be hidden in the field. Even then he managed to spike a finger, which needed bandaging. However, he came in to wrap up the tail with an amazing five wickets for just 9 runs. He had delivered one ball short of seven overs. The Windies lost six for 22 to be removed for 146, which would not have been a good one-day total. Many of the team's batsmen appeared almost fed up. It had been a long tour.

Australia had 186 to make to win and take the series two–nil, with one to play in Perth. Warne noticed that the tension in the dressing room was greater than anything he had experienced. Simpson was telling everyone that all they had to do was bat sensibly and it was theirs. If everyone got 20, then Australia would win.

The start, however, was the worst imaginable. Benjamin removed Taylor, who was having a horror stretch, and Ambrose got Boon lbw for a duck. Mark Waugh looked as if he was going to be more responsible, but he edged Walsh to slip for 26. Ambrose then mopped up the middle order, removing Steve Waugh for 4 and Border for 1. Healy got a pair thanks to Walsh. Hughes received a fast one from Ambrose, lbw for 1. Australia was seven for 74, which Border thought left them with 'no hope'.

Through all this, Langer was playing the innings of his life. Warne, now at the other end, watched him and was inspired. Langer was demonstrating it could be done. A fighter of character, he had a 72-minute partnership with Warne which cobbled 28 runs. Warne planted himself firmly behind each ball in a display of real grit. He stuck to his task until Bishop got one past his bat, lbw for 9. Australia was eight for 102, and the plot still seemed lost.

Again, Langer dug in with his new partner, May, who hid a backbone of steel behind his unprepossessing physique. They put together a solid 42-run partnership, which gave onlookers a ray of hope. Then Langer went for 54, caught behind off Bishop. He had stayed 253 minutes and faced 146 balls. Australia was nine for 144, 42 runs short of victory.

McDermott joined the birthday boy. The Windies tore and roared in at them, but to no avail. They both began hitting the ball in the middle and the runs trickled forth. It looked as if one of the most significant last-wicket stands of the century was taking shape. Both men were being hit and bruised. May took some terror balls on his body and bowling hand, calling for the anaesthetic spray more than once. After an hour he was having trouble holding the bat, but hold it he did.

A greater part of the nation flicked on their TVs and radios as word criss-crossed the country. A real fight was on. The runs began to flow as the 186 needed for victory approached. Then, at 184, Walsh managed to have one rear, which McDermott deflected to the keeper.

Australia was beaten by just one solitary run, the smallest margin in Test cricket history. Before that Australia had beaten England by 3 runs at Manchester in 1902. Eighty years later, England beat Australia by 3, when Border and Jeff Thomson staged a magnificent last-wicket stand to fall just short. There had also been two ties—at Brisbane in 1960 between Australia and the West Indies, and between Australia and India at Madras in 1985–86.

McDermott had made 18 off fifty-seven balls in an 88-minute stay. May remained 42 not out in 135 minutes. They had shown extraordinary guts, but May had paid the price. He couldn't close his bowling hand for days and so missed the Fifth Test in Perth.

In the wash-up, credit went to Ambrose for taking four for 46 and Walsh three for 44. Ambrose, with ten for 120 for the match, was named Man of the Match. It was a top performance from the big man, who showed that at peak form he was the finest speedster in the world. Yet May would have been given the award had he and McDermott managed to score those 2 extra runs …

It was bitter blow for Border. He had come so close. Some in the media wondered if he might retire at the end of the series. They didn't know Border's character. As long as his form held up, he would take the team to New Zealand and then England in 1993. For the moment, it was on to Perth with the score line one-all. The series was still to be won, despite the momentum now being with the tourists. They had won one, and their confidence was high.

And Ambrose was on fire.

Curtly Does It

Mark Taylor's confidence had been so shot by the continual barrage of speed that he was dropped for Perth. Langer's grit in Adelaide saw him pushed even higher to open the innings with Boon, and Martyn returned to bat at five, with Border at six. Steve Waugh was to bat at three and brother Mark four. On paper, it looked like a fair batting line-up.

Jo Angel, aged twenty-four and 198 centimetres tall, was brought in to bolster the attack on his home wicket in place of May, who was not fit enough to hold a cricket ball after his Adelaide battering. The West Indies brought back Adams, and gave paceman Cummins his first Test. They replaced the injured Hooper and Benjamin.

Australia won the toss and batted. Boon and Langer started slowly but well. Then Langer (10) was caught behind off Bishop. Steve Waugh went the same way for 13, and Australia was two for 58. Mark Waugh came and went, again caught Murray. This time the bowler was Ambrose, who was warming to the task. The wicket was bouncy. He and Bishop were now managing to lift a ball just short of a good length to a point between sternum and throat.

By the time Ambrose dismissed Boon for 44, it was clear he was unplayable on such a fast wicket. Australia was four for 90. Border lasted one ball, nicking another superb delivery to Murray, who was loving it behind the stumps.

Healy got his third successive duck, this time caught Lara bowled Ambrose. Then Martyn became yet another Ambrose victim to make it six for 100. Two runs later, Hughes gave Ambrose his sixth scalp, caught for 0.

Warne showed again he had the spirit to resist, but like everyone else seemed uncomfortable against this class of bowling. He was perhaps mercifully run out for 13. No batting line-up on the planet could have held out Ambrose in this form and on this strip. Australia managed just 119, one of its lowest recent scores.

Curtly Ambrose had taken seven for 25, all his wickets coming in one burst of thirty-two deliveries for 1 run. It was one of the most hostile, intimidating and brilliant efforts in Test history. Frank Tyson had done something like it in 1954, taking seven for 27 at Melbourne. So had Sarfraz Nawaz, who took seven for 1 in thirty-three deliveries in Melbourne in 1979, which had won a Test from a near-impossible position. Yet there had been no better performance ever than this one by Ambrose. He had now taken seventeen wickets in three innings.

The Windies replied with one for 135, Haynes being caught behind off Hughes for 24 at stumps on the first day. The tourists were in a dominant position. The next morning McDermott got Richardson quickly for 47. At 184, Simmons (80) became Angel's first wicket in Tests. Lara became another McDermott victim—caught by Warne for just 16. Arthurton found his First Test form and batted well until he, too, fell to McDermott. The Aussie speedster was enjoying the extra pace, as were Hughes and Mark Waugh. However, Murray held them out for 37, and the Windies score of 322 seemed huge by comparison. They had a lead of 203. In the end, Hughes took the bowling honours with four for 71, followed by McDermott with three for 85.

Warne learned early that it wasn't the wicket for spin. The ball bounced, but didn't turn much. He was ineffective with none for 51 off twelve overs.

In the second innings, Boon showed he was in another class playing this speed by staying at the crease for nearly three hours for 52. By comparison, the others seemed perplexed and in a hurry to end the series. Soon the score line was six for 95, almost identical to the first innings. This time Bishop, Cummins and Walsh all pitched in to help Ambrose, with Bishop ending up with six for 40. Border got his first pair in 325 first-class matches as Australia collapsed for a miserable 178 to lose the series two–one.

It was a massive disappointment for Border more than anyone else, although all the team suffered. They had become used to winning one-dayers and Test series. The saddest thing for Border was that he would never have another chance to tackle the Caribbean champions. Not that he could possibly have wanted to face them again for a long time. His batting was shell-shocked in the last two Tests. As he had often said of the Windies, it wasn't enjoyable playing them.

However, he was still captain and there was a three-Test series for him to lead against New Zealand, followed closely by another Ashes tour. The prospect of touring in the home of cricket one more time was the restoration pill Border needed after the Windies. Nothing gave him more satisfaction than beating 'the Poms' in England.

His one consolation was that the Windies had been lucky. Lucky that Warne had not played in the First Test in Brisbane on that last day. Lucky to have had McDermott while still one solitary run ahead. It could so easily have been three–one to Australia. The team had acquitted themselves well, especially in the bowling department, in four of five Tests. They only had their colours lowered in Sydney. The batting had seemed frail at times, yet in the end they were beaten by superior bowling that would have cleaned up against any team of any era. With good reason, Curtly Ambrose was adjudged International Cricketer of the Year and, again, Man of the Match in the Fifth Test.

Warne was caught behind off Ambrose for a duck in his last innings of the series. He left Perth with an abundance of experience. He had faced the world's best with great personal highs and not-so-damaging lows. At no point had he been belted out of the attack. If anything, he had been under-used. He wasn't needed in Adelaide. He was redundant in Perth.

Border had used him judiciously, nurturing his talent now in two series and six Tests. He had shown the talent, aggression and dedication to win matches, a rare capacity for a spinner, and the selectors and the captain had been vindicated in their faith. Warne now had to show consistency over a series. He would not be expected to collect seven wickets every Test innings or every other Test. What was needed was the capacity to add variety to the Australian attack and pick up two or three for not many an innings. He had to be economical, otherwise he would be a liability, which meant he had to work on length and control.

If he sustained his performance over a complete series, he would become a regular member of the team. There was much work to be done. Warne's confidence had gone up a couple of notches. No longer was he doubting his capability at the top level. He had shown himself he had enough skill. Now it was a matter of proving it over time.

All Square in New Zealand

For the first time, Border gave some public clues to his tactical thinking concerning his 'secret weapon' for New Zealand—Warne—just prior to the tour there in February–March 1993.

'My expectation of a leg-spinner is not to bring him on in the first session of the first day to get the gun players out,' he told a media conference. 'As he [Warne] gains confidence, he may be able to do that, but at the moment he is our match-winner in the second innings.'

When Warne gained top confidence, his aggressive style would allow Border or a future captain to use him almost like a first-change strike bowler. When his length and control were considered good enough by selectors—as they were by the end of the West Indian series—he could expect a role in one-day cricket. Warne himself looked forward to this almost as much as Test cricket. His go-ahead, combative style with both bat and ball was expected to make him ideal for the popular, commercial one-dayers. Yet for now, Border, who had handled him faultlessly so far, would use him conservatively.

Martin Crowe, New Zealand's top bat, who ranked with the world's best, faced him in the opening tour game. Crowe was watchful at first of all the Australian bowlers, but was soon into his stride, driving, cutting and pulling. Well into his knock, Border brought Warne on and Crowe was able to get a good look at him. The New Zealand captain decided he could be hit and went about showing how. The spinner watched a lot of balls crashing through the field and over his head. Warne looked anguished every now and again, but generally remained stoic as Border kept tossing him the ball for more punishment.

Warne held back his growing armoury of deliveries, hardly bowling a wrong 'un. Only when Crowe was 120 did the leggie bring out his flipper. The ball pitched perfectly, skidded through low and seemed certain to bowl Crowe. But the star bat jammed his willow down on it and kept it out. Crowe raised his eyebrows and acknowledged the ball, causing Warne to grin. The bowler's expression said: 'You ain't seen nothin' yet.' On that afternoon when the Kiwi skipper sailed on to a magnificent 160, he was only going to see leg breaks.

The word went back out from Crowe and the New Zealand bats that Warne was nothing out of the ordinary. He could turn the ball, but that was about it. Cricketers not present at the opening game read the scores in the papers and the reports of Crowe's mastery.

Australia began the three-Test series well with an excellent team performance at Lancaster Park, Christchurch, scoring 485 in the first innings. The contributions included a return to form by Taylor (82), Langer's patient 63, Steve Waugh's enterprising 62, Healy's rapid-fire 54 and Hughes's thuggish 45 off forty-six balls, including 3 fours and four thumping sixes. The innings highlight, however, was provided by Border (88), who passed Gavaskar as the world's greatest run-scorer. It had taken him

139 Tests and 240 innings for a tally of 10 161 at an average of 51.32 an innings. Border had scored 25 centuries and 59 fifties.

At the end of the second day, McDermott dismissed Greatbatch for 4 and Jones for 8, leaving New Zealand 30 for two at the close. Then, next morning, Hughes removed Crowe for 15, for Rutherford to join the watchful Wright. The two formed a good partnership, with Wright dropping anchor and Rutherford playing his natural attacking game.

Border brought on Warne, who immediately bottled up both players and had them worried with his repertoire, which no New Zealand bat had seen. He removed Wright lbw for 39 and bowled Rutherford with a big break, which virtually broke the Kiwis' back and they were eventually all out for 182. Warne had the best figures, sending down twenty-two overs, including twelve maidens, for three for 23.

New Zealand was forced to follow on and was quickly in trouble, losing 51 for four, with McDermott and Hughes grabbing two each. Hughes again got rid of Crowe (14) cheaply.

The Test looked like folding, when Rutherford got into stride with a thumping 102—his third century in thirty-six Tests. Meanwhile, however, Warne was forcing his way through the middle order, picking up Cairns and Parore.

In came Dilap Patel. Warne decided to try something bold. He would try and hit the little bit of rough on a good length nearly a metre outside the batsman's leg stump. It meant bowling a very wide ball on yorker length fast enough to beat the bat and pad, something out of the question to anyone who was not confident he could really break a ball sharply—at 45 degrees or more.

Warne waited until he had given Patel several deliveries over the wicket and then went round the wicket, making much use of the crease to the right. Patel pushed his leg wide but too late, the ball hit the pitch on yorker length, bit and turned sharply to crash into the stumps, leaving the batsman dumbfounded.

When Rutherford was on strike a magnificent battle ensued. Warne, whose control had been immaculate, would beat him, then the batsman would drive or cut him. At 72, Rutherford was beaten in flight. The ball hit a leading edge and flew to cover just beyond a fielder. Soon after, the batsman cracked Warne for six with a straight drive. It was a tit-for-tat, absorbing contest. Rutherford reached his century, and Warne went round the wicket to him, looking for the rough that had helped remove Patel. But, in fact, he was aiming the ball closer to the stumps, searching for bowlers' footmarks outside leg and on or about a good length, a bowler's equivalent to the erogenous zone.

He got one just on the right spot, turning it sharply across the right-hander. It touched the outside edge of the bat and went on to a grateful Healy, causing him and Warne some ecstasy. Rutherford had faced 215 balls.

Hughes (four for 62) and Warne (four for 63) shared the honours in dismissing New Zealand in their second dig for 243. Australia won by an innings and 62 runs, with Warne being named Man of the Match. He had now been a match-winner in the second innings, to which Border had referred, in three of the nine Tests in which he had played so far. His match figures of seven for 86 were not far short of his best at the MCG against the West Indies.

After the game, the New Zealand media naturally gave Rutherford, now a batting hero, a lot of airplay. He admitted that the Kiwis had underestimated Warne because they knew so little about him.

'When Crowe took him apart [in the opening tour game],' Rutherford commented, 'we thought, you know, he's just another spinner. We weren't prepared for what we got.'

Rutherford went on to explain that there weren't many leggies of quality about. Few played first-class cricket regularly, and they weren't encouraged.

He went on to note that green wickets at the top level did not suit the craft.

'There are a lot of one-day matches in club cricket,' he said. 'Leg-spinners just get slogged. If I was a young leg-spinner, I'd be playing tennis.'

Border read these words later with interest. He was looking ahead to England and the Ashes in a few months time. A strategy on how to present his newish secret weapon had already formed.

Greatbatch and Wright opened with 111 in the Second Test at the Basin Reserve, Wellington, which took the game into the second, rain- and light-affected day before Reiffel sent back Greatbatch and then Jones with a beauty for 4. Then Wright and Crowe built the score to 191 before Wright was caught behind off Hughes.

Rutherford played second fiddle to the captain, who was batting with his fine, upright technique which had won admirers around the world. They took the score to 287 before Hughes had Rutherford pushing forward defensively for a snick to Healy. Then Hughes knocked Blain's off stump out of the ground and it was 288 for five.

As Crowe approached his century, Border brought Warne and McDermott on in tandem to put pressure on the Kiwi captain. He stumbled in the 90s and was completely tied up by Warne, who beat him twice for confident lbw appeals. Another ball which was now becoming a Warne specialty—his 'Cobra'—pitched outside leg. Crowe, thinking he had it covered, lunged defensively, but the ball spun past pads, bat and stumps—just. Crowe was bewildered. Warne beat him again. The batsman tried to cut him and missed.

At the end of the over, Crowe, on 97, shook his head in dismay. He had lost his momentum. Patel took a single off McDermott, giving Crowe the strike. The speedster charged in with extra effort and bowled Crowe, uprooting his off stump, with the star still three short of a century.

After losing its last seven wickets for 42, New Zealand finished with 328. McDermott's figures of three for 66 were the best, with Hughes taking three for 99, Reiffel (two for 55) and Warne (two for 59) helping out.

Australia lost Boon caught-and-bowled Morrison for 37, and Taylor, run out for 50, to reach two for 107 at stumps. The next day, the team struggled towards the New Zealand tally. Only Steve Waugh (75) got past a start and the result was a mediocre 298.

However, the pendulum swung back to the visitors when McDermott got rid of the dangerous Crowe and Greatbatch both for 0, while Reiffel snaffled Rutherford for 11.

Border, contradicting his early remarks about his use of Warne, rushed the spinner into the attack for ten overs, which bamboozled the batsmen so much that they could do little more than prod and push, allowing Warne to dictate terms. He conceded just 7 runs in the spell. New Zealand was left at three for 40 at stumps, after 126 minutes batting.

On the last day, Warne gave Australia some hope by removing Jones lbw for 42, and the fighting Blain caught behind for a well-compiled 51 at 131, but by then it was too late unless the rest collapsed. Wright hung on for 46 not out, while the Kiwis lost two more wickets to be seven for 210 at the end of play in what turned out to be a tame draw. Bowling honours went to McDermott with three for 54, while Warne took two for 49.

Before the Third Test at Auckland, Border—with the previous two Tests in mind—called for the New Zealand umpires to be more positive with lbw decisions and 'give blokes out if they are out'.

He won the toss, batted and wished he hadn't. The unusual cloud cover, a difficult wicket and fine bowling by Morrison (six for 37) reduced Australia to a pathetic 139. Only Steve Waugh (41) and Hughes (33) displayed some fortitude. Australia lost five for 12 off twelve overs in the second hour. The umpires responded to Border's pre-game pleas by giving two doubtful leg-before decisions against Boon and Taylor.

Then the captain himself got a bad decision, which his opposite number confirmed later was not out. Border was given out caught behind to one that threaded between bat and pad, clipped a bail, which was not dislodged, and then went on to keeper Blain. Border began walking, thinking he had been bowled. The umpire put his finger up.

New Zealand started well, but Greatbatch (32), Wright (33), Jones (20), Crowe (31) and Rutherford (43) could not keep on with it, leaving the side vulnerable to Warne, who had them mesmerised. He took three for 5 in ten overs and destroyed the middle order. New Zealand stumbled to 224, and Warne had a staggering four for 8 off fifteen overs. His average of 1 run off every twelve balls demonstrated just what a demon he had transformed into in the eyes of the New Zealand bats.

Australia's batting in the second innings was mixed with Taylor (3), Langer (0 for a pair) and Steve Waugh (0) failing. Boon (53), Martyn (74), Border (71) and Hughes (31) contributed good knocks. Patel took five for 93. The total of 285 left 201 for New Zealand to make to win.

Greatbatch started off slogging and giving Hughes the charge, to which the big fellow didn't take kindly. The two had words, brushed shoulders and generally snarled at each other until Hughes removed his middle stump. New Zealand was one for 44. Wright was run out when the score had reached 65. The decision was referred to the video umpire, who adjudged him out by just 2 centimetres.

Warne then gave Australia some hope by dismissing Jones and Crowe, but New Zealand recovered to be five for 168 at stumps. Rutherford (53 not out) and Blain (24 not out) carried on the next day to reach the required runs without further loss.

The series was over and tied one-all.

Warne came away with the series' best figures of seventeen for 263 at 15.47 runs each, an extraordinary return for a spinner in Tests. He had come a long way in a little over a year since that one for 150 against India. Warne had now experienced four series—against India, Sri Lanka, the West Indies and New Zealand—for a total of thirty-one wickets for 962 at a respectable average of 31.03. If ever anyone had a perfect build-up for an Ashes series, it was Warne, aged twenty-three, who was now a certainty for the big tour.

Hughes, McDermott and Reiffel also looked sure bets, but the batting presented imponderables. Boon, Border, Taylor and

Steve Waugh—because of his form in New Zealand and his record in the 1989 Ashes tour—would get the nod. Martyn had done just enough in New Zealand to make it, but Mark Waugh was doubtful, as was Langer. Tim May was rumoured to be a hot tip as the second spinner. Dashing young openers Slater and Hayden were expected to go, while Healy would keep with Zoehrer as his back-up. Whitney would probably miss out because of injury.

There would have to be a couple of speed back-ups in case Hughes broke down or any of the top quicks lost form. In the end, Wayne Holdsworth and Brendon Julian were chosen amongst a big group of hopefuls. Mark Waugh was fortunate and Langer unlucky, but he joined a long list of batsmen, including Siddons, Jones, Bevan and Darren Lehmann, who could consider themselves victims of opinion, whim and luck. They were certainly no lesser performers than those chosen. Any one of them could step into a Test arena and probably do well (in Jones's case, *again*). It was a question of opportunity, luck and determination for such outsiders as the fortunate ones took off with high hopes to the home of cricket for the battle of the Ashes.

It was Warne's third trip to the UK, but he had never been on the flight in such exalted company. After New Zealand, he felt he belonged. He was living his dreams.

6

England's Nemesis

Hick-ups

On the opening day of the first first-class tour game at Worcester, in the shadow of the Norman cathedral, Border, who was resting from the match, was asked whether Warne would be used against Test player Graeme Hick, the Zimbabwean-born batsman with an awesome capacity for demolishing opposition bowlers in county cricket.

'Yeah, sure.'

'What if he gets a belting?' one journalist wanted to know.

'Well, so be it.'

'Wouldn't that harm his confidence?'

'Maybe, but if he doesn't put the ball on the right spot and a batting talent like Graeme Hick gets a pile of runs off him, then it will give our young leggie a taste of what is going to happen to him if he doesn't get it right.'

His pragmatism had the press silent. Border had made Warne seem like a vulnerable apprentice, but a glance at his record would have given lie to that. He had already played ten Tests and taken thirty-one wickets. He could claim to have been the match-winner in three of them. An apprentice maybe, but he was the Sorcerer's Apprentice.

The English press thought Border had erred for not keeping his leggie hidden until the First Test. They couldn't wait for the confrontation. But there was method in the captain's apparent miscalculation. Border had given Martin Crowe a free first-class dip, without allowing Warne to show him anything but the expected—the big-turning leg break. Now it was time to try the same trick against the even more hard-hitting Hick.

Hick read about Border's hard-headed remarks about Warne having to face the music. He was intrigued, especially as it was in relation to himself. He knew little about Warne, although the reports about his performances in New Zealand had been mentioned in the press.

Hick wanted to get some tips about the bowler, so he planned to phone his all-rounder friend Chris Cairns in New Zealand, who had faced Warne, but there was no time before batting that day. Hick didn't see Warne in his first innings for Worcester, which was dismissed for just 90. Hick himself was removed by Reiffel for 5.

That night Hick spoke with Cairns.

Did he have a good wrong 'un, Hick asked. Cairns said he had picked it. What about a flipper? Cairns couldn't recall it. 'He only got me once,' Cairns said. 'I was caught in slips. He can turn it all right. He's got a good leg break. You've got to watch it. Get to it if you can.'

Hick remarked that Warne had picked up a lot of wickets, and Cairns told him that he thought he had worn some of the New Zealand bats down. He had good length and direction. Hick wanted to know what he was like as a character. How did he take getting hit? Hadn't Rutherford smashed him? Cairns recalled that he had kept coming back. He was 'pretty aggressive' for a spinner.

'Martin Crowe thinks he is better than Mushtaq [the Pakistani leggie],' Cairns remarked. 'But not all the guys agree.'

Hick felt ready for an encounter in his second innings.

Australia scored 262 in its first innings, Boon notching 108 and Steve Waugh 49 not out. On day three Hick and Warne faced each other for the first time. Even before acting-captain Mark Taylor brought the leg-spinner on, Hick was into stride against McDermott and Reiffel. With Warne on, it became Murder at the Cathedral, as Hick laid into him, thrashing fours and sixes at will.

Warne stayed on. After almost each bruising over, Taylor would stand in the slips, his hand over his mouth muttering something to Warne that the batsman could not hear. And the mayhem would continue, much to the joy of the media and the festive crowd. Hick scored 96 in 78 balls from the spinner on his way to a smashing 187. Warne dished up over after over of leg breaks, whether Hick was facing or not, so that all he ever saw of the spinner was his stock ball.

The thing that stuck in Hick's mind was the confirmation of what Cairns had said about Warne. His armoury was limited. There was no wrong 'un to speak of, and no flipper. Yes, he had good control and he could impart slow turn, but he lacked variation and guile. Hick couldn't wait to get at him in the Tests. There had been few run-hungrier figures in first-class cricket than Hick and he had already performed some Bradman-like feats in county games, including one score of 405.

Hick had not yet fulfilled the hopes of the English selectors since they had changed the rules to allow him to play earlier than otherwise because of his Zimbabwean birth. His Test career had started unfortunately against the West Indians, which had been a shocking experience. They knew of his record and went out to strangle him at birth with throat balls. He had been given a torrid time, and had to be dropped after a string of failures.

Hick badly needed to reassert himself with some really big Test innings, having scored his first Test century earlier in the year on the subcontinent. After this first, very satisfying brush with the Aussies, he and many others felt the time had come at last.

The UK media and press reported the destruction of Warne with glee. It was surely a dent in the Aussie camp's composure, wasn't it? Across the nation, English players and supporters were given a boost, and interest in the coming Tests heightened immeasurably. There was going to be a contest this summer, no doubt about it.

The Media Creation

Each summer, England's rapacious tabloids needed to create an image out of a visiting sporting figure to give them a story they could keep running from May to August. He had to be attractive, preferably single, and someone who liked women and partying, especially round the London nightclubs. The dashing Imran Khan and any number of West Indians had had the treatment in the past.

Shane Warne fitted the bill. Even his name had a 'Neighbours' connotation. He wore a diamond earring, appeared to bleach his hair surfie-style, and looked tanned and fit, a sort of antipodean Adonis. Warne was a natural showman. He wasn't media-shy like the Waughs, or terse like 'Capt'n Grumpy', or taciturn like Reiffel or May. He didn't mind the attention and could roll with it.

Border and Simpson were aware of what was happening, but felt certain he could handle the media glare. They were sure that his focus was firmly on helping to win the Ashes. If he could be the team's frontman, it was good for gate-takings.

It didn't matter that Warne's score sheet against Worcestershire read twenty-three overs, six maidens, 122 runs for one wicket. It was his height, weight, chest measurement and romantic attachments in which maidens of a different sort were interested.

Excited reporters, particularly females, lined up to be sent on 'assignment Hollywood', as one tabloid editor dubbed covering the Warne story. It began with a front-page picture of him in one national newspaper, captioned: 'Cricket's sexiest catch'. The *Star* reported Warne as the 'cricket heart-throb who'll be bowling the maidens over'.

Journalist Madelaine Pallas purred: 'As his awesome body powers down the pitch, those 13.5 stones of rippling muscle prompt gasps from female fans. This blond's got bails!'

Just when Barbara Cartland was about to step in and show the reporters how it should done, Warne threw them out of kilter by saying he was 'practically engaged' to Simone

Callahan, 'a blonde promotions manager'. Yet the tabloids were quickly back in stride, with a new, riveting angle about Simone being responsible for his return to form 'after he fell into too many traps partying at nightclubs across Australia'.

'I really wanted to play for Australia,' Warne was reported to have said. 'And I listened to what Simone had to say. She changed my life. Going out with her has done wonders for my cricket.'

The public lapped it up and couldn't get enough of it, long before Warne was to take an Ashes wicket in anger.

Capt'n Disgruntled

Meanwhile back on the field, the media was ready to pounce on any Aussie indiscretion. Channel 7 Australia's TV cameras and sound microphones picked up an on-field confrontation between Border and McDermott. The resultant news item was flashed round the cricket world and picked up on the English networks.

McDermott had just bowled a dreadful spell of no-balls and loose deliveries. Border switched him to the other end and had a word about his performance. McDermott answered back. Border suggested the bowler would be on the next flight home if he continued the way he was going. Border stood in his famous teapot stance—wrists on hips, square-on and a menacing expression on his face.

In the resultant media-created beat-up, sports commentators hinted that the Australians were falling apart, but an undeniable message emerged which chilled the local opposition talent lining up to play the Aussies across the country. It might be fun to portray his men as 'pretty boys and players' off the field. On it, however, Border meant business on this tour, and the business was winning the Ashes.

The skipper was having trouble with his own form and showed his disgust by bashing down his stumps after being dismissed for just 8 by a full toss from Angus Fraser in a one-day game against Middlesex at Lord's. Border was lucky to escape disciplinary action. Again, the picture was flashed round the world of Australia's leader losing his temper.

In the same game, Mike Gatting was run out for 32, just when he looked like firing. He returned to the dressing room and punched his fist through a glass door. Gatting had been hoping for a big score, for he dearly wanted to return to the fray against Australia at Test level. He had been captain of England the last time they won the Ashes in 1986–87 in Australia.

His long exile from the Test arena had been caused by his touring South Africa, arguing vigorously with a Pakistani umpire and enjoying the company of a hotel barmaid. Gatting was fighting his way through the thicket of past misdemeanours in order to return to the England team. He was as single-minded as Border about winning the Ashes.

The media's report of the stump-thumping effort made Border angry, and it seemed that reporters were getting to him. At Hove, he told Meridian TV's Geoff Clark: 'You are all the same, you British media—you are all pricks.' Again, the uncomplimentary appellation was widely reported, and Border realised he had gone too far.

While the media admonished the Australian captain, they were astonished by remarks by Mushtaq Ahmed, who predicted that Warne would win at least one Test in the series. The comment caused surprise after Hick had demolished him under the cathedral.

'I found out last summer that English players don't play leg-spin very well because they don't see much of it,' Mushtaq remarked. 'I found that by pinning them down early, they got to the stage where they were tentative to play a stroke and, when they did open up, it was often to the wrong ball.'

Soon after Warne disappeared from the scene and was not picked for a game for two weeks. He missed selection in the one-dayers. The team line-up in batting order was Hayden, Taylor, Mark Waugh, Boon, Border, Steve Waugh, Healy, Hughes, Reiffel, McDermott and May.

The new face was Hayden, who had hit the ground running with powerful, big scoring from his first game. He jumped Michael Slater, who was slower to find form, but who had begun to collect big scores closer to the First Test. One of them would be chosen to open with Taylor in the Test. Hayden had a chance in the one-dayers to clinch the position.

Australia made a clean sweep of the three-game series, but the undoubted highlight was a breathtaking 167 for England in the second match by Robin Smith, which Border described as 'if not the best one-day innings I have seen, it was in the grand final.'

It was all good psychology to help build the image of the England batsmen as Aussie destroyers. Smith had been inked in next to Hick as a player ready to give the visitors a hiding and get back the Ashes.

Warne was slipped into a game against Surrey after the one-dayers. He bowled well, taking four for 38 off 19.1 overs in the second innings, when he found his rhythm, which had been missing in the first due to his two-week lay-off.

Border then teased the media by telling them: 'There is a temptation to go into the Test with two spinners and we will see how they [Warne and May] go in tandem at Leicester. Tim May has bowled very well and I think we could bowl Warne a little differently if we had May there to bowl the stock overs. If we played two spinners in the Test we would still have Steve and Mark Waugh to handle the donkey work. If Mark hits his straps he can be quite tidy and Steve is also useful.'

However, Border then spoke about Julian and his left-arm bowling that 'we have noticed' troubled some of the English players. It seemed Border was hinting it was between May and Julian for the final undecided spot. Old Trafford, the scene of the First Test, was traditionally the fastest strip in the land, and the money was on Julian.

Just to confuse the opposition, May, Julian and Warne all played in the final pre-Test game against Leicestershire. May took three for 62, Warne three for 31 and Julian one for 19.

The Gatting Special

Australia took a gamble on the morning of the match and went with Julian and not May. Slater pipped the unlucky Hayden, who had muffed his chances in the one-dayers. England chose Gooch, Atherton, Gatting, Smith, Hick, Stewart, Lewis, DeFreitas, Caddick, Such and Tufnell. It, too, had gone for a mixed speed and spin attack. On paper, the English batting looked equal to Australia's, and it was stronger in the spin department having opted for Peter Such and Phil Tufnell. However, Australia's speed attack looked superior with McDermott, Hughes and Julian against Andrew Caddick, Phil DeFreitas and Chris Lewis.

Gooch won the toss and sent Australia in on an under-prepared pitch, which could be good for seamers. It looked a bad decision at first when Taylor and new man Slater started with a 128-run partnership, but the team was out before lunch the next day for 289, thanks to a strong performance by Such, who took six for 67. Only a fine Test knock of 124 by Taylor saved the tourists from severe embarrassment.

England also began well until it lost Atherton for 19, with the score at 71. In came Gatting. Recognised as England's best player of spin, he walked in rolling his head and shoulders, ready to punish. Border, who had spoken much about shielding spinners, immediately sprang Warne on him.

A buzz went round the ground as a surprised crowd realised what was happening. Meanwhile, back in Australia, many fans, supporters and friends grew nervous watching. It was around 1.30 a.m.

Warne's early coach Ron Cantlon was surprised to see him on early. He decided to video-tape the occasion. While he was fiddling with the recorder, he looked up at the TV set to see Warne bowl Gatting. He thought it must have been a replay of an earlier county game.

'How clever,' Cantlon thought, 'replaying that ball just before Gatting started his innings'. Then the actuall ball, the shattered stumps, the Gatting look of utter disbelief, the walk away from the wicket and eleven Aussies in one bear hug around Warne was replayed again and again. Cantlon realised he had just seen his former protégé's first ball in Ashes cricket.

Bob Holland, who had been Australia's leg-spinner on the 1985 Ashes tour, had just sat down after making a cup of coffee in the break following Atherton's dismissal. Like all old leggies, Holland was in raptures over the ball. In calm reflection, he put it down to the *drift* rather than the turn, which got greater with every comment as the days went by.

The drift was away from the direction of the spin. If a bowler could drift or push it further away from the direction of the spin, in other words, away from leg stump, it had a chance of spinning back and taking the off stump. Without that magical drift the ball would pitch about leg, break, miss the bat and stumps, and head off harmlessly towards slips.

Whether drift, turn or darn good luck to land one perfectly first-up, cricket fans from Manchester to Melbourne would forever be able to answer the question 'Where were you when Warne bowled Gatting with that ball in 1993?' Like the Kennedy assassination and the Whitlam dismissal on a larger scale, it would be remembered.

The fact that it was Gatting, the embodiment of the true British bulldog, who had helped destroy Australia in his last two series against them (1985 in England and 1986–87 in Australia) lifted the importance of the moment. He had to be removed as swiftly as possible, to put the whole English team on the psychological defensive against the Australians for the rest of the series.

There were mentions in the press and media of a ball by 'Chuck' Fleetwood-Smith in 1936–37, another ball bowled in anger by Bill O'Reilly in 1938, and Murray Bennett's 'arm-ball' which bowled Viv Richards in Sydney 1984–85. Yet none had the combined impact of coming at such a decisive moment and removing an important batsman.

Perhaps the only other comparable delivery was one bowled by Richie Benaud in the Fourth Test at Old Trafford in 1961.

Thanks to some exceptional Test batting by Bill Lawry, in particular, Australia had clawed its way back from a first-innings deficit of 177 to lead by 255. England began batting with 256 for victory. Ted Dexter smashed his way to a handsome 76, and lived up to his nickname of 'Lord Ted'. England was one for 150.

Benaud, the Australian captain, was in danger of being written off as a flop after a poor bowling and batting performance in the series. He decided to come round the wicket in one last throw of the dice before England coasted to victory in the game and the series, which was then level at one-all. Australia had to get a wicket or go under. First he dismissed Dexter, caught behind by Wally Grout.

Then in came Peter May, the best postwar batsman England has produced. Benaud, showing the qualities of daring that were now evident in Warne in both manner and delivery, made full use of the crease. He pitched it so wide down leg side that May thought it was sweepable. He missed. The ball hit the footmark rough, came back behind his legs and bowled him.

May could not believe he had been bowled. Then he was on his way, and so was England. The jubilant Benaud went on to take six wickets in all and dismiss England for 201. Australia won the match by 54, and took the series two–one.

Warne's Gatting ball was a long way from winning the series, but it was a mighty start. A bowler can't do better than a first-ball wicket. In came Robin Smith, who, together with Hick, had been Australia's main tormentor so far this summer. But Smith had only been the conqueror of the quicks. He was an unknown quantity against top-class spin. For the moment, he remained that way. Warne tied him up and then had him caught in slip by Taylor after a big-turning ball rolled across him. Hick marched to the wicket to join skipper Gooch, who had shown the best technique against the spinner so far. Border brought McDermott on to replace the tiring Hughes. Warne, on the top of his career form so far, was left at the other end.

McDermott followed the game plan to upset Hick with bouncers, glares and generally intimidating bowling. He made it up to the other end, happy to face Warne. That was until he bowled to him. This was not the victim under the Worcester cathedral. This was a demon released from the vault.

He now had a variety of deliveries, including the wrong 'un, and the ball seemed to be breaking twice as much as it had in that early tour game. Hick realised he had been duped. The Australians had actually let him belt Warne around in the early tour game.

Meanwhile, Warne at first confused, then enticed Gooch into lobbing a catch to Julian at mid-on for 65. With Stewart in, there was only Hick left before the home side's tail was exposed. Warne wouldn't let either bat rest or score easily. Hick found no respite with the spinners, while McDermott kept peppering him.

Finally, Border shrewdly brought Hughes in to continue the intimidation. Hick thought he would hit his way out of it, but only succeeded in smashing a long hop to Border, who made a stunning catch at cover. Then Boon took an even more sensational one at short square leg, for what was to be the catch of the summer to dismiss Lewis off Hughes, and Julian bowled Stewart for 27. The rest of England's innings was remarkable only for its ineptness. Warne had them all at sea. He drowned Caddick by getting him to nick one to Healy, who was sharpening skills to spinners that had withered from lack of use over most of his career. England was all out for 210, 79 behind. Warne finished with four for 51 from twenty-four overs, with ten maidens. Once more, he was mean with runs and the opposition bats were cautious with him.

Mid-morning on day three, Australia began again. Taylor looked like repeating his first innings form until Such had him lbw. He then claimed his eighth victim for the game when he had Slater caught for 27 to make Australia two for 46. Boon and Mark Waugh then came together in a timely partnership of 109, in which Mark Waugh showed his class before Tufnell unexpectedly bowled him for 64. Border got himself out caught-and-bowled by Caddick for 31 and Boon drove a catch to cover off DeFreitas when on 93, so denying himself his first

Test century in England. At five for 252, this was where the Aussie largesse ended. Healy and Steve Waugh went on to an unbroken 180-run partnership in just forty overs. After years of rushing into the 20s and departing, Healy completed his first Test century. Few have scored a maiden three figures in better style. He faced just 133 balls and hit 14 fours to remain 102 not out. With Steve Waugh giving solid support at the other end, Border was able to declare at five for 432, a lead of 511.

England had two-and-a-half hours left to bat on the fourth day, and all the fifth. Gooch started as if it was serious about getting them. He and Atherton were scooting along at 4 an over against the quicks, who, like their England counterparts, were finding the pitch unhelpful. Border swung Warne into the attack. He soon beat Atherton, who edged to Taylor at slip. One for 73. Gatting returned for a second chance, but Hughes cut it short when he speared in one on a good length and bowled him neck and crop. England was two for 133 at the close.

On the last day, Robin Smith played safe against the quicks. Border had a word to Taylor and tossed the ball to Warne. Smith immediately became bamboozled. He lunged and padded for a while, then played a forward stroke to a top-spinner. The bat came down across the line, well behind the front pad, and he played on. Warne had got him again.

In came Hick, who also went into his shell, but Hughes gave him no respite, not only with bouncers and rising balls spearing into his sternum, but also verbals—a premeditated but unnecessary tactic and a waste of lung capacity. Then, in the most bizarre incident of the series, Hughes forced Gooch back onto his stumps and as the ball bounced about chest height above the wicket, Gooch instinctively flicked it away with the back of his right hand. The umpire had no choice but to dismiss him handled the ball. Gooch, on 133, was miffed, but the rarely used rule was a sensible one.

England were 223 for four, and Hick was still there. Then Hughes gave him one on a good length, which he edged to Healy at 22. Stewart, tired after long days standing as keeper, batted awkwardly for 11 before Warne forced him to edge another catch behind. Australia was now through to the tail.

Warne had Lewis caught at slip with another big break for 43 and the rest did not last long for England to be all out for 332. Warne ended with another four, this time for 86 from forty-nine overs, with twenty-six maidens.

Australia had won by 179 runs, with Warne Man of the Match for taking eight wickets for 137. Border could be well pleased, for he was a believer in taking the first one of a series. It was the captain's fine tactics in handling Warne long before and during the Test, which had determined the game's destiny.

A series was another matter.

Creating Hollywood

The day after the First Test, Warne took Simone Callahan on a romantic row across Lake Windermere in the picturesque Lake District and proposed to her. This 'event', coupled with his sensational form, opened the floodgates to media madness to such an extent that his Melbourne manager, David Emerson, flew to London to help out the English management firm looking after Warne, Advantage International. It was overloaded with requests and offers.

Emerson managed other big names in Australian cricket, including Merv Hughes, Dean Jones and Simon O'Donnell, but he had never seen anything like this. Warne had gone beyond the pages of the tabloid dailies to become a sex symbol for readers of glossy women's magazines, manufactured by editors needing to create a new image every few weeks. Yet there was something more sustainable about Warne, who was clearly going to run further than flavour of the month.

Most magazines picked up on the 'Larrikin Finds Love' angle, portraying him as either the 'sweet lad' or the 'beach-boy' who had been 'settled down' by his attractive, no-nonsense fiancée.

The less tasteful magazines became involved. One wanted him for an interview 'detailing his love life and what he looks for in female companions'. Not to be outdone, the dailies offered him enticing fees for a column, one of which he took. In desperation to top the Warne stories, the sleazier papers began offering him big money to de-robe. It started with a £15 000 offer to pose bare-chested for a Sunday paper. A tabloid offered a bigger sum for him to be photographed in a jockstrap and some cricket gear, which would have been the village green's answer to the S & M studs-and-leather set.

The dailies were sustaining the momentum by coming up with new pictorial possibilities. Rejected tabloids decided to find ex-girlfriends from his early seasons in Bristol and Lancashire. One woman from the north was well paid for detailing a brief romance she claimed to have had with Warne (but which Warne said was largely fabrication).

The press cover plus his exposure on TV in each of the five Test days was having its effect. Just when he was about to 'dig into a spaghetti bolognaise,' he told the cricket magazine *Inside Edge*, a person would 'stick a piece of paper in my face and say "Sign this"'. He didn't mind 'Hello, well done', but the pushy types were irritating. There were agreeable reactions, too, with taxi drivers waiving fares for an autograph. In Birmingham, a fan delivered a bottle of Möet to his dinner table.

David Emerson, who apart from running his own company, Competitive Edge, was assistant to the cricket manager at the Victorian Cricket Association, was sensitive to the conflict of interest for Warne. It was good for him to be able to make bonuses on top of his $60 000 payment for the tour, but there had to be a limit.

'Warne's highest priority is to play cricket,' Emerson told the press. 'He recognises he's a person in the public spotlight, but cricket comes first, and being a public figure comes second.'

Emerson's remarks were more than endorsed by the Australian team management. They could see it impinging on Warne's performances on the field.

'It's got to the stage where it's getting out of control,' coach Simpson complained. 'There are phone calls getting through at two o'clock and five o'clock in the morning.' The management chaperoned Warne to Bristol for a round of interviews centring on his stay there in 1989, then declared him under media ban until further notice. Warne was given three days off from the touring party and told to disappear with Simone. They spent the time in a quiet village outside London.

Warne returned refreshed for a game against Gloucestershire and caused a sigh of relief amongst the management by continuing his Test form. He collected five wickets in Gloucestershire's first innings, taking his tally to thirty-two wickets for the season so far after a handful of games. Warne had not become sloppy and he didn't need a bigger baggy green. He was keener than ever and hadn't forgotten that the Ashes had yet to be won.

Slatered for Victory

The heavens opened up on London and Lord's in St John's Wood the day before the Second Test, but cleared overnight, leaving the world's most famous ground in fine shape. Australian teams have always attempted to lift a notch for the Lord's Test, because the hallowed turf is the home of cricket. It reeks of tradition from the W. G. Grace gates to the century-old pavilion and Long Room, where the tiny Ashes urn is kept. Australian teams had dominated this Test since 1934, and led eleven–five in Ashes Tests on the 179-year-old ground. The 1993 team was buoyed and ready to make it twelve–five.

It started well when Border won the toss and increased the odds by deciding that England would bat last. This justified the selection of two spinners, Warne and May, the latter having replaced Julian.

Slater drove his first ball for four, then continued with his fellow boy from Wagga Wagga, Taylor. Slater was soon making driving on a slowish pitch look easy, stroking the ball on both sides of the wicket with masterly timing in one of the best innings by an Australian at Lord's in forty years. He reached his landmark 100 by flicking Neil Foster—who replaced Phil DeFreitas in England's XI—to fine leg.

At the other end, Taylor took another ninety minutes to reach his century, which was important for the team. It was his tenth in Tests and his fourth against England, at twenty-eight years of age, bringing up his 1000th Test run against England in fourteen innings, second only to Bradman, who did it in just eight.

The two batted until the last hour when Slater clipped a ball from Lewis to mid-wicket and was caught for 152. The opening stand of 260 was the third highest in Australian Test history and the highest Ashes stand at Lord's, eclipsing that of Woodfull and Bradman in 1930.

Five overs later, Taylor (111) lumbered down the pitch to hit Tufnell and was stumped by Stewart, making up for an earlier bungle when the batsman was on 86. Boon (11 not out) and Mark Waugh (6 not out) were there at stumps with Australia at two for 292. It was déjà vu for England. The score line was looking like the first days in 1989 when Australia went on to 600-plus.

Next day, Boon and Waugh took over from the openers in a stand of 175. Waugh, the team's most elegant stroke-maker, pushed his way to 99. Then he was bowled again by Tufnell, with Australia three for 452. Border came in and batted on remorselessly, while Boon at last brought up his long-overdue first century against England. It was only well into the third day, after having made 77 himself, that Border put the England team out of its suffering and declared at four for 632, with Boon unconquered on 164 and Steve Waugh 13 not out.

McDermott became ill and had to be rushed to hospital for an operation, which finished his summer before he was revved up. It also left Australia one bowler short for this game, and without their best strike bowler for the rest of the series. The burden fell on Hughes, Warne and May, while Border would call on the Waugh twins to provide more than their usual 'stock-and-shock' contributions. Accordingly, Hughes and Mark Waugh opened the bowling. Hughes soon obliged with an early breakthrough by persuading Gooch (12) to hook him to May at deep fine leg.

In strode Gatting. With scores of 4 and 23 behind him, his career as a Test player was on the line. Border brought on May, an unknown quantity for Gatting, and the Adelaide accountant slipped one through him, bowling him for 5. England was two for 50, and in need of some spirited batting to support Atherton, who was playing watchfully and well at the other end. He was taking the taunts from Hughes in his stride, with a few well-chosen rejoinders.

Border was working on the theory of six- to eight-over spells for Hughes, now his main strike bowler, whereas May could bowl in his sleep. Warne had shown in the second innings of the First Test, when he bowled forty-nine overs and conceded less than 2 runs an over, that he, too, had developed into an economical workhorse, when required. Now that he was unlikely to be smacked all over the park, he could bowl all day. His old problem of 'conking out'—that is, becoming fatigued easily—seemed a thing of the past.

Border now had both his spinners on for Smith, who was reduced to an innings of uncertain streaks, dashes and the occasional shot. He tried using his pads. Warne out-thought him with a top-spinner, then a wrong 'un, which caused the batsman to avoid padding up. May had him coming forward until he charged. May tossed one faster and wider, causing Smith to play, miss and scramble. Healy did the rest. Smith had made 22 off forty-three balls. After three failures, his Test place was in doubt. England was three for 84, and 632 looked far away.

Hick joined Atherton, who was playing the spin defensively. Border, not missing a trick or a chance, summoned Hick's nemesis Hughes to the bowling crease. The big fellow roared a couple through him and, after a few overs, had him caught by Healy for 20. It was the third time in three knocks that Hick had fallen to his tormentor.

At four for 123, England was falling. Hughes trapped Stewart lbw for 3. Warne then had Lewis (0) out the same way with a top-spinner that hurried on. At six for 132, England was 500 behind and still with 300 to get to avoid the follow-on. Foster put up token resistance for fifty minutes and 16 runs before Warne deceived him with a turner, which he popped to Border at 167.

Caddick, too, showed spirit in supporting Atherton (80), who looked like carrying his bat until Warne bowled him with a beautiful leg break. It was now only a matter of time. Warne induced Such (7) to nick one to Taylor at slip. The next morning, day four, Caddick had a dip at Hughes, only to see Healy take it, England was all out for a miserable 205.

All bowlers had lifted without spearhead McDermott. Hughes bowled magnificently, despite his verbal attacks, taking four for 52 off 20.5 overs. Warne continued his match-winning First Test form, which was fast looking like his standard for the series, by taking four for 57 off thirty-five overs with twelve maidens. He had bowled more than anyone. Partly because of necessity since McDermott's illness, and partly because of his developing capacities, Border had changed tactics in his use of the spinner. His secret weapon had become exposed as front-line artillery, and was no less effective. Another factor emerging at this point was Warne's ability to remove batsmen.

Hardly a wicket, if any, had fallen to him by a batsman losing patience and having a whack into the outfield, which had been a traditional way of spinners 'buying' a wicket. Warne attacked. He was meaner than the average leggie. He would 'kill' for any wicket, but he would also rather assault the batsman than exchange boundaries for the odd catch at long leg. His length and direction, and sheer capacity to beat the bat, caused him to reduce the number of runs off each over he bowled to about 1.6.

Warne's earlier appearances were also allowing him to bowl more at the top-order bats. They, as much as the middle and lower order, were troubled by him. Only Gooch displayed a comfortable technique based around his eye and timing. He would pick the ball to hit with a firm grip, and the one to caress. Yet even Gooch was still not playing him without problems. He was being beaten enough to see that sooner or later Warne was likely to get him.

Gooch preferred, in the great English tradition, which was copied by purists from Australia to Antigua, to play the spinners from the crease. There was never any attempt to dance down the wicket to smother the spin or crash Warne away. This in essence was the only way to defeat Warne, but there was a catch. One mistake in the waltz forward, one tiny error of judgment, and you were stranded somewhere down the pitch, while the keeper removed the bails in one gleeful swipe.

Only three players in the world could play Warne this way, and one of those was Border. For the moment, he wasn't about to say anything. To watch him play Warne in the nets was a fascinating revelation. No one since Neil Harvey looked as good at that *one-two-one* quick-step to drive in the wide arc between cover and mid-wicket. Warne would frown a lot when bowling to his captain. Border could match him.

While Warne again stole the show in the bowling line-up, Tim May's effort was no less commendable. His two wickets—Gatting and Smith—were struggling for form, but still they were top-order and accomplished. May out-thought them with guile and courage. Once the debits and credits were totted up at the end of the day, on balance, May had summed up his opponents. He would bring them to account before long.

England were some 427 runs in arrears and with nearly two days still to play an Australian victory looked more than likely. Gooch and Atherton commenced England's second effort sedately and made it through to lunch. Then Warne got one on leg stump to spin sharply and catch the edge of Gooch's bat. Healy took the catch and England was one for 71. It was the second time in two Tests that the spinner had dismissed Gooch, the home team's best-equipped and most prolific bat.

Atherton, meanwhile, was batting with common sense and skill in what was his best performance in a Test, at least against Australia. Only Warne had him second-guessing, but Atherton kept taking singles to rotate the strike and avoid being bottled up by the spinner. Like Mark Waugh in the Australian innings, he deserved a Lord's century, but he was run out by a good throw from Hughes on the boundary.

In walked Robin Smith. He hung around for a short time, looking confused and nervous, then popped a catch to the substitute fieldsman Hayden off May and was out of his misery for 5. Gatting and Hick lasted into the fifth day and, with the score past 225, they seemed capable of forcing a draw. Just when this was being contemplated, Warne struck, trapping Gatting lbw for 59. He had batted stoically for 258 minutes, but must have wondered whether he had done enough to make it to the Third Test.

England needed someone to avoid doing things by halves and go on with a solid hundred. Hick and Stewart started to appear as if they might hold out. But just before lunch, Hick failed to pick May's arm-ball from round the wicket and pushed it to Taylor at slip. With both Australian spinners in harness, the in-coming Lewis decided to charge and Healy stumped him for a duck off May.

In the afternoon, with Stewart and Foster at the wicket, another battle of attrition began, but it seemed inevitable that Australia would break through. Even so, Hughes was labouring and Warne was finding the pitch somnolent. His aggression was being blunted as he moulded himself into a stock bowler in a long stint.

Only May looked threatening. Stewart and Foster had decided to avoid putting bat to ball, which meant not playing a shot or padding up. For a while—ninety minutes—it looked uncomfortable but effective. Eventually, the method backfired as May straightened one from around the wicket and Stewart was lbw for 62 after lasting for nearly three hours.

With Hughes clearly spent and Warne needing a break, Border brought himself on and immediately had Foster prodding to Mark Waugh at silly point and on his way for 20. England was eight for 361. After an extended tea break for the two teams to meet the Queen, Border brought back Warne, who decided to experiment. Showing his enormous skills, he bowled Such and Tufnell for ducks round their legs in successive balls to end the match.

These two deliveries were pitched so far from the wicket that had they spun away to leg the umpire would have been compelled to call them wide, but they screwed back and back to take the stumps. Had these two balls been bowled to better bats they would have beaten them and caused a sensation. Instead, they were forgotten in the rush to grab souvenir stumps and decamp the scene. Recognition for this bowling genius would have to wait for another place and another time.

Warne had now taken sixteen wickets in the two Tests, already more than Benaud's fifteen in four Tests in 1961. The next target was Clarrie Grimmett's twenty-nine wickets taken in 1930, a record for an Australian leg-spinner in England. He had bowled a marathon 48.5 overs with seventeen maidens, taking four for 102. May's remarkable effort was even more impressive—four for 81 off fifty-one overs, with nearly half of them maidens. Border chimed in with sixteen overs and took one for 16. England's 365 left them short by 62 runs and the little matter of an innings.

Michael Slater took Man of the Match for his stunning 152 to set Australia on the way to victory. Without McDermott, the ten men left provided even more of a fine team effort than in the first encounter. Everyone contributed.

In the press postmortem, Gooch pledged not to stand down, despite his pre-match threat to do so if England lost again.

'I don't think now is the right time to do so,' he said. 'We're all desperately disappointed but we must stay close together and keep battling away. Our problem is we just can't get wickets. That is where our problems are starting and finishing.'

With that, Foster, Tufnell and Lewis, who were largely to blame for this shortage of wickets, received the chop, as did Gatting and Hick, which represented half the team. Smith kept his place by scoring a hurricane 191 for Hampshire against the Australians at Southampton in a game before the Third Test.

England brought in Mark Lathwell, Mark Ilott, Martin McCague, Nasser Hussain and Graham Thorpe. No one could accuse the selectors of not trying something different. Meanwhile, in the Australian camp, Julian replaced McDermott, who had to return home for further surgery.

A Summer of Sorts

Until late June, it had not been a fine summer in London, with more grey days that threatened cricket than didn't. Then temperatures hit 30 and Wimbledon began in real heat. The Australian team, with their insistence on coloured zinc dabs on the face, stylish mirror-glasses and a variety of headgear, were an odd sight to the sun-starved English, but they were an impressive combination on and off the field. Their fielding, running between the wickets and catching were exceptional, as they held sway against the counties with bat and ball.

No matter whether it was a Test or against the Combined Universities, this team put in, not the least reason being the healthy rivalry within the ranks. Slater had won the right to open with Taylor, but Matthew Hayden was batting with power on his way to a big season even without a Test. If Slater slumped, Hayden would get his chance. The Waughs were performing outstandingly, with Mark showing his great class, and Steve demonstrating his reliability on English wickets. If one of them lost form, Martyn would be in. He had done everything asked of him in his limited chances at the crease.

With McDermott out, the enthusiastic Julian was in ahead of Paul Reiffel, who so far had not lived up to the reason he had been selected. On form, he was a top swing bowler by any standard. Yet he was a 'touch' sportsman. Once it returned, he would be hard to keep out of the team, especially under English conditions of weather and pitch.

As for the spinners, May was making the most of his earned place, and knew that he would be on the fringe of selection when the team returned to Australia. However, he was bowling so well, and had so much respect from Border, that he had a chance to enhance his position. The swing back to spin was catching. If May was taking wickets and helping to win matches, especially in tandem with Warne, then the off-spinner could have a resurgence late in his career. It was keeping him motivated.

Warne was a different proposition. As matters stood after Lord's, he was now certain of selection. Yet it never entered his mind to relax. He was as hungry as any cricketer at the highest level in recent times. He had a lot yet to achieve, and much to prove. He had been conscious of the fact that he had been helped along because Australia needed a leg-spinner. He had no peers in that department. Nor were there any in sight, or at least anyone the selectors would push along so fast.

The odds were that Warne would not have a competitor for his spot for some time, if he held form and fitness. It wasn't player competition that was motivating him. It was the need to prove to himself and the world that he had the right stuff.

The internal jockeying within Border's well-knit touring unit was a positive influence on performance. On the field players concentrated on their best, yet had to be selfless performers. Border wanted winners, but only team winners.

When they arrived at Trent Bridge, Nottingham, there was not the sluggish atmosphere of a team making heavy work of an arduous tour. There was rather an ambience of determination to win the Ashes. A win here would make it three–nil and mean that even if England won the final three games, Australia would retain the little bits of burnt bail.

Trent Bridge was a fitting setting for a contest of such importance, with a history almost as impressive as Lord's. Nottingham had traditionally been a batsman's paradise, but, in recent times, some, like the champion New Zealand all-rounder Richard Hadlee, would disagree. He had little problem taking hundreds of wickets on the Trent Bridge pitch during a decade with Notts in the 1980s. But Hadlee was Hadlee and in a class of his own.

How it would play for bowlers in this Third Test, 1–6 July 1993, was anyone's guess, making this game far less predictable than the previous two in the series.

Backs to the Bridge

The choice of fast bowler Martin McCague in the English team caused controversy before the match. He was born in Essex of an English mother and Irish father, but spent most of his twenty-four years in Australia, where he was given good opportunities in his formative years at the Cricket Academy and through playing for Western Australia in the Sheffield Shield.

Border happened to mention that the Ashes would not be quite the same with someone like McCague coming at him. Border would have preferred Freddie Trueman bowling, giving an English snarl rather than an Aussie one. His comments aroused a furore in the media. He had touched a raw nerve about 'foreigners' playing under the Union Jack. One cricketer wrote an article demanding that all non–English-born players be banned, which would have savagely depleted the English line-up and those awaiting call-up.

McCague had to wait a day to bowl. Gooch won the toss and this time batted. Mark Lathwell opened with Atherton. Gooch dropped down to number five, a strange move considering the earlier combination's good efforts.

Border took Julian off after he was a little loose and nervous in his first few overs and replaced him with Warne. Lathwell (20 off twenty-nine balls) started like a greyhound, but soon fell caught behind to Hughes. Smith came in for what had to be his last chance. He played Warne cautiously, but leant into everyone else, picking up where he left off in his recent county success against the Australians.

Despite losing Atherton, caught by Boon at bat-pad off Warne for 11 at 63, Smith continued with his assault until after lunch, with Stewart in support. Then Warne broke through when Stewart (25) slashed him to Mark Waugh at cover.

England was three for 153 with Gooch at the wicket. Six runs later, Julian disposed of Smith for 86 with a near-miraculous caught-and-bowled, after a strong-arm knock from the batsman which deserved a century. Debutant Graham Thorpe followed soon after for 6, tucked up by a short ball from Hughes.

Gooch and Nasser Hussain, another new boy, restored some hope until Hughes fired a fast one in shortish at Gooch, which the English captain tried to work away on the on side, but only succeeded in spooning a catch to Border at cover. At six for 220, an unlikely stand then began between Hussain and Caddick. The economical Warne should have removed the latter, but if anything bowled too well when he spun a couple of deliveries from outside leg stump, which missed pad, bat, wicket and a stunned keeper. Even Healy could be awe-struck by the leggie's freakish capabilities. The batsmen made it through to stumps for a respectable six for 276, with Hussain on 50 not out.

The night's break stopped their union, and the team lost four for 47. Hussain, wristy in a stylish way, ensured another opportunity in the Fourth Test by scoring 71, caught bat-pad by Boon off Warne, again in form.

Hughes had risen to the occasion, taking five for 92 off thirty-one overs. Warne 'failed' to take four wickets in an innings for the first time in the series, but bowled as well as in the previous four innings. He took three for 74 in his usual long stint of forty overs, and all his wickets—Atherton, Stewart and Hussain—were batsmen.

McCague tore in at the Australian openers, spraying the ball around a bit, but slipping in a few good bouncers and short ones. For the first time, the Aussies were hopping about and the England attack had some fire. He broke through and removed Taylor (28) at 55. Not long after, Slater (40) was lbw to Caddick.

Then Boon and Mark Waugh put things right with a 123-run partnership. Waugh was intent on destruction and was severe on everyone, especially off his legs, in a show-stopping 70 from just sixty-eight balls and he wasn't at the crease for much over an hour and a half.

Brother Steve had a rare failure in England when caught by Stewart off McCague with the score four at 239. Border was suffering from a bad attack of hay fever, and dropped himself down the list to give himself time to recover. Healy and Julian were dismissed cheaply. Hughes found himself batting with Boon, before the latter was out in the pre-lunch session on day three for 101, when he played on to McCague.

It was his second successive Test century following 93 in the second innings of the first Test. Border, still ill, battled on with Hughes until the score was 311. At that point, Ilott slipped one through Hughes and Warne came to the wicket with Australia still 10 in arrears. He batted luckily yet responsibly, picking the right ball to hit and supporting his captain in a handy little venture. It was broken by Such, who had Border (38) caught at wide mid-on at 356. May was lbw to McCague and Warne remained 35 not out in his best-looking Test innings yet. Australia was all out for 373, just 52 ahead. They had raced along at around 3.5 to 4 runs an over for most of the innings and seemed to be heading the game towards a result.

England batted again before tea on the third day and early on lost Atherton, who gloved a ball to Healy off Hughes, bringing the belligerent Smith to the wicket. He was still smarting from his first-innings dismissal, and batted as if determined to make everyone pay with a big, smashing hundred. But he was wary of Warne, using his pads, feet and bat to take on each ball gingerly as if it might somehow explode. Sure enough, when Smith had reached 50 in seventy-one balls, Warne got a faster ball to nick an edge to Healy. England was two for 100 and in trouble considering the 52-run deficit. Then Warne struck again snaring Lathwell, who had never faced a spinner of this calibre, lbw for 33. England was three for 109 and sweating. Then Hughes trapped Stewart lbw for 6, leaving England four for 122 at stumps, with Gooch and night watchman Caddick at the wicket.

This time there was a Sunday rest day—the only one for the series. It seemed to do wonders for England, with Caddick defending stoutly on the Monday morning until Julian had him caught close to the wicket by Boon for 12. England was still just five for 159—a lead of a little over a hundred, with nearly two days to play and not a cloud in sight.

Thorpe, the rookie left-hander, joined the skipper. Gooch settled in for another fine innings of strength, skill and temperament. Thorpe, too, showed mental fortitude as he constructed his innings and the two batted England into a winning position by the time Hughes limped off the ground with a groin injury just before tea. His loss was a blow for the tourists, with McDermott off the scene and Julian not penetrating on English wickets slower than his patch at home in Perth.

It also meant that Warne had to do the heavy work, as May was not proving effective. It was not the way Border would have liked either of his tweakers. Yet there was no choice. The skipper had already called up himself and Mark Waugh. Nevertheless, Warne responded by getting another leg break through Gooch, who helped it along to Taylor.

It was the third time in as many Tests that Warne had got him. The England captain (120 in 324 minutes) wearily removed his gloves and trudged off having played one of his finest innings. He had turned a loss into a chance for a win.

But Gooch was cautious. He let the innings drift on into the fifth morning. It was nice to allow Thorpe (114 not out) to reach a century in his first Test, but it left England with little time to roll Australia and win. He finally declared before lunch at six for 422, with Warne taking three for 108 from fifty overs with twenty-one maidens. He had not caused a crisis, yet he always engendered doubt. Hence his fine economy rate and high percentage of maidens. Australia was left with 371 to make off seventy-seven overs, which was too big a demand on the last day of a Test.

The openers replied as they always did. Taylor put his head down and played the anchor. By contrast, Slater went hell-for-leather, scoring 26 of thirty-six balls with 5 fours, and again too soon and in the wrong situation. This was Test cricket, not park.

Slater swished once too often and Such bowled him. Then the spinner struck again at 74 causing Taylor (28) to edge a catch to Atherton. Mark Waugh went for an irresponsible whack and Caddick bowled him for 1. Border was still unwell and not unexpectedly was caught off Caddick for 2, but Boon surprised with an ambitious half-cut, which flew to the keeper when he was only on 18. It left Australia five for 93. Ian Healy (5) received a fast, straight one from Ilott and was lbw. Australia was six for 115, and staring at defeat.

Julian joined Steve Waugh, who dug in to finish with a characteristically determined 46 not out. This enabled Julian to contribute a bright 56 in a batsman-like performance with one mighty six to bring up his first fifty in Test cricket.

At the end, Australia had six for 202 off seventy-six overs, 169 short of the target. Caddick took the bowling honours at last with three for 32. In the brief patch of true summer, England had risen with the humidity, haze and heat as if inspired by the sun's rays.

However, the forecasters predicted the grey, mixed pre-Wimbledon weather for the rest of July at least. Would Australia's dominance return with it?

Reiffel Fires, Warne Foiled

Rain interrupted much play in the county games in the sixteen days before the Fourth Test at Headingley, and created the incentive Border needed to lift his team out of the mid-tour doldrums. One soggy afternoon they were all in or around a dressing room when the BBC replayed part of the 1981 Headingley Ashes Test. Botham with the bat and Willis with the ball staged one of the most miraculous turnarounds in Ashes history to defeat Australia.

Border was the only current player to have experienced that shameful failure, in which a collective collapse of nerve, tactics, skills and team cohesion let England storm to victory. He used the BBC replay to motivate the team to inflict a crushing victory at Headingley this time. Most of them recalled the 1981 defeat and the feeling of wounded pride.

He also had a new gun in his arsenal to help him. Reiffel had hit form at just the right time. He replaced the injured Julian, who had shown so far he had the temperament, skills and potential to make it at the top. But, even if he had been fit, Border right now needed wickets, not potential. Hughes retained his place by rest, ice-packs, the physio's fingers and sheer will. He would pace himself through another Test with his exceptional endurance.

Border gave him more rest-time by winning the toss and batting on the most enigmatic strip in England. In recent years the pitch at Headingley, in Leeds, Yorkshire, had been much abused for its unreliability. The criticism led to the pitch being dug up and replaced in 1986, but the new turf behaved the same way. At the end of the 1992 season, local groundsmen were given more work in another excavation. The resultant new pitch was now to have its own test.

England dropped Such for Martin Bicknell in anticipation of swing rather than spin working on the bewildering strip. Border won the toss and looked skyward. Clouds over Headingley meant a swerving ball. Noting they had just cleared, the skipper opted to bat first.

Taylor found the pitch was true enough, but started with his usual restraint. His innings ended on 27 when Bicknell secured his first Test wicket, leg before. Slater's raw dash continued, but moments of discretion were detected.

Australia was one for 103 at lunch. Soon after, Slater charitably played across the line to a half-volley from Ilott, which bowled him and put Australia at two for 110. The tourists advanced courtesy of Boon and Mark Waugh until, after a breezy 52, Waugh shouldered arms to a straight ball from Ilott and was bowled. Boon stayed until stumps and reached his century. It was his eighth on tour, his fiftieth in first-class matches, and it took his aggregate for the series to 499 at an average of just under 125.

Border was with him at the close on 38 not out in Australia's ominous-looking two for 307. Next morning, Ilott trapped Boon leg before for 107. In came Steve Waugh, with everything set up for him to make one of his big Ashes hundreds. The weather was fine, the attack controllable and at the other end was the embodiment of cool determination. There was a sense of mission in Border today, and Waugh wanted to be with him, wherever he was going.

The skipper batted patiently, introducing the odd pull, deliciously timed cover drive, cut and on-drive to complement the nudges and pushes. A century came mid-afternoon. It was Border's twenty-sixth Test ton and drew him next to Sobers. Only Bradman with twenty-nine and Gavaskar with thirty-four were ahead of him. But it was clear he was not content with just a century, as he climbed through 140, 150, 160, and settled on 175 for the evening before recommencing on day three to push into the 190s and finally 200 not out, when he declared Australia's innings closed at four for 653. He and Waugh (157 not out) put on an unbroken 332, which ranked eighth in Australia's twelve best-ever partnerships. He had faced 399 balls and had been at the crease for 565 minutes or nearly five sessions. It was his second double century, and only 5 short of his top score in Tests, versus New Zealand.

His partnership with Waugh had put the Ashes out of reach for England in 1993. There could only be an Australian win or a draw now, which meant that even if England won the next two to square the series, Australia would retain cricket's most coveted trophy for the third successive series—all under Border's leadership. Only Bradman had managed to 'hold' the urn for four series in a row.

England came out facing the mountain and stumbled at the first ridge. Lathwell drove flat-footed to Hughes's third ball and it carried to Healy. Robin Smith began pugnaciously with boundaries from his first and third balls, but May soon had him batting more cautiously, calming him to the point where he drove back a return catch.

Stewart pushed across Reiffel's line of fire. His pads were plumb, which meant he was out either lbw or caught by Slater at silly point. Umpire Dickie Bird put his finger up and England was three for 50, still 600 behind. This was too much of a capitulation for Gooch who, with dogged Atherton, recovered England's position by tea, when the score was three for 134. The break lulled his concentration just enough for Reiffel to shoot one into his pads to have him lbw for 59 and England four for 158.

Reiffel, starved of victims all summer, was trigger-happy, removing Gooch, Atherton for 55, Thorpe for a duck and Hussain bowled for 15. England had been massacred and Reiffel had to be restrained from doing more damage.

That was left to Hughes and Warne. Hughes returned three for 47 off 15.5 overs, while Warne had one for 43 off twenty-three overs, with nine maidens. May, with troubled fingers, calloused and bleeding, took one for 33 off fifteen.

Reiffel had the best figures with five for 65 off twenty-six overs, and was always dangerous with his two-way swing. If he wasn't getting them to push at the one going away, he had them missing the one ducking in. It was a first-rate display by a player whose wicket-taking sensitivity had returned.

England had just managed to equal Border's 200. He asked them to follow on. Hughes and Reiffel couldn't break through as Lathwell and Atherton settled in. May and Warne were given the ball and Warne pushed Lathwell into a shell of confusion, then May bowled him for 26. England was one for 60, and still nearly 400 in arrears.

Smith came in and floundered around for some time, trying unsuccessfully to read the spinning ball off the wicket, rather than from the hand. Warne pinned him down, while May provoked the sedate Atherton into leaving his crease and had him stumped. This dismissal only redoubled Smith's uncertainties against Warne. May benefited when he mistimed a lunging drive and it sailed back to May for an easy catch.

Gooch, as usual, stood out for his ability to pierce the field with every loose ball, despite the fact that Warne and May were bowling few bad ones. He moved effortlessly to 26, when May lured him from the crease and Healy had his second stumping for the day. It was a big wicket and Border began to think about a three–nil score line, with England four for 202—250 in arrears—and a day to play.

However, the variable weather on the last morning threatened to stop Australia where England could not. Stewart and Thorpe survived one interruption, but then Reiffel, who had been worrying Thorpe with his line, angled one across the left-hander and he took the bait, nibbling it to Taylor at slip. Reiffel got a nick to Stewart's cutting bat and he was caught one-handed by Mark Waugh. It was Reiffel's eighth wicket and he stood out as the game's best performer with the ball.

Hughes came back before lunch to have a run at Hussain and Caddick, who had resisted for an hour—enough time to make the Australians anxious about victory. Hughes eliminated the threat by having Caddick and Bicknell lbw in successive balls. After the break, he then bowled McCague with a beauty. England was nine for 295, and history. May completed the formalities when Ilott obliged by slogging him high and Border took the catch to finish the game. Australia was the winner by an innings and 148 runs. The series and the Ashes belonged to the tourists three–nil.

May took four for 65 and Hughes and Reiffel three each. Warne did his bit by bowling by far the most overs—forty, with sixteen maidens—and more economically than the others at just 1.5 runs an over. He had taken just one wicket for 106 to add to his one for 43 in the first innings, but the figures were mendacious. Though he was foiled in his hunt for a bigger haul, even his stock bowling bothered every batsman into errors.

Border was named Man of the Match for his 'leadership and unbeaten double century'. He had become the most successful Ashes captain in Australian history with twelve wins to

Bradman's eleven. Indeed, he was arguably second only to the Don as Australia's greatest cricketer.

The media took some gloss off the Australian success by concentrating on Gooch, who resigned as captain now the 1993 Ashes battle was over. There was speculation about his successor. Atherton was the tip. He had the background—Cambridge University, always useful in England—skills and courage. Whether he was a leader or not would be established in the remaining two Tests against Australia and in a series in the Caribbean commencing in January 1994.

Come in Swinger

England once more rearranged the deck chairs on the *Titanic.* For the Fifth Test at the Warwickshire County Cricket Club in Birmingham—or Edgbaston, as it is better known—out went Lathwell (who had not quite done enough for a third chance), McCague (injured and not yet up to Test standard) and Caddick (none for 138 at Headingley). In came Matthew Maynard (rewarded for hammering a brisk hundred off Australia in a county game), Peter Such and John Emburey (the wicket was expected to turn). Australia kept the same force as it had deployed at Trent Bridge.

Edgbaston has been turned into an unprepossessing stadium, with ugly concrete terraces interspersed with unimaginative grandstands. The pavilion is impressive with its portrait gallery and museum of Warwickshire cricket. It was packed with patrons for the opening day, all of whom were hoping for a lift from England, especially with its new young captain.

Michael Atherton, a 25-year-old Lancastrian, had been thrust into the job without ever having captained his county. He was a history graduate, the first 'intellectual' to lead the country since Mike Brearley, who was a cricketer short on talent but long on pedigree, strategy and the capacity to extract the best from lesser minded, more skilled players.

This was a peculiarly English expedient. Never in any other

country would a player be chosen for his captaincy first. In Australia, the best XI was chosen and then the most likely captain selected from among them. This ran the risk of a poor captain, but Australia had had very few duds.

Atherton was a capable Test cricketer, more gifted than Brearley. Whether he was a better thinker in the job was yet to be revealed. He did the right thing by winning the toss and batting. The new skipper then followed through with a defiant innings, despite losing Gooch for 8, Smith for 21 and Maynard for 0 by the time the score had reached 76.

Atherton batted on with Stewart, who once again got more than a good start. Warne was anxious for a wicket after his nil return last time out. He proved he was human by becoming wayward for the first time in nine innings, which in itself said much for his performance over the series. He began bowling the odd loose one, as if he was literally losing his grip—a long hop here, a wide one there. Such were the standards he had set, he became annoyed with himself.

Sections of the crowd heckled him, but before long he found the correct length. Stewart (45) played across the line to give a leading-edge catch back to the bowler. England was four for 156. Without another run being added, Reiffel bowled a fast one which kept unplayably low. Atherton (72) was unlucky and unhappy to hear the death rattle. His dream of a century in his first innings as captain was shattered. Then Reiffel, who was swinging it late and fast, produced a perfect outswinger to bowl Hussain, placing England at six for 160.

The forty-year-old Emburey now joined Thorpe and devised a unique way of playing Warne, basically by standing square-on and holding his bat in front of his legs to keep out the ball, almost like French cricket. What was more, compared with some of the failed efforts of more highly regarded batsmen, it proved effective.

No matter what he tried, Warne couldn't get through. When he bowled a leg break, Emburey would step back on his wicket and cover it with his pads. He could not be out bowled round his legs as Such and Tufnell had been at Lord's, or the way Gatting was at Old Trafford. It also ruled out lbw from a ball pitched outside leg. Warne's other variations also held no terrors and Emburey was able to handle the straight ones or the wrong 'un on the slow pitch.

It was up to May to crack the odd couple. While Warne was tearing his hair out in frustration at the other end, May turned fox to outsmart the young Thorpe, who was well set. At one point between overs, Border asked loudly enough for the batsman to hear if May wanted a sweeper behind point to cut off Thorpe's favourite shot to the boundary. May shook his head.

Border did a teapot.

'Hey?' the captain said. 'You don't want a sweeper?'

'No, no,' May responded dismissively. Border raised his eyebrows as if to say, *OK, don't say I didn't suggest it,* and returned to his position. May then proceeded to starve Thorpe of the shot, pitching on middle and leg for umpteen deliveries. Finally, he pushed one up, wide and drifting away. Sure enough, Thorpe, mindful of that tempting gap behind point, flashed at it—only to get an outside edge to Healy. Thorpe was on his way, *conned* May, 37.

England was seven for 215 and then lost Bicknell and Such to go to stumps at nine for 276, with Ilott on 3 and Emburey, a staunch 55, the not-out batsmen. Next morning, Reiffel had Ilott caught behind with the score unchanged.

Reiffel's six for 71 beat Lillee's haul of five for 15 on an uncovered wicket at Edgbaston in 1975. Lillee's effort was outstanding, but, if anything, Reiffel bowled better. He was straighter and with more control, although Lillee was quicker. Warne's figures were one for 63, from twenty-one overs with seven maidens. He was a little loose. Border used him as more of a stock than a strike bowler.

England came out fighting with the ball. By the time Australia had hit 80, Slater was out for 21, Boon for a duck, Taylor for 19 and Border for 3, leaving the Waugh brothers together. Mark's scores so far had been 6, 64, 99, 70, 1 and 52. It was time for him to come good with a big hundred, and he did. The brothers took the score to 233 before Mark fell to a catch off Ilott. His 137 had taken just four hours, with 18 fours, and was the best and most entertaining innings of the series.

Australia was eight for 258 at the end of day two. Early on day three, Steve Waugh went for a fighting 59 which had pulled the game around after Australia was in danger of collapse. But it was still short of England's 276. Everyone expected Australia to grind out a thin lead, but Healy and Hughes decided otherwise and sailed past England's score to add 107 for the seventh wicket, an Ashes record at Edgbaston. Healy was finally out for 80 and Hughes for 38, leaving Australia eight for 379. Warne and Reiffel helped to take the total to 408, a lead of 132.

Time for the Spin Twins

Gooch and Atherton approached the uphill task with aggression and Border's response was to throw the ball to Warne. It wasn't a moment too soon for the spinner. The young perfectionist had been working overtime in the nets to organise his control and direction.

What a difference a bit of self-belief had made. Less than a year earlier in Sri Lanka, Warne was ambivalent and nervous when Border called him on. Now he pounced on the ball. His powers of direction had returned and he soon had Atherton caught at silly point by Border for 28, with the score at 60.

Smith came in and looked like a blind man with a stick as he poked, hoped and missed. However, Gooch and he made it through to stumps at one for 89, only 43 short of Australia's tally, and still with all but one batsman intact. It augured well for an exciting finish.

Overnight, the Australians discussed tactics. Warne wanted to try bowling Gooch round his legs—the way he had removed Such and Tufnell at Lord's. Some of his team-mates were sceptical. 'Goochie' wasn't like them. He wouldn't fall for it. 'You'll get walloped,' he was told.

The next morning, a sunny Sunday, the crowd streamed in, with high hopes for an England revival. The overnight pair started well enough, with Gooch as solid and comfortable as ever. But soon Smith was in trouble again against Warne. After being beaten by six deliveries, he received a marvellous flipper from him. It pitched short and outside off stump and shot low.

Smith by now had stopped pretending to try to read what was coming. His brain told him that short, out-of-control leg break was coming, which would naturally spin away, and ordered him to gear his wrists and forearms for his favourite shot—a massive cut through cover point.

Smith's worst critic would never accuse him of not having good reflexes. He went through the motions of what would have been a radiant cut. But that rotten ball didn't spin away. It came through dead-straight and flipped the pad of his bent right knee several centimetres outside the line of off stump. Warne went high in appeal—more, one suspects, for the thrill of having delivered such a delivery than in the belief that he had dismissed him. He had bowled Richie Richardson with a flipper in the Boxing Day Test and now he had the hardest ball in cricket working again. His confidence lifted another notch.

The umpire's finger went up. Smith didn't even gasp or protest at the unjustness of the decision. He departed, as if he knew in his heart that he been punished for that most heinous of cricketing sins—deficiency of basic technique.

Maynard came out firing, but still couldn't hide his nerves. It was a tough scene to enter, with Warne bowling a torrid spell—as menacing in its own way as anything dished up by a quick. The batsman thought he might get away from the danger facing May. But he had also been inspired by Warne's bit of magic, in another example of bowlers teasing improvement out of each other in tandem. May bowled one that spun and bounced. Maynard was caught behind and out of his misery for 10.

England was in crisis, but Gooch was still in, looking cool, almost complacent. Warne was feeding him deliveries round the wicket on and just outside leg stump. When the score was three for 124, with Gooch on 48, Warne had a quick chat with Border before he began another over and told him that be was going to attempt to bowl Gooch round his legs.

Warne went around the wicket and gave Gooch twenty balls on about the same spot. The twenty-first ball was another leg break. The batsman gave it a disdainful nudge. Then Warne ran very wide of the stumps, so his feet were only just inside the return crease. He pitchforked the ball wide, long, fast and straight. It landed beyond the popping crease, wide of leg stump. Gooch threw out a protective leg. The ball whizzed past him and spun back into his stumps. There may never have been a better ball bowled by a spinner in a Test. There certainly had never been one as daring or impossible. Yet Warne had done something similar in New Zealand and against Gatting at Lord's.

These incredible deliveries—the flipper, the cobra, the spin back—were not flukes. In future series, Warne would conjure them again. Yet they would be as rare as Penny Blacks. Keeping them that way was part of the secret of their effectiveness.

England four for 124, and all but down for the count. Losing Gooch that way was sure to demoralise the dressing room. It was all right to get a shooter as Atherton had in the first innings from Reiffel. That was bad luck, something to moan about. It was acceptable occasionally to have a rush of blood and flash at a bad ball and be dismissed. But when a bowler was delivering balls no one could play, well, it was best to say nothing extravagant. It would only make matters worse to express awe.

'I got a pretty good one out of the rough,' was all Gooch said to an inquisitor.

Thorpe and Stewart were now together. Warne was circling the latter for a kill. Stewart persisted with using his pads. The Australians appealed for a couple of incautious pushes to balls that were close to being in line with the stumps. He also nicked and nudged and was beaten so many times that it seemed he would have to go any ball.

It was a case of a pad too far. The umpires were fed up and one of them again penalised an English player for a poor performance. The Stewart lbw to Warne decision was a doubtful one. The batsman could count himself unlucky. Five for 124.

Hussain held out for seven balls before May completed the double-act by having him caught behind. Six for 125. England was still 7 runs short of making Australia bat again.

In came Emburey, intent on a repeat performance of his first-innings heroics. The spin twins couldn't remove him or Thorpe. Nor could Hughes, who slowed progress, or Reiffel, who wanted to perform last rites on the pitch. Border had a few overs. So did Mark Waugh.

The runs trickled on. Border became anxious. The crowd grew hopeful. Border rang the changes, but no bell tolled for England for 200 minutes of this partnership. Then, finally, May teased Emburey into nicking one to Healy. Seven for 229, and England was 95 ahead. Not enough, but in front at least. Two balls later, May had Bicknell caught by Steve Waugh for 0. Eight for 229. Realising he was running out of support, Thorpe gave May the charge and was stumped by Healy for 60. Nine for 229.

Unbelievably, a last-wicket stand by Ilott and Such wriggled England up to 251. Then May bowled Ilott for 15, and completed a bag of five for 89 off 42.2 overs with fifteen maidens. Warne took the other five for 82 off forty-nine overs with twenty-three maidens. They had dismissed England between them in one of the best spinning performances since Jim Laker—with Tony Lock assisting at the other end—cleaned up Australia in 1956.

The next morning, there was a bit of a scare for the tourists when Emburey and Such removed Slater and Taylor cheaply, both when the score was 12. But Boon and Mark Waugh handled the turning ball astutely. Waugh thumped and glided his way to 62 not out in eighty-seven balls, while Boon chewed on for 38 not out, ensuring an eight-wicket win. Mark Waugh received the Man of the Match award. Australia went four–nil in the series.

At the post-match media conference, Border suggested that the England team was playing Warne the wrong way. They should be using their feet more, he said. It was not quite like the days when Geoff Boycott would tell the Aussies—Lillee, Ian Chappell and Rod Marsh—after stumps *during* a Test match how to dismiss his fellow England team members, but there was a purpose to the gratuitous advice.

Border knew that the English players were rooted to their creases. If they tried dancing down the wicket in the Sixth Test they would self-destruct. In effect, he was giving nothing away while sowing the seeds of confusion.

After Edgbaston, the tourists would have liked to end the tour. Five games seemed adequate and six a Test too much. Border spoke of going to five–nil, but wasn't as convincing as before. His expression was drained of all challenge and he needed a rest. However, for a chance to go five–nil, which no one had done since 1921, he and Simpson would use the short break before the Sixth Test at the Oval to rekindle desire.

Oval and Out

England let the *Titanic* sink and constructed a new ship. The speed-bowling line-up was the problem. It had been incapable of getting Australia out twice in all five Tests, so the last remnants of earlier failures—Ilott and Bicknell—were replaced by Devon Malcolm, Angus Fraser and Steve Watkin.

Emburey made way, too, but Such was retained. In batting, Maynard held on to his place but Smith was given his marching orders, further admonition for his failure against spin. Mark Ramprakash made a last-minute dash to the Oval from his county game to replace Thorpe, who was injured in the hour before the game started. Australia held on to the same XI, when it perhaps could have rewarded Hayden and Martyn. But its problem was, who to drop?

The Oval has generally been kinder to batsmen than bowlers. It looked as if it might continue the tradition when Atherton won the toss and batted. He and Gooch got off to a rapid start. It took Steve Waugh to break the 88-run opening partnership when he had Gooch caught for 56. Hick came in, looking streaky and uncomfortable, but scoring fast. At 139, Waugh struck again to trap Atherton lbw for 50.

Maynard came to the wicket. Border introduced Warne to exploit his weakness against spin. In his first two overs, Warne gave him leg breaks, then in his third over he delivered a disguised top-spinner, to which Maynard used braille and was bowled. It was Warne's thirtieth wicket of the series, which surpassed Clarrie Grimmett's twenty-nine in 1930.

Hick kept hammering the quicker bowlers, taking 17 from one over off Mark Waugh. Border soon had both Warne and May on against him. They combined to get rid of him when May induced a catch to his spin partner. England was four for 231.

Stewart, too, had taken up the cudgel and, for the first time in eleven innings, England was really carrying the attack to the opposition. Then Warne had Hussain caught by Taylor at slip for 30 and England was five for 253. It wasn't long after tea and England were on target for a big first-day score.

Wickets were falling, but the runs were coming fast. Hughes, who had been smashed for 80 in his first fifteen overs, was called on for another spell and had Ramprakash caught at the wicket for 6.

At six for 272, Fraser joined Stewart and Hughes's volatile temper flared, not for the first time that day or during the series. In a senseless act, at the end of one over, he threw the ball to Healy, narrowly missing Fraser. Soon afterwards, he settled another argument by removing the rampaging Stewart—with whom he had also clashed earlier—caught behind for 76 off only ninety-four balls. Fraser and Watkin were there at stumps with England seven for 353.

It was one of the two or three best day's entertainment of the twenty-six days so far, with 57 fours and 2 sixes being hit. Next morning, Reiffel cleaned up the rest to complete what was the most shared bowling performance of the series—all the bowlers took a pasting and a couple of wickets. Hughes had three for 121 to take his tally to twenty-eight. Warne took two for 70 from twenty overs with five maidens. England had its best first-innings score of the series at 380, and Australia was in for a fight.

The crowd cheered Malcolm from the first ball that sailed past Taylor's head, as the West Indian–born speedster bowled the most hostile spell of the series, removing Slater (4) and Boon (13), both caught by Gooch close to the wicket.

Fraser, also quick but thoughtful, had Mark Waugh caught behind for 10 and Australia was in trouble at three for 53. Border and Taylor carried on doggedly until Malcolm came back to have Taylor caught for a well-made 70. Fraser then bowled Steve Waugh for 20 and Australia stood at five for 164.

The progression thereafter was steady. Fraser had Border caught behind for 48. Hughes was soon caught off Watkin for 7, who then removed Reiffel for a duck, leaving Australia eight for 196. The steadfast Healy was joined by Warne, who showed once more that he could bat more than a bit, as they put on 52 for the ninth wicket. It took a good swinging ball to remove the spinner, caught by Stewart off Fraser for 16 at 248.

May joined Healy for another fine stand, this time of 55, lifting Australia's score to 303 before Fraser found the edge of May's bat for a catch to the keeper. Healy remained 83 not out. Malcolm, the wayward destroyer, took three for 86. Fraser, on his return to Test cricket after a long break caused by hip problems, took five for 87.

The Oval was packed on Saturday when Gooch drove Reiffel to the long-off boundary to pass David Gower (8231) as England's greatest run-maker. He and Atherton exactly doubled the 77-run lead, batting aggressively until Reiffel broke through at 77 to remove Atherton, caught by Warne for 42.

By tea, England was one for 127, which stretched the lead to 204. Hick and Gooch took the score to 157 before Hick bat-padded to Boon off May for 36. Hughes came back to remove the tentative Maynard for 9 and then had Hussain caught in the slips for a duck. England was four for 180.

Warne, who had been working hard and economically, came on to bowl to Gooch. Their six-match contest had been the main battle of the series—England's best bat versus Australia's best bowler. So far, Warne had removed Gooch four times. Both men seemed to lift when facing each other. This final confrontation was no less keen, for Warne wanted his wicket one last time, and Gooch wanted to preserve it. They were like two jousting knights, each determined to knock the other off his steed.

At 186, Warne pushed through a leg break that tickled the edge. Healy leapt high in appeal. Gooch was already on his way knowing that his combat with Australia was over forever. He had made 79 in fourteen minutes short of four hours. When he departed, England was 261 ahead with five wickets still intact. It was England's best chance yet to roll Australia after seven years of trying.

Day four, Sunday, was wet early, forcing a delay, and many feared England could be robbed of its chance for victory. When play resumed, Stewart and Ramprakash continued on until Reiffel had Stewart out for 36 and England was six for 254. Then, at 276, Reiffel removed the stubborn Fraser.

Warne was fortunate to have Watkin out lbw when for some reason he failed to offer a shot to a full toss. A half-hour later, the spinner was bowling to Such, who was happy not to face the pacier bowling. Warne gave him a series of leg breaks, which the Scot fended off more or less competently.

Then came the flipper. Such did everything right as he pushed forward, head down, eyes over the ball. But he was a week late. The ball skidded into his pads. By the time the umpire had adjudicated in Warne's favour and his team-mates had congratulated him, Such had just finished his stroke.

It was the leggie's thirty-fourth wicket, at 25.7 runs each, a long way past his modest aim of taking twenty wickets in the series. His final figures of three for 78, from forty overs with fifteen maidens, touched almost his average and demonstrated his remarkable consistency. He just kept coming at the batsmen, showing his youthful fitness and strength, which he had honed since those days of hard training more than a year earlier at the Cricket Academy. There was no more 'conking out' for him. Rather, it was the batsmen all over England who were worn down into error. Warne ended up taking seventy-five first-class wickets at 22.64 for the season, more than any other player in the country.

Hughes wrapped up England's twelfth innings at 313 when he had Ramprakash caught by Slater for 64. It was Hughes's thirty-first wicket in the six Tests at an average of 27. He and Warne thus joined Lillee and Alderman as the only Australians to take more than thirty wickets in a series in England. Lillee and Alderman performed the feat twice each. Hughes was unlikely to tour again, but Warne could look forward to at least two more tours, if his form and fitness held.

In the background, the reticent Reiffel collected nineteen wickets in only three Tests at just 20.84, which stole the figures from the others. May chimed in with twenty-one at 28.19. It was some time since four bowlers had served any country so well in a series.

While these figures were being analysed and compared, Australia still had a job to do to draw the Sixth Test. They were 375 in arrears on the morning of the fifth day, with all wickets intact. Early on it seemed that the England umpires were almost bending over backwards to please the England media and fans, such were the bad decisions.

Slater received a shocker and was given out caught behind for 12 off Watkin. Boon (0) then got a doubtful lbw decision off Watkin. Taylor was bowled for 8 and Australia three for 30. Then, at 17, Border poked his willow cross-bat at a wide one from Malcolm. The awful shot was very late and, to the naked eye and in replays, the ball was well past the bat when Border pushed forward. The umpire put his finger up without hesitation. Maybe this was a rebuke for the excessive appealing and bad temper of the Australians at times through the series.

But there was no such excuse for Mark Waugh when, after a spanking 49, he hooked a bouncer from Malcolm high to deep backward square for Ramprakash to run in and take an easy catch. This lapse left Australia at five for 95. Healy made another when he also hooked and was caught for 5 off Watkin. Australia was six for 106.

Steve Waugh had been jumping and struggling against the ferocious Malcolm, who finally trapped him lbw for 20, leaving Australia seven for 142 and facing defeat. Hughes went for 12 after a patient eighty-six minutes at the crease and Warne came in at eight for 143. An irritating partnership for England commenced between him and Reiffel. They had done enough bowling to put their feet up. Yet both remained determined to bat well.

Reiffel soon showed just how single-minded he was when Malcolm hit him a fearful blow behind the ear. The batsman went down. He seemed to be semi-conscious as an England fielder tried to lift him to his feet. He recovered, but would not leave the field. After some medical assistance, deep breaths and head-shaking, he returned to the crease, showing his nerve by getting behind every delivery. Up the other end, Warne was inspired by this show of resilience. He demonstrated just how far he had come in confidence against Malcolm, who was bowling as fast as the West Indians at Perth earlier in the year. The ball was pounding into Stewart's gloves and sending his hands back, a sure sign of an express delivery.

Back and across went Warne, solid in defence. Atherton had nothing to lose by bringing the field up. Both bats became cheeky and began to play attacking shots. The partnership lingered. The big crowd, expecting an England victory, became worried. Was England destined not to take one in this series?

At 217, it was the thinker Fraser, not the furious Malcolm, who gave the answer when he caught and bowled Reiffel for 42. In came the redoubtable May. No one in the Aussie camp doubted he would fight, having seen his guts in Adelaide when the West Indies had pulverised his fingers and body. Could the last pair stay long enough to force a draw?

Into the last hour, at 229, Fraser turned Warne square and had him lbw for 37, his highest Test score. England had won by 161 runs. Malcolm took three for 84, Watkin four for 65, and Fraser three for 44, in an even effort. Fraser was made Man of the Match. In the series, only Such got more than eight wickets for England—sixteen at 33.81—which highlighted its lack of penetration.

As the players left the field, Gooch threw out a hand to shake with Warne, but the Australian walked right past, oblivious of the gesture. He had not seen it, so steeped was he in the disappointment of having been dismissed last. Warne felt that he had let the team down. It was another indication of how he would rise to the many challenges to come, with ball and bat.

He was adjudged Man of the Series by the English. The Australians gave their award to Gooch. Former England Test all-rounder Trevor Bailey and others in the opposing camp went further. Warne was the best leg-spinner they had ever seen.

Warne's Ashes batting finished with a respectable 113 at 37.67, which would be tough to keep up. He had now taken sixty-five Test wickets and would be looking to top one hundred during the coming 1993–94 summer in Australia in six Tests against New Zealand and South Africa.

7

Kiwis and Proteas

In the Glittering Firmament

Warne grabbed the football, charged the goal and let fly with a 50-metre kick that bounced through the posts. The 100 000-strong Grand Final crowd roared. Unfortunately for Shane—in a smart green suit—it was only kick-to-kick with Merv Hughes at half-time in the 1993 Essendon versus Carlton battle. Yet it was still a thrill

It always would be on the MCG's hallowed turf. Warne felt lifted by the occasion. It stiffened his resolve to do great cricketing deeds there on every occasion he appeared. The post-Ashes highs continued.

Warne's feats in England had preceded him and he came back to news that Nike, the mighty US sportswear company, were interested in offering him a contract. Henselite, the Australian distributor of Gunn and Moore bats, renewed a three-year sponsorship. The *Cricketer* magazine signed him up, as did radio station Triple M-FM. Just Jeans stepped in with a promotional and endorsement deal. Its managing director, Craig Kimberley, explained why in fulsome praise capturing the true S. K. Warne:

'He's good-looking, has a good build. The fact that he's a great Australian sportsman and doesn't carry any baggage helps. He has Australia-wide appeal and relates so well to our consumer. He's a good, regular guy. He doesn't big-note. He's great to do business with.'

Warne was now an advertising product and loving it. He was in the money and going some way to assuring his future, at just twenty-four. Mindful of the importance of 'the good build' image and the challenges of the up-coming season, he went straight into a routine of running on Melbourne's bayside beach tracks and working out at the King Club guided by former St Kilda high-flyer and personal hero Trevor Barker. He even began turning up at the nets for state practice earlier than most. Warne wanted a full summer playing for his country and a break into international one-day cricket. So far he had been kept out of yellow pyjamas, but for one game in Wellington. The attitude had been that he should be saved for the Tests. Besides, so the recent philosophy had it, leggies were too expensive, too *risky* for big-time one-dayers.

Warne had two months to run into peak form and fitness after a post-Ashes holiday with his now-fiancée Simone in Venice and the Algarve in Portugal. He was 88 kilograms and he wanted to slide down again to about 83 or 84 kilograms, at which he felt slim, comfortable and fit. A perfect weight would have been a bit lighter still, but that would have seen him giving up pizza, toasted cheese sandwiches, chocolate bars and the odd beer completely. Warne, the junk-food addict, would have been miserable at such deprivation. He felt he was making enough sacrifices already without making life unbearable. There was always a packet of cigarettes hidden in his pocket or kit. That was another pleasure he was damned if he were going to give up, at least while he was out of the public eye. He was going beyond the call of duty in terms of public accessibility and endearment. No need to take away delights that he thought would never interfere with his on-field performances.

As expected, Warne's form was ordinary in the early-season district games for St Kilda, but even then he was fiery and competitive. The spirit was willing despite the extra flesh. And he took wickets. His first real test came in a one-day Mercantile

Cup game for Victoria against Queensland. Warne set himself to do well, especially against Border. If he performed, it would be hard to keep him out of international one-day contention.

Victoria made 220-odd and Warne came on for his ten overs with Stuart Law batting well. Dean Jones, the new state captain, was energetic and enthusiastic in the field, but he had much to learn about handling the young champion.

Warne bowled without a close-to-the-wicket fieldsman. It meant that there was no real threat to the batsman, even though Warne was not yet anywhere near top form. It made no sense not to have even a slip, who would have made his big-turning stock leg break so much more dangerous. But Warne didn't appear to protest and it became the norm for one-dayers during the summer, no matter for whom he played.

If any ball strayed from perfect line and length on the docile MCG strip, it was going to be hit by Law, who was in early-season form, and later Border, who once more showed how adept he was at playing spin.

Warne was despatched and all but demolished, returning figures of none for 60 off his ten overs. But, as usual, he learnt from the experience. If making the international one-dayers meant bowling defensively and relying on unerring line and length, without that important man in slip to give him wicket-taking options, he would do it.

Next time out in the Mercantile competition against South Australia in Adelaide he bowled with extraordinary control, again without close fielders, and returned none for 24 off ten. In blustery, difficult conditions, he put the ball precisely on a spot and delivered only his leggie, just varying the amount of break on a slow-turning wicket. It was a pointer for things to come and the national selectors took note. Warne could bowl tighter than tight in this format of the game. Slowly but surely he was eliminating the excuses for not playing him in the pyjama game.

It was important to Warne to be selected in the big one-day competition. First, he loved the faster game. Secondly, he enjoyed performing in front of the big crowds. Thirdly, playing in them made him more commercially marketable than the Tests. If he was going to earn as much as he could from cricket, he needed to succeed in both its formats.

In Shield games, he wore the opposition down, demonstrating an even greater consistency than before. He might go wicketless for a day, but in the fourth or fifth session, he would break through. As important as his skill was his staying power. The Shield competition had been scheduled to give Test players as much opportunity to find form as possible. Warne played in four of the first five Victorian games, taking twenty-seven wickets, including fourteen in two matches against the powerful New South Wales side. He was ready to enter the fray against that season's dual visitors, New Zealand and then South Africa.

One-Way Traffic

New Zealand arrived in Australia to a moderate build-up and began its campaign with an injured Martin Crowe and a thin bowling line-up. Border, coach Simpson and Warne himself played up the 'amazing new balls' he was going to serve up against the Kiwis. No longer did Border feel constrained to keep feeding the media his unconvincing line about having to 'protect' his white-haired boy.

Now Warne was the unplayable winner. It was good marketing. The Aussies had to 'sell' something different to whip up interest in the New Zealanders, who had never really captured the Australian public's imagination. Even after drawing the three-match series in New Zealand eight months previously, they had respect but not much more. Apart from that, the mind games between the two sides were only a way of establishing psychological superiority. The 'mystery ball' talk was just that. Warne had five basic deliveries, the leg break, the top-spinner, the flipper, the wrong 'un and the zooter. Everything else was a variation of these five.

On the first day of the Perth Test beginning on 12 November 1993, Border called correctly and batted. There was a two-hour delay due to rain before Taylor and Slater got going, slowly. Chris Cairns, who looked to have improved in pace and length since earlier in the year, broke through when he had Slater fending a rising ball to Patel at square leg for 10. Boon shocked by parrying at another lifter from Cairns and was on his way for a 'golden' duck. Australia was two for 37 and hadn't yet seen out an hour's play.

Mark Waugh came in and made a bright 36 before Danny Morrison got him with one that slipped through embarrassingly low for a first-day pitch. Border came in and scratched around uncharacteristically until Morrison induced a biggish edge to second slip. Taylor ground to a halt after four hours and chopped Cairns onto his stumps, leaving the home side at a modest five for 164. Suddenly, the Ashes were a dim memory. The Aussies were struggling against a foe playing above itself.

Steve Waugh restored the situation somewhat with 44, after which Healy and Reiffel took the score to six for 229 at stumps. Next day, they slammed on another 62 in quick time before Reiffel departed for a fine 51. Warne came in at seven for 298 and departed for 11, followed by McDermott with some big hitting to collect 35 off only thirty-three balls. Healy remained unbeaten on 113 and Australia was all out for 398.

New Zealand replied with nine for 419 declared, Jones plundering a fine 143 and Cairns 78. Warne suffered from Jones's sweeping and Cairns's one big six over mid-off onto the corner of the Farley Stand roof. The latter was Warne's only victim for the match. The wicket had been the slowest at the WACA for decades and Warne's one for 90 return did away with any further 'pysche' talk about mystery balls, which had preceded the game. He found some bounce, but little spin in the WACA pitch, which was never a happy hunting ground for him. Australia's second dig saw them notch one for 323, with Taylor not out on 142, Slater making 99, and Boon 67 not out. The visitors replied with four for 166, leaving the game a dull draw.

It was then on to Bellerive Oval, Hobart, for the Second Test, which began on 26 November. Border won the toss and batted. Australia ran up six for 544 declared, now a familiar performance, with Slater crashing a first-rate 168, Boon a solid 106 and Mark Waugh a stylish 111. Border himself made 60. Then it was May and Warne in tandem who destroyed undermanned New Zealand, dismissing it for 161. May took five for 65 and Warne three for 36. In went the Kiwis once more and again they could only muster 161. The game, hardly a match, was over in three and a half days. This time Warne took six for 31, and May two for 45.

Warne was brought on after only ten overs, and was used as a strike bowler. And strike he did. He fooled Pocock (9) with a faster ball as the batsman left his crease to go after him and Healy had him neatly stumped. In a short space of time, he clean bowled Rutherford (55), Su'a (5) and Morrison (0). It was a classic case of Warne at his best, creating havoc among the opposition and breaking through regularly.

Australia's reliance on spin seemed entrenched. The combination was convincing. In their past seven Tests working together, Warne and May had taken seventy-one wickets—Warne thirty-six and May thirty-five. It had started in January at Adelaide when May took seven for 50 and Warne one for 29. In England in the last five Tests, it was Warne eight for 159, May six for 145 at Lord's; Warne six for 182, May one for 143 at Trent Bridge; Warne one for 106, May five for 98 at Headingley; Warne six for 145, May seven for 121 at Edgbaston; and Warne five for 148, May two for 85 at the Oval. And now Warne nine for 67, May seven for 110 at Hobart.

Warne spoke effusively about his relationship with the off-spinner: 'Maysie is a great partner. His dry humour keeps me going in the lulls—when we are containing rather than blasting through. He's always on hand for advice. It really helps my bowling rhythm to have him wheeling away at the other end. In tandem, we keep the pressure on by attacking and getting through our overs quickly.'

The Third Test at Brisbane saw the New Zealanders fare better when they batted first and reached 233. McDermott was at his near-best with four for 39. Warne was well in the wickets again, getting rid of the dangerous Jones, whom he bowled for 53. He took four for 66, while May's figures were one for 51.

Australia showed no mercy in reply, scoring six for 607 before declaring. No one missed out in the run feast. Slater, 28, Taylor, 53, and Boon, 89, set the foundations and Border returned to the century lists with 105, while Steve Waugh was unbeaten on 147. He and Warne shared an unbroken seventh-wicket partnership of 142, with Warne hitting his highest Test score yet of 74 not out.

His batting seemed at last to be realising some of its potential, especially when he curbed the need to swat every ball. He had still not learnt to measure an innings and concentrate, but this performance was encouraging. He had a technique which looked good when he used it and avoided the urge to let the back foot drift towards square leg against faster bowlers. His ability to hit straight and hard, coupled with his superb eye, was enough to enable him to become a bowling all-rounder, if he wished. So far, the desire had not manifested itself. Perhaps there was too much to concentrate on with his bowling. There was also the worry while batting that a paceman would send a ball bashing into his spinning finger, which was already tender and showing signs of wear. This made him wary of speed. It was not a matter of courage, which Warne never lacked, but commonsense. A damaged spinning finger would end his Test career.

In its second innings, New Zealand seemed more determined than ever not to capitulate. Young resisted until Warne bowled him for 53. Captain Ken Rutherford showed grit after blasting his players for their lack of effort in the Second Test, but, on 86, was induced by McDermott to slash a ball to Warne in the gully and the resistance was thereafter limited. The side was all out for 278, leaving Australia victors by an innings and 96 runs. Warne collected another bag of four for 59, with a new, young fast bowler named Glenn McGrath offering best support with three for 66.

Before the lopsided series ended, the media was speculating on the first tour of a South African side in thirty years. New Zealand would have to be happy with a token performance in the one-dayers. It would see better teams develop.

Rutherford made comment on Warne and his eighteen wickets, and his dominance over New Zealand in two successive series:

'He's the most demanding spinner I've ever faced. Everyone goes on about how far he spins his stock ball, the orthodox leg break. I think his greatest asset is his line and length. He drops onto it pretty quickly and really doesn't give many bad balls to hit. So when you have to face five or six good deliveries per over, you've nowhere to go. The pressure is relentless. You go searching for the bad one—the half-tracker or the full toss. That's when the batsman gets into trouble. You try to go down the wicket or maybe back too far, desperate in looking for a way to make runs and break the hold he has on you. That's when you go out.'

Warne had taken his overall Test-wicket tally to eighty-three, having captured sixty-eight in calendar year 1993 alone. This surpassed the previous record for Australian spinners of fifty-five, set by Arthur Mailey in 1921 and equalled by Richie Benaud in 1959. The challenges ahead meant he would build on that figure. South Africa was next.

One-Day Wonder

By December 1993, Allan Border had become Warne's key minder in and out of cricket. He knew what he had in the young blond freak: a character of strength, will and exceptional ability. Border knew a match-winner when he stumbled on one. Recently, he had stubbed his toe on Glenn McGrath. Border had tested McGrath mid-pitch in a Shield game with some verbal abuse to see what this beanstalk was made of. The country lad had responded in kind with mouth and ball in a way that impressed the Aussie skipper. The selectors were tipped off. The raw-boned speedster had what it took in the skill and mental stakes at the top level. Similarly, Border had pushed Warne, especially in the nets where he noticed the spinner tended at first to be not slack, but unfocused. He watched Warne bowling medium-pacers and off-spinners. Then, when it was Border's turn to bat, he challenged Warne to dismiss him.

'See if you can put one, *just one*, past me,' Border told him in the nets during one of Warne's early Tests. 'Because you won't get me out. Not the way you shape up in the nets.'

This was a typical stirring from Border, who believed in practising with the same sharpness and determination as in the middle in a Test. He asked Geoff Marsh to 'umpire' while Warne bowled to him. In a twenty-minute session, in which Border faced about 100 deliveries, there was dispute over an lbw decision, and one other ball that shot past Border's probing blade. The point was made. The batsman defended most, but hammered anything loose, often using his feet to drive, several times out of the nets and into the deep country. Border would call 'four' or 'lazy three' when he got onto one. Warne responded to the challenge. It touched his competitive spirit. He disputed Border's 'scoring' now and again, saying that a shot would be covered by fielders. Warne's attitude to the way he practised changed forever. He only ever bowled mediums again when he needed to rest his shoulder, fingers and wrist from the rigours of spinning.

Border knew he had a 'winner', a bowler to match Lillee in his capacity to strike fear and doubt in the hearts of opponents. Not because the spinner could hurt them, but rather because he could demoralise them when breaking through an opposition.

The skipper's protection ran to keeping him out of one-day cricket and ripe for Tests. The selectors seemed to agree with Border. And Warne, who was most eager to play in the exciting short game, accepted the judgment. Yet deep down he wanted to be out there, especially at the MCG in front of the home spectators, who were more like an AFL crowd than Test supporters. They were far bigger too. A one-dayer might attract 80 000 where an average Test day attendance might slip to fewer than 20 000 after day one. Warne, like all top sportspeople, preferred to perform in front of a big house. There was also more money for him if he played international one-dayers. Yet he didn't gripe or complain about Border's desire to conserve the performances of his new top gun. Instead, he made it known that he wanted to play and left it to form and providence.

Border made the point after Warne's second successive destruction of New Zealand at Brisbane when responding to media questions about when the leggie would put on pyjamas.

'Warne can play a role in one-day cricket,' Border said circumspectly, 'but I see him as a real bonus for us in Test cricket. Test cricket is more important for us at the moment. We don't want to overexpose and overburden him.'

Border bemoaned the fact that he had seen 'a couple of other really good leg-spinners turn into stock bowlers'. He went on: 'I think Mushtaq [Ahmed] is not as effective in Test cricket as he was, but is a tremendous one-day bowler. And the same for Pakistan's Abdul Qadir. You don't want to give the batsmen an edge by having them belt you all over the place in a one-day game and the next day they play you in a Test match. At this stage, I think we're better off holding him back a little bit.'

Reacting to a question about Warne's inclusion in the World Series Cricket one-day squad at the end of 1993, the captain said he was being kept fresh. In other words, he would be training hard with the other team members, but not playing many games, if any. Warne, Border implied, would be having enough of a run at the state level in the one-dayers and Shield games, especially with Dean Jones as captain.

Providence and luck then stepped in and changed Border's thinking. Injury-prone Tim May hurt his hamstring and Australia was forced to pick Warne to play WSC games against the South

Africans in Melbourne and Sydney. First-up, Border held his star back to the twenty-fifth over when Kepler Wessels and Hansie Cronje were well set. But later he managed to bowl Daryll Cullinan with a terrific flipper. Cullinan, many astute observers in South Africa opined, was the Proteas' best bat, and he would prove it on this tour. The encounter proved nothing, except that Warne had not been plastered. He could bowl tight in this format.

He next bowled in two one-dayers against the New Zealanders and continued his dominance over the unfortunate Kiwis with four for 25 off ten overs, and four for 19. His other one-day encounter with South Africa saw them crash for 69. He wasn't needed to bowl.

Border's fear that Warne might be hammered had been allayed. Yet the verdict on his other point about overusing him would not be in for some time.

Meanwhile, Warne was keeping his eye in with Victoria in the Sheffield Shield. In the return game against New South Wales in Sydney, just before the First Test with South Africa in December 1993, Warne was pitted against a better batting side in the host team. It boasted Slater, Taylor, the Waughs and Bevan. The finest combat in the game was between Warne and his close friend Mark Waugh. The latter started cautiously and took nineteen balls to score against the spinner. Warne was using the same method he had employed so successfully in England—aiming most deliveries into the rough outside leg stump. Waugh did his impression of a Spanish dancer, kick-flicking the ball away, an ugly method allowed by the outmoded lbw law. Warne persevered. He slipped one through his opponent and appealed for a catch behind, as did keeper Darren Berry. Umpire Darrell Hair turned down the wild appeal, much to the histrionic Warne's chagrin.

'You touched that!' Warne said at the end of the over.

'No, you know I didn't,' Waugh responded.

'We all heard it, mate.'

'Wishful thinking.'

'We heard it, didn't we, Darren?'

'In your dreams,' Waugh said with a tough grin before Berry could back up his bowler.

And so the banter went for much of Waugh's great innings of 119 in 270 minutes—later compared to his brilliant knocks against South Africa in 1997 as among the best he has played—on a turning wicket which offered Warne considerable help. He remarked that Waugh's performance on such a wicket ranked him above all other batsmen to whom he had ever bowled.

Warne finished with an equally impressive five for 77 off forty overs, which made him only the eleventh player to pass forty first-class wickets in an Australian season before the end of December. He took forty-six in all before the end of December, just five less than Clarrie Grimmett's all-time record of fifty-one wickets in 1934, nearly six decades earlier.

The two friends fought out one of the finest Shield contests ever, rivalling that of Bradman against Grimmett and Bradman against O'Reilly in the 1920s and 1930s. Warne dismissed Waugh cheaply in the second innings. New South Wales managed to hold on for a draw in the game in fading light, which saved it from outright defeat.

The battle's intensity was not lost on the 5000 spectators, the biggest Shield crowd for the summer in an atmosphere that brought a taste of the glory decades from the 1920s to the 1960s when crowds of 30 000-plus turned up to watch Victoria play New South Wales in Melbourne and Sydney. Warne and the other Test players could not have had a more competitive build-up for the First Test in Melbourne against South Africa.

Rain and Pain

It's risky ever to plan an outdoor party in Melbourne, even at the height of summer. The weather can change so quickly that locals might start the day in sun-hat and glasses, move under an umbrella and end up putting on the sun-hat again. And so it was for the renewal of Test battles between South Africa and

Australia at Christmas 1993. The temperature was 14.9 degrees Celsius—the coldest Boxing Day since 1924—when the rain-delayed day began at 5 p.m. Less than sixteen hours of play for the entire match ensured a tame draw, with Australia scoring seven declared for 342, and South Africa replying with three for 258. Taylor top-scored for Australia with 170 and Mark Waugh made 84 with characteristic fluency. Alan Donald bowled with a hostility that was not reflected in his one for 108 off thirty overs. He had three catches dropped and struck Taylor and Waugh with such force that onlookers, huddled in the stands, winced. It was a triumph for Taylor, who became only the second batsman behind New Zealand's Martin Crowe to score a century against seven opponents in Test cricket. It was also the fourth time Taylor had scored a hundred on debut against an opponent in fifty Tests and he became the twelfth Australian to pass 4000 runs in Tests.

During the Australian innings, Test newcomer Daryll Cullinan dropped four catches. According to Warne, he never stopped abusing Australia's batsmen and caused them to question his right to be so 'chirpy' since he was new to Test cricket. Much was said between the two teams on the field.

Warne bowled tidily, troubling every batsman for thirty overs and one for 63, having Hansie Cronje caught in close by Boon for 71. It was the beginning of a tremendous battle between the spinner and South Africa's most reliable bat which would continue for the rest of the 1990s and go a long way to determining which country held the upper hand. Andrew Hudson (retired hurt for 64) and Kepler Wessels (63 not out) were the other players to show form and resistance to the speed of McDermott and the guile of Warne.

Wessels's effort was notable, given that he had a knee injury which would have forced lesser men not to play. He showed the same defiance against Australia that he had demonstrated for them as a limited, yet gutsy opener in the 1980s when he took Australian nationality in order to be able to play at the highest level of the game.

Sydney provided good weather and a far better Test—in fact, one of the most thrilling since such matches began in 1877. South Africa had never won in Sydney and only achieved a draw in 1963–64 under Trevor Goddard, having lost four previous Tests there by big margins. Australia had had great success in Sydney over the years, invariably picking two spinners to take advantage of the slow, bare pitches that had been known to turn on the second day, if not the first.

Even Allan Border, a modest orthodox left-armer, had snared eleven West Indies wickets on a pitch typical of those prepared by Peter Leroy, the local ground supervisor. Murray Bennett, another left-armer, was picked several times for Sydney to partner Bob Holland, but could not maintain his place away from the SCG. However, Warne, who had started his career ingloriously at Sydney against India, was yet to take advantage of Sydney's rich offerings. A year earlier he had run into a brilliant Lara (277) and had only managed one for 116 off forty-one overs. He was economical, but shell-shocked like all the bowlers by the West Indian dominance as they racked up 606.

Warne was ready and aware that the Proteas would never have faced anyone like him at his best. They had played against Anil Kumble, but in South Africa and not on India's turners. Again, Kumble was different from Warne in that the Indian relied on pace and bounce more than Warne's variation, loop and spin.

A big Sydney crowd of 32 681 turned up on day one at an SCG bathed in sunshine. South Africa batted first and quickly lost Hudson, lbw to McGrath, who with McDermott gave Australia's speed attack new venom. With Cronje and Kirsten travelling well at one for 23, Border threw the ball to Warne. McDermott had Cronje caught close to the wicket for 41. Then in Warne's twelfth over, the mayhem began. He bowled the new batsman Daryll Cullinan with a magnificent flipper. There was already a 'bit of aggro' between these two as Cullinan had 'verballed' the Australians, particularly Warne, during the Melbourne Test. As Cullinan walked away from the wicket, Warne and he had 'words'. The spinner had just humiliated his opponent in the best way possible and his 'send-off' was undisciplined. No one, however, officially penalised or warned him. The excess was lost in the flurry of his ensuing performance, as he helped roll South Africa for 169, taking seven for 22 in seventy-eight balls, to finish with seven for 56. Sydneysiders who remembered Grimmett and O'Reilly could not recall such beguiling spin. Three fell to the flipper that had rocketed him to stardom in Melbourne a year earlier. Each dismissal was different: Cullinan was bowled, Jonty Rhodes was lbw and Gary Kirsten stumped by Healy. Was it the surprise of this 'hit-me' ball, or had Warne imparted something special to it? Time would tell.

Australia replied with 292. Slater (92), Damien Martyn (59) and Border (49) provided resistance against not great spin, but speed. Fanie de Villiers (four for 80) and Donald (four for 83) overcame the wicket's slowness and used its low bounce to good effect. Slater's innings was notable. He showed unusual restraint and picked the right shot to hit rather than displaying his hallmark impetuosity. Border, for a long time at the other end, cajoled and guided Slater into a responsible knock. Slater only lasted nine balls after his skipper, suggesting that he needed his support.

The second time around it was McDermott who removed Hudson (1) early by having him caught behind, then Cronje (38) by bowling him. Warne then trapped the hapless Cullinan lbw for just 2, giving him 0, 0 and 2 for an average of less than 1 so far. Warne this time glared and restrained his apparent contempt for the now less cocky batsman. Channel Nine TV commentator Tony Greig went round to see the South African coach Mike Procter and Cullinan to offer some advice on how to play the flipper. Greig was astonished to learn that neither of them knew what a flipper was or how it came out of the hand. Greig suggested they find a local leg-spinner who could bowl it and use him in the nets to familiarise the team with it.

South Africa slumped to five for 110, still 16 runs behind, thanks mainly to McDermott. Rhodes then led a brave recovery in a stand of 72 with keeper Richardson, who contributed 24. Rhodes remained not out on 76 and was helped by Donald in a last-wicket stand of 30 runs off thirty-nine balls in forty-two minutes, statistics that were to have a bearing on the final result. South Africa was all out for 239, Warne taking the bowling honours with five for 72 of forty-two overs, including seventeen maidens. He was nudged rather than hit for less than 2 runs an over, making him both an economical bowler who could tie up an end and a strike bowler as destructive as any quick in history. His overall figures of twelve for 127 from sixty-nine overs were his finest and worthy of the Man of the Match award. Scorers had to go back 107 years to find a better effort at the SCG when Charles 'The Terror' Turner snared twelve for 87 with his medium-pace off cutters against England. Warne's tightness and strike rate had worked in well with McDermott, who took four for 62 off twenty-eight overs.

Australia was left with a paltry 117 to make to win, but given recent history, a fear crept into the home camp. Eight of the players in the team performed in the side that lost by 1 run to the Windies a year earlier in Adelaide. One player, captain Border, was involved in the shocker at Headingley in 1981 when Australia managed just 111 pursuing 130 for victory. Could that happen again now?

Sure enough, de Villiers struck early, removing Slater for 1. Then Taylor and Boon steadied, taking the score to one for 51—just 66 short of victory. De Villiers hit back, taking Boon, night watchman Tim May and Taylor in five balls, leaving Australia at a perilous four for 62 overnight on day four. Still victory seemed probable given the batting strength.

De Villiers told journalists that he still thought South Africa had a good chance of victory, warning the Aussies to 'watch out'.

'If we can get a breakthrough in the first seven overs and get two guys out then the pressure is really going to be on them,' he said. 'I don't think they're going to play any big shots. They'll try to get them in singles … it's definitely still on … we've always shown character in that sense.'

This was bluff and bravado, yet useful propaganda in the psychological sense, with the implication being that Australia did not show character and that they might choke. When not two but four wickets fell cheaply the next morning, de Villiers was hailed as a prophet, while his partner Donald revved up and trapped Mark Waugh lbw for 11 and bowled Border for 7. Healy for once stumbled in a crisis and unluckily played on to de Villiers for 1. Warne was then run out for 1 by a brilliant piece of fielding by Cronje. Australia crashed to eight for 75 and faced defeat.

Martyn, who seemed paralysed by what he was viewing at the other end, was joined by McDermott. He had often been criticised for backing away from the pacemen, but when it really counted in Adelaide a year ago against the Windies, the big fast bowler had shown grit with Tim May in a last-ditch stand that all but paid off. They then scored 40 in a last-wicket stand.

Now McDermott decided to retaliate, with a series of boundaries that put the game in the balance again. Then Martyn, who had hung around for 106 minutes for his 6, decided to strike out. He drove Donald to Hudson in the covers and was caught. It was the shot that unfairly shattered his Test career. He would never be forgiven by selectors. Australia was nine for 110, still needing 7 runs for victory. A run later, last man in McGrath popped a soft caught-and-bowled back to de Villiers and Australia was beaten by 5 runs. McDermott was left on 29 not out, the only batsman to go for his shots.

In the end, it was de Villiers and not Warne who took the Man of the Match award, with ten for 123 and the performance that did most to give his team a win. After the prolonged lapse of decades, the inexperienced, undertalented yet fiercely determined South African combination had drawn first Test blood, against all the odds.

All Square

A dispirited Aussie team regrouped in Adelaide at the end of January for one chance to level the series. The injured Steve Waugh returned for the hapless Martyn, and Reiffel replaced

McGrath. The South Africans omitted off-spinner Pat Symcox, in favour of four specialist seam and fast bowlers.

Border won the toss and batted. Australia grafted to four for 240 after losing Slater (53) caught off Donald, Taylor (62), Boon (50) and Mark Waugh (2). On day two, Border (84) and Steve Waugh (164) brought back memories of their recent dominance over England with a partnership of 208 to take Australia to nine for 469.

The South African response was solid, if uninspired, as they trotted to two for 173 at tea on day three. Warne and May had failed to make a breakthrough and Australia's decision to pick two spinners seemed a misjudgment. Then Steve Waugh broke through with a vengeance to take four for 15 by his ninth over and the 38-year-old Peter Kirsten only just managed to steer his team clear of the follow-on when they were all out for 273. Warne took just one for 79, but again tied up one end with 44.2 overs, with fifteen maidens at less than 2 runs an over. No one was either equipped or inclined to take him on. Waugh's four for 26 off eighteen overs saw him take bowling honours and complete a fine double with bat and ball.

Australia batted for 164 minutes before declaring at six for 124, giving it a lead of just 320. Border's declaration was generous. He wanted to tempt the South Africans into chasing at less than 3 an over at the end of day four and into the fifth.

Border gambled with Warne just before stumps after McDermott had dismissed Hudson for 2. The spinner bowled Gary Kirsten (7) and trapped Cronje (3) lbw in just twelve deliveries, leaving the visitors three for 18 at stumps in twenty-one overs. It had been stubborn, tense Test cricket at its best.

Night watchman de Villiers, sporting a broken thumb from McDermott in the first innings, buckled down to the countdown of the day's ninety overs with the dependable Peter Kirsten at the other end. They grafted until lunch and the score trickled to 100 by the middle of the afternoon session. Then de Villiers (30) lashed at McDermott and was caught by Reiffel in the covers. South Africa was four for 100 and still with a chance to

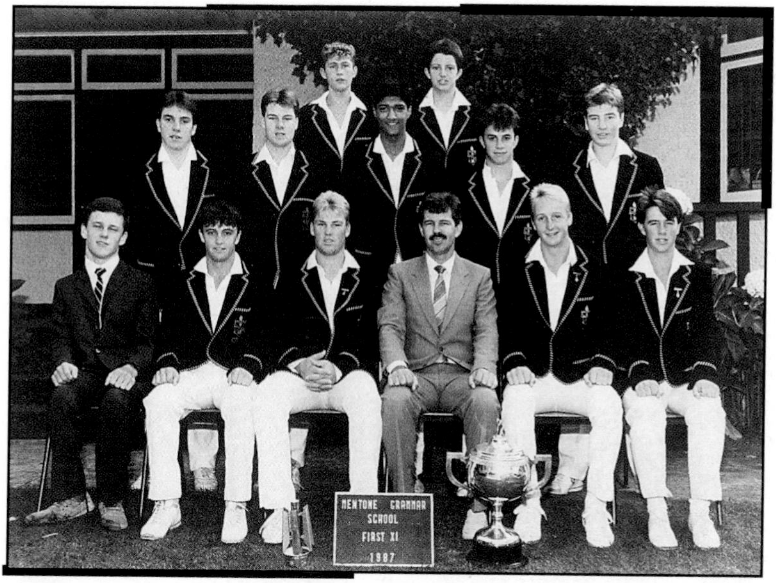

Natural leader. At school, Warne (front row, third from left) showed the lead-from-the-front attacking style that is apparent now in his play and captaincy.

Happy and hirsute. Warne's happy-go-lucky approach was apparent in his early career before his Test debut. When he realised he just might maintain a place at the top, he got serious and shed kilos.

Bagging the baggy green. Warne tries on his Aussie Test cap for the first time in January 1992.

The pay-off. Border with Warne after the spinner destroyed the West Indies at Melbourne on 30 December 1992. It was his first match-winning effort.

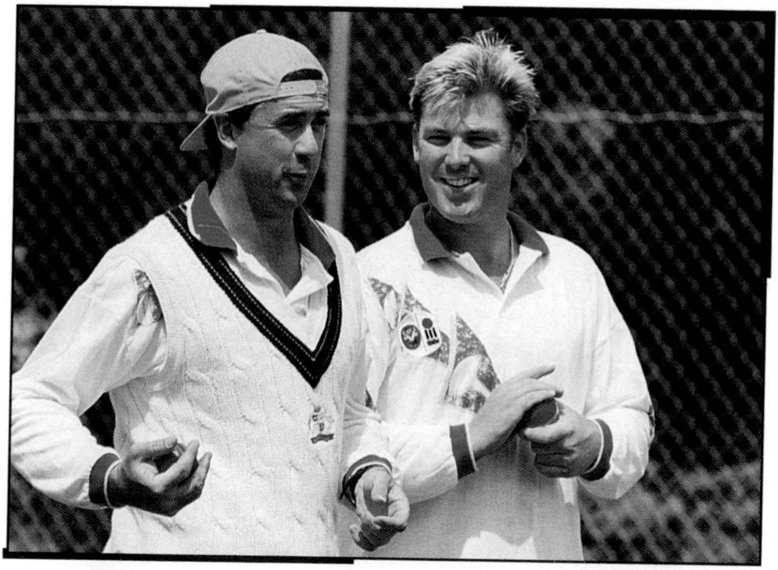

May the spinning begin. Warne with his spin partner Tim May in October 1993. They proved a strong combination for several series.

Shouldering responsibility. Warne gives it everything in South Africa, March 1994. David Boon is the fielder.

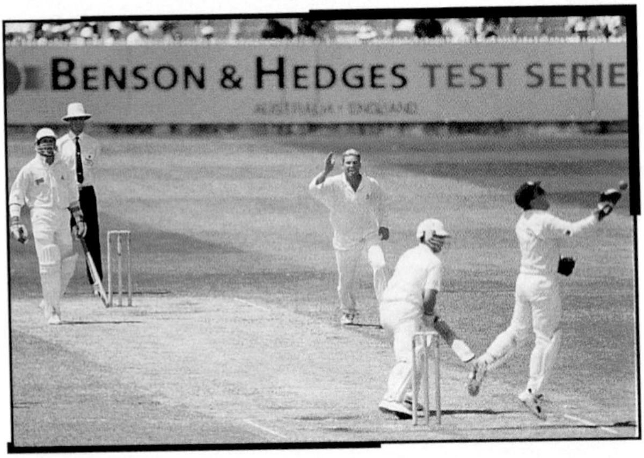

Chapeau magic. Warne dismisses DeFreitas (lbw), Gough (caught behind) and Malcolm (caught by Boon) for a Test hat-trick against England at the MCG on 29 December 1994.

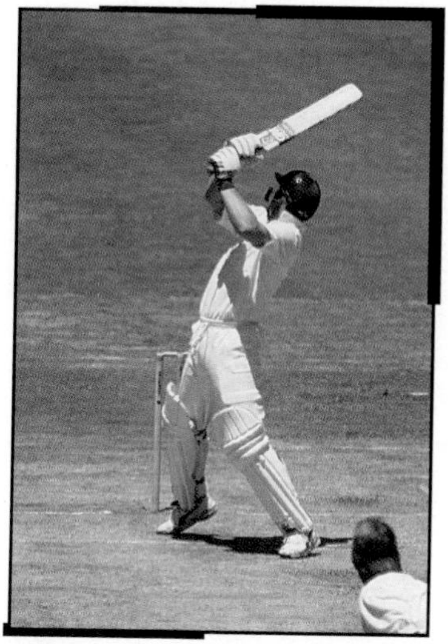

Upper cut. Warne goes for an up-and-under shot against England in 1994–95.

Mirror image. Warne with his wife Simone. They married in September 1995.

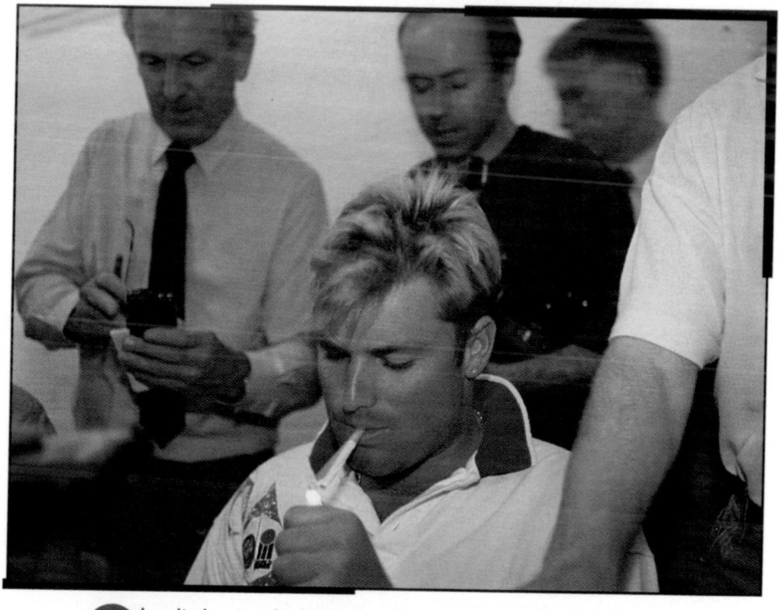

That little vice. Lighting up after a media conference. Warne refused to give up this private pleasure until January 1999, when paid $200 000 to do so.

Spinning Jenner. Former Australian spinner Terry Jenner gives Warne some advice after his comeback from finger surgery in 1996. It helped him regain confidence.

When we were mates. Warne with Brian Lara at the Eden Gardens cricket ground in Calcutta in February 1996. Warne went more than halfway for a friendship with one of his biggest rivals in world cricket. Later, their relationship deteriorated after allegations of sledging against Warne.

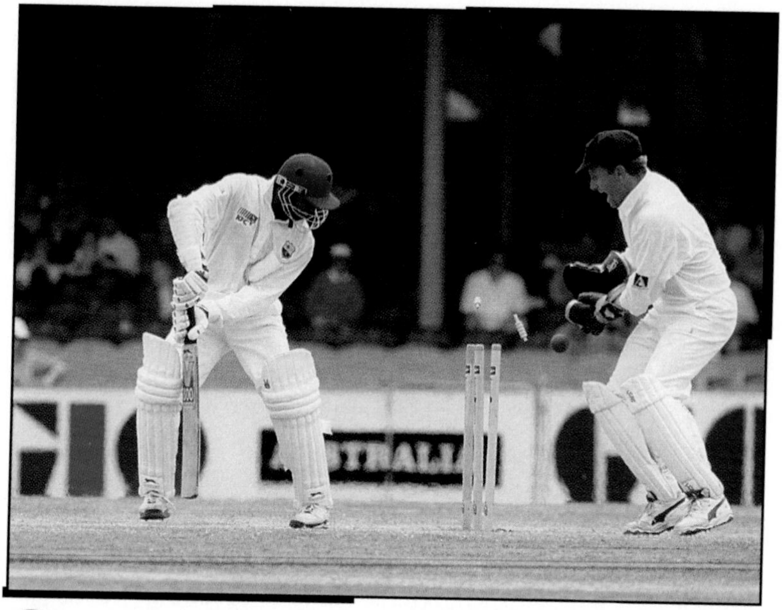

The Chanderpaul ball. Warne bowls the rampant Shivnarine Chanderpaul on the last ball before lunch on the final day of the Second Test at Sydney, 1996–97. This delivery, one of the finest ever bowled in Test cricket, swung the game Australia's way.

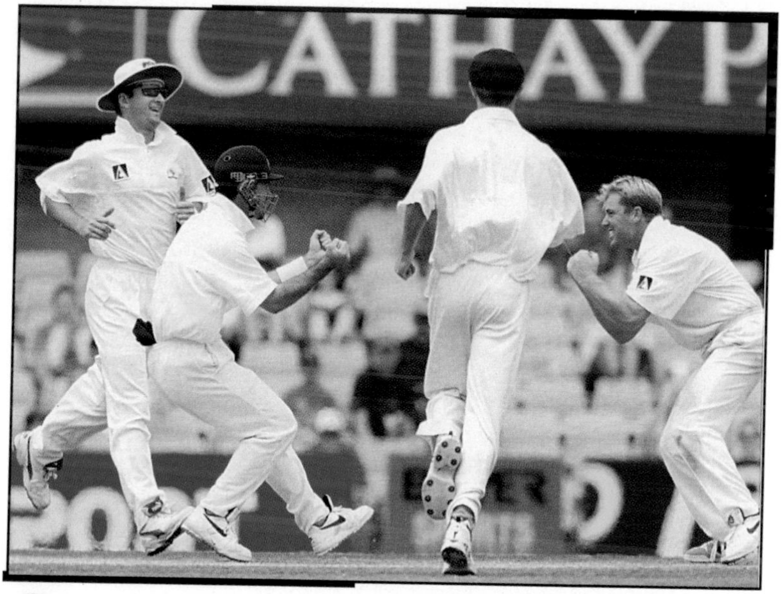

The punter rap. Ricky Ponting and Warne go into a spontaneous dance of delight after Warne removes Chanderpaul on the last day of the Sydney Test in December 1996.

Body speak. Vice-captain Steve Waugh, skipper Mark Taylor and Warne seem to be struggling to think of ways to stop England during the First Test at Edgbaston in 1997. England won.

A Saint at Lord's. Warne wearing a St Kilda Football Club jumper on the balcony at Lord's during the Second Test. Australia outplayed England, but the game was drawn.

Praying or appealing? Warne puts the pressure on during the vital Old Trafford Test in 1997.

Dance of the *derrière*. Warne celebrates on the balcony of the pavilion at Old Trafford in 1997, after Australia's fifth successive Ashes victory. His action was wrongly seen as a dance of derision for the vanquished foe.

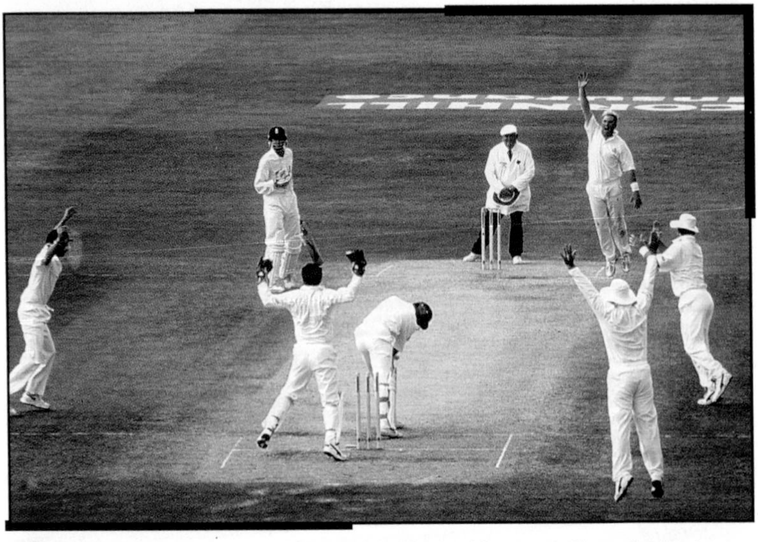

The taming of Hussein. Warne bowls Nasser Hussain at Trent Bridge in August 1997 and spins out England's hopes of winning its first Ashes series in five attempts.

I'm no dummy. A few seconds after this shot was taken in late 1997, Warne walked out of a 'photo opportunity' upset by remarks pertaining to his weight compared to the wax replica destined for Madame Tussaud's.

Mark's catch. Mark Waugh demonstrates the top-drawer fielding back-up for Australia's bowlers as he takes this one off Warne against New Zealand in November 1997.

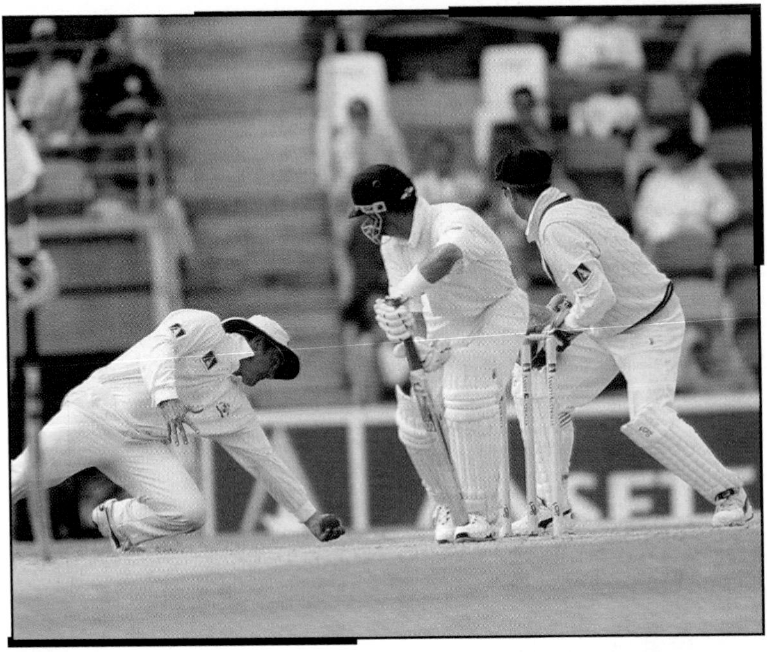

The great slipper skipper. Mark Taylor shows why the scorecard 'caught Taylor bowled Warne' has become a regular line. This time New Zealand's Adam Parore is the victim, in November 1997.

Wicket fever. Warne catches Richardson off his own bowling in the Second Test versus South Africa at the SCG, 5 January 1998. This was his 299th Test wicket.

Three hundred and climbing. Warne celebrates his 300th Test wicket by bowling Kallis at Sydney on 5 January 1998. The spinner's six for 34 and eleven for 109 for the match were a big factor in the win.

Meeting his match. The dashing Indian Sachin Tendulkar hits out against Warne during the First Test in 1998 at Madras, India. Tendulkar became the first player in Warne's six-year career at the top to dominate him.

Which delivery? Warne contemplates which ball he will send down in the first game—at the MCG—of the one-day finals against South Africa, 1998. Australia won the series against the odds.

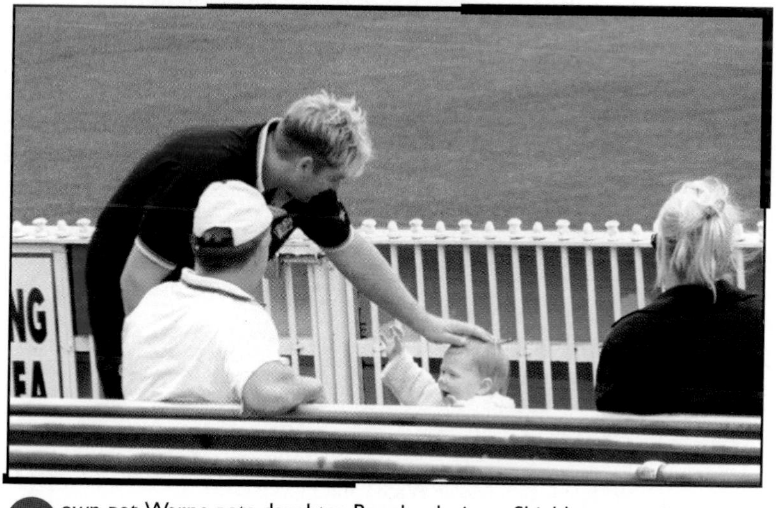

Down pat. Warne pats daughter Brooke during a Shield game against Queensland in December 1998, while Simone looks on. Given the stark choice, Warne said he would opt for his family over the game.

A kiss for the girl in his life. Warne blows a kiss to daughter Brooke during a Shield game in December 1998. He withdrew to family and friends during the bookie scandal.

Birds of a flutter. Warne and Mark Waugh at the nets together. Their off-field, 'naïve and stupid' dealings with an Indian bookie got them into more trouble than they ever gambled on.

force a draw, but it collapsed to be seven for 116 by tea and then all out for 129, giving Australia victory by 191 runs. The series was squared at one-all. Warne came in for the kill to capture McMillan (4) lbw and hold a caught-and-bowled from Snell (1).

He also took bowling honours with four for 31 off 30.5 overs, including fifteen maidens. It was a perfect situation for him with the opposition freezing up and on the defence. He could force errors and create a crisis that panicked the batsmen, who had no relief even when they got away from him and found themselves facing men like May and McDermott at the other end. Warne reached the 100-wicket mark with Brian McMillan's wicket and took his tally in all to 101, with eighteen against South Africa in this series and another eighteen in the previous one against New Zealand. Since his triumph in England, where he had taken thirty-four wickets in six Tests, Warne had taken no fewer than thirty-six in the next six, with remarkable consistency and economy. He was not your average leggie who 'bought' wickets, but a spinner who could tighten or attack at will. Warne had bowled 30 per cent of all Australian Test overs during the summer. No wonder Border kept saying he ought to be carefully looked after. No wonder, too, that he was named the Benson & Hedges International Cricketer of the Year.

Although the series was over, it was not the last the Australian saw of the South Africans. In only a few weeks time, they were to meet them again in another three-match rubber, this time on the Proteas' home turf, that would mark the end of an era—Allan Border's retirement from the Test scene.

8

From Border to Taylor

Return Bouts

Australia arrived for the First Test at the Wanderers ground in Johannesburg early in March 1994, chastened from a three–one deficit in the one-day series to that point. The team morale was low, with injury and illness problems affecting Border, Taylor, Mark Waugh, McDermott and Merv Hughes, who was recovering from knee surgery. Matters were not helped by being centre-stage as soon as their plane touched down. It was a new type of attention for many of the team, who found the crowds intense and ill-mannered. Warne was the focus of most attention with people demanding autographs with no beg pardon, please or thank you. It upset him. He objected to people pushing and shoving and making rude demands.

Abusive and threatening phone calls to players at the hotel worsened the team's mood, particularly Warne who had little sleep during the Test. Boon noticed his grumpy manner. Twelfth man Reiffel was stunned when, before play, Warne snapped at him, 'Get me some balls will you, so I can roll my arm over.'

It was an un–Warne-like, arrogant command.

Wessels won the toss and batted. His team began as if in one-day combat, led by Cronje until he tried his luck once too often and edged to Border at slip in place of the ill Taylor. South Africa posted 251 in 80.2 overs, with Rhodes (69), Gary Kirsten

(47) and McMillan (31) the main contributors. Warne, feeling out of sorts, only delivered fourteen overs and took just one for 42—Richardson, whom he trapped lbw. McDermott (three for 63), Hughes (two for 59) and May (two for 62) were the main wicket-takers.

Australia replied as if it was still in the same frame of mind and was consequently lucky to get within only three runs of the visitors' total. Mark Waugh (42), Border (34) and McDermott with another solid offering of 31 played the only innings of any significance.

In South Africa's second effort, Cronje made up for his earlier indiscretion and batted with application and style when he came to the wicket at one for 76 on the fourth day. It was a good start and Australia began to flag in the field. Warne on the fence at fine leg livened the Sunday crowd. Someone called out:

'Warne, show us your mystery ball.'

He looked down his trousers.

Another yelled:

'Pull up your pants.'

He again obliged by hitching his trousers high. It was all good fun. Then one or two members of the crowd turned nasty and made abusive remarks. Warne stopped responding. An orange was hurled out and hit him on the back. The crowd roared their approval. Warne looked across at security guards squatting by the fence. They thought it a huge joke, too, and were laughing. Warne was incensed. He couldn't wait to get into the action and prove a few points. The abuse kept coming. He had, to a point, erred in encouraging the crowd, some of whom were a little less than couth. Now he was paying the price for being the entertainer.

At last, after forty-four overs, Border came over and tossed him the ball.

'C'mon Warnie,' he said, 'get us a wicket.'

The revved-up crowd cat-called, yelled, clapped and screamed. They wanted to see him walloped. Warne was fired up for something else. He dropped straight onto a length. His third ball was pitched some way outside leg stump. It turned behind opener Andrew Hudson's legs and bowled him. Warne was cock-a-hoop at having shown the crowd a thing or two and answering his skipper's call. He screamed at the departing Hudson:

'Fuck off! Go on, Hudson, fuck off out of here!'

Warne gesticulated and advanced towards the batsman. If the crowd could not hear his words, like Hudson, they got the ugly message. Healy quickly moved towards Warne to stop him getting any closer to Hudson and making matters worse. Border joined in as well, wagging his finger at the wayward leggie, and eventually things calmed down.

Wessels came in and defied Australia, while Cronje (122) skipped on to a great century. By the time Warne broke through at 258 by having Wessels (50) caught by Border, the game was out of the visitors' reach. Peter Kirsten (53) and Richardson (31 not out) also helped lift the South Africans to an invincible nine declared for 450, an hour after lunch, leaving Australia 133 overs either to get the 454 required to win or stay at the crease. The tourists' state of mind in this game suggested that only Bradman could save them, and he wasn't about to pad up.

Despite the disruptions and the hostile crowd in the 'Bullring', as the ground is known, Warne put in a sustained performance, returning four for 86 off 44.5 overs. His victims included McMillan, who was fast becoming a 'bunny'—someone whom he had bamboozled so much he thought he could dismiss him almost at will, as he had poor Daryll Cullinan, now banished from the Test scene as a result, at least for the time being. At the other end of the scale there was Cronje, who had taken liberties with him in the one-dayers in Australia. Warne regarded him as his biggest challenge among the South Africans. He was no bunny, but Warne would lift against him in their Test and one-day encounters. Removing Cronje early, or at least subduing him, the Australians felt, was vital in their South African clashes.

While the Australian team manager, Dr Cam Battersby, and coach Bobby Simpson did their best to mollify an angry Australian Cricket Board in Sydney and a hungry international media over the Hudson incident, Slater and Hayden walked out to bat.

Hayden, under pressure to perform in his first Test after coming in for Taylor, received a brute of a ball second-up from the fiery Donald which crushed his thumb. Though he could hardly hold his bat, Hayden carried on with courage, but was soon bowled by de Villiers. He trudged off the field to learn his thumb had been fractured in two places, thus ending his tour.

Slater and Boon carried on until de Villiers bowled Slater (41) at 95. Mark Waugh (28) fell caught behind to Donald and Border (14) was caught off McMillan. When Boon (83) was bowled just before lunch on the fifth day, Australia was six for 194, still 260 short of victory and sixty overs adrift of salvation. Hughes joined Healy as darker clouds massed overhead. However, Donald caught-and-bowled Healy (30). McMillan got Warne lbw for 1 and bowled McDermott for 10, leaving Australia at nine for 236.

The light faded and drops of rain began to fall. Umpires David Shepherd and Barry Lambson conferred twice about the light, but decided to carry on. The third time, not long before tea, saw them leading the players back to the pavilion. The crowd bayed for their blood and more play. As Hughes and May entered the race, a spectator howled abuse at Hughes and he crashed his bat against an advertising hoarding. The spectator continued his invective and Hughes reached over the hoarding as if he was about to deliver a fierce cut for more than four. The spectator cringed as Hughes swore back at him and then joined May, who had ducked when spat at and hit in the face, in heading for the dressing room. TV cameras captured the whole unsavoury incident.

Soon afterwards, the rain eased, the covers came off and the Australian last-wicket defenders were on their way out again to more abuse. This time Hughes ignored it and concentrated on the job with May. They did well for sixty-six minutes as more rain threatened, but eventually Cronje had May caught at short leg by Gary Kirsten for a stubborn 11. Hughes was left dangling on a meritorious 36 not out.

Victory was South Africa's by 197. The team was ecstatic and the fans delirious. With two Tests to play and Australia's form so far down on tour, the locals were now confident they could win both the one-dayers and the series, thus earning South Africa clear superiority over the Australians in their first series in South Africa in a quarter-century.

Warne's Woes

Warne was fined $1000 by the ICC match referee, Donald Carr, for the Hudson episode. He apologised to the South African opener, who seemed to hold no grudge. Yet the damage was done in front of TV cameras that brought Warne's lack of self-control to the world. Warne had appeared like a crude hothead, an Australian 'yobbo'. He would have to work hard to restore his image, as would Hughes, who was also fined $1000 by Carr for his actions when coming off the field. Carr at first regarded the Hughes incident as minor, but on reviewing TV videos of what he had done decided it was bad enough to penalise him.

At the end of the game, Hughes and Warne received a further $4000 fine each by the Australian Cricket Board for their indiscretions, imposed by two board members, Alan Crompton and Graham Halbish, who flew over to South Africa after the match.

Warne and Hughes were upset because they did not receive a hearing on the matter. Their excuse was that they had been provoked by the abuse and attacks by the crowd. Crompton would no doubt have dismissed this even if there had been a formal hearing. Most observers and commentators had found their actions inexcusable.

English writer Peter Roebuck said Warne should be sent home if he repeated the misdemeanour.

'If he arrived here as a saint,' Roebuck wrote, 'he is rapidly losing his halo. Although the earring remains and has been joined by a goatee beard, the boyish innocence of yesterday has disappeared and his face has developed a disturbing snarl.'

Victorian team-mate Dean Jones thought the incident ugly and unnecessary. Warne heard second-hand that Tim Lane, an ABC radio and sometime TV commentator, said he was 'ashamed to be an Australian' after Warne abused Hudson. Lane later denied he had said it. Back in Australia, Derryn Hinch on Channel Nine's 'Midday' show thought Warne's lack of control 'an absolute disgrace'. Hinch, known as the 'human headline' for his sensational reporting and comments, went over the top by saying that Warne 'obviously had no mind of his own'. He added that Warne simply followed Hughes's lead in his antics on the field in general. This got under Warne's skin, but he was even more irritated by former Australian batsman David Hookes, who asked if Australia needed him and Hughes.

With a piece of questionable logic, Hookes said that 'Australia has lost the Test with them, so why should they be kept over there?'

Warne crossed Hookes, Lane and Hinch off his list of acceptable interviewers if there should be requests from them in the foreseeable future. His mood didn't improve, but was helped by a chat with Mark Taylor and an angry team discussion of the two men's alleged 'victimisation'. There was talk about boycotting the next tour game against Boland. Eventually, Warne was finally calmed down by his father, Keith, who fortuitously arrived in South Africa to watch the rest of the tour.

'Learn from it [the Hudson incident], put it behind you and get on with the rest of the tour,' Warne senior told him. Shane, as ever, took the advice.

Bouncing Back

Warne felt it necessary to do some remedial work with his born-again Christian friend, Jonty Rhodes, in the form of coaching kids in the black townships before the Second Test at Newlands, Cape Town. But the headlines that greeted the tourists when they arrived on 17 March showed that it would take more than image repair to undo the damage done at the Bullring. The Cape Town *Weekend Argus* blazoned its Test preview, 'And now for the Boor War', adding 'Shell-shocked Australia approach the crossroads.'

The players may have shrugged and drawn up the drawbridge in order to play better cricket. Yet it may have been sinking into a few of the more enlightened minds in the team that they had a long tradition of honour to uphold stretching back to the end of the Boer War in 1902. In that year, Joe Darling turned up at Newlands along with other Aussie great players *and sportsmen* such as Victor Trumper, Clem Hill, Warwick Armstrong, Monty Noble and Syd Gregory. None of these would have brooked the exhibition in the First Test.

Warne was among those now imbued with an awareness of their broader responsibilities. With his father's advice and some direct words from vice-captain Mark Taylor ringing in his ears, he spoke contritely to the kids in Cape Town at a mini-festival put on by the United Cricket Board of South Africa (UCBSA). He urged the wriggling but attentive children to practise their skills and warned them 'not to develop bad habits'.

Security was beefed up for the Test to make sure there was no repeat of the missile-throwing at Johannesburg. Stiff-armed staff held several fierce Alsatians, Dobermanns and Rottweilers on leashes inside the fence on the field itself. This did not stop the crowd taunting Warne with insulting remarks and banners that screamed 'Shame Shane' and 'The Match isn't over until the fat boy spins.' Hughes received the less offensive 'The Good, the Bad and the Merv Hughes' and 'Merv Hughes with a Short Fuse'. All this and no Bill Lawry in sight to defend his beloved Victorians.

The extent of Warne's refreshed change of heart was fully evidenced as he hardly rejected an autograph seeker on the fence while all eyes drifted between balls to him, by now the most talked about, analysed and scrutinised Australian cricketer since Bradman, who never made it to South Africa.

The Proteas had decided not to play shots to him, a ploy that was more or less effective at first as Hudson (102 run out), Gary Kirsten (29 run out), and Peter Kirsten pushed, prodded and padded him away. Meanwhile, McGrath rose to the occasion by bowling Cronje for 2 and McDermott dismissed the dogged Wessels. Then Warne, whom the South Africans had turned into a stock bowler on the unhelpful pitch, struck back. He dismissed Peter Kirsten, whom he had tied down, lbw for 70, and McMillan, whom he had tied up, bowled for 74, just when they looked like taking the game away from the Australians.

Warne bowled with pinpoint accuracy, conceding a miserly 1.65 runs an over in a marathon stint of forty-seven overs. What was more, he behaved himself impeccably despite continued provocation from the crowd who now seemed to dislike the skill of his bowling as much as his new image. Even when Hudson was given not out on 68 to an lbw appeal when a superb wrong 'un trapped him dead in front and on the back foot, Warne did little more than squint back down the wicket. There was not even a shake of the head, but a wry smile did crease his zinc-smeared lips. His reward was a yeoman-like three for 78, ably backed by McGrath with three for 65, as South Africa collected 361. It may have seemed enough after the First Test. But Border had other ideas as Australia put in a team effort. Slater (26), Taylor (70), Boon (96), Border (45), Steve Waugh (86) and Healy (61) combined to build 435 in reply, leaving them with a handy 74-run lead. Australia's *bête noire*, de Villiers, took four for 117, though Matthews registered the best figures of five for 80.

In South Africa's second innings, Border used Warne as a strike bowler and he broke through early to capture Gary Kirsten lbw for 10 at 33. Then Steve Waugh got rid of Cronje for 19 and Border ran out Wessels for just 9 when he was looking solid. From that point, three for 94, it was all Steve Waugh and Warne as they returned five for 28 and three for 38, respectively, to dismiss South Africa for just 164, leaving Australia with just 91 to pick up. There were jitters in the tourists' camp nonetheless, given the horrors of Sydney just a few weeks earlier. Donald broke through Taylor (14) to bowl him with the score at 30, but Slater attacked sensibly, while Boon was solid in seeing Australia through to a nine-wicket victory. In the space of less than two months, they had squared a second successive series. After the calamity at Johannesburg, the team had pulled itself together. The aggression was there, but the sledging was mild. Wessels commented that his old team-mates were more focused and that 'there was less chitchat on the field'.

The Warne and Waugh Show

The tourists arrived at Kingsmead in the port of Durban for the Third Test and replaced the injured Hughes with the reliable Reiffel. There was an air of hope in the squad, despite the political turmoil throughout the country, which caused the UCBSA's managing director, Dr Ali Bacher, to reassure them they were not in danger. Police in vehicles marked 'Tourist Support Unit' patrolled the nearby foreshore of the Indian Ocean, just a kilometre from the ground.

The tense atmosphere probably caused the fall-off in spectators with just 2000 on hand for the first ball, perhaps because Australia batted. As the home side moved through the opposition, only Boon (37), Mark Waugh (43), Steve Waugh (64) and Healy (55) showed some fight as Australia struggled to an unconvincing 269. Donald bowled his quickest for the summer and dealt blows to several Australians, including Boon, who felt the impact of a ball that destroyed his protector and put him in hospital. While Donald added new meaning to the word 'strike bowler', it was his partner Matthews who again took the honours with the ball, returning four for 65 off twenty-seven overs.

South Africa began well in reply with an opening century stand between Hudson and Kirsten before Reiffel removed Hudson lbw for 65 and then sent back his partner caught behind for 41. The scoreboard looked good for Australia when Warne caused Cronje to push a catch to Steve Waugh for a disappointing 26. The rivalry between these two was building, with Warne just holding an edge with this dismissal at a critical time. Cronje's scores for the series had been 21, 122, 2, 19 and 26. Warne took his wicket just once, but his presence and pressure affected the South African.

When McDermott hit Wessels's pads plumb in front for 1, the Proteas were four for 155. But once more Rhodes (78) led a recovery supported by McMillan (84) and Richardson (59) as South Africa constructed a laborious 422 in 832 minutes off 205.2 overs, which looked enough to keep the crowds low for the rest of the game, and to avoid defeat. Warne again came home with the figures, taking four for 92 off a marathon fifty-five overs, including twenty maidens. He beat his friend Rhodes with a terrific flipper just before tea on day three after some defiant batting. He had taken fifteen wickets at his usual economic rate of around 24 runs per wicket, and would have had a chance of keeping up his average of six wickets per Test if South Africa batted a second time. Steve Waugh, showing good form with his swinging deliveries once more, backed up the spinner with three for 40 off 27.2 overs.

Australia's response to South Africa's spiritless performance was to mix aggression with defence to avoid being bogged down in reducing its deficit of 153. There were wobbles early as Taylor (12), Boon (12) and night watchman Warne (12) fell in the battle to get ahead. Then Mark Waugh (113 not out) and Border (42 not out) batted the team into an unbeatable position at four for 297 and the game fizzled out to a draw.

It was fitting in a way that Border should end his career in yet another back-to-the-wall fight, of the sort that typified his enormous value to Australia and his place in cricketing fame. He was now to bow out reluctantly after one of the longest careers in Test history, with a breathtaking record of 11 174 runs in 265 innings at an average of 50.56. He had scored twenty-seven centuries—including two doubles, with a top score of

205—and 63 fifties. He took 156 catches and thirty-nine wickets at 39.10. It was a sad moment and a poignant one for Warne, whom he had nurtured, protected, pushed and inspired.

The series ended with the two teams level again at one-all. They would have to wait three years to find out who had the upper hand in the new era of South Africa's return to international competition.

One-Day Struggle

With the Tests now over, the spotlight swung on to a series of eight one-day internationals between the two teams. They had already played seven times in Australia, with the home team winning four games and also taking the WSC cup. In the South African leg in April 1994, Australia won the final game at Bloemfontein by a solitary run to make it four-all, giving it an eight–seven edge in the fifteen games between the two sides in both countries.

One of the most fascinating features of these clashes was the continuing struggle for supremacy between Warne and the rising South African star Hansie Cronje. It reached a new peak of intensity in South Africa when Cronje made 112, 97, 45 and 50 not out to give his team a three–one lead in the first four games. Despite Warne's ascendancy in Australia in both the Tests and the one-dayers, Cronje struck back in the opening game in Johannesburg hitting Warne for 33 in twenty-one deliveries, including three towering sixes. The batsman cheekily opened his stance and employed the odd reverse sweep. In the second game at Pretoria, Cronje helped take 5 an over off the spinner.

He subsequently faced the media and told them of his method in combating Warne:

'My stock shot [against leg-spin] is the sweep ... I'm quite prepared to slog-sweep over mid-wicket. You can't allow him to dictate terms—rather you must look to dominate him. By sweeping or using your feet to go down the wicket to him, you also increase the chances of him bowling bad balls; then you look to cut or pull.'

Cronje was confident—sweep, slog and dance to well-up balls, then wait for the short ones and cut and pull. All very easy, really—except for one thing: no one yet had been able to tame Warne in the long game or in the other games that counted, such as a one-day final. Fine batsman from several countries now had been trying all those things and getting out to him, early and often. Forcing him to bowl short balls, even in the one-dayers, was fraught with risk. Warne was learning to slide balls past advancing batsmen for a stumping or miscue and catch.

In the third game, at Port Elizabeth, Warne took four for 36 and was in improved form. Cronje had not been able to collar him a third time.

Border joined in the propaganda war and implied that Cronje's earlier big-hitting at Centurion Park was risky and lucky.

'There will be a few difficult periods [for Warne],' Border said. 'It's just a matter of hanging in there ... they're obviously attacking him, and the crowds are getting into him, too.'

Warne defended himself in press interviews:

'My day's going to come, sooner hopefully than later. I think I'm going OK. It's not as if I'm bowling half-trackers or full tosses. Hansie is getting away with a bit, I suppose. From my limited experience in one-day cricket, anything can happen. If an attempted six goes up in the air, it's a different ball game ...'

By the third encounter, Warne was especially tight and effective, underlining the point that he was on the comeback trail.

The last four one-dayers were played under lights and Cronje was inconspicuous, failing to have any further influence on the series, while Warne continued to bowl economically. Australia took this block three–one, the highlight involving Warne not with the ball, but the bat. At St George's Park, Port Elizabeth, he (55) and Reiffel (58) combined with the score at seven for 77 in a world-record eighth-wicket partnership of 119 off 116 balls.

At the end, Warne had returned to form and Australia just held the upper hand in the competition in both countries.

Bribing Their Time

Mark Taylor took over from Border as captain of Australia on the toughest assignment of all: a short one-day tournament in Sri Lanka followed by a tour of Pakistan for three Tests and a series of one-dayers from September to November 1994. The new skipper prepared well during the winter with meetings of the team's most influential players: himself, Craig McDermott, David Boon, Shane Warne, Ian Healy and the Waugh brothers. They felt confident that they could win the three-match Test series and also the one-dayers. First up was the Singer four-team one-day competition against Sri Lanka, India and Pakistan in Colombo, Sri Lanka.

The team stayed at the Oberoi Hotel and, in time off, Warne and Mark Waugh liked to visit a casino in a dimly lit street nearby. One night, Warne got caught up playing roulette, winning and losing. After a few hours, he was down $US5000. At the time, Warne was introduced by Waugh to an illegal Indian bookmaker called 'John', whom he had just met. 'John' watched Warne lose. The three later chatted about cricket for about half an hour.

The next day, Warne was contacted by John, who was also staying at the Oberoi. John invited Warne to his hotel room and told him he was a 'big fan', flattering him in a way in which the cricketer was now familiar.

'It was an honour to meet you last night,' 'John' said. 'I've won lots of money on Australia. They are winning all the time. You have won plenty of Tests.' The bookie took an envelope containing $US5000 from his jacket pocket. 'I saw you lose last night.' He handed the envelope to Warne. 'Here's a token of my appreciation. You're my favourite player.'

'What's this?' Warne asked, noticing the money.

'Please accept it ... I appreciate you taking time to meet me.'

'Thanks very much, but I've got my own money. I'm fine, thanks.'

'Please take it. There are no strings attached. I don't want anything in return ... please ...'

'I really don't want the money,' Warne repeated.

'I'm a very wealthy man. Please accept it.'

Warne shook his head.

'Please,' the Indian bookie said again, this time with his hands on his heart, 'I would be very offended if you didn't accept my gift.'

Warne relented and took the envelope.

'OK,' he said, 'thank you very much.'

Later that day, he went back to the casino and lost the lot on roulette. (Warne later said he received calls from 'John' in Sydney, Melbourne and Perth during the 1994–95 season. The bookie, according to Warne, asked for weather reports and pitch conditions, and was given information such as whether the pitch was conducive to spin or speed. At no point did Warne discuss team tactics or selections.)

'John' also gave Waugh $US4000 for similar reports. 'John' had asked Waugh for other 'intelligence' such as team selection, tactics, details about individuals and 'the general feeling in the team', but Waugh refused to give any of this. The two cricketers did not tell their team-mates or management, knowing that it would be frowned upon and disallowed. Their consciences were apparently clear, however, because they were not giving any intelligence that would be harmful to the team's chances of winning, such as match-fixing. There had been no betrayal.

Waugh and Warne, perhaps too quick to accept an easy buck, did not stop to consider that 'John' could be a match-fixer and how it might affect them later. They did not seem to realise that once they accepted money from someone involved in illegal activity, even for innocuous information, they were compromised and even susceptible to blackmail attempts. It did not seem to occur to them that 'John' just might be making suckers out of them—today, an envelope for pitch information;

tomorrow, a cake tin full of dollars to play poorly.

Soon after these payments were made, they were in the Australian team for a one-day game at the SSC Ground, Colombo, against Pakistan. An early burst by Wasim Akram that put Taylor and Slater back in the pavilion and the team on the back foot. Mark Waugh steadied the position with 23, then Bevan (37), Healy (30 not out) and Warne (30) completed a partial recovery, leaving Australia with seven for 179 at the close of their fifty overs. Neither Waugh nor Warne played poorly. They aimed to win.

Pakistan seemed to suffer a setback before the game when their listed number-three batsman, Asif Mutjaba, split the webbing in his hand and had to bat last. Pakistan started well, but were curtailed by Steve Waugh bowling his swingers. Then Saeed Anwar (46) retired hurt with a hamstring strain with the score at 77. Warne then came on and, with Waugh, broke through Pakistan to change the course of the game. Warne had hard-hitting Inzamam-ul-Haq (29) stumped by Healy, and next caught and bowled Basit Ali (0). Waugh dismissed Salim Malik, who had pottered about for an extraordinarily long time, facing eighty-four balls and making just 22 runs. Soon after, Rashid Latif was caught in the slips for 7. From then on, there was a steady progression back to the pavilion, as Pakistan collapsed for 150, giving Australia a comfortable victory after it looked beaten halfway through the Pakistani innings. Warne, with 30 runs and three wickets, was awarded Man of the Match. As ever, he had done his best to win for Australia, as had Mark Waugh. (Later, allegations were made about Pakistani players, including Salim, deliberately playing poorly so that Pakistan was sure to lose. None of the Australian team was aware of this.)

Australia travelled to the Premadassa International Stadium for a match against India. India batted first. With Sachin Tendulkar (110) in scintillating form against speed and spin, it managed an even top-order effort of eight for 246. Warne (two for 50 off ten overs) was expensive, as were all the bowlers with the exception of May (one for 35 off ten). Australia batted evenly, with Taylor (22), Mark Waugh (61), Boon (40), Steve Waugh (22) and Bevan (26) all contributing—but not enough. Australia was all out in 47.4 overs for 215 and beaten by 31 runs.

Three days later, the Australians played Sri Lanka. Again, the team batted evenly after a slow start by Taylor (41) and Slater (24 run out). Mark Waugh (24) looked in good form, but did not go on with it. Again, important contributions were left to Steve Waugh (30), Bevan (47 not out) and Healy (28), who added respectability in reaching six for 225. Rain fell in the evening and the game was reduced in over numbers. Sri Lanka scored four for 164 and made the allotted target without much trouble, with captain Ranatunga sledging and hitting his way to a spirited 59.

The Australians arrived in Karachi for the First Test against Pakistan, beginning on 28 September, with a different bowling line-up. They were without the services of McDermott (on tour, but injured) and Hughes (injured and left at home). Jo Angel and Tim May joined Warne and McGrath as the four specialist bowlers. Taylor won the toss, batted and promptly started his career as Test captain with a duck, when he was caught and bowled by Wasim Akram. Bevan came to the rescue with a sound 82, along with Steve Waugh (73) and Healy (57). On day two, the tail failed to wag against the tail-smashing specialists, Wasim Akram and Waqar Younis. The last four wickets fell for 12. Australia reached 337 on a 400-run 'belter' of a wicket that had nothing much in it for the bowlers. Akram, Waqar and spinner Mushtaq Ahmed took three wickets each.

Pakistan's openers, Saeed Anwar and Aamir Sohail, started well. They saw off McGrath and Angel, leaving it to Warne to break through at 90, when he had Sohail (36) caught by Bevan. Then May got into the act by inducing close-to-the-wicket catches from Anwar (86) and Zahid Fazal (27). Angel returned for a second spell to remove Salim lbw for 36. Not to be outdone, McGrath had Basit Ali caught by Bevan for a duck. Warne came back to remove Inzamam-ul-Haq (9) and Rashid Latif (2), which left the home team at seven for 209 at stumps on day two, after being one for 150. Akram came out the next morning for a bit of controlled slather and whack, making 39 and lifting Pakistan to 256. Australia's reply was another poor start by Taylor, who collected a pair courtesy of Waqar. The skipper nicked a low, slow one to the keeper Latif. Boon and Slater looked to be taking the game away from Pakistan, until Mushtaq trapped Slater lbw for 23 when the score was on 49. Boon and Mark Waugh then slipped into gear, taking the score to 171, a lead of 252 with seven wickets in hand.

In the dressing room, some of the Australians were talking cockily about the game now being just a formality. Taylor told the players to stop the overconfident chat and to concentrate on doing their best. His words of caution were well placed. In the next half hour, the game made its first fateful twist as Mark Waugh (61) was bowled by Waqar. Three for 171 looked healthy enough, but then Akram had Steve Waugh lbw and bowled Bevan, both for first-ball ducks, reducing Australia to five for 174. Boon and Healy held out until stumps for five for 181, a lead of 262. The odds were still with Australia if its tail could wag. Boon was the anchor and the best of the Pakistani speedsters could not remove him. They gave up and concentrated on the others. Again, Waqar and Akram did the job, mopping up the rest for 47, with Boon remaining 114 not out. Akram took five for 64 and Waqar four for 69.

Pakistan had 314 to get in a day and a half. It started promisingly and reached 45 before Sohail was run out for 34. Warne came on early and Taylor crowded Fazal (3) and had him caught by Boon. With two batsmen removed for just 64, the pendulum swung to the tourists. Anwar and Salim Malik batted cautiously. At 148, Angel's slower ball caused Anwar to hit one back at him. Raza came in as night watchman, leaving Pakistan on three for 157 at stumps. The game was on a knife edge. Seven wickets left and halfway to the target. Odds had to be with the Australians, given that 300-plus was a formidable fourth-innings target. Betting plunges began in the Pakistani underworld. It seemed that the big money would be on the home side or a draw, but not the Australians, if certain matters could be arranged.

That night at about 10.30 p.m., at the Pearl Continental hotel, Warne received a phone call from Salim, whose nickname among the Australians was 'the Rat'. He wanted the Australian to join him in Salim's hotel room. Warne was surprised. The Pakistani seemed a stand-offish, distant character, whom Warne would never feel comfortable about approaching after a game's play. Salim greeted him in a long, white robe. They chatted about the tough battle of the first four days. Then Salim said:

'You know, we cannot lose.'

Warne shook his head and laughed.

'Don't know about that, mate. We can still do it.'

'We cannot lose,' Salim repeated.

'I think we can still win it,' Warne replied.

'You don't understand. We cannot lose,' Salim repeated with emphasis. Warne held his gaze.

'What do you mean?' the Australian asked. 'I tell you we are going to go out and beat you tomorrow.'

'No, no. I'm telling you that you and Tim May are the two key bowlers tomorrow. There will be $200 000 cash in your room in half an hour if you don't bowl well tomorrow.'

'What do you mean?'

'Both of you bowl outside off stump and it will be a draw,' Salim added. (Given this was the way May usually bowled, Salim probably meant that May should bowl *well* wide of the off stump.)

'Are you serious?'

'Yes, if you agree.'

'As far as I'm concerned,' Warne said, getting up to leave, 'you can get stuffed. But I'll talk to Maysie ...'

The Rat did not seem to be kidding. The request to Warne to bowl outside off stump was pertinent. Warne's line was around leg stump, with his stock ball spinning across the right-hander. If he shifted his line to outside off stump, he would be ineffective and belted to the point and cover point boundary, unless he bowled wrong 'uns, which he rarely did.

Warne was sharing a room with Tim May. He told his partner about the approach.

'If we played doggo,' May said, 'it wouldn't be a draw. They'd beat us. They've only got 157 to get. They're not going to take three sessions to get them.'

'Do you reckon he could get that sort of money on the spot?' Warne asked.

May then mockingly showed interest.

'Two hundred thousand, eh?'

'That's what he said. It's crazy.'

'In half an hour?'

Warne nodded.

May began laughing.

'Ring the Rat and tell him to get fucked ... Tell him we are going to beat them tomorrow.'

Warne rang Salim.

'Maysie says to get fucked, we're going to beat you tomorrow.' Salim did not react and rang off.

May and Warne speculated that there would have to be a huge, gangster-driven local betting plunge on Pakistan or, if Salim were serious, a draw. They told Taylor, who informed coach Bob Simpson and manager Col Egar. Egar reported the approach to match referee John Reid. The matter would later be taken higher, but not in the middle of the competition. The Australian team resolved to do everything to win.

The next morning, Warne quickly disposed of Raza (2) by cornering him lbw, making the home team four for 157. Soon after, Angel induced a nick from Salim (43) to Taylor at slip. The Rat had been forced to abandon ship. At five for 174, Pakistan was reeling. The Australians, however, seemed to be pushing too hard. McGrath tore his hamstring and couldn't bowl. May was on and off the ground with a strained neck. Angel and Warne were the only two front-line bowlers left. Warne lifted his effort even further and had Basit Ali lbw for 12 and caught and bowled Akram for 4. Pakistan had slumped to seven for 184. They were still 130 from victory, which was now looking improbable. Then Inzamam and Latif (35) staged a recovery, taking the score to 236 before Steve Waugh got an inswinger past Latif's bat and trapped him dead in front. Eight wickets were down and the home side still needed 78. Imzamam took charge, but couldn't shield Waqar from Warne, who had him caught behind for 7. With 56 to get and one wicket left, Pakistan looked beaten. But Inzamam and Ahmed struggled on, helped by two lbw appeals and a catch behind that were rejected when they seemed undeniably out. This and some good luck helped them to nine for 311, only 3 runs short.

Warne, who had given everything for victory, was now bowling to Inzamam. The heavy-hitting batsman, on 58, suddenly charged several metres down the wicket to him and swung hard, trying to hit the ball over mid-wicket, but missed. With Inzamam stranded a long way out of his crease, however, the ball kept low and went through Healy's legs to the boundary for four leg byes. The anguish of the Australians was obvious as Healy, down on one knee, watched the ball reach the boundary. Warne held his head. Taylor at slip threw his hands high. Instead of a stumping that would have given Australia a 2-run victory, Pakistan, at nine for 315, had won by one wicket. Warne's great effort to win was reflected in his figures of five for 89 off 36.1 overs, with twelve maidens. He won the Man of the Match.

The Australians, particularly Healy, were shattered, having come so far and so close in a game they controlled for all but the last hour on the fifth day. It was especially disappointing for Taylor, with a 'pair' and a loss in his first Test as captain. But as his team-mates well knew, he was fundamentally up to the task. Just as whenever he batted he could put the last ball behind him, no matter how close he was to being out, or how badly he had been beaten, so he was capable of doing the same on a bigger scale after an unfortunate Test.

•••

That night at the teams' hotel, Salim ran into Warne and took him aside.

'You were stupid,' Salim said. 'You lost.'

'You were very, very lucky, mate.'

'You lost. You could have had the money, but you can't now.'

'There are still two Tests,' Warne retorted. 'We're going to win them.'

They parted, Warne uncomfortable with the Pakistani captain's insulting attitude. Salim subsequently kept up his approaches during the triangular one-day series involving South Africa between the Second and Third Tests. Warne and the other cricketers ignored his overtures and concentrated on their task of achieving success in a region where wins were few.

Days of the Rat

Australia had to recover its equilibrium in just three days before the commencement of the Second Test, beginning on 5 October at Pinda Stadium, Rawalpindi. McDermott and Damien Fleming replaced May and the injured McGrath on a wicket that was expected to help the pace bowlers and leave little for the spinners.

Salim's behind-the-scenes activity gave the tourists plenty to fight for, despite the big let-down of the First Test. Captain Taylor had a personal problem of dried-up runs and was nervous when he decided to bat after winning the toss. But he came through, as did all batsman except Boon, who had been a stubborn hero of the first encounter. Taylor (69) and Slater (110) gave the side a great start of 176, but they then slid to three for 198. Yet with Akram and Waqar neutralised by the bland pitch, Australia recovered thanks to Mark Waugh (68) and Bevan (70), who added 124 to make it four for 322. At 347 for five, Healy (58) and Steve Waugh (98) were joined in the third big partnership of the innings that took the score on by another 119 to 456. Taylor was in a position to make a rare first-innings declaration at nine for 521, a total that meant Australia could not lose.

His bowlers, particularly McDermott (four for 74) and Damien Fleming (four for 75), then ran through Pakistan. Warne also played a part by trapping the ever-dangerous

Inzamam (14) lbw with a top-spinner that came on quickly and thus prevented a repeat of his rear-guard effort in the previous match. But if it wasn't Inzamam holding up the Aussies with some power batting, it was the brutal Akram, who crashed 45 and lifted his team from eight for 198 to 260 all out. Warne, with no help from the pitch, managed one for 58 off an economical 21.4 overs.

Taylor was left with his first major decision during a game. With a lead of 261, one more than the home team had managed in its first effort, he was tempted to put them straight back in, as was his right with a 200-run lead. There was half an hour to go on the third day. He consulted his bowlers. They were tired, but with the prospect of a good night's rest they indicated they were ready. Against instinct, Taylor asked Pakistan to bat again.

He set a trap for the hard-hitting Sohail with two fielders at deep backward square leg. Angel gave him something hookable and he launched into it. Warne, usually a reliable fielder anywhere, positioned himself, but spilt the chance.

The next morning Sohail, with a life behind him and his luck running, attacked until he was out for 72, bringing Salim in. He and Anwar made it to lunch without much trouble. After the break, Taylor got Angel to bowl around the wicket aiming at Salim's ribcage and again put two men out for the hook to tempt him. If he didn't take the bait, he might then lash at a wider ball and get himself caught behind. Angel did as Taylor directed, sending down a bouncer which Salim, then on just 20, evaded, followed by one right into his ribs which he managed to fend away. The next one was wider and, sure enough, Salim fenced at it, sending it flying straight to Taylor at first slip. One of the game's best-ever slips fielders promptly dropped it. If he had snaffled it, Pakistan would have been two for 120 and still 141 behind. Instead Salim went on, and on.

Warne was challenged by the brash batsman and threw everything he had at him. Salim used his feet rather than letting Warne dictate to him and was also able to pick every delivery out of Warne's hand, a rare feat managed by only a few outstanding players such as Brian Lara, Sachin Tendulkar and Mark Waugh. Rather than trying to blast Warne as Tendulkar had, Salim selected the gaps in the field with wristy glides. His quick eye and hands allowed him to change his shots late and guide the ball to places where fieldsmen were not, as he moved on through one hundred and into the next.

Salim went on to a magnificent double century, saving the game for his country. It was the 'match of the Rat' and he had every bowler's measure in an innings that stretched from before lunch on day four to around tea on day five. Despite the attitude of the Australians towards him, Salim was unruffled. Warne and he bickered and bantered their way through two days on the field, the bowler frequently reminding him of his ill-judged fiscal incentives and the batsman answering with his blade and tongue, in about equal measure.

With the score at 469, Fleming induced a nick to Healy and Salim was on his way for 237 in one of the finest innings ever played for Pakistan. Fleming then removed Inzamam lbw for a duck and had Aamir Malik (65) caught by Bevan, giving him a hat-trick to liven up what was then a dead game, with Pakistan more than 200 ahead. The home team rattled on to 537 and Australia was forced to bat for half an hour, losing Slater for one. The game ended in a tame draw. Two dropped catches may well have lost a golden opportunity for Australia, although the fielders concerned were among the game's best.

Again, Taylor had to lift the spirits of the side, which now realised it could not win the Test series. It could only draw level. The skipper also had to maintain the team incentive as it changed its mind-set for the new round of one-day games, which would be on them once more in a few days.

•••

Australia first took on South Africa at the Gaddafi Stadium in Lahore, and scraped in with a 6-run win, scoring six for 207 to South Africa's eight for 201. Taylor batted stolidly for his 56, as did Slater (44) in an opening partnership of 98. Only Steve Waugh (56) among the rest contributed. Boon and Bevan were run out cheaply, perhaps forgetting the skill of the Proteas in the field. Cronje was the mainstay of the South Africans with 98 not out. He and Rhodes (42) had a threatening 76-run fourth-wicket stand.

Warne was steady with none for 39 off ten. He contained Cronje in their continuing star wars. McDermott, bowling his heart out on unresponsive pitches, took three for 32, and was well supported by Fleming with two for 29 and Steve Waugh with two for 35. The victory lifted the morale of the Aussie camp. The evenness of the battle between these two meant any win was a boost. Two days later at the Qasim-a-Bagh Stadium at Multan, Pakistan struggled to eight for 200, with Inzamam (59 run out) in superb touch. Fleming again bowled well, taking four wickets, but he was expensive, going for nearly five an over. Although he only took one for 29, Warne was just as effective because of his economy rate of less than 3 an over in his ten-over spell. He gained great satisfaction when he had Salim caught behind for 32.

Less than a week later at the Iqbal Stadium, Faisalabad, Australia fought to six for 208 against South Africa again, with even performances from Slater (38), Mark Waugh (38), Boon (43) and Bevan (36 not out). Cronje once more was the South Africans' backbone with 64. They looked to have a good chance at six for 156, but then Warne struck, luring batsmen from their crease for an exceptional and unusual three stumpings by Healy and the Proteas collapsed to 186 all out in 48.2 overs, 22 short. Warne's four for 40 off 9.2 overs was not his best rate, but the wickets came at a critical time and gave Australia victory.

The Australians moved on to Rawalpindi on 21 October in preparation for a game against Pakistan the next day. At an evening reception for the two teams and their officials, Salim approached his former team-mate from Essex, Mark Waugh, who was talking to Warne. After a short chat to Waugh, the Pakistani asked him if 'four or five' of the Australian players would like to make some easy money. Perhaps Salim knew that Waugh and Warne had entered into a deal with 'John', the illegal Indian bookmaker. Certainly he was aware that these two were the keenest on a bet amongst the Australians, and therefore possibly open to making easy money.

Waugh asked what it was to do with.

'Gambling,' Salim replied. The Australian shrugged, inviting Salim to explain.

'There's $50 000 each in it for you, your brother, May and Warne, if you're interested.'

'In what?' Waugh asked.

'There's a lot riding on tomorrow's game.'

'So?' Waugh asked.

'All you have to do is play badly.'

'What? Throw the game?'

'Just don't play well,' Salim said, with his little half grin. 'That should be enough.'

'None of the guys are into that,' a shocked Waugh replied.

'Just think about it,' Salim said, 'and let me know tonight.'

Warne overheard the conversation and was surprised that Salim had the gall to approach him—through Waugh—again, especially after he had been rejected in no uncertain terms during the First Test in Karachi.

Waugh took time to recover from the shock and decide what to do. About an hour and a half later, he spoke again with Salim and made it clear that he rejected the offer.

The next day, Mark Waugh batted as if he were making a point to Salim, stroking his way to a master innings of 121 not out, as the team reached six for 250. Pakistan then sent shock waves through the tourists, cracking three for 251 off just thirty-nine overs at a rate of more than 6 runs an over. Aamir Sohail slammed 45 in the opening stand of 91, then Inzamam, promoted up the order for some killer blows, crunched 91 not out in a 160-run partnership with the steady Saeed Anwar, who reached 104 not out.

The Australian team was stunned. Back in the dressing room after the game, Waugh joked: 'We would have been better off taking the bribe, guys.' Some of the others laughed and agreed.

'What are you talking about?' Egar asked.

The players then told Egar and coach Bob Simpson of the bribery offer. Warne and Mark Waugh said nothing then about the easy dollars they had picked up from 'John'. It was not for match-fixing, they justified to themselves, it was just for a simple report on conditions.

Pakistan had won two of the three encounters. Taylor and his men were now aware they could not expect to win a final if they batted stodgily for 200 and then attempted to contain the opposition. The batting would have to be more productive and aggressive. The next game at the Arbab Niaz Stadium in Peshawar against South Africa gave Australia a chance to test its new resolve. South Africa scored six for 251, with Cronje (100 not out) again dominant. With the exception of McGrath, who took two for 22 off ten overs, he was severe on all the bowlers, including Warne (one for 51 off ten overs), and clearly took the honours. Warne, however, had the consolation prize of Cullinan, his bunny, whom he bowled for 36.

Australia replied with another even performance by Slater (54 run out), Mark Waugh (43), Boon (39 run out), Bevan (45) and Langer (33 not out), which saw it win on the third-last ball. The Australians chased with panache and commitment, and, in scoring 252, gave themselves the confidence needed for even tougher encounters against the host team.

The tourists assembled again at the Gaddafi Stadium for the final against Pakistan on 30 October. Taylor won the toss and then took part in the best opening stand of the series—122 from twenty-five overs. At that point, 300 was not out of the question, but then Taylor (56) and Slater (66) were dismissed and Australia set its sights at 250. Mark Waugh (38) and Boon (21) put in steady performances, but the pace slowed until Bevan took control, pacing his way with power to 53 in forty balls. Akram and Waqar were brought back at the end of the innings to roll the middle and lower order, but they could not get through Bevan, who attacked and drove Australia's score up to a formidable 269 for five.

Fleming and McGrath put paid to any thoughts of a serious challenge when they crashed through the Pakistani top order. It left the home team on four for 64 and defending rather than attempting 6 an over as in the previous game, which was now needed. The rate required jumped to more than 8 by the time the fifth wicket fell at 112. Salim (35) and Basit Ali (63) helped Pakistan recover, but it could only manage 205. McGrath, though expensive, took five wickets for 52. Fleming was also a match-winner with three for 32 off eight overs. Warne showed his versatility by bowling steadily to return none for 32 off ten and acting as a stock bowler in the middle of the innings in between bursts by the speedsters.

The Australians were happy to come away with the one-day series. It was a minor consolation under the less-than-happy circumstances of the tour. Yet, to a man, they wanted to take the Third Test, to be on even terms in the more respected and challenging form of the game.

Tossing away a Series

Taylor was willing the coin to come down his way at Lahore on 1 November. He needed to bat first on a hard, flat grassless wicket, especially as Waqar Younis and Wasim Akram were out injured. Unfortunately, he called wrongly and Pakistan went out to bat for as long as possible in the knowledge that a draw would give them the series. McGrath broke through early by having Sohail (1) nick one to new keeper Phil Emery, in for the injured Healy. Warne lifted Australia's hopes further by bowling Anwar (30) with a superb leg break, leaving Pakistan at two for 34. Then Inzamam and Salim settled in for a risk-free display of fine batting. May trapped Inzamam (66) lbw with the score at 157. At 204, May struck again, forcing a catch from Salim (75). Warne then had Basit Ali (0) caught bat-pad by Mark Waugh and the home team was five for 209, and in trouble. However, Ijaz and Moin Khan, the replacement keeper, took the innings on into day two before another Warne purple patch. At 294, he had Ijaz (48) caught close to the wicket and then bowled Akram Raza for a duck. From then on, Moin (115 not out) dominated the strike and took his team on to 373. Warne's display of six for 136 off 41.5 overs was one of his best, considering the conditions were against him and the batting was top-class. May, with his guileful off-spinners, was steady with three for 69 off twenty-nine overs. They both showed stamina and purpose through the innings.

After their long stint in the field, Australia's bats put in a steady effort for the team. Slater (74), Taylor (32), Mark Waugh (71), Bevan (91), Langer (69), Warne (33) and McDermott (29) all assisted in raising the score to 455, a lead of 82. It was enough to give them thoughts of victory. When Basit Ali (2) and Inzamam were caught behind off McGrath and McDermott with just 28 on the board, a win was a serious possibility. Salim came in and steadied things up, although Pakistan kept losing wickets until it was five for 107. The lead was just 25 and half the side was back in the pavilion. Salim (143) and Sohail (105) then settled in to take the game from Australia's grasp with a depressing partnership for the fielding side of 196. Pakistan rumbled on to 404 and the match fizzled out to an ordinary draw. McGrath was in top form with four for 92 and Warne (three for 104) was steady, taking his tally to nine for 240 for the match.

The difference in the game, and indeed the series, which Pakistan won one–nil, was Salim Malik, who scored 557 at an average of 92.83. Despite Warne's distaste for him, he respected him as a batsman and regarded him as perhaps the toughest in the world to dismiss next to Tendulkar and Lara. Pakistan's two best bowlers, Akram (nine wickets at 22.22) and Waqar (ten at 25.80), were strong but not dominant, while Warne proved to be the best bowler of the series. He took eighteen wickets at 28.00, bowling sixty more overs than anyone else and keeping up his average of six wickets a Test. His endurance was remarkable given the pressure on his right shoulder and spinning finger. Experts were predicting that Warne, now twenty-five, would begin to suffer sooner rather than later because of his heavy workload. He had been bowling much more than the quicks now for two years, and they had been breaking down regularly. The strains and stresses were more in the legs for the faster bowlers, but spinners were troubled at the same rate in the shoulder and fingers.

With 134 Test wickets to his name, Warne went home, like the rest of the Australians, better equipped for the experience. New skipper Taylor left Pakistan confident of leading his team to an Ashes victory in the 1994–95 Australian summer.

9

Atherton's Challenge

Brisbane Triumph

Warne and his team-mates arrived back in Australia on 5 November 1994 and within a few days were out in the middle again playing first-class matches. Less than three weeks after the Third Test in Pakistan, they were lining up at the Gabba in Brisbane for the first of a five-Test series against England. Such was the intensity of international cricket in the 1990s. The rush and unending run of big matches put tremendous pressure on players, who were expected to perform at their best every time they stepped onto a cricket field.

At the beginning of events in the 1994–95 season, the Australians were living on inspiration as they approached another Ashes series. There was enough 'needle' between the two countries to ensure both would lift to somewhere near their best. The home team had to defend its hold on the Ashes for the fourth successive time. The visitors had more to play for. Only a series win would boost morale and appease severe English critics.

The Australians gained a premeditated psychological advantage in a clash between New South Wales and England at Newcastle in the run-up to the Test. Taylor and Slater went out to attack Derek Malcolm, the speedster being touted as the big hope by the British media. Taylor led the way with a strong

150, supported by an elegant 80 from Mark Waugh. In the second innings Slater cracked 94 in fine style and Taylor hit another 47. Three of Australia's front-line batsmen had gained an advantage before a ball had been bowled at Brisbane. Malcolm had been nullified.

At the Gabba on 25 November, England went in with a good, balanced team of Atherton, Stewart, Hick, Thorpe, Gooch, Gatting, McCague, Rhodes, DeFreitas, Gough and Tufnell. They were missing Malcolm, who was stricken with chickenpox.

Australia's squad looked strong. The batting order was Taylor, Slater, Boon, Mark Waugh, Steve Waugh, Bevan, Healy, Warne, McDermott, May and McGrath. In theory it had two quicks, three spinners (if Bevan was used), and Steve Waugh to fill in with his effective medium pace if required.

Taylor won the toss and led the way again in a partnership of 98 with Slater before being run out for 59. Slater dashed on to 176. None of the front-line bowlers could remove him and it took Gooch's innocuous slow-mediums to do the job. Australia reached four for 329 at stumps with Mark Waugh on 82 not. On day two, Waugh went on to 140, his seventh Test century and his highest Test score. Australia reached 426, with Gough by far the most effective bowler, taking four for 107. Warne and the rest of the Australians respected his aggression. He was similar in style to Botham, the gifted all-rounder who had been one of Warne's cricketing heroes as a boy. Warne's batting, with its characteristic flourish, seemed modelled on that of the Englishman, though more modest in quality.

Gough, with both bat and ball, seemed to be Botham personified. 'His [Gough's] approach to the game was more like ours,' Warne remarked after the first day. He was one of Gough's victims, caught going for a big drive for just 2.

England's reply was unconvincing as they scrambled to six for 133 at stumps with Atherton hanging on with his usual grit for 49 not out off 151 balls. There was no more resistance early on day three when they crumbled to all out for 167. McDermott dismissed Atherton for 54 and came in with the best figures of six for 53 off nineteen overs. He was assisted by Warne, who caught and bowled Graham Thorpe (28), England's most dangerous bat next to Gooch, and helped clean up the tail with three for 39 off 21.2 overs.

In the eighteen months since last facing Warne in a Test, the Englishmen seemed not to have learnt anything about playing him. They refused to come down the pitch to him and at times considered their pads more useful than their bats in dealing with him. Only Gooch, with his soft hands, seemed to have a clue.

With England dismissed and ripe for a follow-on, Taylor was in two minds about what to do next, but ultimately decided to bat again and set up England for Warne and May on a deteriorating last-day wicket. He and Slater started at a fair rate of about 3 an over for a strong partnership of 109. Australia then led by 368 with ten wickets still intact. However, when they were out, the team went into a slow drift with Boon the main culprit scoring just 20 in nearly three hours.

At eight for 248 and a lead of 507, Taylor called a halt to the dreariness fifty minutes into day four. The target was 103 more than the biggest last-innings score ever made to win a Test. There were eleven hours of cricket left.

Stewart began as if bent on scoring the 508 in record time before Warne fooled him with a terrific flipper and bowled him after he had made 33. England went to lunch on one for 59. Warne again bowled a flipper on the first ball after the break and trapped Atherton lbw. Hick and Thorpe then staged a recovery, with Hick, usually such an attractive stroke-maker, using his pads in an ugly manner to keep out Warne. But it was effective cricket when his team could not afford to lose wickets. The unbroken partnership put on 152 in four hours, taking England to two for 211 at stumps. It was still 297 from victory with eight wickets in hand.

England's management told the media it had not discounted a victory.

Taylor was worried, but did not let his squad know. He called the team together after the fourth day's play and told them not to get frustrated or upset. 'Let's just keep going the way we're going and the breaks will come our way,' were his most mortal words. The next morning, he took Warne aside. He told him to relax and keep bowling as well as he could.

'I was beginning to lose it yesterday,' Warne said, admitting his frustration, particularly with Hick's tactics. The left–right batting combination of Thorpe and Hick had not helped his line either. Warne had to keep switching where he placed the ball. It threw his rhythm during the long partnership.

'Just stay cool and things will go your way,' Taylor repeated.

'I'll get down to it,' Warne replied with conviction.

His first ball to Thorpe (65) on day five was a low full toss pitched at the footmarks outside the left-hander's off stump. Thorpe's normal reaction would have been to belt it to the cover fence, and perhaps he would have the day before. But in the morning his mind was on defence. The left-hander was caught in indecision, a split-second that had been fatal for even Bradman. He pushed and missed. The ball spun out of the footmarks and into his stumps. Minutes later Hick (80) tried to let one go. The ball spun into his pads, bounced, hit his bat and was caught by Healy diving forward.

Fifteen minutes into the last day's play victory was not an option for England, on four for 220. Gooch then stood between Australia and victory as he and Gatting struggled the score on to 250. McDermott then removed Gatting (13) for the second time in the match, having him caught behind.

Soon after this, Atherton and Gatting were spotted watching Warne with binoculars from a vantage point high above the wicket. They were picked out by TV cameras in earnest discussion and only served to make the point that England had not done its homework on Warne. The 1993 obsession with him had been swept under the carpet rather than regarding him as a problem to be faced, tackled and overcome. It was too little, too late. An Ashes series might be won and lost before they had come to terms with how to approach his spinning subtleties.

As if aware of this special audience, Warne lifted a notch and finished the game by taking three wickets in four balls. First he had Gooch (56), defiant for 150 minutes, caught behind off a cross-batted swipe. He then bowled DeFreitas (11) and trapped McCague lbw first ball. Tufnell provided comic relief by imitating Hick's padding away, only to fall on his *derrière*. England was all out for a creditable 323, having lost eight for 112 on day five, thus going down by 184 runs. Warne's figures, his best ever, were eight for 71 off 50.2 overs. He conceded just 1.4 runs an over. His match statistics were eleven for 110 off 71.4 overs.

He had been the difference between the two sides. After the game, Australian journalist Phil Wilkins asked Taylor at the media conference:

'What did you say to Shane before the ball before he dismissed Thorpe?'

Taylor tilted his head whimsically and replied:

'I told him to bowl a full toss because he'd be bound to miss it.'

Almost no one laughed. It was some time before Taylor got the chance to inform the more gullible members of the media throng that he was joking. The next day some Australian papers and at least one tabloid in England reported his remark as if he were serious. Such was the mythology built around Warne and Taylor's invincibility as captain with him. It all helped to confuse and demoralise the opposition.

Hat-Tricker

In December, the two teams had to adjust to the most illogical cricket timetable in the world, switching in mid-stream from the demands of five-day Tests to the hit-and-giggle of the fickle shorter game, which could be won or lost on a missed catch, an unlucky run out or even a mishit for four.

In every other cricketing nation's schedule, the one-dayers either preceded or followed the Tests, thus making adjustment one-way and easier. Australian administrators had yet to find a way of accommodating the Shield competition, the Tests and the one-dayers, which meant that after the initial burst of qualifying games in December, it would be back to the Second and Third Tests, then more one-days in January and the finals, followed once more by the two final Tests. Players would just become used to their bright pyjamas, then they would be pulling on whites. It all played havoc with the players' technique and mental attitude as they tried to adapt from one to the other.

The shorter playing time and the various restrictions of the one-day format meant that, in any particular game, a weak team could account for a stronger one. So it was with Zimbabwe, which managed just nine for 166 against Australia on 2 December at the WACA. Warne (two for 27) and McGrath (two for 23) bowled well, only for the batsmen to struggle to eight for 167 off 47.5 overs.

Four days later against England at the SCG, Australia batted stodgily, apart from a bright, late 46 by Bevan, to reach four for 224. England's initial reply was a 100-run opening partnership before May put the brakes on, collecting the first three wickets. Warne had Gooch (21) caught by McDermott in an attempt to blast him out of the attack. It didn't quite work. Warne's one for 46 was worse than his average, but May (three for 35) evened out the spinners' combined effort as England slid to 196 all out.

A few days later, against Zimbabwe again at Bellerive in Hobart, Australia was more aggressive, notching three for 254, with Law making a strong 110 and Boon a diligent 98 not out. Zimbabwe replied with eight for 170. Warne contained the battling visitors with one for 23 off nine overs, as did all the other bowlers.

On 11 December, at Adelaide, Australia played the Australia 'A' team in a game dreaded and regretted by Taylor. He didn't like the idea of this style of game with 'A'—the underdog—inevitably receiving more support. He also disliked what was in essence a 'trial match', allowing several players to display their skills in front of selectors in pressure situations, as well as the fierce competition this style of game engendered.

Taylor did little to help his personal cause as a one-dayer with a staid 44. Slater (64) was not much more productive, and Boon (39) was consistent but again uninspiring as the number-one side limped to all out for 202 in 48.3 overs. 'A' responded with 196 off 47.3. Warne avoided embarrassment for current team-mates by dismissing Martyn (37), Langer (1) and Ponting (42) before they could get on top of the bowling. Hayden (45) also failed to go on with it. Yet it was a reminder to all observers of Australia's great batting depth in the 1990s.

Several players had a chance to extricate themselves from the one-day mode with four-day Shield games before the Second Test beginning on Christmas Eve, with Christmas Day off. Damien Fleming replaced McGrath, while for England Devon Malcolm came back for Martin McCague. Ex-Australian McCague had a torrid time with verbal volleys from the Australians, and a horrid time with bat and ball. He made 0 and 1, and went for 5 an over in taking two for 96. A stomach upset allowed him to avoid more humiliation in Australia's second innings.

Atherton won the toss. Earlier rain and an uncertain forecast caused him to send Australia in for the start of the fiftieth Anglo–Australian contest at the MCG, the world's oldest Test match venue. Fired up by manager Ray Illingworth's pep-talk at the previous night's dinner, England began well, thanks to DeFreitas, who ran out Slater (3) going for an unnecessary run, and then had Taylor (9) lbw. Australia was two for 39. The home team struggled to a boring seven for 220 by stumps, with only the Waugh brothers standing tall. Mark delivered one of his cameo gems of 71 before DeFreitas had him caught by Thorpe.

Both teams celebrated on Christmas Day—England in fancy dress and Australia in more sombre mood—before re-engaging on Boxing Day. Australia carried on to 279 thanks to a last-wicket stand of 37 between Steve Waugh (94 not out) and Fleming (16). Darren Gough took another haul of four wickets, picking up his 'soul-mate' Warne caught by Hick at slip for 6.

England was soon struggling, not against speed, but spin. A broken finger to Stewart saw Hick and Atherton opening. After

McDermott had Hick (23) adjudged caught behind, Warne snared Atherton lbw for 44. Mark Waugh at silly point then grabbed a bat-pad from a disgruntled Thorpe (51 in two hours), again off Warne. The spinner had turned sniper, picking off hapless English bats when they popped their heads up. Gatting top-edged one from Warne and Steve Waugh took an acrobatic catch at backward square. The bowler was thrilled with this wicket, for he and McDermott, who had dismissed him twice in the First Test, were keeping the pressure on a beloved foe. Gatting's Test career was teetering. The Australians, after disposing of McCague's self-confidence, were undermining the Gatt's. The home team was demonstrating that there was no room for sentiment in top cricket.

Warne had taken three in an hour, leaving England 4 for 148 at stumps and with their Yuletide cheer now a hangover. Night watchman Gough joined Gooch with hopes for some bulldog belligerence next morning. McDermott's first-ball full toss came straight back to him from Gooch (15) and he swallowed it. Gough punched back for a bright 20 before McDermott had him caught behind, then Stewart fought one-handed with his broken finger for 16 before hitting against Warne's spin and skying a catch back to him. It was the bowler's 150th Test wicket, and his fiftieth against England. He had taken thirty-one Tests to get there. He was moving on average at five wickets per Test, putting him in the same company as Lillee (355 wickets) and Hadlee (431). At twenty-five years of age, Warne had every chance of overhauling both, barring major injury.

Australian ABC radio commentator Neville Oliver opined that England's approach showed 'the never-say-die attitude of a Kamikaze pilot'. Perhaps this mass suicide batting was induced by the one-day mode. But over and above any excuse was the side's inability to play Warne. Someone had whispered in the ear of DeFreitas (14) that the way to play him was by the 'down-the-wicket dance'. He tried it and was stumped by Healy. It would ensure that most of the other bats would stay rooted behind the popping crease. England compiled just 212 and lost six for 64 in the morning, which by coincidence were Warne's final figures. He bowled 27.4 overs, including eight maidens. McDermott backed up with three for 72, taking him to 249 wickets in Tests and ahead of Richie Benaud.

Australia batted again with resolve and was three for 170 at stumps, with Boon reaching his 50th fifty and partnered by Bevan. The lead was 237 and the pitch deteriorating. The odds were firmly in the home side's favour.

On day four, Boon (131) held the innings together as Australia drove on to seven for 320 before Taylor thought the 387-run lead was enough. England lost four for 79 by stumps, thanks to Fleming and McDermott. Gatting was caught off the first ball of day five from McDermott, leaving England on five for 81. It never recovered and slid steadily to oblivion in 77 balls, losing six for 13. McDermott took three to make his figures five for 42. It seemed at one point that Warne would not be needed, but Taylor, keeping the pressure up, brought him on with England six wickets down.

He trapped DeFreitas lbw on the back foot, making England seven for 91. In marched Gough, swinging his blade like an axe as he reached the wicket. Warne wheeled in, delivering a regulation leg break. Gough prodded and edged to Healy for the fourth of his five catches. The Australians gathered around Warne. Two wickets in two balls meant he was on a hat-trick. The players watched the video screen of the dismissal. All eyes then turned to the pavilion. Second-last man in was big Derek Malcolm, a tailender's tailender. Warne knew that if ever he was going to get a Test hat-trick, this was it. Before he bowled, he spoke to Damien Fleming, the only player in the team to have performed the feat.

'What do you reckon, Flemmo?' Warne asked.

'Bowl your stock ball,' Fleming replied. That would be a perfectly pitched leg break.

'Right,' Warne nodded. Taylor brought the field in with several men around the bat. Warne took a breath. He paused to eyeball the uncomfortable Malcolm, then moved in and pitched the ball straight on leg stump. Malcolm groped forward. The ball hit his glove and flew low to the right hand of Boon at short leg. The Tasmanian held it centimetres off the turf. Warne raced down the wicket to embrace him as the rest of the team gathered round to offer their congratulations. Warne had his hat-trick.

In came Tufnell, perhaps a little put out to be following Malcolm in the order. McDermott put the spinner out of his misery early by having him caught behind by Healy. England were all out for 92, and Australia had won the game by a whopping 295 runs.

Warne had three for 16 off thirteen overs, with six maidens, giving him nine for 80 from 40.4 overs for the match. He and McDermott (eight for 114) had once more destroyed England. It was looking like a very tired, ragged old enemy.

Life in the Old Lion

The England team was pilloried in its home press, with *The Times* even writing an editorial calling for more 'guts and determination'. It was doubtful that the team needed this. A bit more application, perhaps, but not courage. When they arrived in Sydney with an extra afternoon's grace after the early finish on day five, they headed for the beaches and Sydney's North Shore shops for post-Christmas bargains. The nets at the cricket ground could have been used, but they stood empty.

The Third Test started on Sunday 1 January, after both teams had celebrated New Year in their hotels. Atherton resolved to bat in 1995 as well as he had in 1994 when he had made more Test runs than any other player. He started the new year in keeping with his resolution as he won the toss and dug in for a 'captain's knock' of 88 after a bad beginning. In the first hour, the tourists were three for 20, with Fleming and McDermott doing the damage. But Atherton and Crawley (72) combined for a long, gritty partnership of 174. They were helped by McDermott's absence from the field with a stomach complaint, and Warne's indifferent form. The latter was economical, but occasionally wayward. It was thought that the Sydney pitch would help him the way it did a year earlier when he ran through the South Africans, who played him a similar way to the Englishmen. But there was none of his usual rip of the leg break. The flipper wasn't working and the ball seemed to be turning slowly, more like an Indian wicket.

Taylor took the new ball thirty minutes before stumps and both batsmen fell to McDermott and Fleming. England ended the day at seven for 198, having lost three wickets in the first hour, four in the last and nothing in between. An odd day's cricket in anyone's language. Australia's champion was McDermott, who, despite his illness, returned figures of four for 42 off twenty overs, with seven maidens.

Australia should have knocked off the English tail, but Gough and Fraser partnered well. Gough employed the long handle for 50 in forty-five balls, while Fraser preferred solid defence. He was a good foil for his partner. Then Malcolm, unaccustomed as he was to successful hitting, went after Warne with sixes and fours. He collected a more-than-useful 29 before Warne bowled him for his only wicket, at the cost of 88 from thirty-six overs, with ten maidens. McDermott's figures were more bloated than he deserved at five for 101 with support from Fleming (two for 59). The upshot was England making it to an unlikely 309, a respectable score.

Australia had lost none for 4 when rain stopped play for the rest of the day. Day three started in ideal conditions for bowling. The pitch was damp with a tinge of green here and there, and there was heavy cloud cover—perfect for the swing and speed employed by Fraser, Gough and Malcolm. Accordingly, these three took advantage and ran through the Aussies, with only Taylor (49) being able to cope. They were six for 65 at lunch. Minutes after the break, Australia was eight for 65. McDermott (21) struck out at the end of the innings when there was nothing to lose, except the fact that failure meant Australia would follow on. It managed to avoid that ignominy.

The final tally of 116 was paltry. Gough, the star with the bat, showed even more aggression and ability with the ball in registering six for 49. Fraser (two for 26) and Malcolm (two for 34) did the rest.

England's lead of 193 was 283 at stumps with only Gooch out, lbw to Fleming for 29. Atherton (67), Hick (98 not out) and Thorpe (47 not out) batted on to a declaration at two for 255 on day four. Warne ended with none for 48, giving him one for 136 for the match in a performance he would rather forget, at least from a bowling perspective.

Atherton wanted to have a go at Australia before tea and so ended the innings at 2.57 p.m., stranding Hick just 2 short of his first century against Australia. Hick was favoured by fortune, particularly a caught-behind by Healy off Warne, which was turned down. Yet he and his career deserved the reward of three figures. As it turned out, declaring before tea gave England no advantage as Taylor and Slater were still on song at stumps with a partnership of 139 after a blistering start. Australia still needed 310 on the final day to win. Clearly, it intended to chase.

On the last day, the openers continued on, more circumspectly, until lunch with the score at none for 206. They now needed 243 runs to win in two sessions and about sixty overs. If Australia were to succeed it would need to score the highest ever last-innings tally to win a Test. Another big crowd, this time more than 25 000, built in anticipation of a terrific victory. Then rain again intervened for another ninety minutes. Under the playing rules, only seven overs were lost. However, changes in calibrations touch the thinking of skippers. Taylor, instead of contemplating that 4 an hour was gettable with ten wickets in hand, now saw closer to 5 an hour as too much, especially as the pitch was damp. He was never going to risk throwing away a Test, at least when a series was not yet secured. Consequently, batting for a draw become the order of the afternoon, and perhaps to Australia's peril rather than glory. Slater (103) was caught off a poor shot hooking by a running

Tufnell at deep square leg. This delighted the English supporters, rightly called the 'Barmy Army', who had followed the team around the country. They broke into their favourite ditty:

We came over on a jet plane
You came over wiv a ball and chain

Devastating stuff. Malcolm was more penetrating. He bowled Taylor for 113, his finest Test hundred to date. Thereafter, wickets fell to Fraser until well after tea when Australia reached seven for 292. At that point, only England could win.

May joined Warne at the wicket. These two had just one wicket between them for the match. Now they had a chance to save it with the bat and become heroes. They dropped anchor and counted down the overs after 5 p.m., along with the big crowd and an even larger one tuned in to TVs around the nation and abroad to see the rear-guard action. As Atherton crowded them, Warne and May pushed, probed, padded and went back on their stumps. It was as riveting as it would have been had Australia stroked its way to a win. Every ball counted. A player's deep, true power of concentration was tested. Atherton knew that if he brought on the quicks in the poor light, the umpires would have offered the Australians a chance to leave the field and call it quits, which they would have taken. Warne demonstrated that if he ever combined his aggressive technique with his sound defence, he would score a Test century in the style of Botham.

With 36 and 10 not out, respectively, he and May saw the home side through to a draw at seven for 344. Fraser took five for 73 in a sustained display of top-class swing. Australia was slightly more than 100 short of England for the game, but a long way shy of it in terms of the merits for the match. Unfortunately, the tourists would have to endure another change of pace and game just when their Test match momentum had begun to build.

Much to Taylor's annoyance, it was back to the uncertainties of the one-day game—against Australia 'A' at the Gabba on 8 January. He won the toss and his senior squad crunched out a convincing five for 252. Mark Waugh delivered another great cameo of 93, and Boon, more belligerent than normal, reached 86 not out. The 'A' team responded well at the top of the order with Hayden (51), Blewett (63) and Ponting (run out 39) doing much to push their cases for higher selection. Apart from them, there was little to impress as the 'A's crumpled to all out for 218 in 47.5 overs, giving the number-one team victory by 34. Law was the best of the bowlers with three for 46, while Warne was rested.

He returned two days later at the MCG in front of a huge home crowd and bowled with his usual control and impact, taking two for 37 off ten. He dismissed England's two most dangerous bats in the game (Hick for 91 and Fairbrother for 35), while McGrath bowled brilliantly, taking four for 25 off ten. Only Gough (45) at the end of the innings added to a disappointing effort by the tourists. Australia's response lacked fire and enthusiasm as Fraser matched McGrath with even better figures of four for 22 off ten. The home team was at one point three for 19. Only Mark Waugh (41), Healy (56) and Warne (21) showed any form as Australia crumbled to all out for 188. England won by 37 runs and maintained its improved form and drive from the Third Test at Sydney.

It was not enough, however, to put them into the finals and Australia had to face the 'A' side in Sydney on 15 January, in the first of a best-of-three last round. Reiffel was 'promoted' from the 'A' side to the senior team, but, in an odd move, was relegated to twelfth man. He had been the 'A's' best and most consistent performer. Now he had removed from the competition.

The 'A' side won the toss and batted ordinarily to eight for 209. Hayden again staked a claim for top national selection with 50, while Bevan, who was having a poor Test series, demonstrated his one-day skills with 73. Warne put a clamp on the middle-order scoring, with one for 37 off ten, while McDermott did the damage with four for 25.

The senior team bumbled its way to an unconvincing but thrilling last-ball win, with Slater (92) leading the tortuous way home. The packed, boorish crowd of 36 000 had little interest in the uninspiring cricket, being far more interested in distractions such as the inevitable stripper and yobbo fights. Yet even the worst of them turned their eyes to the field when Greg Rowell ran in to deliver the last ball, overpitched and was cracked over point by Healy for a face-saving four that gave the seniors a win.

Two days later, at the MCG, there was a similar story with the 'A' side doing better when batting first again with 226. The crowd of 53 765 was good for mid-week and were baying for 'Warnie', who took only one wicket—Martyn, lbw for 54. By the end of the innings, he had taken a hammering, which his figures of one for 55 off ten overs reflected.

This time the Australian team coasted to a victory in forty-nine overs, scoring four for 229. Taylor (50), Slater (56 run out) and Steve Waugh (56 not out) made it a comfortable win. It had not been an uplifting event. But the two–nil lead in the final series meant a third contest was not necessary. Taylor and his team moved to Adelaide for the resumption of the longer and more challenging game.

Fade in Adelaide

Australia brought in Blewett and leg-spinner Peter McIntyre to replace Bevan and the injured May for the Fourth Test, starting on Australia Day at the Adelaide Oval. The England camp suffered the great loss of Gough with a stress fracture of the foot and Hick with a back injury, while Stewart remained unavailable with his broken finger.

After winning the toss and batting, Atherton went on to a typical 80 following an opening stand of 93 with Gooch (47), who to that point had been a disappointment. England battled to two for 196 in a rain-interrupted day, with Gatting beginning to show the form that so far had eluded him in the Tests, in which he had made just 57 from five innings. The next day, he crawled to his first century since 1987 at the Oval.

Earlier, Thorpe (26) had been deceived by a Warne wrong 'un to be caught by Taylor at slip, leaving Gatting as the

England backbone as Crawley—bowled by Warne for 28—and DeFreitas added to the resistance. England held on till after tea for 353. Its batsman seemed incapable of scoring against McDermott, who sent down forty-one overs with fifteen maidens for figures of three for 66. In his first Test, McIntyre returned two for 51 off 19.3, which was statistically similar to his spin partner Warne, whose figures were two for 72 off thirty-one overs. The fortunes of these two talented leggies had diverged after the Australian 'A' tour of Zimbabwe in September 1991. Then, selectors such as John Benaud thought they were on a par. It took another three-and-a-half years before they played together in a Test. Warne had been fast-tracked to a permanent Test place, whereas McIntyre had struggled at the state level.

Slater and Taylor looked sure and aggressive in pursuit at none for 81 at stumps from just twenty-two overs. They went on next day until 128, when Slater (67) fell to DeFreitas, who also dismissed Boon caught behind for a duck. Taylor then dug in with Mark Waugh until, at 202, he was trapped lbw for a strong 90. Mark Waugh contributed a sparkling 49, but his brother managed only 19 before nicking one off all-rounder Chris Lewis. Australia was four for 232, and in need of steadying. The firm hands came from rookie Greg Blewett and Healy, who took the score to a healthy five for 394 at stumps, 41 ahead. Blewett was on 91 at stumps and Healy 72.

The third day, however, saw another England fightback. Blewett made 102 not out, but unfortunately he was the lone ranger, as Australia collapsed to be all out for 419, adding just 25 for the loss of five wickets early in the morning session. Blewett joined an elite of fourteen other Australians who had scored a century on Test debut. They stretched back to Charles Bannerman's 165 in the first-ever Test in 1877.

The lead of 66 was *just* a lead, not a match-winning break over the opposition. However, when Atherton (14) and Gatting (0) were back in the pavilion with the score at 30, both unlikely victims to part-time leg cutter and occasional off-spinner Mark

Waugh, it appeared a lot more. At three for 83 and Gooch out for 34, Australia seemed in the box seat. Yet stubborness by Thorpe and Crawley took them to 154, when McDermott removed Thorpe (84) caught by Warne. At stumps, Crawley was still hanging on with 49 not out and DeFreitas 20 not out, with England on six for 220, just 154 ahead.

The media suggested it was just a matter of Australia turning up on the last day for its third win in four Tests. DeFreitas changed all that in the morning and crashed his way to a magnificent 88, taking the England total to 328. Mark Waugh astonished himself by taking the bowling honors with five for 40 off fourteen overs.

Warne was steady with two for 82 from 30.5 overs, with nine maidens. He was not taking the big hauls of the first two Tests, but he was still a threat to the English bats, who treated him with due respect. Their method of playing him was obvious, simple and more effective than previous approaches—it was to play him from the other end. Batsmen defended or went for singles to rotate the strike and limit his ability to pin them down and dismiss them. If the bowler could deliver six balls to one batsman, the odds were than he would get at least one through him which would yield a chance or a wicket. It was Warne's way. He created worry or confusion in the batsman's mind, then took advantage of his concerns with consistent, good-length bowling and a variety of balls. If he couldn't get more than two or three deliveries at a player intent on singles that put him at the bowler's end, he was thwarted and could become frustrated. His spell would come to an end and the batsmen would win a minor round. This strategy saw him taking two wickets an innings rather a more penetrating four or more.

Australia needed 263 to win in sixty-seven overs—a rate of just less than 4 an over. Taylor was confident his strong batting line-up could achieve that rate and told his squad that they were going for a win. It stirred the dressing room. At none for 16 at lunch, all looked possible. Forty minutes after the break, however, Australia was four for 23, and all looked lost, thanks to Malcolm. He got rid of Slater, Taylor and Steve Waugh in a fierce spell, while Fraser removed Boon.

Mark Waugh (24) led Blewett on a different mission than in the first innings, but the debutant was caught behind for 12, leaving Australia five for 64. That transformed to seven for 83 at tea, with Warne lbw to Lewis for 2. This left Healy and McDermott to carry on, but McDermott went straight after and it was eight for 83. Fleming then joined Healy in a courageous rear-guard action lasting 113 minutes, before Fleming fell lbw to Lewis.

The partnership of 67 had taken Australia to nine for 152, but the score was academic. It was still 110 runs shy of England, with only a faint hope of stealing a draw. The crowd of more than 12 000 was not leaving as the last fifteen overs whittled down. McIntyre was out of his depth with Malcolm, who trapped him for his second duck in the match at 156. England had won a shock victory by 106 runs. Malcolm had at last fulfilled his promise on Australian wickets with four for 39 and Lewis had risen above himself by taking four for 24.

The series was now two–one in Australia's favour. But the tide was moving the tourists' way. Perth would provide a fast, hard wicket, suitable for Malcolm. Consequently, Australia brought in McGrath and local speedster Jo Angel for Fleming and McIntyre. England seconded Mark Ramprakash from a tour of India.

A Crusher at the WACA

England arrived in Perth for the final Test, beginning on 3 February, with high hopes of levelling the series after the euphoria of its unexpected Fourth Test victory. Taylor won the toss and batted, only to go for 9, caught behind. However, Slater rode his luck to hit his third belligerent century of the series. Only Bradman with four in 1930 had hit more.

Boon (1) continued his mixed form, but Slater and Mark Waugh took over with a partnership of 183. Waugh again was destined to go before a century when he was caught at 88 off

Lewis. At stumps, Australia was a strong four for 283, with Steve Waugh and Blewett still in.

Next morning, Malcolm, who had been over-testing both batsmen with short balls, again went head-hunting, but to no avail. Fraser, bowling with more intelligence, induced a nick to Rhodes from Blewett (20), bringing Healy in. Just when he was set and seeing well, he tore a calf muscle and DeFreitas had him caught for 12. Warne made just 1 before providing Rhodes with another catch off DeFreitas.

At lunch, Australia had lumbered on to seven for 345. In a bizarre end to the innings, which appeared as if the batsmen were still in one-day mode, the last three in—Angel, McGrath and McDermott—were all run out, leaving Steve Waugh stranded on 99 not out.

England began after an early tea and was soon two for 5, courtesy of McGrath, who had stepped up to take over as the number-one striker with McDermott in hospital for checks, but still likely to bowl again in the match. The speedster had Atherton (4) on his way gloving one to Healy, and next ball caused Gatting to play on.

England recovered via Gooch and Thorpe, and Taylor gambled with Mark Waugh and his leg cutters again. After 11 runs were collected from his first over, Waugh trapped his Essex team-mate Gooch lbw for 37. A few balls later, he now had Crawley edge a leg cutter to Warne at slip. The part-time bowler had helped make England almost capitulate at four for 77.

Thorpe set about rebuilding England's position and was 54 not out at stumps, with Mark Ramprakash on 14 not out. Next morning, a recovered McDermott returned and joined McGrath in attacking the batsmen, but they pushed the score up 158 by mid-afternoon, before Warne bowled a wrong 'un to Thorpe, on 123. It turned away from him and left him stranded for a stumping by Healy. Soon afterwards, Warne bowled Ramprakash (72) and England was six for 246. Lewis then cracked 40 from sixty-two balls that took England to 295 all out, 107 short of Australia.

Angel justified the selectors' faith in him with three for 65, while McGrath finished with three for 88 and Waugh took two for 29. Warne's two for 58 off twenty-three overs was about par for him for the past three Tests. He was never going to manage a bagful on the WACA and his figures were pleasing enough.

Australia had twenty-four overs to face in the rest of day three. Slater raced out of the blocks and helped put the score past 50 in eleven overs, obviously aiming to hit Malcolm out of the attack. It was a risky method for a Test and he was lucky that he did not come unstuck. Malcolm again sprayed some; but many also beat the bat, and he was very, very quick. At 75, the steadier Fraser replaced him and first ball removed Slater for 45. Angel came in as night watchman to protect Boon and Taylor promptly ran him out for a duck, so that Boon had to come in anyway. Australia was two for 87 at stumps, with a handy 194-run lead.

Next day, however, Australia stumbled, losing three quick wickets—Boon for 18, Mark Waugh for 1 and Taylor for 52. The score was an unhealthy five for 123, with a modest lead of 230 and more than five sessions to play. If England could run through the other half by lunch, it would be looking at a chase of around 300, or only 2 runs an over—a doddle, provided wickets were intact.

Any such optimistic expectations were soon dashed by Steve Waugh and Blewett, who, by lunch, had added 63, with Blewett on 37 and Waugh on 22. Blewett then went on and reached his second century in as many Tests on the last ball before tea. He became only the third Australian—and fifth batsman in the history of Tests—to score a century in each of his first two Tests. This one had come in just 135 balls. After tea, Blewett (115) holed out off Lewis to Malcolm at long-on, Waugh (80) was caught in the slips off Lewis and Taylor decided to declare at eight for 345. The lead was 452. England's great duo of Gooch and Gatting, who had both now announced their retirement from Test cricket, would have to bat at their peak for victory, and for both that was now safely behind them.

Gooch (4) was dropped twice before he was caught and bowled by McDermott. The crowd of 10 000 stood to cheer Gooch all the way from the crease for a fine career of 8900 Test runs at 42.58. He had scored twenty centuries, with a highest score of 333.

Gatting came in and fiddled against genuine, accurate speed from McGrath and McDermott before the latter bowled him neck and crop for 8. He, too, received a thunderous ovation for a top career of 4409 runs at 35.55, with ten centuries and a highest score of 207.

England was two for 17 and in need of more than crowd sentiment now to recover. Fraser was sent in as night watchman, only to fall lbw to McGrath for 5. It was now three for 26. Thorpe came in, but McGrath got one to move away from him and he was caught for a duck by Taylor at slip. England was now a shocking four for 26 and McGrath was on a hat-trick. Crawley came to the wicket on a pair and, while McGrath missed him, McDermott did not, having him caught by Mark Waugh. Crawley had avoided the hat-trick, but not the dreaded pair of noughts.

England went to stumps a miserable five for 27, with Atherton on a resolute 8 not out. But the next morning, the England skipper was caught behind off McGrath without addition to the overnight tally. Ramprakash and Rhodes began to restore a little pride, but, at 95, Mark Waugh was cut by Ramprakash (42) to brother Steve for a superb catch. The rest then rolled over to the fearsome McDermott, who took the last three wickets, to be all out for 123. McDermott ended with six for 38, supported by McGrath with three for 40. Warne was needed for just seven overs. He sent down three maidens and took none for 11. The spinner was happy to accept his back-seat role as the fast men wrapped up the game. He had had his chances on more suitable wickets at Brisbane and Sydney, and he had taken them.

Australia had won by a massive 329 runs, giving it a convincing three–one series win to retain the Ashes. Warne, with twenty-seven wickets at 20.33, shared bowling honours for the series with the more consistent McDermott (thirty-two at 21.09) and Gough (twenty at 21.25). Michael Slater was the outstanding bat of either side with 623 runs at 62.30, while Greg Blewett (249 at 83.00) made a big late contribution. Thorpe (444 at 49.33), Steve Waugh (345 at 49.29), Mark Taylor (471 at 47.10) and Mark Waugh (435 at 43.50) were consistent and productive.

In 1993, Warne had been the main difference between the two sides. In 1994–95, it had been the combination of his guile and McDermott's power and accuracy that had done most to secure the Ashes for Australia.

Post-Ashes Dashers

The *Sydney Morning Herald* did the Australian team a favour by not breaking the Pakistan bribery story of September 1994 until after the Ashes. The team was having four days off after the Fifth Test when the newspaper revealed the incident. It ran hot through February while the team was in New Zealand for a one-day tournament with the Kiwis, South Africa and India. Team members took their families with them in what Warne told friends was a 'very relaxed' atmosphere. 'Practice was optional and the guys had a bit of fun after the pressures and rush of the summer at home,' he said.

Taylor made it clear that the players should still strive to win. Warne and company needed no motivation to step up a gear in the first game against South Africa at the Basin Reserve, Wellington, on 15 February. He and the rest of the team now regarded the Proteas as a greater challenge than England, who had become less difficult to overcome in the 1990s. Games against South Africa consequently became gritty affairs and enterprise went out the window, as the South African innings demonstrated. It struggled to 123 all out in 46.2 overs—less than 3 runs an over. The smallish crowd was kept from a collective yawn by the steady fall of wickets.

Much interest in the local media centred on Warne, especially his battles with Cullinan, whom Taylor brought Warne on to bowl against as soon as he appeared. Warne duly tied him up and the frustrated Cullinan moved out of his crease to drive him, missed and was stumped by Healy for 0. Yet another round of many between these two went the bowler's way. Cronje (22) was caught by Taylor in slips off Blewett before he could lock horns with Warne, who delivered his ten in succession without challenge. The South African bats were content to see him off rather than belt him out of the attack and he returned two for 18 off ten overs, with three maidens.

These were remarkable figures—just 1.8 runs an over—as a result of his tight, on-the-spot performance. Yet much of it was to do with the leaden-footed South African bats who, like the Englishmen, had decided to play him from the other end—that is, by rotating the strike. Yet it was more sensible in Tests than one-dayers, when attack more often than not was more profitable than defence. Australia caught the contagion in compiling seven for 124 in 43.2 overs and at one point even looked like going under. Steve Waugh hung on for 44 not out and saved the day. Warne (2 not out) was there for the winning run.

It was on to Eden Park, Auckland, four days later for a more entertaining encounter with New Zealand. Australia batted first and Taylor had a rare foray in this form of the game by pushing near a century, being caught and bowled for a creditable 97. Mark Waugh (74) produced yet another gem of speed and grace. Australia's total of five for 254 meant New Zealand was forced to chase at more than 5 an over, a tough assignment against one of the best one-day attacks in the world. After Mark Greatbatch, the hard-hitting opener, was dismissed for a strong 74, only Stephen Fleming (53) could sustain the challenge. Warne tempted the aggressive Rutherford (7) from his crease for a good stumping by Healy in taking one for 40 as New Zealand struggled to nine for 227.

Despite the comfortable win, the Australians could not relax against the enterprising India in the next game at Dunedin on

22 February. Taylor dropped down the list and let Boon (32) open with Blewett (46). Ponting (62) showed the attacking form needed in the middle order and was supported by Steve Waugh (23) and brother Mark (48) as Australia reached six for 250. This left India with much the same challenge set New Zealand. The difference was a more powerful, attacking batting line-up, beginning with Prabhakar (50) and the dashing Sachin Tendulkar, still only twenty-one years old, with 47.

He and the steady-eyed Sidhu (54 run out) took to Warne in a manner he had not experienced since he entered Test cricket early in 1992—also against India. He returned none for 61 off ten overs, which was a rude shock as India coasted to an easy win, scoring five for 252 off 47.2 overs. No bowler escaped the onslaught. Some of the Australians realised that to give bowlers a chance against such batting, they would have to post scores nearer 300 than 250, which was another dimension in one-day cricket.

That problem would be faced at another time. India did not make the final, which was fought out by New Zealand and Australia at Eden Park on 26 February. New Zealand won the toss and batted. After Reiffel removed Greatbach (8) and Douglas (2), only Rutherford (46) put up any real resistance. Warne bowled at his best, taking two for 21 off his ten overs. He put a block on the middle order and any thoughts of the Kiwis compiling something competitive by removing Thomson (9) caught-and-bowled, and Parore (0), caught by Taylor at slip, in quick succession, reducing them to eight for 106. They lasted the fifty overs to reach nine for 137. Australia then put them out of their misery in just 31.1 overs, losing only four wickets in overhauling the target. Taylor (44) and Mark Waugh (46) led the way.

The 1995 New Zealand tournament was a nice, successful 'vacation'—a busman's holiday, when most players would prefer to have been with families or elsewhere relaxing before a tour to the West Indies, which was of enormous importance to them. It turned into a disturbing time for Warne and Mark Waugh—off the field. The revelations in the media that they and Tim May had been offered bribes by Salim Malik forced the

Australian Cricket Board's Alan Crompton and Graham Halbish to check if any players had been 'involved' with bookmakers. This was done in New Zealand by Australian team manager, Ian McDonald. He spoke individually to each player. Warne and Mark Waugh owned up to taking $US5000 and $AUD6000 respectively from 'John', the illegal Indian bookmaker. (The ACB apparently mistook Waugh's $AUD6000 to be $US6000.)

McDonald rang Crompton and Halbish, who faced a tough decision. If they made it public that two of Salim's accusers—Warne and Mark Waugh—had dealt with 'John', there was sure to be a huge, worldwide media and public outcry. The building heat in the issue, plus the fact that Salim's accusers had suddenly become the accused, meant the two culprits would receive wide censure. The ACB may have been forced to take severe action—perhaps banning them from the game for a year or two, or even finishing their careers. Partly in sympathy with the players' plight and partly because the board's own intransience had forced it into a corner, Crompton and Halbish decided on a cover-up.

Warne and Waugh were fined $8000 and $10 000, roughly the amount in Australian dollars they were thought to have taken from 'John'. (Waugh claimed he had taken $US4000, roughly equivalent to $AUD6000, at the time. Accordingly, he should only have been fined $AUD6000. In effect, the ACB owes him $AUD4000.) The fines would not hurt either of these two, particularly Warne, who, apart from his substantial salary as a contracted Test player, was earning plenty from his deals with Nike and other companies. Yet the fines were in line with the 'in-house' traditional system of discipline.

The board informed two senior International Cricket Council (ICC) members—chairman Sir Clyde Walcott and chief executive David Richards—who happened to be in Sydney at the time. The other board members were presented with a *fait accompli*, despite a few of them being uncomfortable with the way the matter had been handled and the fact that they had not been consulted.

The small-time but potentially dangerous business of giving innocuous intelligence to a bookie was now a 'secret' known by other members of the team, the ACB and the ICC. Despite it being tidied up on the one-night stop-over in Sydney on the way back from New Zealand en route to the West Indies, it was now a time-bomb for everyone concerned. With so many people knowing about it, the odds were that somebody with a grievance, an agenda or simply a loose tongue would one day leak the story.

10

Caribbean Conquest

Shortcomings

Warne was once more the centre of media attention when the team reached Barbados on 3 March 1995 for their five one-dayers and four Tests against the West Indies. He was in the background as Taylor handled a positive press conference, but the local media wanted Warne's thoughts on his coming encounters with Brian Lara. Warne said he was looking forward to it. He was quick to emphasise the team element in the encounter. It wasn't Warne versus Lara. It was Lara and any other West Indian against a finely tuned unit. A big factor in Warne's success was his team-consciousness, despite his individual brilliance. This was appreciated by his team-mates, who realised his popularity with the media and public, but were not resentful of it because of his attitude. He enjoyed the mateship that came with being part of this elite group. Warne inspired and supported them on the field and had fun with them off it.

When he arrived late at the races for the Barbados Cup the next day with Steve Waugh and Justin Langer, they remembered that Mark Waugh, the team's top gambler, had the guest passes. He and Ricky Ponting had arrived eager for the first race and were already busy in the betting ring. Undaunted, the trio jumped the fence and walked over the course itself to the winning post. They expected to be grabbed and tossed out. To their surprise, they were met by an effusive club president and directed to the hospitality area, where they found Mark Waugh and Ponting buried in their race guides.

Warne did not bother about the races so much. He went around with his video camera filming the crowd and the activities in the middle of the course, where every kind of gambling—including on the forthcoming cricket—was going on, along with calypso bands and dancing. He and Steve Waugh didn't go unnoticed. Locals called out for the bowler to watch out for Lara and Richardson, who would 'blow you away, *mun*'.

'Hey, there's Shane Warne, the mystery *mun*,' one said, 'and Steve Waugh, the best slower ball bowler and fearsome cover-driver.'

Another laughed at the zinc on Warne's face:

'Hey, *mun*, you look like an Indian.'

They all wanted to be in Warne's 'movie'. 'Hey, *mun*,' they asked him excitedly, is this going to be on TV?'

Waugh, Ponting and Warne had so much fun that they missed the big race, the Barbados Cup, but promised themselves they would see it next time they came over.

A couple of days later, the team was on the local beach, Accra, where the people were playing soccer, volleyball, cricket, paddle ball and sundry other sports on the sand. For once, Warne didn't join in.

'Warney [sic] had two photographers in the palm of his hand as if he were auditioning for the swimsuit cover of *Sports Illustrated*,' Steve Waugh noted in his *West Indies Tour Diary*. 'It was quite a sight to see Shane discover poses that involved beautiful muscles held taut, backed up with that smile that sends schoolgirls' hearts a-flutter.'

One pose made Waugh double up with laughter, when the photographers had Warne gripping the top of a surfboard. 'Warney has never ridden a surfboard in his life!' he observed.

Taylor's leadership, along with the resort-like conditions of their hotel, soon made the team buoyant with confidence. They were looking forward to playing good, winning cricket.

The first chance for this came in the opening one-day game at Kensington Oval in Bridgetown, the island's capital, on 8 March. The Windies won the toss and batted at their usual rapid rate until newcomer Stuart Williams (11) was caught behind off Reiffel. Lara came to the wicket and seemed nervous at first, for all his swagger. His form had not been brilliant of late and he needed a big series to consolidate his ranking as the world's premier batsman. There were political problems to do with local cricket preying on his mind and, since setting world records for the highest scores in first-class cricket of 501 and 375 in Tests in the previous year, he had been even more of a target for opposition sides.

He soon settled down, however, and batted with authority for 56, although he faced little of Warne, which gave no clues as to how they would fare against each other in the Tests. Hooper scored a mercurial 84 at a run a ball in setting up a final total of 257, and was severe on both Warne and May.

McDermott's three for 25 off ten overs was the best bowling performance. Warne dismissed the dangerous Simmons (37), but was not yet on song in taking one for 56. More perhaps from bravado than sound reasoning, he predicted after watching Lara that he would not make more than 220 in the four Tests, averaging around 30. It was a good thing he kept this bit of soothsaying to himself and a few close team-mates. Needling Lara, a competitive sort of chap at the best of times, was not a sport to be encouraged.

Australia chased, but perhaps not hard enough at the start—although taking on the Windies quicks was always a tough assignment—and fell short by 7 runs at the end of their fifty overs, with four wickets in hand. A little more enterprise should have won it.

The team attempted to put this to rights three days later at Queens Park Oval in Port of Spain, Trinidad. Slater and Taylor began with 37 in ten overs, before Ambrose dismissed Taylor (16). Again there was an even contribution from several batsmen—Slater (55), Boon (48), Steve Waugh (58) and Healy (51)—without anyone taking the opposition apart for a long period. Still, eight for 260 was enough to put pressure on the pursuers.

Lara and Hooper led the effort. They both went after Warne and dispatched him to all points of the compass until he dismissed Hooper (55) at 175 after Blewett had got rid of Lara (62), for the second time, at 121. Lara had the upper hand in the early psychological stakes, although the Windies went down in this one, finishing 24 runs short of the Australian total, mainly due to the accurate, nagging bowling of Reiffel (three for 32). Warne returned his worst-ever one-day figures of one for 63, surpassing his none for 61 against India less than three weeks earlier at Dunedin. He had now been collared by both Tendulkar and Lara in a short time. Still, he took heart from his vital dismissal of Hooper and the team's victory.

Next morning, the two sides were at it again. The Windies batted first, only for Fleming to dismiss Simmons for 6. Not long after this Fleming left the field with a shoulder injury that would send him home. With him, it seemed, went Aussie fortunes as, for the third successive time, Lara and Hooper embarked on a strong partnership, putting on 99. Hooper made only 41, but Lara wound up for the type of innings that crushed the opposition. Warne (none for 52) was not his only target this time. Steve Waugh, standing in for Fleming, collected two wickets but went for 61 runs off 9.3 overs and even McGrath (none for 57) was smashed as Lara crunched 139 from 125 balls. Jimmy Adams played a strong second fiddle with 51 not out as the Windies finished with five for 282.

Australia had to manage just less than 6 an over or almost a run a ball as it went for the chase, but both Taylor and Slater were run out by the time the total was 50. Only Steve Waugh (44) and Ponting (43) fought back as Australia crumbled to 149 all out. Simmons bowled above himself in collecting four for 18 off only 4.5 overs.

Taylor won the toss and batted on a good wicket in the fourth contest, at Arnos Vale, St Vincent, only to be met by a souped-up Ambrose, whose return of none for 22 off eight overs belied the menace of his actual performance. Walsh, bowling as fast as anyone had ever seen him, took three for 30 off nine overs as Australia struggled to nine for 210 from a rain-reduced forty-eight overs. Further rain reduced the Windies' allocation to forty-six.

The West Indies struck hard and fast against McDermott, Reiffel and McGrath in its chase for the runs and Taylor was forced to try Warne earlier than intended. The spinner lifted at a critical moment, dropping the ball straight on the spot. Frustrated opener Stuart Campbell tried to jump into him and was smartly stumped by Healy. Then a controlled partnership by Simmons (86) and Hooper (60 not out), the most consistent player on either side, made it easy for the Windies, who coasted to victory in 43.1 overs.

Warne's form was the only positive to come out of the match. He troubled and contained every batsman and had Hooper vigilant when he could have been vicious. Taylor made a rare error in taking Warne off after half his allotted ten when the spinner's form and the Windies' performance dictated leaving him on for ten in a row. But Taylor's faulty mathematics meant that he juggled his bowlers badly in the weather-shortened game.

When Warne was brought back to complete his spell it was too late. As if to make the point to his skipper he delivered a 'pearler' to remove Simmons. It snaked away from the probing bat of the opener, who was seeing the ball like a pumpkin, and he edged it to Healy. Warne's two for 33 off 9.1 overs did not tell the tale of his impact.

Nevertheless, the loss of the series, which now stood at three–one in the Windies' favour, killed the Australians' early self-confidence. The soul-searching was evident, from the captain down to the physio.

'Better now than in the middle of the Tests,' was Warne's private reaction.

A reassessment of attitude was now required in the shell-shocked Aussie camp. Warne, May and Mark Waugh were unsettled by news that an investigating committee in Pakistan ruled that Salim Malik was innocent of attempting to bribe the Australians until 'conclusive' proof was presented to the contrary. There were suggestions that the world body governing cricket, the ICC, would somehow investigate the matter further or even adjudicate. This would probably mean that the Australians would have to present evidence or submit themselves for questioning. It was not a comforting thought, especially as death threats could follow exposure on such a contentious issue.

There was also the matter of the cover-up concerning the deals with the illegal bookmaker 'John' in Sri Lanka, which would make Warne and Mark Waugh uncomfortable facing any probe. Taylor counselled the three men and told them to forget the controversy and say nothing to the media. He was concerned that they should focus on the job ahead of them.

'Certainly nothing to do with that is going to interrupt this tour,' he told them. His words comforted his charges, who were able to push the matter aside for the time being and concentrate on their cricket.

•••

On 16 March, it was on to Georgetown, capital of Guyana on the South American mainland, via Trinidad, and team morale slipped into grumbling because of the inevitable lost luggage. Georgetown's unprepossessing grubbiness didn't help the team spirit. Nor did the usual search for a half-decent restaurant, which proved fruitless until members of the 1991 tour remembered the Palm Court.

Warne was one of the discontented. He was missing his favourite tinned spaghetti and there wasn't a McDonald's in sight. His lack of gourmet adventurism worried his team-mates, who thought he might waste away if he couldn't receive a Big Mac fix from time to time.

Dripping with sweat in the humidity after practice at the Bouda Oval, the bad temper of the players was exacerbated by the showers at their hotel. The water was brown in colour with an odd odour. Some of the tourists wondered if the hotel's sewage was circulated where it should not be. They were fascinated by the depreciation of the local currency, with 150 Guyanese dollars now buying one US dollar. On the last tour, it was four to one. Players joked they would need a truck to carry the money to pay for a team dinner at the Palm Court, where the local head gangster, Big Daddy, played host. As long as this Rasta man was known to be 'close' to the team, they were not likely to be mugged or robbed of their huge wads of local notes.

For the moment, the team was preoccupied with the Sheffield Shield competition back home where South Australia would be playing Queensland in the final at the Gabba. It was the talk at breakfast, lunch and dinner and a further distraction from depressing Georgetown. There was little to do but relax by the pool, especially on Sunday when the town shut down for a Hindu festival.

With nothing hinging on the final one-day game, Australia rested McDermott, whose shoulder was troubling him, along with Warne, Boon and Blewett. Into the side came Ponting, May, Langer and Brendon Julian, who had just arrived to replace Fleming. The Windies stood down Lara and Ambrose and brought back Stuart Williams, together with paceman Vernon Drakes.

Taylor won the toss and, along with Slater, got Australia off to an impressive start, which hushed the vocal Bouda crowd. They only found voice when Drakes had Slater (41) caught. Taylor went on to a fastish, solid 66 and Mark Waugh delivered a superb 70. Healy hit form again with a bright 36 as the tail wagged the score up to nine for 286, only a reasonable effort considering the small ground.

How reasonable was soon emphasised by the withering Windies bats as Williams (45), Simmons (70), Hooper (50), Adams (60 not out) and Holder (34 not out), racked up the runs in just 47.2 overs for the loss of five wickets. It was another comprehensive win, establishing the home one-day side as superior with bat and ball over the five games by a margin of four–one. Only Reiffel bowled with any sense of containment given the short route to the boundary, taking two for 48 off ten. Julian outstripped Warne with the most expensive ten overs of the competition, returning none for 66.

Team morale was now at its lowest of the tour. A win was needed in the three-day, first-class game against Guyana from 20 to 22 March. Guyana began poorly and never recovered as McGrath (five for 47) and Julian (two for 23) ran through the locals with sheer pace. Warne's form, however, provided the major interest of the game. He came on early and tied up every batsman in a mesmerising spell as he collected three for 21 off eleven overs, with six maidens. Most important was his handling of the little dasher Chanderpaul, a Test prospect, whom he tied down, beat and then dismissed by enticing him out of his ground to a ball that curled past his bat into Healy's quick hands for a stumping. He also caught and bowled the hard-hitting former Test player Roger Harper for 2. Guyana reached a risible 105.

Australia's response looked like being even more laughable when both openers were back in the pavilion with the score at 7. But Mark Waugh thrashed 75 before Harper caught-and-bowled him. Blewett hit his fourth consecutive first-class hundred before being caught on the mid-wicket fence for 116, while Langer collected a smooth 55 in a much-needed stay in the middle. The team tallied 373.

Guyana went in again and did nearly twice as well in scoring 207, which still gave Australia a big innings win. Warne again dismissed Chanderpaul—this time with a skidding flipper—and continued his good form in taking three for 42 off fifteen overs. He had his flipper working well, taking two wickets with it, a sure sign that he was running into top form. This ball had failed him during the summer against England and he had not revved it up in any of the one-dayers.

Julian showed he had recovered from his round-the-world rush to Guyana by taking five for 45. He sprayed a few, but was quick. McGrath continued his progress with two for 49.

Both developments were opportune in view of an accident to McDermott, when he tore ligaments in his ankle on a run from the Bouda ground to the hotel. His tour was finished.

The news kept team spirits at a low ebb as Australia's chances of taking the series nose-dived long before the first ball of the First Test. Some players were down with a flu virus that had been circulating since the New Zealand trip and there were worries about malaria in Guyana, where disease-carrying mosquitoes were prevalent.

The tourists were now without their two front-line speedsters. Second-stringers—McGrath, Reiffel and Julian—had to step up in a hurry to support Warne, on whose shoulders Australia's chances seemed to rest. Yet one wouldn't know it from his demeanour. The spinner was in upbeat mood. He had two garish gold earrings made in Guyana—one in the form of the Nike logo and the other as '23', the number worn by his football hero and also his favorite roulette number—and displayed them to the team over the last breakfast in Guyana. He persuaded the undemonstrative Reiffel to do the same and he paraded a pistol earring to the surprised team. It was a 'coming out' in personality for Reiffel and suggested he was relaxed for the task ahead.

Meanwhile, the Windies camp was elated with the news that McDermott was on his way. He had been determined to settle a few scores from the 1992–93 series, and some of their key bats were resigned to a barrage or two from him. He had arrived in the Windies at the peak of his career. Now he was out of the contest.

The West Indies had won the one-day competition comprehensively. Australia's attack was depleted. The home team were preparing for a quick kill in the First Test.

•••

Before that encounter there was a game against the President's XI, a Windies second XI made up of past Test players and young prospects, on the beautiful island of St Lucia. The weather disrupted the game, reducing it to two inconclusive days. But there was still much-needed time in the middle, as Slater with 90 and the Waugh twins with 73 apiece ran into great touch to lead Australia to five for 322 declared.

The President's XI fared well in its limited reply with five for 261. Warne was given a real working over by Arthurton (75 not out) and D. A. Joseph (83) in his second spell, which saw him return two for 84 from fourteen overs for the innings. But there was an encouraging note about his top-class first spell, in which he captured the wicket of the team's captain, Roland Holder, and also that of Chanderpaul (caught and bowled for 2) for the third time in three encounters. It stopped the latter's chance of Test selection for the time being. Warne was adept at killing off or pushing back careers in his unending battles with the world's leading batsmen.

Barbed in Barbados

The media descended on Barbados, island of the First Test, days before the tourists did, pleased to spend a few days in the sun before 'work' covering the Test cricket, commencing on 31 March. TV networks from Australia, Asia and the UK were there along with innumerable journalists and writers. This series was being billed as the 'heavyweight championship of cricket'. The implicit reason for the huge interest was the belief that Taylor's team was strong enough to inflict a series defeat on the West Indies for the first time in twenty years.

Weaknesses, however, were not apparent from the bearing of Richie Richardson and his squad, who seemed as eager and ready as any of the Windies' previous teams. Most eyes were on the visitors as the media looked for some sign that the Aussies might crack or that they lacked the will to beat the home team. Instead, they saw a vibrant Ian Healy, thrilled that Queensland had at last won the Shield competition; an 'in-control' skipper, realistic in his goals 'to play good cricket and win the series'; a diplomatic Warne, himself acting as a commentator/interviewer for TV's Channel 9; a quiet Steve

Waugh, still recovering from the flu and absorbed in his diary of the tour; a fit Julian spending more time in the water than the nets. It was evident to journalists that this team was happy and united, welded together by Taylor's dedicated leadership.

At last, on 31 March, the strength of their resolve was to be tried. The crowd was growing as the visitors came out to begin their warm-up routines and pre-match fielding practice. A big cheer went up from the Australian contingent of about 1000, who had come expecting an Aussie win, nothing less, at a spectacular one-handed stop by Warne. He waved and bowed. It was a warm-up for Warne the showman. The crowd, especially the Aussies, loved the response. The special 'character' of the team looked primed and punchy, fit not fat. 'Warnie' would give it everything from his waddling run after a ball to his belligerent hitting with the bat to his mighty shoulder heave when bowling. The bottle-blond had brought an excitement to the bowling scene in world cricket that had been missing until he appeared in earnest in 1992. Not only did he get through an over in rapid time, but also his leggies caused more confusion and fear—albeit of a slightly different kind—than any of the great quick bowlers at several times the pace. He coped happily with public attention, but did not crave it. Warne could live with or without it. He cared most for performance on the field.

Talyor lost the toss and the Australians were bowling. Fifteen minutes into the West Indian innings, Julian, bowling with great pace and surprising bounce, sent back Williams (1) and Richardson (0) while Reiffel removed Campbell (0). The Windies were reeling at three for 6. Lara nearly made it four down when he edged Reiffel just short of the slips. Then the brilliant left-hander, accompanied by the in-form Hooper, counterattacked when Warne was brought on early. Hooper stepped into Warne's first three deliveries for fours. It was a brave yet risky approach. The batsman was lucky not to be stumped on his second advance down the wicket. A Windies game plan to blast Warne out of the attack was now laid bare.

Warne went round the wicket, gambling on his judgment that any player who tried to hit him would lose his wicket when he bowled this way into a bit of pitch wear, even early on. However, Hooper didn't think so and continued to wallop him. The fightback sparked an avalanche as all bowlers suffered until lunch when the Windies reached three for 116.

Taylor was glad of the break, reminding the players that three wickets were a good haul and another one now would put them on top again. Sure enough, at 130, Julian induced an edge from Hooper (60) to Taylor and then McGrath got Adams to half-push, half-cut at one for Warne to hold a good catch at third slip and make it five for 152.

Four runs later, Lara cut at Julian and Steve Waugh took a tough, juggling catch in the gully. Everyone on the field with a view of it, including Lara and both umpires, thought Waugh had taken the ball and that it had not touched the ground. The crowd and the media contingent were stunned. Lara was travelling so well that a big hundred seemed likely. Now he was on his way for an ordinary, for him, 65. The shock would later translate into some mischief-making from some journalists and commentators. A video replay was interpreted by some as suggesting the ball *may* have touched the turf and Waugh, who had displayed the highest sportsmanship in such matters throughout his career, found himself being vilified.

Meanwhile, McGrath attacked the Windies' tail of fast bowlers with surprising venom, causing Ambrose, Walsh and the two Benjamins—Winston and Kenneth—to squirm, jump, sidestep and back away. After Ambrose decided he had had enough and lashed out to be caught, Taylor brought Warne on at the other end to bowl to Winston Benjamin and Walsh. Warne soon removed both. His guile and McGrath's fire ended the Windies' innings at 195. Julian's superb four for 36 start was finished off by McGrath's three for 46, and Warne, whose wickets saved his figures (two for 57 off 12.2 overs) and some face.

Australia's reply was solid and slow as the Windies bowled without their expected brutality and enthusiasm. Taylor hung on to be 42 not out at stumps, though Slater (18) and Boon (20) fell in taking the total to two for 91. The tourists' talk at dinner bordered on bombast, but Taylor reminded them that they were still 100 short.

In the morning, Bob Simpson was about to conduct some catching practice when he asked Alcott to look at a swollen leg. The physio examined it and sent him straight to a doctor. The swelling had been caused by a blood clot in his upper left calf. Simpson was rushed to intensive care at a local hospital.

Unaware of the seriousness of the coach's problem, the Australians resumed their innings. Taylor, wanting a team 350 to 400 and a big hundred from someone, battled on to 55 before he edged Kenny Benjamin to slip. That brought Steve Waugh to join his brother and they added 45 before Mark (40) was caught behind. Blewett came out blasting in an effort to notch his third hundred in his first three Tests, but ran into a pumped-up Ambrose and was caught behind for 14.

Steve Waugh battled on against the unrelenting pace to be 44 not out at lunch and Australia five for 197—2 runs ahead. Then after lunch, Waugh fended at a short one from Kenny Benjamin he could have left and was one his way for 65. Australia was six for 230 and shaky. Julian joined Healy and made 31 in an inspiring partnership of 60 against a second new ball. From 290, Healy took over and guided the team to 346, remaining unconquered on 74.

The lead of 151 had been reduced by 13 at stumps. On day three, McGrath struck and removed Williams (10) caught behind. Warne was on early to put pressure on Lara. The champion bat-padded his second ball to Mark Waugh. The Australians went up in unison. Umpire Lloyd Barker raised his arm to give Lara out. Warne charged towards Waugh, only to look back and see the umpire shaking his hands and his head to indicate not out. He had changed his mind. The spinner swallowed his disappointment and soon after had Campbell (6) caught by Steve Waugh trying to slash his way out of a runs trough. McGrath then found a faint edge from Lara (9), putting the Windies at three for 31. The back of the world's best bat so early was a delightful sight for the Aussies.

Taylor kept the pressure on, rotating his bowlers, with Warne and McGrath being used most. At 51, Hooper (16) on-drove Julian to Reiffel at cover and Richardson decided to counter-attack, but, just before lunch, drove at the accurate Reiffel who removed his off stump. The Windies were a tottering four for 91.

Adams and Murray fought until Warne out-thought the keeper. Warne looped a ball and tempted Murray into a big hit over mid-wicket, which was unpatrolled territory. The batsman connected, but not the way he would have wished, and the ball soared high in the air. Steve Waugh at short mid-wicket turned and dashed towards the boundary. He looked up into the sun and could just make out a golden dot high overhead. Waugh seemed to stretch out as the ball descended and clutched at it as came over his right shoulder. It stuck as he tumbled over. A roar went up from the Australian supporters, while the locals sat stunned. It was a sensational and perhaps match-winning catch. The Windies were five for 136, still 15 runs short of making Australia bat again.

McGrath returned to the bowling crease with more brimstone for the tail, trapping Benjamin, Ambrose and Walsh in an inspired spell to take his figures to five for 68 off twenty-two overs. Warne bowled Kenny Benjamin to finish the innings and give him three for 64 off 26.3 overs, with five maidens.

Slater and Taylor crashed the 39 to win in just 6.5 overs and then grabbed the stumps as souvenirs. All but one of them was wrestled away from them by an overenthusiastic crowd.

A grinning McGrath stepped forward to receive the Man of the Match award and then the celebrations began, with some players taking time off to visit the ailing but happy Simpson in hospital. His spirits were lifted by the win in three days and the cheerful entourage. They didn't heed his warning to 'take it easy and don't imbibe too much' as the merriment continued. It was not until the following evening that they surfaced with any normal signs of life at Shakey's Pizza Parlour. Warne had 'dined' there for the last six nights, eating the same meal each time: two serves of garlic bread, spaghetti bolognaise and a large Sprite. The restaurant was his idea of culinary heaven and the best place for him to celebrate Australia's early edge.

Taylor sobered everyone by recalling that the Windies had been behind in eight of their past twenty-eight Test series, but had not lost any of them. Richie Richardson reinforced the point by reminding the media of the Windies' comeback in Australia in 1992–93.

Nex day, Warne and Lara played a cheerful game of golf. Despite their on-field rivalry, Warne had succeeded in creating a friendship between them. It was his approach with all his international opponents whom he liked and respected, and who would meet him halfway. To Warne, such links were a big part of the reward for the sacrifices to compete at this level.

Bad Vibes and Bribes

Unwanted rewards were on Warne's mind, however, as he, Mark Waugh and Tim May were forced to face up to the consequences of Salim Malik's bribery overtures. Graeme Johnson, the ACB solicitor, flew to the West Indies to get them to sign sworn statements about the Salim approaches, which were forwarded to the International Cricket Council. On 10 April, the ACB announced that the trio would not be flying to Pakistan for an inquiry into the scam due to fears for their safety. The ICC washed its hands of the affair by saying it could not charge Salim under its Code of Conduct because the allegations came to light after the series was completed.

Salim's response was to call the Australians' accusations 'viciously false and unfounded allegations'. He sent a legal statement to the Pakistan Cricket Board (PCB), which was leaked to the Pakistan media. It included irrelevant attacks on the 'overseas press' and the 'scurrilous manner' in which Pakistan's leading cricketers were 'lampooned and libelled time and again'. The legal statement went on:

'For them, a Lillee or a Marsh who confessed to betting against their own team [in England in 1981] and whose team then lost the match [a game that Australia looked certain to win] can be excused; as can Atherton, who found some dirt in his pockets. But not a Miandad who dared raise his bat to defend himself.'

The PCB reacted by suspending Salim for seven days, sacking him from the captaincy and not selecting him for a tour of Sri Lanka. However, under pressure from Pakistan's President, who was the patron of the PCB, and other influential quarters, officials decided not to make any further comment about the scandal as it would damage the national image.

There was no inquiry into big betting in cricket despite many serious allegations about its extent. Three, in particular, obviously required further investigation, but were ignored. First, Pakistan's opener Aamir Sohail was reported in the Pakistani media on 16 February as saying illegal betting involving his team was rife. Two days later, he denied saying any such thing. Second, on the same day, former captain Imran Khan said he was aware of heavy betting in cricket. He urged a swift inquiry and no cover-ups. Third, an article in the mass-circulation Indian magazine *Sportworld*, in March, reported how an Indian journalist interviewing Salim in a room at the Hotel Lanka Oberoi in Colombo overheard his Pakistani team-mate Akram Raza and another man discussing some heavy betting. Akram and his companion were speaking in their local dialect and did not realise that the Indian journalist understood what they were saying. As the journalist left the room, he heard Salim 'severely chastise' Akram and his companion for talking so openly in front of him.

Salim kept up his pressure to be reinstated in September 1995 by filing a petition against the PCB challenging his exclusion from the Pakistan team. The Lahore High Court rejected Salim's plea. He did not go to Sri Lanka.

The end result was a PCB whitewash and in effect, a clearance for Salim to continue to play international cricket. It decided it was better to sweep the bribery business under the carpet and avoid more public acrimony from Salim by selecting him for the 1995–96 tour of Australia. But this was several months down the track from the Australian tour of the West Indies early in 1995.

The Master-Blaster Squeaks

Viv Richards tried, in the press, to stir up the Australians when they landed in Antigua by saying Lara was 'robbed' of a century because of Waugh's poor sportsmanship. This was hypocrisy of the highest order considering Richards's failure to call back Dean Jones after he was 'bowled' on a no-ball and then 'run out' in 1991. But Richards was in his home island of Antigua for the Second Test and here he was *the man.* He planned, he said, to confront Waugh during the Test and tell him what he thought of him. This was bluff. Richards knew better than anyone that he would make a fool of himself in any verbal contest. But his frothing was designed to whip up ill-feeling towards the Australians and unsettle them. It was also meant to return the 'master-blaster' to centre stage for a moment. Richards was finding it much harder than most to be out of the limelight since his retirement.

His intervention had an impact only on the media and was soon forgotten on the first day of the Test on 8 April at the Recreation Ground, St John's. Taylor lost the toss and was asked to bat by an uncertain Richardson. Australia began well against some uninspired bowling, except from Walsh, who looked dangerous, but lost Taylor (37), hooking, just before lunch with the score at 82. After lunch, Slater (41) and Mark Waugh (4) were back in the pavilion before the others could digest their meals. There was a steady decline for the rest of the day until they were all out for 216. Many had starts, but did nothing with them as Walsh scythed his way through the team, taking six for 54.

The Windies survived with all wickets intact at stumps. The next morning the Australians speedsters could make no impact.

Taylor called Warne to the crease and he obliged his skipper's request to 'Get us a breakthrough, will you?'

Williams drove at one he should have blocked and Boon took the catch at mid-wicket. Richardson, who had opened, was joined by Lara. The new man got into stride with alacrity and raced to 50 as Richardson held up the other end, intent on partnering Lara en route to a massive score, similar to his 375 at this ground against England a year earlier. However, the skipper was dismissed by Julian for 37. In the afternoon session, Lara continued on, happily hitting across the line.

Warne came on for a second bout with him, but instead dismissed Adams (22) lbw with a top-spinner. The score was three for 168, with Hooper now in. Steve Waugh came on to bowl and Lara (88) drove at one which Boon, stationed just to the left of the pitch at the bowler's end, leapt to catch one-handed. Waugh had once more 'robbed' the crowd and Lara of something huge, and in so doing had turned the Test in Australia's favour. Viv Richards was sought for a comment by journalists, but could not be found. He was either hiding or elsewhere.

Soon afterwards, Waugh also had Hooper caught by Julian at mid-wicket for 11 and the Windies were five for 187. Then at 240, three fell for nought as Warne had Arthurton (26) caught in slips by Taylor, and Reiffel dismissed Murray (26) and Ambrose.

The final tally of 260 meant a lead of just 44 for the Windies and, with the wicket showing signs of deteriorating, Australia's position was good. Warne bowled more than anyone and returned three for 83 off 26.3 overs. It was none for 16 at stumps, thanks to the courage of Taylor and Slater, who endured bodyline in every respect except for the field placement. Half the balls delivered were short-pitched and several hit their mark.

The two men sat stunned in the dressing room wearing ice-packs, and feeling unhappy about the tactics. Slater perhaps had made a mistake in saying earlier that the Windies pacemen held no terrors for them. Ambrose responded tersely that there would be plenty of ambulances waiting for Slater the next day.

The openers' bruises were given time to heal as the rain tumbled down on day three and it was half an hour before lunch when they were called to the wicket. Walsh sent them both back before the 44-run deficit had been removed. But then Boon and Mark Waugh set about restoring Australia's position in the middle and last sessions, taking the score to two for 134—a lead of 90—at stumps, with a welcome rest day following.

On day four of the Test, with the score at 149, Boon shouldered arms to Winston Benjamin and was trapped lbw for 67. Steve Waugh came in and received the now expected 'throat ticklers' from the speed men. It was wasted effort, and seemed to galvanise the batsman, who, after losing brother Mark Waugh for 61 and three other partners during the rest of the day, saw the Australians beyond danger to seven for 273 at stumps, a lead of 229.

Day five disappointed with more rain, and play could not resume until the middle session. Taylor declared at seven for 300 with Waugh unbeaten on 65 and the lead 256. The Windies had thirty-seven overs in which to get them, at an impossible 7 runs an over. The Windies managed two for 80 off thirty overs. Reiffel bowled Richardson for 2, keeping the pressure on the Windies leader, who was coming in for local media criticism.

All the Australians except Blewett, who failed twice with the bat, contributed in a strong team effort, with Steve Waugh the main Aussie influence with bat and ball, and in the field.

A game against the Windies Cricket Board XI at Basseterre, St Kitts, offered useful bowling time in the middle for Tim May and McDermott's newly arrived replacement, Carl Rackemann, while Slater (60), Taylor (62) and Blewett (93) got some solid batting practice. It was then on to Trinidad for the Third Test and the business end of the whole tour.

If Australia could win, it would take the series. If the Windies won, their tails would be up for a fourth and final decider in Jamaica.

Beaten by the Toss

As soon as the Australians inspected the wicket before play in the Third Test, beginning on 21 April, they realised it was so bad that the toss could well decide the game. It was grassy and excess moisture meant that it was far below Test standard. Taylor again called wrongly and rued it in less than half an hour as Australian wickets tumbled. The noise of kettle drums and conches was deafening as the West Indian crowd urged on the speedsters to do physical damage to the visitors on the problematic pitch. The ball was flying at various heights.

At three for 14, Ambrose had removed Taylor and Mark Waugh, both for 2, while a Walsh lifter had sent back Slater for a duck. Steve Waugh was booed on his way to the wicket to join Boon. Both defended with grit in between breaks caused by rain. Ambrose was boosted by the ball darting off the seam. His previous lethargy had gone. He was all fire, glares and stares, and after hurling down one steepling bouncer at Waugh, he clashed with the Australian batsman verbally and almost physically in the middle of the pitch. He kept trying to bounce Waugh again, but failed to dislodge him.

Australia missed an hour's batting due to rain before lunch, when the score was three for 31. Boon (18) didn't last long after the break, as Ambrose continued his more controlled rampage. Only Waugh resisted en route to 50. Rain stopped play again at seven for 112 and he was booed all the way from the wicket to the pavilion. The mob's response was ugly and upset Waugh. It had been the hardest fifty of his career. He had welts and bruises on his right arm and body that would remind him of his courage. The next day, nothing could hold up the Windies' assault as Australia capitulated for 128. Ambrose returned five for 45 and Walsh three for 50.

Now it was the Australian pacemen's turn. McGrath, lifted by the pitch and what he had seen from Ambrose, bowled equally aggressively and just as fast. After Reiffel had bored in with the wicket of Williams (0), McGrath sent back Richardson (2) caught behind and then had Lara (24) caught by Taylor. Adams went on to 42, but after Steve Waugh dismissed Hooper for 21, the Windies' tail fell apart and they were all out for 136.

McGrath finished with the magnificent figures of six for 47, supported once more by the control of Reiffel, who took two for 26 off sixteen overs. Warne backed them both by bottling up one end in taking one for 16 off twelve overs.

Australia was none for 20 at stumps—12 runs ahead—and full of hope, with a real feeling the game could be won. It needed 200 to make it tough for the Windies, and 250 to make it nigh impossible.

The Australians were travelling with promise at one point on three for 85 with the Waughs together. A few minutes later, there was chaos as Australia slid to eight for 87. Five wickets fell for just 2 runs as players came and went in a hurried procession which left the dressing room in more turmoil than any member of the team could recall. And with the collapse went the Australians' chances of wrapping up the series.

Ambrose (four for 20), Walsh (three for 35) and Kenny Benjamin (three for 32) swung it the home side's way as Australia struggled to just 105 off just 36.1 overs. Only Taylor (30) and Steve Waugh (21) looked as if they could hold out.

Warne was given some rough treatment, sending down 3.5 overs without a maiden or a wicket, and going for 26 as the Windies chased down the small target of 98. They decided not to get bogged down and hit the runs at nearly 5 an over, thus squaring the series one-all.

The mood in the Australian dressing room was depressed. It wasn't helped when Steve Waugh was again booed when he was mentioned as a candidate for Man of the Match. It hurt him. His mood was smoothed just a fraction by learning that his 63 not out was judged by Deloitte, the officially recognised sports rating agency, as equivalent to a double century in degree of difficulty, placing him as the number-two bat in the world behind Jimmy Adams.

Warne was out of sorts, too, with a badly bruised thumb. It would take some hard work by him and Alcott to get him right for the final showdown in Kingston, Jamaica. The winner would take the series.

The momentum was with the home team.

High Noon in Jamaica

The team was up at 5 a.m. on 27 April for a fatiguing flight from Trinidad, via Barbados, Antigua and St Martin's to Kingston in Jamaica. They arrived early afternoon to inspect Sabina Park, which looked like a chocolate lake. It was hard and grass-less.

Warne was the only injury worry. Taylor took him aside at the ground while the others were practising.

'How's the thumb?' the skipper asked, examining Warne's hand.

'Bloody sore,' he said. 'I don't know how it will come up, Tubs.'

'We want you there, Warnie. Got to have you, mate.'

'I can't grip the ball properly.'

'What's Errol say?'

'Says I've a got a good chance. He's worked on it a bit.'

'We really need you. I don't want them to get a lift by being told you're out. You're absolutely essential to winning this.'

'I'll do my best, Tubs,' Warne assured him. 'I reckon I'll make it.'

Taylor worked on Warne's confidence the next day and he made an effort at practice, rolling his arm over and loosening up. The thumb was painful and, coupled with wear and tear to his spinning finger, was a big threat to his playing. But he was determined to compete. When selection time came around, Warne declared himself fit and was chosen ahead of the disappointed May.

Taylor, as usual, lost the toss and the Windies batted. Reiffel excited the Australians by removing Williams with a superb second ball which hit his glove, cannoned into his chest and bounced to a diving Blewett at short point for a catch. But then Lara joined Richardson and led the charge, attacking everything with such fury that he threatened to take the game away from

Australia. Taylor tried every trick he knew, rotating Reiffel, McGrath, Julian and Warne, while slipping the Waugh brothers on for relief and something different. Lara was taking no prisoners as he drove, cut and pulled his way past 50, with his captain as ever playing second fiddle, but not far behind.

They crashed the score to 103. Then, in the last over before lunch, Warne kept his nerve and length despite Lara's ruthlessness and gave him a leg break that turned more than the batsman anticipated. He edged it to Healy, who took a brilliant diving catch. Lara was out for 65 before he could deliver a knock-out blow. Instead, Warne had managed a sharp counter-punch that kept the Australians in the contest.

Adams—a Jamaican—joined Richardson after lunch and they began to swing the game the Windies' way once more until, at 131, Adams misjudged one from Julian and went for 20. Hooper and his skipper nudged the score up to three for 188. Then Hooper (23) again played one of his 'soft' shots to be caught by Mark Waugh.

Richardson reached his century, but then fell lbw to Reiffel and the game turned once more. Steve Waugh took the new ball after Warne had dismissed replacement keeper Courtney Brown, caught by Boon for 1, and enjoyed shaking up the tail with the odd bouncer before the other pacemen wrapped up the innings for 265. Reiffel had been a model of accuracy in taking three for 48, while Julian had worked up a troubling pace for his two for 31. Warne had been steady in collecting two for 72 off twenty-five overs, but those modest figures did not reflect his dedication and discipline against a strong Test line-up, especially with his aching thumb making it tough to grip the ball. Most importantly, he had snared Lara at a critical moment. That in itself was worth three or four wickets.

Australia's start on day two was not encouraging, as first Taylor (8) fell to a freakish catch by Adams at short leg, then Boon (17) was given out caught behind when the ball brushed his helmet, not his bat. At 73, the over-adventurous Slater was removed by Lara, who took a flying catch at deep backward square leg. It was fifteen minutes to lunch when the Waugh brothers came together in the most critical moment of the series.

They saw the Australian innings through to the break. Both remarked that the pitch was like a WACA wicket to bat on—hard and bouncy—just what these two shot-makers loved. This may have been their way of saying they could be in for a big partnership. The WACA was where they had put together 464 in a Shield game for New South Wales against Western Australia a few seasons earlier.

Ambrose, Walsh and the Benjamins came out firing after the break and threw everything at the twins. About four balls an over shot over shoulder height. The other few balls were often misdirected as all bowlers lost their way. The Windies' approach from the beginning was to try to bounce the Waughs. It was the major strategic error of the series, as the brothers ducked and weaved, dodging or absorbing the bouncers while taking short, sharp singles to keep the scoreboard moving.

The Windies became frustrated with the Australians' tactics. As they both crept into the 20s and 30s, Kenny Benjamin twice threw four overthrows, which lifted the tally by 10 in a couple of balls. The fielders' heads drooped and the Waughs could feel themselves getting on top as the score steadily mounted. Australia went to tea at three for 192. It was 72 in arrears and back in the match.

Back in Australia, Sir Donald Bradman was watching the partnership on TV in the middle of the night and loving it.

'You could see the Windies bowlers falling apart after tea,' the Don told me next day. 'Too much short-pitching had taken its toll. The Waughs really got on top then.'

Bradman and countless other Australian supporters applauded when Mark Waugh reached a century—his eighth in Tests—with the score at three for 248. It triggered a pitch invasion.

'It was the finest innings I'd seen Mark play,' Bradman remarked. Steve Waugh concurred.

'He showed a steely resolve not to get out,' Steve noted in his diary of the tour. '[He] weathered the short stuff and punished anything remotely off line. It was a superb all-round display of batsmanship.'

Hooper came on and soon managed some sharp turn. The score reached 265, with Mark on 107 and Steve on 83. Steve crept into the 90s and then also reached his eighth Test century. Another pitch invasion held up play, but not the scoring. Shortly afterwards, at 304 and with the lead at just 39, Mark (126) popped up a gloved catch to Adams at short leg. The partnership of 231 had come in 233 minutes. The Australians now really had the upper hand. Blewett hung in with Steve Waugh until stumps at four for 321—a lead of 56, with six wickets in hand and three days to play.

At the beginning of day three, the Windies came out firing with the new ball, knowing that a breakthrough was imperative to lurch them back into the match. Failure to do so, however, would see the game slip away. Blewett survived the onslaught and came back counter-punching until he was out for 69, with the score five for 417 and the lead 152. Waugh was fatigued, but made it through to lunch on 141 not out. He remained disciplined throughout the middle session and went to tea on 177. Wickets fell until Reiffel (23) helped him put on 73 runs before being bowled. Warne came to the wicket and realised that the grille on his helmet had been twisted—perhaps by a prowler who had been disturbed in his hotel room two nights earlier, he thought. Warne couldn't see properly through the grille and blamed his dismissal—caught by Lara off Kenny Benjamin for a duck—on this possible sabotage.

It left Australia on nine for 522, and Waugh on 195 with Glenn McGrath as his partner. McGrath seemed determined to see Waugh through to a double century, which the weary batsman duly brought up with a four all-run, the first time he had reached 200 in Test cricket. Four balls later, he received a bouncer from Kenny Benjamin which he could not keep down and was caught off his glove by Lara after 555 minutes or nearly five sessions at the wicket, during which he had faced 425 balls.

Australia had reached 531—a lead of 266. With more than two days to go, it could not now lose the game, but had every chance to win it. Before long, that chance began to look like a certainty.

Reiffel, the quiet achiever who had risen to the occasion so often before, bowled Williams (20) at 37, just when the Windies looked as if they would sneak through to stumps without loss. Lara came in looking as if the weight of the Windies, if not the cricketing world, was on his trim shoulders. Reiffel bowled one that kept low. It trapped the pocket dynamo right in front for a duck. The Australians were ecstatic.

Reiffel was not done yet. He induced a caught-and-bowled from Richardson (14) with a slower ball. The Windies were three for 63 at stumps and reeling. The only thing that could stop Australia now was the weather.

Right on cue, it poured next day, but, as luck would have it, that was the rest day, 2 May. Day four saw night watchman Winston Benjamin stay until lunch and in the first session the Windies only lost Adams for 18. Soon after the break, Benjamin (51) was cornered by an inswinger from the irrepressible Reiffel. Hooper (13) ran himself out, sending the Windies to six for 140, still 116 short of making the visitors bat again.

Arthurton came in blazing against Warne—who, despite his throbbing thumb, was hungry for wickets to finish the match—and connected with a huge six into the newly constructed stand. Warne, unfazed and even encouraged by this desire to take him on, tossed one into the rough. The left-handed Arthurton went back on his stumps, half lifting his bat in a 'leave'. The ball struck him dead in front, giving the umpire an easy lbw decision.

Ambrose came in and showed he didn't really want to stay. It wasn't long before he was stumped by Healy off Warne for five. Walsh joined Browne, who was resisting well with a mix of defence and good shots, and collected a rapid 14 before holing out to Blewett off Warne. The spinner now had three wickets as he wrapped up the innings. He tied the bow of victory with a tremendous leg break to Kenny Benjamin, which he edged to Taylor at slip. The Australian skipper would not let the ball go until it was in the hands of a recovering Bob Simpson, who had presided over his nation's gradual rise to the very top of world cricket over a tough decade.

Browne remained a stoic 31 not out as the Windies in the end only mustered 213, giving Australia a win by a whopping innings and 53 runs.

Warne ended with four for 70 off 23.4 overs, with eight maidens, giving him a creditable fifteen wickets in the four matches at 27.07, which was not his 'usual' performance of five or six wickets a Test. Yet he was invaluable in the mix of the series victory, as was Reiffel who took four for 74, giving him fifteen wickets at 17.53 overall. McGrath took one for 28, leaving him with seventeen wickets at 21.71 all told.

Undoubtedly, it was Steve Waugh's series. He even took five wickets at 12.40, more than useful for a part-timer who loved to deliver a bouncer. His batting was the difference between the two teams. He hit 429 runs at 107.25, eclipsing Lara who hit 308 at 44.00.

Australia had taken the series two–one and had become the first team to beat the West Indies in eighteen attempts by all the world's leading cricket nations. With Border, Dean Jones, Geoff Lawson and David Hookes joining in the celebrations at this historic sporting achievement, there was extra verve and emotion in a stirring rendition of the victory chant, 'Under the Southern Cross I Stand', led as always by David Boon.

A Private Affair

Shane and Simone Callahan spent the few months after the successful West Indies tour preparing for the biggest day of their lives—their wedding—planned for 1 September 1995, twelve days short of Warne's twenty-sixth birthday.

He had rested from cricket during the Australian winter months of June, July and August 1995, while keeping fit with gym activity and continuing physio work on his spinning finger and right shoulder. He was able to watch some footy, but it was not the restful, private period he craved. When word seeped out about the wedding, which both parties wanted to be a private affair, efforts were made to make it a media event. Magazines and newspaper offered money for exclusive rights to feature it and take photo portraits. It was going to be one of the most glittering unions of the year with many 'name' sports stars and others in attendance.

He turned down an offer, believed to be at least $200 000, from an English film and TV group to film the wedding. The producers had seen the success of 'Sylvania Waters', a BBC documentary series portraying the daily lives of a supposed 'typical' Australian family. They wanted to film the wedding in the same style, with the added bonus of highlighting such characters as Merv Hughes and Allan Border. Warne and his bride-to-be would have none of it.

'Both were appalled by such an invasion,' a close friend of both commented. 'Remember Shane was now no ordinary Oz, no matter what his upbringing and experience before he became a Test cricketer. Sport had brought out his showmanship, which combined with his love of the simple pleasures—sport, drinks with mates, gambling, partying, and so on—made him an attractive figure. He was only superficially now like the members of the family in "Sylvania Waters". Shane was a modern superstar on and off the field, moving with fellow superstars in a social world of endless invitations to be seen at this and that function. He had no need for nosy film crews, or photographers or journalists on the job at his most important day. Nor did he need the dough. His agent could tomorrow pick him up an extra advertising or promotion job for the sort of money being offered [by the TV company] if that's what he needed.'

Warne prepared a wedding speech in the days before the event. He was most grateful for his father Keith's advice:

'Whatever you do, don't forget to say how nice Simone looks. I didn't do it at my wedding. Your mother has never forgiven me.'

Later, his mother said much the same thing.

On the day, Warne was more nervous than anyone had ever seen him, even when bowling at a critical point in a Test when a big performance was needed to win. Fellow players noticed his hands shaking when they were greeted at the reception at Melbourne's Como House, a classic, white colonial-style building.

'Hey, Warnie,' more than one asked, thrusting a glass of beer at him, 'how about a drink?' They just wanted to see him spill it.

Among the guests were Allan Border, Dean Jones, Craig McDermott, Ian Healy, Merv Hughes, Rod Marsh, Simon O'Donnell, the Waugh brothers, Tony Dodemaide and Brendon Julian. They gathered in the garden by the fountain, under a big old fig tree, while the chaplain of the Victorian Shield team, Rev. Barrie Sutton, performed the ceremony. Once Shane and Simone were formally husband and wife, the song 'Finally' was played as the guests stepped forward to congratulate the smiling couple.

They then moved into a huge white marquee to continue the celebration. Warne's speech, while amusing, was sincere and humble. He thanked his parents and best man brother Jason for their great support early in his career, and mentioned unsung heroes, mates such as Rick Gough, who had encouraged him to go to England and play League cricket there in 1989. It was an impressive effort for a man who had at times given the false impression of being 'big-headed'. His words made it clear he was grateful for the opportunities life had presented and would do again in the future with his new bride.

He didn't forget his parents' advice either. He commented on how terrific Simone looked. He drew a laugh when he added: 'At my father's wedding, he forgot to say it and Mum has never forgiven him for it.'

The only sour note came later when the 18 September 1995 edition of *Woman's Day* carried a two-page picture spread entitled 'Shane's Wedding Panic', written by Patrice Fidgeon. The seven photographs had been stolen—allegedly—by a Rabbit Photo employee and sold to the magazine. The Warnes were incensed.

They had hired security guards to keep unwanted photographers away, as well as refusing a tidy sum for media coverage. The Warnes and a wedding guest, Mrs Jennifer Cottrell, who took the photographs, sued. But Rabbit Photo, not *Woman's Day*, became the bunny. Perhaps Warne didn't wish to antagonise the magazine's owner, who just happened to be his own most important employer, Kerry Packer.

Mrs Cottrell had placed the negatives for processing at Rabbit's Cranbourne Park, Victoria, outlet. She gave an employee at Rabbit three rolls of film. Later, Mrs Cottrell found she was seven prints short. Claims for rights worth up to $150 000—'unlawfully exploited and appropriated'—were made against the photo outlet. This was the sort of money the Warnes reckoned they could have picked up by selling the photos themselves. The legal battle dragged on until an out-of-court settlement, with both parties signing a confidentiality agreement not to disclose the result.

The Shane Show

For all his love of privacy in other respects, late in 1995 Warne took the step of becoming a fully fledged TV personality. Australia's highest profile cricketer since Don Bradman widened his public reach even further by working for cable TV's Optus and commercial TV's Channel Nine. Optus's use of Warne was a smart marketing ploy, as it screened more than 600 hours of cricket during the summer, including live coverage of Sheffield Shield games.

'It's an exciting time for Shield cricket,' Warne remarked at the media conference announcing the deal in August 1995. 'I remember watching it on TV [on the ABC] as a kid when I came home from school. It was something I looked forward to and I'm sure the new coverage will tap into the huge interest there is out there in Shield cricket.'

Warne now had to juggle his responsibilities to the Victorian Shield team with his new commitment to Optus, where his fellow commentators were Greg Chappell, Greg Ritchie and Simon O'Donnell.

Warne already had a contract with Nine and this saw him continue his Test-eve reports, which he had begun in the West Indies, for Nine News. He also acted as a co-host on 'The Cricket Show', with O'Donnell and Michael Slater, another contemporary player with the personality and communication skills to succeed on TV.

A thirty-minute magazine-style show screened at lunchtimes during Nine's Test coverage, its breezy format was a ratings winner, keeping cricket fans entertained during the lunch break. The items covered anything of interest to do with cricket, from selecting the right gear to the memories of former players. The Nine Network wanted it to win the same ratings support as 'The Footy Show', but without the slapstick. There were, however, light-hearted items and graphics to balance the more informative sequences.

Warne's new manager, Austin Robertson, gave more than a hint of Warne's future at the media conference. 'I think, down the track,' he said, 'TV is where Shane will finish up.'

These new links with that medium would give him the experience to take on TV full-time after his retirement. In some ways, Warne's situation was similar to that of Richie Benaud, who was groomed by the BBC in the 1960s and went on to be the most accomplished and long-lasting cricketer–commentator in television.

Warne's accumulating knowledge, in addition to writing and broadcasting experience would mean that by the time he retired, perhaps in his mid-thirties, he would already be a solid media professional.

But that was looking far ahead. The most important thing on his mind as the 1995–96 season approached was the visit of Pakistan for a three-Test series, followed by Sri Lanka for yet another round of Tests and a set of three-sided one-day internationals with Australia and the West Indies.

11

Sugar and Spice

Spin Fever

Salim Malik surprised the cricket world by being selected to tour Australia with the Pakistani team for the three-Test series in November and December 1995. He had been dumped as captain of Pakistan not, it was claimed, because of the bribery allegations, but the ill-discipline of his squad on tour in South Africa and Zimbabwe. However, he had been dropped for Pakistan's recent visit to Sri Lanka. Now he had been reinstated.

This was face-saving by the Pakistani authorities. It would be a public relations disaster to have Salim lead the side down under, especially as his relationship with several Australians was beyond repair. Now he had been selected as just another player. He was sure to keep a low profile—so low, in fact, that he was not with the team when it arrived in Perth in October to begin its tour. Salim arrived alone later and refused any media comment.

The heat of the bribery issue seemed to have been diffused in the month before the First Test. The controversy had consumed media attention so much that by the time of the opening day at the Brisbane ground, it had been played out. Furthermore, the no-nonsense yet diplomatic approach of the two captains, Taylor and Wasim Akram, had done much to avoid conflict and concentrate on cricket. All eyes turned to the on-field contest, with much interest centred on the confrontation between Warne and Salim out in the middle. The Pakistanis were confident they could 'tame' Warne and said so. They argued that they were used to leg-spin on the sub-continent and would not be mesmerised by him as the English and the South Africans had been. They also had Mushtaq Ahmed to practise against in the nets. He had a good wrong 'un, a useful flipper and a vicious top-spinner. They had seen it all. Warne presented no fears or major problems.

Australia made only one change from its team in the great victory at Sabina Park back in May, now half a year ago, bringing in McDermott for Julian, who was made twelfth man. Pakistan made five changes from its last Test side, which lost by 144 runs to Sri Lanka at Sialkot in September. It introduced eighteen-year-old right-hand opening bat Saleem Elahi, whose 102 not out against Sri Lanka in a one-day international had earned him the reward of his first Test. The tourists surprised by leaving out Mushtaq Ahmed in favour of the right-hand off-spin of Saqlain Mushtaq, another eighteen-year-old and the youngest member of the squad.

Taylor was pleased to reverse his horror stretch with the coin toss in the West Indies and bat first. He and Slater put on a stand of 107—their eighth century opening in twenty-eight Tests—before Taylor (69) was dismissed pulling a long hop from Saqlain to Salim Malik at mid-wicket, who split the webbing in his hand. It required six stitches and put him off the field and perhaps out of the game. The big face-off between Warne and Malik might have to wait, possibly until the next Test.

Slater (42) followed soon after courtesy of Akram. Boon and Mark Waugh then took over, the latter making 59 off ninety-six balls, including 8 fours and 2 sixes, before being caught off Saqlain to give the delighted young bowler two great scalps to boast about. Boon was more than an hour slower in reaching his fifty, but his 54 helped the team reach four for 262 at stumps. Steve Waugh was looking solid on 24 and Blewett was also there on 0 not out. Next day, they took the score from 135 to five for 385, before Waqar Younis deceived Blewett (57) with reverse swing as he played across the line. Australia's lower order rolled over in the face of a combination of pace and left-arm finger-spin from vice-captain and opening bat Aamir Sohail, who ended with the best figures of two for 43. It was left to Waugh (112 not out in 366 minutes) to battle the final tally up to 463—an effort, against arguably the world's best speed attack, which would keep him on top of the Deloitte ratings.

The Pakistanis had an hour or so to bat before stumps and lost young Saleem Elahi (11) at 20, bowled by McDermott. Taylor brought Warne on for a few overs to test Rameez Raja, a noted one-day hard-hitter, and the spinner had him groping and fumbling until he edged one to Taylor and the tourists were two for 37. Akram sent in the young Saqlain Mushtaq to see the day out, but McGrath trapped him lbw for a duck and Pakistan was three for 40 at stumps.

First thing next morning, Taylor had Warne on at one end and speed from McDermott and McGrath at the other. The Pakistanis decided on reckless adventure in jumping into Warne and he was through the middle order before they had realised their folly. The spinner was in an aggressive enough mood to test his sore shoulder and finger with huge spinning leggies. They worked.

He had Inzamam-ul-Haq groping and missing. The big fellow liked to get on top early, but Warne bamboozled him with big breaks that were impossible to play and smaller ones of which he was unsure. Inzamam fumbled to 5 in thirty-three balls and thirty-seven minutes, before lashing out and being well caught by Steve Waugh at point.

Aamir Sohail was the only batsman to use his feet to Warne. The bowler enticed him out of his crease twice then ripped in a big turner that left him stranded. Healy, waiting and ready, whipped off the bails. The dashing opener, Pakistan's main hope of combating Warne this day, was on his way for a bright 32. Basit Ali was soon under Warne's spell for an agonising fifty-three minutes and thirty-two balls in which he made a solitary run, in such a state of paralysis that he was using his pads rather than the bat. Warne was more than confident—he was in command. He brought his top-spinner into play, induced an edge and Taylor did the rest.

Pakistan was six for 70. Moin Khan (4) came in to do some more groping, decided it was against his nature and drove to McDermott. Warne had five of the seven wickets to fall and he was all over Pakistan, more like a fever than a rash, forcing the tourists to bat out of character. Wasim Akram, like Inzamam, loved to stroke and whack bowlers into submission. This morning he fiddled, swung at and missed a couple, then used his pads. After seventeen balls of batting he would as soon gloss over, he bat-padded Warne to Boon at short leg.

The score was a rare eight for 80. Waqar Younis gave his first name resonance by going for his shots and collecting 19 from twenty-seven balls before Mohammad Akram (1) submitted to Warne's vigour, leaving Pakistan on nine for 97. Salim did not appear at the gate. The crowd and a warmed-up Warne were disappointed. Like the other Australians, he understood that the Pakistani's injury must have been severe for him not to come out. Salim had been accused of much, but no one doubted his commitment and courage.

The Pakistani innings had ended with a wimper at 97. Warne had taken six for 10 from fifty-six balls in one of the finest exhibitions of spin and control ever seen. His overall figures were seven for 23 from just 16.1 overs.

With a lead of 366, Taylor this time didn't hesitate about asking the opposition to bat again. Aamir Sohail decided on attack and began well. Saleem Elahi lasted thirty-five balls for just 2 in a Test start he would rather forget when he edged one to Healy off McGrath. Rameez Raja, more subdued than normal, suffered Elahi's fate for 16 and Pakistan was two for 88. Sohail continued with abandon, flaying the bowlers for 15 fours in facing 159 balls. Warne tried everything against him, even the flipper, which the batsman picked and the bowler put back in his locker for another day or another batsman. Sohail deserved at least one more than his 99, when McGrath yorked him.

Warne enjoyed taking on the big, heavy-hitting Inzamam-ul-Haq, who was in good form. The bowler dished up leg breaks, but slipped him a wrong 'un, which the batsman put his 188 cm of power into and pulled through mid-wicket for four. Warne tried another wrong 'un in the last over of the day and was unlucky not to obtain Inzamam's wicket lbw, when he refused to play a shot. The ball was so good it seemed to surprise the umpire as much as the batsman. Inzamam was 56 not out at stumps with Pakistan on three for 197.

They had Sunday 12 November to mull over their plight, still 169 runs in arrears.

On day four, Warne again relied on his 'stock' leg break, but with variations in the way he imparted side-spin (often announced with more *grunt*), or pushed the ball out the front of his hand. The latter often meant less spin and the possibility of finding the edge or inducing a mishit.

Taylor, however, again pulled a trick out of the box by bringing on Mark Waugh when the batsmen expected Warne. The part-time off-spinner had Inzamam caught for 62, leaving Pakistan at four for 217, still 149 short of making the home side bat again.

Taylor then reverted to Warne at one end and McGrath and Reiffel at the other. Basit Ali decided to offer his pad to most deliveries. Warne's delight was obvious as he crowded in on the batsman. He glided through his overs, slipping in one maiden in only sixty-eight seconds. He noticed Basit Ali's gloves were low as he pushed forward, feigning a shot. That caused Warne to try more top-spinners to induce a catch to Mark Waugh at silly point or Boon at short leg. There was also more chance of an lbw with the 'toppie' working well. Basit was relieved to be up the other end, where he felt more comfortable. This was when McGrath struck, capturing him lbw for 26.

Reiffel snaffled Moin Khan (9) caught behind and brought Salim to the wicket, his hand strapped and his head down. He looked uncertain as Warne circled him. There would be no sympathy here for an injured foe. The bowler was extra-keen to 'get' Salim. It would be his way of delivering the 'justice' that did not seem to be coming from the courts. The Australians gave him the 'cold shoulder' and treatment. It prompted Salim to tell one umpire: 'Nice to have someone to talk to.'

Salim, hesitant and dour, poked at three balls before lifting Warne towards mid-off. McDermott ran in, dived and took a first-rate catch. Warne was jubilant, but there were no macho stares or sneers as the batsman headed off after a four-ball duck, although Warne remarked later at a press conference that he thought justice had been done. The Pakistanis were seven for 233.

The spinner then went into overdrive, nailing the tail in another world-class display. Wasim Akram chanced his arm and slammed him down the ground, not quite getting to the pitch of the ball. A few deliveries later, he mishit another drive and was caught by Slater for 6. With Waqar Younis and Saqlain at the wicket, Warne changed his strategy. He pinned them both down with faster leg breaks. This had both in confusion, the bowler's favourite condition for batsmen. Their indecision led to the flipper, which he bowled full and fast, searching for a clean-bowled or an lbw. He soon had Waqar leg before with one which was perfectly pitched. He repeated the tactic by pinning down Mohammad Akram and elicited the same score line—lbw bowled Warne 0.

Warne finished with four for 54 off 27.5 overs, including ten maidens. Only seven boundaries were struck off him, five of them from short-pitched deliveries. In the two Pakistani innings, the bulk of the runs scored from him came from players going on to the back foot or sweeping. Otherwise, there was a notable lack of shot production, initiative or attack down the wicket.

Warne hardly allowed a square cut against him, demonstrating that he had the stamina to keep the ball up, particularly at the end of spells. There were no long hops or loose balls due to fatigue, which kept every batsman under great pressure. The slightest lapse in concentration meant death at the wicket. The

Pakistanis, like most other teams, were not confident about driving him off the front foot. For the right-hander, this meant attacking a ball that might spin hard across the bat, demanding a perfect eye and footwork for execution through the off side. A marginal mishit would see a ball flying to Taylor or the covers. The left-hander trying to drive Warne's stock leggie would have to be very quick-footed against the spin. Perhaps only Allan Border, Brian Lara, Neil Harvey and Gary Sobers in recent decades could have contemplated such adventure.

Warne's match figures of eleven for 77 broke Carl Rackemann's thirteen-year record against Pakistan and earned him the Man of the Match award in Australia's victory by an innings and 126 runs. Taylor could not have asked for a more dominant start to a series against a very strong side, on paper at least.

Toed Off

The Second Test at Hobart began four days after Brisbane on 17 November and was preceded by a reunion of the first-ever Australian team to play Pakistan in a Test match. It was contested at the National Stadium, Karachi, from 11 to 17 October 1956, and the Australians were led by Ian Johnson. Apart from him, Colin McDonald, Neil Harvey, Ian Craig, Ron Archer, Alan Davidson and Ray Lindwall were present from that side at a dinner before the match with the two current teams. The old-timers mingled with the new boys. Wasim Akram and Waqar Younis, for instance, took time with Lindwall and Davidson to discuss reverse swing. The Pakistanis were delighted to learn their side had won that first game by nine wickets. They were wanting a repeat of this at Hobart and brought in Mushtaq Ahmed in place of Saqlain Mushtaq, and the newly arrived Ijaz Ahmed for the injured Salim.

On day one, it looked as if the tourists might get their wish as Australia battled from the start. It lost Slater for a duck, lbw to Wasim Akram on the sixth ball of the first over. Boon (34) was run out just when he was settled and looking solid. Taylor

(40) played a typically determined yet unenterprising knock before being bowled by Akram twenty-five minutes into the afternoon session.

It was spin not pace that was Australia's undoing as Mushtaq Ahmed ran through the middle order in the middle and last sessions. Only Mark Waugh looked likely to develop the Australian innings beyond the ordinary, as the 25-year-old Ahmed put his fine skills on display to show that Warne was not the only spinner who could destroy an innings. He collected Steve Waugh (7) caught behind, bowled Blewett for a duck, and had Reiffel (14), Healy (37) and Mark Waugh (88) caught.

Warne, in belligerent mood, belted 27 not out from twenty balls in half an hour of mayhem, in which he lifted Ahmed for three leg-side sixes. This lifted Australia to a not-so-respectable 267. Ahmed took five for 115—his best Test bowling figures—while Wasim Akram returned three for 42.

Back in the dressing rooms, Warne found that a brutal yorker from Waqar may have broken the big toe of his left foot. X-rays later confirmed that it was indeed a fracture. It put Warne out for the rest of the game. He could only look on in pain and frustration as Pakistan reached two for 33 at stumps, thanks to McGrath, who dismissed Saleem Elahi (13) and night watchman Mushtaq Ahmed (0) with successive balls. The next day the pacemen, Reiffel (four for 38), McGrath (three for 46) and McDermott (two for 72) covered well for the loss of Warne and dismissed Pakistan for 198. It again collapsed, losing its last six wickets for just 48. Only Rameez Raja (59) managed a half-century in another insipid display by the tourists.

Taylor (42) and Slater (62) took full advantage in putting together their ninth century opening stand, taking the score to none for 107 at stumps. The lead was 176 and the game seemed in Australia's grasp. Slater continued to hit freely the next morning until Ahmed took him out lbw for a dashing 73 with the score at 120. Taylor, with 123 in just under a day's batting, hung on for a big innings. Wickets fell steadily through the day until a final score of nine for 306, without Warne's appearance at the crease. Mushtaq Ahmed's four for 83 raised the question again of why he had been left out of the First Test. His match figures were nine for 198. Wasim Akram again took three wickets, this time for 72. The Australians' lead was 375 and Taylor was reasonably sure it was enough, even without his top striker in Warne.

Pakistan made it through without loss at stumps on day three with none for 15. However, Aamir Sohail was forced to retire hurt with a strain. He resumed at 27 the next day when McGrath removed the hapless Saleem Elahi (17) caught in close by Boon. Reiffel struck twice with lbws (Rameez Raja for 25 and Inzamam for 40) and helped precipitate a steady decline. Sohail (57) chipped Blewett to Julian substituting for Warne at square leg. McGrath (five for 61) picked up where he left off the night before in wrapping up the tail and ending the Pakistani innings at 220. Reiffel returned three for 42 and Blewett two for 25 as Australia—with Taylor adjudged Man of the Match—running out easy winners by 155 runs and taking the series.

The Mushtaq–Warne Show

Warne surprised by declaring himself fit to play in the Third Test at Sydney beginning on 30 November despite his fractured big toe of just ten days ago. He was soon put to an examination on the field of battle when Taylor lost the toss. Pakistan batted with a new line-up, bringing in Malik for Saleem Elahi, and Latif as keeper in place of Moin. Saqlain took over from Mohammad Akram. Australia remained unchanged when it could have done with another spinner on the turning Sydney wicket.

Aamir Sohail decided to attack from the first ball, hitting a four off McDermott, but the tall Queenslander struck back two balls later and had him caught in the slips. Ijaz Ahmed joined Rameez Raja in a promising stand, which ended when Warne, brought on early again, enticed him to hit a catch to Slater. Inzamam was once more in trouble against Warne's prodigious first-day tweaking on a wicket that was underdone due to the stormy weather of the previous two weeks. In contrast to the last time he played Warne, he went for his shots and notched 39. It worked for a while until the leggie had him slicing a catch to Healy. Pakistan was three for 141 when Salim marched to the wicket through a thicket of booing.

Warne could not snare him this time and that was left to McGrath, who had him lbw for 36. Salim had acquitted himself well in a 107-minute stay at the wicket, showing that, like his 'enemy' Warne, he could carry on with an injury that would put less hardy men out of action.

Pakistan was four for 231 at stumps with the battling Ijaz Ahmed 101 not out and Basit Ali 8 not out. The next day saw a different story, although the rapidity of the fall of wickets had a familiar ring about it. McDermott was on fire, sending back Basit Ali for 17 and Rashid Latif for 1 with the score at 263. Wasim Akram (21) put up some resistance, but Warne wrapped the innings with the wickets of Ijaz for 137 and Mushtaq Ahmed for a duck.

Pakistan had lost six for 68 in the morning, bringing its innings to an ignoble end once more at 299. Warne returned to the top of the bowling honours with four for 55 off thirty-four overs with twenty maidens. McDermott was also in good form with three for 72.

Wasim Akram bowled Slater in the first over of two before lunch, but it was the spinners who did more damage afterwards. Saqlain had Taylor (47) caught by Latif and the keeper repeated the feat off Mushtaq to send back Boon (16), leaving Australia three for 91 and in trouble. The Waugh twins, however, were disposed towards a fight and stayed until stumps, with Mark on 54 not out and Steve 26, and Australia at three for 151. The next morning Mushtaq soon struck, first having Steve Waugh (38) stumped and then breaking through Blewett for 5, exposing the South Australian's flawed technique against top-class spin.

Only Mark Waugh could resist with a conscientious 116, his ninth Test century. Australia lost its last five wickets for 31 to reach just 257 and trail by 42. Mushtaq took five for 95 and Wasim Akram four for 50, in a bowling tale similar to the first Australian innings of the previous Test.

McDermott broke through early having the dangerous Aamir Sohail caught by Boon for 9 at 18. Forty runs later, when the game seemed to be slipping from Australia a little, Warne deceived Ijaz Ahmed (15) with a top-spinner that caught him leg before.

Salim strode to the wicket and was booed a second time. He began sedately and was content to watch Warne weave his magic once more, as he induced a bat-pad from Rameez Raja (39) to put Pakistan at three for 82. The lead was 124 and the game was in the balance. With every run now, the game moved more into Pakistan's grasp.

Warne bowled the last over of the day, but, after five deliveries, he paused and had a long talk with Healy mid-pitch, which held up play for two minutes. The umpires glanced at each other as the discussion went on. The main object was to make the batsman, Basit Ali, nervous and unsure, but Warne also told Healy that he would try to bowl Basit round his legs, a ploy he had used before on the last ball of a session.

Warne wasted more time by motioning he was going to bowl around the wicket, a method that had been successful in the last two Ashes series, but which he had not resorted to in this series. Basit waited for the sightscreen and took block. Warne strolled in, threw his right foot as far right as he dared and heaved the ball up the pitch. Basit anticipated the big turning ball round his legs and did what most batsman normally did—he *thought* about pushing a leg at it. But the ball had been delivered faster. It drifted, deceived Basit in the fraction of a second of its flight, and landed between his legs. Then it bit and spun hard into the stumps.

Warne was embraced by the team. This delivery would rank in the top ten of his entire career. Basit wandered off a shattered batsman and Pakistan was four for 101—a lead of 143, with Salim on 21 not out and seemingly in no trouble. It was not enough for the Pakistanis to feel safe, but enough to make the Australians realise they would have an extra tough challenge to win the game.

Next morning, Inzamam joined Salim in the walk to the wicket to quiet applause. The Sydney crowd had decided to give Salim a 'fair go', which may or may not have been deserved for his actions off the field, but was for his performance on it. He set about building the score on the fourth day until Mark Waugh had him lbw for 45 in the middle session with the score at five for 163 and the Pakistani lead at 205. Then once McDermott dismissed Inzamam (59) caught in the slips, the Pakistanis again crumbled to all out for 204. Warne captured four for 66 off thirty-seven overs, including thirteen maidens. McDermott, steady, accurate and always menacing, had the best figures with five for 49.

Australia had a target of 247 to win. It began with some promise, but then lost Slater (23), who padded up to a wrong 'un from Mushtaq Ahmed at 42, and Boon (6) to Saqlain at 69. Healy came in as night watchman after Mark Waugh (34) was caught behind chasing runs when he perhaps could have played as he did in the first innings. At stumps, Australia was three for 117, with Taylor solid on 49 not out and Healy 4 not out.

Time was no trouble as Australia set out on day five to score another 130 runs with seven wickets still standing. It seemed to be anyone's game until a few minutes into the morning when Healy (5) was caught behind again off Wasim Akram. When Taylor (59) was stumped off Mushtaq trying to loft him at 146, the equation looked bad for the home side. It was still more than 100 short and only an injured Steve Waugh with Blewett left to take Australia home. Waugh had a groin strain that would not allow him to stretch against the spinners and it was no shock to see him play on to one from Mushtaq for 14. Blewett's confidence was down and he looked uncomfortable against everyone. He was soon bowled by Waqar Younis for 14 and the side collapsed to be all out for 172, losing its last seven for 46. Mushtaq, although expensive at times, was the destroyer with four for 91, giving him his best-ever Test figures of nine for 186.

Waqar Younis took three for 15 in a devastating spell and Wasim Akram two for 25.

Pakistan's well-deserved win by 74 runs brought the series to a more realistic two–one victory for Australia. Mushtaq Ahmed was Man of the Match for the Third Test, while Warne took the Man of the Series. He took nineteen wickets at just 10.42 runs per wicket, compared with Mushtaq's excellent eighteen wickets at 21.33.

In just four Tests between them, these two had taken thirty-seven wickets, demonstrating that leg-spin was now a major force in Test cricket. Teams that didn't have such a bowler would be looking for one and nurturing the art. Blewett, who could not handle it, was banished to the Sheffield Shield to regain confidence and form, while the rest of the side looked forward to three more Tests against Sri Lanka. It had been sweet revenge to beat Pakistan after the bitterness of the Salim Malik controversy, and now the Australians were to face a series with some unexpected spice of a different variety.

No Match in Perth

Australia made three changes for the First Test against Sri Lanka, starting at Perth on 8 December 1995. It brought in Law (aged twenty-eight) and Ponting (aged twenty) for their first Tests, and Julian—for Blewett, Steve Waugh, whose groin was still a problem, and Reiffel, who had torn a hamstring in Sydney. Only two members of the Sri Lankan team, Dharmasena and Chaminda Vaas, had not played in the last series between the two countries in 1992.

Arjuna Ranatunga won the toss at the WACA and batted on what appeared to be a good pitch. The tourists, who had just two weeks preparation in Australia, didn't take advantage of it and were two for 46—with McDermott and McGrath dismissing an opener each.

Warne prepared to bowl the last over before lunch. Aravinda de Silva, Sri Lanka's batting champion, looked as if he wanted to live up to this billing by slamming him for two risky fours. He went for a third and hit the ball back to the spinner for a caught-and-bowled. Sri Lanka was three for 54 at lunch and de Silva back in the pavilion for just 10.

After lunch, Gurusinha and Ranatunga restored the position until McGrath induced an edge to Healy to remove the skipper for 32. Tillakeratne, another batsman of quality in an impressive first-six line-up, was lbw to McDermott for 6, leaving the team a disappointing five for 132. The keeper, Kaluwitharne, came in and smacked a team-lifting 50 in seventy-four balls, losing Gurusinha (46) bowled by McGrath. Warne put an end to Kaluwitharne through an edge to Taylor at slip. With Wickramasinghe at number ten crunching 28 from thirty-two balls, Sri Lanka managed to scramble 251 by the close of play.

The visitors treated Warne like any other bowler and looked the least fearful of him since he had established himself in the Australian team in the summer of 1992–93 against the West Indies. He went for nearly 3 an over in taking three for 75 off twenty-seven overs, with eight maidens, when his average was more like 2. The tourists had more trouble with the fast, accurate McGrath, who took four for 81, although he too was not spared some hitting off his twenty-four overs. They were more respectful of McDermott, who took three for 44 off 18.4.

Slater and Taylor responded next day by attempting to wipe out the entire Sri Lankan score by themselves. They nearly succeeded, only losing Taylor (96) lbw to de Silva at 228, sixteen minutes before tea. Slater was playing the innings of his life as he and Taylor hit their tenth opening of a century or more, surpassing the nine such innings by Simpson and Lawry.

After seventeen overs, umpire Khizar of Pakistan held up play and called for Australian umpire Peter Parker to examine the ball. They agreed that it had been interfered with, although Ranatunga was adamant it had not. If the umpires were serious about the problem they made an error in not replacing the ball. The batsmen seemed to back Ranatunga in the way they were hitting it.

Boon came and went for 13 in half an hour. Mark Waugh joined the carefree Slater for the fun until stumps when the score was two for 358, a lead of 207 with almost all wickets still intact. Slater was 189 not out and Waugh 36 not out. Day three saw more of the same, with both players in superb touch. Slater reached his first double century in Tests and then, at 219, was caught-and-bowled by Muttiah Muralitharan, the 23-year-old right-arm off-spinner with the contentious arm action.

Australia was three for 422 as Ricky Ponting strode to the wicket and seemed born to rule in Test cricket as he set about building a big debut innings. He and Waugh took the score to 496 before Waugh (111) was out caught behind. Ponting (96) looked certain to reach a century in his first-ever Test innings until a lazy lbw decision by umpire Hayat, TV replays of which showed the ball would have missed the stumps by about 30 centimetres. The score was five for 617 with Law on a comfortable, accomplished 54 not out in his first-up innings, when Taylor declared.

Muralitharan finished with two for 224, the worst figures in a Test since Clarrie Grimmett returned two for 191 against England in 1928–29. Perhaps the calls for the Sri Lankan's action to be changed might have helped his figures as well. However, he had seventy-eight Test wickets, more than any of his team-mates, and he was coming off a fifteen-wicket haul in three successful Tests against Pakistan.

Sri Lanka went to lunch at none for 13 on day four as they set out to run down the deficit of 366. McGrath broke through soon afterwards and Warne again dismissed de Silva, one of the players touted with the skill to play out a huge knock that could save the game, caught for 10 by Ponting in the covers. Tillakeratne showed the way with a great exhibition of Test refinement as he climbed to 119 in 267 minutes before he, too, was snapped up by Ponting off the persistent Warne.

However, Sri Lanka was all out for 330 by day's end. McGrath took three for 86 and took the crucial wicket of Ranatunga (46) just before lunch, while McDermott managed three for 73.

Warne sent down 29.4 overs with just six maidens in securing three for 96. He had been effective and bowled well, yet his returns for the match of six for 171 hinted that he was not the force he had been against the Pakistanis. His control was not the same, leading to a higher run rate per over against him. At no moment in the WACA Test was Warne able to swarm all over his opponents with pinpoint precision and 'rip' his big leg-spinner. An explanation could be found in his fitness. His spinning finger—the fourth on the hand, which straightens in order to flick the ball out hard—was very sore at the end of each day in the field.

Warne was forced to have cortisone injections into the knuckle, which required a wriggling of the needle to make the drug effective. Such painful insertions were normally not needed more than every six weeks. By the end of the WACA Test, Warne was requiring one every two weeks to avoid pain and disability.

One Chucker to Sri Lanka

Apart from his troublesome digit, Warne looked unlikely to play in the Boxing Day Test at Melbourne because of a viral infection over Christmas, but the Australians gambled on selecting him and hopefully batting first, thus giving him another day or so to recover.

Australia brought back Steve Waugh and Reiffel for Law and Julian. Sri Lanka dropped Dharmasena for Jayantha Silva, a 22-year-old left-arm spinner.

Taylor lost another toss, but was sent in by Ranatunga on what looked like a fair Melbourne wicket which proved to be hard and even-bouncing. Wickramasinghe bowled Taylor (7) with a beauty that pitched on leg and took off stump when the score was 14. Slater was dropped and then Boon on 0 padded up to a ball from Vaas that seemed on-line. New Zealand umpire Steve Dunn said not out. Boon was then dropped in the gully on 6. Two lives were enough for this batsman and he proceeded to eke out an innings that bored most of the big holiday crowd of 55 000 in the sun. Australia went quietly to lunch on one for 63.

Perhaps Darrell Hair, the other umpire, felt Boon had offered him a chance to liven up events, for into the afternoon session he stood 5 metres back from the stumps at the bowler's end to scrutinise the bowling of Muralitharan. Hair judged that sometimes his right elbow was crooked at the moment of delivery. This made it an 'unfair' delivery, or more prosaically, the spinner was seen to be a 'chucker'. Hair called 'no ball'. The match had bogged down to a point where the crowd's concentration was on other matters. Hair kept calling Muralitharan, not every ball, but seven times in four overs. It was intolerable to continue, at least at Hair's end.

By the completion of the fourth over, spectators realised what was happening. They began to react. A buzz went round the ground every time Hair's right arm went out. Victorian cricket fans with long memories recalled that one of their favorite sons, left-arm paceman Ian Meckiff, was the last player to be called in a Test, in 1963–64 at Brisbane. Meckiff did not bowl another ball in the match after one humiliating over and never played cricket again.

Ranatunga, not one to bow to anyone, particularly umpires, switched his spinner to the other end. Steve Dunne didn't agree with Hair and didn't call him. Hair, a strong-minded umpire who would never be intimidated out of an opinion, decided that he had made his point. The crowd was now watching the umpire's arm with more concentration than the bowler's delivery itself.

Slater (62) was unable to get on top and surrendered his wicket to Vaas to bring Mark Waugh to the wicket at two for 116 after 196 minutes. Waugh proceeded at last to entertain the crowd with some dash and, together with Boon, posted a 103-run partnership in just 100 minutes before Waugh (61) played across one from Muralitharan and was bowled. Steve Waugh replaced his brother to be 2 not out at stumps, with Boon 93 not out after batting for 330 minutes.

The next morning, in front of a much smaller crowd, he dallied in the 90s for fifty-two minutes before reaching the three figures he obviously craved, to be finally out for 110, his twenty-first Test century. It took 408 minutes and he faced 312 balls. Ponting replaced Boon at four for 280 and went for his strokes straight away, cutting, driving and pulling with equal facility in compiling 71 from just ninety-four balls in 125 minutes, before being caught off de Silva, with Australia five for 395. Healy (41) then joined Waugh for a 93-run partnership that demoralised the Sri Lankans and saw Waugh reach his tenth century.

At tea, Hair told the Sri Lankans that he would no-ball Muralitharan from either end if they persisted in bowling him. In other words, he would call him from square leg as well. Ranatunga did not risk aggravating the problem and used Aravinda de Silva instead as Australia sailed on. Waugh remained unconquered on 131 when Taylor called him in with the score at six for 500.

Warne did not bat. He still felt weakened from the effects of the virus that threatened his participation. He took the field with his team-mates late in the afternoon of day two and was there to congratulate McGrath as he caused opener Mahanama to edge one to Taylor at slip. Sri Lanka was one for 33 at stumps.

Taylor, for reasons known only to him, decided early on the overcast third morning, 28 December, to throw Ponting and not Warne the ball after McGrath, McDermott and Reiffel had failed to remove the opener Hathurusinghe and Gurusinha. The Tasmanian bowled medium-pace swingers and sure enough immediately got a nick behind off Gurusinha (27). It was only his third first-class wicket.

A steady fall of wickets through the day, mainly perpetrated by the forceful McGrath, led to a total of 233. Keeper Romesh Kaluwitharana again belted a refreshing 50 from just fifty-nine balls, while Ranatunga struggled to 51 with a finger injury before McDermott had him pushing to Warne for a catch in the gully.

McGrath took five for 40 of 23.4 overs. None of the tourists seemed to be at ease with his express pace and accuracy.

Warne took the valuable wicket of Tillakaratne, beating him with a leg-spinner that he edged to Taylor. His figures were ordinary at one for 49 off eighteen overs, with five maidens, and reflected the deterioration of his finger. He was not able to grip the ball without discomfort.

The number of left-hand batsmen in Sri Lanka's line-up—Gurusinha, Ranatunga, Tillarakatne and Vaas—didn't help Warne, as his big leg break was less effective against them. He was forced to bowl more top-spinners and wrong 'uns to them, and if the batsmen could share the strike with singles, it threw his line a fraction. Warne preferred to have one player face every ball in an over. He could then encircle, corner and defeat them. If that wasn't possible it was still better that he bowled continuously to right-handers rather than a left–right combination.

Early in Sri Lanka's follow-on, Reiffel cajoled Mahanama into a half-drive, which he sent to Warne's safe hands in the gully. This left the tourists one for 29 at stumps, with Hathurusinghe on 20 not out and Gurusinha on 8 not out.

On day four, the pacemen found it difficult to penetrate on a slowish pitch. Gurusinha moved into top gear with an attractive 65 in the pre-lunch session, including a soaring six wide of mid-on off Warne. Unfazed, Warne retaliated by trapping Hathurusinghe (39) lbw, making Sri Lanka two for 97. It went to lunch on a fighting two for 133.

Gurusinha—nicknamed 'the Guru'—showed unshakeable concentration as he reached his highest Test score of 143, before Reiffel ended his brave knock.

Warne prevented the aggressive activities of Kaluwitharana, who liked to attack without notice, by teasing him just out of his crease for a flash stumping by Healy. It even looked quick on the slow-motion replay. Ranatunga, who normally batted at number five, dropped himself down to seven. He plonked himself at the wicket, determined to stay there until the death. He was unconquered at stumps on 6, with Vaas on 5 and the score at six for 284.

The Sri Lankan lead was just 17. Taylor urged his troops to blast out the last four so that they could 'get in some golf' on the last afternoon. McGrath heeded his leader's words. His first ball the next morning was a ferocious lifter at Vaas's throat. The night watchman fended it off and Boon snaffled the catch at short leg. That brought a collapse. Warne was all over the opposition, having Wickramasinghe out of his ground for Healy to whip off the bails. The next ball, Muralitharan poked at a leg break and Taylor snapped up the resulting edge. McGrath then bowled Silva to end the innings on 307, with Ranatunga not out on 11 after resisting doggedly for nearly two hours.

Despite his finger problems, Warne returned the best figures of four for 70 from thirty-seven overs, with ten maidens. Man of the Match McGrath took two for 92 and Reiffel two for 59.

Slater (13 not out) and Taylor (25 not out) knocked off the required 41 in eight overs before lunch to give Australia a ten-wicket win and the series, so far, two–nil.

The players now had that golfing option.

World Series Wonders

The 1995–96 World Series competition between Australia, Sri Lanka and the West Indies that followed the Second Test was perhaps the most exciting and exceptional one-day competition played in Australia. It had surprises, shock finishes, fierce attacking batting, superb bowling—particularly from Shane Warne in the finals—amazing fielding and controversy.

Sri Lanka was in the thick of all the highlights and lowlights, with its irritating, talented but unfit skipper Arjuna Ranatunga leading his team in all the right and wrong directions. His team had been brilliant in beating Pakistan in a recent one-day series and the Australian team was prepared for a tough competition in December 1995 and January 1996, with no guarantees that it would make the finals.

The public and the media, unaware of the Sri Lankan winning style in one-dayers, were surprised in the early games as the West Indies dropped off the pace and lost their first four games.

Match five on New Year's Day 1996, a day–nighter in Sydney, was the highlight of the entire competition. Its outcome was dominated by Warne and Michael Bevan, who did more than any other bowler or batsman of the three sides to influence the course of events at critical moments.

The weather was dull and wet, 104 minutes being lost due to a thunderstorm during the Windies' knock in the afternoon, reducing the game to forty-three overs a side. Still, 37 562 holiday fans stayed on in the uncertain conditions.

The Windies were in trouble in the eighteenth over at five for 54, thanks to some outstanding fast swing from Reiffel, who returned the best figures for the match of four for 29. Then the mercurial Hooper (93 not out from 99 balls) pulled his team out of trouble with Roger Harper (28) in a partnership of 81 for the sixth wicket. Warne, under pressure, bowled with the control he had shown in the First Test against Pakistan and returned three for 30 off nine overs. He kept the lid on the Windies' fightback, restricting them to only slightly more than 3 an over when they needed 6, while still taking vital wickets.

Australia replied and fell in a hole, losing six for 38 as Walsh, Ambrose (three for 20) and Otis Gibson (two for 40) bowled fast and tight. But Bevan, who had established himself as the best-ever one-day innovator, turned things around with Reiffel (34) until the score was 162 and Australia was in sight of a miraculous victory with a couple of overs to go. It then lost three wickets and stumbled to nine for 168, with Bevan still in on 74 not out. McGrath came to the wicket with three balls to go in the last over and 5 runs required for victory. He and Bevan scrambled a single, leaving 4 to win with two balls left. After being forced to block the next one, Bevan then coolly smashed the last delivery into the sightscreen before the fieldsmen at deep mid-on and mid-off could make a step towards it. Australia, nine for 173, had won, with Bevan collecting 78 off eighty-nine balls.

Despite this loss, the Windies' form improved with three wins in the last four games, but it was too little too late. The Sri Lankans, who had captured the cricketing world with their attack from the first over, played Australia for a place in the finals in an MCG day–nighter on 9 January before a crowd of 60 110. Australia batted first, struggling to five for 213, with Ponting (123) early and Bevan (65 not out) later saving their team from humiliation.

Sri Lanka surprised by opening with keeper Kaluwitharana, who raced out of the blocks. At one point it was two for 83 off sixteen overs, then slumped to six for 147, losing Kaluwitharana for 77 off just seventy-nine balls. But solid batting by Mahanama (51) and de Silva (35) got them home in 47.3 overs. The result gave them a superior run rate to the Windies and put them in the finals.

The first game, in Melbourne, pulled in a crowd of 72 614 on 18 January for a day–nighter. Again, the Australians started poorly, slumping to four for 34. It took the efforts of Ponting (51), Bevan (59) and Healy (50 not out) to drag the home team up to a still-lowly seven for 201.

Sri Lanka once more got away to a blistering opening and at one stage was two for 110, thanks to Gurusinha (47) and de Silva (34). Warne (two for 29 from ten overs) then changed the game in five balls, in which he collected the wickets of de Silva and Tillarkeratne. Sri Lanka turned defensive before the focused accuracy of Warne, McDermott, McGrath and Reiffel, who were so mean that it could only manage 183 from 48.1 overs.

'I guess we got out of jail with this one,' a relieved Mark Taylor told the media after the game. He mentioned that the Australians would have to improve in Sydney or face defeat in the second final.

True to his word, Taylor (82 from ninety-six balls) led the way with Mark Waugh (73 from eighty-two balls) in an opening of 135 in front of 39 223 spectators jammed into the SCG on 20 January. Healy (40 not out from just twenty-eight balls) and

Bevan (32 not from thirty-five balls) carried on to take Australia to a series best of five for 273.

The Sri Lankans would have to score at 5.5 an over under lights, in front of a crowd wanting serious action, but thunderstorms delayed play until just before the cut-off time of 8.45 p.m. that would have seen the game abandoned. The Sri Lankans' innings was reduced to twenty-five overs and it needed 168 to win. This was at a rate of 6.72 runs an over.

Tempers frayed early as McGrath clashed with Jayasuriya mid-pitch. Both sides were capable of belligerence, but Ranatunga caused most trouble and upset the Australians. He took drinks at every over, and played for breathing space by also demanding new gloves and a new bat.

At one point, he demanded a runner, when he only seemed out of breath from his obvious lack of condition and umpire Steve Randell refused the request. Then Ranatunga complained about a leg injury and started limping. After further debate, the umpire allowed the runner.

Meanwhile, Warne closed in on the middle order with the best bowling spell of either side for the finals. He took three wickets in his maximum five-over spell, including that of Ranatunga for 41. It was the wicket that won the match and the final series, as Sri Lanka was caught short by just 9 runs on eight for 159.

Warne and Taylor shared the Man of the Finals award.

In an act of poor sportsmanship, Ranatunga—along with de Silva and the team coach, Duleep Mendis—refused to shake hands with Mark Taylor when he offered his hand after the game. The ill-feeling had heightened with the calling of Muralitharan in the Melbourne Test, and had nothing to do with the Australians. In fact, it was the Sri Lankans who had flouted the spirit of the game by not doing something about the spinner's action. Instead, their administrators and team management had attempted to call the cricket world's bluff, banking on the goodwill extended to Sri Lanka as the 'new team on the block'.

The cricket world welcomed and encouraged this team of genuine class. Nevertheless, there were rules and regulations which kept the game at a high level of goodwill and sportsmanship. One problem would always be that of 'cheating' to gain an advantage. Throwing was a time-tested method of bending the rules beyond the spirit of the game. It had to be stopped. Umpire Hair's action in Melbourne was a courageous, if belated, act to correct a wrong that should have been handled with far more toughness and alacrity earlier by the ICC and the Sri Lankans themselves.

The result of the festering problem was continued bad feeling between the Australians and Sri Lankans. Fortunately, however, it didn't manifest itself in the concluding Test of the series, which was not played until after the one-day competition.

Star Waugh

The home side made no changes for the Third Test at Adelaide over the Australia Day weekend, beginning on 25 January 1996. Sri Lanka, by contrast, thought it was time to blood players. There was nothing to lose by leaving out Muralitharan, for obvious reasons, as well as young Silva. Ranatunga, whose hand injury was still causing him problems, could not play and nor could Mahanama, who had a torn hamstring.

In came Saneth Jayasuriya, a left-hand orthodox spinner; Sanjeeva Ranatunga, Arjuna's brother, a left-hand bat and right-arm medium-pacer; and Ravindra Pushpakumara, right-arm fast-medium, while Dharmasena was recalled.

Boon announced his retirement from Test cricket before play, but was soon batting after Taylor won the toss when Slater was caught behind off Vaas from the first ball he faced. At 36, Taylor (21) went the same way and this brought Mark Waugh in. Where Boon was dour, Waugh was dashing as they put on 60 before Boon (43) was bowled after lunch by Pushpakumara.

At four for 181, Mark Waugh was dismissed for a delightful 71, made in 199 minutes, which had pulled Australia out of trouble. At stumps, it was a just-respectable five for 239, having lost Ponting for 6, with Steve Waugh 71 not out, accompanied by Healy on 21.

Sri Lanka thought it had a real chance to dismiss Australia for a more modest score when play began on day two. But Waugh and Healy had other ideas. They plundered on into the morning until the score was 326, when Healy departed for 70 after two hours of entertainment. Reiffel joined Waugh for another crushing partnership that took the score on by 117 to 443, before Waugh was bowled for 170, his eleventh Test hundred.

Reiffel continued on to 56, his highest Test score. Warne came to the wicket and went after almost everything in compiling 33 off thirty-nine balls in a 63-minute stay at the wicket before Taylor called a halt at nine for 502, the team's third huge 500-plus innings of the series.

Sri Lanka's reply was a confident none for 80 off just sixteen overs—a rate of 5 per over—at stumps on day two. Warne looked out of sorts and had rare trouble with his line. His finger was now at its worst for the summer and his shoulder was also sore.

The next morning, Reiffel struck Jayasuriya on the back of the head. The batsman was shaken and, in the next over, Reiffel removed him for 48, caught behind, and then the other opener—Hathurusinghe (28)—caught by Mark Waugh. It put Sri Lanka on the back foot for the rest of the day as it lost wickets at regular intervals after partnerships that showed promise, but then fizzled. Sanjeeva Ranatunga showed some of his brother's grit in compiling 60 and Tillakaratne battled with determination for his 65.

Reiffel, having a match he would remember, captured five for 39 and McGrath four for 91. Warne, for reasons hidden from the media and opposition, disappointed with none for 74 off twenty-six overs. He looked frustrated when he bowled, but was not about to tell the world why.

Sri Lanka's best score of the series—317—just avoided the follow-on. Taylor and Slater negotiated the few overs to stumps on day three, but not many more on day four when they were both back in the pavilion cheaply. However, with the 185 lead, there was no danger. The side cruised to six for 215 after tea, a lead of 400, before Taylor waved his hand in declaration for the fourth time in the series.

Steve Waugh batted with usual assurance and application for 61 not out, bringing his tally for the series to 362 for once out. Boon ended his outstanding 107-Test career with 35 in sixty-six minutes, taking his final tally to 7422 runs at 43.65. Only Border (11 174 in 156 Tests) had made more runs for Australia. It was a dignified end for a champion.

Sri Lanka replied with one for 69 at stumps on its forlorn chase of 400 in 112 overs. On paper, this ask of less than 4 an over could be conceived as obtainable. But on turf it was nigh impossible, although not perhaps in the mind of the enterprising Jayasiriya, who had produced 50 not out at stumps. He continued on the fifth morning as if there had been no break.

Midway through the middle session, Sri Lanka was cruising towards saving the game when Taylor tossed the ball to Steve Waugh. He had bowled only sixteen overs for the summer, but now had the responsibility of winning a Test, which was slipping towards a tame draw. Warne was not his vital self and the wicket was unhelpful to speed. Waugh bowled his seamers and dismissed Jayasuriya caught behind for a superb 112, and then in the same over sent back Kaluwitharane, bowled for a duck. Sri Lanka was four for 195 and still twenty minutes from tea. Then McGrath removed Tillakaratne (3) caught behind. Next, Mark Waugh, like his brother covering for Warne, then had de Silva (3) caught in slip by Taylor. Sri Lanka went to tea on a disappointing six for 208.

After the break, Steve Waugh soon removed Dharmasena (2) and then the defiant Sanjeeva Ranatunga (65), placing the tourists on a precarious eight for 215. A little happy hooking by Vaas (26 off thirty-two deliveries) was not enough to put off McGrath who had him caught behind, while Warne bowled Wickramasinghe for a duck. Sri Lanka was all out for 252, giving Australia victory by 148 and the series three–nil.

Steve Waugh surprised even himself by taking four for 34 off nineteen overs. McGrath took three for 48 and brought his series total to twenty-one wickets at 20.85.

Warne again failed to impress, although he was economical. He returned one for 68 off twenty overs, including eleven maidens. His series figures were modest for him, twelve wickets at 36.08.

Healy took eight catches in the match to bring his number of dismissals to 275. But it was Steve Waugh who stole the show with three awards: Man of the Match, Man of the Series and International Cricketer of 1995.

•••

The feeling between the two teams had been good in the Third Test, but poor in the first two, partly due to the unfortunate ball-tampering and throwing incidents, and also because Ranatunga's abrasive 'style' was not liked by the Australians. He made pathetic but disturbing noises about playing Australia in his country, implying that Sri Lanka had been treated unfairly on the just-completed tour. This attitude made the entire squad wary of the first game against Sri Lanka in the forthcoming World Cup one-day series on the subcontinent. The contest was scheduled to be played in turbulent Colombo, where terrorist unrest was ongoing.

On top of this, Warne, McDermott and coach Bob Simpson had received death threats that mentioned what might happen to them if they toured Sri Lanka. There was even a fax to the ACB which said the team would be met by a suicide bomber on arrival in Colombo. The ACB reassured the team and gave guarantees about security.

Then, in late January 1996, a bomb went off in that city and killed a hundred people. The ACB met and decided to abort the Sri Lankan leg of the World Cup. Opprobrium was heaped on the Australians as they forfeited two points to the Sri Lankans before a ball was bowled. But the individual players were relieved they would not have to concern themselves with the possibility of attempts on their lives, and bombs in their hotels.

12

World Cup Blues

Kenya Keen

Australia's pulling out of the game against Sri Lanka in the World Cup, scheduled for 17 February in Colombo, made it a target for upstart politicians on the subcontinent looking for a headline and every tabloid journalist searching for a team to attack. Bad or negative news was always preferable to positive news, and the Australian team, far more than the West Indies combination which also would not play in Colombo, was just right for the fickle British papers in particular.

The Australian squad arrived in Calcutta on 11 February for the World Cup's opening ceremony at Eden Gardens in front of 120 000 fans. Any apprehension about the reaction to its stand evaporated with the enthusiastic reception the players were accorded by the crowd. They were relieved they did not have to worry quite as much about bombs and death threats. They shut themselves away at first in their hotel rooms watching videos, but when they were out in public they soon realised that the goodwill of the Indian people towards them was stronger than ever. Despite some sections of the world media portraying the Australians as 'villains', the masses revered them as near-gods of cricket.

Missing the game against Sri Lanka gave the Australians a twelve-day build-up to a match against Kenya that they were expected to win without too much difficulty on 23 February at Visakhapatnam. The long run-up provided a near-perfect acclimatisation and preparation for the tougher competition ahead.

Physiotherapist Errol Alcott, assisted by Michael Bevan and Craig McDermott, two experienced gymnasium enthusiasts, directed the rest of the players' fitness programs. They included swimming and physical jerks, such as sprints alternated with sit-ups, push-ups, burpees, squats, jumps and boxing. This was all in addition to normal net practice.

By 16 February, when the team reached Bombay, Warne, who had been unable to find his favourite toasted cheese sandwich anywhere, came down with a stomach virus which meant he could eat nothing. Ponting soon joined him in the sickbay. The next day, room-mates Steve Waugh and Glenn McGrath were down with a stomach bug, depleting the squad for a practice match at the Bombay Gymkhana Club on 18 February.

By 22 February, however, the eve of the game against Kenya, the team was pretty well intact. They may have been training hard, yet there was no shortage of enjoyment on tour, which helped shape their minds for the tense times ahead on the field. They could drink as much alcohol as they wanted—admittedly in private, because they were in a 'dry' area—and eat a variety of meals at the top-class hotels, in between sightseeing and playing roulette and blackjack in their own private-room casinos. Only Warne was disgruntled. His search for a decent toasted cheese sandwich had proved fruitless.

The Australian squad was as united as any that ever toured, thanks to Taylor's sensible 'control' of the team and his encouraging attitude to each member, backed up by coach Bob Simpson, Alcott, manager Col Egar and media manager Ian McDonald.

The team in batting order at Visakhapatnam, on India's east coast, was Taylor, Mark Waugh, Ponting, Steve Waugh, Law, Bevan, Healy, Warne, Reiffel, McDermott and McGrath. Shane Lee, a surprise selection for the tour, was twelfth man. Others to miss out were Fleming and Slater.

The Kenyans won the toss and sent Australia in. One reason was the heat. It was stifling, and would be more so bowling and fielding in the afternoon. Australia went into the game with only McDermott worried about a sore calf muscle. Steve Waugh had stomach cramps, but decided to play. Warne was 'comfortable' with his finger—although still needing cortisone injections every two weeks—and his shoulder, which had benefited from rest since the Adelaide Third Test against Sri Lanka, now three weeks away.

The Kenyans soon shocked by sending back Taylor and Ponting for 6 apiece, which brought the Waugh brothers together. They were in no mood for a humiliating collapse against this talented group of tyros. At times, the Keynans were so strong in delivery and swift at fielding that both Waughs had to remind themselves that they were not playing the West Indies. Nevertheless, the twins added 207, a new World Cup record, and steered Australia to seven for 304. Mark, in magnificent form, notched 130. Steve, also in touch, managed 82 in eighty-eight balls.

Kenya's reply was aided by McDermott tearing that troublesome calf muscle and putting him out of the cup altogether. It was the last in a string of injuries that had hampered and frustrated the champion speedster for four years. Kenya built a respectable reply that was up to the Australian run rate in the twenty-fifth over, the halfway mark. It took Bevan, with his well-flighted spinners, to remove the carefree skipper, Maurice Odumbe (50), caught by Reiffel.

The opener–keeper, Kennedy Otieno (85), was bowled by McGrath and unlucky not to reach a century. Severe cramps restricted him and led to his dismissal. Kenya was all out for 207, and certain, as the football cliché goes, to 'worry a lot of top sides'.

Reiffel (two for 18 off seven overs) and Warne (one for 25 off ten) bowled best in terms of what mattered most in one-dayers—pinpoint accuracy and economy.

Australia's Day in Bombay

The team moved on to Bombay on 25 February, via the 'milk run' taking in Patna and Calcutta, arriving after a day's flying when a direct route would have made it in two-and-a-half hours. The team was a little irritated by the long flight, but fascinated by this city of contrasts, with its immense poverty on the one hand and ostentatious opulence on the other, the latter exemplified by gleaming skyscrapers, top-class hotels and expensive apartment blocks. The team hotel, the Taj, was a lavish example of the city's contradictions.

Those interested in the big game between India and Australia in two days time, who numbered most of the population, were fixed on the one-on-one combat expected between Warne and Sachin Tendulkar, the batting genius who was the most revered god in India's cricketing pantheon. Just twenty-three years old, Tendulkar was already ranked with Brian Lara as the most exciting batsman in the world. The Australians were fully conscious of his popularity, not least because of his ubiquitous presence in TV ads and on huge billboards for Pepsi alongside fellow star Vinod Kambli. Most were aware of his skills from first-hand experience in the 1991–92 Test series in Australia when he smashed two outstanding centuries.

The Bombay ground, which unfortunately could only take 40 000 people for its first-ever day–night game, had an atmosphere all of its own because of the close proximity of its steep stands to the playing field. Reiffel's hamstring was playing up and he was left out in favour of Shane Lee, while McDermott went home and was replaced by Fleming. Jason Gillespie was on his way to join the squad.

Practice the night before on the clay-based surface suited Warne, who was all but unplayable as he ripped his leg-spinners and smacked his lips at the thought of his bowling prospects the next day.

Taylor and Mark Waugh got the team off to an ideal start, attacking at just less than 5 an over with the skipper leading the way. Anything wayward or loose was dealt with as the score reached 103 in twenty-two overs. The fun for the Australians ended when the frail-looking left-arm spinner Raju had Taylor (59) caught in the deep by Srinath. Then Ponting (12) was out to a brilliant one-handed catch by Manjreker, again off the deceptive Raju. Steve Waugh (7) was run out when Raju deflected a return hit from Mark Waugh onto the stumps at the bowler's end, leaving Australia three for 157.

With Law (21) in a supporting role, Waugh steadied Australia until he was out in the forty-third over for 126, with the score at four for 232. It was his second successive ton in the series and he had given the team a great start. A disappointing string of dismissals—including the run-outs of Bevan (6) and Lee (9)—saw just 26 more added as Australia struggled up to 258, when 275 should have been the minimum given the early and middle-order efforts.

The buzz-name in the stands and among the media was *Tendulkar*. But it was Fleming who stole the early show in India's innings by removing Jadeja (1) lbw and bowling Kambli for a duck.

McGrath then dropped a caught-and-bowled from Tendulkar that he should have taken, demonstrating the thin line between success and failure in a one-day game, even for someone of Tendulkar's brilliance. Part of his glitter was caused by his desire to smash or dominate a bowler from the first ball. It gave bowlers a chance, albeit a low-percentage one. Risk-taking was part of his spectacular appeal. It was also going to cause his downfall from time to time. His breathtaking, precise power-hitting was based on utter split-second timing. One miscalculation could lead to a dismissal.

Taylor introduced Warne after Tendulkar had wrought mayhem with the quicks, slamming McGrath for 3 fours in one over with an on-drive, a hook off the front foot and a cover drive. Warne's first delivery was smashed straight back over the bowler's head for four. Soon after that he attempted a six over wide mid-off, but instead got under it too much and skied a tough chance to Law, who dropped it. The crowd was loving its hero's good fortune, yet Warne calmed him down with some accurate big breaks that were turning so much they were in danger of being called wide. Fleming struck again, bowling skipper Mohammad Azharuddin for 10, and placing India on three for 70. After this minor interruption, the Tendulkar matinee continued as he crashed his way to 90 out of 143, outscoring the other batsmen and the extras by more than two to one.

Taylor had taken Warne off after the spinner had held his line and length despite Tendulkar's attempts to destroy them. Mark Waugh came on to bowl his innocuous off-spin and was treated with scant respect. But he soon hit back. Tendulkar, anxious to reach a century, ran down the wicket to him. Waugh managed to slip it wide. Healy dragged it in and tore off the bails. The umpire at square leg signalled 'out', while the umpire at the bowler's end threw his arms out, signalling a wide. The former prevailed and Tendulkar was out for 90, a half-hour short of a stay that would have assured victory for India.

Manjrekar carried on with Mongia, the keeper, and looked like taking India home until Warne was re-introduced. He beat Mongia with flight and spin and had him caught by Taylor at slip. Then Steve Waugh came on and induced a snick from Manjrekar (62) to Healy.

Fleming then sliced into the tail for two more wickets and India crumbled from six for 201 to all out 242 in forty-eight overs. Fleming was superb and never flagged despite some stick early on from Tendulkar, taking five for 36 off nine overs, while Steve Waugh got two for 22, but unfortunately from only three overs. Warne was the meanest of all, taking one for 28 off ten. Despite Tendulkar's assault, he went for less than 3 an over.

The Australians were delighted, if not a little surprised, by their win. Most of the team considered themselves now a serious threat to win the cup, although the West Indies and India remained favourites with the bookmakers.

The players adjourned to the hotel bar for much rum and a few punchlines. They were disappointed when it closed early.

The next day, 28 February, the team flew to Nagpur in central India for a game against Zimbabwe, no longer an easy-beat of world cricket. There was a slight air of tension when they arrived. A year earlier a wall at this ground had collapsed, killing thirteen people, and there was talk of demonstrations as compensation had yet to be paid to the families of the victims. However, the game at the small venue was not interrupted.

The wicket was dry and crumbling, just right for Warne. He took full advantage of it once McGrath and Steve Waugh had made inroads, sending Zimbabwe to three for 55. Warne at times was unplayable. He turned the ball prodigiously and gave his shoulder and finger its toughest work-out for some time. He crashed through the middle order and tail, taking four for 34 off 9.3 overs—a performance that won him the Man of the Match award—as the Zimbabweans surrendered for just 154 off forty-five overs. Steve Waugh took two for 22 again, but this time from seven overs, and looked in form with the ball. Australia (two for 158) had no trouble winning. Mark Waugh slipped into fine form with 76 not out.

Windies' Woes

The Australians had a three-day break before the next game in Jaipur in northern central India against the West Indies. They considered this to be the biggest contest for them so far. The lads wondered what to expect from the cricket ground as they made their way through the poverty-stricken throng of people in the streets interspersed with emaciated camels, cows, donkeys, buffaloes and horses. They were surprised to see a rock-hard pitch in the centre of a bigger-than-average ground, which was well grassed.

The night before the game the players socialised at their 'hotel', the former Jai Mahal Palace, with the West Indians, who were feeling stale after a humiliating defeat by the Kenyans. The Windies, only half-jokingly, remarked that they were frightened to go home. They expected a lynching unless they did far better. That was not a good sign for the Australians, who knew that it meant they would come out desperate and firing.

The Australians won the toss and batted against the fearsome, fast and straight bowling of Walsh and Ambrose, who made it tough to score early. After eight overs, Walsh got through Taylor (9) for a catch behind, and out marched Ponting minus his helmet. The Windies had never been treated with such disdain since protective headgear was introduced two decades previously, mainly to combat their four-man pace attack.

They lifted plenty of deliveries into his ribcage and throat, inviting the umpires to call them, but Ponting was very much in the mould of Viv Richards, who also didn't bother with steel hats. He was untroubled as he took the pacemen on and began to gain ascendancy over them. At 84 in the twenty-fifth over, it was spin from Harper than broke through when he removed Mark Waugh (30) stumped.

Steve Waugh joined Ponting and they embarked on what seemed like a match-winning partnership of 110 at nearly a run a ball. At first, Waugh only had to cope with spin from Harper, Adams and Athurton, but Walsh came back on and bowled him, though not before he had collected 57 from sixty-four balls. Then Ponting was run out for 102 off 111 balls. Bevan followed soon afterwards in the same ignominious way for his second low score of the series, as did Healy in like manner. Australia stumbled to six for 229, not a bad score considering the opposition and the formidable bowling early by Walsh and Ambrose. Nevertheless, it was about 30 short of what might have been had the run-outs not occurred.

Fleming continued with his wonderful starts by getting rid of Campbell (1) caught behind, then Browne caught the running disease and was on his way for just 10. This brought Lara and Richardson together and they proceeded to turn the game around without any special fireworks. They preferred, like the Kenyans, Indians and Zimbabweans before them, to treat Australia's number-one striker, Warne (none for 30 off ten), with respect and not go after him. It worked as they chased the other bowlers and collected the runs, putting them at three for 113 when Lara (60) misjudged Mark Waugh and holed out to McGrath. Richardson, under enormous pressure from the media and influential figures in cricket officialdom back in the West Indies, showed great application and courage in accumulating 93 not out, guiding his team home to a four-wicket victory with seven balls to spare.

The Australians were a little subdued after the loss. They went back to the Palace and watched a video of *The Shawshank Redemption*, about an amazing jailbreak. The team knew it would have to show the ingenuity, if not genius, of the main character if it were to win this tight, fierce tournament.

Australia, with three wins, a loss and a default, made the quarter-finals and was drawn to meet New Zealand on the southern coast at Madras.

Fingered

Warne had felt reasonably comfortable with his injuries in the run-up to the finals. He was only required to bowl ten overs in the one-dayers, compared with fifty or more in a Test, and this reduced workload was helping. But he was needed at practice between the matches when he would rather have rested his body, particularly the spinning finger, which was worrying him again. He also had a strained hamstring.

In the build-up to the quarter-final against New Zealand on 11 March, Simpson asked for three days of intense training, similar to finals conditions. On the last day Warne's finger swelled. The ligaments had stretched due to his knuckle joints loosening up, causing veins to emerge through the knuckle. Alcott massaged his forearm and hand and managed to relieve the tightness in them.

At the final practice, Warne tried about six deliveries, but the pain was too much. He gave up and headed for the dressing rooms. He assured Taylor that he would play the next day. It was better to rest it for another half-day before putting pressure on it. In the back of his mind now, he knew that he would have to tackle the growing problem one way or the other after the tournament.

For the moment, he once again had to rise above his physical ailments to compete. Warne could not face sitting on the sidelines while the national side battled out a final in front of a big crowd. The desire to be in the thick of the action would override the pain.

Taylor lost the toss and New Zealand batted in the stifling afternoon heat made worse by a stench from a creek running round the Madras ground. The 45 000 fans who packed the stadium for the day–nighter soon found voice as the Kiwis attacked and took 15 off Reiffel's first over. Then Fleming removed Nathan Astle caught behind for 1. He was swinging the ball well, whereas Reiffel was having trouble with his line. He was still having difficulty when Chris Spearman (12) slashed at a wide ball and was also caught behind.

At 44, McGrath caused Stephen Fleming (8) to hit one straight to Steve Waugh. New Zealand was in trouble. Everything seemed to be going nicely for Australia. Then captain Lee Germon was joined by Chris Harris. They played above their usual reach for an outstanding 168-run partnership that shook Taylor and his men, who had flashes of going home from the cup a few games earlier than expected.

Warne overcame his nagging pain, but couldn't maintain his usual immaculate length and was belted for the first time in the competition. But he wasn't alone as these two hopped into all the bowlers. McGrath came back earlier than Taylor would have liked to end the mayhem at 212 when he had Germon (89) caught.

Taylor gambled on Warne for most of the final overs and he kept the lid on New Zealand, while removing Harris (130) caught by Reiffel in the deep. He was aided by Mark Waugh, who took the vital wicket of Chris Cairns, one player who could have improved New Zealand's score by a hundred rather than 57 in the last ten overs. Bevan also chimed in for a wicket and some tighter bowling. The Kiwis finished pleased with their efforts. They felt the score of nine for 286 was nigh-on insurmountable.

With sheer grit, Warne recovered to two for 52 from his ten, but without a maiden. The New Zealanders had been humbled many times by him in the past four years, and they were lifted by their own ability to attack him. They were unaware of his injury handicap, which the Australians kept secret. They did not want any opposition side gaining an advantage by knowing that their main striker was in trouble.

The rest of the bowling figures showed that Warne was not alone in bearing the force of New Zealand's fury. Reiffel took one for 38 off just four overs, McGrath two for 50 off nine, Mark Waugh one for 43 off eight, Bevan one for 52 off ten, Steve Waugh none for 25 off four, and Fleming one for 20 off five.

The Aussies left the field with their heads down. It would take a tremendous effort to top that score under lights and in the sweltering conditions. Yet this was what the game was all about—accepting and overcoming near-impossible challenges. The team's despondency was not helped by seeing Steve Waugh on the massage table, his lower legs swathed in ice-packs. He had gone over on both ankles on the rock-hard surface. Next to him was Warne, who waited for further treatment from Alcott for his finger.

The mood turned pensive in the dressing rooms as players took showers and cooled down. Taylor moved among his charges and in his bouncy manner revved them up. 'We can do it,' they told each other.

All eyes turned to Mark Waugh as he strode out with Taylor to begin the chase. He was the in-form player of the tournament with two centuries under his belt. Something in the order of 6 an over, or a run a ball, was needed to win. Few Australian one-day teams had ever achieved anything like it.

Spinner Dilip Patel caused Taylor (10) to tickle one down the leg side while attempting a leg glance with the score at 19. Ponting joined Mark Waugh and they kept the run rate up. Back in the dressing room, Steve Waugh, padded-up ready to go in, suggested to vice-captain Healy that it might not be a bad idea to send in a pinch-hitter—a player who would go in and blast 20 or more, lift the scoring rate and upset the fielding side. There was nothing to lose if the batsman was dismissed for a duck, and much to gain if he managed a few. Healy duly informed Taylor of Waugh's idea. He liked it. When Ponting (31) hit out and was caught at 84, Warne, his fingers strapped, marched out in a new role.

Warne delivered, smacking 24 off fifteen balls in a 43-run partnership in four-and-a-half overs, before Astle trapped him lbw. Australia was three for 127 after twenty-five overs—a run rate of 5-plus—and left with 162 to make from twenty-five overs, or 6.48 an over. The pinch-hitter move paid off. Still, the task was a big one. Anything more than 6 to get at the halfway mark—in ninety-nine out of one hundred one-day internationals—meant defeat for the chasing team.

Steve Waugh joined his twin brother for an 86-run link of quality and power that put Australia ahead of the run rate required. At 213 in the thirty-eighth over, an exhausted Mark was out for 110, his third century in the tournament, which delivered him his third Man of the Match award. Australia now needed 76 from seventy balls, a much more manageable challenge. Law came in and, with some judicious placement, reached 42 not out in helping Steve Waugh (59 not out) to steer Australia comfortably home at four for 289 in 47.5 overs.

The team spirit rose to a new level, something like that of a year ago when it won the Fourth Test at Sabina Park. It was an appropriate mood. The Windies had just beaten South Africa in another quarter-final. The Caribbean lads would be Australia's opponents in a semi-final in Chandigarh in India's north.

The Miracle of Chandigarh

The morning after Australia's great win against New Zealand, Warne, doing his daily stint on TV for the Nine Network, asked Steve Waugh, the originator of the pinch-hitting idea, if he could do it again against the Windies. It sounded like a request. Waugh thought it would be most unlikely.

'We wouldn't be able to coax you out of the toilet,' he replied. The response was lost on the Channel Nine audience in Australia. It was Waugh's oblique way of comparing New Zealand's mediocre pair of pacemen—Astle and Thompson—to Ambrose and Walsh. The joking implication was that Warne would be locked away in the small room, too frightened to face the big men from the Caribbean. But beyond that, of course, this would be a much tougher game.

Taylor won the toss and Australia batted, or at least tried to. Ambrose was devastating, cornering Mark Waugh lbw for a duck, second ball. Soon he and Bishop had Australia on its knees with Taylor, Ponting and Steve Waugh also back in the pavilion. The score was four for just 15 off 9.1 overs.

The full import of Waugh's joke with Warne was now apparent. There would be no request for a pinch-hitter today. The lower order would be in soon enough, or so it seemed. Australia's batting depth was now tested as Law and Bevan settled in as if it were a Test. The emphasis was on defence. It would be nice to score a team hundred. It would be better to reach 150 and make a contest of it. They succeeded in playing Test-style in a 138-run partnership. At the moment Law decided to return to the one-day mode by hitting out and taking quick singles, he was run out for 72.

Bevan, the best placer of the ball in the short game, continued on to 69 before being caught trying to scramble Australia to 200, an amazing recovery. That task was left to Healy, who collected 31 at a run a ball before he was run out. Australia reached eight for 207, with Ambrose (two for 26) and Bishop (one for 35) the best for the Windies.

The Australian team was buoyant after overcoming the disaster of the first ten overs. Taylor hoped the momentum would follow through into a few quick wickets. They didn't come. The skipper, always proactive rather than waiting for something to happen, tossed the ball to Warne after the eighth over, with the score at none for 25. The spinner rose to the occasion and enticed Browne to hit hard, which he did, straight back to Warne.

Lara came in and after Warne failed to snare him early, Taylor put his main weapon back in the cupboard. It was a toss-up whether to leave him on or not. The Australian skipper thought 207 gave him some runs and overs to play with. Better to hold Warne back, he decided. It looked as if it were the wrong option as Lara and Chanderpaul moved the Windies' score along without problems to 93 in twenty-three overs.

Steve Waugh was doing the stock spell, bowling without extending himself, but accurately enough to keep the run rate at four. Yet 4 an over without wickets being lost would bring the West Indies home at a canter. Waugh, bowling round the wicket to Lara (45) to restrict him, bent his back with a quicker one, which clipped the left-hander's off stump.

It was a huge moment for the Australians. Lara, along with Tendulkar and Mark Waugh, was the big wicket of the tournament.

Richardson came to the crease and looked like a hero on a mission. He had announced his retirement after two years of harassment and criticism from those who wanted his head for the Windies' fall from power. This tournament would be his last. He wanted to go out with a big victory.

It looked like it was his as he and Chanderpaul raced the score to two for 165 in the forty-second over. There were only 43 to get from fifty-four balls and eight wickets were in hand. The game was as good as over. Then Chanderpaul (80) attempted to loft McGrath and was caught by Fleming. In came Harper. McGrath got him leg before, and the game was still a contest, although the odds were still with the Windies. They were four for 173. There were still forty-one balls to get 35 runs and six wickets in hand, including that of Richardson.

Taylor signalled for Warne to return. It was Australia's last throw of the dice. He deceived Otis Gibson twice, then beat him with a faster leg break, which was snicked behind. The

Windies had slumped to five for 178. Jimmy Adams, usually a cool cricketer, came to the wicket. Warne caused him to push, probe and miss before bowling a fast top-spinner, which caught him on the pads dead in front, neither forward or back, making the umpire's adjudication easy. The score was now six for 183, and Warne was on fire, revelling in the crisis that he and McGrath, with two for 30, had created. Each ball now was a hand grenade to the Windies. Richardson was defensive, but intact. The others were nowhere.

Taylor flipped the ball to Fleming, who soon had Arthurton (0) caught behind, making it seven for 187. The Windies had 21 to make at a run a ball.

In the forty-eighth over—from Fleming—Ponting saved a four with a dive at the boundary which typified the Aussies' fighting spirit as Richardson kept punching. In the forty-ninth over, Warne had Bishop leg before. The West Indies was eight for 194.

Ambrose strolled to the wicket looking as if he would like to be far away. He scrambled a single, and Richardson sliced a three, leaving the score at eight for 198 at the end of the forty-ninth. Warne, his finger raw and sore, took his cap from the umpire, satisifed he had done his very best at the crease with four for 36 off nine. His effort would be later acknowledged in winning the Man of the Match award.

There was one Fleming over to bowl, 10 runs to win and two wickets in hand. Richardson had to go for the boundary, which he did off the first ball and collected four. There were now just 6 to get from five balls. Richardson bottom-edged one to Healy behind the stumps. Ambrose called for the run. Healy hurled the ball and hit the wicket, stranding Ambrose out of his ground. The video was called for and the stadium waited for two minutes. The red light flashed. Ambrose put his head down and wandered off. Four balls were left with still 6 to win.

Walsh was the last man in. He and Richardson had two discussions before Walsh faced Fleming. The lean Victorian paceman ran in and delivered a straight ball, well up. Walsh swung at it, missed and was bowled. The Australians did a delirious dance for about two minutes, such was the shock at coming back from the dead twice.

This was the miracle of Chandigarh.

No More in Lahore

Sri Lanka won its way into the final against Australia with a win against India in Calcutta. It scored eight for 251, with de Silva (66) and Manahama (58 retired hurt) starring. India was eight for 120 after 34.1 overs. Soon after Tendulkar (65) was dismissed stumped off Jayasuriya, rioting Indian supporters torched sections of the wooden stands and threw bottles and rocks onto the field. The game was abandoned. Given that India had only two wickets in hand and 15.5 overs to score 131 to win, at a rate of more than 8 an over, the match referee awarded the game to Sri Lanka by default. It would now meet Australia in Lahore.

The Australians reacted with mixed feelings towards facing Sri Lanka. If anything, they were more confident about winning. India would have been more problematic, depending on the performance of Tendulkar. There was no one of his stature in the Sri Lankan line-up. Furthermore, Australia had crushed the Sri Lankans in the Tests and World Series Cup only a matter of a few months earlier. Yet there was an antipathy between the two squads that would add needle, and perhaps nastiness, to the contest.

Euphoric over their win against the Windies, the Australians were looking for ways to motivate themselves. The word was that they wanted to teach the Sri Lankans—particularly Ranatunga—a lesson after their display of poor sportsmanship in the World Series. Ranatunga continued the 'war' between the two combatants by telling the media that Warne was overrated—an insinuation used by the English, the South Africans and the West Indians in other series. He also claimed that the Waugh brothers had been given 'far too much good press of late'.

The Australians didn't react. They could not be provoked any more by the Sri Lankan skipper, who was doing his best to stir up support for his team. It was a waste of breath. Most of the 800 million watchers of the game on the subcontinent would be hoping for a 'local' side to win. Taylor and his men knew that their opponents—as the Asian underdogs—would have 99 per cent of the support at the ground, which held 50 000.

Australia batted first in the afternoon and started well until Mark Waugh (12) flicked a ball from Vaas straight to Jayasuriya at square leg. Ponting and Taylor restored the moment with an excellent partnership, crashing fours to all parts of the ground. Taylor, much-maligned for his perceived unsuitability for the one-day game, was making a mockery of such criticism. The partnership reached 101 and the score 137 off just twenty-five overs (at 5.5 an over) when part-timer Arivinda de Silva spun out Taylor for 74 and Ponting for 45.

The complexion of the game changed further when Steve Waugh (13) tried to lift a ball from off-spinner Dharmasena over the infield, but only succeeded in hitting a simple catch to mid-on. It was most unusual for both Waughs to fail in any game, let alone a final. Still, on paper, three for 156 was a base for 260.

Warne came in at number six, again as a pinch-hitter. This time it failed when he was stumped on 2 going for a big one off Muralitharan, whose action was deemed legitimate by the umpires in this contest. The scoreboard read four for 170.

Bevan and Law were capable of restoration, but were pegged down. Jayasuriya—the hero of the previous match against India bowling his orthodox left-arm spinners—had Law caught for 22. Healy arrived at the crease with the score on six for 202. De Silva shocked by bowling him for 2, making Australia seven for 205. Bevan (36 not out from 50 balls) and Reiffel (13 not out) managed to wriggle the score up to a far-from-satisfactory seven for 241.

The Sri Lankan spin contingent of Muralitharan (one for 31 off ten overs), Jayasuriya (one for 43 off eight), Dharmasena (one for 47 off ten) and de Silva (three for 42 off nine) were steady and tight enough to restrict Australia's attacking batting line-up. If the Sri Lankans were to win, they would be congratulated for their dogged performances.

Taylor looked on the positive side. His team had won defending 207 against the Windies. 241 was better.

The Australians were disconcerted by the outfield, which turned damp after sundown. It would mean that the ball would be difficult for Fleming, Steve Waugh and Reiffel to seam, and Warne, Bevan and Mark Waugh to grip for spin, thus giving Sri Lanka an unforeseen advantage batting second. This seemed irrelevant early when Jayasuriya was run out brilliantly by Healy for 9, and early heavy-hitter Kaluwitharana (6) was caught by Bevan off Fleming. Sri Lanka was two for 23 off 5.1 overs.

De Silva was joined by Gurusinha for an important partnership of 125. They batted resolutely but were let off by three dropped catches and some poor outfielding, which was uncharacteristic of this Australian unit. It was if they were playing in 1986, not 1996. Warne's spinning finger was giving him hell, but he suffered as much from the wet ball. He was wiping it, but could not grip it. Yet even if it were bone-dry, there would be no ripping leg breaks on this black night. The finger would not allow this delivery. His length, direction and spin suffered and the batsmen took advantage. Australia's main weapon was defused.

Reiffel blasted through to bowl Gurusinha (65), making the score line three for 148. Ranatunga waddled to the wicket with a bat twirl and a few comments. The Australians were on their toes. They wanted him out early as much as they had ever wanted to see the backs of Lara or Tendulkar.

Warne tried everything he knew to secure the wicket, even the flipper. It slipped out short and off-line. Ranatunga smashed it for six. Warne rubbed the back of his neck and looked up the wicket to see what the cameras had captured for the 800 million watching on TV—a cheeky tongue poked out at him.

Warne (none for 58 off ten) grimaced, yet could do nothing to stop the haemorrhaging of runs that stopped at 46.2 overs and the score of three for 245. Sri Lanka had won by seven wickets.

The favourites had been crushed. Yet they didn't blame the umpires or sneer at the opposition. Instead, they shook hands with their grinning conquerors. They then returned to the dressing room and the hotel to savour defeat and the inevitable what-might-have-beens.

The loss had to be viewed in the context of a magnificent eighteen-month run for this sterling combination, which had taken all before it in one-dayers and Tests. Even then, it had made the final ahead of ten other international teams in the World Cup. The question was whether it could learn from such a defeat and create a side that would go one better in England in 1999. Australian cricket's continual rise since the low point of 1986–87 suggested it would.

Yet there was much cricket and many hurdles to get over before that. Warne, in particular, had another more immediate problem that threatened to finish his career prematurely.

A Winter of Discontent

Warne returned to Melbourne with the possibility of surgery on his shoulder and/or his finger. He couldn't make a decision, realising that either operation could reduce his capacities and end his career. He took off for the United States with Simone on a holiday that included a visit to the US Masters, and consulted medical specialists in Los Angeles about his injuries.

The shoulder specialist suggested surgery and warned him it would have to come sooner or later. Why not have it now? Warne was not convinced. For one thing, he felt he could carry on with physical management and physio treatment for up to two years. He ignored the advice and heeded his own counsel. After all, it was his body and his career.

The LA finger specialist had a good look, took into account that Warne could still bowl, albeit it at a reduced skill level, and recommended he rest the offending digit for four months over winter and see how it came up. This was tempting, but avoided Warne's own feeling that sooner rather than later he would not be able to bowl a leg break at all. He felt this was possible inside a year—before the Ashes trip in 1997.

He inquired about the recuperation period if he opted for the knife and was told it would be two to three months, with added time for physio work on the finger after it had healed. That would take him through to August or September and the beginning of the Australian cricket summer. He would miss a tour to Sri Lanka for a one-day tournament in August. He hoped to be fit for a second tour for one Test and the Titan Cup one-day competition in India in October.

Yet missing both tours was a small price to pay—*if* the operation was a success. The big 'if' played on the star's mind, but he had always been one for facing reality. If he played on, he would be finished as a player far earlier—perhaps in eight years—than he would expect. If he had the operation and it failed, he would be finished as a cricketer a few months earlier than if he did not have it.

Cold logic dictated the knife from surgeon Greg Hoy at a private sports clinic. The operation took place on 21 May 1996, the same day that knives of a different sort had found their way into the back of Dean Jones as Victoria's state cricket captain. He was dumped in favour of Warne.

The fickle finger of fate was pointed at Warne. He was being handed one of his greatest dreams—the captaincy of his state—on the day that surgery could take the dream away just as fast as it had been given.

Dr Hoy felt the operation had been successful technically, from his professional point of view as a surgeon. The finger would function normally again. But whether it had succeeded from the professional cricketer's view was another matter.

Warne's rehabilitation included several physio treatments a week and seemed to be going well. As the winter months slipped by and the home cricket season of 1996–97 loomed, Warne began to prepare himself psychologically. He needed to muster no greater incentive than the thought of the West Indies coming for a series of five Tests. Warne wished to be part of an Australian team that aimed to prove its two–one win in the Caribbean early in 1995 was no fluke, but a true measure of superiority.

13

Windies Again

Finger Faults

Warne's finger responded slowly to treatment because of the build-up of stiff scar tissue and he was forced to miss the tour of India in October, which disappointed him. It was the first Test he had missed since being dropped for the first match of the 1992–93 series against the West Indies. It also hurt because the pitches would suit him. He had something to prove against the Indians since his initial game against them in January 1992.

Warne had to remain in Melbourne and continue his finger treatment, following the tour from reports in the papers. It was a frustrating and depressing time. Hoy reassured him that the stiffness of the scar tissue was an excellent sign. The finger would be better for it in the long run. Warne passed this on to the media and the countless fans and acquaintances who inquired about the troublesome digit until it drove him to distraction.

'It's taking a little bit longer,' he told *Australian Cricket* magazine, 'but they say it's a good thing as it's healing nice and strong. Hopefully, it'll last longer.'

Notwithstanding this optimistic prognosis, however, the finger remained puffy despite massaging it regularly with ultra-soft Plasticine.

The media picked up on this and the general uncertainty surrounding his recovery. The questions they put to him reflected the fact that they were preparing the fans for an Australian team without Warne. He was asked if he would be forced to bowl fewer overs in the summer.

'I hope not,' Warne replied. 'I'm hoping to have a good year. I want to be part of the Australian side again. Otherwise, I don't know what I'm doing all this training for.'

The words 'hope' and 'want' alerted observers. Nowhere was Warne saying 'I expect' or 'I will' with his usual frankness. In the back of his mind was the feeling that if he didn't come up as the old Shane Warne, or if he were forced to put away his big, ripping leg break forever, then he would give the game away. Period.

In practice sessions at the beginning of the 1996–97 season in late September, the stiff and puffy finger made Warne uncertain how to bowl. He agreed to play in a club game for St Kilda, but was still unsure how to let the ball leave his hand. If he bowled a flipper, there was too much stress. The huge breakers were not even considered. He didn't know what would happen if he tried to deliver a wrong 'un. He was all over the place in the match and was smashed around the park. His confidence had been down, but this put it at rock bottom. In early October 1996, the career of Shane Warne, champion Test bowler with 207 wickets, was in the balance.

His ambition to lead the Bushrangers, as the Victorian state team had now styled itself, saw him suppress his doubts about his fitness and take the field as skipper for the first time in a one-day game against South Australia. This was a better performance, but the ball was still not coming out the way he wanted it to. He was still worried about the soreness and stiffness. He took only one wicket, albeit a good one in Jamie Siddons, who charged him, missed and was stumped. He didn't take the hammering he had in the club game, yet he was dispirited by his effort. If ever a sportsman was doing everything to come back after injury and surgery it was Shane Keith Warne. He was bursting to do well by his standards. It was not yet coming off.

Then came a breakthrough. The venue was the Optus Oval, Carlton, on 27 October, in a one-dayer against Tasmania. Warne won the toss and batted. Dean Jones (100 not out) set up a good score of four for 250, which would be competitive against Tasmania's strong batting line-up led by David Boon. Warne had a serious challenge on his hands and rose to the occasion. He took five for 35, his best-ever limited-overs effort and held three catches as his team dismissed Tasmania for 192.

Suddenly, that most vital of factors in a sportsperson's make-up, self-confidence, was back. He had won one as state skipper and he had bowled with more control, despite the lack of turn and dip. He had managed to retrieve some basic 'form', but some questions still remained. How would he fare in a four-day Shield game, where he would be required to bowl far more than the standard one-day ten overs?

While Warne was pondering this, Australia had performed poorly in India, after a bad one-day tour of Sri Lanka. It lost the one-off Test and all the one-dayers. Taylor stated frankly in his book, *A Captain's Year*, how he and his team felt about Warne not being with them in India. The skipper noted their dependence on him as a bowler, character and team-man:

> *We missed Warnie a great deal... He brings so many pluses to a tour—on and off the field. He's a funny bloke to have around the change room—a lifter of spirits—and he's a big wicket-taker out in the middle. The conditions in Delhi [for the Test] would have been to his liking—that dusty, turning wicket on which he would have got bounce and bite. Our two spinners, Bradley Hogg and Peter McIntyre, did their utmost to fill the gap, despite their relative inexperience at that level... neither is at Shane Warne standard at this stage. Who is? Because of their slower pace through the air and off*

> *the wicket, neither applied the sort of pressure that India's Kumble, Joshi and Kapoor were able to maintain as they fizzed the ball through.*
>
> *Ian Healy especially missed Shane Warne throughout the campaign. The pair of them seem to have been a double act for some time—Heals taking the catches, making the stumpings, cajoling… encouraging… the Australian cricket team is a lesser entity without Shane Warne, whether it's in Bombay, Brisbane or Birmingham.*

Meanwhile, back in Brighton, Victoria, the finger was becoming less puffy, and Warne was learning to live with the stiffness, especially as his line and length were improving with every stint at the crease. Twelve days after his five-wicket haul against Tasmania, he travelled to Sydney for the biggest test of his recovery yet—a Shield game against a full-strength New South Wales team in Sydney. Warne wondered if his finger would stand the strain, but was lifted again by getting through forty-five overs in two innings and overcoming the throbbing pain. There still wasn't the old Warne turn or dip, which needed extra pressure on shoulder and hand, but he was on-line most of the time and was able to bowl an eight-over spell. Captain Warne was gaining confidence every session with his star spinner. He was also not unhappy with his team's effort and his own leadership. In a tight game, Victoria had gone down by 58 runs.

Four days after this, beginning on 15 November, Warne was on the MCG in another Shield game, against South Australia. He took three for 25 in South Australia's first innings and had another long stint bowling in the second as Victoria won its first Shield game under its new captain.

The finger had now stood up to several strenuous match sessions in the space of just ten days. Warne felt in his heart that he was ready to return to the Test scene, although he was honest about still being a little tentative and was not yet fully confident. However, he convinced Errol Alcott, new Test team coach Geoff Marsh and chairman of selectors Trevor Hohns that he would be right for the First Test against the West Indies beginning on 22 November at Brisbane.

Gabba Comeback

The Brisbane wicket looked flat yet grassy and Australia was not surprised to be sent in first by West Indies captain Courtney Walsh. This was when a new player, the 25-year-old Victorian opening bat Matthew Elliott, had an attack of nerves in the dressing room, a problem that afflicted most top batsmen, and not just in their first Test innings. He turned to Warne, who had given up a single room to be with him on Test eve, and said:

'Jeez, I thought I was going really well but now my legs won't stop shaking.'

'You'll be right, mate,' Warne assured him. 'Everyone feels like that before the first big one.'

Elliott carried his jitters to the middle and looked frozen in facing a few deliveries until he was given out caught behind for a duck off Ambrose from a ball that touched his shirt, not his bat. Perhaps the umpire had taken pity on him. Taylor and Ponting recovered the situation by lunch at one for 82, with Ponting crashing his way to 88—including one mighty six off Kenny Benjamin—before being caught hooking. Taylor (43) was bowled by Walsh and Australia was three for 146. Fifty runs later, at 196, Mark Waugh (38) was caught behind, also off Walsh, who then removed Bevan caught for a golden duck. Walsh was having an inspired start to the series and Australia was reeling with half the side out. However, Steve Waugh (48 not out) and Healy (47 not out) rattled the score up to a healthy-looking five for 282 at stumps on day one.

The next day Healy lost Waugh for 66, but soon went on to his third Test century while Reiffel (20) and Warne (24) stayed with him for about an hour each, taking the score well into

400s. Eventually, he ran out of partners at 479 with his score on 161 not out, in what was arguably the most accomplished innings ever by an Australian keeper.

The Windies batted in the final session to be two for 61 at stumps, with Lara looking dangerous on 19 not out and Hooper 4 not out. But next morning McGrath picked up Lara for 26 with the total at 77, and the Windies were in deep trouble.

Hooper was then joined by the tenacious Shivnarine Chanderpaul for a 172-run recovery, during which Warne was put through a stiff test. He turned the ball little and looked steady but, for him, innocuous. Neither batsman was able to dominate him, but nor could he make an impression on them as they rolled on past tea and well into the last session. Then just after Hooper reached his century, Steve Waugh had him caught at leg slip by Ponting. Chanderpaul (82) was snaffled close to the wicket by Mark Waugh off Reiffel, making it five for 255.

Adams went soon after for a duck and Reiffel and Warne swarmed all over the vulnerable tail. Warne, restricted to top-spinners and just rolling out the leg break with no extreme or quick spin, had to be content with straighter deliveries, capturing both Bishop (0) and Benjamin (9) lbw. He helped wrap up the Windies' innings at 277, 3 runs short of avoiding the follow-on. His figures at one point read none for 80, but he went into the sheds with a more respectable two for 88 off twenty-seven overs, with three maidens. He had at least justified his selection. He and the team selectors knew that only by bowling at this level could he restore himself fully to its standards. Those figures showed he was on the way. Warne had been neither penetrating nor threatening, but he had been economical.

Taylor decided not to enforce the follow-on as he wanted the Windies to face Warne on the last day. Australia went to stumps at none for 8 and the next morning Elliott mastered his nerves in a stubborn 98-minute stay for 21. Taylor (36), Mark Waugh (57) and Healy (45 not out) pushed the second innings to six for 217 before Taylor declared, leaving the Windies 420 to get from 120 overs. At stumps on day four, the tourists were one for 89, with Warne managing to catch the edge of Samuels's bat. The ball flew to Taylor at slip.

The next morning, day five, after Reiffel had got rid of Lara for 44, Taylor introduced both his spinners, Warne and Bevan, and it was apparent that Bevan's left-arm wrist-breaks were turning well. He had Hooper (23) caught behind. Then McGrath returned and bowled Chanderpaul (14).

Adams (2) pushed forward at Warne after being beaten several times and was trapped in front, leg before. There seemed little doubt his leg was *before* the wicket, but there were questions about how far forward he was. It was one that could have gone either way, depending on the umpire's mood and method. This time it went against Adams.

Warne still seemed to be just bringing the ball out, rather than propelling it, and it was reflected in his figures of two for 92. The good news was that he stood up well to a stock-bowling effort of forty-one overs, with sixteen maidens. But where Warne waned, Bevan boomed, breaking his chinamen and wrong 'uns prodigiously. He assisted McGrath (four for 60) in dismissing the tail as the West Indies were all out for 296, the opener Campbell top-scoring with 113. Bevan's figures were a more than commendable three for 46.

Taylor had the luxury of two effective spinners in winning this Brisbane Test by 123 with fifty-three minutes to spare, whereas in the corresponding Test against the Windies in 1992–93, Border did not and the Windies had hung on for a draw when Australia should have won. Warne was brought back for the next Test that season and was never left out when fit again.

Old Warne, Reborn

Warne wasn't happy with his form in Brisbane. He couldn't comprehend why he had not been able to bowl at his top form. He sought help and it came from former Test leg-spinner Terry Jenner, a good coach who had the knack of being able to cut straight to the heart of a bowler's problem. He had watched Warne on TV and noticed a few faults, which they worked on together in the nets in Sydney two days before the Second Test. Jenner thought Warne was tentative and bowling too many loose balls. He knew 'the finger' was causing Warne psychological problems. He did not have the confidence to propel the ball, rather than just push it out of his hand. Warne didn't know how to correct this.

With a few journalists and a small crowd watching, Jenner asked Warne to bowl to him without a run-up. With forward steps and body momentum, Warne was forced to use his shoulder and hand to thrust the ball with greater force. Soon his hand became more of the source of power required to launch the ball.

When he later bowled in the nets with his normal run-up, his old zip returned. He had more confidence in his spinning finger. The ball began to dip in the air. Warne started spinning it back with a bit of fire. He could not wait to bowl in the middle.

Two days later, on 29 November, Jenner retired to the grandstand to commentate on ABC radio as Taylor won the toss and batted on a dry, bare Sydney strip. Elliott continued his progress and looked the goods in his 78-minute stay, hitting 5 fours in his 29 off forty-five balls until Bishop caused him to edge one to slip. Soon after, Taylor was also caught off Bishop for 27 and Australia was two for 68. Then, just on lunch, Ponting departed for 9, leaving Australia on three for 73. After the break, Mark Waugh (19) never got going, though Bevan lasted more than two hours for 16 before Benjamin had him caught.

Just after tea, Australia was five for 131. Blewett, who had come back into the Australian team for this Test when Steve Waugh's dicey groin kept him out, went on to be 58 not out at stumps, with Healy 44 not out and the score a fair five for 229. Healy failed to add to his score next morning, however, and Blewett, too, was soon dismissed for 69, placing Australia on six for 245.

Warne, batting at eight, enjoyed the responsibility of lifting Australia's tally without applying his pinch-hitter methods as he and Queenslander Michael Kasprowicz added a valuable 38. Kasprowicz was next to go, followed by Warne (28), who was ninth out at 288. He had batted well, demonstrating his capacity for 20 or 30 when he put his mind to it. That Test century still eluded him and looked further away than two years ago. Yet he had shown that, after five years of top cricket, he could deliver a rear-guard performance to save a Test, and had done so several times. The grit and defensive skills were there, while he had the strokes, temperament and powers of concentration to deliver a hundred. All it needed was for the planets to align the right way and Warne would do it.

The lanky South Australian quick Jason Gillespie, in his First Test, and team bunny McGrath amazed everyone, including themselves—especially so, in McGrath's case, as he reached his highest score of 24—by combining in a seventy-minute last-wicket stand of 43. Australia's innings ended at 331—50 more than the Windies would have been entitled to think was a likely score.

Campbell and Samuels began as if the Windies thought that 331 was surpassable before McGrath broke through at 92 and had Samuels lbw for 35. McGrath immediately went up a notch and got one through Lara (2) for an edge to Healy. Campbell, the mainstay in Brisbane, was then bowled for 77. The Windies were three for 156 at stumps, with Hooper on 27 not out and Chanderpaul 3.

Warne had bowled well during the second afternoon. Commentators noted he was achieving more turn and had delivered just one bad ball in a spell. Jenner, speaking on the ABC, predicted Warne would have an impact on the game.

Taylor opened with him on the morning of the third day. He soon manoeuvred Hooper into error and had him lbw without addition to his overnight score. Chanderpaul and Adams (30) resisted well until McGrath dismissed Adams, followed by Browne for a duck. Bishop held up the tail for a well-compiled 48, and was last man out when he misjudged Warne's flight for a catch to Elliott. Gillespie picked up his first Test wickets by bowling Ambrose and Benjamin.

The Windies reached 304. McGrath bowled with fire for his four for 82, while Warne returned to something like his old self with three for 62 off 35.2 overs, which included thirteen maidens, reflecting his hold on the batsmen and his accuracy. He had bowled perhaps three bad balls in a sustained spell. Terry Jenner's diagnosis of his bowling problems had proved more than helpful. Warne seemed confident. There was more bounce in his step and movement, and spin in his well-flighted deliveries. What's more, he was having an influence in a Test, rather than being a player making up the numbers.

Australia batted again after tea on day three and again lost Taylor (16) and Ponting (4) cheaply, both to Bishop, to go to stumps at two for 77—104 runs on with eight wickets in hand.

The next morning would be remembered for a disastrous accident when Elliott and Mark Waugh collided in mid-pitch going for a second run. Elliott had to be taken from the ground on the drinks cart, retired hurt for 78 after suffering torn knee ligaments which would put him out of action for the rest of the series. Waugh batted into the afternoon for 67, after which Bevan (52), Blewett (47 not out) and Healy (22 not out) enhanced the score to four for 312 before Taylor declared, giving Australia a lead of 339.

The Windies negotiated the last forty minutes before stumps without loss. The score of none for 29 and target of 311 to win from ninety overs at around 3.3 on over had many people speculating that the visitors could take it next day—if Lara struck form. But it was McGrath who struck first when he removed Campbell lbw for 15 and, next over, Warne had Samuels, also lbw. Then came one of the most sensational incidents of the series.

Lara had only been in for a couple of overs when he got a nick off McGrath, which fell low into a jubilant Healy's gloves. English umpire David Shepherd was unsighted. He asked his Australian colleague Darrell Hair if the ball had carried. Hair indicated that it had. Lara (2) was out and the score-sheet read three for 35. TV replays were inconclusive, although it seemed that the ball had carried. The disgruntled Lara, harbouring a deeper grievance caused by his failure in the series so far, reluctantly left the field and stormed into the Australian dressing room to announce to team manager Ian McDonald and coach Geoff Marsh: 'Ian Healy is no longer welcome in our dressing room. I think you're all cheats!'

Back on the field, Chanderpaul was playing the best innings of his short career for the West Indies, cutting and driving everyone. He was severe on Warne as he carved a brilliant 71, including 10 fours in just sixty-eight balls in the pre-lunch session. Taylor persisted with Warne, despite the hammering, which threatened to turn the game as the Windies reached three for 152 with two balls until lunch. At that moment, they had 188 to get in sixty overs, with seven wickets in hand. Hooper was playing a good support role.

Warne had been shredded so badly that it wouldn't have mattered if he bowled a bouncer. He couldn't do any worse against this left-hander, who was wreaking such havoc on the Australian attack. There was nothing for it but to go for broke. He was bowling round the wicket. He stepped up to the crease and catapulted the ball hard and straight down the wicket towards the rough outside the left-hander's off stump.

Remembering his lesson from Jenner in the nets, he let his fingers make all the running and corkscrewed the ball from his hand, imparting a mighty spin on it. The ball hit the deck in the middle of the rough, bit and spun back a metre at an angle of about 60 degrees. Chanderpaul scrambled his feet desperately to try to keep it out with bat and pads, but had no chance as the ball crashed past him. He looked round in disbelief to see his off stump tipping back and the bails go flying as Healy yelled in glee.

That Ball to Mike Gatting in the First Test of the 1993 Ashes had a psychological impact for the rest of the series. The one that bowled Graham Gooch round his legs at Edgbaston in the Fifth Test of the same series confirmed Warne's genius and gave Australia a big boost in the game.

But this ball to Chanderpaul turned a contest. One moment, the Windies were on their way to an historic victory. The next, they were dumbstruck by the sheer magical force of that one delivery. No West Indian bat in history could have done better in that awesome hour before lunch than young Shivnarine Chanderpaul, and yet Warne had managed to wipe out his performance in one masterstroke. It ranked in impact with the mighty flipper with which he bowled Richie Richardson in the Second Test in 1992–93. It was one of Warne's greatest deliveries at a critical moment and meant the Australians were the ones to go to the break with the momentum and mind to win it from there.

McGrath came out after lunch determined to steal the show by having the hapless Adams caught by Blewett for 5, leaving the Windies five for 157. Then Bevan tricked Hooper (57) with a wrong 'un. The ball clipped Healy's leg and flew to Taylor, who fell trying to grab it. He ended up like a turtle on its back juggling the ball with hands and a foot, which kicked it up to his hands again for a catch.

It was the sort of effort not long after the Chanderpaul dismissal that electrified the whole Australian outfit. Bishop (0) was run out and then Bevan bowled Ambrose. Warne then swooped in and improved his figures, having Taylor catch Benjamin (4) and McGrath catch Walsh (18).

Browne remained 25 not out as the West Indies lost its last six for 63, collapsing for a tally of 215. Australia had won by 124 runs, one more than at Brisbane.

Warne looked up at the scoreboard to note his analysis of four for 95 off 27.4 overs. He still managed six maidens outside of the Chanderpaul onslaught. McGrath took three for 36 (seven for 118 for the match) and was adjudged Man of the Match, which would have been a close decision ahead of Warne's effort of seven for 160. Warne now had taken 218 Test wickets at 23.89 in forty-six Tests. Bevan's two for 40 in the second was a strong back-up to Warne and gave Taylor an option with spin.

Australia led two–nil in the series. It was in the prime position to win the competition in Melbourne at the Boxing Day Test.

The Windies' Fightback

Curtly Ambrose had reached the lowest ebb in his great career, taking just two wickets for 279 in the first two Tests. He had the one-dayers in December to sharpen up and he worked up a sweat in the nets fine-tuning his line and length. By Christmas, this laconic loner reacted to media comment that he was on the decline as a speed force, claiming he was back to his best and boasting that he would take ten wickets in the game.

Ambrose was pleased to see Junior Murray return as keeper in place of the athletic yet erratic Courtney Browne, who was likely to drop the easy ones and swallow those considered nigh impossible. Australia brought back Steve Waugh, Paul Reiffel and Matthew Hayden in place of Bevan (twelfth man), Kasprowicz and the injured Elliott.

Taylor won the toss and batted on what he thought was a good wicket. It was, for fast bowlers. It had plenty of unpredictable bounce, which was just right for Ambrose, who worked up great pace and fine rhythm in the first hour, bowling Taylor (5), having Hayden caught by Hooper and trapping Mark Waugh lbw for a golden duck.

The run-out of Langer (12) saw Australia four for 27. Ambrose's figures at that point were three for 5 off eight overs. It was not the start most of the 72 821 fans would like to have witnessed as the biggest Boxing Day crowd since 1975. In that game, a much happier 85 661 turned up to see Lillee (four for 56) and Thomson (five for 62) roll a strong Windies line-up for 224.

Steve Waugh (58) and Blewett (62 run out) restored the innings with a 102-run partnership before Bishop moved one through Waugh for a catch behind. Healy batted with confidence for an hour for 36, before becoming Ambrose's fourth victim. Warne managed 10 and showed promise until

Bishop had him caught by Campbell, and McGrath was caught by Hooper off Ambrose from his batting helmet grille for nought. Australia luckily reached 219.

McGrath opened as if trying to show that he was faster than Ambrose by bowling a fearful bouncer at Campbell. Two balls later he had him lbw for 7 at 12. The Windies were one for 29 at stumps, with Samuels on a shaky 10 not out and Chanderpaul 11.

Despite some hostile bowling by Gillespie until he went off injured, the partnership looked promising until Warne found an edge from Samuels (17) to Taylor, making the Windies two for 62 and bringing Lara to the wicket. There was much feeling between the Australians and the champion since his petulant outburst in Sydney, for which he had yet to apologise. Team manager, Clive Lloyd, had apologised to coach Geoff Marsh and captain Taylor. But the team wanted a direct apology from Lara to Healy.

It was not forthcoming. Until it was, Lara would be open to the obvious sledge about his sportsmanship. It did not come in 'direct' words to him in the field. Yet 'asides' within earshot would refer to it, and get under his skin. It made the batsman extra determined to make the Australians suffer. This was not the wicket to do it on, nor the attack that would wither easily.

Lara scratched around for twenty minutes against McGrath and Warne. The speedster appeared to go up a gear, cramping the left-hander round the wicket and tempting him to be himself and stroke his way out of a trough. McGrath's tactics were fairly easy to comprehend. He bowled three dead straight and then one that lifted outside the off stump. Lara fell for the trap, one of the most tried and tested in all cricket, and steered it to Warne at about a fourth slip position. He held it and broke into a wide grin of satisfaction. Warne would like to have taken the wicket as the bowler, but holding one was pleasing, especially from this number-one Windies scalp.

McGrath had now dismissed him four times in five innings and six times in seven Tests. He still had another chance in the second innings. The Lara-versus-Warne title fight for the second series had become Lara versus McGrath, who was making his name at the expense of this great batsman. The pressure of the two Australians, often bowling in tandem at him, was proving too much and so assisted the home team towards a series win.

McGrath's efforts didn't end with Lara, as he caught-and-bowled Chanderpaul for 58 and ran out Hooper for 7. Adams (74 not out) sustained one end, while Junior Murray (53) hoicked his way to 53 until McGrath came back with the new ball to have him caught and then trap Bishop (0) lbw. This paved the way for Warne to bowl Ambrose (8) and have Walsh (14) caught by Mark Waugh to end the Windies' effort at 255, early on day three.

McGrath took five for 50 off thirty overs, with eleven maidens, in a top performance of sustained speed. Warne was serviceable and unlucky not to have a couple of lbw decisions go his way. He returned three for 72 off 28.1 overs, with three maidens.

Australia began disastrously in front of the big Saturday crowd, losing Hayden and Langer for ducks to Ambrose in the first three overs. Taylor (10) and Mark Waugh (19) showed some pluck against the dangerous bounce but were no match on the day for the speed generated as Walsh put them both back in the pavilion by the time the score was 47. It was five for 64 when Walsh had Blewett (7) caught behind. One run later, Healy was bowled by Benjamin for a duck.

There was now some doubt about Australia reaching a hundred, but a mini-stand between Waugh and Warne took the score to 107, when Benjamin broke through and bowled Waugh (37). Shortly afterwards, Warne surrendered to Ambrose, caught by Adams, for a bright 18 off twenty-eight balls. Australia was all out at 122 after 45.5 overs. Ambrose took four for 17 to give him nine (not his predicted ten) for 72 for the game. He was well supported by Benjamin with three for 34 and Walsh with three for 41.

The Windies managed the 87 to win, but not before a pronounced stutter caused by McGrath, who dismissed

Campbell (0) with his fourth ball caught in the slips, Samuels (13) leg before and then the big one of Lara, yet again, caught from a lifter outside off stump for 2. This was now McGrath's fifth dismissal of Lara in six innings. Reiffel bowled Chanderpaul for 40 as Hooper saw the tourists home for a comfortable six-wicket win.

If McGrath had had more runs to play with, he may have challenged Ambrose for the Man of the Match. But he had to be content with three for 41 and a tally of eight for 91 for the game.

Australia now led two–one with two Tests to play. The history of Windies' fightbacks in their long pre-1995 reign indicated that the series was very much alive as the teams headed for the Fourth Test in Adelaide.

One-Day Success in a Failed Side

Before the Adelaide Test began, however, towards the end of January, Australia had been eliminated from the CUB one-day international series against the West Indies and Pakistan. Warne's performances in that series were one of the few success stories in a side that failed to make the finals for the first time since the competition's inception in 1979–80. Warne took the most wickets of any player involved—seventeen at 17.10—despite taking part in only six games when others such Curtly Ambrose and Pakistan's Wasim Akram appeared in ten.

Warne's form was good from the first game against the West Indies at the MCG on 6 December 1996 in front of 42 442 fans, when he took two for 34 from ten overs and collected his one hundredth one-day international wicket, the fifth Australian to reach that landmark, as Australia won easily by five wickets.

Australia's next game was against the Windies at the SCG on 8 December, in front of another bumper crowd of 35 860. Warne showed the cricket world how well he had recovered from his finger surgery by taking his best short-game international figures of five for 33. This fine effort gained him the Man of the Match award. All his wickets were taken in a devastating fifteen-ball spell in which he wove his web of spin around a panicky group of batsmen, who had little idea of how to play him in such circumstances. Some tried it from the crease and were bowled or caught, while others attempted to charge him and were trapped out of their ground. Their main problem was that—except for Lara and Hooper—they were not reading Warne out of his hand and could not pick the kind of ball he was delivering. This meant they were watching to see which way it turned—or didn't—once it hit the pitch. This method needed a terrific 'eye' and very quick hand- and footwork, which seemed beyond them.

The Pakistanis seemed no more adept at playing Warne when they faced him at the Adelaide Oval on 12 December. He took four for 52 in restricting Pakistan to 223 in one ball fewer than the full fifty overs. This time he was more expensive, going for 5 an over as against a little more than 3 in the first two games, due to the aggression of Aamir Sohail (67), Muhammad Wasin (44) and Inzamam-ul-Haq (34).

Australia only managed 211 in response, losing by 12 runs. While the speedsters restricted them, the destroyer was young off-spinner Saqlain Mushtaq, who took five for 29 off 8.5 overs. He bowled a good length to intelligent fields, showing the capacity to drift the ball and make it drop. Only Steve Waugh, out for 57, and Michael Bevan with 30 handled him with any authority.

Two weeks later at the SCG on New Year's Day 1997, Australia batted first and could only manage 199 in 47.1 overs. Steve Waugh (42) and Blewett (33) were the batsmen among the runs, while Saqlain continued his dominance with three for 23. He was backed up by Aamir Sohail, with two for 33.

Pakistan gathered the runs in 45.3 overs, losing six wickets. Ijaz Ahmed with 58, Aamir Sohail with 52 and the dashing Shahid Afridi with 34 led the way, which was only blocked by Warne. He took four for 37 off ten overs, with one maiden. The judges were so impressed by the spinner's control and sharp turn in tying up every Pakistani bat that they awarded him the Man of the Match award ahead of Sohail.

Owing to a groin strain problem, Warne did not play in Australia's fifth game on 5 January at Brisbane against the West Indies. Despite Mark Waugh's 102 and Law's 93 in a score of four for 281, the Windies ran riot to amass three for 284 in 48.5 overs. Lara also hit 102, and Hooper 110 not out. Warne's form against them in every game and the Tests suggested he may have changed the course of this match and given the Australians victory.

However, he did turn out two days later at Bellerive Oval, Hobart, and helped put Australia into a winning position by returning two for 35 against Pakistan, while Andy Bichel managed a tight three for 17. Pakistan slumped to all out for 149 in 45.2 overs, but Australia's batsmen let the bowlers down as it collapsed to be all out for 120. Wasim Akram proved even more frugal than Bichel with three for 13.

This failure meant the home team had to win its final preliminary-round match against the Windies at the WACA ground in Perth on 12 January. Australia batted first and hit seven for 267, with Mark Waugh scoring 92 and Bevan 35. Ambrose was expensive with two for 53, while part-timer Chanderpaul collected two for 16.

The Windies replied with six for 269 in 49.2 overs. Lara belted 90 with Junior Murray (56) and Chanderpaul (49) in support. Australia seemed to have the game in its keeping when the Windies needed 66 to win from forty-two balls. Lara then turned the game around, belting Warne for two sixes in succession, and led the charge to victory. (It was one of only two occasions in the entire 1996–97 summer that Lara had the upper hand in their encounters, the other being the Fifth Test in Perth. Otherwise, Warne held sway in their titanic encounters.) Despite this blast from Lara, Warne still took the figures of two for 46, along with Tom Moody, also two for 46.

Pakistan went on to beat the Windies in the first final in Sydney by four wickets and the second in Melbourne by

62 runs, thus taking the series. Lara, with two centuries and a 90, won the Man of the Series award, while Shahid Afridi of Pakistan was named Man of the Finals.

The postmortems on Australia's poor showing began when it was eliminated. Some reassessment and restructuring was necessary after it lost five successive games in the CUB series and the previous one-day tournaments in Sri Lanka and India. The finger was pointed at Mark Taylor, who failed to score 30 in any of his eight CUB games. He had never come to grips with the short version of the game and was often not aggressive enough early in an innings. It was fashionable now to attempt 80 or 90 in the first fifteen overs, when 50 used to be the Aussie target. Taylor was better suited to the latter approach, when the team went for a slow build and big finish. He was not right for the slather-and-whack start.

There was talk in cricket circles now about the need for two distinct teams—one for Tests, the other for one-dayers. Players would be groomed as specialists for the short game. Taylor would not be the only established Test star to be left out of the new strategy. However, Shane Warne was likely to retain his place in both forms of the game. He thrived in both his ten-over spells and the longer options in Tests.

Larrikin, Leader or Both?

Warne loved playing at the MCG, his home turf, more than any other cricket ground, especially in front of a big crowd. He had missed out on making it as a footballer for St Kilda and playing in a Grand Final, his main sporting dream. This was the next best thing, made more uplifting by his popularity as a performer and character.

Warne often played up to the crowd, acknowledging 'requests' for waves and so forth from the fans, if they were good-natured. But his antics in the field in a one-day international in the 1996–97 CUB series drew some criticism from top-rating Melbourne radio personality and journalist, Neil

Mitchell. While fielding near the boundary, Warne made a jerking motion with his hand, a gesture usually taken to stand for the colloquial term 'wanker'.

Mitchell editorialised on station 3AW about Warne's behaviour and put sports commentator and former Australian Rules 'Great' Ron Barassi on the spot by asking him for his views on Warne's alleged 'yobbo' exhibitionism. Barassi refused to express an opinion as he hadn't witnessed the incident. Mitchell kept pressing Barassi, trying to elicit a comment about 'yobbo' behaviour in general.

At that point, Warne, who had been listening at home, rang in to defend himself, saying: 'I thought you were a good bloke, Ron ... Don't let him [Mitchell] put words into your mouth.'

Warne was not pleased with Mitchell and placed him on his banned list of media interviewees, along with the ABC's Tim Lane, broadcaster Derryn Hinch and former Test cricketer David Hookes. They had upset him over the incident in South Africa when he gave Andrew Hudson a vicious verbal send-off after dismissing him. Dean Jones told Mitchell that Warne had urged his Victorian state team-mates also to boycott Mitchell, but they took no notice.

The broader issue for Warne from this unwanted publicity was his new status as a state captain. His larrikin image would have to be modified if he was going to fulfil the responsibility. The problem was that his exuberant behaviour was so much part of his nature that he would have to make a special effort to restrict it.

He had always liked blending in as 'one of the boys'. However, his continued success got ahead of his personal maturity. Warne experienced the common problem of the sportsperson who goes on from school to top-level international competition. There is less chance for 'normal' development as he or she lives out of a suitcase in shared hotel rooms and spends the rest of their time in locker rooms or grandstands for a decade or two, often cocooned as 'stars' and insulated from the real world.

Warne's behaviour problems were complicated by his innate leadership skills. Not only was he an unselfish, strong team man. His ability to rise to the big occasion and often win matches by his own efforts had developed the raw leadership qualities that had been apparent since his school days.

The nearest equivalent to Warne would be former Australian captain Ian Chappell. They both were portrayed as larrikins, whether justifiably or not. This was part of their popular appeal in Australia, where most people seem prepared to accept boorish behaviour by prominent public figures from political leaders to sports stars.

Chappell was a born leader with a fierce determination to win who liked being 'one of the boys', when the image of touring Australians in the 1970s—justified or not—was that of beer-guzzling, profane yobbos. The difference is that Chappell took over as Australian captain at a comparatively young twenty-four years of age, while Warne was somewhat older when he assumed the responsibilities of captaincy at a senior level.

Warne was fortunate to take the Victorian top job when he did, at the age of twenty-six. It gave him useful experience should he ever aspire to go higher (and from all he has said, he does).

But captaining a state was low profile and undemanding in comparison to leading the national team, the most prestigious and scrutinised sports job in Australia. If he wished to impress the ACB enough to influence it to make him Australian captain after Taylor and Steve Waugh, there could be no more jerking of the hand, wiggling of the *derrière* on pavilion balconies after victories, abuse of opposition players, or sledging of batsmen. Modification of his behaviour whenever in public view, however galling for him, would be essential.

Warne's choice of direction would depend on how much he wanted the country's number-one sporting job, which had made demands on the character of every leader up to Mark Taylor, Don Bradman included.

Lara's Folly

Jason Gillespie's side strain did not improve enough in the month following the Melbourne game and he was left out of the Adelaide Test beginning on 25 January 1997, as was Reiffel, who was named twelfth man. In came the 26-year-old Queensland paceman Andy Bichel. The inclusion of Bevan, regarded as a genuine all-rounder, gave Australia a different look, with two quicks, two spinners and seven specialist batsmen. The Windies brought in 25-year-old Barbados opening bat Adrian Griffith, who replaced Robert Samuels. Ambrose had strained a hamstring in the one-dayers and Kenny Benjamin had already flown home with a side strain. Their places were filled by Patterson Thompson and Cameron Cuffy.

The Adelaide wicket was flat with a tinge of grass and Taylor was disappointed to lose the toss and bowl. Not too long into the morning he had changed his mind. McGrath had Campbell caught edging an outswinger behind for a duck, and new man Griffith was leg before to equally new man Bichel, leaving the Windies on two for 22.

Taylor took advice from local spectators and brought Warne on early to try out the Adelaide wicket, which was said to be more conducive to spin than speed in recent seasons. Lara had been at the wicket for forty minutes, batting with caution, but no trouble, against McGrath for the first time in the series.

Warne spent an inordinate amount of time setting the field and busying himself for his first over to Lara, who looked agitated by the wait. His friendship with Warne had waned and was at breaking point after the Healy incident in the Sydney Test two months earlier. It was obvious he wanted to assert himself from the first ball. He tapped the crease with more vigour than usual, as if he had made up his mind about how he was going to deal with the first ball no matter how it came to him. As it happened, it was well up and on the stumps. Lara launched into it, hitting it straight to Blewett at mid-on for a regulation catch. Warne was amazed at this woeful effort, which even tail-enders Walsh and Ambrose would disdain. He clapped Lara as he departed the scene, an action that would be sure to upset the little star even more.

This adolescent indiscretion by a batting master sent shock waves through the Windies camp. Just when it needed a dedicated performance from him, Lara had thrown his wicket away to leave the Windies reeling at three for 45. It seemed to upset Chanderpaul, who was doing a degree of shuffling of pads and feet to counter Warne and remain at the wicket now that more responsibility had fallen on his shoulders. He misjudged one too many and edged to Taylor who held a reflex grab. The score was four for 58.

Hooper came out blazing like a one-day slogger and cracked a quick 17 before pushing one to Mark Waugh off McGrath, leaving the Windies five for 72. The Australians were jubilant and looking for a quick kill, unable to believe their good fortune on the first morning of a Test on a very good batting wicket.

Only the defiant but out-of-touch Adams, Junior Murray and the tail stood between Australia and a complete crushing of the Windies by mid-afternoon. Warne elicited a caught-and-bowled from Adams (10) after he had been at the wicket seventy-three minutes. This left just Murray, who had decided to wallop his way out of the mess. Bevan was bowling at the other end after lunch and took some stick from the keeper, but then had him caught for a pugnacious 34. Bevan bowled his chinaman and wrong 'un with pace and bite as he removed Walsh (0), Bishop (1) and Cuffy (2), all caught behind. In a 28-ball spell, he took four for 1, returning him final figures of four for 31.

The Windies' one-day effort had brought them just 130 in 47.5 overs in 195 minutes. Warne had done most to break their backbone, taking three for 42 off sixteen overs, with four maidens, supported by McGrath with two for 21 and Bevan running through the brittle tail with those impressive final figures of four for 31 off 9.5 overs.

Australia took advantage of this unexpected windfall, reaching none for 29 at tea and adding 110 for the loss of two wickets in the final session to be 139 at stumps, the out-of-form Taylor

(11) going lbw to Bishop and Langer (19) being caught behind off Cuffy. Hayden was on 66 not out and Mark Waugh 31.

They went on the next day into the second session before Mark Waugh was caught behind off Hooper for 82, while Hayden, dogged and watchful, proceeded to record his first Test century with 125. Blewett, 81 not out at stumps on day two, moved watchfully to 99 not out, but then played on to Cuffy to become the fourteenth Australian to be dismissed just one short of three-figure glory. Bevan soldiered on for 85 not out as Australia totalled 517, a mammoth lead of 387.

Taylor didn't waste much time in bringing Bevan into the attack in the Windies' second effort after McGrath had Griffith out caught for 1. The spinner justified the move by having Chanderpaul (8) caught at slip, leaving the Windies two for 22. Lara came out and started blazing away, lashing a six each off Bevan and Warne. This time he was luckier and more fruitful, but couldn't find a staying partner as Bevan had Campbell (24) caught in the slips and Warne claimed Hooper (45) lbw. Adams came in at four for 138 and lasted eight balls before Bevan had him caught close to the wicket for 0. Bishop lasted only five balls as night watchman before Warne had him caught by Bevan, leaving the Windies on a lamentable six for 154 at stumps, with Lara on 65 not out. The lead had been reduced to 233.

With four wickets in hand, it seemed the Windies would be certain to be beaten in less than four days, a big Lara innings notwithstanding. However, next morning, Lara was galled to be dismissed caught by Healy off a bottom edge from Warne for 78. The only consolation as he trudged off the field was that McGrath had not got him in either innings in this Test. But Warne dismissed him both times, which hurt Lara just as much.

Bevan again romped through the tail, taking the last three—Murray (25), Walsh (1) and Thompson (6)—to end the Windies' innings at 204. Australia had won by an innings and 183 runs, and retained the Frank Worrell Trophy. The series victory was the first against this great amalgam of small Caribbean islands and nations in Australia in twenty-two years. Bevan's whippy action earned him six for 82 off 22.4 overs with three maidens on the second innings, giving him ten for 113 for the game. This plus his 85 not out ensured his Man of the Match award.

Warne took three for 68 off twenty with four maidens, a total of seven for 110. He was competitive with Bevan for wickets and disappointed he couldn't take more, but delighted to have a spin partner of note after May's retirement. He was also thrilled to be a significant part of Australia's win for the second time in three Tests. At the critical times, he again took the big wickets. His spinning finger problem was now manageable with Alcott massaging him each night after play to ease the tension from his shoulder to his fingers.

Warne knew he was not the force he had been. He had doubts that this would return in full, but, as long as he could take five and more wickets a game, he could still be a match-winner at the top level.

No Mirth in Perth

Taylor won the toss at Perth in the so-called 'dead rubber' Fifth Test and batted in a game that had nothing hinging on it except pride. Australia had swapped Langer for Reiffel in its only change, while the Windies brought back Ambrose, Browne and Samuels to replace Thompson, the injured Murray and Griffith.

The Windies had just three fast bowlers for the first time in the series, and that was all they needed on the cracking, dry pitch as Australia slumped early to four for 59 at lunch in a heatwave. Mark Waugh and Bevan restored some shape to the innings until Ambrose had Waugh (79) in the slips for 79. They had put on 120 to make the score five for 169. Ambrose and Bishop ploughed through the tail, with only Bevan being able to resist in his best Test innings of 87 not out in just less than four hours, as Australia scrambled to 243 all out. Ambrose took five for 43 and Bishop three for 54.

The Windies kept all wickets intact in reaching 25 at stumps, but early next morning, it lost Campbell for 21 and

Chanderpaul for 3 to be two for 43. Samuels dug in at one end to let Lara have full reign. He continued where he had left off in the Adelaide Test and crashed Australia's attack to all points. As the partnership built, the fielding side began to sledge Samuels, calling him a 'loser'. Lara snapped back, protecting his junior partner, and confronted some of the Australian antagonists, primarily Warne.

Lara answered with the bat as well by banishing Bevan, the hero of Adelaide, to the deep country after five overs that yielded 31 runs. Not even Warne threatened him. The spinner bowled a tight first spell and then came back for a second, where he took time to land them on the right spot. Lara attacked and won this battle in his war with Warne, which had hotted up from intense champion rivalry to something more personal.

It was Lara's day as he slammed 22 fours in 132 off just 185 balls in a 223-minute stay. Despite this, Warne was still happy to be the bowler to remove him, caught behind. He also had Samuels (76) caught by Mark Waugh. At stumps, the Windies was seven for 353, with Hooper on 57 not out and Bishop on 5.

At that night's press conference, Lara blasted the Australian sledgers for picking on Samuels and named Warne as the ringleader.

'Australia have won the series and good luck to them,' Lara remarked, 'but they seem to be rubbing it in at this point in time. With a youngster who is trying his best and whose Test future is in a bit of doubt and he's working as hard as possible, I was a bit disappointed with the Australian approach to him.'

Lara added that the umpires intervened and 'tried to calm things down', and then went on:

'When there is an all-day sledging and stuff like that of one particular player [Samuels], it's unnecessary. When I asked one of the guys [Warne] to cool out, he said he wouldn't say anything to me, but only to "that loser" [Samuels] up there.'

The Australians were annoyed by his comments, feeling that he had broken the players' code of 'what's said on the field, stays on the field'. The unprecedented outburst portrayed

Warne as a bully-boy and poor sportsman. Since this kind of public reporting of sledging had never happened before, it isolated him as an offender when verbal ping-pong of this kind had been a part of the game at least since the mid-1970s.

Lara may have shredded the already damaged friendship between him and Warne. He finished with a warning for the Australians.

'We're going to bounce back,' he claimed. 'We've got them in two years time [early 1999 in the West Indies] and, I promise you, we'll not be losing.'

Taylor hit back at Lara at his post-match conference and the ill-feeling between the teams was further exacerbated. Matters were brought to a head the next morning on the pitch when Reiffel had Hooper (57) caught behind and then Bishop (13) caught by Taylor at slip, making the score line nine for 367.

Walsh, with Lara out on the field as his runner, and Ambrose were at the wicket. The comments were flying between Lara and fielders. Umpires Darrell Hair and Peter Willey called Walsh and Taylor to a mid-pitch conference, and ordered them to control their players or face the consequences.

Ambrose (15) was run out soon afterwards with the Windies at 384. Reiffel made a welcome return, taking five for 73, while Warne bowled his best so far at Perth in a Test, taking two for 55 off nineteen overs with eight maidens.

Australia batted again in the morning, facing a 139 deficit. It then lost eight wickets clearing it. Walsh and Ambrose were rampant in their last Tests in Australia. Only Hayden (47) stood up to the barrage of uneven bounce, which saw balls flying overhead or shooting low, with Blewett getting an absolute 'grubber', which shot along the ground and smashed into his stumps.

After Healy whacked 29 in thirty-one balls, Warne (30 from fifty-three balls in seventy-seven minutes) and Bichel (18) decided on some feisty late resistance. A frustrated Ambrose began cribbing over the mark round the wicket in order to land one on Warne. In so doing, he bowled nine no-balls in his last over before limping from the crease. It was a pathetic end to his outstanding run of successes against Australia. However, his final return was two for 50 gave him seven for 93 in the game and was good enough to earn him the Man of the Match award. Walsh dominated in the Australian second innings, taking five for 74.

Australia reached 194 and the West Indies openers soon knocked up the 56 runs required, giving it a ten-wicket win. Australia had won the series three–two and could now claim a definite ascendancy over their rivals.

Glenn McGrath took the Man of the Series award with twenty-six wickets at 17.42. Warne was not far behind him with twenty-two wickets at 27, while Reiffel, as ever, was more than a contributor with twelve at 25.41. Bevan with fifteen wickets at 17.66 and 275 runs at 55 could be considered to be unlucky not to take the Man of the Series award. Only Healy, with 356 at 59.33, was ahead of him in the batting averages for both sides. Blewett with 301 at 50.16 was the only other batsman of the series to average 50 or more.

For the Windies, Ambrose with nineteen at 23.36 was a sensation later in the series, while Bishop did well with twenty at 25.20. Walsh was expensive with nineteen wickets at 31.15, but once again effective. He blamed the West Indies' failure in the series on its batsmen.

Before the summer analysis was over, the Australians were packing their bags for a tour of South Africa. Warne was aiming to return to his blistering best against these rivals, whom he liked and admired as characters more than any other Test team. It was always an exalted feeling to do well against them.

14

Veldt Victorious

First Blood at The Wanderers

Shane Warne had trouble with his run-up in his first game on the 1997 tour of South Africa against Boland at Paarl, north of Cape Town. It was just a little thing, which showed even someone of his experience could lose touch after a few weeks lay-off. His line and length were not up to his usual perfection and he went for a few sixes against a modest batting line-up in front of a crowd of about 8000.

Yet he enjoyed the work-out, running the stiffness out of his fingers and right shoulder in the pleasant surroundings of vineyards in the Drakenstein Range. Warne and the rest of the squad were pleased to see a majority of black faces through the smoke, not from bombs or gunfire, but the locals cooking their sausage lunches. The relaxed atmosphere was a welcome change from the chilling isolation that faced the team in city hotels amid tight security, especially in places such as Johannesburg, the location of the First Test, where murder was common and violent crime rampant.

By the time the Australians lined up at the Wanderers on 28 February 1997, every player except the unfit Reiffel had managed a fair effort in the middle in at least one of the four warm-up games. The squad was fitter than any Australian tourists before it, thanks to its new trainer, the tattooed ex–Navy-man Steve Smith, a former Aussie Rules football coach from Western Australia. He ran a Perth gym and was a personal fitness adviser to leading Western Australian sportspeople.

Smith had the team doing rigorous routines of walking, running, weights, exercises and boxing to increase stamina, and sharpen and hone skills. This was all embraced by fitness fanatics in the squad such as younger members like Hayden, Blewett and Bevan, who were unabashed 'gym junkies'. The older members such as the Waugh brothers and Warne were not enamoured with the idea of pre-breakfast work-outs on tour. Yet all players began to feel the benefits after a short time. While difficult to measure, it would show in a batsman's ability to concentrate longer, stay at the wicket, run with less puff. Bowlers would find over time that their stamina allowed them to maintain a top performance for a complete spell, without tiring or tapering off after five or six overs. The benefits in the field over time would show, too.

It was a far cry from the days of Rod Marsh and David Boon in setting beer-drinking records on long flights. The drinking culture was still prevalent as an acceptable form of relaxation. Even excessive drinking bouts during major victory celebrations were not considered harmful. Yet such was the competition for places that younger players were now more diet-conscious and wary of overdoing the alcohol consumption.

Warne felt his best for the entire summer and was focused on even bigger performances than he had been against the West Indies. He also knew that the South Africans were likely to fight harder than the Caribbean squad, whose members were not yet used to their slip from the top of world cricket and the hard work needed to claw back. The difference in the Australian mentality since the last tour here under Border early in 1994 was that the unit felt confident about winning. It had established itself as the team to be beaten for the world crown.

The team—with Matthew Elliott and Jason Gillespie in for Andy Bichel and Reiffel—had the right attitude if it wished to maintain its run of series wins. It was mentally prepared when

Taylor lost the toss in the opening encounter and Australia was forced to bowl first on a good batting wicket, which would turn more as the game progressed.

McGrath, finding more lift that was decent on such a placid-looking pitch, soon had Hudson (0) and Kirsten (9) both caught by Healy, and Kallis (6) snapped up by Mark Waugh in slips. South Africa, who had never before sighted McGrath, was three for 25.

Daryll Cullinan appeared and Warne's fingers became twitchy, ready to render him his bunny once more. However, there was little chance for this encounter to test either of them, as McGrath had him out, again caught by Healy, for 27. Gillespie, working up speed to give the home team no respite, helped Healy to his fourth catch for the innings when Rhodes (22) edged one. The score line read five for 115.

While Cronje dug in at one end, taking more than half an hour to get off the mark, Bevan removed the heavy-hitting Klusener (9) caught by Taylor at slip. Shaun Pollock came out blasting in his first Test against Australia, slamming 8 fours in his 35, before Bevan caused him to hit a catch to Steve Waugh.

Bevan was managing slow turn, while Warne was tight, not letting more than 2 an over through the field. Once more, the South Africans decided they must play the spinners from the crease. Bevan was more loose, going for nearly 4 an over, but his unorthodox left-armers confused the batsmen. They had just been introduced to him and had no prepared answers. It was a new problem playing on minds in the home dressing room. The squad had Warnophobia before the game. Cullinan and Richardson tried to play him down, telling the media how ordinary a bowler he was. Now here was a different kind of spinner whom they would have no time to work out.

If that was not bad enough, the Proteas were apprehensive about the new speed attack of the tourists, which had real venom. The Indians had told the Australians that Cronje didn't like the short stuff and they tested him. He was defensive and unconvincing, but eventually got to 76 when Warne had him driving to short cover where Mark Waugh took the ball in front of his face.

South Africa was a disappointing eight for 195 at stumps. Australia did not relax the next morning, but it could not stop the tenacious keeper Richardson from accumulating 72 not out. He was well supported by Donald (21), who liked to say South Africa batted to number ten. He was Gillespie's second victim and Healy's fifth catch-behind.

Little Paul Adams marched in, all offensive mouth at Warne and McGrath. He pulled faces and poked his tongue out. It didn't impress his opponents.

'Listen, champ,' Mark Waugh said to him, 'you better be able to bowl.'

McGrath let go a vicious bouncer that slammed into his helmet. It didn't shut him up and he annoyed the fielding side more by partnering Richardson in a last-wicket stand of 49. He tried the reverse sweep against Warne, a shot that had been discarded as too tough and dangerous by the world's best bats. Warne finally trapped him leg before for 15, ending the South African innings at 302, a sobering score for the Australians. They had visions of being in shortly after play resumed, chasing not many more than 200.

McGrath continued his role of number-one striker, taking four for 77. He had steady back-up from Gillespie with two for 66, Bevan two for 64 and Warne two for 68 off 27.4 overs, with nine maidens.

Taylor's sorry run continued with a bit of bad luck when, on 16, he played an ordinary Pollock delivery on to his stumps. Elliott came out to join Hayden and looked as if he were making up time for his ten-week enforced lay-off. He lost Hayden (40) caught off Pollock along the way at 115 while crashing 85, including a hooked six off Donald, who eventually had him caught by Adams. The Australian dressing room was stirred by his powerful hitting and it set a pattern, not so much of pace, but of determination to accumulate and do well.

Mark Waugh, batting as usual at four, looked good for a

while and no bowler troubled him until, on 26, he played a low, wide ball from Donald which hit the bottom of the bat and went through to keeper Richardson. This brought Blewett to the wicket, with the score at four for 179. Steve Waugh was already in and conscious that he was due for a big hundred. He had failed to reach three figures against the Windies, even though his form was always fair to good.

Rain robbed Australia of the last session, leaving the score at four for 191. Blewett and Waugh were slow early on when they resumed next morning, but did not hesitate to despatch any bad balls. Blewett was not tempted to blast his way out of trouble, thanks to the calming words of Steve Waugh, who kept telling the young South Australian that, if he kept his head down, he could make a big score on the friendly wicket.

Blewett's confidence accordingly grew and grew as he began to play his shots freely, as he and Waugh batted through the first two sessions without the South Africans being able to make any impression upon them.

Late in the afternoon, as the partnership reached 300, statisticians began reaching for the record books. The big one was the sixth-wicket stand of 405 in the Ashes series of 1946–47 between Bradman and Sid Barnes. At stumps, the score had climbed to four for 479, with Blewett on a fine 156 not out and Steve Waugh on 130 not out. The partnership had continued through a complete day—a rare event in any form of cricket, let alone Tests. Geoff Marsh and Taylor had done it last, in a 1989 Ashes Test.

The Waugh–Blewett stand was worth 305, just 100 short of the record. Australia was 177 ahead and in control of the game. South Africa, to its credit, had kept up the pressure without wilting. Their fielding never slackened off the way the West Indies' did when up against it. If anything, the Proteas saved 50 to 60 runs in a day of efficient, tidy and, at times, brilliant outfielding.

Blewett partied that night and was so pumped up, according to Mark Waugh in his book, *A Year to Remember*, that he had only ninety minutes sleep before resuming the next day. It showed. His timing was out and he seemed sluggish and risky. Donald beat him three or four times outside the off stump and then hit him on the helmet. That seemed to stir Blewett, who up to then had been batting on remote control.

The solid, gritty Waugh was first to go, caught behind off Kallis for 160. The score was five for 559. They had added 80 in the morning and the stand had been worth 385, just 20 short of the Bradman–Barnes effort half a century previously.

Blewett reached the coveted 200 and went on to a career-best 214 before he hit a catch off Klusener. But the carnage didn't stop there. Bevan (37 not out), Healy (11) and Warne (9) crunched the score up to eight for 628 before Taylor declared. The lead was 326, with a day and a half left to dismiss South Africa.

After so long in the field, the South African bats stumbled early, as teams so often do when facing a huge total. Fatigue after many sessions in the field took its toll on top of the side's low morale.

Sensing the wicket might be turning more, Taylor brought on Warne early against batsmen who would not expect to see him at the crease for a couple of hours. He replaced Gillespie and soon had Kirsten (8) groping until he bowled him. With the score at 46, Hudson was run out for 31.

Cullinan was in. Warne told Mark Waugh that he was going to have him for breakfast, when he should have said 'dinner'. If he had him for breakfast, then Cullinan would be in overnight, which was unlikely to be Warne's intention. He had the batsman playing and edging to Healy for 0, thus maintaining him as his very favourite bunny. Rabbit and duck were on the menu.

At 90, Steve Waugh had Cronje (22) out caught behind. The South Africans reached four for 99 at stumps, still 277 in arrears and the game looking as if it would be in Australia's safekeeping.

Next morning, Warne bowled Kallis (39) at 108 and touched off another landslide of wickets. First he had his good friend

Rhodes (8) lbw. In the past, Warne would have now gone on to collect a bag of six or seven on his own. But Taylor brought Bevan on to make a spin duo that destroyed South Africa. Bevan rolled up the innings in the space of a few runs and overs for a miserable 130, taking the last four wickets in succession. He managed as much turn as Warne and bamboozled the tail with loop, bounce and spin.

Bevan's figures were four for 32 from fifteen overs, with three maidens, as against Warne's of four for 43 off twenty-eight, with a remarkable fifteen maidens.

Australia's win by an innings and 194 runs was as huge as it was unexpected. The tourists celebrated long and hard, with Taylor and other older hands in the team warning that South Africa would come back. This was the biggest walloping they'd had since returning to the international scene and it hurt. They would respond.

The Mother of All Comebacks

South African commentators poured scorn on the home side, which put undue pressure on Cronje and his players. Expectations were high before the Tests that they would win the series, and with ease. Ex-players such as Kepler Wessels compared the current Australian side with Border's team and concluded that Taylor's squad was much weaker. This was not the case. If anything, the batting was stronger, more enterprising and just as resilient with the maturity of the Waugh brothers—who rarely both failed in a Test—and the introduction of new blood such as Blewett and Elliott. The basic bowling combination of McGrath, Gillespie, Reiffel, Warne and Bevan was potentially the best, and best balanced, in the world. Taylor's squad was capable of bigger things than Border's, as it had proved in toppling the Windies in two successive series.

In their efforts to promote the Proteas' cause, local commentators such as Wessels ignored this fairly obvious fact.

The size of the First Test defeat was a shock. Instead of accepting the fact that Australia might have a superior outfit, the South Africans ended up attacking their own for lack of courage and commitment, a ridiculous criticism when considering Cronje, Donald, Klusener, Richardson and the rest. This carping approach placed impossible expectations on the home team, which now had to scramble a new strategy for winning together at a time when group confidence was at a low ebb.

By contrast, Taylor's men sailed on with victories against the Eastern Province Invitation XI at Zwide, a black township outside Port Elizabeth, and Border in East London. Their form was encouraging with Blewett hitting another ton, Gillespie taking seven for 34 and Warne snaring three wickets in four balls. Consequently, the Australians made no change for the Second Test at Port Elizabeth, while South Africa made three. In came Herschelle Gibbs, Brian McMillan and Adam Bacher for Hudson, Rhodes and Klusener.

The wicket at St George's Park on 14 March was an underprepared grass top set up for exploitation by South Africa's Donald, Pollock and McMillan, and to nullify Australia's spin combination of Warne and Bevan. This blatant doctoring would stand a big chance of success if the Proteas bowled first. If they didn't, they would face the wrath of McGrath and Gillespie, when both were clocking deliveries as fast as anything Donald could deliver. There did not seem much sense in relying on the flip of a coin to decide the course of a game.

The ploy backfired when Taylor won the toss and had no hesitation in sending in the opposition for the first time in his career as captain. In the first hour, Gillespie and McGrath ripped through the early order, taking two wickets each and reducing South Africa to four for 22. The four batsmen back in the pavilion—Kirsten, Kallis and Cronje, all for 0, and Bacher for 11—could only feel that they had been hard done by, having to face genuine Test speed on such a substandard wicket.

Cullinan (34) and new man Gibbs (31) managed to survive until Gillespie forced a deflection from Cullinan to Warne, who held it with glee. It seemed that if he wasn't bowling the poor man out, he was catching him. Gillespie, now in full flight, bowled Gibbs at 95 and then trapped Pollock (0) lbw to put the score line at seven for 95. However, the lucky Richardson (47) and the plucky McMillan (55) made it look healthier as they fought back to add 85.

It took a sterling spell by Warne to finish off South Africa for 209. He had McMillan caught by Steve Waugh, Richardson snaffled by McGrath in the deep and Donald caught-and-bowled. This was a fair score on such a wicket. Gillespie starred with the ball, taking five for 54, while Warne returned three for 62 off 23.4 overs, with five maidens.

South Africa went into the field feeling somewhat happier than it had been half an hour after the game started, and even more so when Pollock had Hayden caught by Cullinan in the slips for a duck, leaving Australia one for 10 at stumps.

The next day was one of Australia's worst in recent times as it laboured for seventy overs in scratching up just 108 runs. Only Elliott (23), Mark Waugh (20) and Warne (lbw to Adams for 18) looked at all comfortable. Donald, Pollock, Adams, McMillan, Cronje and Kallis shared the wickets in a disciplined team effort.

South Africa reached 83 without loss at the end of day two, giving it a 184-run lead with ten wickets in hand and three days to go. The critics went full-circle and began to speak of a South African recovery and inevitable victory.

Taylor called a team meeting at the hotel and the consensus was that 108 in seventy overs had hardly done them justice. The batsmen undertook to go for their shots in the second innings. In the meantime, the bowlers were asked for an extra effort early on the third morning. If South Africa was able to notch another 120—a lead of 304—then the game would most probably be lost. This meant it had to be dismissed for a very low score.

Gillespie did his part by beating Kirsten (43) with sheer pace and bowling him at 87. Eleven runs later, Kallis was smartly run out by Blewett. Moments later, Gillespie had Bacher caught for

49 and Cullinan lbw for 2, which meant South Africa had lost four for 7. With the lead, it was effectively four for 201. Thanks to this 'Dizzy' spell, Australia was in with a slim chance.

Cronje and Gibbs held up proceedings with a partnership of 22 until McGrath had Gibbs for 7. Taylor turned to an all-spin last-ditch effort. It paid off as Bevan soon trapped McMillan lbw for 2 and removed the stubborn Cronje (27) caught behind. Warne had the dangerous Pollock (17) out lbw to a top-spinner. He then caught Donald (7) off Bevan and caused the cheeky Adams to lob one to Taylor at slip when trying to reverse sweep.

Warne's dismissal of Adams brought an exaggerated laugh of derision from the Australian. It was a reminder of his Hudson send-off at the Wanderers in 1994. Warne was rebuked by South African coach and former England player Bob Woolmer in a newspaper article. There was no need to mock Adams, he said. Warne felt differently, having been the object of much mouthing-off by Adams, but he would have done better to ignore the provocation and not react the way he did to Adams's silly shot. This would have meant more focus on Adams's folly and not on Warne's.

As it was, Adams's indiscretion ended the South African innings on 168. Australia had captured ten wickets for 81 in a stunning fightback. Gillespie had been the blaster of the early order with three for 49, while Bevan's three for 18 had broken through the middle, leaving the tail for Warne (two for 20 off 17.4 overs, including seven maidens) to tidy up.

The Australians began their chase of 270 to win and were soon in trouble when Taylor (13) was lbw to McMillan at 23. It was two for 30 when Elliott and Hayden ended up racing to the same end. Hayden was run out for 14. Mark Waugh came to the wicket due for a hundred and prepared to dig in for it. He and Elliott added 83 before Elliott (44) pushed one back to Adams for a caught-and-bowled. Australia was three for 113. The Test was on a knife edge as Steve Waugh joined his twin. By stumps, they had taken the score to three for 145, with Mark on 54 not out and Steve on 11.

Twenty runs into the morning of day three, Kallis removed Steve (18) and Australia was four for 167, still 103 short. At 192, Adams bowled Blewett for 7. Bevan then settled in with Mark Waugh for the most vital stand of the two Tests. At 226, Donald took the new ball and built up to his fastest, but couldn't dislodge them. Then Kallis broke through and bowled Waugh for 116. The score line was six for 258. He and Bevan had put on a vital 66. Healy came in and immediately lost Bevan (24). It was seven for 258, with only 12 runs to win.

Warne was on edge when he came to the wicket, a not-unusual state for him when batting. But there was an extra pressure now. He was unsure of what tactics to employ and approached Healy for a mid-wicket conference.

'What are we going to do, Heals?' he asked.

In his book, *A Captain's Year*, Mark Taylor reported that Healy, who had only faced a few balls himself, replied:

'I don't know. I haven't worked it out for myself yet. How can I let *you* know what to do?'

'Well,' Warne said, adjusting his pad, 'I can't feel my legs.'

But Kallis could. Seven runs later, he rapped Warne on the pads and he was out—*jelly pins before wicket*, it might be said.

Gillespie came in. Healy's head was clearer now. He had to take the initiative and told Gillespie to 'hang in there'. The number ten got behind the remaining balls of Kallis's over. This left Healy to face Cronje, with only 5 runs to get.

Cronje's third delivery veered into Healy's pads. Healy picked up the movement and swung, hoping to lift it into the outfield for a single or possibly two. He connected and set off for the run, then looked up to see it sail over the square-leg fence for a mighty six. The hit—the best and most important of Healy's career—took Australia to eight for 271 and a two-wicket victory.

Healy and Gillespie embraced. The Aussies in the dressing room danced in celebration of a great victory, which gave them the series two–nil. Mark Waugh was the obvious choice for Man of the Match with his second-innings century. He was pleased for another reason. Australia had come from behind in a much tougher assignment than the one against South Africa at Sydney early in 1994. No longer could scribes write that this side always collapsed in a run chase.

Back to Earth at Centurion Park

Australia was keen to make it a clean sweep in the Third Test at Centurion Park in Pretoria, beginning on 21 March. Taylor started well by winning the toss and staying at the crease for more than three hours. However, his poor return of just 38 runs did little for his personal morale after nineteen innings without a Test half-century.

Hayden (10) was bowled by new inclusion Brad Shultz, a fast left-armer who was in the action again when Elliott (18) hit a catch to him off Donald, who then bowled Mark Waugh (5), thus preventing any repetition of his previous match-winning effort. It took Steve Waugh and Blewett to restore order as they took the score from 110 to 190. Waugh (67) was then adjudged caught behind down the leg side. Blewett (37) went soon afterwards, caught behind from off-spinner Pat Symcox, and the rest collapsed for Australia to go down for a disappointing 227. Donald's three for 60 and Shultz's four for 52 did the damage.

South Africa's reply was all unconvincing resolution as they played and missed their way through the second day to be three for 240 at stumps, with Bacher on 94 not out. McGrath put the crowd and those watching or listening on TV or radio out of their misery by getting him lbw next morning after he had added 2 more runs at about the same rate.

McMillan plodded, too, for his 55 before Mark Waugh had him caught by Hayden. Cullinan was more watchful against Warne and managed to avoid too much contact by rotating the strike. McGrath bowled him for 47 in the batsman's best effort in several Tests against Australia. Cronje (79 not out) and

Klusener (30) made sure that his side squeezed out every run possible as it climbed to 384.

McGrath's marathon performance returned six for 86 off 40.4 overs, with fifteen maidens. It was the sixth time in twenty-eight Tests he had taken five or more in an innings. Gillespie was more erratic, but managed the good figures of three for 75 off thirty-one overs. Warne was steady, but not as penetrating as usual. His figures of none for 89 off thirty-six overs, with eleven maidens, did not reflect his form. Like McGrath, he beat the bat often.

Australia faced a daunting deficit of 157 as it began its second innings before tea on day three. There was talk in the dressing room about another comeback similar to the Second Test effort. By stumps there were just mumbles about 'rear-guard fights'. Taylor's horrors continued as he pushed forward to Donald and was caught behind for 5. His form was unsettling the players around him. Hayden was lbw to Shultz for a duck and Donald, bowling at his best for the season, crashed down Elliott's stumps when he was just 12, leaving Australia a pitiful three for 28.

The Waugh brothers seemed as if they might turn the game around. Mark relished seeing Symcox on, for he had slapped a big hundred off him at Natal earlier on the tour. But the aggressive right-hand offie had a last laugh when he bowled him for 42 right on stumps.

At four for 94, Australia was still 63 in arrears with six wickets in hand. Next morning, Donald bowled Blewett (0) with a fast beauty. Symcox bowled Bevan (5), whose dismissal left Australia on six for 108. Healy marched in, ready for a real scrap, and made a watchful 12 before he got a poor ball from Shultz down the leg side which clipped his pad on the way through. The keeper appealed and umpire Cyril Mitchley gave what even South African commentators said was the worst decision of the series. Healy stayed at the crease for longer than he should, open-mouthed in anger and surprise. Finally, he stomped off, knowing that he was taking with him any chance of Australia saving the game.

In a moment of frustration, he tossed the bat up the dressing-room steps, an action picked up by everyone watching TV and the match referee, Raman Subba Row. He found Healy guilty of dissent and gave him a two-match suspension. However, Mitchley, the worse offender, was free to umpire again without penalty.

Steve Waugh completed a fine double for the match with 60 not out, but could not beat the continued substandard umpiring as he lost Warne to another dubious lbw decision. The umpires were not biased, but their fingers were going up with an unusual frequency, possibly because they were paying undue attention to the position of the bowler's front foot in enforcing the no-ball rule. This suggested they were cutting the time for observing the ball when it reached the batsman. Eight poor decisions were the result.

The Australian total was 185, with Man of the Match Donald taking five for 36 and living up to his reputation. South Africa clipped off the runs needed while losing two for 32. Its eight-wicket win was a fair result and reflected the difference between the two sides for the game.

On reflection, the Australians were content with a two–one series win. It was made sweeter by Steve Waugh taking the Man of the Series award. He hit 313 at 78.25. Gillespie showed what a find he was by taking fourteen wickets at 20.50, just pipping McGrath with thirteen wickets at 22.23.

Warne was not far behind with eleven wickets at 25.63. He did not take a big bag of wickets, yet he snared crucial ones at critical moments and was thus still a force. His hold over Cullinan early in the series thwarted a fine player who had shown potential, but only this, against Australia.

Seven of the Best

Australia started underdogs in the one-day series of seven matches, beginning on 29 March at Buffalo Park, East London. South Africa and its supporters were feverish in their desire to see the home side conquer the Australians. The tourists had their problems. Taylor was so out of form it was cruel to have him playing on when he needed a break from cricket. Healy was under suspension for the first two one-day games.

Australia brought across Adam Dale, Stuart Law, Brendon Julian, Adam Gilchrist and Michael Di Venuto as specialists for the one-dayers and sent home Langer, Hayden and Elliott. Gilchrist, picked as a batsman first, found himself in the side as an all-rounder—keeper and batsman—which was an opportunity to exhibit his exceptional skills.

The Australian selectors had never before gone for such wholesale changes from one form of the game to the next. The more specialised outlook came from the poor showing of the one-day side in the last year. However, few expected the new look to shake South Africa, which had won its last thirteen internationals.

Australia began well with two for 125 in the first twenty-five overs, but then run-outs of Steve Waugh and Blewett slowed the run rate. Law, Steve Waugh and Bevan all reached fifty, but the side then lost five for 15 and ended up nine for 223.

South Africa was down three for 50 at one point in reply, but the Australians' fielding let them down. Catches were dropped that should have been taken and run-out chances went begging. Kallis (63) and Cullinan (85) joined in for a 122-run fourth-wicket partnership which turned the game the Proteas' way. After many fruitless efforts in Test and one-day cricket against Australia, Cullinan lived up to his potential to be South Africa's best bat. For once, Warne had not been able to disrupt him before he could settle in. The honours went to the batsman.

•••

Mark Waugh, who had missed the first game because of a back injury, returned for the second game at Port Elizabeth and was the match-winner with 115.

South Africa batted first and lost three early wickets before the in-form Kallis (82) and Rhodes (57) lifted the total to eight for 221. Adam Dale, with his medium-pace swingers, at one stage had three for 5.

The Proteas' score made it a similar game to the first one, but with the Australians chasing. Taylor began flailing at everything in an effort to change his fortune. His timing was out as he hit just 17.

The Waughs were in touch as Steve (50 off fifty-two balls) and Mark (115 off 125 balls) steered the tourists home to a seven-wicket victory with five overs to spare and South Africa's first defeat in fifteen contests. The game's highlight was provided by Mark Waugh who, when he was 91, hit 2 sixes to pass his century.

•••

After much agonising and consultation, Taylor dropped himself from the team. His form had not merited selection and he made way for Healy who returned as skipper for game three at Cape Town on 2 April. Rhodes's 83 not out was the highlight of the South African innings of 245. The home team managed 45 runs from the last three overs as the wheels fell off for Australia.

Warne took some stick from his mate Rhodes, including a six, much to the delight of the crowd who focused their verbal abuse on the spinner. The mob element in the Cape Town crowd was unforgiving when it came to Warne. The reason for their abuse of him was said to be his 'send-off' of Hudson in 1993–94, and his mocking of Adams in the recent Tests. But a more pertinent reason was his dominance of South Africa. His 'style' in keeping the upper hand over the key Proteas' bats now over three Test series and one-day competitions seemed arrogant to the local fans. Furthermore, the brash Aussie larrikin did not go down well with people used to South Africa's less flamboyant outfit. However, fans everywhere looked out for players in visiting teams to jeer. With Merv Hughes out of international cricket, Warne was the obvious target.

Mark Waugh split his hand while going for a catch in the slips off Gillespie. It needed six stitches and put him out of the game. He was to bat only if Australia reached eight for 200.

The tourists slumped to four for 25 in the eighth over in reply. Bevan relished being in early and took over for a typical 82 of 'hit and dash', converting many shots into an extra run where it did not seem possible against the brilliant arms of the South Africans. His was the eighth wicket to fall at 170. Mark Waugh was not required and Australia's chase ended at nine for 199.

South Africa now led two–one. Most observers predicted it would win the series.

•••

Australia batted first at Kingsmead in the fourth contest and Adam Gilchrist showed why selectors had so much faith in him. He came in when Australia was in another run-out mess at four for 50, slamming a superb 77 from eighty-eight balls. His clean striking was a feature as he launched into the opposition, including Donald, whom he clouted for six. Australia collected nine for 211, another ordinary total made more respectable later in the innings by Healy and the hard-hitting Bichel.

South Africa began soundly, hitting one for 81 in the first thirty overs. Then Warne broke through, dismissing Cullinan to begin a slump, with Bichel cutting into the middle order. In twenty balls, South Africa lost four wickets to be five for 89. Pollock looked like twisting the game back with a dashing 41 off thirty-seven balls. But it wasn't enough and South Africa fell 15 runs short at 196, despite a last-wicket stand of 31.

The two-all score line reflected the evenness of the teams.

•••

Australia lifted its rating in the fifth game at the Wanderers, Johannesburg, thanks to another 'newcomer' to the side, Di Venuto, who opened and crashed a quick 89, thus setting up a total of seven for 258.

The final result was in doubt to the end as the game see-sawed. However, South Africa's steady fall of wickets left it without out the firepower to win and it ended 8 runs short at eight for 250. Australia now led three–two.

•••

The sixth game was at Centurion Park, Pretoria, and South Africa made its highest-ever score against Australia of 284. The tourists had to make more than 5.5 an over to win—a daunting task even on this small ground. The chase was made tougher by the poor lighting and barbecue smoke emanating from the terraces.

The cause looked lost when Mark Waugh went for a duck on the third ball. But the fortunes of the one-day game were unpredictable. Steve Waugh and Bevan lifted for the big occasion as they had many times before. They put on a crushing 189-run stand for the fourth wicket with Bevan carving his way to 103 off just ninety-five balls and Waugh 80 off one hundred balls.

Australia reached the target with five wickets intact and an over to spare.

The tourists' four–two lead could not be overtaken and, against all predictions, they had won the one-day series.

•••

Neither side was keen to front for game seven at Bloemfontein, a dead rubber. South Africa rocketed to six for 310, thanks to a fast opening by Lance Klusener of 92. It was the highest one-day effort by the Proteas against Australia.

The asking rate of 6-plus an over for victory was never a serious proposition and Australia collapsed to be all out for 210—109 short—despite a fighting 91 by Steve Waugh.

The tourists had to be content with a four–three win. Yet no one was disappointed. Any series win against this proud, tight and skilful South African combination was fulfilling. Warne, Taylor and co. were most satisfied to leave South Africa knowing they had competed in six series against this super-competitive country and not lost one of them.

Warne was satisfied with his tour. In the three Tests, he took eleven wickets at 25.63, with a best of four for 43. In six one-dayers, he took ten wickets at 27.20, with a best of two for 36. On the surface, these figures appeared modest by Warne's high standards. Yet he took 'big' wickets and the honours against Cullinan and Cronje when it counted, thus helping to swing both series Australia's way.

15

Ashes and Ashes

Shot down in May

The four-week lay-off after six months of intense cricket was not enough to prepare the Australians for the concentrated four-month Ashes tour of England beginning in the second week of May 1997. The short break had seen Taylor confirmed as skipper for the tour while Steve Waugh took over from Healy as vice-captain. There was no doubt that Healy's bat-throwing had cost him the leadership role and any chance he had of captaining Australia.

Taylor was so out of form that if he continued his run of low scores he would be dropped from the side, even during the Ashes Tests. It put unprecedented pressure on Taylor, an individual with character, courage and outstanding leadership skills. The situation was also bad for all team members, who needed a skipper leading from the front and not offering himself as a sacrifice for the opposition.

Taylor's neck had been saved by Australia's continued success and its position as the top side in the world. If the side slipped, he would have to go. Even if it kept winning, there was a limit to the selectors' patience, especially with the media, public and ex-players of influence calling for his sacking.

Taylor was seen as stubborn and selfish by some for staying on. But who could blame him for wanting to keep his position?

The Australian captaincy was the most publicised and coveted in sport, involving the leadership of such a talented group of fine Australians who were 'winners'. On top of this, of course, was the salary of around $500 000 a year from the ACB, with other additional endorsement contracts, which lifted his annual income to around $1 million. This was about five times that of the Prime Minister, who might on average last at The Lodge about as long as the Australia captain would occupy his office.

Taylor's woes were pounced upon by the brutal English media, particularly the tabloids, who could see a possible chink to the Australians' armour which they planned to widen. Anything that dampened the tourists' morale would help England's cricket fortunes. Constant speculation could not help but damage the tourists' spirit.

It was already causing problems within the side's hierarchy. Taylor, Steve Waugh and Geoff Marsh made up the selection panel on tour. If Marsh wanted to drop Taylor (as his public utterances were suggesting if Taylor didn't score runs) and Taylor wanted to play, then the casting vote would be left with Steve Waugh. He would have the unenviable task of ending the career of a good friend of fifteen years.

This dilemma was in the back of the selectors' minds on 15 May as the tour began against the Duke of Norfolk's XI in front of 10 000 packed into the grounds of Arundel Castle. Australia hit five for 235, with Slater (50 not out), Mark Waugh (46), Taylor (45) and Steve Waugh (27) getting in some useful practice. The Duke's XI crumbled for 122, with Gillespie taking four for 21.

Taylor's innings was a relief. Thoughts of dumping him were pushed back in the minds of his fellow selectors.

Warne came into the side for the one-day game against Northamptonshire on 17 May. Australia batted first and Taylor hit 76, while Gilchrist (40) grabbed his chance with the bat as Australia compiled five for 232. The skipper's knock ensured he would captain the side in the first two one-dayers in the Texaco Cup competition.

Northampton's reply was rain-reduced to five for 134, in which Warne returned the best figures of two for 21 from six overs, including one brilliant stumping by Gilchrist.

The next day the team took their tour bus, with its three TVs, microwave and fridge, to Worcester. The players either read books, played cards or watched the box as they relaxed en route. Perhaps they were a little too laid-back on arrival as they were run-through by medium-pacers for just 121.

Worcester, captained and led well by Tom Moody (32), collected the runs with five wickets in hand. One positive to come out of the game for Australia was Warne's form. He took two for 36 off ten and snapped up three catches—thus taking part in each dismissal.

The next game against Durham was washed out as cold and wet weather settled in over England, and left the team without a useful tune-up before the first one-day international at Headingley, Leeds, on 22 May. Under grey skies and in front of a capacity crowd, the Australians were kept down to eight for 170 thanks to the speed of Darren Gough (two for 32) and swing of Mark Ealham (two for 21). The new-look English team featured players unsighted by the Australians before: Dean Headley, Graham Lloyd, Adam Hollioake and Mark Ealham. The 'old' faces were Nick Knight, captain Mike Atherton, vice-captain Alec Stewart, Graham Thorpe, Philip DeFreitas, Robert Croft and Darren Gough.

England began poorly, losing four for 40 before Thorpe (75 not out) and the Melbourne-born Adam Hollioake (66 not out) slammed home a win in just 40.1 overs. Hollioake, who had learned his cricket in Australia, pulled Gillespie for six to win the game and take the Man of the Match award ahead of Thorpe, who was equally, if not more, impressive. McGrath (two for 34) was in form, but the other bowlers, including Warne (none for 46 off ten), had an ordinary day.

The England press had a field day, with jingoistic fervour reaching an hysterical pitch following the victory. The mischievous probing about Taylor continued and kept the Australians distracted from their recovery task. A member of the 'home' selection panel, Steve Bernard, was known to be following the team everywhere. It was thought that he might be needed to persuade Taylor to make a critical decision if his form did not pick up. But Bernard did not go near the dressing room, leaving Taylor, Marsh and Waugh to stew in their own dilemmas.

Injuries to Julian, Bichel and Blewett reduced the squad to fourteen as the team prepared for the second game at the Oval, London, on 24 May. The selectors brought in Gilchrist for Blewett, leaving Elliott, Ponting and Langer to cool their heels.

Atherton won the toss and sent Australia in. Both Taylor (11) and Mark Waugh were run out before Bevan came to the rescue with 108 not out, well supported by a dashing 53 in forty-eight balls by Gilchrist as Australia reached a respectable six for 249.

Atherton then batted through the 48.2 overs it took to overhaul Australia after a power-laden start with Stewart (40). Hollioake again excelled with 53 not out.

Australia appeared 'soft' in the field, missing catches. No bowlers seemed capable of maintaining line and length, and there was not the usual spirit in the fielding. Warne was pleased to bowl Stewart, but that was his only bright spot as he toiled for his one for 39 off ten overs. The tour seemed hardly to have begun and already a cup—the Texaco Trophy—had been lost.

The team trudged across town to Lord's on Sunday 25 May for the dead rubber with plenty to play for. A win would send Australia in a good mood towards the Tests and quell some of the hysteria in the tabloids. A loss would maintain the 'Aussie-bashing' which was being pursued by the *Sun* and *Mirror*.

Taylor saved the other selectors some heartache by dropping himself from the side. Slater, who had failed twice, was also left out. In came Elliott and Langer. England experimented with Adam Hollioake's nineteen-year-old brother Ben, John Crawley and Chris Silverwood.

Atherton won the toss and again put Australia in first. It looked to be the wrong move as the tourists notched 269 in 49.2 overs with Mark Waugh leading the way with a brilliant 95, supported by Gilchrist (33), Healy (27) and Kasprowicz (28 not out). England took on the challenge with verve, led by Stewart, in his best form, with 79, and the debutant Ben Hollioake with a spanking 63. It won by six wickets and completed a three–nil whitewash of the competition.

The tourists, who were cock-a-hoop in April after beating the South Africans in the one-dayers, had been shot down in May. There would be more soul-searching by Warne and his team-mates in the next few days than at any time pre-series since he first made the team in 1992.

County Matters

Taylor pre-empted his sacking by telling his fellow selectors he would give himself two county games and the First Test to recover some form, or he would stand down. This decision was kept secret and took the pressure off Steve Waugh, who now would not have to drop his long-standing mate. It would have a been an awful way for Waugh to take over as captain. If Taylor did fail, there would not be any stigma attached to Waugh's accession.

With that out of the way, Taylor made a duck against Gloucestershire at Bristol on 27 May. The *Daily Mirror* tried to obtain a picture of him with a metre-wide bat. The skipper refused. The photo was taken anyway, and the photographer found himself facing an irate Steve Waugh. Manager Alan Crompton stepped forward to seize the film. He later phoned the *Mirror* to complain. The paper played out the journalism axiom of *run it if you can't lose a defamation case.* A story the next day was headlined 'Batman and Sobbin'.

In the match itself, Australia scrambled to 249 with Mark Waugh cracking 66 and Steve 92. Gloucester replied with 350, of which the opener Nick Trainor scored 121, his maiden first-class century, while Warne began to hit the right spot with authority for the first time on tour. He sent down 35.2 overs, including ten maidens, in a sustained stint, taking four for 97.

It was a good omen for the six Ashes Tests in which Warne's form would be vital. There had been much chatter in the press and among England supporters at large about his supposed decline. Wishful thinking had become myth.

In Australia's second innings, Elliott hit top form, cracking 124, while Langer hit 152 not out as the side reached four for 354. Warne was promoted for a bit of afternoon pinch-hitting, but was bowled for a duck. Taylor's opening 30 was thirty-five minutes of insecurity as his timing was still out. But an attacking thirty was far better for him than his brief first-innings stay.

Two days later, against Dean Jones's Derbyshire at Derby, Taylor won the toss and was out for 5. He had to watch Elliott (67), Blewett (121), Steve Waugh (43), Bevan (56) and Healy (40 not out) acquire some useful batting practice in the middle, compiling six for 362 declared.

Jones was furious that the England selectors asked speedster Devon Malcolm to stand down for the game. He wanted a victory, just to prove a few points. Derby replied with nine declared for 257. Jones enjoyed his battle with the Australians, but not being bowled for 31 by his Victorian team-mate—the man who relieved him of the state captaincy—Warne. Warne's figures of two for 45 off fourteen overs, with two maidens, implied his form was 'steady'.

Australia batted again. When Taylor was on 1, he nicked an easy one to Jones in the slips. The former Test champion, a superb fielder, grassed it. There was speculation among watching English journalists that he may have done it on purpose. Australian scribes shook their heads. It wasn't like Deano: he was a competitor and this was a genuine contest. The question of whether he spilled it because something deep down in his psyche was sympathetic to the struggling, deflated Aussie skipper would be left to the psychoanalysts.

Taylor's reaction showed he was in need of counselling when he met Langer mid-wicket and told him he was ready to 'give up'. Langer, a scrapper who would never throw in the towel in a fight of any kind, reprimanded his captain and told him to keep his eye on the ball. Taylor obeyed and made it to tea on 9 not out.

He went on to 59 not out at stumps and out on the third morning for 63. The remnants of a confident 'Tub' were noticed in some of his strokes and his score was a goodish one at last. Meanwhile, Bevan stroked a fine 104 not out while Julian thrashed 62 as Australia declared at four for 265.

Derby was set 371 runs off sixty-nine overs—a tough task for the chasers. But Bichel had a back injury and Gillespie a sore foot. The bowling attack was depleted. Much rested on Warne's ample shoulders.

Jones instructed his batsmen to 'go for it'. It was soon a battle between Warne and his capacity to take wickets, and eleven players charging for victory. Rollins (66), Adams (91) and Jones himself (56) led from the front against him, as the leg-spinner scythed his way through the line-up. But Derby scraped in for a win with three balls to spare, reaching nine for 371 off 68.3 overs.

Warne took a wicket every three overs and ended with seven for 103 from twenty-three overs, including two maidens. It was a classic, sustained display of spin-bowling. He was rewarded with the Man of the Match award.

But it went unnoticed. The hype in the media after the game swamped his performance. The focus was on Australia's defeat. Again, the English media did its team a disservice. It ignored the two most important factors to come out of the game as far as the Ashes were concerned: Taylor was far from spent and Warne would be a force in the Tests.

Collapse at Edgbaston

Taylor won the toss and did not hesitate to bat first on a fair Test wicket at Edgbaston, Birmingham, on 5 June. Gough started well by bowling Elliott (6) with the score at 11. Taylor (6) followed by nicking to second slip Butcher off Malcolm and the rot set in as Australia collapsed to seven for 48.

Warne strode in, looking less nervous than usual when batting. He soon lost Gillespie (4) leg before to Caddick and the score was eight for 54. This was the signal for Warne to go for everything. Partnered by the straight-hitting Kasprowicz, he crashed his way into the 40s in a stand of 56. Warne played the 'inside-out' cover drive with rare success and had the English fielders floundering a fraction in an outstanding performance. He was severe on Gough, sending him to the boundary for several fours and out of the attack.

The fun ended when Kasprowicz (17) was caught in the slips and became Caddick's fifth victim. At 118 and six overs after lunch, Warne skied one too many and was caught by Malcolm at third man. This was Warne's best form with the bat in many Tests, and showed yet again that he might just hit a three-figure score, one day. Caddick took five for 50, Gough three for 43 and Malcolm two for 25. The Englishmen surprised the Australians with their devil and skill in the field. Australia's 'old-timers', Steve Waugh, Healy and Taylor, had never seen such eagerness from them before.

They continued this purpose in their batting, reaching three for 200 at stumps, with Hussain 80 not out and Thorpe 83 not out, to take a lead of 120 on the first day after a shaky start which saw England three for 50 at one stage. Hussain and Thorpe carried on until after lunch on day two until Thorpe was caught off McGrath for 138 after a partnership of 288. The score was four for 338 and the lead 220 with six wickets in hand.

The main disappointment for Australia was Warne's form as he turned in his worst performance in a Test since his first-ever effort against the Indians. He couldn't get his length on a slow pitch that gave him no assistance.

Hussain reached a top-class double hundred by cracking Warne for three consecutive fours and impressed with his impeccable placement and clean hitting. Then, when he was 207, Warne finally turned one with some force and induced an edge from him to Healy. The bowler was grateful but unhappy. It had been another day of cricket hell for the Aussies. At stumps, England was six for 449. The lead was 331. For the second successive day, Australia had been outplayed and thumped.

On day three, the home side lost three wickets and declared at nine for 478. Warne's figures of one for 110 off thirty-five overs, with eight maidens, reflected his below-par performance, though his stock-bowling effort saw him going for just 3 an over.

Now it was Australia's turn again. Taylor knew he had come to the end of the line as he marched out to bat with Elliott. If he failed, he would drop himself for the Second Test at Lord's and that would mean he would probably not get back in the side. But he hit some sweet shots early and before long was 50 in just sixty-nine balls. He and Elliott made it to lunch still together. Afterwards, Taylor went into his shell and Elliott took over. The off-spinner Croft broke through and bowled Elliott for 66. He and Taylor had put on 133, the sort of start they both would have settled for before the day began. Yet Australia was still 227 behind.

Blewett, the man who had scored two centuries in his first two Tests against England in Australia in 1994–95, came in and played sensibly, while Taylor dragged himself through the final two sessions to 99, then a single for an easy dash to a hundred. He pointed his bat to the dressing room as his team jumped to their feet and cheered and clapped him.

Taylor slumped in the dressing room at the end of the day with 108 not out and Blewett looking in top form on 61 not out. Their partnership was worth 123 and the score was one for 256, still 104 short. But next morning, after reaching 129, Taylor played a lazy, perhaps tired, drive at Croft and the bowler held an easy one. It was a poor end to a fighting knock, with the score at 327, just 33 behind. The second-wicket stand had registered 194.

Blewett brought up his hundred and had now scored a century in each of his first three Ashes Tests, a feat no player of either nation had ever before achieved. He reached 125 when, with the score at 354, he was caught bat-padding to Butcher off Croft. This brought Bevan in to join Steve Waugh and together they took Australia into the lead with seven wickets in hand. Then, at 393, Bevan (24) tried to evade a bouncer from Gough and was caught by Hussain. The lead was 33 with six wickets left.

Mark Waugh, who had been ill with suspected appendicitis, came and went, and Australia had slumped to five for 399. Brother Steve and Healy battled on to 431 when Waugh (33) went lbw to Gough. This brought Warne to the wicket and he attacked. He was determined to keep the scoreboard moving.

At 465, Healy (30) was caught off Ealham. Kasprowicz joined Warne, but didn't last long. Warne swung lustily for a while, but was out caught and bowled by Ealham. Australia's fight was over at 477, leaving an unusual symmetry of 118 for victory—Australia's score in the first innings.

England lost Butcher (14) lbw to Kasprowicz along the way, but Atherton (57 not out) and Stewart (40 not out) slammed 119 runs in 21.2 overs—nearly 6 an over—to win inside four days by nine wickets. Stewart brought up the winning runs with a fine cover drive for four off Warne, a piece of play that seemed apt after the unfolding of events over four days.

The spinner's figures were 7.3 overs, no maidens, none for 27. His match figures were one for 137. England's senior cricket scribes claimed he was no longer a threat. England's conqueror in 1993 had been vanquished.

The home team was strong and dominated most of the Test. The local press went into overdrive about 'new eras' and 'new attitudes'. The Ashes were the home side's for the picking, if you believed the broadsheets. According to the tabloids, the tourists were a spent force and the Ashes were already England's. Very few consulted Taylor and his men for their thoughts.

Rain Dance at Lord's

The Australians had two county games before the Second Test at Lord's, the first against Nottinghamshire and the other against Leicestershire.

Net practice was not compulsory when they arrived at Nottingham on 10 June, yet Warne turned out for not one session but two. He wanted to straighten out some problems he was having with his big leg break and his wrong 'un. Warne didn't have to be taken aside by Taylor and Steve Waugh to be told he had to lift. He was keener than anyone to bounce back. For someone who was not enamoured with practice, there was a real spring in his step as he kept coming in at Steve Waugh with all his old vigour and determination.

A second net session lasted 45 minutes. Warne came in from all angles with every type of delivery in an effort to beat Waugh, who danced down the wicket to meet him and keep him out. For any aficionados watching, it was a wonderful exhibition of champion bowler versus champion batsman at their best.

It was also a useful tune-up for Waugh, who was due to captain Australia for the first time next day. But it was washed out as England's miserable summer weather continued with temperatures low and skies etched a permanent grey.

When play got under way the following day, Notts was all out for 239, with McGrath getting four for 63 and Paul Reiffel—who had just arrived as a replacement for the injured Andy Bichel—hitting his straps immediately with three for 15. Australia replied with five for 398 at a fair clip to win. Elliott (127) continued his rise in form, while Steve Waugh celebrated his first turn at the helm with 115.

On 14 June, at Grace Road, Leicester, Australia was sent in on a difficult wicket and declared at eight for 220. With rain threatening to ruin the game, Leicester responded by declaring at four for 62. Reiffel once more hit an immaculate line and length for another fine result of three for 12. He was clearly making a bid for immediate Test selection at Lord's.

Warne, too, seemed to have turned the corner in his limited spell of five overs. He took only one for 20, but it was remarked how he was now managing to make the ball dip from above the batsman's eye level, something which had been missing on tour so far. Now it was back and fooling batsmen who stepped into the ball only to lose it as it dropped under or past the bat.

Taylor stood in the slips, chewing, stroking his chin, clapping and nodding his head to Healy's chant:

'Bowled Warnie ... Like it Shane ... Great bowling Warnie.'

Leicester skipper, James Whittaker, had suggested to Taylor that they engineer a result, no doubt to keep the pressure on the tourists if they maintained their losing streak. Taylor, never one to shirk such a challenge, agreed and declared at three for 105—the skipper himself showing his form was holding with 57.

Leicester was set 264 to win from seventy overs, a more than fair offer from Taylor. Warne showed that his good form of the brief first innings was still with him as he took five for 42 from 16.4 overs, as Leicester was all out 84 runs short. The win gave Australia a much-needed boost.

Reiffel took three for 49 and, only a few weeks after threatening to retire from cricket when he was left out of the Ashes tour, was chosen to replace Gillespie—still recovering from his torn hamstring—for the Lord's Test.

Rain fell incessantly on the scheduled opening day and, at 5 p.m., play was officially abandoned. The Test was now reduced to four days, and this limited the chance for a result. England could relax a fraction. It was more important for the Australians to win and draw level. On day two, Taylor looked at the cloud cover, examined the wicket and decided to send England in if he won the toss. This he did and his thinking proved correct as the home side were soon in trouble, losing Butcher (5), Atherton (1), and Stewart (1), all to McGrath. The score was three for 13. Thorpe and Hussain struggled on to three for 38 after twenty-one overs. Then the rain returned, and didn't stop. Again the fans waited, read the papers and hoped. Day two also succumbed to the weather, and a dismal draw loomed.

Day three, Saturday, got underway on schedule and, at 47, Reiffel removed Thorpe, caught by Blewett. Then McGrath removed Crawley (1) caught behind and cleaned up Hussain lbw with a great in-dipper to make it six for 62. Croft became

McGrath's sixth victim when he left his bat out to dry for another edge to Healy. Gough tried to hit his way out of trouble, but was also caught behind off McGrath for 10 and England was eight for 76. One run later, Reiffel disposed of Ealham (7) and, at the same score, McGrath had Caddick (1) lbw.

England was all out for 77. Apart from 52 at the Oval in 1948 against Bradman's 'Invincibles', this was the lowest score by an England team since early in the century. McGrath's eight for 38 was the best-ever figures by an Australian in one innings at Lord's and one of the great bowling performances of all time.

Taylor urged his men to seize the day, but was out for 1 chopping the ball onto his stumps, his most common form of dismissal in recent seasons. Elliott and Blewett consolidated until Blewett (45) was caught off Croft at 73. Mark Waugh came in to be 26 not out at stumps, with Elliott 55 not out. Australia had made two for 131 in the sixty-five overs managed in the rain-interrupted day. The lead was 54, with just two days to go.

Australia's hopes were further frustrated on day four, Sunday. Play didn't get going until 5.50 p.m., when all but the true cricket faithful had gone home. They must have wished they had stayed. There was something in the seventeen overs played for everyone. After Mark Waugh was dismissed for 33, Warne went in at number five as a pinch-hitter. The Australians were plainly out to 'have a go'. They wanted to force a win.

Warne's form with the bat had been encouraging at Edgbaston, and he was keen to get into the game after bowling only two overs in England's innings. But Taylor's plans and his hopes were disappointed. He tried a big hook off Gough, mishit and was caught in the slips for a duck. Steve Waugh went for the same score immediately afterwards, lbw to Caddick, followed by Bevan for 4, both also trying to force the pace.

Australia went to stumps at seven for 213, mainly due to a powerful 112 by Elliott, his first Test century after a short career which had seen more than its share of ups and downs, and unexpected setbacks. The team's rush of blood had added 82 in those seventeen overs—a rate of nearly 5 an over—for the loss of five wickets. Taylor kept England guessing overnight, but declared in the morning of the fifth day, with a lead of 136. But it was a declaration made more in hope than certainty as England soon put any chance of an Australian victory out of the question. It wasn't until the score was 162 that Atherton was the first out, hit-wicket for 77, when he stepped back onto his stumps to Kasprowicz.

By then Warne was on in a performance which was the only real plus to come out of the last day for the tourists. His line was good and he was extracting turn, even trying one or two of his big, rolling leg breaks. His loop and dip also came into play so that he had all the English batsmen watching him carefully and, at times, apprehensively.

After Stewart was out caught hooking off McGrath for 13, with the score at two for 189, Hussain came in. Following his treatment of Warne on their last encounter—in the First Test—he was clearly keen to assert his dominance again. But this was a different game and a more confident Warne. The bowler made Hussain wait while he set his field, then hurled a tempting leg break up to him. Hussain came forward to despatch it over the bowler's head. But the big dipper, missing at Edgbaston, Hussain's fun-park, was back. The ball dropped on him sharply at the last moment, causing him to hit early and loft it straight back to Warne. He caught it and hurled it high.

Warne perhaps now had a slight mental edge over the double centurion, having dismissed him in both his last two innings, and especially first-ball this time. The two methods of dismissal—this caught-and-bowled and the caught-behind from a big turner at Edgbaston—would not be forgotten by bowler or batsman. How the dismissals would affect each of them would go a long way towards deciding the Ashes outcome. If England's number-one striker prevailed, the home team would probably win the series. If Australia's match-winner managed to get the better of him, the tourists would most likely retain the precious urn.

Warne had made a habit of arrowing in on the opposition team's most dangerous batsmen. Against South Africa, it was

Cullinan and Cronje; the Windies, Lara and Richardson; India, Tendulkar and Azharuddin; Pakistan, Salim; Sri Lanka, Ranatunga; and New Zealand, Martin Crowe and later Stephen Fleming. Hussain and Thorpe were the biggest threats among the current English batsmen, followed by Atherton and Stewart if they were given the chance. Warne would be summoning up that extra effort against them.

But, for the moment, it was back to this match. The left-handed Butcher had batted with too much confidence for the Australians' liking. But when he was 87, his confidence was shaken by a big-turning leg break from Warne which snapped out of the bowlers' footmarks outside the off stump and bowled him. It turned so viciously it was unplayable for a left-hander and possibly for any right-hander, too, unless he was uncommonly speedy with his pads.

Two England batsmen had now left the wicket frowning. They had not been dismissed due to silly shots or lapses of concentration. They had been beaten. Maybe it would not worry them overmuch until they faced Warne again in two weeks time. Then the doubts would creep in.

England cruised to four for 266 and the game fizzled out. Warne's figures were two for 47 from nineteen overs, with four maidens. Not surprisingly after his eight-wicket haul in England's first innings, McGrath took the Man of the Match award, with game figures of nine for 103.

The Australian camp went away talking about a 'moral victory'. The tourists felt they had outplayed England, yet the game had not run long enough to quite judge it that way. The fact was that England was one-up in the Ashes series, with four to play. The onus was on the Australians to claw one back.

The New Girl in Shane's Life

By mid-June, halfway through the tour, Warne had become edgy. His wife, Simone, was due to give birth to their first child in Melbourne, 20 000 kilometres away. He felt helpless at such a distance only being able to offer platitudes of support over his mobile phone. He wanted to be close to Simone. Other fathers in the team, such as Steve Waugh, Healy and Taylor, were sympathetic, assuring him everything would be fine.

His team-mates humoured him and asked what the baby's name would be.

'I don't know,' Warne mumbled, 'probably Duke.'

That brought some incredulous looks.

When one of them asked what it would be called if it was a girl, he replied: 'Not sure. Jordan maybe.' After Michael Jordan, the US champion basketballer? Or perhaps Air Jordan?

'Hope it's a girl,' someone quipped.

On 27 June, while the Australians were at their hotel in Oxford sitting out a rain-abandoned game against British Universities, Warne was told that Simone had opted to have a Caesarean section. He had been reassured that this procedure was a routine alternative to normal delivery, but the news only made him feel like fathers of another generation, who were not expected to be present at the birth of a child, but were left in a waiting room to smoke, sweat and worry, rather than be right there and 'assist' in the delivery, which was the current fashion.

At least Shane had his parents, Keith and Brigitte, with him as he chain-smoked, waited and clutched his mobile. Most members of the team were close by. The phone rang at 10.30 a.m. in England—7.30 p.m. in the evening in Melbourne. Warne punched the answer button and hurried to a quiet room. He emerged a few minutes later and announced:

'It's a girl! Brooke! She weighs 9 lb 6 oz and she's 56 centimetres long.'

A cheer went up. Warne was slapped on the back, his hand pumped. He embraced his parents.

'She looks like me!' Warne said.

'Poor kid!' someone called.

A beaming Warne produced a box of cigars. Champagne appeared from nowhere. Corks popped and a dozen men, along with Brigitte, were soon lighting and puffing cigars.

Cameras clicked for a group photo to record the moment—for a new dad. If he couldn't be with Simone, then this was the next best thing, surrounded by family and good mates—comrades in arms, an Ashes Test team in the middle of a campaign.

Within minutes of the celebration, the media were there snapping photos and rolling TV cameras for sixty-second 'sound bites' for British and Australian TV news bulletins.

'I'm not sure if Warnie fully realises what has happened,' Steve Waugh noted in his *1997 Ashes Diary*, 'and how much it will change his life from now on. No doubt he'll be a good father, and I bet he can't wait to get home to see what his daughter looks like.'

Warne was relieved after the ordeal of waiting and pleased also that the game against the Combined Universities was washed out and abandoned. He was excused from all duties so that he could celebrate. It meant that, by the time the Third Test at Manchester came around on 3 July, he was free of cares and in the right frame of mind to turn in one of the finest performances of his career.

Third Time Lucky

The tourists were relieved to find a break in the weather that allowed some cricket on 28 June against Hampshire at Southampton. Warne celebrated the birth of his baby girl Brooke the day before by taking three for 30 as the county collapsed for 156. He had the hard-hitting, talented Robin Smith caught behind for 22, reviving memories of the last Ashes campaign of 1993, of which Warne's embarrassing destruction of this top-class batsman had been such a feature. Smith's career never quite recovered from the experience.

Australia replied with eight for 465. Elliott continued in 'hungry' form with a quick 61, while Taylor with a solid 109 and Mark Waugh with a dashing 173 showed welcome returns to form. Warne's revived capacity with the bat was maintained as he belted a boisterous 38.

Hampshire batted again and was sent back for 176, mainly due to Gillespie, who was in devastating form with five for 33. Warne took one for 26 from nineteen overs, with three maidens. His economy rate of a little more than 1 an over exemplified his accuracy and control in the run-up to the Old Trafford Test, beginning on 3 July.

Taylor made the most courageous decision of his captaincy in winning the toss and batting on a grassy, moist wicket under an overcast sky. His thinking was based on his previous experiences in Manchester when the wicket had deteriorated after day one. Better to bat first and battle for 200 than bat second and fourth and struggle for 150, he reasoned.

Soon his judgment was questioned as new England speedster, Dean Headley, who replaced Devon Malcolm, removed him for 2, caught by Thorpe at first slip. At 22, Blewett (8) was bowled by Gough. At 42, Mark Waugh (12) was caught behind off Ealham. Steve Waugh joined the in-form Elliott and they dug in against the seaming and swinging.

Then, soon after lunch, Elliott (40) was given out caught to Headley, making Australia four for 85, although replays showed that he hadn't touched the ball. Waugh settled in, but had difficulty finding anyone to stay with him. Bevan came in and was soon on his way, caught behind for 7 off Headley, making the score five for 115. Healy (9) managed to stay for a valuable 37-run partnership with Waugh, who was now in control at one end, but Warne (3) fell caught behind to Ealham, leaving Australia seven for 160. Reiffel joined Waugh and the rain came down, delaying play for two frustrating hours. They then batted courageously despite several other breaks for bad light until, in the last over before stumps, Waugh aptly brought up his century with a boundary and Australia went in for the night at seven for 224.

Next morning, however, England wrapped up the Australian innings with ease, with Reiffel (31) and Waugh (108) both falling to Gough. Headley (four for 72) completed a dream first-up performance by having Gillespie (0) caught behind.

Australia's 235 was fair, but it left the bowlers with little room for error. Atherton (5), however, assisted with the first mistake by edging McGrath down the leg side with the score at 8. Warne failed to make a run-out of Stewart, allowing England to sneak to lunch at one for 37. The home side travelled well after the break and reached 74, before Warne beat Stewart (30) with a sharp turner that he nicked to Taylor.

The skipper brought Bevan on at the other end for an all-spin attack that had England floundering. Warne, bowling from the Warwick Road end, was turning the ball and beating the bat, while the batsmen were finding Bevan hard to score from. Left-hander Butcher received a faster ball down the leg side from Bevan that he played at and missed. Despite being unsighted, Healy gathered it and lifted the bails almost in the one speedy action. No one except Healy was certain if it was a dismissal or not. Everyone waited for the verdict of the third umpire up in the stands, who examined the video. Replays showed the keeper's amazing skill in notching his one hundredth Ashes wicket. Butcher (51) was on his way, the score three for 94.

Before and after the tea break, England crumbled to Warne. At 101, he dismissed Thorpe (3), caught edging a top-spinner to Taylor at slip. The batsman stood his ground, apparently from shock. The replay was explicit. His bat had deflected the ball to the fieldsman. It was a most gratifying wicket for Warne. The champion left-hander had troubled him in the First Test, and Warne had the highest regard for his ability.

Now all Warne's histrionics, which had so annoyed the English and thrilled the Australian supporters, were back. There was the confident body language, the querying looks down the wicket, the stroking of the chin as he considered how a batsman had or had not played him, the grins, frowns and grimaces, the charges down the wicket after an appeal, the chitchat with Healy—'You were right about that, Heals'—and the chirpy remarks for the ears of the batsmen at either end—'Bit of a turner now.'

With the score at 110, he rolled another fast break past Hussain (13), who nicked it to Healy. In the space of fifteen balls bowled to Hussain in three successive innings, Warne had dismissed him three times. In a huge sea change from the period in the First Test when Hussain had swamped the bowler with some great hitting, Warne now was his master at a critical time in the series.

Boosted by these big wickets, Warne forced Crawley (4) to edge another to Healy, giving the bowler his fourth wicket. England was six for 111 and Taylor's brave decision to bat first seemed justified. McGrath worried Croft (7) out, caught by Steve Waugh at 122. One run later, Warne bluffed Gough into a tentative push. He missed and was lbw. It was Warne's fifth scalp, and he was now level with Richie Benaud on 248 Test wickets, the most by an Australian spinner.

Ealham and Caddick then produced an unbroken 38-run stand for the ninth wicket, bringing England to eight for 161 at stumps. They were just 74 runs short and the game was tight. On the third morning, Warne crowded the batsmen and produced his sixth wicket—Caddick, caught by Mark Waugh. McGrath then bowled Headley (0) and England was all out 162.

Warne returned six for 48 from thirty overs, with fourteen maidens. He now had the highest number of wickets by an Australian spinner at 249. McGrath continued as the most consistent and dominant bowler of the series with three for 40, while Bevan did his bit with one for 14.

The Australian lead was 73, but it was soon squandered by some inept batting by Taylor (1) caught in the slips off Headley at 5. Blewett (19) was then the victim of a more than dubious catch claimed by Hussain off Croft. The position worsened to three for 39 when Elliott was caught off Headley for 11, but the Waugh brothers then came together and took the score to 131 before Mark was bowled by Ealham for 55. One run later, Bevan, shell-shocked from a barrage of short balls, departed for a duck. Steve Waugh was again in need of a partner while he held up one end as well as he could with an injured hand which restricted his scoring. He found one in Healy, who contributed a solid 47 before edging Croft to slip. The score was now six for 210, a lead of 283, and the game was slipping beyond England's reach, especially with Warne in form with the ball.

He was in next and from the start showed he was also in good touch with the bat and determined to lift Australia to a winning position as he went for his shots. Yet he was fortunate there was no catch-replay adjudicator when he jammed down on a ball that went to a close-in fielder. The umpire considered it a bump-ball. The TV replay suggested it was a legitimate catch. Warne rode his luck to be 33 not out, while Waugh, his injured hand swollen to twice normal size, struggled on gallantly to be 82 not out at stumps with the score at six for 262. The lead was 335, with four wickets in hand.

The next morning, day four, Warne and Waugh began the best way possible with 20 runs in three overs. Warne reached his second Test half-century. He was striking the ball so well that his batting partner and others wondered if this could be the day for his first hundred. However, at 53, and with the score on 298, he edged one behind off Caddick. That elusive three figures would again have to wait.

All interest centred on Waugh's tortured effort to reach a century himself as he crawled through the 90s. On 99, he stroked the ball through mid-wicket to reach his second century for the Test. He battled on to 116, when he gloved a lifter from Headley to end a great double by any standards.

Australia was eight for 333, but Reiffel proceeded to belt a confident 45 not out, supported by Gillespie with a competent 28 not out, so that Taylor had the unexpected luxury of having enough runs and time to declare at eight for 395.

Australia was 468 runs ahead with England having 141 overs to get them. At 3.5 an over, it wasn't impossible, but England had a one in a thousand chance of making the runs. No team had ever chased so many and succeeded in the last innings of a Test.

Gillespie made the first breakthrough, trapping Atherton (21) lbw. Taylor soon brought Warne on and he bowled Stewart for

1—his 250th victim. The score was two for 45. Hussain (1) had not been in long when Gillespie cornered him lbw as well, making England three for 50. Hussain's confidence had dipped since his First Test double century and, with Warne on, he seemed edgy, only to fall to Gillespie, who was bowling with speed and accuracy.

Butcher (28) then top-edged a hook off Gillespie for a fine running, one-handed catch by McGrath at fine leg. It brought England to its knees at four for 55. Warne had Thorpe struggling with his regulation breaks that speared in from the rough outside the left-hander's off stump. He bowled him several, easing the line closer and closer to the stumps while changing the delivery to a top-spinner. Satisfied he had Thorpe pushing forward for the straight one or a turner, he slipped in a wrong 'un. Thorpe lunged and edged to Healy. Warne had the prize scalp cheaply (7) for the second time in the game. England was five for 84. Crawley hung on with Ealham to be 53 not out at stumps, with England five for 130. The next morning, day five, Warne bowled at his best, but it was McGrath who broke through with the wickets of Ealham for 9, Croft for 7, Crawley for 83, hit-wicket, and Gough for 6. Warne snaffled Caddick (17) caught by Gillespie and England was all out for 200. Australia had won by 268 runs.

McGrath took four for 46, Gillespie three for 31 and Warne three for 63 from 30.4 overs, with eight maidens. Warne's top match figures of nine for 111 were not enough to give him the Man of the Match, which went to Steve Waugh for his two fighting centuries.

Australia was now back in the Ashes war at one-all, with three Tests to play.

In the Lead at Leeds

A few days after the Third Test, Warne was given a week off by the team management to fly home to see his new baby daughter Brooke, thus missing exhibition games at Edinburgh against Scotland, at Ibstone against J. P. Getty's XI, and a county game versus Glamorgan. He was back and bouncy for a further county game at Lord's against Middlesex, needing a bowl to run the stiffness out of his shoulder and fingers. He returned just one for 76 off twenty-three overs, with four maidens, as Middlesex succeeded in scoring 305, which was better than England had managed in all but one innings of the series so far.

It was shown how by Test selector Mike Gatting (85), who handled Warne as well as any other batsman for the season, and Mark Ramprakash (76). Australia replied with seven for 432 (Mark Waugh 142 not out, Elliott 83 and Steve Waugh 57). Warne showed that his pre-trip form had returned by taking the first three wickets of the Middlesex second innings and ending with three for 55 from twenty-one overs, with six maidens, in the county's six for 201.

He lost his spin partner, Bevan, dumped for the Fourth Test after his inept display with the bat at Manchester and his failure so far to make much impact with the ball. He was replaced by Ponting, from whom he could learn something about handling bouncers. England's only change for the match, beginning at Headingley, Leeds, on 24 July, was to drop the unlucky Caddick for Mike Smith.

However, it took some more extreme precautions with one of the most blatant examples of 'doctoring' a wicket when, three days before the game was due to commence, its chairman of selectors, Tom Graveney, ordered that the pitch be changed. It was too dry and lacking grass, he decided, which would have given Warne an advantage. It was too much for the England camp after his performance at Manchester.

Claiming that even he would have managed to 'turn it square' on the spurned pitch, Graveney made sure that the new wicket was prepared green and well grassed, obviously to benefit the English seamers, But this interference had more than a 50 per cent chance of backfiring. The fixation about Warne seemed to blind England to the fact that Australia had two exceptional pacemen in McGrath and Gillespie. They were just as likely as Warne to take a big haul of wickets if presented with a pitch that suited them.

Taylor again won the toss, but this time he did not hesitate to send England in. The game was interrupted by rain until late in the day when Atherton and Butcher saw off Gillespie, who was replaced by Reiffel. He soon removed Butcher (24) at 43 and Stewart (7) at 58. Even when Hussain came to the wicket, Taylor held back Warne, judging the pitch to be for the fast men only. Sure enough, at 103, Hussain (26) edged one from McGrath to the skipper himself at second slip. Night watchman Headley stayed with the defiant Atherton (34 not out) to stumps, with the score three for 106.

Headley stayed a decent time into the second morning to reach 22 before he was caught in the gully off Gillespie, who was working up a formidable pace. At 154, Atherton (41) was also caught, hooking McGrath.

Thorpe came in and Warne had to look on in admiration as Gillespie bowled him comprehensively. Healy judged Gillespie's speed the fastest he had ever kept to, which was high praise, given that McGrath could rip them through if he wished. If anything, he stepped up a notch in the next few overs as he polished off the final four wickets cheaply, having Crawley caught by Blewett, Croft caught protecting his body rather than his wicket and clean-bowling Gough and new man Mike Smith, as England crumbled to just 172. Gillespie finished with seven for 37 off 13.4 overs, with one maiden, while McGrath took two for 67. Warne was given one over for two runs.

When Australia began its reply, Taylor failed yet again, this time with a duck, retreating from a Gough short snorter which touched his glove. Apart from his 129, Taylor had now scored 7, 1, 2, 1 and 0. Any other player—except for the Waughs—with this sort of return would, like Bevan, be given his marching orders. The opposition pacemen now had an early go at Blewett, who was soon out for 1, nicking one to Stewart off Gough. Mark Waugh (8) was then caught-and-bowled by Headley, while Steve Waugh (1) was out when he pushed an ordinary ball from Headley to Crawley at bat-pad. The score was four for 50, with only Elliott standing tall.

The opener was joined by Ponting. They both began to develop their innings with sound techniques and a natural aggression that gradually made the England attack wilt. Elliott reached his second century in three Tests and went on to be 134 not out at stumps, with Ponting 86 not out. Australia was four for 258—86 runs ahead with six wickets in hand.

Next day, Ponting reached a masterly century and continued on to 127, when he miscued a hook off Gough and was caught at point. The score was five for 318, and the partnership had reached 268. At stumps, Australia was five for 373, with Elliott on 164 not out and Healy 27. There were still two days to go and England was 201 in arrears.

Early on the morning of day four, however, Healy was bowled by Ealham for 31 and Warne followed without troubling the scorer for Australia to be seven for 382. Then Elliott found a partner in Reiffel to take the score to 444, at which point Gough knocked back Elliott's off stump when he was on 199. He walked off feeling a little cheated. As a minor consolation, he was the first Ashes player to be dismissed one short of his double century.

England's agony continued. Gough bowled Gillespie for 3, but McGrath (20 not out) then surprised everyone again by staying with the dashing Reiffel (54 not out from just seventy-two balls) for an unbeaten tenth-wicket stand off 40, which again allowed Taylor the extravagance of being able to declare, this time with the score on nine for 501. The skipper judged that 329 was too much for England. Besides, he couldn't trust the Leeds weather. Five sessions to get ten wickets was good insurance.

His judgment again proved correct as England soon lost Butcher (19) to McGrath, who then had Atherton caught by Warne in the gully. At 57, Reiffel slid a ball under Stewart's bat to bowl him for 16. Gillespie chimed in with an express ball to Thorpe, which ended in Mark Waugh's safe hands in the slips. England was four for 89 and looked like folding, but Hussain and Crawley fought an encouraging rear-guard stand of 123 unfinished by stumps. Hussain reverted to his First Test form, defying Warne and building an excellent innings of 101 not out, while Crawley was on a fighting 48. At four for 212, England was just 117 short.

Warne bowled without fireworks and did not receive any help at all from the wicket, which was Graveney's expectation. It took the spinner until the next morning to remove Hussain for 105 when he lobbed a straightforward catch to Gillespie at mid-off. That loose shot would haunt him, as would the knowledge that Warne had now snared him four times in the series. Even if he managed a score, the spinner was there to stalk him.

Ealham (4) held up proceedings with Crawley for an hour, until, at 252, Reiffel found the edge of Ealham's bat and Mark Waugh took a 'blinder' at second slip. Reiffel then bowled Crawley (72) and England were done, almost, at seven for 256. Reiffel and Gillespie wrapped up the remaining three between them and, after lunch, England capitulated for 268, giving Australia a win by an innings and 61 runs.

Reiffel took a fine five for 49 off 21.1 overs, with two maidens. McGrath (two for 80) and Gillespie (two for 65) bowled up to standard. Warne was limited to one for 53 from twenty-one overs, with six maidens.

Australia was now up two–one in the series. With two Tests to play, England would have to win both to take back the Ashes that had now resided with the Australians since 1989. Taylor and his men had fought hard to restore themselves after a poor start in the one-dayers and the First Test. Those shock days were now faded memories as the team looked forward to the Fifth Test at Trent Bridge, beginning in ten days time.

More than Taunts at Taunton

Warne was keen to have a good work-out in the only game—against Somerset—before the Fifth Test, after bowling about half his normal quota at Headingley. There was a full house at the Taunton ground on 1 August, the biggest attendance since Bradman's 1938 team. It inspired the county batsmen on the first morning to blast the tourists, scoring none for 72 in the first thirty-five minutes in the morning session. Captain Steve Waugh brought on Warne, in tandem with McGrath, to put the brakes on.

Warne thrived on the challenge to put the county in its place and maintain his reputation as the scourge of England's bats. He loved taking on players who had never faced him and those who had not survived when he caused such havoc in England in 1993. One victim was Somerset's Mark Lathwell, once hailed as a potential star, whose promise had been dealt a blow by Warne and his fellow bowlers on that tour. His Test scores of 20, 33, 0 and 25 had not been enough to earn him a third Test. Hughes had roughed him up twice and then took his wicket, while Warne and May had cast doubts on his capacity to handle the spinners. Now, in the summer of 1997, he again ran into Warne, who sensed his apprehension.

Lathwell pushed and prodded for half an hour before Warne had him caught by Mark Waugh close to the wicket. It was a cruel game at times, but every batsman in first-class cricket who faced Warne dreamt of dominating him. In the 1920s, 1930s and 1940s, the biggest boast in world cricket was 'I got Bradman.' In the 1990s, the equivalent was, 'I smashed Warne.'

No one at Somerset in August 1997, least of all Lathwell, would be able to make it as he carved his way through the line-up to claim five for 57 from 18.3 overs, with seven maidens, as the county managed 284. Australia's reply at stumps was four for 182—for a day's tally of fourteen wickets for 466, with seventy boundaries. The big crowd had been treated to the best day's entertainment of the season.

On day two—Saturday—the Australians went on to 323, with Steve Waugh hitting 62. Andy Caddick took five for 54, making a point after being dropped from the line-up for the Fourth Test.

Somerset batted again in warm sunshine for three for 147, but without the fervour of the first morning. Warne again removed Lathwell, this time working a leg break around him as he launched himself at it and was stumped by Healy. Warne's stint at the crease was nothing more than a useful tune-up as he took one for 26 from eleven overs, with three maidens.

The slower pace of the run-getting, the beer and the heat brought out a pathetic yet ugly side of one section of the crowd, who focused on Warne, non-stop.

He had learned to live with some of the taunts, such as:

> *Warnie… Warnie… you fat bastard, you*
> *fat bastard…*
> *You ate all your pies…*

And:

> *He's fat, he's round, he bounces on the*
> *ground …*
> *Shane Warne … Shane Warne …*

Waugh brought him on to bowl with this latter chant ringing out. It was repetitive and boring, so the drunken slob element, a group of about twenty shirtless wonders, turned nasty with:

> *Warne takes it up the arse; Warne is a*
> *poofter;*
> *… We own your country, we own your arse…*

If it had been sung once or twice, it would have still been a chorus too much. But the offenders went on and on. The words reverberated around the small ground. Warne hesitated before bowling another over. He looked across to his captain, Steve Waugh, who had stepped in to stop the humiliation of Taylor earlier in the tour. He spoke to the umpires.

'It's too much,' he told them. 'I don't think we should play on with that…'

The umpires conferred with the Somerset chief executive. Security men were sent to the terraces. They soon ascertained who the two ringleaders were. They were escorted, protesting, out of the ground, to mild applause from real fans, who had come to watch good cricket, not hear foul abuse.

At the post-play press conference, Waugh was forced to defend his actions when reporters pointed out that the crowd's behaviour was no different to anything else in other parts of the world. This was true. In South Africa, New Zealanders and Australians were called 'sheep-shaggers' at the Wanderers stadium. At the MCG, the outer section, formerly 'Bay 13', would muster: 'So-and-so *is a wanker.*' In Sydney, there was more aggressive language accompanied by missile throwing. In India, it was less abuse and more projectiles, and the occasional ill-timed pitch invasion that threatened a game, if India was losing.

But Waugh's response was right. It should not be tolerated. He asked the reporters if they would bring their wives and children to the game if they were subjected to 'loutish behaviour'. The silence from the inquisitors told Waugh that he would receive no support in the papers the next morning.

Sure enough, the reports next day implied that the tourists couldn't take it. Perhaps the tabloids were worried about losing some of their loyal readers, who supported the jingoistic 'journalism' proffered in their sensational pages.

Nor did the more responsible papers come out in support of Waugh's action. This reflected their resentment of Warne's domination of England over three Ashes campaigns. They would love to see the back of him forever. Sadly for England, if Warne could overcome his shoulder injury, there were at least two more campaigns of big-turning torment in wait for them.

Showdown at the Bridge

Mark Taylor called tails for the fifth time in the Tests and again won the toss at Trent Bridge, Nottingham. The wicket was good and he had no hesitation in batting with an unchanged line-up. England had been forced to replace the injured Gough. It also dropped Butcher, Smith, and Ealham and brought in the Hollioake brothers, Adam and Ben. Caddick and Malcolm regained their places.

Taylor and Elliott took advantage of the even pace and began with 117 before Elliott (69) was caught behind off Headley. At age thirty-one, the Victorian had reached 1000 runs for the tour, a milestone that registered his stamp on the season. Taylor passed 6000 in Test cricket en route to 76, when he was bowled by Caddick. Blewett stroked an impressive 50 before playing a loose drive off Ben Hollioake. Australia reached three for 302 at stumps, with the Waughs—Mark on 60 not out and Steve 38 not out—in great touch.

However, they did not last long together next day. Mark was first to go, lbw to Caddick for 68. Steve was subsequently bowled by Malcolm for 75. From then on, the middle and late order made a rare collapse, as Australia lost its last seven wickets for 125 to be all out for 427, forty-five minutes after lunch.

England began at a pace mid-afternoon and cracked 76 before tea and without losing a wicket. Stewart's 50 came up in just sixty-one deliveries as he launched into all bowlers, including Warne, who began a 22-over spell before tea.

The small break didn't seem to slow Stewart, but Atherton was vulnerable to Warne, who asked Taylor for more close-to-the-wicket fieldsman. A few balls later at 106, he had the England skipper caught behind for 27. Stewart crashed on to 87, including 18 off one over from Gillespie, while Taylor persevered with his ace spinner. At 129, Stewart punched at a Warne turner. It skidded off the bat, clipping Healy's glove and popping up over his head. The keeper threw himself back to catch the ball, sending his England counterpart on his way for the best innings of the match so far.

Hussain came in and looked tentative having to face Warne first-up. He flicked a two and then received a sensational ball that was a nearly as good as *That Ball* which dismissed Gatting in 1993. It turned prodigiously from the line of leg stump to cannon into off. Warne had thus captured the first three wickets and put Australia back in control of the game. It was the fifth time he had dismissed Hussain in the series.

Healy then pulled off a superb catch down the leg side to remove Crawley (18) off McGrath. England was four for 141.

Thorpe and Adam Hollioake then retrieved the situation to take the score to four for 188 at stumps.

Next morning, it took Australia another 55 runs before it broke through when Hollioake (45) edged Reiffel to Taylor. At the same score, 243, Warne had Thorpe (53) probing forward. The ball hit his glove then his front pad for an easy catch to Blewett at forward short leg.

Croft came in, thankful he was not facing speed. He launched into Warne for a six and collected 18 before Taylor brought on McGrath, who soon put an end to his jinks, leaving England seven for 272 at the lunch interval. After the break, Reiffel bowled the composed younger Hollioake for an impressive 28.

McGrath rolled up the tail with two wickets to take the figures with four for 71 as England finished with 313. But it was Warne's burst that had done the damage with the key England bats at the critical moments. He took four for 86 from thirty-two overs, with eight maidens.

Elliott gave Australia's second innings a heady start by blazing 37 in an hour, but just before tea he was out to a fine running catch by Crawley on the square-leg boundary. The happy hooking continued with Taylor (45) lobbing an easy catch to Hussain, leaving Australia two for 105, and 219 ahead. At 134, Mark Waugh was lbw to Headley for just 7, while Blewett put together a patient 60 before departing at 156. Ponting joined Steve Waugh and was still there at stumps with the score on four for 167—a lead of 281. Taylor said he wanted at least 100 more.

On day four, after Steve Waugh went early for 14, Healy came in and put the series in Australia's hands by smashing 50 in forty-nine balls. He added another 13 before exiting, with Australia six for 278 and 402 ahead. The rest of the Australian innings wagged on 58 more runs, with Ponting going for 45, Warne for 20—including a retaliatory six off Croft—and Reiffel for 22. The final total of 336 meant a lead of 450—exactly the figure that Taylor had in mind as 'enough'.

England responded by losing Atherton on tea for 8, caught behind off McGrath at 25, which was England's score at tea. After the break, England's top order batted as if it had fifty overs to get the runs, but Stewart went for 16 and Gillespie then bowled Hussain for 21.

The score was three for 75 and the English bats were now in full suicidal mode. Crawley made a rapid 33 runs, but he was no match for Gillespie, who beat him with sheer pace and had him caught behind down the leg side. It was four for 99, and some of the Australians began to wonder if it would be all over by the end of the day's play.

With this in mind, there was an extra pep in Warne's step as he took on Thorpe. The left-hander seemed to be trying to reach a personal hundred before his team-mates deserted him as he cut and drove with panache.

The terraces were full of Warne-taunters, some of them decidedly overweight, chanting their 'fatboy' lines and lyrics. He began conducting their efforts from the slips, as if to show his contempt. Perhaps driven by the yobbos, he was in a mood to swarm, removing Ben Hollioake—whose brother had already gone for the same score and the same way to Gillespie—lbw for 2. Warne waved to his tormenters, who returned a bleary-eyed cheer, or was it a jeer? No matter. He was just too good.

Croft was there to make modest hay again while he could. He had in mind Warne's smashing him for six in the last innings. Croft replied in kind and was soon caught by McGrath attempting another. Caddick had no idea how to play a Warne top-spinner and was lbw for a duck, making England eight for 166. Thorpe (82 not out) kept playing his shots but McGrath made sure he ran out of partners by taking the last two wickets at 186. The innings was over after forty-nine overs, one less than a one-day innings.

McGrath (three for 34), Gillespie (three for 65, off just eight overs) and Warne (three for 43 off sixteen overs, with four maidens) shared the wickets. Warne's overall seven for 129 just pipped McGrath (seven for 107) for importance in the game, but Healy's keeping and his second-innings batting display earned him Man of the Match.

Australia had won by 264 runs, which gave it an unbeatable three–one series lead. Taylor and his men celebrated appropriately. They had now defended the Ashes on five consecutive occasions. It was going to be hard to whip up team enthusiasm for the remaining Test at the Oval in eleven days time. Could they overcome those hideous 'dead-rubber blues' that had dogged the victorious Australians for four years now?

Dance of the Derrière

The Australians celebrated their fifth successive winning of the Ashes more like a soccer team taking the World Cup than a dignified national cricket squad. Yet it was entitled to. It was a sporting feat of historic importance. The cameras picked up Shane Warne's victory dance on the dressing-room balcony at the Oval. He held a stump over his head and swung his hips, responding at once to the English yobbos, who continued their insulting chants, and the large contingent of ecstatic Australians.

Warne's reaction was at the same time a reaction to all the heckling he had received around England, and an exhibition of his delight at winning after a hard-fought comeback. The cameras captured his antics for TV news items in the UK and Australia, and stills shots in the morning papers. Most of the English papers featured him on their front pages. His swinging *derrière* became symbolic of England's humiliation. The headlines and editorials delighted in masochistic attacks on the losing home team, as the British papers love to do. Captain Atherton took the brunt of the brutal put-downs. He was the scapegoat. Journalists called for his sacking as captain.

Warne's dance of derision was not aimed at the England team, writhing in the agony of defeat in the other dressing room. He felt for the opposition. Earlier in the season, he and his team-mates had been there on five notable occasions—in the three one-dayers, the game against Dean Jones's Derbyshire and the First Test. Then the British media had been merciless in their attempt to crush the spirits of the tourists by writing them off as second-rate, has-beens and losers. Warne, in particular, along with Taylor, came in for fierce criticism.

Yet it was noteworthy that Warne was the only one of the tourists who made a public reply, which meant that it was observed in countless living rooms around the world through the all-seeing eye of television.

It was not the image that the ACB wished to portray of Australian supremacy in the sport, even if it reflected the unfair pressures placed on the nation's star cricketing attraction. Warne's action, like his send-off of Andrew Hudson at the Wanderers in 1994, would not help his chances of one day leading the Australian team, if he wanted this honour.

Did it seriously harm his possibility of gaining the captaincy? Probably not, if it was the last such exhibition, no matter what the provocation. Yet the spinner would have to wait his turn. Once Taylor stepped down, Steve Waugh would be the logical choice to replace him, especially after he had taken the brunt of the tough press conferences in England on the 1997 tour.

Déjà Vu All Over Again, Once More

Warne was allowed to miss an exhibition match against Ireland at Eglinton and the final county game versus Kent at Canterbury. He had been carefully handled by the team management to keep him fit and fresh for the Tests. He and McGrath were the only front-line bowlers in working order for the Sixth Test, beginning at the Oval on 21 August. Gillespie's back put him out of consideration and Reiffel was forced home when his wife developed complications with the birth of their child. In came Shaun Young, the Tasmanian all-rounder, and Michael Kasprowicz.

England experimented and played musical chairs at the same time. It dropped Crawley, Ben Hollioake and Croft, while Headley was injured. In came batsman Mark Ramprakash, paceman Peter Martin and Philip Tufnell. Mark Butcher also returned for a game on his home turf.

Atherton at last won the toss and batted on a dryish wicket. McGrath bowled Butcher (5) early and soon after removed Atherton for the seventh time, caught by Healy. Stewart and Hussain attacked Kasprowicz, who was despatched for several fours. Taylor brought on Warne. His first ball turned and sent a buzz through the crowd. Within minutes, he had put the batsmen back in a containable box.

England was two for 97 at lunch, but straight after began batting the way it did in the last innings at Trent Bridge. McGrath trapped Stewart (36) lbw and, at 128, had Hussain (35) caught and then bowled Thorpe for England to be five for 131. McGrath had all five wickets.

Warne was on at the other end worrying all batsmen with his accuracy and occasional big turn. He cornered Adam Hollioake, rolling big breaks past him, which the batsman pushed a pad at or tried to ignore. Then Warne bowled a straight one, which was also left alone. It bowled him, and left Hollioake (0) looking foolish. The score was six for 132.

Ramprakash (4) tamely bat-padded one from McGrath to Blewett. Martin (20) showed spirit, hitting McGrath for six. Next ball, McGrath bowled him and nodded towards the pavilion. Caddick (26 not out), hit Warne for another six, but soon after the spinner had Tufnell (1) caught by Blewett. Malcolm (0) was lbw to Kasprowicz and England was all out for 180 at tea.

McGrath's figures were seven for 76 off twenty-one overs, with four maidens. Warne took two for 32 from seventeen overs, with eight maidens, but only McGrath's exceptional bowling prevented the spinner from a haul himself.

Taylor led the way in Australia's reply by smashing 3 fours off one over from Malcolm, then two more from Martin. Atherton was forced to bring Tufnell into the picture early and it soon paid dividends when Elliott played all over one to be bowled for 12 with the score at 49. Taylor (38) went soon after, but Mark Waugh and Blewett made it safely to stumps at two for 77, and the Australians looked forward to taking a 150-run lead and wrapping up the match in three days. This overconfidence showed up in the batting on day two.

At 94, Mark Waugh (19) became Tufnell's third victim. Then, at 140, Caddick trapped Steve Waugh (20) lbw for 20. But it was Tufnell who was the main threat. Only Warne (30) resisted the English spinner's grip, smashing him for a mighty, straight six before playing on to Caddick, while Ponting battled on to 40 until he, too, fell to Tufnell's guile.

Australia reached a disappointing 220, when 320 would have just about sealed the game. Tufnell upstaged his counterpart Warne and matched McGrath's dominance with seven for 66 from 34.3 overs, with sixteen maidens. The tabloids recorded that the Aussies had been given 'a dose of their own medicine'. They looked as inept at handling spin as the England batsmen had at any time in the series.

Michael Kasprowicz broke through in England's second effort by removing Atherton for 8, then Stewart for 3. Taylor then produced one of his magic tricks by bringing on Mark Waugh to bowl his innocuous off-spin when everyone expected Warne. Before long, he had Butcher on his way lbw, placing England on a precarious three for 26. Hussain and Thorpe stuck together until stumps with the scorecard reading three for 52, or in actuality, three for 12.

Taylor rallied his men for one last mighty effort in the field on day three and Warne obliged. Hussain (2), rattled at having to face the spinner early, had a go at his third ball and sliced it to Elliott at short third man, who took a tidy catch. Warne had had Hussain six times in the series. Thorpe, England's lone batting ranger, was joined for a vital stand by Ramprakash that looked like taking the game away from Australia until Thorpe was caught by Taylor off Kasprowicz, who then claimed Hollioake lbw for 4, sending England to lunch on a shaky six for 145.

After the interval, Ramprakash (48) danced down the pitch to a Warne delivery. It looked neat, but Warne saw him coming and speared the ball in quicker. The batsman missed. Healy gathered and knocked off the bails.

Warne was now limping. A groin injury had recurred and was hampering his delivery. Mercifully for him, Kasprowicz closed England's innings by taking the last three wickets with the score at 163, taking his figures to seven for 36 from 15.5 overs, with five maidens, a better result than either McGrath's or Tufnell's. Warne's figures of two for 57 from twenty-six overs, with nine maidens, were a commendable end to his Ashes bowling campaign.

Australia had a mere 124 to rake up to win. It was the sort of score that gave recent Aussie teams the jitters. It should not have, but it did. To say this one batted mindlessly would be too harsh, but there was a certain lack of application and concentration evident. Malcolm began the rot by trapping Elliott (4) lbw at 5. Taylor (18) at 36 followed the same way, this time to Caddick. Mark Waugh (1) was caught behind off Tufnell, reducing Australia to three for 42. Steve Waugh struggled through to tea with Blewett at three for 49. Soon after, Blewett (19) was given out caught behind off Caddick, who then had Waugh (6) caught by Thorpe at slip to make Australia five for 54.

Ponting and Healy then staged a 34-run partnership that should have turned the game, but for a poor lbw decision to Tufnell against Ponting when he was on 20. At 92, Healy thrashed a ball back to bowler Caddick, who juggled and then snaffled it.

Warne, who had proved a good rear-guard fighter with the blade, but not yet a match-winner, came to the wicket to find himself with novice Shaun Young. Warne's legs may well have been jellied, for the game was now on the knife edge it should never have been. The batsmen had let down the bowlers, who had done their jobs with steadiness in the past five Tests with rarely a faltering step. Now here was the leg-spinner, forced into a tough position as a batsman that he had rarely been in before. There wasn't even a Healy to ask what to do. Young was defending grimly, but not experienced enough to take the game in hand.

Warne's dilemma was whether to defend and take the game in pushed singles, or open up the shoulders for some big hits. There were just 32 measly runs to get with three wickets in hand. Warne decided to lash out in a do-or-die effort and he died, with a catch to Martin off Tufnell for 3. He left the field to the roar of a crowd stunned by what it was witnessing. Australia was choking again at the death in a Test, as it had done twice in 1981 when facing Willis and Botham. Now the England heroes were Caddick and Tufnell. Kasprowicz (4) was soon caught by Hollioake off Caddick at 99.

Young met McGrath for a chat they would never remember verbatim, if they heard it above the din at the Oval as England's win was now the obvious bet. McGrath (1) prodded at Tufnell and was caught at slip by Thorpe. The score was 104. England had won a heart-stopper by 19 runs.

Caddick's five for 42 demonstrated that he should never have been dropped, and Tufnell's four for 27—eleven for 93 for the match—raised the question of his non-selection in the other five Tests.

The Australians suffered in the dressing room, as they always did when defeated. Yet the series was theirs three–two, which was infinitely better than two–three. They had been clearly dominant in the business part, winning three Tests by huge margins when it counted. The discrepancy between the teams was as marked now as it had been in the four previous series.

A big crowd of fans gathered for the final presentations. Tufnell, the only player to take a 'ten-for' in a Test, was Man of the Match. The team coaches awarded their opposition Man of the Series awards. That was easy enough. Thorpe (453 runs at 50.33) was outstanding for England, while McGrath (thirty-six wickets at 19.47) was even more prominent for the winning side.

Taylor was presented with the Ashes urn replica, which was what all the fuss had been about. The next time these two sides met in England—2001—it would be the third century in which the battle had been waged.

Caddick (twenty-four at 26.42) was England's top bowler, but was equalled by Warne's effort in also taking twenty-four wickets (at 24.04). Warne's performances with the bat (188 at 18.50) did not reflect his occasional good form and the potential to lift his average into the 20s. He could not claim all-rounder status, but still his record was impressive. When he reached 6 in the first innings of the Sixth Test, he became the ninth Australian to make 1000 Test runs and take one hundred wickets, the fourth to score 1000 and take two hundred wickets (after Richie Benaud, Ray Lindwall and Merv Hughes), and the first ever to hit 1000 and take 250 wickets. He now had taken 264 wickets at an average hovering around 24 runs a wicket, as it had for his entire Test career.

He packed his bags for the long plane trip home to see Simone and Brooke. Like all the tourists, he had earned a prolonged break that would take him through to September.

16

Two for a Treat

Kiwi Entree

Once over the shock loss of St Kilda to Adelaide in the 1997 AFL Grand Final, Warne turned his mind to a warm-up Shield game, against New South Wales in late October, in preparation for three Tests against the touring Kiwis. It could not have been a more combative contest. The mighty New South Wales batting line-up had to chase Victoria's six for 509 declared (Elliott 187, Laurie Harper 160), and it spared Warne nothing in collecting four for 407 (Steve Waugh 202 not out) declared. He sent down thirty-three overs with just three maidens and returned figures of one for 117, his solitary victim being a good one, however, in Michael Bevan.

Warne bowled better in New South Wales's second innings, taking two for 78 from twenty-five overs with six maidens. His wickets this time were Taylor and Mark Waugh. Victoria took just first-innings points in the drawn game, but skipper Warne was pleased enough with his form and the ascendancy over New South Wales. He felt a great deal better than a year earlier when overcoming finger surgery. His shoulder was holding up, although he would need concentrated physio work to keep him going as the season progressed.

The Tests against New Zealand, beginning on 7 November at the Gabba, were the perfect preparation for the main contest later in the summer, a three-Test series against South Africa. By the first day, Warne was fired up as ever for a professional performance. The Kiwis may not have been world-beaters, but they would like to be. It was up to the Australians to make sure there were no upsets. They brought back Reiffel for Young from the team at the Oval Test in late August. The Australian team was at full strength but for Gillespie, whose stress fracture to his back would keep him out for the entire season.

Kiwi skipper Stephen Fleming won the toss and invited Australia to bat on a green wicket. It looked a smart move when the first four batsmen (Elliott for 18, Blewett 7, Mark Waugh 3 and Steve Waugh 2) fell to Chris Cairns for just 53. It should have been five for 54. TV replays showed that Ponting had tickled one down the leg side to keeper Parore, but the umpire said not out. Cairns had taken just six for 477 in his previous five Tests against Australia.

Taylor was unmoved by this onslaught. He found a partner in Healy at 108, after Ponting had gone for 26, and they added 117 until Taylor was out for 112 late in the day. It was his sixteenth Test century. At stumps, Healy was on 62 not out and Reiffel 23, with Australia six for 269.

Although Healy was out early next day for 68, Reiffel continued his fine form in England to compile 77—his highest Test score—from 113 balls. Warne joined his Victorian team-mate for some controlled mayhem before he was caught on 21 going for a big hit. The Australians were content with 373 after the poor start.

After Blair Pocock had made a neat 57 before being bottled up and then dismissed by Warne, New Zealand reached three for 134 at the end of day two, with Fleming on 49 not out. Fleming went on in fine style the next morning to make 91. Chris Cairns then joined promising newcomer Craig McMillan, who straight-hit Warne for six to reach his fifty. Moments afterwards, however, the spinner gained revenge by trapping the young bat lbw for a commendable 54. The score was six for 279, and it took McGrath's bowling of Cairns (64) at 317 to put the brakes on. Warne came back to grab two quick wickets and make sure New Zealand didn't overtake the home side's first-innings score. Still, the reply of 349 made the 24-run lead negligible. Warne took the figures with four for 106, sending down a shoulder-testing forty-two overs with thirteen maidens to demonstrate he could still deliver long spells.

Australia batted again and lost Taylor for 16 to be one for 25 at stumps. Next morning, Elliott soon departed and when the Waugh twins and Healy all went cheaply, Australia was four for 105 and in a spot of bother. Blewett and Ponting then pulled their team out of a hole with 91 and 73 not out, respectively, to allow Taylor to declare late on day four at six for 294.

New Zealand made it to stumps safely to be none for 4. It would have ninety overs on the final day to make 315, at the not-impossible rate of 3.4 an over.

The next morning, however, McGrath sent back the first five batsmen for 69, at one stage taking four wickets for 4 runs as New Zealand declined from one for 55.

Warne again chipped in to polish off the tail as New Zealand crashed to 132 all out, giving Australia a comprehensive win by 186 runs. McGrath ended with five for 32 (seven for 128 for the match), while Warne took three for 54 from twenty-five overs with six maidens (seven for 160). Taylor took the Man of the Match award for his 112, his innovative captaincy and five catches, including his fortieth catch off Warne. This broke Gary Sobers's record of thirty-nine off Lance Gibbs.

New Zealand repeated its second-innings collapse nine days later in the Second Test, at the WACA ground in Perth—only this time in the first innings—as it slumped to five for 87 on the opening morning. Cairns and McMillan fought back aggressively to add 74, but Kasprowicz first broke McMillan's thumb and then had him caught for 54. Then with the score at 187, Warne tossed one high to Cairns (52). It dipped, but the batsman latched on to it, flicking it hard to mid-wicket. Mark Waugh launched himself sideways and grabbed a 'screamer' horizontal in mid-air. It was the catch of the summer so far.

This effort exposed the tail and Warne duly proceeded to chop it off, to finish with four for 83 from 22.4 overs with three maidens, his third successive top bowling performance, bringing his Test wicket tally for the summer to eleven.

Taylor's day was soured in Australia's first innings when he was lbw for 2 to left-arm quick Shayne O'Connor, who early next morning also removed Blewett for 14. However, when Elliott departed soon afterwards for 42, placing Australia on three for 71, the Waugh twins came together to put on 153, with Mark Waugh, in particular, in aggressive mood for his 86. Steve, with 79 not out, and Healy, 3 not out, were there at stumps with the score at four for 235.

Taylor urged a lead of 200 as the pair went out to bat on the third morning, but Waugh was bowled by O'Connor for 96, with the score at 262. Healy then took charge to run up 85 and was helped in the run feast by Reiffel with 54 in eighty-eight balls. Warne was not to be outdone and he went for big shots that came off, ripping 36 off just twenty-five balls to assist Australia's tally up to 461. At 244 ahead, Taylor had his desired lead.

New Zealand soon lost Pocock for 1, and then Young for 23, making the score two for 53. The young spinner Daniel Vettori came in as night watchman. Warne came on and snared him for 1, caught by Taylor. New Zealand went to stumps an uncomfortable three for 69, with batsman–keeper Adam Parore 42 not out and Fleming 0.

Early next morning, Warne caused Fleming (4) to pop one to Blewett close to the wicket, making it four for 84. The spinner relished the prospect of a big haul, but he was thwarted by the unlikely figure of New South Wales paceman Simon Cook, replacing the injured McGrath, who aimed his deliveries at the notorious WACA pitch cracks and took five of the next six wickets as the Kiwis crumbled again for 172. He ended with five for 39—his best first-class figures.

Warne had to be content with two for 64 off twenty-six overs, with four maidens, giving him six for 147 for the game. Steve Waugh was Man of the Match.

Australia had won the trans-Tasman series two–nil.

Taylor ushered his troops down to Hobart for the back-to-back Third Test, commencing on 27 November. The main interest left in a contest that had not fired the public imagination was whether the Australians could break their bad habit of capitulating in a final Test that did not matter.

Taylor won the toss and batted in cold, wet conditions at Bellerive Oval. Only fifteen overs were bowled on the first day, and Taylor and Elliott were still together at stumps, with the score on none for 39. Taylor was first to go on day two, bowled by O'Connor for 18. Blewett then began a long stand with Elliott, who reached his third Test hundred—all in 1997—and looked likely to settle in for a second when he was caught for 114 with the score at 238. At the same score, Blewett played all over one from Doull to be bowled for 99. Steve Waugh (7) and Ponting (4) then went quickly and, at stumps, Australia was five for 273, with Mark Waugh 21 not out and Healy 3.

On the morning of day three, Mark Waugh gave another of his exhibitions of artistry. He reached 81, in yet another too-short display that was worth paying the entry fee for alone. He was supported in short bursts by Healy with 16 and Reiffel with 19. Warne came in, pottered about for twenty minutes or so, then tried to hit Vettori into the Derwent, missed and was stumped for 14. Kasprowicz added a useful 20 to help land Australia on 400.

New Zealand faced just thirty-seven balls in its first innings before rain stopped play for the day in mid-afternoon, with the score at none for 15. With three days now gone, there would have to be some imaginative captaincy to avoid a Test fizzle.

Next morning, Reiffel broke through at 60 to bowl Young for 31, but Horne, who replaced the injured Pocock, was unstoppable in making the most of his chance. He outpaced Parore in a fine stand of 132 before Steve Waugh had Parore lbw for 44 at 192. Next ball, Waugh had Fleming caught behind for a golden duck. At the other end, Warne cornered new man Roger Twose lbw for two. Steve Waugh then deceived McMillan with pace to trap him lbw, also for 2. New Zealand was five for 198, still less than half Australia's score.

Reiffel finally had Horne (133) caught by Elliott after a top innings and Fleming showed he was a captain with verve by declaring at six for 229. He had nothing to lose. To bat on would mean a certain draw. By declaring, he threw the initiative into Taylor's court and opened up the possibility of a result.

Steve Waugh took the bowling honours with three for 20 off nine overs. Reiffel returned two for 27, while Warne had a lean time with one for 81. It could easily have been three wickets, but for some lbw denials which could have gone either way.

Taylor opened the run-chase with Mark Waugh, presumably because Waugh was more of an attack specialist than Elliott. It seemed an odd move. Elliott was more likely to thrash a fast 50 than Taylor, who perhaps should have dropped himself down the list. The score was none for 14 at stumps.

On the final day, Waugh was lbw to O'Connor for 9 without addition to the overnight score. Blewett then came in and proceeded to annihilate the bowling, scoring 56 in sixty-five balls. Taylor, by contrast played a sheet-anchor role when it wasn't needed. He ended on 66 not out in 143 minutes, having scored at about half Blewett's pace, and then declared at lunch on two for 138, leaving New Zealand to score 288 to win in sixty overs.

Fleming and co. clearly fancied their chances. The Kiwi skipper changed the batting order, lifting Astle to the opening spot and promoting Cairns to number three. A dead game in a dead rubber was now full of life.

New Zealand's moves came off as Horne and Astle led a ferocious charge, picking up 72 in thirty-nine minutes, until Reiffel broke through by capturing Horne lbw for 31, off just twenty-seven balls. Cairns came in and began by slamming sixes off Warne. But this was what the Australians wanted. Warne kept tossing the ball up, tempting more. Cairns was suckered into a dash too many and Healy stumped him with the score at 93.

Reiffel soon struck again, this time having Astle caught by Ponting for 40. New Zealand was soon four for 95, when Warne slipped one past Fleming before he had scored for Healy to effect another speedy stumping.

McMillan and Young combined for a useful 42 before Young also succumbed to Warne and New Zealand was five for 137. Parore joined McMillan only for Warne to roll a near unplayable ball past the latter, which he edged to Taylor after making a valuable 41. The score was six for 152.

It didn't deter Parore, who kept attacking. He and Twose lifted the Kiwi tally to 218. There was 70 to get at less than a run a ball with four wickets still in hand.

But then the Warne factor came into play. The spinner tempted Parore, who had collected a bright 41 in just fifty-five balls. He took the bait and sent a catch to Elliott. A few minutes later, Twose was run out for 29. It was eight for 221. The target now looked a bridge too far and when Steve Waugh removed Vettori caught behind, making it nine for 222, it looked utterly unreachable. However, the last pair in—Doull and O'Connor—then made themselves heroes across the Tasman by defending for thirty-eight minutes in facing sixty-four balls to prevent an Australian win. New Zealand remained on nine for 223 and forced an honourable draw.

Warne ended with five for 88 off twenty-eight overs with six maidens. It was his twelfth 'five-for' in Tests and took his series tally to nineteen wickets at 25.05, beating his own record against New Zealand of eighteen at 16.94 in Australia in 1993–94.

Greg Blewett was made Man of the Match, and surprisingly Taylor (214 runs at 53.53) received the Man of the Series award ahead of Warne.

The three Tests had been a financial flop and made observers wonder why New Zealand was preferred over India, which was long overdue for an extended series in Australia. Tendulkar versus Warne would be just one battle among many that would cause Australian fans to turn up in their droves.

New Zealand, however, provided the perfect build-up for the three Tests against South Africa, commencing on 24 December—four weeks away. All the Australians seemed to have run into form, with the injured McGrath ready to return in place of Cook.

Perhaps the preparation against New Zealand was the ACB's intention.

One-Day Dips

Before those Tests, however, the first stanza of the usual triangular one-day international series began, this time between Australia, South Africa and New Zealand.

The Australian selectors at last made a move to improve the performances of the national one-day team by selecting the best eleven short-game players, with Steve Waugh as captain and Warne as vice-captain. Only they and Ponting, McGrath and Gillespie of the Test team would remain as regulars in the one-day side. Out went Taylor, Healy, Elliott, Blewett and MacGill. Healy was justified in feeling aggrieved. He had done nothing wrong as either keeper or a late middle-order batsman. However, Australia lost nothing with Adam Gilchrist as a keeper and he was a better bat, especially in the bursts needed up the order.

Andy Bichel, Michael Kasprowicz, Paul Reiffel, Paul Wilson, Tom Moody, Ian Harvey, Adam Dale and Gavin Robertson would not be automatic choices, but would get opportunities during the series due to injuries and form fluctuations.

The players to join the one-day regulars would be Gilchrist, Darren Lehmann and Michael Bevan, with Michael Di Venuto being given the chance at the top of the order.

The new one-day leadership of Steve Waugh and Warne (with Mark Waugh making up the 'brains trust') was a clear pointer to the future. It was all a radical departure from the past—more a revolution than an evolution. It caused some discontent among those who missed out, particularly Taylor, who felt slighted that he had lost control of 'his' men. The problem was that he was not as equipped for the short, sharp innings as the others. While he would be one of the first aboard for a long time in the Tests, retaining him as a slow passenger in the short game was not tenable.

The selectors knew that their would be teething troubles early, and they had to risk that this new outfit under Waugh would be slaughtered by the tough one-day unit South Africa had put together. Nevertheless, the selectors were taking the long view. They were doing the best as they saw it in terms of winning the World Cup in England in May–June 1999.

Australia's traditional approach had not been good enough since winning the World Cup a decade ago under Border. Something fresh and innovative was required.

As most observers predicted, South Africa was too strong in the first game against the new home-team combination in a day–nighter in Sydney on 4 December. The tourists scored a modest 200 with Kirsten (44) continuing his long-game form. Australia collapsed from one for 61 to seven for 92, thanks mainly to Man of the Match Pat Symcox, who took four for 28 and scored 27 not out. The final total of 133 in thirty-eight overs was a miserable start for Steve Waugh, made worse by the crowd misbehaviour which caused a five-minute break in play when the South Africans were subjected to unacceptable abuse from a drunken element among the spectators. Symcox, who fielded on the boundary, was the main target. He complained it was the worst abuse he had experienced.

The second game against New Zealand on 7 December—the first day–nighter staged in Adelaide—was more encouraging. The Kiwis caught Steve Waugh and his men by surprise, charging out of the blocks with McGrath conceding 32 runs from his first four overs. Astle (66), Fleming (61) and McMillan (43) contributed to the competitive score of seven for 260. Despite the onslaught, Warne managed three for 48 to be the best of the bowlers—all of whom were under siege from the enterprising New Zealand effort. The Kiwis were smarting from their humiliation during the Tests. A one-day win against Australia would restore pride. They had already beaten South Africa.

Man of the Match Mark Waugh (104) answered the challenge with his eleventh one-day century and a 156-run opening stand in twenty-six overs with Di Venuto (77). It was enough to push on to victory on the third-last ball of the night with seven for 263. Bichel guided a shot through third man for four to win the game after a worrying stutter in the middle order. The big crowd for Adelaide of 30 049 loved the entertainment and suggested future day–nighters there would be a big success.

South Africa began poorly in a day–nighter at the MCG on 9 December, due to a brilliant fielding display by the Australians, who secured four run-outs. Only Rhodes (42) got going in the Proteas' eight for 170, while Mark Waugh was the best of the bowlers with two for 39. Australia's middle order again fell apart—from three for 79 to eight for 104—and the team struggled to 125 all out in 39.1 overs. Man of the Match Klusener ruined the night for the 55 673 fans, taking an outstanding five for 24.

South Africa continued its winning form with a tight win over New Zealand at Bellerive Oval. The Kiwis needed a six to win off the last ball, which Harris could only hit for four.

The MCG again played host on 17 December in a day–nighter between Australia and New Zealand attended by 31 097. The Kiwis scored just 141 in 49.3 overs, thanks to an even bowling display by Paul Wilson (three for 39), Dale (two for 22) and Bevan (two for 26). At one point, the tourists were six for 45, before Harris (62 not out) came to the rescue. Australia began badly thanks to Cairns (four for 40) and were three for 22 before Ponting (60 not out) and Bevan (42) put on 95 for the fourth wicket.

Australia's six-wicket win kept the critics from baying for blood, although some were already suggesting the selectors' gamble with a new-look team was a failure. The proof of the cake, however, would only come when the series resumed early in January after the first two Tests against South Africa.

Main Course

The biggest crowd for a Test in twenty-two years—73 812—settled at the MCG on 26 December, ready for the start of the fourth series between Australia and South Africa in the new era. They were disappointed as Elliott (6) tried a big pull shot off Klusener which went straight up in the air for an easy catch to keeper Richardson. Taylor stayed, but couldn't move the runs along against some accurate bowling on a slowish wicket, and he was caught for 20 off the medium-pacer McMillan. Two for 42 became three for 44 at lunch when Mark Waugh was caught behind off Donald for a duck.

The post-lunch session was not much better as Australia crawled to four for 92, losing Blewett stumped off Symcox for 26. After tea it was a different game as Steve Waugh and Ponting opened up and took control of the game. The stumps score was four for 206, with Waugh 87 not out and Ponting on 56.

Next day, Waugh (96) was caught off Donald for 96, his eighth time out in the 90s—in his ninety-ninth Test. Healy (16) came and went quickly, but Ponting went on to 105 before Symcox bowled him. At 309, Reiffel (27) was bowled by Symcox, Warne was caught and bowled by Pollock, and Kasprowicz (0) was caught by Bacher off Symcox to end the Australian effort, which was mediocre at best.

South Africa replied in kind, losing Bacher (3) and Kallis (15) early. At 75, Cullinan (5) was run out before his battle with Warne could warm up. He was nervous and too keen to avoid his tormentor.

Cronje then came to the wicket. Taylor crowded him and Warne had him pushing to Blewett close to the wicket for a bat-pad catch for a duck from the second ball he faced. The Australians were delighted to have South Africa four for 92 at stumps, after a day in which just 195 runs were scored.

On day three, the slow pattern continued until Kirsten was caught off Mark Waugh. Pollock, a natural attacker, didn't appear comfortable and pottered about against Warne, who sensed a kill. He delivered a wrong 'un, several stock leg breaks and then a top-spinner that broke through Pollock to have him lbw for 7. Pollock, who padded up and didn't play a shot, seemed miffed at the decision and received grunts of commiseration in the South African dressing room. It was a dangerous if not ill-advised way to play the spinner, who over the years had relied on this folly as a steady wicket-taker.

Warne was in top form and loving his stint in front of a 'home' crowd, who were enjoying his typical show. The batting was costive, but the bowling action was swift, with Warne sometimes slipping through an over in less than two minutes. He was catching the edge of the bat and causing all who faced him to play and miss so much that the crowd were waiting for a wicket every ball. He was often unplayable and raised expectations with frequent and enthusiastic appeals.

No matter how often they were turned down, he kept smiling and trying. The only thing missing from a complete effort was the flipper. It hadn't been coming out that well in net practice in the morning. Warne didn't see the need to give the tourists a free hit to deep mid-wicket or through cover point. It was all part of a well-tried strategy: starve the batsman of runs and make him hungry, then anxious and finally desperate.

In the event, he finished with three for 64 from forty-two overs, including fifteen maidens—more than twice as long a stint as any other bowler—as the South Africans folded for 186. His figures did not reflect his control over the Proteas. On other occasions, he had bowled less efficiently and taken twice the number of wickets.

In keeping with the match's trend, the Australian top order again collapsed. Elliott (4) was perhaps unfortunate to be given out lbw to Donald, who then had Blewett caught in the slips for 6 and bowled Mark Waugh for 1. Australia was three for 12 and South Africa was back in the game. Pollock helped by removing Steve Waugh (17) at 44, but Ponting stayed with Taylor through to stumps, with Australia four for 67 and 190 ahead.

Ponting (32) was first to go next morning, followed by Taylor to a huge Symcox break that seemed to go straight to Cullinan at slip without the batsman tickling it. Donald then bowled Healy for 4 to make Australia seven for 128—a lead of only 251. But Reiffel unleashed one of the best straight-hitting cameos at the MCG in many seasons to pull the game clear of South Africa's reach. Warne (10), Kasprowicz (19) and McGrath (18) stayed long enough for him to reach 79 not out, his highest Test score, as Australia reached 257, a lead of 380. Reiffel had now lifted his Test average in eight months from 18.04 to 28.24. As Taylor later quipped: 'A few more wickets and we'll call you an all-rounder.'

Reiffel was soon in the action again in the Proteas' second innings when he clean-bowled Kirsten for a duck. They recovered to be one for 79 at stumps, with Bacher 34 not out and Jacques Kallis on 40. The last day's equation was intriguing. South Africa had 302 to make to win from ninety overs—at 3.3 runs an over. If Kallis, Cullinan, Cronje and Pollock could get starts, anything was possible. However, the Australians remained favourites to win.

Next morning, Warne broke through to remove the stubborn Bacher for 39, having him caught brilliantly one-handed by Taylor. Cullinan came in and the spinner's movements were noticeably sharper. Warne delighted in this rivalry, which the batsman tried to play down but could not. On this day, it was not a fair contest as Warne beat him a couple of times before bowling him for a duck. He now had two wickets in the first forty minutes and South Africa was three for 89.

Cronje joined Kallis for a fine stand of 122 before the South African skipper, on 70, edged Steve Waugh to be caught by Taylor. The Proteas were four for 211. Cronje had handled all bowlers with conviction except Warne. During the long stand, he beat the bat no fewer than thirty-one times, but couldn't find an edge, prompting Taylor to remark later: 'On another day, he'd get a few more nicks. He'd bowl the same way and get six or seven.'

Kallis rode his luck to reach a well-deserved, fighting 101 when Reiffel bowled him, making South Africa five for 229.

Warne then offered some hope when he had McMillan caught by Taylor, and McGrath trapped Richardson lbw for 11, making it seven for 260. But Pollock and Klusener hung on until stumps and save the game with the score at seven for 273—107 behind.

Warne's prolonged effort of forty-four overs, with eleven maidens, returned him three for 97. His match marathon read eighty-six overs, twenty-six maidens, six for 161. Taylor had used him both as a strike and stock bowler at different times during the Test. He was to reap far greater rewards in the Second Test, beginning in just two days time, on 2 January 1998.

Rich Desserts

Both teams anticipated a turning wicket as usual in Sydney and chose an extra spinner each—Bevan in place of Kasprowicz, and Paul Adams for Lance Klusener. Cullinan paid the price of his Warne hoodoo once more when he was dropped for Herschelle Gibbs. The spinner was sorry not to see his bunny there, mainly because he wanted his wicket. The banishment was a small victory. Cullinan was a top bat against anyone except the Australians.

Cronje won the toss and decided to bat in what turned out to be a dreary day's play. The Australian bowlers looked jaded as they toiled again after only forty hours break from the long, unfulfilled last day in Melbourne. Taylor rang the changes to try to engender some freshness in the bowlers, using eight of his men in seeking to break through, but with only occasional success. The South African batsmen were equally sluggish, with only Gibbs showing any real enterprise for his 54. Cronje was the main offender in a long but plodding occupation of the crease. The South African skipper's approach seemed too negative, if he wished to push for a win. The Proteas crawled to five for 197 at stumps, with Cronje on 56 not out and Pollock on 1.

The next morning was all Warne's. First, with the score at 228, he induced an edge from Pollock to Taylor to send him on his way for 18. Richardson (6) didn't last long as Warne worked well with the breeze to drift one past his bat and into his stumps. Symcox joined Cronje and dominated a 40-run partnership. Taylor tried a few tricks, but couldn't budge them until he switched Warne to the Bradman Stand end, into the breeze.

His first ball drifted and dropped, catching Cronje (88) in two minds, propped at the crease. He edged it to Taylor for a catch to make South Africa eight for 287. In his next over, Warne had the hard-hitting Symcox (29) caught behind. The score remained on 287 and stayed there when Adams lasted only three balls before he gave Steve Waugh a catch.

Warne had taken five for 29 in the morning to give him five for 75 off 32.1 overs, with eight maidens. Bevan backed him up with two for 56.

Australia started after lunch again to lose Taylor for 11 and Elliott for 32, followed by Blewett for 28, before the Waugh brothers came together and saw the side through to three for 174 at stumps, with Mark on 78 and Steve 18.

Day three saw the Waughs working in tandem at their best as they took the full force of Donald at his top pace. Mark overcame the onslaught to post a fine century, but was out shortly after to Pollock with the score at 219.

Ponting joined Steve Waugh for a partnership of 98, which took Australia into the lead. Then, at 317, Donald came back to bowl Waugh for 85. Australia eventually went to stumps at nine for 392, with Healy on 31 not out and McGrath 3.

Next morning, South Africa took the new ball, but it didn't stop Healy and McGrath collecting another 29 runs to reach 421, when Donald wrapped up the innings by having McGrath caught behind for 14, leaving Healy 46 not out.

Australia's lead was 134. South Africa's hopes for survival were slim, but they were keen to give Australia a chase—Cronje spoke of 150—in order to exploit the myth of the home team's vulnerability in pursuit of a small score.

The speed men had Australia off to a good start by dismissing Kirsten for 0 and Bacher for just 3. After lunch, Taylor used Warne and Mark Waugh, but it was the leggie who was once again to be the destroyer. At 21, Cronje was facing Warne after playing him defensively with soft hands. Warne floated one up, which seemed to drift into the right-hander's pads. The batsman appeared to lose the line, pushed at the ball as it dipped and sent a catch to Blewett at short leg.

This was a major blow, leaving South Africa on three for 21. Then, at 27, Gibbs pushed forward in a similar fashion to Cronje and Blewett took another one-hander. At 41, McMillan became the fifth wicket to fall and Warne's third victim when he went back to protect his stumps from a ball turning into him. It snapped past and clipped the off bail. Pollock seemed even more tentative when facing the spinner and prodded at a turner which snaked to Taylor for his fiftieth catch from Warne's bowling.

South Africa was six for 55, and the spinner was in familiar territory with batsmen who had caught a contagious rash. Warne was all over them, swaggering with the certainty of success. The opposition was so down he could afford to experiment with balls that in other situations might be risky. Even a flipper was tried, but quickly abandoned when it didn't pitch correctly.

Still on 55, Richardson spooned back a caught-and-bowled to Warne. Kallis was the only batsman to approach him with any assurance as he employed soft hands for forward prods, and strong forearms for sweeps. He was joined by Symcox, in for a bit of fun and mayhem when only the weather could save South Africa. They took the score to seven for 85 in mid-afternoon, when the heavens opened up and delayed the game. It resumed under floodlights after 6 p.m. in front of a small crowd.

Just after 6.30 p.m., Warne was on bowling to Kallis, who had been at the crease for 155 minutes for his 45. Warne rolled a quicker leg break down, catching Kallis in two minds. He hesitated for a fraction of a second, unsure whether to use bat or pad. The ball defied all geometric possibilities to squeeze through between his bat and pads to bowl him.

Warne stood mid-pitch, threw his hands heavenward and yelled his delight. He now had 300 Test wickets and few were sweeter or cleaner in execution than this.

Warne was the thirteenth man to reach the 300-wicket milestone in the game's history, and the fourth fastest to get there behind Lillee, Hadlee and Malcolm Marshall. At twenty-eight, he was the second youngest behind Kapil Dev, the world record holder with 434 wickets. He was also the first leg-spinner to reach 300. Only Lance Gibbs, the West Indian off-spinner, had more, with 309 wickets. At 112, Symcox's merriment ended when Reiffel bowled him for 38. One run later, Reiffel dismissed Donald. Australia had won by an innings and 21 runs.

Warne's figures were six for 34 from twenty-one overs, with nine maidens. He had taken eleven for 109 for the match. Warne said afterwards that this match went a long way to avenging the defeat suffered by Australia in the corresponding Sydney game in 1994, when it was set 117 to win and reached only 111. This was after Warne had taken twelve wickets in the game. In that contest, he missed receiving the Man of the Match award. This time, because of the victory, it was his.

Australia now broke up as a unit for the rest of the one-day series. They would reconvene under Taylor at the end of January at Adelaide for one last tilt at South Africa. The one–nil lead at least ensured it could not lose a series against the visitors, who had failed to defeat Australia now in four successive series since the new era of South African participation in world cricket.

Fast-Food Finals

The one-day series resumed on 9 January when South Africa scraped in for a 2-run win against New Zealand in a day–nighter in Brisbane. Two days later, the Proteas took on Australia again. This time the home team batted first and looked a little better in reaching eight for 235, thanks to useful efforts by Bevan (45 not out), Mark Waugh (37), Lehmann (34) and Ponting (31). Donald (three for 37) as ever caused the batting order trouble. South Africa replied with five for 236 in 47.3 overs to score an easy five-wicket win.

South Africa was in the finals, having beaten Australia in all three games between them. The critics now went after Steve Waugh, who was still not getting runs. Waugh refused to buckle. 'It'll be alright on the night,' was his stock reply. The selectors' 'bold gamble' was now being described as a 'failed experiment'.

The Australians' next game was a day–nighter against New Zealand in Sydney on 14 January 1998 without the Waugh brothers. Steve had an injured hip and Mark was suffering from flu. Warne became captain of Australia for the first time, judged by a huge TV audience and a crowd of 36 476. Few had formed a firm view on his skills. As the game progressed, his capacity to lead was put under the microscope.

Ponting (84 from 103 balls) and Lehmann (52) combined again for a 132-run fourth-wicket stand after Australia had been restricted to three for 36 in the first ten overs. The result was a fair score of 250.

Warne led the side onto the field and looked as 'pumped' as any leader of a football team. It was clear from his body language and air of authority that he had the confidence of all around him as he directed his bowlers and fielders—a fact that was not lost on the national selectors. His style was different from that of the laconic, cool-headed Steve Waugh. As wickets fell, the crowd enjoyed the game and got behind the Australians. Warne himself bowled as tightly as he had all summer in any form of cricket, with two for 19, and demonstrated that he thrived on the added pressure of leadership. New Zealand crumbled to 119 all out in just 33.1 overs.

Warne had a major supporter in former Australian captain Greg Chappell, who was impressed with his temperament and composure. Chappell thought Warne's behaviour in England in 1997 was taken out of context and nothing more than 'letting off steam' after all the concerted barracking he suffered.

'In many ways he's a big kid, enjoys a laugh and a good time,' Chappell wrote in *Australian Cricket.* 'And that's so important when it comes to striking a balance between cricket and normal life.'

Chappell recommended Warne as Taylor's successor because he was positive and aggressive.

Meanwhile, the Proteas won against the Kiwis at the WACA on 16 January to eliminate New Zealand and make it a South Africa versus Australia final series. However, there were still a few 'dead' one-day preliminary-round games to go. The first was a day–nighter two days later at the WACA between Australia and South Africa.

Australia's 165 in 48.2 overs was another disappointing effort with only Harvey (43) and Bichel (27 not out) managing some fight. South Africa coasted to three for 170, with Kirsten (44), Cronje (39 not out) and Kallis (38) doing the damage. It now had four straight wins against Australia.

In the last preliminary-round game, between Australia and New Zealand at the MCG on 21 January, the home team gave an improved batting performance, highlight by an even 100 from Ponting, as it compiled four for 251, only for Kiwi skipper Fleming to hit 116 not out and take his team to victory by four wickets. The game didn't count, but a loss did nothing for the Australians' morale as they prepared to tackle South Africa in the best of three finals beginning two days later at the MCG.

South Africa won the toss and batted in the first clash at the MCG on 23 January in front of a crowd of 44 321. Kirsten and Cullinan got away to a bright start and Steve Waugh was forced to bring on Warne earlier than planned to stem the run flow. After a bit of lusty hitting, Warne speared one past the advancing Cullinan (26) for a stumping, after having unsettled him again.

Kirsten (70), with Pollock (36) and Kallis (33) in support, helped South Africa reach nine for 241. Warne was expensive but effective in taking vital wickets with three for 52.

The Australians looked 'home' when Steve Waugh (53) and Bevan (57) added 101 for the fourth wicket to take the score to four for 206. But then six wickets fell for 29 in an insipid finish and Australia was dismissed for 235 on the second-last ball of the allotted fifty overs. Donald was again a problem for the Australians, taking three for 36.

After this, the fifth successive loss to South Africa, the critics were writing Australia off for the series. They included Ian Chappell, who wrote a damning piece about the captain and his side in the *Bulletin* magazine that hit news stands during the finals. Unperturbed, Waugh replied that he expected South Africa to 'choke' in the last two games. It was a bold comment that could come back to haunt him.

South Africa batted first in the day–nighter at Sydney on 26 January—after play on the scheduled date the day before had been washed out—and soon lost Cullinan for 3, caught by Warne off Mark Waugh. Then big Paul Wilson had danger-man Kirsten caught behind for 14, leaving South Africa two for 35. Klusener went soon after for 31, but Cronje and Rhodes took the score from four for 64 to 192, when Cronje slammed a huge six off Warne that landed on top of the Bill O'Reilly stand. Next ball, the Proteas' skipper went for another, but was caught in front of the stand by the running Bevan for 73. At five for 206, the game was evenly balanced.

Rhodes (82 not out) helped it along to a total of six for 228. Reiffel rose to the occasion with some tight bowling, taking three for 32, but Warne was expensive, with one for 52. It was the third successive time he had been carted for 50 or more. Nevertheless, his claiming of Cronje before he could go on to a match-winning score was a critical moment. It helped restrict the Proteas to a 'gettable' tally, provided the Australians didn't collapse in the same brittle manner as earlier in the series.

Waugh decided to promote the underused Gilchrist to the opening spot with his brother and the move paid off. The left-hander hit a century in 102 balls in front of an enthralled crowd of 26 293. He was supported by Ponting (47) and Harvey as Australia cruised to a win in 41.5 overs.

It had taken the Australians six games to win one, but they chose the most important moment to do so. Steve Waugh still expected the Proteas to crack in the last game. 'It's down to one game now,' he told the media, 'and we can win it.'

Donald was unfit for the 'grand' final at Sydney next day and was replaced by Paul Adams. The hapless Cullinan, still with Warnitis, was not risked in the big game. In came Bacher. Australia steadied with the same combination.

Waugh won the toss and batted, so as to have the opposition batting under lights. This time Gilchrist managed only 6. Ponting then took hold of the game, despite losing Mark Waugh (21) and Lehmann (10). At three for 79, he was joined by Steve Waugh, who proceeded to make a superb 71, while Ponting slammed 76. Bevan remained 36 not out as Australia climbed to seven for 247 at the close.

South Africa's reply began badly when Kirsten was beautifully run out by Ponting for 3. Reiffel then settled on a line that worried Bacher and Kallis, until he removed both of them within four balls for South Africa to be three for 64, with Cronje and Rhodes now together at the crease. Steve Waugh then shrewdly brought on Warne, who tied Cronje up for four balls and kept him waiting between a couple of deliveries, just for effect. Cronje, who had dominated in the second game, wanted to assert his influence early, knowing that otherwise Warne could end the game in a short spell.

The batsman came down the wicket to his fifth ball and missed it, only to have Gilchrist whip off the bails with a flourish. Cronje was caught so far out of his crease that he he just kept walking. Warne had taken a belting or two from him in the one-dayers, but got his revenge when it counted.

South Africa was four for 72, but not yet beaten. Rhodes went for 29, but Klusener proved a major stumbling block, collecting 46 in forty-one balls until Steve Waugh took a sensational catch over his shoulder running back at mid-wicket to dismiss him. Bevan had the dangerous Pollock stumped for 28 and Australia was on top with the Proteas on seven for 191.

When Symcox was run out for 22 and Richardson followed caught by Ponting for 1 to make the score nine for 204, it seemed all over. However, things quickly changed through the unlikely figure of Adams, who managed to hit Warne for 14 in an over. South Africa was up to 233, just 14 short with two overs to go—one each from Warne and Tom Moody. McMillan and Adams now had to go for everything. Warne's first ball was pushed to Steve Waugh at cover. He swooped and returned to Gilchrist, who ran out McMillan for 15.

Australia had won a wonderful, see-sawing game in front of a disappointing crowd of only 19 008 to take the series two–one. Reiffel again took bowling honours with three for 40, while Warne was steady with one for 43 off 9.1 overs. Gary Kirsten was given the Man of the Series award.

South Africa's shock defeat left them empty-handed in both the one-dayers and the Tests—so far—but they were fine, tough and skilled competitors.

Australia's one-day 'experiment' had worked and was a personal triumph for Steve Waugh. The side was now somewhere on track for success in the 1999 World Cup with experienced and confident leaders in Steve Waugh and his deputy, Shane Warne.

For the moment, however, it was back to what many might consider the more serious business of Test cricket.

Back for More

Two days after South Africa's defeat in the one-dayers, Cronje regrouped his men for one last blast at Australia in Adelaide, commencing on 30 January. A Test win would level the series and restore some prestige to the tourists. They made two changes. Donald, who was injured in the second one-day final, was replaced by Lance Klusener. Adams, who took just one for 66 at Sydney, was dumped in favour of batsman Jonty Rhodes.

Australia dropped Bevan. It had to replace McGrath and Reiffel, both injured, and brought in 26-year-old debutant leg-spinner Stuart MacGill, Michael Kasprowicz and Andy Bichel.

Cronje did the right thing by winning the toss and batting on a wicket that begged for runs. South Africa was well on the way early with the openers putting on 140 before Bichel had Bacher (64) caught by Warne, who also caught Kirsten for 77 at 148 off

Kasprowicz. Kallis then fell lbw to MacGill, making it three for 160, but Cronje and Gibbs fought back to put on 109 before Blewett had Gibbs (37) caught behind right on stumps, leaving South Africa on four for 269, with Cronje 70 not out and Richardson, in as night watchman, on 0.

Taylor opened the next morning with Warne, who promptly bowled Cronje for 73. The spinner had removed the South African skipper at critical times in both the Tests and one-dayers. If he didn't get Cronje early, Warne would stalk him and win his wicket before he could turn the game. Their personal battle was a key to the fortunes of the summer. Cronje's average in this series would be 40, whereas without Warne to combat him, it would probably have been more like 70 or 80.

Rhodes went cheaply, followed by Richardson, caught by Taylor off Warne for 15 and seven were down for 305. But the South African tail wagged as McMillan and Pollock lifted the tally to 374, whereupon Klusener (38) helped McMillan put on another 69 before he was caught by Warne off MacGill with the score at nine for 443. Symcox then added insult to injury by crashing 54 from forty-two balls in just forty-seven minutes before Steve Waugh trapped him lbw, leaving McMillan on 87 not out. South Africa's 517 was the highest score of the series. Kasprowicz took three for 125, while MacGill returned two for 112. Warne managed two for 95 from thirty-three overs, with six maidens. He also took three catches.

Elliott was soon out for 8 when Australia began its long chase, but Taylor played doggedly to be 26 not out at the end of the day, with Blewett on 31 and the scorecard reading one for 71. Blewett didn't add to his score next morning, giving way to Mark Waugh, who helped Taylor put on 126 before being caught off Pollock for 63. Steve Waugh didn't last long and, at four for 207, Australia was in danger of being asked to follow on. While wickets fell around him, however, Taylor brought up his seventeenth Test hundred and stayed on like an immovable rock until he and Kasprowicz saw the side through to 317, thus evading the ignominy of being ordered to bat again. He was still there on 157 at the close of day three, with MacGill on 2 and the score at nine for 327.

Next morning, MacGill clattered his way to 10 as he helped Taylor edge the score up to 350. The skipper was left on 169 not out—the highest score by any player carrying his bat through an innings in a Test in Australia. The effort fully restored him as an opener after the horrors of the previous season against the West Indies. It eclipsed Shaun Pollock's feat with the ball of seven for 87, his best Test figures.

South Africa's second innings was full of the enterprise lacking in its previous five innings as it strove for quick runs. Another good opening stand, this time of 80, got them firing before Warne had Bacher caught by MacGill for 41. Kirsten was in fair touch, but couldn't find a partner en route to 108 not out. MacGill took over from a jaded Warne, who was limping and had a groin strain. His shoulder was also giving him concern. The physio work to allow him to function was becoming more frequent and urgent.

South Africa finally declared at six for 193. Warne took one for 52 from fifteen overs, with eight maidens. MacGill, who ended with the fine figures of three for 22, showed he had a big leg break and would be dangerous on turning wickets. He didn't have Warne's variety or pinpoint accuracy, but that might come as he developed. He displayed a good temperament at the top level, but whether Australia could afford the luxury of two leg-spinners was questionable. The sameness of such bowling might allow opposition batsmen too much familiarity. Better, in theory at least, to have a top off-spinner as an alternative. However, performance would count for everything. If MacGill took enough wickets, then he could not be denied a place.

Cronje had left Australia 361 to chase for a win. The seventeen overs remaining to be bowled on day four meant 107 in all were available—at a rate of 3.37 an over. But Pollock's dismissal of Elliott caught behind for just 4 jolted Australia. When Klusener bowled Taylor for 6, the score became two for 17 and a win already looked out of the question. Australia stumbled to two for 32 at stumps, with Blewett on 9 not out and Mark Waugh 11. The equation now read 329 to win at 3.65 runs an over, with eight wickets in hand.

Pollock bowled Blewett (16) at 54 next morning and so reduced Australia's options to a draw, a loss or a suicidal rush for runs. Mark Waugh was joined once again by brother Steve and together they carried the score to 112, when Steve was caught behind off Klusener. By now, Australia had fallen so far behind the required run rate that survival was the only thing in mind.

Mark Waugh obviously had his head down for an all-day stay. Ponting stayed with him for just less than two hours for 23 before Klusener had him caught. Australia was five for 185. Healy was at the wicket, and playing his natural game as Cronje crowded him, when Waugh at last brought up his thirteenth Test century. He had already been dropped twice and now, after Healy was dismissed and Bichel came to the crease, he was involved in a controversial incident when he was hit on the shoulder by a bouncer from Pollock and, as he turned away from the wicket in pain, dropped his bat, which crashed into the stumps. The South Africans went up for hit-wicket.

Umpire Steve Randell did not see the wicket being hit and referred the appeal to the third umpire up in the stand, Steve Davis, who re-ran the video several times from different angles and determined that Waugh had finished his shot when the bat hit the stumps, meaning that he was not out. But Cronje would not accept the ruling and play was held up for several minutes while he argued with ground umpires about it. His passion for beating Australia was admirable, but he was taking it too far.

Shortly after play resumed, Waugh was dropped by Symcox. Then Klusenser had Bichel lbw for 7 and Australia was seven for 215. Warne came out and met Mark Waugh for a quick conference. They had six overs to negotiate. Warne got in behind every one of the thirteen deliveries he faced, while Waugh steeled himself for the last twenty minutes. At the end, Waugh was 115 not out and Warne 4 not out as Australia reached seven for 227. The home team had achieved a remarkable draw, thanks to Waugh, whose unbeaten innings lasted 404 minutes. He faced 305 balls.

Cronje grabbed a stump and, once in the pavilion, speared it into door of the umpires' room. It was a stupid act, compounding his childish turn on the field. The South African skipper later 'confessed' to his action, but received no penalty. A similar action by an Australian would have received a swift and tough penalty from the ACB, as exemplified by the harsh rebuke for Healy, who was demoted from his position as vice-captain.

Australia had won the series one–nil. Pollock was named Man of the Match. Warne's twenty wickets at 20.85 earned him the Man of the Series award. Mark Waugh topped the batting average with 279 at 69.75, while Taylor collected 265 at 66.25.

Warne was happy to miss a short tour of New Zealand for four one-dayers in February. He was wanting to get over a niggling groin strain, and his shoulder was now giving him serious trouble after a long, hard summer, in which he had bowled twice as many overs as any other Australian in the six Tests. He was looking forward to a tour of India beginning in less then four weeks. But he was being nagged by the growing realisation that he would have to face shoulder surgery. The battle to recover from the finger operation seemed like a lot less than a year ago. It was not easy for him to gear his mind to more pain and the tedious months of rehabilitation. Always with him, too, was the worry that surgery would reduce his capacity to perform as he had just done with distinction over six Tests in which he had taken thirty-nine wickets.

Warne now had 303 Test wickets. There was much talk about him taking 500, even 600 wickets. The bowler himself would just be happy to make it through three Tests in India without breaking down.

17

Shane versus Sachin

A Score to Settle

Some weeks before the Australians arrived in India for their tour from February to April 1998, Sachin Tendulkar spent four days preparing for his clash with Warne by having three leg-spinners bowl at him. The dashing Indian batsman, whom Bradman said was his nearest modern incarnation with the bat, had watched most of the Australia's recent Test matches against the South Africans on television in order to learn as much as he could about his main opponent.

Tendulkar had two of the bowlers send down flippers to him until he felt sure he was playing the delivery properly, while the third bowler mainly served up wrong 'uns and top-spinners. He had seen how the South Africans floundered against the ball that Warne pitched into the rough outside the right-hander's leg stump, so he scuffed up an area around that spot and asked all the bowlers to aim at it with leg breaks. Tendulkar pushed and swept, and used his pads until again he felt he knew how to play such a ball.

He was bowled once and tickled another onto his stumps, and miscued the sweep about three times. The rest of the deliveries, literally hundreds of them, were handled with increasing skill and confidence. When he walked away from the last of these exacting sessions, Tendulkar felt he had done as much as possible in schooling himself for the forthcoming contest.

By contrast, although every Australian player had something to prove in the tour, none of them had done their homework on the Indians. They had not seen them on cable TV. Nor had they watched any videos to see how the spinners operated or Srinath bowled his deadly inswinger, taught to him by that finest of teachers, D. K. Lillee.

Warne had played against Tendulkar before, of course, first when the Indian was a brilliant teenager during that first horror series of 1991–92 and then in the World Cup in 1996. The bowler felt he was ready for him, as he had been for all the top bats around the cricketing world. Warne had vivid memories of his opening Test against the Indians in January 1992, when he had been destroyed and left with the miserable figures of one for 150. He wanted to show them just how far he had come in the context of a five-day Test series. Also on his mind was a chance to take a bagful of wickets on the subcontinent's turners. The flat, dry tracks helped the ball to turn, but much slower than in Australia. Spinners had to consider pushing the ball through quicker or face being belted by the locals with their experience on home pitches. India was a spinner's paradise, if they bowled well enough. The only problem was that Indian batsmen shared this heaven and played them better than any other nation.

The team as a whole had a broader challenge. Australia had a poor record on the subcontinent. The India tour had always been stereotyped behind Pakistan as the toughest because of the different culture and food, the third-rate hotels, the risk of illness and security problems. But the quality of hotels and the range of food available were far better at the end of the twentieth century than they were in the middle of it when Ian Johnson led a winning side there, as was the medical treatment for players who fell ill. Security would always be a problem, especially with the fanatical attitude of cricket followers in India. Players were mobbed when they were recognised in the street, and this forced many to restrict their movements outside the hotels. But with gyms, indoor pools, TV, computer games, organised tours and high-quality hotel restaurants, players could find a variety of ways to relax and avoid the crowds. Adventurous souls such as Steve Waugh could even slip out the back of a hotel and explore the city or surrounding region. He made such tours enjoyable and memorable with the odd high point, such as his meeting with Mother Teresa during the 1996 World Cup.

Waugh was the only survivor from the 1986 three-Test series, which did not see a result. He scored 12 not out, 2 not out, 39 not out and 6, giving him a flattering average of 59, and also captured two wickets with his medium-pace swingers. That series was highlighted by the tied Test at Madras, in which Dean Jones scored 210 in one of the most courageous innings in Test history.

Bill Lawry last led a winning side (three–one) in India in 1969–70 in a five-Test series. Since then, Kim Hughes had captained Australia to a two–nil defeat in a six-Test series in 1979–80. Border's team in 1986 drew two Tests and tied a third. The two nations played one Test, won by India, in 1996. Nearly three decades after Lawry's success, Taylor very much wanted a series win in both India and Pakistan to prove he was captain of the world's number-one side. The Australians made no secret of their desire to take over the mantle worn by the West Indies since the 1980s.

The team was better and more seasoned than the last challenge under Border in 1986, when he was in the process of rebuilding the side and its pride after beltings from England and the West Indies.

India had to start favourite despite struggling in recent times. Warne was expected to be the key. It was his first exposure to Indian Test wickets, which tended to crumble into dust by the end of a match. Warne was encouraged by looking at Richie Benaud's record in India. He took fifty-two wickets in eight Tests in the 1950s. In October 1956, he took a career-best seven for 27 at Madras, and followed it up two Tests later in Calcutta with his best-ever match figures, six for 52 and five for 53. In December 1959, at Delhi, he took three for 0 and five for 76, then four for 63 at Kampur. In January 1960, at Madras, he took a further five for 43 and three for 43, and in the same month, at Calcutta, managed three for 59 and four for 103.

The message was that Benaud had been brilliant almost everywhere, only missing out in one Test, at Bombay. Warne would be most satisfied to do as well at an average of six or seven wickets per Test.

Much was made of the battle between Warne and Tendulkar, one of the two best batsmen—the other being Brian Lara—Warne might ever face at the international level, given that the Waugh twins would always be playing with him.

There were many similarities between Warne and Tendulkar in terms of their fame. But while Warne was perceived in his home country as a hero with a larrikin streak, the Indian was regarded as a god. At twenty-four, Tendulkar was forced by the Indian fascination with cricket almost to lead a double life. Whereas Warne might wear wrap-around sunglasses and a cap to avoid being recognised at the movies, Tendulkar would dress like a street urchin to go to the theatre in his home city. Soon after he entered the Test scene at the age of seventeen, he started to wear ragged clothes, a false grey beard, dark glasses and a hat in public. In the seven years since then, during which he played in fifty-six Tests and boasted an average of 51.71, he had never been left alone by mobs in Bombay, and indeed everywhere in India. Along the way, like Warne, he cashed in on his fame. He accepted a $4 million deal with Adidas, though he rejected millions more to promote cigarettes. Tendulkar's face was always on TV signing a Visa card, eating a new muesli breakfast cereal and drinking Pepsi. Nevertheless, he wanted to remain invisible in the flesh, to limit the pressures brought by exposure and fame.

Whenever he batted, so much was expected of him. While Warne made no secret of his desire to conquer this champion,

Tendulkar played down the element of personal combat. It was not 'Tendulkar v. Warne', but 'India v. Australia', he reminded the media, as if it were not as important as it was being pumped up to be. Journalists ignored this. They knew a super-contest when they saw one. Tendulkar was primed and ready. Warne, more than any other bowler he had every faced, was uppermost in his thoughts. It would be the biggest spinner-versus-batsman contest since O'Reilly bowled to Bradman in the 1920s and 1930s.

The media, despite Tendulkar's public disclaimer, still billed the first game of the tour against Mumbai (Bombay) in late February as a major clash between these cricketing titans. Slater, with a handsome 98, Ponting 53 and Blewett 47 began well in Australia's eight for 305 declared. Then came Tendulkar batting at two down for Mumbai. He proceeded to demolish the Aussie attack, smashing 204 not out off just 192 balls with 25 fours and a six. He was especially harsh on Warne, who was given a solid working-over and finished with his most unflattering figures of none for 111 off sixteen overs.

Tendulkar was nervous when he arrived at the wicket, but soon eased tensions by lifting Warne's second ball to him for six. The 204 not out, in Mumbai's score of six for 410 declared, was his best-ever first-class score, surpassing his 179 against the West Indies in 1995. Having dreamed and practised this contest in the mind and actuality for months, he was satisfied he could take whatever Warne tossed up at him. Demoralised by this unrelenting onslaught, Australia crumbled for 135 in its second dig. Mumbai wrapped up the game by ten wickets.

It seemed that Tendulkar had drawn first blood. Some in the Australian media said it would be different in the Tests. Warne was not himself in the Mumbai game. It was noticeable that he delivered no flipper and perhaps only one wrong 'un, and that was not to Tendulkar, who received only the stock leg break with the occasional top-spinner. Warne had played this withholding game successfully everywhere, first in New Zealand in 1993 against Martin Crowe, who also belted him in a build-up game to the Test series. In the Tests, it was different and Warne worried the Kiwi skipper at every encounter and ran through his team-mates. They may have been lulled into a false sense of security after the initial shellacking by Crowe and his report that Warne 'only had an ordinary leg break'. It was all he saw before the Tests.

Again, a few months later in 1993, Warne was hammered into submission by Hick under the cathedral at Worcester. But in the Tests Warne dominated. It happened once more with South Africa and Cronje. Now Warne had been seemingly embarrassed by Tendulkar. Had the bowler not heeded coach Marsh's dictum that it was vital he and the team start the tour well? Was he holding back his range of deliveries for the Tests?

In the next game against the President's XI at Visakhapatnam, he bowled better, taking two for 88 off twenty-six overs in the home team's four for 329 declared. Notable were his dismissals of Laxman and Dravid, who would be in the twelve in the First Test at Chennai (Madras). Slater continued his great form with a dashing 207, with excellent support from Ponting with 155. The match was drawn.

Operation Bean Drop

Warniemania reached a new height of banality two days before the First Test when a media story broke about Shane's apparent desperation for tinned baked beans and spaghetti. Robert Craddock, in the Melbourne *Herald Sun*, reported that Australia would rush 'emergency supplies' of the food to India to save Warne from undernourishment.

'Warne is not a great lover of Indian food,' Craddock reported, 'and the Australian hierarchy is concerned he's not eating enough to sustain him through the marathon spells he faces in the three-Test series.'

Australian physio Errol Alcott had faxed the Australian Cricket Board asking for baked beans and spaghetti. It seemed that with skipper Mark Taylor, Steve Waugh and Ricky Ponting sick, Australia wanted to make sure Warne stayed well with the First Test about to commence. He had been getting by on a stock of beans and spaghetti coach Geoff Marsh had brought with him, but it had proved so popular it was now all gone. Warne was down to Vegemite on naan bread and supplementing his diet with vitamin capsules, along with tomato soup for dinner.

Back in Australia the ACB pondered the problem of 'Operation Bean Drop', as it was dubbed. They first considered asking the Australian High Commission in India to help out and then decided to send the products by air. The ACB approached the task with the determination of a wartime exercise. The beans had to get through, and on time. Warne had to be stuffed with carbohydrates so his energy levels would be high for the punishing heat and humidity of Chennai that a decade earlier had nearly killed Dean Jones when he made his great 210 in the 1986 tied Test.

The food company Heinz came to the rescue and announced in Melbourne that it was sending 1900 cans of baked beans, one per day for the rest of the tour for each of the nineteen members of the touring party. TV news clips showed boxes of cans being loaded into a plane's cargo hold. They were marked: 'For Shane Warne, Heinz Beans'.

The 'issue' became a lead news item in Australia on all media networks and generated the usual round of bean-eating jokes. An ABC TV news reporter, for instance, noted that Warne might have to fly home on his own after the Tests if he polished off all the beans that were being rushed to him. In India, a TV cricket commentator spoke of one of the Indian spinners in the First Test looking like Mr Bean, played by Rowan Atkinson.

'I think Warne is now a rival for that title,' he remarked.

The Melbourne *Sunday Age* commented that the secret to Warne's success could be put down to his being 'full of beans'. In ensuing days, scores of Warne–bean jokes sprang up across Australia and the world.

The whole matter was blown out of proportion because of the December 1997 media 'event' when Warne seemed insulted by a press question about his weight when, at the time, he was standing next to a Madame Tussaud's wax dummy of himself. His reaction led to much speculation about his fitness. Since then he had worked hard over January and February 1998 to drop a few kilos. In the first twelve days of the Indian tour, his weight fell to around 84 kilograms, the lightest he had been for two years.

The bean plea from India brought the usual response. Heinz and other companies rushed to capitalise on the publicity. Media commentators spoke about Warne's eating habits. Former Test player David Hookes noted that during a recent dinner with Warne he had only eaten 'plain meat'. Hookes was unimpressed by Warne's detestation of 'vegies'. An Indian restaurant owner was wheeled out for the TV cameras to talk of a visit by Warne to his Melbourne restaurant. The Indian had prepared an Indian-style curry pizza for him, given Warne's penchant for Italian food, including spaghetti bolognese, lasagne and pizza. Another representative of the Indian community in Australia made indignant noises for the cameras about the way in which Warne had insulted their culture.

The issue was getting a 'politically correct' ethnic spotlight thrown on it. The question was asked of how Australians would like it if touring Indian cricketers in Australia refused to touch local food and demanded Indian food to be flown in. It was exacerbated by Errol Alcott's diktat that, while in India, the players should 'look at the meal, touch it to ensure it is piping hot, smell it and then taste it'.

Alcott ordered players not to put ice in their drinks. 'When you're in a restaurant, watch the food when it's brought to you,' he was said to have told them. 'If a waiter touches the food with his hands or touches part of the utensils that touch the food, reject it.' Players wondered whether he was overreacting, but when Taylor and Ponting fell ill, the fears about 'Delhi belly' seemed justified.

After that, all meals eaten by the team on match days would be specially prepared by chefs at Taj hotels where the players were staying. The favourites for the lads were rice meals or Chinese and pasta dishes. They would only drink bottled water. They had been 'warned off salads because they are washed in local water', it was reported.

Seafood was also to be rejected because the local refrigeration was not up to standard. Steve Waugh, who liked to pass the time sightseeing and getting about rather than playing computer games in hotel rooms, noted how fish at the Vishakhapatnam market was dumped on a dirty floor. His report led to the tourists avoiding delicious-looking seafood delicacies at a barbecue put on by tour sponsors Fosters.

Warne responded to the bean storm the day after the news item by suggesting that everyone was overreacting.

'There's no big deal,' he told Mark Ray of the *Age*. 'There's no emergency, but I do struggle to find food I like over here. Like most of the guys, I enjoy baked beans and spaghetti on toast for breakfast and we'll enjoy it when more arrives.'

Warne added that he had a 'good' margherita pizza in the Madras hotel restaurant. He said that he and the other players preferred to only eat ice cream at the ground during a day's play. Journalists speculated that Warne would be signed up for sponsorship by Heinz when he returned to Australia.

Into the Cauldron

Taylor lost the toss in the First Test in the cauldron of Chennai and Australia suffered as Indian openers Mayam Mongia and Navjot Sidhu put together 122. Both batsmen went after Gavin Robertson, the 31-year-old off-spinner, and gave him a rude introduction to Test cricket. Then Mongia (58) swished at a lifting ball from Kasprowicz and was caught behind by Healy.

Sidhu had been advancing to both Robertson and Warne, and blocking the ball metres from his crease rather than stroking it. Warne tempted him again and Sidhu played the ball to Mark Waugh at silly mid-off, who flicked it back to the base of the stumps and Sidhu was run out for 62.

The score was two for 126, and Australia had squeezed back into the game.

Tendulkar strode to the wicket. He drove his first ball from Warne straight and a little uppishly for four. Two balls later, Warne spun one past his bat. Then another. Next ball, Tendulkar tried to cover-drive, but got an edge and was caught head-high by Taylor at slip, making up in part for having dropped Sidhu off Warne. Tendulkar had looked nervous in his short stay. The build-up after his great double in the opening match may have been too much. Warne was pleased, but not crowing. Tendulkar could have up to five more innings and his moment could come in any or all of those innings.

India looked vulnerable at three for 130, but captain Mohammad Azharuddin and Rahul Dravid added 56 before Azharuddin (26) top-edged a lazy cut off Warne to Reiffel at point. Then, at 189, Robertson trapped Saurav Ganguly lbw for his first Test wicket. At stumps, India was five for 232, with honours about even after the Australians had toiled hard in the oppressive heat.

Next morning, two hours before the game started, Tendulkar had net bowlers deliver leg breaks to him outside his off stump, which he crashed off the back foot until he was satisfied he had fixed the problem, if there were one in the first place. His obsession with beating Warne had reached an unprecedented level.

A slight breeze drifting across the ground gave Australia's bowlers some hope early on day two. They capitalised with Robertson bowling tightly and Warne also lifting his rating. Five Indian wickets fell for 25 and they were all out for 257. Robertson ended with four for 72, a top debut, and he took a catch. Warne finished with four for 85, taking his Test wicket tally to 307.

Now it was Australia's turn to face India's answer to Warne, the loose-limbed Anil Kumble, whose fast leg breaks and wrong 'uns reminded many observers of Bill O'Reilly, Australia's star of the 1930s. First he had Slater caught close-in for 11 and then trapped Steve Waugh for 12 when he shouldered arms and watched a wrong 'un slam into his stumps. Ponting was given out caught behind just on tea off Venkatapathy Raju, the left-arm finger-spinner, for 18, while Blewett (9) could consider himself unlucky to be lbw to Rajesh Chauhan, the right-hand off-spinner, whose questionable action had aroused much adverse comment. At stumps on day two, Australia was four for 193 with Healy and Warne both looking solid.

Warne was 13 not out and started next morning responsibly enough until he got out to a fine ball from Kumble that ballooned to Tendulkar at slip. In came Robertson for his first innings in a Test. He showed sound defence as he and Healy dragged Australia out of a nasty hole with a record ninth-wicket partnership against India of 96 before Healy was out for 90. When Robertson was finally out for 57, Australia had reached 328 and a lead of 71.

India's openers responded well until Blewett came on to trap Mongia for 18 with the score at 43. Then Sidhu took to Warne, belting 4 fours and a six off him in two overs. The bowler, with his shirtsleeves ripped off at the biceps for some relief from the clamminess, seemed out of sorts, perhaps ill and ill-tempered. He appeared to have a gastric problem on day one when he dashed from the field. Perhaps more than remnants of it were still with him. He was no-balled three times and Sidhu was caught in close by Mark Waugh off one of them. This did not improve the bowler's temper as he watched balls sailing over the boundary to the appreciation of the 40 000 trumpeting, whistling, conch-blowing and cheering Indian spectators. India finished at one for 100 and on top after a day that had seen it lose the initiative and then win it back.

On day four, India took control of the game with Tendulkar leading the way with a magnificent 155 not out, his third century against Australia. The diminutive right-hander faced just 191 balls in 286 minutes at the crease. He hit 14 fours and 4 sixes—one off each of four bowlers—and won the battle against all the Australians. Warne finished with one for 122 off thirty overs, including seven maidens. These were his third-worst Test figures since his first-ever Test. But he went for just 4 an over in Tendulkar's controlled onslaught and several times beat the Indian star, giving him more than hope that in future encounters he would break through again. With one Test gone, honours were even between the two, except that Tendulkar's performance had put India on top.

Warne would have preferred to be facing him on Australian pitches where there was more pace and he could attempt to dictate terms as he had against all comers. He resorted to round the wicket to Tendulkar, trying to bowl him round his legs or induce a catch by pitching the ball very wide. He achieved some bounce that was awkward and was twice unlucky not to have him caught with it, yet the tactic proved defensive rather than offensive, as the batsman responded by fending off the ball with his left pad. It nearly worked when Tendulkar, on 60, decided to hit against the spin and Ponting just missed a difficult chance at mid-wicket. Tendulkar now felt confident that all his preparation had paid off, but he would not be satisfied until he had taken many more runs off Warne. The other bowlers held no terrors for him.

Warne's only victim was Dravid (56), who took evasive action from a vicious turner out of the rough outside the leg stump. The ball popped up from his bat and Healy took his 350th Test victim. The leggie bowled sixty-five overs in the match. After many of them, he bent over with his hands on his knees, distressed by the heat and his workload.

Azharuddin (64) and Ganguly (30 not out) gave Tendulkar support as India climbed to four for 418 declared, giving Australia fifteen overs to negotiate before stumps. Slater (13) was out playing on to Srinath, then Blewett (5) and Taylor (13) were caught in close off Kumble, leaving Australia a miserable three for 31 at stumps, still 317 runs behind.

The next morning a combination of tenacious spin-bowling, the hellish heat, bad umpiring and weak batting put India on the right track by lunch time. Mark Waugh was given out caught at bat-pad for 18 to a ball which missed his bat by several centimetres, followed by Reiffel, supposedly caught off one which hit his boot and not his bat, and then Ponting, confusingly ruled lbw to a ball he snicked just short of slip.

Then, at 96, just on lunch, Steve Waugh (27) received the fourth bad decision of the morning, though, to be fair, only a replay could determine that he, too, had not hit the leather in a flurry of bat, pads and ball. None of the decisions was 'home-town' or biased—particularly with one of the offending parties being a top-class 'neutral' umpire—but they had all helped to give the Test to India.

After lunch, Warne wandered out and attacked. It seemed a pointless way to approach the situation. Healy was sitting at the other end as unmovable as he was in the first innings. If Warne had shown more restraint while still picking the bad ones for treatment, he might have lasted longer, given his good technique. Perhaps he was trying to 'get back' at the Indians for slopping him around the park the day before, but, if so, it was wrong-headed, given the situation of the game. At any rate, when the score was 153 and he was on 35, Warne holed out to deep mid-wicket Srinath off Chauhan after swatting him for a mighty six the ball before. He left the field with just a hint of relief on his face through the shroud of disappointment. He could have a cold shower and beer, after a job half-done and not thoughtfully executed.

Robertson arrived at the crease, but was unable to replicate his sterling first-innings effort. Kumble 'flicked' him a faster, lower off break that crashed into the stumps less than 30 centimetres up. It was a stinker. Robertson slinked off with a first-ball duck. Kasprowicz lasted a bit longer, but soon holed out, leaving Healy marooned at the other end on a typically determined 32 not out as Australia folded to an ignominious 168. Kumble completed a convincing double with four for 46 after his four for 103 in the first innings. Raju backed him up with three for 31 after three for 54. Only Chauhan with one for 90 and two for 66 would be in doubt for the next Test, not so much because of his figures as his arm action.

India ended up the winner by 179 runs and led the best-of-three Tests one–nil. Their victory was set up neither by bad umpiring nor a weak opposition, but by a great batsman—Tendulkar—playing towards the peak of his form and riding his good fortune. Australia was now being written off for this series by Indian and Australian commentators alike. It would take a strong skipper to shake off the 'the world is against us' mentality that must have crept into the dressing room on the rotten fifth morning.

Taylor was the man for the task, despite his own slipping form with the bat. Yet the question was, could Australia's modest attack led by Warne lift above the trying conditions and win in Calcutta in ten days time? It would take more than the character that this team had in abundance. A little luck and some batting with resolve by all the team would be a necessity.

Out of Eden

The Australian Cricket Board and its team selection panel made a blunder in announcing the one-day squad to follow the Tests on the morning of the Second Test at the mighty Eden Gardens stadium in Calcutta. It would not have helped the already fragile team morale to learn that Taylor, Slater, Blewett, Healy, Reiffel, Stuart MacGill and Adam Dale would be on their way home in two weeks to be replaced by Damien Martyn, Damien Fleming, Michael Bevan, Adam Gilchrist and Tom Moody.

The best time would have been before the team left Australia, even if it might be premature. Instead, the first three batsmen in would have had their departure in mind. They batted as if it were preoccupying them. On the sixth ball of Srinath's first over, Slater pushed forward and bat-padded a ball to forward short leg for a duck.

Azharuddin attacked, bringing in an extra gully and leaving just two men on the leg side. Blewett took the bait. He aimed to hit the ball on the on side, played all around an inswinging yorker and was bowled middle stump. Australia was two for 0.

The 50 000-plus pro-Indian crowd was making the 120 000-capacity Eden Gardens rock.

Mark Waugh (10) looked in command, but received a good inswinger from Srinath and was plumb in front. Australia was three for 15 and in trouble. At 29, Taylor (3) played at an away swinger from Ganguly that he could have left and was caught behind. Ponting joined Steve Waugh, who was batting freely, having returned to form with a century in the tour match between the Tests. He and Ponting stayed until lunch with the score at four for 67. They continued after the long break until 141, when Ponting (60) tried to hook at a shortish top-spinner from Kumble and was bowled.

Again the pendulum swung hard India's way when Healy was caught bat-pad at short leg by Laxman off Kumble for just 1, leaving Australia six for 151. Warne was at the wicket with Waugh and needed to buckle down, but instead swung at a leg break from Kumble and was caught at slip for 11. He walked off the field angry with himself for his irresponsibility, but he had done the same thing in the First Test. It seemed that the team coach and captain were failing to impress upon him the importance of showing some true grit.

At tea, Australia was seven for 175, with Waugh on 79 and using a runner because of a groin injury. Straight afterwards, however, a mix-up occurred and Waugh was run out, but then Robertson and Kasprowicz combined in an enterprising 54-run partnership that allowed Australia to reach 233 all out, just on stumps. Srinath, Ganguly and Kumble took three wickets apiece and kept the pressure on throughout the day. Honours were clearly with India.

Day two saw the home side take the game right away from Australia with some magnificent batting in which it compiled three for 369, scoring at a rare rate of 4 an over. The opening stand by Laxman and Sidhu was 191 before Sidhu (97) was trapped lbw by Mark Waugh, while Laxman hammered 95 before Robertson had him caught behind. India was two for 207, 26 short of Australia and set to deliver the *coup de grâce.*

This was accomplished by Tendulkar, who pounded 79 in just 109 minutes with 12 fours and two walloping sixes. Dravid (86) and Azhuraddin continued on into day three, which proved equally horrific for the toiling, lacklustre Australians as the India skipper made a magnificent 163 not out and India climbed to a mammoth five for 633. Azharuddin then stopped the slaughter and declared, 400 ahead of Australia.

Warne's miserable Test, indeed tour, continued as he returned his worst-ever Test figures of none for 147 off forty-two overs. Nonetheless, he did not bowl badly in comparative terms, as the Indians took only 3.5 runs an over off him. His problems were many. First, the Australian batting was so feeble that he had no reasonable score to bowl against. Second, there was no speedster of the calibre of McDermott, Hughes or McGrath to open up the opposition so that he could then scythe into the middle and late order. Third, he was facing five top-class Test batsmen, including two champions—Tendulkar and Azharuddin—playing on their own pitches, which were very different to those in Australia, South Africa, England, the West Indies and New Zealand, where Warne had reaped rich harvests.

These factors had reduced him from 'world's best bowler' to just an ordinary battler in two demoralising Tests. In turn, his performance had lowered his confidence. This had affected his batting, which lacked direction and conviction. Yet Warne and the bowlers were not the main culprits in India. They ranked well behind several batsmen—Slater, Taylor and Blewett, in particular—who lacked application and conviction in their work.

True to form, Slater (5) dragged one onto his stumps off Srinath and left Australia dangling at one for 38 at the end of the third day. Next morning, a Saturday, India broke the backbone of Australia's batting, reducing it to five for 97 at lunch. Healy and Steve Waugh, batting this time without a runner, battled on between lunch and tea until Healy was adjudged lbw in another poor decision to make Australia six for 138. Warne came to the wicket and seemed intent this time on a little more defence, but, in Kumble's first over after tea, was out caught-and-bowled for just 9. He seemed a dejected figure as he walked off.

The end was not long coming, with only Steve Waugh offering any resistance in nearly three hours of determined effort for his 33. Australia was all out for 181, beaten by a massive innings and 219 runs, its fourth-heaviest defeat ever. Kumble bowled consistently to claim five for 62, and was well backed up by Srinath, who took three for 44. These two bowlers were most responsible for giving India the series two–nil.

That night, most of the Australian team gathered in a bar at the team hotel, the Taj Bengal, to watch the Aussie Rules pre-season grand final between North Melbourne and St Kilda. A few of them, including Ricky Ponting, went out to party on at a local nightclub where, in the early hours of Sunday morning, Ponting got into a row with the bouncers after a female Indian journalist complained that he had pushed her.

After a second incident, Ponting was escorted from the club. The management called the police, but they did not arrive until an hour after Ponting had left. Australia's team officials—tour manager Steve Bernard, tour director Cam Battersby and captain Mark Taylor—read about the incidents in the Calcutta *Statesman* on Monday morning. They had a hearing and imposed a fine of $2000 on Ponting, who admitted the scuffle with the bouncers, but denied he had pushed the woman.

The news evoked considerable criticism from the Indian media, with some journalists rounding on the Australians for their attitude to India and its culture. The baked beans report, the apparent paranoia about local food, the pettiness of the team insisting on a plane rather than taking a five-hour train trip between the Tests and Ponting's behaviour were just a few incidents that the media seized on to go on the attack, particularly after the tourists had taken such a drubbing on the field.

Punch-drunk and reeling, Australia gathered together for the last Test at Bangalore with speedster Damien Fleming and all-rounder Michael Bevan arriving well before the one-day matches, ready for possible selection in the depleted team, while injured players Paul Wilson and Reiffel were sent home. There was only to be four days break before the two ill-matched teams played again. The Australians were flat after coming to the end of a long run of Tests and one-dayers that started in November and would end in April. There were also rumblings in the team about the splitting of the Test and one-day sides. The main culprit was Mark Taylor, who made his feelings public. It seems he had never come to terms with being dumped from the one-day team. He was supported by Reiffel when he arrived home in Melbourne.

Team morale was split, he said, 'with half the one-day side going and the other half coming'. Reiffel added philosophically that 'I suppose you have to go with the way the selectors had gone', which was the only attitude to take. The day of the specialist cricketer was well under way, despite the strong argument that good players could adapt to any form of the game. Evidence suggested that some were better suited to one form than another.

Considering the team's mood, it would be a surprise if Australia was competitive, as India seemed determined to make it a three–nil clean sweep.

More of the Same in Bangalore

Darren Lehmann and Adam Dale were brought in for their first Tests at Bangalore. Lehmann had waited ten years for his Test cap and had paid one of the most biggest dues in first-class cricket while accumulating more than 8000 runs. Dale, who had himself been ill for most of the tour, got his chance when Fleming picked up a respiratory infection on arrival at Bangalore. Most Indian observers were surprised that Bevan was not selected, a choice that would have given Australia three spinners with Slater being dropped and Blewett opening. Alternatively, Robertson could have been left out and Slater retained. In the end, Bevan, rushed over by the national selectors, was ignored by the tour selectors.

India was forced to make two changes, replacing the suspect Chauhan with the seventeen-year-old off-spinner Harbhajan Singh for his first Test, and bringing back Harvinder Singh for injured Srinath.

Taylor lost the toss and India batted. Kasprowicz broke through to have Laxman (6) caught in the slips at 24. Dale backed up his Queensland team-mate with tight bowling before Warne came on to a big cheer after an hour of the first session. He bowled a great line and kept Sidhu and Dravid quiet. Before the game, he spoke to travelling journalists and was circumspect about his form.

'I'm putting it down to experience,' he said, 'and will be a better bowler for it.' He reminded them that his flat performances had only come in the last two Tests. Sources close to the tourists reckoned that his mind was right for Bangalore and his first spell sugggested this was so. However, Robertson was loose at the other end and Sidhu took to him, taking the score at lunch to one for 96.

After the break, Warne struck back and showed India why he was regarded everywhere else in the world as cricket's best wrist-spinner. He bowled Sidhu round his legs for 74 at 109, just when he was looking dangerous. One run later, he bowled Dravid (23) with a fine leg break, which pitched centimetres outside leg and took off stump, making India three for 110. Then Tendulkar, with Azharuddin in the support role, took the game back with a 139-run partnership before Lehmann, bowling his orthodox left-arm finger-spinners, had Azharuddin (40) caught behind. Meanwhile, Tendulkar crashed his way to his sixteenth Test century in 107 balls and 164 minutes of superb power hitting. His hundred included 18 fours and 2 sixes—84 in boundaries. The average Test player would bring up a ton with about half his runs in boundaries, but the Indian champion charged the ropes with cuts and back cuts. It was an even better innings than his 155 not out at Chennai.

At stumps on day one, India was well on top at four for 290, with Tendulkar on 117 not out. Warne had taken two for 66 off twenty-seven overs and was the best of the bowlers. Dravid was his 310th wicket, making him the most successful spin-bowler in Test history. The West Indian off-spinner Lance Gibbs took 309 wickets.

Adam Dale broke through for his first Test wicket on day two by cornering Ganguly lbw for 17. Tendulkar then took over, smashing fours with improvised drives down on one knee and contemptuous back-foot shots through the on side. Even Warne, who continued his economy rate, was taken to, with 11 off one over including one towering straight six. The spinner struck back against Mongia (18), who had started to emulate the little master with his drives, but, unlike Tendulkar, could not control his impulses. He drove at a leg break pitching outside off stump and drifting away, only to pop it to the diving Ponting.

Tendulkar reached 177 and records were falling. He was aiming at Sunil Gavaskar's highest Test score by an Indian—236. Dale then stopped the rout by bowling him. Tendulkar had faced only 207 balls—a run rate of 85.5—in just short of five scintillating hours at the crease. He crashed 29 fours and 3 sixes, a remarkable 144 runs out of 177—or nearly 82 per cent—from boundaries. Had anyone ever collected better rates in a Test innings of more than 150? Only Bradman. He had performed better and for longer. Yet Tendulkar had scored 4, 155 not out, 79 and 177 for a tally of 415 at an average of 138.3, which was indeed Bradmanesque.

Harvinder Singh came in and was given out lbw to Dale first ball in another terrible decision and then Robertson had Raju caught at bat-pad, leaving India nine for 415. It had been a well-balanced, exciting session, in which five wickets fell for 125.

Robertson also picked up Kumble for 39 and India was all out for 424, the third time it had reached 400 in the series. Dale took the figures with three for 71. Warne was close behind with three for 104 off thirty-nine overs. His wicket tally was now 311 and he had Lillee's 355 next in his sights. Warne was 'honoured' to have taken Gibbs's record, he told the media, but disappointed that it had 'not come sooner in the series'.

Slater shot out of the blocks and gave India back some of its own exciting medicine against a weakened attack, but, at 68, Taylor (14) nicked one from Kumble to the keeper. He had now scored 12, 13, 3, 45 and 14 for an aggregate of 87 and an average of 17.4, raising the inevitable question of how long he could hope to retain his place in the team. A similar query hung over the mercurial Slater as he powered to 91 off 117 balls in 140 minutes of exhibition batting. It had all been too late, or had it? However, nothing could save out-of-sorts Greg Blewett, who managed just 4 before teenager Harbhajan Singh baffled him with spin and turn and bowled him.

After Slater left at three for 143, Mark Waugh (58 not out) and the first-up Lehmann (35 not out) took the score to 209 at stumps. Next morning, Lehmann picked up where he had left off the night before until, when he was 52, he pushed forward to Harbhajan and gloved one to silly mid-off. Ponting made 16 before nicking one off Kumble, but Healy was the victim of another doubtful decision when he was given out caught behind to the same bowler for only 4.

Warne joined the ailing Waugh—who had been ill overnight—and proceeded to bat as normal, unable to resist having a lofty waft that woke up the outfielders. By good luck rather than good judgment, along with his sound defensive technique when he applied it, Warne made it through to lunch on 22 not out. Waugh struggled to the break at 110 not out, his fourteenth Test century.

Australia was now six for 325, having lost three for 116 in a second successive pre-lunch session of fine Test entertainment. On the resumption, Warne kept up his usual belligerent mood and was out once more giving catching practice to fielders in the deep for 33. Lately, his luck seemed to be running out when he reached the 30s. One day soon a catch would be dropped when he was in that region and Warne would put his head down for a big one. This time it was the young Harbajhan who took a good catch from a high hit off Raju to long-off. Robertson came in and defended for a while and was then caught at bat-pad for 4, with Australia eight for 380, still 44 runs short. The score dribbled on to 394, when Kasprowicz pushed down the wicket and found himself lbw to Kumble, giving the Indian his fifth wicket for the innings, with Dale adding another one shortly afterwards when he was caught off the same bowler for 4. Kumble finished with six for 98, bringing his tally to a remarkable twenty-three wickets at 18.6 for the series. Waugh remained 153 not out, having 13 fours and 4 sixes, and facing 267 deliveries in a 375-minute stay at the crease.

Tea was taken early, leaving a long final session of thirty-six overs. Sidhu started blasting and Taylor brought Warne on to put pressure on the dasher. He responded by taking 14, including a straight six, off Warne's first over. The pitch was beginning to turn, albeit slowly, and Warne fought back, getting rid of Laxman (15) who drove him to Ponting at mid-off for an easy catch. The spinner then focused on Sidhu and quietened him with two consecutive maidens, switching from over to round the wicket to take advantage of the rough. This was classic Warne.

Frustrated at being so tied down, Sidhu attempted to sweep the spinner, only for the ball to run off his glove and up his forearm to Lehmann at bat-pad. India was two for 61. Meanwhile, Tendulkar was moving along, but only sedately for him. Warne thwarted his on-side hitting by tossing the ball straight at Tendulkar's leg stump, making it fizz into his pads and forcing him to cover up to keep it out. He was having difficulty for the second time in the series. Dravid (6) was defensive, but couldn't resist cutting at Robertson for an edge to Healy. India was three for 95 and 119 ahead. Tendulkar (27 not out) and Azharuddin (4 not out) played out time, as India bogged down to three for 99 at stumps. Warne took two for 42 off thirteen overs in a powerful display of leg-spinning.

The next morning belonged to Michael Kasprowicz, who ran through the Indian line-up, starting with the prize wickets of Tendulkar, caught-and-bowled for 31, and then Azharuddin, bowled for 16, to end the Indian innings just after lunch for

169. His effort of five for 28 was well supported by Robertson with three for 28, giving him twelve wickets at 34.42 for the series, as against Shane Warne with just ten at 54.00.

It was Warne's least effective series performance since he toured Sri Lanka in 1993, yet his bowling in both the last Test innings was top class. He ended with two for 80 off twenty-five overs in India's second innings, giving him five for 184 off sixty-four overs for the match, which meant he had contained the Indians to less than 3 runs an over—respectable economy considering Tendulkar's plunderings in the first innings and Sidhu's at the beginning of the second. Tendulkar's 31, only his second low score for the series, left him with 446 runs at an average of 111.25. He was the difference between the two teams. When he made runs India scored more than 400. When he failed, India managed 257 and 169.

Australia now had to make 194 runs to win and a little short of five sessions of 148 overs in which to get them. It was a testing target. The previous highest fourth-innings total to win a Test at Bangalore had been 151, made by India against New Zealand in 1995–96. The Australians had to prove that their alleged problems chasing smallish targets were more myth than reality. Media commentators were murmuring about the alleged 'mental hurdle', but the side in recent years had proved more times than not it could mount a rear-guard fight or score enough to win in the fourth innings.

The message now was to 'go for your shots where possible', and Taylor and Slater went on the attack from the start, forcing their way to 91 before Slater was out, on the last ball before tea, for 42. Alongside his first-innings effort, this performance may just have saved him from a second chop. Blewett (5) came in and struggled against Kumble until the bowler had him lbw. The axe was now sure to fall on him. Forty-eight runs at an average of 8 in six innings left him with no plea for a reprieve.

The now 'reliable' Mark Waugh (33 not out) joined his skipper for a safe partnership as Australia reached the target for a comfortable eight-wicket win. Waugh topped the tourists' Test averages with 280 runs at 70.00. Taylor cruised to 102 not out, taking his tally for the series to a more or less respectable 189 runs at 37.8. Once more, he may have done enough to let him continue on to Pakistan, although the fact remained that he had now led a losing side.

Kasprowicz was named Man of the Match, the logic being that his second-innings spell set up a win. Tendulkar took the Man of the Series award.

Captain Who?

Speculation mounted after the game concerning the leadership of Australian cricket. Taylor skilfully parried the question of his own form by noting that Australia had won its first Test in India in twenty-nine years. He also touched on the problem that was vexing to him concerning the 'two captains—two teams' attitude now prevalent in Australian cricket. Taylor felt it was divisive and should be abandoned in favour of one captain for both teams.

But this would mean he would have to stand down, for there was no justification for his returning to the one-day captaincy. His batting style was not suited to international one-day cricket. This opened up the debate on his successor, if the selectors agreed with him and decided he should stand down—as captain, but not necessarily as a player—for the three-Test Pakistan series in six months time.

The selectors' first choice would be Steve Waugh, who had started well as a one-day captain after the initial struggle to weld a new team over the past Australian summer. Waugh was a leader by example in the Bradman and Border tradition rather than an inspirer of men like Ian Chappell and Richie Benaud. The disadvantages for Waugh were his proneness to injury and, at thirty-two years old, the possibility that he would have no more than three or four summers ahead. Another choice would be the contrite and 'reformed' Healy, who had paid his penance for the bat-throwing incident in South Africa a year previously.

It was likely, however, that the selectors would be unforgiving.

The third choice under the circumstances was Warne. His ability to inspire and lift a team was established in both the one-day and Test arenas, and he was only twenty-eight. If he could conserve his bowling arm, he had anything from four to eight years left at the top. Australian selectors had always aimed for a longer term captaincy, as had proved successful with Bradman, Benaud, Lawry, Chappell, Border and Taylor.

Warne had already shown his abilities in captaining Victoria, and the Australian one-day side in Waugh's absence through injury late in 1997. His accession to the national leadership would curb any minor excesses in his exuberant character.

At the end of the disappointing India series which ended Taylor's nine-series winning streak, the problem rested with the ACB and the selectors. They met with Taylor and Steve Waugh after the players returned to Australia.

Taylor accepted that Steve Waugh would continue as one-day skipper and he would carry on in charge of the Test team. This would be made more palatable to both during the 1998–99 Australian summer when—for the first time—the Tests would be completed before the one-day series.

Consolation Prize

Australia still had to play two one-day series in April 1998, the first in India with Zimbabwe also playing, and the other the Coca-Cola Cup in Sharjah, including New Zealand.

Australia's first game, on 1 April, was against India at Cochin in Kerala. India showed the way, despite losing its two most powerful batsmen, Sidhu and Tendulkar. However, India's most celebrated one-day specialist, Ajaz Jadeja, demonstrated why he had so many supporters by crafting 105 not out from 109 balls, well supported by Azharuddin (82), Hrishikesh Kanitar (57) and Kumble (33), as the side dashed to five for 309. Warne was wicketless, but by far the most economical bowler, conceding only 42 runs in the onslaught.

Australia replied with an 11.2-over opening stand of 101 between Mark Waugh and Gilchrist. After twenty overs, it only had to make 108 from seventeen overs with seven wickets in hand when Tendulkar was brought on to bowl his mixed bag of leggies and offies and an assortment of other odd balls. The tiny champion had fun destroying the middle with ten overs in succession that yielded the next five Australian wickets.

Warne came to the wicket at a point where Australia had a faint hope of victory. A controlled 25 from him was required, but he was caught at long-on off his opposite number, Kumble. Tendulkar's five for 32 earned him the Man of the Match award and the game for India when Australia's innings closed at 268, 42 runs short of victory.

Two days later, Australia had to muster enthusiasm for its game against Zimbabwe in Ammedabad, where the temperature soared to 43 degrees Celsius. Waugh won the toss and led from the front with 49, supported by Bevan with a quick 65 and Ponting with 53, as Australia finished with a respectable but not exceptional seven for 252.

Zimbabwe looked like taking it when it needed only 110 off twenty overs with eight wickets remaining intact, but Fleming pushed the game back to Australia with a fine second spell which held Zimbabwe to 239, just 13 runs short. He took the bowling honours with three for 30 off ten overs, followed by Moody with three for 39 off 9.5.

Warne was serviceable with two for 45 off ten. He produced some magic by bowling the dangerous Goodwin, who had played for Western Australia, around his legs. Again, he had been steady under fire without being a match-winner, which seemed to be the story of his tour.

Australia's second encounter against India—at Kanpur on 7 April—ended with another host victory. Waugh won the toss and batted on a good wicket that demanded 280 runs. Instead, the tourists bumbled along to just nine for 222. Only Ponting with a strong 84 and Moody (44) succeeded. Twenty-year-old Ait Agarkar took four for 46. India's reply was to lose its first wicket—Tendulkar for an even hundred—at 175. It took the little master just eighty-eight balls, off which he hit a one-day record 7 sixes. After he departed, India cruised to an easy six-wicket win.

Warne's form was fair, with one for 43 off nine overs. He came on when the openers were in full flight and bore the brunt of their blows well, beating the bat often without luck. His only wicket was Tendulkar with a delivery that Warne had been waiting to take effect. Tendulkar was dancing down the wicket and driving straight, without missing. Warne looped one a fraction more, causing the advancing batsman to mishit the ball to cover. Warne's reasoning was that Tendulkar's daring would cause him to make an error at some stage. This time it had come at 100. His hitting was immaculate. Once he got to the ball, he seemed like a champion golfer teeing off.

Australia now had to win again against Zimbabwe at Delhi on 11 April to make the final with India. Australia batted first and Ponting turned on his best one-day performance with 145 from 157 balls, allowing Australia to amass seven for 294. Mark Waugh, in consistent form, made 87 in a record second-wicket stand of 219 with Ponting.

Zimbabwe replied with nine for 278. At one stage, it was two for 219 and looked as if it could take the game, after Gary and Andy Flower had put on 121 in 18.4 overs for the third wicket. Then Warne struck in the forty-first over with a good flipper that took out Gary Flower's leg stump on 84. Wickets fell regularly until Zimbabwe ran out of time just 16 runs short.

Warne returned one for 55 off ten, one of his worst economy rates, though he did not bowl poorly. But he flexed his shoulder more often than usual and seemed to be in some trouble with it. Fears were confirmed after the game with the news that he had injured ligaments in his right shoulder when diving for a catch at cover. However, he was expected to play against India in the final in Delhi three days later on 14 April, especially as his presence always provided something of a psychological advantage over the home team.

Azharuddin won the toss and batted on a fine morning in front of a full house and a TV audience of several hundred million on the subcontinent and round the world. The Australian game plan was to rock the early Indian batting order with short balls aimed at the ribcage.

It worked from the start as Fleming and Kasprowicz put Ganguly and Tendulkar on the back foot and made them uncertain. Tendulkar, in particular, seemed nervous, playing and missing several times as he fumbled his way to 15, when Fleming had him fencing at a ball to be brilliantly caught by Gilchrist. Ganguly (29) was next to go, leaving India at two for 58, and then three for 128 when Azharuddin went for 44, followed by Sidhu for 38. Four were now down for 144.

From then on, there was a steady trudge of Indians back to the pavilion, with the innings petering out to 227 from 49.3 overs. Fleming (three for 47 off ten overs) and Kasprowicz (two for 43 off 9.3) did all that was asked of them. Warne only took one wicket, but conceded just 35 off ten overs in an exhibition of controlled leg-spin under pressure.

Round one had gone to Australia, leaving it with a run rate of 4.5 an over to win. Gilchrist was out for 1 and Mark Waugh for 20, making it two for 56, but Ponting and Bevan fought back until Ponting was stumped for 41, with the score at three for 84.

Waugh then gambled again with Warne as pinch-hitter to see if he could get a quick 15 or 20, lift the run rate and upset the Indians with his strong-arm tactics. Warne obliged by striking 14 in as many balls before receiving a full toss, which he edged into his stumps. Warne appealed to the umpires for a no-ball, but the Indian umpires didn't see fit to call it. The move had unbalanced the Indians and lifted the run rate with no real loss.

With the score at four for 111, Waugh now settled in with the busy Bevan, and together they pushed it up to 167, 60 runs short of victory with ten overs to go. Waugh launched himself into an over from the youngster Hrishikesh Kanitkar and, with the aid of a wide and a no-ball, nine overs were left to collect 42 for victory and the game was all but over. Waugh was bowled by Kumble for 57 with the score at 218, but, in the forty-eighth over, Bevan crashed the ball over mid-wicket for four to win the game, after making a determined 75 not out from 127 balls. Australia had won the final against the odds.

Tendulkar the Terrible

The team continued on to Sharjah, Dubai, for the opening match of the Coca-Cola Cup against New Zealand. The Kiwis batted first and only captain Stephen Fleming (59) and Chris Harris (26) resisted in a weak total of 159 off 48.4 overs. Fleming bagged four for 28 and the Man of the Match award, with Warne securing the next best figures of two for 28. Once more, he dominated the New Zealanders. His two victims, McMillan (1) and Martin Horne (14), had troubled Australia in recent times, but his control and economy were first-rate, despite his obvious discomfort with his shoulder. The Australians replied with four for 160 off 36.5 overs, headed by Gilchrist with 57 and Ponting with 52.

They maintained the pressure next day against India. The Australians started well, winning the toss and compiling nine for 264 in an excellent all-round effort in which Bevan top-scored with 58. India started at a rate that suggested it would win, if it could be maintained. Tendulkar came back to form, crashing his way to 80 off just sixty-six balls in another great knock. But when he and Jadeja (35) were out at 161, the game swung Australia's way. The push came from Steve Waugh, who took four for 40 as he wrapped up India's innings for 206 off forty-four overs, supported by Fleming (two for 35), Kasprowicz (two for 40) and Warne (one for 37 off eight overs), despite Tendulkar's early onslaught.

New Zealand won its first game of the Sharjah series when it rolled India by four wickets on 20 April, thus making its game the following day against Australia a vital one. Both teams had to win. The Kiwis batted first and hit an impressive seven for 259, Nathan Astle (78) playing the sheet anchor after a hefty start, and Chris Cairns hammering 56 in fifty balls before being stumped off Warne.

The spinner's figures were one for 56 off ten overs, his worst ever against New Zealand. His line and length were mostly impeccable as usual, but there was nothing of the old zip and rip. The flipper was kept in the closet, but not because he wished to pull it out later in the final. The reason for its omission was pain and strain on his shoulder.

The Kiwi bats took advantage of this rare moment when their nemesis of recent years was reduced to being playable and hittable. It reinforced in Warne's mind the need for surgery.

Australia's replied with five for 261, giving it a comfortable five-wicket victory thirteen balls short of the fifty overs. Moody crashed 63 off seventy-four balls, including a towering six, while Bevan showed remarkable consistency by notching another 57 in just sixty-four balls and Mark Waugh enjoyed himself in chalking up 34 off twenty-eight balls.

Australia played India next day in what was far from a 'dead' match. Australia's place in the final was assured, but it could keep India out by scoring around 270 and winning by 20 or more. Gilchrist looked as if he was aiming at getting half of 300-odd required, but was soon out caught behind for 11. The innings was then dominated by Mark Waugh, who made a superb 81 from ninety-eight balls, and Bevan, who continued his outstanding form to make 101 not out from 103 balls as Australia finished with seven for 284. India now had to collect 265 to have a run rate that would secure the other place in the final. If it scored less than that, New Zealand would make it.

Tendulkar began as if he intended to not just help India qualify, but win. The game was stopped after thirty-one overs by a night dust storm that had players and spectators covering their faces. The score was then four for 143, with Tendulkar unconquered on 68. India's over allotment was therefore reduced to forty-six and it needed 276 to win and 240 to make the final. Tendulkar resumed with his own kind of storm in a furious performance that convinced the crowd, the commentators, the Australians and the Indians alike that he could achieve victory on his own. The diminutive dynamo didn't quite reach his goal, but he did do the most to push India to five for 250—enough to see it sneak into the finals on run rate ahead of New Zealand.

Most observers rated Tendulkar's century his best-ever one-day innings under pressure. Coca-Cola was among them, awarding him a special prize of £20 000 pounds ($A45 000) for his astonishing performance in front of a packed house of wild supporters. No Indian crowd had been more ecstatic at its team losing a game. Tendulkar at least, however, steered his side into a final.

When the dust settled, Australia had still won the match. It was its sixth successive one-day victory. Waugh had welded a fine combination, prepared for a creditable climax on 24 April.

Azharuddin won the toss in the match and surprised by sending Australia in. It looked a good move twenty minutes into the Australian innings when three batsmen—Mark Waugh, Ponting and Moody—were back in the pavilion with just 26 runs on the board. Gilchrist and Bevan set about restoring the Australian position until the score was 85, when Gilchrist was caught behind for 45. Steve Waugh and Bevan then put on a century partnership which ended when Bevan was run out, also for 45. Australia was five for 187 and travelling at 5 an over. Lehmann, who had had a quiet series, now picked up the baton and came good with 70 in just fifty-nine balls to see Australia through to a fine nine for 272. Only Tendulkar stood between it and victory. That was the whisper at the ground and probably, too, among fans watching worldwide on TV. If he were dismissed early, Australia would most likely win.

Tendulkar bided his time while first Ganguly and then Mongia were dismissed. Then, at 128, Azharuddin joined Tendulkar and this formidable batting combination could not be broken. Tendulkar sailed on to 100 when the score was 190 after 36.2 overs. It was his fifteenth century in one-day internationals. India needed just 83 from eighty-two balls.

Warne had no impact. Both batsmen treated him like a club spinner, belting anything loose. However, an ounce of luck would have had both of them. The Indian skipper was clearly lbw to Warne early in his innings, but the umpire said not out. The bowler was giving it everything, but seemed not to have the zest needed to challenge the attackers. There was never the vicious bounce and spin that had been a feature of his game. But no one could doubt his will from a mighty effort he made to catch Tendulkar from a mishit to mid-off, as he launched himself backwards and hit the ground hard, just failing to reach the ball.

Tendulkar's power was illustrated by one drive in particular which came back so fast that Warne either couldn't get to it or didn't wish to see his fingers go with it. The umpire ducked and the pickets were rattled. But the hardest hit of all came after Tendulkar and Azharuddin had reached their century partnership. Tendulkar—the smallest player of either side—crashed Moody—the biggest—straight over mid-off. It hit a wall and bounced 30 metres back into the field.

The fun and carnage ended after he had made 134 off 131 balls when Kasprowicz had him lbw in a doubtful decision. India was three for 248, just 25 short of almost certain victory. At 261, Azharuddin (58) was caught behind off Kasprowicz, but it was all over as India coasted to a six-wicket victory in 48.3 overs.

India's strong win ended the Australians' winning streak of six in a row. The difference in this series, as it had been in the Tests, amounted to the formidable batting of Sachin Tendulkar. He won the Man of the Match and the Tournament awards. This last innings took his plundering against Australia to 1130 runs from twelve innings. His average was 113 against the tourists since they arrived in India on 24 February.

After the game, Steve Waugh said: 'You take Bradman away, and he is next up, I reckon.'

Comparisons in style, begun by Donald Bradman himself, had now stepped up to ranking the Indian the best since the

Don. Tendulkar, at twenty-five, would have every chance in the next decade to see if he could live up to that daunting epithet.

He had scored one first-class double century, for Mumbai against the Australians on tour in February 1998, but was yet to score a double in Tests. At the same age, Bradman had scored twenty-one first-class double centuries. On four occasions he went on to a triple century and once a quadruple. The Australian had scored eight double centuries in Tests and had gone on to triples twice.

Tendulkar's Test average at twenty-five years is about 55. Bradman's was 100. What does it mean in comparing performances on the field at similar stages in their careers? Given that both players were or are entertainers who wherever possible set out to attack and dominate the opposition, Bradman could concentrate in sustaining a top-class performance twice as long as Tendulkar.

•••

In the Sharjah final, Fleming (two for 47) and Kasprowicz (two for 48) bowled respectably, while Warne returned one of his worst-ever one-day figures in any competition of none for 61 off ten overs. He had been treated with contempt on the field. It was hurtful and humiliating. Yet he took the hammering in the best spirit possible.

In a game where character is tested more than most, Warne had come through his toughest examination. In the context of his fabulous career it was one blip, not helped by an injury that had rendered him less than fully armed against the one-man blitzkrieg that was Tendulkar. For the moment, the batsman had settled the argument of dominance in a top contest between bat and ball.

Warne, for the first time, was momentarily diminished in the eyes of the cricketing world. Yet he had grown in experience. Once over the delayed shock of the Indian summer, he would be an even more determined cricketer. Warne would survive to battle Tendulkar again in a couple of seasons' time, and on Australian soil.

The Don on Warne and Tendulkar

Just before the First Test in India at Chennai in March 1998, I rang Sir Donald Bradman to get his assessment of the long-awaited battle between Warne and Tendulkar. Did he think Warne and the Australians had been foxing Tendulkar when he scored 204 not out in the first game of the tour playing for Mumbai, in which Warne returned none for 111 off sixteen overs?

'No, I don't think so,' Bradman replied. 'The Australians would, I feel, have been trying to gain an advantage early, given the shortness of the tour. However, Test-match cricket is vastly different. It will be a fascinating contest.'

I had the impression that he expected Tendulkar to come out on top in the Tests.

In 1996, Bradman paid Tendulkar the ultimate batting compliment when he said the Indian was the nearest performer to him in style he had seen. It was his 'stroke production' that brought the comparison from Bradman. Tendulkar reacted with humility to this, saying it was the greatest compliment he had ever had in his life. ('It still is,' he remarked, two years later.)

The Don also paid Warne an enormous tribute during my interviews with him in 1995 by saying he ranked him with Bill O'Reilly, 'the finest bowler I ever faced,' and the other great Australian leggie of the 1920s and 1930s, Clarrie Grimmett.

Bradman brightened when we spoke of Warne. He loved watching him and what he had brought to the game. Bradman considered his emergence one of the most important things to have happened to the game in the modern era. His style was right for the age and he made the turnstiles click. Bradman liked the way he speeded up the game and brought the fine art of leg-spinning back to the fore. The Don had been irritated about fast bowlers taking six minutes to complete an over, whereas Warne could often do it in less than two minutes.

'He challenges the world's best batsmen like no one else,' Bradman observed, 'and that can only serve to improve cricket as a spectacle.'

When we spoke in 1995, Bradman expressed concern that Warne was playing too much cricket. 'His shoulder and spinning finger won't be able to take it,' he observed. He predicted that Warne would struggle to play after he reached the age of twenty-eight.

The Warne–Tendulkar clash was the nearest thing to imagining how Bradman would play Warne, given Tendulkar's quality against the spinning ball. Bradman intended to watch the contest, reliving old battles with the great spinners of his time, such as Bill O'Reilly, with his quick leggies that came at you, as Bradman noted, 'like a swarm of bees'; Clarrie Grimmett's slow mixed bag; R. W. V. Robins with his brilliant wrong 'un; England's Doug Wright with his tempting spin; and the sharp orthodox off-spin of England's Jim Laker.

The 1970s and 1980s produced a range of speed men such as Lillee, Thompson, Hadlee, Marshall, Garner, Willis and Ambrose. Those decades all but killed off the art of leg-spinning, particularly as the West Indies, with its line-up of four fast men, dominated world cricket and ruined the art of front-foot driving. It gave batsmen nothing to hit forward of the wicket, slowed down the game and forced the cutters and hookers to take risks. It decreased crowd numbers. The era of the fast men also terminated the art of playing spin. Gone was the *one-two-one* skip down the wicket. Except for teams on the subcontinent, wrist-spinners took not second but fourth fiddle, if they were even selected. Opposing batsmen muddled through against them, playing from the crease and never venturing out to take them on.

When Warne and India's Anil Kumble arrived on the scene in the 1990s, they flummoxed the world's average Test batsmen and troubled the best, with the exception of a few such as Tendulkar, Border, Mark Waugh, Lara and Martin Crowe. Tendulkar even more than the rest was prepared to dance down the wicket. This was the way Bradman tamed the best bowlers of his era. He lifted to the big occasion against them and set out to destroy them at every opportunity. Bradman regarded O'Reilly as the best of all and he targeted him for special treatment. It began at Bowral Oval in 1925, when Bradman walloped 234 in 167 minutes against O'Reilly and Wingello, and continued in the same manner at almost every other encounter over the better part of two decades. It was no wonder that O'Reilly held a huge grudge against the Don.

The method of Bradman and Tendulkar was to glide the ball around for ones and twos, if a boundary was not an option. This plays havoc with a bowler's line, as Warne found from his first game in India in 1998, and the field. All great bowlers prefer order and to have a scheme. If this is thrown out by successful batting tactics they become unsettled, frustrated and thwarted.

In the 1998 encounters, for instance, Tendulkar forced Warne off his leg-stump line, by swatting the ball to mid-on and over mid-wicket, and on to an unnatural off-stump line that allowed the batsman to cut the ball spinning away. Warne also seemed to slow his deliveries early, whereas the faster, less-turning ball worked for his opposite number Kumble.

Warne has spoken wistfully about bowling to recent champions he had just missed such as Botham and Richards. He admired their brilliance, swagger and aggression. It's probable that Warne would have dominated Botham and had even tussles against Richards, as he does against Cronje and Lara, with the odds in Warne's favour over time.

Bradman and his modern proxy, Tendulkar, are a different proposition. Almost fifty years ago, another fine purveyor of leg-spin, Richie Benaud, expressed his disappointment to Keith Miller that he had just missed bowling to Bradman, who retired in 1948.

'It's better that you did miss him,' Miller replied ominously. He felt the experience may have damaged the young Benaud's confidence. A more mature Benaud later bowled to the great Gary Sobers in full flight and had enough guile and skill by then to avoid too much embarassment.

Warne, in his very first Test, and again in 1998, experienced what it is like to bowl to the finest batsman since Bradman himself.

18

The Knife and Life After

Nightmare Time

After the Sharjah tournament, Warne told the media contigent who greeted him at Melbourne airport that all he was looking forward to in the next few days were some fish and chips, and 'a few beers,' as well as watching a few Saints' games.

'I think I'll have nightmares about Tendulkar hitting me over my head for six,' he said, but added with one eye on future encounters: 'He is an outstanding batsman who is a good challenge to bowl to.'

Causing Warne nightmares of a different sort was a dreaded second visit to his Melbourne surgeon, this time for arthroscopic work on his shoulder. It was overdue, if he was to continue his cricket career. The wear and tear had been making it tougher in preparation before games and maintenance after them for three years now. Errol Alcott had helped keep him going without having to face the knife again. But enough was enough.

On the bright side, it was an enforced break that would avoid the cricket tour routines that had, in part, enslaved him. He could watch a lot of his beloved Saints. It was good that Warne could enjoy his football team's season, for his own sporting pleasures would be out. There would be no golf or anything else that engaged the shoulder for several months.

Deep down, Warne was a little concerned. With Alcott's guidance, he had managed the shoulder with physio work as if he had had an operation. Now there was no way of acting as if there were a phantom surgeon in the operating room. This time he would face a real one. Older bowlers who'd had surgery scared him with tales of never returning to the pre-knife days.

Warne spoke to Richie Benaud about his shoulder problems, which may have caused him to retire earlier than he wished. His injury became pronounced on the tour of England in 1961. After that Ashes conquest, he was never the same bowler and retired after the 1963–64 season.

The two bowlers compared injuries, and Warne asked Benaud how he got over them.

'I retired,' Benaud replied.

But that was thirty-five years ago. Surgical techniques had improved beyond recognition. Warne was reassured that with proper physiotherapy and dedication after the operation, he would be back.

Off the Cuff

Days before the operation, a small camera was inserted into Warne's shoulder joint that showed internal tearing of the rotator cuff. This had not been evident on preliminary investigation. On 6 May 1998, he had surgery on the cuff. Torn fibres were cut away from within and would scar. Surgery was also undertaken on the torn cartilage in the shoulder labrum, which was stitched. (The labrum is an important structure in the shoulder joint. It surrounds the socket, stabilising the joint.)

The operation took longer than planned and the damage done was worse than expected. Doctors told Warne after the surgery that if he had played a few more games on the tour of India and Sharjah the shoulder may have fallen apart completely. His career would have been finished.

Warne would have his shoulder in a sling for four to six weeks, and then would have to spend between five and eleven months in rehabilitation. His return would depend on the natural processes of his recovery, particularly concerning scar tissue. Warne's scar tissue tended to be very stiff. This, doctors said, was an advantage for his long-term prognosis. But it could delay his recovering his full range of joint management.

Translated, this meant Warne's shoulder would recover well enough not to interfere with the length of his career. He would either retire when he wanted to, or be forced to if his form fell away.

After the operation, Warne met the media wearing a Victorian navy-blue and white tracksuit and a different hairstyle, with his unblonded hair cut short on top and brushed forward. He said that he would have to do 'all the right things to get it right and get back on the field'. He added: 'If I have to put most of my life on hold, then I'll do that to get back again, but it's not going to be easy, especially on my wife and daughter.'

Doctors told Warne that if the rehab went well the shoulder would eventually be better than brand new. There was no reason why he couldn't have another five years playing for Australia as long as his form was good enough.

Warne was hopeful of returning for the 1998–99 Tests against England. He enjoyed the Ashes contests and with good reason. He had been a series winner in 1993, dominant in the first two Tests of 1994–95 and a major influence in the last three Tests of 1997. In the three series, he had taken eighty-five wickets at 23.57 in seventeen matches, and these figures included his only hat-trick. With his great career on hold in mid-1998, he had taken 313 wickets at 24.78 in sixty-seven matches.

Confessions and Solutions

Warne 'confessed' in an article for the Melbourne *Age* in April 1998 that he had been 'selfish' in playing on with an injured shoulder. He feared that if he stood down, his replacement might do so well that Warne would not get back into the Australian team.

'No one wants to sit out a game and watch your replacement take five wickets or make a century,' he wrote candidly. 'But we are human and often feel that way about our careers.'

His remarks reflected every sportsman's fear at every level of any sport.

Warne added that he kept bowling when his shoulder was sore because he 'just wanted to be out there every time I was selected. We all see it as an honour to play for our country and it is not something we want to give up easily.'

More to the point, Warne was needed in the front line of Australia's attack, not just because of his exceptional skills, but also for psychological reasons. All opposition players either feared his ability or focused on combating him. This often took pressure off Australia's other key bowlers and led to their gaining the wickets of batsmen who lapsed in concentration when facing them after getting away from Warne.

Nevertheless, he may have gone one series too far in playing in India. He took half his normal quota of wickets and did not dominate one Indian innings in three Tests. Nor did he have his normal impact in the one-day tournaments. A break from the game and surgery were overdue.

Warne's solution to the handling of Australia's main bowlers was not necessarily the rotation of players in the Tests and other first-class matches, but less practice. He didn't completely support the view that out-of-form bowlers should iron out problems in the nets with hard work.

'You can become bored with it all,' he said, 'and that can lead to laziness and bad habits.'

A small problem since the game began was the fact that batsmen always loved 'nets', whereas bowlers could be less enthusiastic. They often felt they were there to service the batsman. Bowlers grumbled about this over the years, particularly on long tours.

Warne suggested that local bowlers not in the Test side should be seconded to bowl to the batsmen and that more attention be paid to bowlers' problems.

Just Your Average Vocal Fan

In May 1998, Shane Warne took a holiday on the Gold Coast, where he met up with his good mate Merv Hughes. Then he returned south to Melbourne's cold, damp winter. He filled in the idle months with three physiotherapy sessions a week, and exercises he had to do four times a day.

Warne circled Friday, 20 November 1998 in his diary—the first day of the first Ashes Test at Brisbane. He wanted to be ready for that, which meant solid preparation, including games for St Kilda and Victoria. Yet in mid-1998, he had no idea whether that was a realistic aim. Like Golfer Greg Norman, who had a similar operation at the same time, he could only hope that his body would be restored to its former physical capacity.

Warne's first major pleasure in the rehabilitation program would be swinging a golf club himself. Each week, whenever possible, he would watch St Kilda in the AFL and become just your average vocal fan, cheering ('Go Sainters!') and jeering the opposition and its supporters. In fact, Shane ended up something like the fan who had given him more than a merry time in England in 1997, except that he was not foul or abusive. He enjoyed giving and receiving the odd jibe, as long as it was good-natured and not personal.

He reported after a game against Collingwood:

'I can be as loud and passionate for my team as any footy fan. Some things in football haven't changed. It's not that hard to get under the skin of Collingwood fans ... If they [football administrators] bring in those new rules about stopping loud barracking, I might end up leaving games in handcuffs.'

Warne's loyalty to the Saints was extraordinary. He sometimes watched training. He often visited the dressing room at half-time during matches where his presence was an inspiration to the players he admired so much, such as Peter Everitt, Robert Harvey, Nathan Burke and Nicky Winmar.

His main sporting regret was his failure to make the grade as a footballer in the AFL. Given his determination and success in top cricket, it often crossed his mind that he should have persevered after the Saints dumped him early in 1989. *Perhaps, maybe, if only*... But whenever he thought about it, he realised that he could never have combined cricket and football at the top level. That possibility went out with in the 1970s with Max Walker, who played Test cricket for Australia and football for the Melbourne club. Demands at the top in both sports would make it impossible. Players gifted in the two sports had to make a choice. His failure at St Kilda made the choice for him.

Warne's greatest dream was to play for St Kilda in a Grand Final on the MCG in front of 100 000 people. The next best thing was watching them play in one and win, which he had yet to do. He was born three years after St Kilda's only premiership win in 1966. In 1997, it was a hot favourite, but lost to Adelaide, much to Warne's chagrin. He cheered himself hoarse to no avail.

In the meantime, during the winter months Warne turned up at the odd celebrity function, such as the opening of football commentator Rex Hunt's D'lish Fish café in Melbourne. In July, he was interviewed by Ray Martin and did some TV commentating on Foxtel covering the Malaysian Super 8s tournament. Later in the month, there was a $65-a-head 'tribute' night for Warne at the Crown Casino. He made headlines the next day after suggesting there was a slim chance he would never play again. His supporters hoped his shoulder would recover and that this was not his farewell.

Nappy Rash

In August, Warne appeared in a TV special featuring interviews by and with top Aussie Rules player, Wayne Carey. In a mutual back-slapping exercise, the two indulged in a 'What do you have for breakfast?' trivia fest, which their fans, but no one else, lapped up. Warne seemed to feel that the smaller Foxtel viewer numbers meant he could be a little more loose and relaxed than on Nine, the top-rating commercial network. He spoke of his ineptitude as a father, at least in his first attempt at changing a nappy on daughter Brooke—in a disabled bathroom at the MCG. Carey and viewers were treated to a blow-by-blow description of the event that took him fifty-five minutes.

'I feel sorry for the next person [who entered the bathroom],' Warne remarked, adding a few choice remarks about tissues stuck on walls.

His sensitivity about his weight was drawn out by the more subtle Carey when they discussed the time Warne walked out of a media conference at which a journalist made a jibe about his weight, comparing his actual shape with that of the sleeker-looking wax dummy on display at Madame Tussaud's.

'If people like me, that's great,' Warne added. 'If they don't, I'm not going to loose any sleep over it.'

Carey thought this was a fine approach. He now used it himself in handling critics and any bad press he received.

Warne further remarked that the media had a responsibility to report the 'good' stories, and demonstrated a misunderstanding of how the media and fame, fickle bedfellows, work together. Ninety per cent of articles and comment about him would be favourable, while the rest would be less so on occasions, such as his send-off of a batsman in South Africa. There would be some journalists who would always look for the negative or the 'knock'. But they were few and far between. The more astute commentators were objective. For instance, Melbourne journalist Caroline Wilson wrote in the *Age* that Warne was 'insincere' in the Foxtel interview in saying that he was 'so accessible—people can just ring you up on the mobile'.

'Any sports journalist will tell you that Warne's mobile telephone answer machine is notorious for the dozens of messages which remain unanswered,' Wilson noted.

She attacked him for wearing 'ridiculous sunglasses' when interviewed on TV news. Warne implied that he had to wear them, presumably because of a deal with a manufacturer.

'At least in the Fox interviews [with Carey], we get to see Warne's face and his smile,' Wilson added, 'both of which are wonderful to look at.'

The Greats and the Greatest

Warne received the invitation of a lifetime to join Sachin Tendulkar for a meeting with Don Bradman at his Kensington Park home in Adelaide on the Don's ninetieth birthday on 27 August 1998.

Warne, looking somewhat awed and humble, was nervous—as was Tendulkar—as they were driven to Bradman's home on the leafy outskirts of the city.

The friendly host, in an open-necked shirt and grey cardigan, put the two suited visitors at ease. Warne found him mentally sharp and in the mood to deliver the odd joke. They sat in the floral living room overlooked by the big portrait of Bradman and chatted about the game. Bradman said Tendulkar was today's best batsman. Sachin was 'very honoured' by the remark. The Indian asked him who was the best cricketer Bradman ever saw.

'Sir Garfield Sobers,' Bradman said. 'He is the greatest player of all time. He was five cricketers in one.'

Bradman was referring to Sobers's capacities as a left-arm seam bowler, who could turn his hand to wrist and finger spin—making him a triple-purpose performer with the ball. He was also one of the best batsmen of all time, a top-rank fielder anywhere and a fine skipper.

Warne asked his host whom he considered the best bowler he ever saw.

'Bill O'Reilly,' Bradman replied without hesitation. Warne was not upset. He knew this answer before he asked it. In my interviews with Bradman, it was clear that he ranked Warne almost in the same bracket.

'You bowl slower than O'Reilly,' the Don added, 'but you spin the ball more. Bill's strengths were his pace and bounce. He always had two short legs and got a lot of close catches with his extra bounce.'

Bradman described O'Reilly as a middle-finger spinner and saw Warne as a third-finger spinner. O'Reilly had a well-concealed wrong 'un. He held the ball closer to the palm than the fingers, whereas Warne used his fingers more than the palm and thus imparted more spin. Both bowlers' strong wrists gained them accuracy. O'Reilly's unusual style allowed for an effective change of pace. Both Warne and O'Reilly flighted the ball deceptively. Bradman remarked that O'Reilly's height aided him in extracting life from the pitch, especially with his faster ball.

'Sir Donald, what were your movements just before the bowler delivered the ball?' Tendulkar asked Bradman.

'I moved back and across to the off side before delivery,' the Don replied. 'I thought I could move quickly in any direction from there.'

'How did you prepare for a game?' Tendulkar inquired. Bradman explained that he was an amateur. If he was playing in Adelaide, he would go to work at the broking house early in the morning and would arrive in a suit to toss the coin to begin the match.

'After play,' Bradman added, 'I'd go back to work for several hours.' He had to work to make ends meet.

The three discussed the mental strain of the popularity they had experienced. Bradman commented that living up to his reputation had been 'enormously difficult'. The others, fresher to being exalted as gods, concurred with his anguish.

At the end of the hour's chat, Bradman walked them down his drive to the gate in front of several TV camerapeople and journalists. He shook hands with Warne and Tendulkar and bid them good luck.

'How do you feel?' a journalist asked Bradman as he turned to go inside.

'I'd feel a lot better without all the cameras around,' he replied. 'It's all a bit too much.'

Bradman had met Warne before and thought him a 'very nice chap'. He was familiar with him as a performer on TV on and off the field. But he had not met the Indian. After the meeting, Bradman told me he was 'very impressed' with Tendulkar. 'Even at this stage of his career, he was willing to ask questions,' he said. He expected him to go on to even greater achievements. Bradman, like many cricket fans, hoped Warne would return and add to his magnificent record.

Crunch Time

Warne spent the next three months until mid-December 1998 juggling his comeback and media work, and keeping up psychological pressure on the visiting Englishmen. They still had Warnophobia. It showed embarrassingly when they hired former Australian leggie Peter Philpott to educate them about leg-spin. Yet, for the first three Tests of the five-Test Ashes series, fears about Shane Warne, their conqueror in several previous contests, were an illusion. Their bogeyman didn't make an appearance.

The conjuring trick was exposed by early December when he pulled out of the Victorian side to play England at the MCG. The tourists' former nemesis was a paper tiger.

Warne said he wouldn't play because he wanted to maintain his five-year mental grip on them.

'Why should I let the Poms have a go at me when I am honestly nothing like 100 per cent spot on with my bowling,' he told England's *Daily Mirror.* His form suggested discretion was the better part of valour. In games for St Kilda and Victoria—Sheffield Shield and one-dayers— until the end of 1998, he took a handful of wickets for twice as many runs as his usual average. He was about half as good—statistically, physically and formwise—as he was a year earlier.

The last few months of the year were worrying. He had sleepless nights before state games because of concern about how he would perform, knowing thal all eyes would be on every ball. His competitive spirit meant that he wanted to leap back into the Test side and secure his place in it by rolling England. His confidence in his shoulder and form, however, did not warrant it. His flipper was not working. He had to work hard on it, along with his wrong 'un, top-spinner, back-spinner and zooter. Warne had watched Australia beat Pakistan for the first time in decades in both Tests and one-dayers. He had witnessed Australia's continued dominance of England in the 1998–99 Ashes contest. The victories pleased him, but it hurt that he was not part of it—and he was not missed. His understudy, Stuart MacGill, had maintained Warne-like returns, averaging just less than six wickets a Test.

The knowledge that he was not indispensable nor needed to beat the traditional enemy, and the pressures of a nation's expectations, tested his character daily. His frustration showed as he faced the prospect of not returning to the Test side for some time. He was failing to produce his special magic with a cricket ball and found himself leading a losing team in close Shield games. An umpire received a blast in one and Warne was fined. Yet he somehow kept up a cool and contented public image off the field, mainly through TV appearances—such as '60 Minutes', 'The Panel' and commentating on the Tests—that would have convinced other than cricket fans that he was still playing for Australia. He never seemed out of the news, as the media played up the *would he* or *wouldn't he* make it back in the national side for the summer.

If this was not front-page speculation, he was seen everywhere in advertisements for Nicorette. Warne was being paid $200 000 to give up smoking by 1 January 1999. Smokers around Australia were heard to grumble that they would like to be offered such a sum to give up smoking. But they were not Shane Warne. His reason for taking on the challenge—that he was doing it for the health of his young daughter and a future child now that Simone was again pregnant—seemed dubious. Why, the critics asked, would he not give up without a money incentive if that were the reason? Yet critics and controversy were now part of Warne's incident-prone career. He could roll with them.

Then, in one week, his world seemed to collapse around a money scandal. On 9 December 1998, David Hookes reported on radio station 3AW in Melbourne that Warne and Mark Waugh had, in September 1994, taken money from an illegal Indian bookmaker ('John') in Sri Lanka. Overnight, the images of these two were turned from heroes to demons. Warne's major sponsors considered whether or not to continue with him, while his main newspaper writing outlets—England's *Mirror* and Australia's *Age* and *Sydney Morning Herald*—dumped him. Former Test great Neil Harvey wanted him and Waugh either banned for two years or kicked out of the game. Others said that Warne should never captain Australia. The Pakistani judge investigating bribery in cricket in that country demanded that he and Mark Waugh return to Pakistan for further questioning.

Looking like guilty schoolboys, the pair read statements at a press conference in Adelaide before the Third Test against England, where, in synchronised fashion, they both admitted that had been 'naïve and stupid'. Questions were not allowed. This fuelled discontent in the Fourth Estate. The media outpouring was relentless, as journalist after journalist in Australia's leading dailies attacked. The main accusation against Warne seemed to be that he did not return calls on his mobile with alacrity.

Warwick Hadfield and Brian Woodley, in the *Weekend Australian* of 12 December, editorialised: '... Warne is in need of some good advice, but not from business managers and PR folk too happy to tell him how wonderful he is in order to flog a few more videos, books, pairs of duds, sports shoes or anti-smoking ads.'

They suggested that since he had been out of the Test team he was missing wise counsel from Mark Taylor and coach Geoff Marsh. This may have been so, yet Warne was twenty-nine years of age, a state captain and a team leader when he was in the Australian side. His 'naïve and stupid' act in Sri Lanka occurred more than four years ago. A chastened Warne had since then been appointed captain of Victoria and vice-captain of the Australian side by ACB people aware of his indiscretion. On top of that, all national selectors—especially Allan Border—maintained him in the highest regard, and not just for his on-field performances. His professionalism and ability in recent

ACB–first-class player payment negotiations had impressed Border, the most important mentor in Warne's career.

Border had been most responsible for bringing Warne on quickly and in nurturing him to a point where he felt confident of launching him on any opposition as a strike bowler. The former Test skipper would stand by him now in a crisis. Richie Benaud was also an important supporter, while Don Bradman's view that Warne was the best thing to happen to Australian cricket in decades had not changed after the illegal bookie revelation. Mark Taylor said publicly that the affair should not affect Warne's chances for higher responsibilities and endorsed him as a strong option to follow him as Test captain.

During that feverish week in December—and after it—Warne was disappointed yet not remorseful. He coped with the pressures by staying close to his family and friends, and temporarily out of the spotlight. Those phone calls would continue to be ignored for the time being.

'I'm still the same person I've been for twenty-nine years,' he told the media. 'I think the people close to me know what sort of person I am.'

Provided there were no more acts that would bring him into disrepute, he would not be short of support for higher appointments in Australian cricket once Mark Taylor stepped down. Yet Warne's immediate concerns were form and fitness.

In a Shield game held on 19–22 December in Sydney, against a near full-strength New South Wales team, he sent down 29.3 overs for a return of two for 80 in New South Wales's first innings. The Waugh brothers treated him with caution and Warne bowled his best for the season. No flipper or wrong 'un was sighted and he was slower through the air than before the shoulder operation. Yet there was a little of the old rip and zest. His hallmark late (last metre) dip and swerve in the air were on the way back. He was accurate and confident, and delivered few loose deliveries. In New South Wales's second dig, Warne took none for 64, but bowled superbly against Mark Waugh and Slater, who both notched centuries. Again, the flipper and wrong' un were not in evidence, but Warne was rolling over big leg breaks and ripping the occasional one with that characteristic grunt. Waugh took most of the strike from him and only someone with Waugh's unmatched technique against spin could have kept him out.

After the game, Warne asked the Waugh brothers and Mark Taylor how they thought he bowled. All replied it was as good as anything he had delivered before. That was enough for Warne. He let the selectors (Border, Andrew Hilditch and Trevor Hohns), Mark Taylor and Geoff Marsh know that he was available for selection. It was too late to make the Boxing Day Test in Melbourne and he would not have been chosen anyway because there would be room for just one spinner—Stuart MacGill. Warne watched some of the exciting game as MacGill consolidated his place with four for 61 and three for 81, and Australia lost a thriller by 12 runs, leaving it with a two–one lead in the series.

During Victorian practice on Tuesday, 29 December, Warne learned that he would, in June 1999, be the father of a baby boy. He was excited. He bowled in the nets with extra zip and even let go several flippers and wrong 'uns. Later that evening, he was surprised to learn he had been selected in the Australian team for the Fifth Test at Sydney, replacing Western Australian speedster Matthew Nicholson, who had made his debut in Melbourne with a creditable one for 59 and three for 56. It had been a good day for Warne and marked the turning point in his recent fortunes, which had seen his image take a battering over the bookie scandal.

'My life has become a soap opera in recent times,' a happy, if not slightly bemused Warne, who loves to watch 'Melrose Place', told the media on learning of his recall. In many ways, it had been a melodrama since even before he was a sports superstar. He appeared more pleased about Simone carrying a boy than his return to Test cricket.

Warne unwittingly delivered a variation on American writer Ernest Hemingway's dictum 'A man is not a man until he has a son' with the comment: 'It makes you feel a bit like a man.'

The next day, further buoyed by the good news, he made his first steps in repairing his image by taking six cricket writers—whom he regarded as 'negative' or highly critical of him—to lunch in a Chinese restaurant at the Crown Casino in Melbourne. Warne made the lunch convivial, drinking wine and enjoying several cigarettes for the last time before his much-publicised effort to give them away. Warne spoke off-the-record about the bookie scandal and informed the journalists that he and Mark Waugh would give evidence in public in Melbourne (on Friday, 8 January 1999) before representatives of Pakistan's judicial inquiry into match-fixing. This unexpected public relations assault by Warne was the beginning of several more moves devised by him and his agent–manager, Austin Robertson, which they hoped would swing public opinion back his way. Much was at stake in the medium term (a year or so), including future sponsor contracts and Warne's chances of winning the Australian captaincy.

He then set aside all else in preparation for his return to Test cricket, beginning with a link-up with the team at a Sydney harbourside hotel on New Year's Eve. Warne was already plotting to present the England batsmen with a different kind of delivery to that coming from MacGill, who imparted great side-spin. If and when they were bowling in tandem, Warne would opt more for over-spin, thus keeping the opposition under pressure from both ends and preventing them from becoming familiar with the same kind of delivery every over. This would prevent skilled players such as Nasser Hussain and potential destroyers such as Alec Stewart and Graeme Hick from adapting to leg-spin sameness.

Comeback

The sell-out Sydney crowd of 42 124 was abuzz with anticipation at 12.25 p.m. on 3 January 1999—day two of the Fifth Test—as Warne began his warm-up exercises at mid-wicket.

England was one for 42 and recovering from the early loss of skipper Stewart, nicely caught by Warne above his head in slips off the bowling of McGrath. The catch had helped ease the anxiety Warne felt about bowling again in a Test. The day before, he had received a mixed reception from a late-afternoon crowd, including some abuse and catcalling from a sprinkling of pious Sydney members, drunken yobs and England supporters.

It was a blunt reminder that he had much work to do to overcome the effects of the bookie scandal. Nevertheless, he was aware that some successful big hitting could have turned fickle spectators his way. But his chance to achieve this was thwarted by Darren Gough taking a hat-trick—Healy caught behind, MacGill and Colin Miller clean bowled—leaving Warne watching on 2 not out as Australia was rolled for 322. He could only wink his congratulations to his mate Gough, the gutsy Yorkshire speedster.

Yet that was yesterday. Now skipper Taylor was retiring Miller from the bowling crease, after good spells of medium-pace and off spin, by raising his arms high—like an umpire registering a six. The skipper then gave Warne the nod to bowl. Warne was the fifth bowler used, allowing for Miller being effectively two men. Taylor had demonstrated that MacGill was his key leggie at this point and Warne his second choice. The crowd cheered and clapped. It was what they had been waiting for. At 12.27 p.m., in warm, sunny conditions, he stepped up to bowl to left-hander Mark Butcher—Warne's first time at the bowling crease in a Test for nine months.

The batsman smashed a short second ball through mid-wicket for four, then blocked a third. The fourth Warne delivery was a marginally faster leg break (off break to the left-hander), which caught Butcher back on his wicket and plumb lbw. Warne ran down the wicket celebrating and only as an afterthought turned to see confirmation of his appeal from the umpire. The team descended on him and the crowd erupted. He had made the breakthrough. Reprimanded by some sections of the crowd the day before, he was once again an instant hero.

Warne bowled steadily from then on, but it was MacGill who took the honours with five for 57, as opposed to Warne's one for 67 off twenty overs with four maidens. England collapsed to be all out for 220 under the weight of top-class spinning (Miller took two for 45) which caused eight wickets to fall. None of its batsmen was confident against the sharply turning ball on the typical Sydney turner.

Only Hussain (42) and John Crawley (44) had any clues and even they seemed to have developed techniques built around combating the ball off the pitch, rather than making decisions on what was coming out of the bowler's hand.

Australia was only saved from humiliation on day three by a great innings from Michael Slater (123), as it stumbled to be all out for 184. Slater's knock was equal to anything achieved by India's Sachin Tendulkar and not for the first time. His size, fleetness of foot and preparedness to hit over the top made him—at his best—just as exciting as the Indian champion. Australia had been hampered by a hamstring injury to the in-form Steve Waugh (8)—later awarded Man of the Series—who had scored 96 in the first innings and 122 not out and 30 not out in Melbourne. Only brother Mark (24), who had scored a fine, disciplined 121 in the first innings, could handle the impressive bowling by England's speedsters and off-spinner Peter Such (five for 81), before falling to a brilliant one-handed leap at square leg by Mark Ramprakash off Dean Headley (four for 40).

England was left with two days and thirty overs on day three to collect 287 to win. In theory, it looked gettable—210 overs to score the runs at 1.37 an over. Yet no team had scored this many runs in the fourth innings of a Test in Sydney, which on the final days would prove a haven for spinners. Stewart and Butcher attacked with the bat in their usual way and gave no thought to attempting to nudge the runs along at 1 or 2 an over. Butcher belted 12 off McGrath's first over and gave notice of England's intention to win. Taylor rang the changes and again turned to Warne last among his bowlers, as England powered its way to 57 without loss. Warne then did it again, this time with the sixth ball of his first over, as he drew Butcher from his crease. The batsman, expecting a leggie (an offie to him), received a top-spinner that drifted and went straight on to Healy for a swift stumping. Inspired, Warne's spin partner MacGill soon afterwards similarly enticed Stewart from the crease for another Healy stumping.

England went to stumps at two for 104, but never looked like challenging on day four. The heavy roller flattened the pitch for the first hour when McGrath and Warne opened up. MacGill then came on when the pitch was turning more and ran steadily through England, who were all out for 188, giving Australia a 98-run win. MacGill took seven for 50, a performance equal to anything Warne had ever achieved. This effort made sure that the plucky English revival late in the Ashes series did not turn into a victory as the tourists went down three–one.

While Warne toiled manfully without luck or success for one for 34 off nineteen overs, with three maidens, MacGill spun the ball viciously and delivered the occasional superb wrong 'un. Warne was slower than MacGill and his famed 'drift' was not as evident as two years earlier. It was obvious that Warne's confidence was not yet fully restored and he grimaced at his bad luck as England's inept batsmen prodded and missed. MacGill, previously known for his impatience, kept his cool. Where Warne could not take a trick, MacGill's luck was running, exemplified by the final dismissal of Such, who belted the ball to Langer at silly mid-off. The ball bounced off Langer's legs and into MacGill's hand 10 metres away for a caught-and-bowled.

Yet Warne bowled very well and England's batsmen had nowhere to hide from the leg break, which was literally turning square, the wrong 'un and the top-spinner. With spinners coming at them from both ends and a delivery received every 18 seconds on average (compared with twice that length of time between deliveries with pace bowling), there was no relief against such stinging quality and eventually nine of the ten batsmen cracked and fell to the turning ball.

Taylor, chewing away at slip, hand on chin, revelled in the moment and the capacity to produce such firepower and so relentlessly. And just for something different there was biting off-spin from Miller, who seemed to be improving every Test. His two for 45 and one for 50 would do him no harm when selectors sat down to consider the squad for the West Indies in February.

During and after the Fifth Test, Warne was magnanimous in his support for MacGill. MacGill's twelve for 107 were the second-best figures ever on the SCG behind Charles 'Terror' Turner, who took twelve for 87 against England in 1888. These returns gave MacGill the Man of the Match award. His effort on this notorious spinners' paradise was in line with Warne's twelve for 127 against South Africa in 1993–94 and eleven for 109, again against South Africa, a year earlier in 1997–98. The big haul allowed MacGill to head the Ashes bowling figures for both sides, with twenty-seven wickets at 17.7 in just four Tests.

Without detracting from MacGill's performance in Sydney, skipper Taylor put matters in perspective:

'I thought both the leg-spinners bowled well. It was one of those things where Stuart got the wickets. He bowled fractionally better than Warnie, but I didn't think there was that much difference between twelve wickets and two.'

More importantly, Taylor gave a glimpse of things to come as the nation savoured the possibility of the finest spin combination since O'Reilly and Grimmett in the 1930s:

'It just shows that if you've got two of them working together, you can apply a lot of pressure.'

The upshot of MacGill's remarkable emergence (eight Tests and forty-seven wickets at 21.77) meant Australia had two outstanding leg-spinners to call on for the tour of the West Indies from February to April 1999 and to exploit even more than before the Caribbean weakness against spin. The forgotten cricket art of the 1980s would now be a great strength for Australia into the new century. It would give it the potential for the best bowling attack in decades and the opportunity to maintain its number-one ranking in Test cricket—a position it has held for four years since first beating the West Indies in May 1995.

The return of Warne at age twenty-nine to the Test arena, exactly seven years after he first appeared, marked the beginning of the second phase of his cricket career, which could even run another seven years, given form, fitness and desire.

Warne's fine Sydney Test form was as good as could be expected considering his recovery from shoulder surgery. He would not be at full strength and top form until the 1999–2000 Australian season, including a demanding six Tests against India and Pakistan, and which would be a better gauge of his recovery and future. In the short term, he was given an important endorsement by the ACB on 6 January when he was again appointed vice-captain of the Australian one-day international team for the January–February triangular contest with England and Sri Lanka. This effectively gave him the chance to captain again because of Steve Waugh's withdrawal from the first few games with a hamstring injury.

It was a reprieve of significance for Warne, who once more was presented with a forum to exhibit his outstanding skills as a leader, which had first been noted as a twelve-year-old. The others under him in the one-day squad for the first game against England at Brisbane on 10 January 1999 were Mark Waugh, Adam Gilchrist, Greg Blewett, Ricky Ponting, Darren Lehmann, Damien Martyn, Michael Bevan, Adam Dale, Damien Fleming, Brendon Julian, Glenn McGrath and Brad Young. This one-day series would be followed by a four-Test tour of the Caribbean, the one-day World Cup campaign in England in May–June 1999 and tours to Sri Lanka and Zimbabwe.

Hearings and Tribulations

While preparing for his second game as Australian captain, Warne had to take time off with Mark Waugh to face the Pakistan Judicial Commission Hearing into bribery and match-fixing. It was held in a tribunal courtroom in King Street,

Melbourne, on 8 January 1999. On the wall was a portrait of Mohammad Ali Jinnah, the founder of Pakistan. A small Pakistani flag sat on the bench. The judge in charge of the hearing, Abdul Salam Khawar, began with a short prayer to 'the almighty Allah' for the fifty or so present—most of them media. The two cricketers had demanded that the hearing be public. Warne's father, Keith; his wife, Simone; and his agent, Austin Robertson, were present. Each witness swore an oath and told the court his father's name, in keeping with Pakistani law.

First Waugh, then Warne was cross-examined at length by the Pakistani lawyer Ali Sibtain Fazli and his assistant Ali Sajjad, followed by Salim Malik's counsel, Azmat Saeed. At one point, Azmat made a telling slip, referring to the hearing as a 'trial', and had to correct himself. At times, Waugh's counsel, barrister Michael Shatin QC, had to step in to stop the Pakistanis pushing into irrelevant areas as they thrashed around trying to find holes in the sworn statements by the cricketers. Waugh looked uncertain and nervous, just as if he were beginning a difficult innings against bouncers, but he showed his faculties were as acute as ever when he pointed out a major mistake by the Pakistanis. Azmat tried to make much of a statement—a summary of Waugh's evidence presented in Pakistan in September 1998. The Pakistani lawyers had prepared this summary. Waugh said:

'Everything is correct except for two sentences where it appears the language barrier … everything is mixed up …'

The Pakistani version suggested that Waugh and Salim spoke for an hour and a half at the reception in Rawalpindi on 21 October 1994 when Salim attempted to bribe him. Waugh denied the length of time they chatted. Salim spoke briefly to Waugh, with Warne within earshot, at the reception and offered him the $US200 000 bribe. An hour and a half later (not after an hour-and-a-half's discussion, which would suggest something conspiratorial), a still-shocked Waugh made it clear in another even shorter conversation with Salim that he rejected the offer.

Azmat, who had a disconcerting and sometimes abrupt manner on his feet, went through a few histrionics, approaching Waugh in the witness box and pushing the statement under his nose. But Shatin was alert, pulling out the original transcript covering what Waugh had actually testified in Pakistan. The barrister went one better and produced the tape for the judge from which the full transcript—not the Pakistani summary—was made. Shatin told Judge Khawar that he (Khawar) could verify the authenticity of the tape by recognising his own voice on it.

Warne, looking suitably sombre in a dark suit and conservative tie, performed as he had promised before the hearing when he said he looked forward to giving evidence. It was vintage Warne—direct, ingenuous and confident. He pitched his responses at just the right level, neither being disrespectful nor genuflecting towards the at times aggressive Pakistan Cricket Board lawyers, who seemed intent on tripping up the Australians rather than accepting evidence and asking for expansions. Fazli and Sajjad were almost indistinguishable in their approach from Salim's counsel Azmat. If anything, the hearing appeared to drift into a showdown between two nations as intense as any Test match, with attack and defence from both sides.

The grilling of the players (Waugh about eighty minutes, Warne about forty-five minutes) led nowhere, as their responses remained consistent and, on the whole, credible. Neither was remotely near cracking on any point. In fact, they enhanced their positions without dissembling.

Both were asked about the one-day game in Colombo on 7 September 1994, which Australia won, scoring seven for 179, with Pakistan managing just nine for 151. The Pakistani lawyers suggested that they had evidence that this match was fixed. Waugh and Warne knew nothing about it.

'We only ever play to win,' Warne said with certitude. He pointed out that he won the Man of the Match award in that game, hardly the performance of someone who had been bribed. The allegation was that a couple of the key Pakistanis deliberately played poorly in the game.

On a couple of occasions, the Pakistani legal contingent went further and alluded to the possibility that the Australians may have thrown the First Test in Karachi, played from 28 September to 2 October 1994, when, at the end of the fourth day, Pakistan was three for 157 and the game was on a knife edge. That night, Salim made his $US200 000 offer to Warne and May to throw the game the next day by bowling badly (outside the off stump). May had a neck injury, but Warne bowled at his best and helped reduce Pakistan to nine for 258.

The home team seemed beaten, but a last-wicket stand between the hard-hitting Inzamam-ul-Haq and Mustaq Ahmed turned the game around. Warne bowled to Inzamam in what became the last over. The batsman lunged and missed the ball. Healy missed a tough stumping and the ball went for four leg byes, giving Pakistan a one-wicket victory in one of the closest, most thrilling Test finishes in history. Harold 'Dickie' Bird umpired the game and said it was the best match he ever saw. Warne took five for 89 off 36.1 overs, with twelve maidens, one of his finest performances considering the tightness of the game. He was awarded Man of the Match for this, too. To suggest that the Australians would throw the match, or that they could contrive to lose it with such a good delivery and a tough missed stumping, was absurd. Shatin picked up on this and intervened when the question arose a second time.

'It's outrageous to make any allegation of that nature without any warning or notice,' the QC railed indignantly. 'Everyone who loves cricket saw that incident and saw the ball beat both the batsman and the keeper, and those of us who were Australians were disappointed and those who were Pakistanis were happy.'

It was not clear where Fazli and Sajjad were heading with this. Were they implying that Salim had actually bribed May and Warne, or even the whole team seeing that Healy missed the stumping? If this were the case, many of the Australians would be better giving away cricket and taking up careers as thespians or, at least, American professional wrestlers. It appeared that the Pakistani lawyers were intent on casting doubt on as many Australian names as possible without a shred of evidence or plausibility, knowing full well that the media worldwide would pick and run with any name or hint of wrongdoing. It was mischievous and foolish, and demonstrated the feeble position the Pakistanis were in when dealing with the inquiry into their fellow countrymen.

If ever there were the need for the world cricketing body, the ICC, to have powers in matters such as match-fixing, it was now. There was some hope here. Its member countries' chief representatives were currently assembling in New Zealand to consider how much power the ICC could exercise in this area.

The next day, 9 January, Tim May gave evidence. Fazli struggled to make much of the mention of Steve Waugh's name. May had said he had heard from Warne that he and Warne, and the Waugh brothers, were offered collectively $US200 000 to throw the one-day game between Australia and Pakistan on 22 October 1994. Steve Waugh did not hear of the offer directly, but was made aware of it through press items late in 1998. He reacted by saying he 'would knock the block off' anyone approaching him directly with a bribe offer. (Pakistan won this game, scoring one for 251 in just thirty-nine overs, after Australia had made six for 250. Mark Waugh scored a brilliant 121 not out. Warne took none for 47 off nine overs, with one maiden, and May none for 65 off nine.)

Fazli seemed unable to grasp the reason for May assuming that the bribe offers to the four Australians would amount to $US50 000 each. May said he had made the simple long division in his head and assumed the $US200 000 would be offered in equal parts.

'I am an accountant,' May said without bombast, as he shifted in his seat. The remark and the fiddling around the non-issue by the Pakistani lawyers caused another amused stir among the mainly Australian media, who were enjoying the theatre. A few of them giggled when Shatin's seven-year-old son, James, who was sitting in the audience during the second morning of the hearing, yawned audibly. Was he bored? Not for long. His father jumped to his feet during a prolonged interrogation of May by the earnest Sajjad.

'If he [Sajjad] wants a job as a junior on the O'Regan Inquiry [into possible bribery in Australia],' Shatin remarked. 'I'm sure something can be arranged ...'

It was a scathing yet appropriate put-down. May was being treated as if the hearing were an inquisition into his activities, not as a helpful witness to corruption in Pakistani cricket.

The hearing was studded with humour. Azmat asked Warne what Salim's hotel room number was during the First Test in Karachi in September 1994 when the attempted bribe took place. This ridiculous question drew a titter, but Azmat no doubt would have made much of it, had Warne remembered. (I later rang Azmat, an engaging figure when not involved with courtroom theatrics, at his hotel and asked him for his room number. Fortunately for him, he could recall it.)

Azmat asked Warne why he referred to Salim as 'the Rat'.

'Because that's his nickname with the Australians.' Warne replied. 'Some of them think he looks like a rat.'

Both Australians admitted liking a bet.

'I own horses,' Waugh said, 'and I like to bet on the races, golf and Rugby.'

'On cricket?' Azmat asked.

'Never on cricket,' Waugh replied.

'You say you took money [from the illegal Indian bookie "John" for weather and pitch reports],' Azmat said. 'Did you ever give money *to* a bookmaker?'

'Most of the time,' Waugh responded, again getting a laugh from the audience.

Azmat tried to make something of Waugh having an account with Centrebet, the legal Darwin-based betting operation, but this also led up another blind alley.

Waugh did revise the number of times he gave 'John', the Indian bookie, weather and pitch information from 'a handful' to 'about ten times'.

When Waugh's interrogation—for that was what it seemed—was over, Judge Khawar released him, but ordered that he make no contact with Warne, then corrected himself and said no *immediate* contact.

Shatin, showing humour and a knowledge of cricket, remarked:

'Good, I was beginning to worry about Sunday.' (Sunday, 10 January 1999, was the day when Warne and Waugh would need to communicate in the one-day international against England.)

Warne admitted liking blackjack and roulette, and the occasional bet on Australian Rules football.

'Do you bet on cricket?' Azmat asked again.

'No, never,' Warne replied.

Warne did elaborate on his discussions with 'John', who had given him $5000 at his Colombo hotel in September 1994, which Warne claimed had 'no strings attached'. He apparently, however, felt obligated to give him some information about later matches. He heard from 'John' again in early December 1994, just before the one-day game against England in Sydney.

'He telephoned me at the hotel,' Warne testified. 'He asked me the make-up of the team. I said, "I don't know. That's up to the selectors and the captain, but in Sydney we always play two spinners." He asked me what the pitch was like and I said I hadn't seen it. He said, "Good luck. Do you think you'll win?" I said, "Bloody oath, we will."'

Warne next heard from 'John' just before the Boxing Day Test later in 1994. He phoned him at the team hotel in Melbourne, congratulated him on his form and asked what the pitch was like.

Warne replied:

'Mate, it's a typical MCG pitch. It should be a good batting wicket. It should turn a bit and keep a bit low towards the end of the game."

'John' asked whether it was going to rain. Warne replied that 'you could never tell in Melbourne, but I don't think so'. 'John' wished Warne a merry Christmas.

The third and last time Warne heard from 'John' was in Perth in February 1995. The player informed the bookie that it was hot in Perth and that the wicket was a normal WACA pitch—'fast and bouncy'.

'Is the pitch going to crack up?' the bookie asked.

'No,' Warne responded, 'it's got a good coverage of grass. It should hold together.'

Warne said he had not spoken to 'John' since February 1995, which was the month the Salim bribery allegations became public, and when he was fined in private by the ACB for his dealings with the Indian bookmaker.

Shatin brought the hearing back into perspective by asking both cricketers at the end of their questioning if Salim Malik had ever challenged them face-to-face about their allegations. There were chances during the Pakistani visit to Australia for three Tests in the 1995–96 season and when the World Cup was played in 1996. Both Waugh and Warne were adamant. He had never confronted them. They had not exchanged a word with him since October 1994, not even when he batted against them. In fact, the whole Australian team refused to speak to him, giving him a frigid reception. This was quite an admission, given their penchant for sledging.

The firm-jawed Alan Crompton, now a solicitor with the Supreme Court of New South Wales and the ACB chairman during the time the illegal bookie payments were made to Warne and Waugh, made the most definitive statements yet in defence of the Australian cricketers. He was the last witness at the hearing and took the stand after May on Saturday, 9 January. It was clear in this articulate lawyer's mind that they had done nothing beyond give weather and pitch reports to the Indian bookie. The conduct of Warne and Mark Waugh 'amounted to a breach of the players' contract in that it brought the game of cricket into disrepute'. Crompton stuck to a clear enunciation of the ACB's attitude, punctuating his sentences with 'aarhs', which, coming from him, sounded precise. The matter was handled in private, as were all such matters of the breach of the players' contract in off-the-field incidents. On-the-field incidents were dealt with in public.

Crompton would not be budged from this, as the Pakistani lawyers variously tried to characterise the ACB's actions as 'sweeping it under the carpet' and amateurish in that it did not keep detailed written notes on the procedures for discipline. The Pakistanis picked on the apparent dictatorial approach of Crompton and Graham Halbish, the then chief executive officer at the ACB. They took action against Warne and Waugh, then reported the incident to twelve of the other fourteen board directors at a Sydney meeting on 28 February 1995. In effect, Crompton and Halbish presented the board with a *fait accompli.* Yet none of the twelve expressed any disagreement with the action. Crompton pointed out that this approach—of chief executives making decisions quickly in time-restricted, critical circumstances, and then presenting them for ratification or otherwise to a board—was the way most businesses operated.

While denying a cover-up, the former ACB chairman admitted he was concerned that, if the off-the-field transgressions of Warne and Waugh were made public at the time, they could be confused with the then (February 1995) public problems facing Salim involving match-fixing and bribery. The blow-up four years later seemed to confirm Crompton's concern. It's probable that, had the dealings of Warne and Mark Waugh been made public when discovered in late February 1995, far more drastic action would have been forced on the conservative ACB by the media and the Australian public. It may be that the ACB's approach, whether viewed as appropriate or not, saved the players' careers.

In quizzing Crompton, Sajjad said that Warne and Waugh were effectively charged by the ACB with bribery. The witness's jaw extended in the Pakistani lawyer's direction.

'They were not charged with bribery,' he said firmly. 'Bribery has nothing to do with this matter ... had I thought it had anything to do with bribery, I would have viewed these whole circumstances quite differently and I would have handled them quite differently.'

Warne and Waugh were disappointed that their 'stupidity' in taking money from the bookie for innocent information about the weather had been confused, it seemed, in the public mind, with the bribery and match-fixing allegations aimed at several Pakistani players. It had been a diversion by Salim's counsel, in particular, in an effort to have Salim exonerated from wrongdoing.

Some sections of the media did nothing to prevent the confusion and seemed to blur the two distinct issues. It annoyed the players. Both were incensed after the hearing at the front-page headline in the Melbourne *Herald-Sun*'s p.m. edition of 8 January. It screamed 'MATCH FIX' and featured photographs of Warne and Waugh. Both players told the media door-stopping them at the hearing that 'the matter [of the paper's report] was in the hands of their lawyers'. The next morning, the paper's headline read 'INNOCENT', with bigger shots of the two players. The accompanying story was much clearer in its reporting of the players' positions.

Bold Capt'n Warnie

With this unsettling experience behind them for the time being, both players, captain and vice-captain in Steve Waugh's absence, flew to Brisbane for the start of the one-day international series to concentrate on what they did best—playing cricket.

The opening game of the three-team (Australia, England and Sri Lanka) CUB Series was between Australia and England at the Gabba on 10 January. England batted first and was kept down to eight for 178 thanks in no small measure to Warne's captaincy. Australia's bowling and fielding was inspired. McGrath (two for 24) was used in bursts at key moments, while the reliable Fleming (two for 33) and Dale (two for 25) were also used in tight spells. Warne ignored the mixed reception from the crowd and was all inspiration. He remained on top, thinking through every move and riding the game's rhythms, which had largely been dictated by him. He was always there with the right word to a bowler at the end of an over, and the first to congratulate a successful wicket-taker. With a bum-pat here, a hug there, Warne often seemed more of an Aussie Rules football skipper, such was the energy and enthusiasm he brought to leadership.

He bowled well, bringing back the flipper, a sure sign that he was running up to peak form and fitness. It was hardly seen in 1997. In the early part of 1998—his previous stint in the international arena—it was non-existent. His shoulder could not stand the extra strain. After surgery, he had kept it in the locker as his shoulder strengthened. Now this most demanding delivery in cricket was back. Warne's figures of none for 44 did justice to his accuracy, but not his form and contribution, as he took responsibility for bowling in the last few overs.

Australia's batsmen let the skipper down by stumbling in the rain-reduced game to nine for 145 in thirty-six overs, not enough for a win. The left-arm quick Alan Mullally was the destroyer for England with a brilliant burst, taking four for 18.

Warne lost the toss again in Sydney on 13 January, and Sri Lanka batted and charged out of the blocks with 95 before Julian removed the rampaging Sanath Jayasuriya (65). Warne bravely brought himself on before the first fifteen overs were up, a time when spinners are vulnerable to being belted over the top with most of the field forced inside the circle. He immediately changed the pace of the game and, in his fourth over, bowled the dangerous opener Kaluwitharana round his legs. Soon after, he showed that the all-important 'dip' was back in his deliveries when he deceived Marvan Atapattu into driving an easy catch to Mark Waugh at short cover. Warne's two for 44 helped contain the Sri Lankans to nine for 259. Australia responded with two for 260 (a record for chasing at the SCG) in just 46.1 overs, thanks to a clean-hitting yet brutal 131 in 118 balls by Adam Gilchrist. Mark Waugh (63) showed that his confidence following the Pakistani hearing was back. The bribery story was not going to fade and it was important that Waugh managed to minimise the effect on his game.

Warne, for his part, seemed to have decomparmentalised the off-field dramas. He was revelling in his chance for quick redemption with sections of the Australian public. The captaincy and his bowling in the high-profile one-day international presented timely opportunities for exhibitions of the 'true' Warne. There was a perfect forum two days later on 16 January in Melbourne, when a massive 82 299-strong MCG crowd assembled to see Australia do battle with England. Melburnians felt starved after the disaster of the opening of the Boxing Day Test. Perhaps they were also out in force to support their favourite son, 'Warnie'.

He lost the toss for the third successive time, and this forced Australia into the field in 37-degree heat. He kept his troops alert, however, and England could only manage 178. McGrath was expensive yet penetrating with four for 54, while Warne, with one for 44, once more bowled well, breaking through in his first over to have Nick Knight (27) spectacularly caught by Mark Waugh at short cover. Warne had again brought himself on before the first fifteen overs were up.

Australia lapped up the runs, losing just one wicket in making 182 in 39.2 overs. Waugh's confidence was again evident as he stroked a controlled 83 not out. The big crowd became distracted during Australia's innings. A Mexican wave washed around the stadium and the outfield became strewn with rubbish, including the odd beer bottle. A golf ball struck Mark Ealham on the knee. He complained to umpire Darrell Hair. England skipper Alec Stewart beckoned Warne onto the arena. He wandered onto the MCG wearing a tracksuit and thongs.

'You're the god of Melbourne,' Stewart told him, indicating the old Bay 13 area where some of the 'yobbos' were found. 'Can you calm them down?'

'I don't know what I'm going to do,' Warne replied, bemused. He was not yet sure of crowd reaction to him, despite it being his home ground. In a spontaneous act of good-humoured inspiration, he picked up Mark Waugh's helmet. 'I'll put this on. I might get a bit thrown at me, too.'

The two skippers walked over to the offending area, at one point putting their arms around each other. It was a gesture to indicate the good feeling between the teams and the stupidity of the tiny disruptive element. Warne gestured for the crowd to stop. The unruly spectators calmed down. His job done, Warne trotted back to the dressing room and the game continued. That night and for the next two days, Warne was seen on TV wearing the helmet and carrying out his good-natured placation. It was another useful moment in his rehabilitation.

Warne's captaincy record now read three wins and one loss, and his credentials for future leadership duties were enhanced. On Sunday, 17 January 1999, he handed back the one-day captaincy to Steve Waugh, for a third match against England. Stewart won the toss and England compiled four for 282 in batting first. Hick (108 from 129 balls) and Hussain (93 from 114 balls) put on 190 and all Australian bowlers—with the exception of Adam Dale, who took none for 26 off ten overs—took some stick. Warne (none for 57) tried hard, but ran into some powerful batting on a surprisingly unresponsive pitch. In a clear plan to put Warne off his line and length, Hick and Hussain swept at more than 50 per cent of his deliveries. Warne swapped to around the wicket and back to over in an effort to thwart the English pair. He experimented with a sliding top-spinner from out of the front of the hand and still beat the bat. But his couple of flippers were not on target and he was a fraction short in general. It was a very rare victory for England's bats against the leg-spinner.

Australia was set 5.66 runs an over to win, by far the toughest assignment ever at the SCG. Mark Waugh (85 from ninety-five balls) and Darren Lehmann (76 from eight-seven balls), back from injury, gave the home team a chance. But the task was always uphill, especially with Gough bowling superbly (one for 40 off ten overs), backed up by Mullally (one for 45) and Adam Hollioake (two for 48). Bevan and Blewett put on a 50-plus partnership before Ashley Giles bowled Blewett (32 from thirty-three balls). Shane Warne strode in to a big reception from an excited crowd. This was the kind of adrenalin-pumping situation that made all the abuse, criticism, pain, surgery and hard work to get back on top worthwhile. This was what it was all about. The score was six for 263. There were just twelve balls to go and 20 runs to get. Bevan and Warne could only scramble 5 runs off the forty-ninth over, from Ealham. This left 15 to get off the last over, bowled by Giles. The first three balls yielded just 4 runs, when a spectator rushed on to the ground. There was a break of a minute with three balls to go and 11 runs to win. The batsman could only manage singles, as Australia reached six for 275, falling 7 runs short.

England had thrown down the gauntlet for the rest of the CUB Series, and perhaps the more important World Cup on its home turf only four months away. Two days later, on 19 January, the English team easily disposed of Sri Lanka at the MCG and moved to the top of the competition.

The next day, Australia's stocks were down further with the news that Ricky Ponting had been involved in a fracas in a Sydney nightclub after the 17 January loss to England. Sporting a black eye, the 24-year-old told the media he had a drinking problem that he intended to address. He was pilloried in the press, which was revelling in the continued woes of Australian players in off-field incidents.

In the next game at Hobart, Australia could only manage nine for 210 on a difficult, slow wicket, which only Mark Waugh (65) and Darren Lehmann (51) could handle. Steve Waugh aggravated his troublesome hamstring and Warne took over as skipper when Australia fielded.

Kaluwitharana (54), Atapattu (82) and captain Ranatunga (45 not out), with his usual runner because of alleged injury, took Sri Lanka to victory at seven for 211. Warne's performance—three for 45—was encouraging, but he still wasn't landing his flipper well. It was falling short. Nevertheless, he skippered the team with energy and thought. Warne would never die wondering while in charge. He tried everything and anything to break through. Waugh's injury was later found to be bad enough to threaten his participation in the rest of the one-day series. Warne would continue as skipper.

Saturday 23 January put cricket on the front pages around the cricketing world, again for all the wrong reasons, as England did battle with Sri Lanka during the Australia Day triple-header in Adelaide. It was a great game. England belted 302, with Graeme Hick (125 not out), the best bat of the series, and Neil Fairbrother (78 not out) starring. Sri Lanka responded with nine for 303, thanks to a fine 120 by Jayawardene. Yet the score line was reduced to small print under the main story of umpire Ross Emerson calling off-spinner Muttiah Muralitharan for throwing, and the subsequent reprehensible actions of Sri Lankan captain Ranatunga, who abused the umpires and his right to be playing the game itself.

Late in the thrilling match, tempers raised by the earlier fiasco flared. Mahanama, when going for a quick run, stepped sideways into Darren Gough as he attempted to field the ball. Alec Stewart then shouldered Mahanama as they walked past each other at the end of the over. The tight game seemed temporarily like an Australian Rules contest, where such body contact is within the law.

The next day, 24 January, Sri Lanka, buoyed by their terrific victory, reduced Australia to 270 on the good Adelaide wicket. Mark Waugh (75) gave his team another fine start. Skipper Warne worked on a plan to have McGrath blitz the Sri Lankan batsmen with chest and throat balls, even if it meant conceding a few no-balls. It was typical of Warne's aggressive leadership. The boldness paid off. McGrath took five for 40 and Sri Lanka was never in the game as it scraped up to 190. McGrath bowled beautifully, making deliveries rear in a way not expected in one-day cricket, which forced batsmen to fend off balls for easy close-to-the-wicket catches.

Warne himself bowled poorly, taking none for 53 off nine overs, but there was no pressure in the game when he was on. Appropriately, he lifted when it counted on Australia Day, 26 January, with a match-winning effort against England as both skipper and bowler. Australia batted first, scoring a mediocre eight for 239. Mark Waugh (65) collected his sixth successive one-day fifty and was assisted by Lehmann (51) and Martyn (59 not out).

Hick (109) racked up his third century of the tournament, but Warne, in easily his best effort since his return from shoulder injury, took three for 39 off ten overs. He was supported by his trump card, McGrath, with three for 40.

England looked to have the game, but lost seven for 47 thanks to the pressure Warne applied at the crease and in the field. Hick deserved his Man of the Match award, but Warne should have been given it because of his performance at the death. His courage, cool and bold style were proving to be his key assets as bowler and captain. He was on track to reach his peak again, possibly for the World Cup and almost certainly for the next Australian summer.

During this challenging time, Shane Warne enjoyed being back on the field. And cricket fans everywhere were again being inspired by his deeds with the spinning ball, and the cry from behind the stumps of:

'Bowled, Warnie!'

SHANE WARNE

Career Statistics

As at 6 January 1999

Compiled by Ross Dundas

Test Cricket

Debut: 1991–92 Australia v India, Sydney

Bowling

Series	Opponent	Venue	M	Balls	Mdns	Runs	Wkts	Avrge	5	10	Best	Stk/Rt
1991–92	India	Australia	2	408	9	228	1	228.00	–	–	1/150	408.00
1992–93	Sri Lanka	Sri Lanka	2	229	8	158	3	52.67	–	–	3/11	76.33
1992–93	West Indies	Australia	4	650	23	313	10	31.30	1	–	7/52	65.00
1992–93	New Zealand	New Zealand	3	954	73	256	17	15.06	–	–	4/8	56.11
1993	England	England	6	2639	178	877	34	25.79	1	–	5/82	77.61
1993–94	New Zealand	Australia	3	909	49	305	18	16.94	1	–	6/31	50.50
1993–94	South Africa	Australia	3	1051	63	307	18	17.06	2	1	7/56	58.38
1993–94	South Africa	South Africa	3	1145	69	336	15	22.40	–	–	4/86	76.33
1994–95	Pakistan	Pakistan	3	1090	50	504	18	28.00	2	–	6/136	60.55
1994–95	England	Australia	5	1537	84	549	27	20.33	2	1	8/71	56.92
1994–95	West Indies	West Indies	4	828	35	406	15	27.07	–	–	4/70	55.20
1995–96	Pakistan	Australia	3	690	52	198	19	10.42	1	1	7/23	36.31
1995–96	Sri Lanka	Australia	3	988	43	433	12	36.08	–	–	4/71	82.33
1996–97	West Indies	Australia	5	1303	56	594	22	27.00	–	–	4/95	59.22
1996–97	South Africa	South Africa	3	798	47	282	11	25.64	–	–	4/43	72.54
1997	England	England	6	1423	69	577	24	24.04	1	–	6/48	59.29
1997–98	New Zealand	Australia	3	1024	36	476	19	25.05	1	–	5/88	53.89
1997–98	South Africa	Australia	3	1123	51	417	20	20.85	2	1	6/34	56.15
1997–98	India	India	3	1002	37	540	10	54.00	–	–	4/85	100.20
1998–99	England	Australia	1	234	7	110	2	55.00	–	–	1/43	117.00
Total			**68**	**20025**	**1039**	**7866**	**315**	**24.97**	**14**	**4**	**8/71**	**63.57**

Bowling record against each country

Opponents	Debut	M	Balls	Mdns	Runs	Wkts	Avrge	5	10	Best	Stk/Rt
India	1991–92	5	1410	46	768	11	69.82	–	–	4/85	128.18
Sri Lanka	1992–93	5	1217	51	591	15	39.40	–	–	4/71	81.13
West Indies	1992–93	13	2781	114	1313	47	27.94	1	–	7/52	59.17
New Zealand	1992–93	9	2887	158	1037	54	19.20	2	–	6/31	53.46
England	1993	18	5833	338	2113	87	24.29	4	1	8/71	67.05
South Africa	1993–94	12	4117	230	1342	64	20.97	4	2	7/56	64.33
Pakistan	1994–95	6	1780	102	702	37	18.97	3	1	7/23	48.11

Innings of match comparison

	Balls	Mdns	Runs	Wkts	Avrge	5	10	Best	Stk/Rt
First innings	6617	316	2698	86	31.37	3	–	7/23	76.94
Second innings	4083	209	1733	71	24.41	3	–	7/56	57.51
Third innings	3303	180	1235	61	20.25	4	–	8/71	54.15
Fourth innings	6022	334	2200	97	22.68	4	–	6/31	62.08

Record in each country

Opponents	Debut	M	Balls	Mdns	Runs	Wkts	Avrge	5	10	Best	Stk/Rt
Australia	1991–92	35	9917	473	3930	168	23.39	10	4	8/71	59.03
Sri Lanka	1992–93	2	229	8	158	3	52.67	–	–	3/11	76.33
New Zealand	1992–93	3	954	73	256	17	15.06	–	–	4/8	56.11
England	1993	12	4062	247	1454	58	25.07	2	–	6/48	70.03
South Africa	1993–94	6	1943	116	618	26	23.77	–	–	4/43	74.73
Pakistan	1994–95	3	1090	50	504	18	28.00	2	–	6/136	60.55
West Indies	1994–95	4	828	35	406	15	27.07	–	–	4/70	55.20
India	1997–98	3	1002	37	540	10	54.00	–	–	4/85	100.20

Fifty-wicket comparison

Opponents		M	Balls	Mdns	Runs	Wkts	Avrge	5	10	Best	Stk/Rt
2 Jul 1993	N Hussain (Eng)	14	3421	194	1325	50	26.50	1	-	7/52	68.42
1 Feb 1994	BM McMillan (SAF)	23	6832	402	2444	100	24.44	5	1	7/52	68.32
27 Dec 1994	AJ Stewart (Eng)	31	9650	559	3445	150	22.96	9	2	8/71	64.33
12 Dec 1995	HP Tillakaratne (SL)	42	12460	706	4600	200	23.00	10	3	8/71	62.30
6 Jul 1997	AJ Stewart (Eng)	51	15789	866	5992	250	23.96	11	3	8/71	63.15
5 Jan 1998	JH Kallis (SAF)	63	18475	983	7066	300	23.55	14	4	8/71	61.58

Venues

	Debut	M	Balls	Mdns	Runs	Wkts	Avrge	5	10	Best	Stk/Rt
IN AUSTRALIA											
Sydney	1991–92	8	2599	125	1030	43	23.95	4	2	7/56	60.44
Adelaide	1991–92	7	1830	83	776	20	38.80	–	–	4/31	91.50
Melbourne	1992–93	6	1747	81	630	32	19.69	2	–	7/52	54.59
Perth	1992–93	6	1299	51	606	17	35.65	–	–	4/83	76.41
Hobart	1993–94	3	557	24	236	15	15.73	2	–	6/31	37.13
Brisbane	1993–94	5	1885	109	652	41	15.90	2	2	8/71	45.98
IN SRI LANKA											
Colombo	1992–93	1	163	5	118	3	39.33	–	–	3/11	54.33
Moratuwa	1992–93	1	66	3	40	–	–	–	–	–	–
IN NEW ZEALAND											
Christchurch	1992–93	1	288	19	86	7	12.29	–	–	4/63	41.14
Wellington	1992–93	1	414	34	108	4	27.00	–	–	2/49	103.50
Auckland	1992–93	1	252	20	62	6	10.33	–	–	4/8	42.00
IN ENGLAND											
Manchester	1993	2	802	58	248	17	14.59	1	–	6/48	47.18
Lord's	1993	2	629	33	215	10	21.50	–	–	4/57	62.90
Nottingham	1993	2	828	50	311	13	23.92	–	–	4/86	63.69
Leeds	1993	2	510	31	161	2	80.50	–	–	1/43	255.00
Birmingham	1993	2	675	38	282	7	40.29	1	–	5/82	96.43
The Oval	1993	2	618	37	237	9	26.33	–	–	3/78	68.67
IN SOUTH AFRICA											
Johannesburg	1993–94	2	687	42	239	11	21.73	–	–	4/43	62.45
Cape Town	1993–94	1	462	31	116	6	19.33	–	–	3/38	77.00
Durban	1993–94	1	330	20	92	4	23.00	–	–	4/92	82.50
Centurion	1996–97	1	216	11	89	–	–	–	–	–	–
Port Elizabeth	1996–97	1	248	12	82	5	16.40	–	–	3/62	49.60
IN PAKISTAN											
Karachi	1994–95	1	379	22	150	8	18.75	1	–	5/89	47.37
Rawalpindi	1994–95	1	280	14	114	1	114.00	–	–	1/58	280.00
Lahore	1994–95	1	431	14	240	9	26.67	1	–	6/136	47.88
IN WEST INDIES											
Bridgetown	1994–95	1	231	7	121	5	24.20	–	–	3/64	46.20
St John's	1994–95	1	210	9	101	3	33.67	–	–	3/83	70.00
Port-of-Spain	1994–95	1	95	5	42	1	42.00	–	–	1/16	95.00
Kingston	1994–95	1	292	14	142	6	23.67	–	–	4/70	48.66
IN INDIA											
Chennai	1997–98	1	390	18	207	5	41.40	–	–	4/85	78.00
Calcutta	1997–98	1	252	4	147	–	–	–	–	–	–
Bangalore	1997–98	1	360	15	186	5	37.20	–	–	3/106	72.00

Wickets taken

How Out	Wkts	%
Caught	171	54.28
(ct MA Taylor)	51	16.19
(ct IA Healy)	31	9.84
(ct ME Waugh)	17	5.39
(cgt and bwd)	14	4.44
(ct DC Boon)	11	3.49
LBW	56	17.77
Bowled	58	18.41
Stumped	16	5.07
(st IA Healy)	15	4.76
(st PA Emery)	1	0.31

Batsmen dismissed

Position	Wkts	%
Openers	47	14.92
Number 3	27	8.57
Number 4	38	12.06
Number 5	34	10.79
Number 6	30	9.52
Number 7	28	8.88
Number 8	31	9.84
Number 9	28	8.88
Number 10	32	10.15
Number 11	20	6.34
Numbers 1–6	176	55.87
Number 7–11	139	44.12

Batsman		Wkts
AJ Stewart	(England)	9
GP Thorpe	(England)	9
N Hussain	(England)	8
WJ Cronje	(South Africa)	8
DJ Richardson	(South Africa)	8
MA Atherton	(England)	7
GA Gooch	(England)	6
BM McMillan	(South Africa)	6
CA Walsh	(West Indies)	5
DJ Richardson	(South Africa)	5
CL Cairns	(New Zealand)	5

Five wickets in an innings

Wkts	Opponent	Venue	Series
7/52	West Indies	Melbourne	1992–93
5/82	England	Birmingham	1993
6/31	New Zealand	Hobart	1993–94
7/56	South Africa	Sydney	1993–94
5/72	South Africa	Sydney	1993–94
5/89	Pakistan	Karachi	1994–95
6/136	Pakistan	Lahore	1994–95
8/71	England	Brisbane	1994–95
6/64	England	Melbourne	1994–95
7/23	Pakistan	Brisbane	1995–96
6/48	England	Manchester	1997
5/88	New Zealand	Hobart	1997–98
5/75	South Africa	Sydney	1997–98
6/34	South Africa	Sydney	1997–98

Innings by innings

Test	Inn	Venue	Ovrs	Md	Rns	Wk	Batsman	How Out	Wkt	Balls	Mdns	Runs	Avrge	5	10	Stk/Rt
1991–92 v India in Australia																
1	1	Sydney	40.3	7	133	1	RJ Shastri	ct DM Jones	1	243	7	133	133.00	–	–	243.00
			45.0	7	150	1			1	270	7	150	150.00	–	–	270.00
2	2	Adelaide	7.0	1	18	–			1	312	8	168	168.00	–	–	312.00
	3		16.0	1	60	–			1	408	9	228	228.00	–	–	408.00
1992–93 v Sri Lanka in Sri Lanka																
3	4	Colombo (SSC)	22.0	2	107	–			1	540	11	335	335.00	–	–	540.00
	5		3.1	1	11	1	GP Wickramasinghe	ct ME Waugh	2	559	12	346	173.00	–	–	279.50
			4.5	2	11	2	SD Anurasiri	ct ME Waugh	3	589	13	346	115.33	–	–	196.33
			5.1	3	11	3	MAWR Madurasinghe	ct GRJ Matthews	4	571	14	346	86.50	–	–	142.75
4	6	Moratuwa	11.0	3	40	–			4	637	17	386	96.50	–	–	159.25
1992–93 v West Indies in Australia																
5	7	Melbourne	23.3	6	65	1	CEL Ambrose	ct CJ McDermott	5	778	23	451	90.20	–	–	155.60
			24.0	7	65	1			5	781	24	451	90.20	–	–	156.20
	8		8.5	–	32	1	RB Richardson	bowled	6	834	24	483	80.50	–	–	139.00
			12.4	2	41	2	KLT Arthurton	stp IA Healy	7	857	26	492	70.28	–	–	122.42
			14.3	3	45	3	CL Hooper	ct MR Whitney	8	868	27	496	62.00	–	–	108.50
			18.1	5	49	4	PV Simmons	ct DC Boon	9	890	29	500	55.55	–	–	98.88
			21.4	8	51	5	D Williams	ct ME Waugh	10	911	32	502	50.20	1	–	91.10
			23.1	8	52	6	IR Bishop	ct MA Taylor	11	920	32	502	45.63	1	–	83.63
			23.2	8	52	7	CA Walsh	ct MG Hughes	12	921	32	503	41.92	1	–	76.75
6	9	Sydney	33.3	4	99	1	CL Hooper	bowled	13	1122	36	602	46.30	1	–	86.30
			41.0	6	116	1			13	1167	38	619	47.62	1	–	89.77
7	10	Adelaide	2.0	–	11	–			13	1179	38	630	48.46	1	–	90.69
	11		4.2	2	17	1	RB Richardson	ct IA Healy	14	1205	38	647	46.21	1	–	86.07
			6.0	2	18	1			14	1215	40	648	46.29	1	–	86.79
8	12	Perth	12.0	–	51	–			14	1287	40	699	49.93	1	–	91.93
1992–93 v New Zealand in New Zealand																
9	13	Christchurch	8.4	7	2	1	JG Wright	lbw	15	1339	47	701	46.73	1	–	89.26
			11.3	7	6	2	KR Rutherford	bowled	16	1356	47	705	44.06	1	–	84.75
			21.5	12	23	3	MB Owens	lbw	17	1418	52	722	42.47	1	–	83.41
			22.0	12	23	3			17	1419	52	722	42.47	1	–	83.47
	14		4.1	1	5	1	CL Cairns	ct MA Taylor	18	1444	53	727	40.38	1	–	80.22
			9.5	3	14	2	AC Parore	ct DC Boon	19	1503	55	736	38.73	1	–	79.12
			15.5	4	24	3	DN Patel	bowled	20	1509	56	746	37.30	1	–	75.45
			22.3	5	48	4	KR Rutherford	ct IA Healy	21	1554	57	770	36.66	1	–	74.00
			26.0	7	63	4			21	1575	59	785	37.38	1	–	75.00
10	15	Wellington	28.5	9	59	2	W Watson	ct MA Taylor	22	1748	68	844	36.70	1	–	76.00
			29.0	9	59	2	MB Owens	bowled	23	1749	68	844	36.70	1	–	76.04
	16		19.2	11	29	1	AH Jones	lbw	24	1865	79	873	36.37	1	–	77.70
			29.1	19	37	2	TE Blain	ct IA Healy	25	1924	87	881	35.24	1	–	76.96
			40.0	25	49	2			25	1989	93	893	35.72	1	–	79.56

Test	Inn	Venue	Ovrs	Md	Rns	Wk	Batsman	How Out	Wkt	Balls	Mdns	Runs	Avrge	5	10	Stk/Rt
1992–93 v New Zealand in New Zealand (cont'd)																
11	17	Auckland	1.2	1	0	1	KR Rutherford	stp IA Healy	26	1997	94	893	34.34	1	–	76.80
			8.3	6	5	2	DN Patel	ct IA Healy	27	2040	99	898	33.25	1	–	75.55
			9.4	7	5	3	CZ Harris	ct MA Taylor	28	2047	100	898	32.07	1	–	73.10
			15.0	12	8	4	ML Su'a	ct SR Waugh	29	2079	105	901	31.07	1	–	71.69
	18		11.2	5	17	1	MD Crowe	ct JL Langer	30	2147	110	918	30.60	1	–	71.56
			16.1	5	24	2	AH Jones	bowled	31	2176	110	925	29.83	1	–	70.19
			27.0	8	54	2			31	2241	113	955	30.81	1	–	72.29
1993 v England in England																
12	19	Manchester	0.1	–	0	1	MW Gatting	bowled	32	2242	113	955	29.84	1	–	70.06
			1.1	–	4	2	RA Smith	ct MA Taylor	33	2248	113	959	29.06	1	–	68.12
			9.0	5	14	3	GA Gooch	ct BP Julian	34	2295	118	969	28.50	1	–	67.50
			21.2	7	51	4	AR Caddick	ct IA Healy	35	2369	120	1006	28.74	1	–	67.68
			24.0	10	51	4			35	2385	123	1006	28.74	1	–	68.14
	20		5.5	4	4	1	MA Atherton	ct MA Taylor	36	2420	127	1010	28.05	1	–	67.22
			22.4	12	46	2	RA Smith	bowled	37	2521	135	1052	28.43	1	–	68.13
			37.2	18	70	3	AJ Stewart	ct IA Healy	38	2607	141	1076	28.31	1	–	68.60
			45.2	25	74	4	CC Lewis	ct MA Taylor	39	2657	158	1080	27.69	1	–	68.12
			49.0	26	86	4			39	2679	149	1092	28.00	1	–	68.69
13	21	Lord's	14.0	3	35	1	CC Lewis	lbw	40	2763	152	1127	28.17	1	–	69.07
			20.5	3	45	2	NA Foster	ct AR Border	41	2804	152	1137	27.73	1	–	68.39
			23.0	4	50	3	MA Atherton	bowled	42	2817	153	1142	27.19	1	–	67.07
			29.2	8	54	4	PM Such	ct MA Taylor	43	2855	157	1146	26.65	1	–	66.39
			35.0	12	57	4			43	2889	161	1149	26.72	1	–	67.19
	22		5.0	2	8	1	GA Gooch	ct IA Healy	44	2919	163	1157	26.29	1	—	66.34
			34.0	11	64	2	MW Gatting	lbw	45	3093	172	1213	26.95	1	–	68.73
			48.4	17	102	3	PM Such	bowled	46	3181	178	1251	26.62	1	–	69.15
			48.5	17	102	4	PCR Tufnell	bowled	47	3182	178	1251	26.62	1	–	67.70
14	23	Nottingham	3.4	2	5	1	MA Atherton	ct DC Boon	48	3204	180	1256	26.16	1	–	66.75
			14.4	6	36	2	AJ Stewart	ct ME Waugh	49	3270	186	1287	26.26	1	–	66.73
			39.5	16	74	3	N Hussain	ct DC Boon	50	3421	194	1325	26.50	1	–	68.42
			40.0	17	74	3			50	3422	195	1325	26.50	1	–	68.44
	24		7.0	2	25	1	RA Smith	ct IA Healy	51	3464	197	1350	26.47	1	–	67.92
			8.1	2	29	2	MN Lathwell	lbw	52	3471	197	1354	26.02	1	–	66.75
			39.0	18	77	3	GA Gooch	ct MA Taylor	53	3656	213	1402	26.45	1	–	68.98
			50.0	21	108	3			53	3722	216	1433	27.04	1	–	70.23
15	25	Leeds	22.1	8	43	1	MJ McCague	ct MA Taylor	54	3855	224	1476	27.33	1	–	71.38
			23.0	9	43	1			54	3860	225	1476	27.33	1	–	71.48
	26		40.0	16	63	–			54	4100	241	1539	28.50	1	–	75.93
16	27	Birmingham	6.0	2	21	1	AJ Stewart	cght & bwld	55	4136	243	1560	28.36	1	–	75.20
			21.0	7	63	1			55	4226	248	1602	29.13	1	–	76.84
	28		3.4	2	6	1	MA Atherton	ct AR Border	56	4248	250	1608	28.71	1	–	75.85
			15.0	7	33	2	RA Smith	lbw	57	4316	257	1635	28.68	1	–	75.71
			17.2	8	34	3	GA Gooch	bowled	58	4330	256	1636	28.20	1	–	74.65

Test	Inn	Venue	Ovrs	Md	Rns	Wk	Batsman	How Out	Wkt	Balls	Mdns	Runs	Avrge	5	10	Stk/Rt
1993 v England in England (cont'd)																
			20.3	9	39	4	AJ Stewart	lbw	59	4349	257	1641	27.81	1	–	73.71
			46.0	23	68	5	GP Thorpe	stp IA Healy	60	4502	271	1670	27.83	2	–	75.03
			49.0	23	82	5			60	4520	271	1684	28.07	2	–	75.33
17	29	The Oval	2.5	1	9	1	MP Maynard	bowled	61	4537	272	1693	27.75	2	–	74.37
			10.3	2	36	2	N Hussain	ct MA Taylor	62	4583	273	1720	27.74	2	–	73.91
			20.0	5	70	2			62	4640	276	1754	28.29	2	–	74.84
	30		15.3	6	33	1	GA Gooch	ct IA Healy	63	4733	282	1787	28.36	2	–	28.36
			33.0	13	66	2	SL Watkin	lbw	64	4838	289	1820	28.43	2	–	75.59
			39.2	14	78	3	PM Such	lbw	65	4876	290	1832	28.18	2	–	75.01
			40.0	15	78	3			65	4880	291	1832	28.18	2	–	75.08
1993–94 v New Zealand in Australia																
18	31	Perth	33.3	4	86	1	CL Cairns	bowled	66	5081	295	1918	29.06	2	–	76.98
			37.1	6	90	1			66	5103	297	1922	29.12	2	–	77.32
	32		13.0	6	23	–			66	5181	303	1945	29.47	2	–	78.50
19	33	Hobart	8.1	1	16	1	DN Patel	ct MA Taylor	67	5230	304	1961	29.26	2	–	78.05
			14.5	4	30	2	ML Su'a	ct MA Taylor	68	5270	307	1975	29.04	2	–	77.50
			15.5	4	31	3	SB Doull	lbw	69	5276	307	1976	28.63	2	–	76.46
			18.0	5	36	3			69	5289	308	1981	28.71	2	–	76.65
	34		10.1	5	15	1	BA Pocock	stp IA Healy	70	5350	313	1996	28.51	2	–	76.42
			12.4	5	25	2	KR Rutherford	bowled	71	5365	313	2006	28.25	2	–	75.56
			17.4	7	28	3	ML Su'a	bowled	72	5395	315	2009	27.90	2	–	74.93
			18.0	8	28	4	DK Morrison	bowled	73	5397	316	2009	27.52	2	–	73.93
			19.1	9	28	5	TE Blain	cght & bwld	74	5404	317	2009	27.14	3	–	73.02
			19.5	9	31	6	SB Doull	ct TBA May	75	5408	317	2012	26.83	3	–	72.11
20	35	Brisbane	8.3	4	16	1	AH Jones	bowled	76	5459	321	2028	26.68	3	–	71.82
			20.0	9	45	2	CL Cairns	cght & bwld	77	5528	321	2057	26.71	3	–	71.79
			23.1	12	49	3	DK Morrison	ct IA Healy	78	5547	329	2061	26.42	3	–	71.11
			28.3	12	66	4	RP De Groen	ct AR Border	79	5579	329	2078	26.30	3	–	70.62
	36		6.5	2	8	1	AH Jones	ct AR Border	80	5620	331	2086	26.07	3	–	70.25
			7.3	3	8	2	BA Young	bowled	81	5624	334	2086	25.75	3	–	69.43
			28.0	10	43	3	DN Patel	bowled	82	5747	339	2121	25.86	3	–	70.08
			33.1	10	55	4	SB Doull	ct MA Taylor	83	5778	339	2133	25.69	3	–	69.61
			35.0	11	59	4			83	5789	340	2137	25.75	3	–	69.75
1993–94 v South Africa in Australia																
21	37	Melbourne	18.0	5	42	1	WJ Cronje	ct DC Boon	84	5897	345	2179	25.94	3	–	70.20
			31.0	8	63	1			84	5975	348	2200	26.19	3	–	71.13
22	38	Sydney	12.0	4	28	1	DJ Cullinan	bowled	85	6047	352	2228	26.21	3	–	71.14
			16.0	5	37	2	JN Rhodes	lbw	86	6071	353	2237	26.01	3	–	70.59
			16.2	5	37	3	G Kirsten	stp IA Healy	87	6073	353	2237	25.71	3	–	69.80
			17.3	5	42	4	DJ Richardson	ct MA Taylor	88	6080	353	2242	25.47	3	–	69.09
			18.5	6	42	5	KC Wessels	cght & bwld	89	6088	354	2242	25.19	4	–	68.40
			19.3	7	42	6	CR Matthews	ct MA Taylor	90	6092	355	2242	24.91	4	–	67.68

Test	Inn	Venue	Ovrs	Md	Rns	Wk	Batsman	How Out	Wkt	Balls	Mdns	Runs	Avrge	5	10	Stk/Rt
1993–94 v South Africa in Australia (cont'd)																
			24.4	8	50	7	PL Symcox	bowled	91	6123	356	2250	24.72	4	–	67.28
			27.0	8	56	7			91	6137	356	2256	24.79	4	–	67.43
	39		18.5	9	31	1	KC Wessels	bowled	92	6250	365	2287	24.85	4	–	67.93
			19.3	9	31	2	DJ Cullinan	lbw	93	6254	365	2287	24.59	4	–	67.24
			33.4	14	59	3	CR Matthews	ct ME Waugh	94	6339	370	2315	24.62	4	–	67.43
			35.4	15	64	4	PS De Villiers	lbw	95	6347	371	2320	24.42	4	–	66.81
			42.0	17	72	5	AA Donald	ct IA Healy	96	6389	373	2328	24.25	5	1	66.55
23	40	Adelaide	43.3	14	84	1	PN Kirsten	ct ME Waugh	97	6650	387	2412	24.86	5	1	68.55
			44.2	15	85	1			97	6655	388	2413	24.87	5	1	68.60
	41		2.4	1	1	1	WJ Cronje	lbw	98	6405	389	2414	24.63	5	1	65.35
			4.2	2	2	2	G Kirsten	bowled	99	6681	390	2415	24.39	5	1	67.48
			29.3	14	31	3	BM McMillan	lbw	100	6832	402	2444	24.44	5	1	68.32
			30.5	15	31	4	RP Snell	cght & bwld	101	6840	403	2444	24.20	5	1	67.72
1993–94 v South Africa in South Africa																
24	42	Johannesburg	4.2	–	20	1	DJ Richardson	lbw	102	6866	403	2464	24.15	5	1	67.31
			14.0	4	42	1			102	6924	407	2486	24.37	5	1	67.88
	43		0.3	–	0	1	AC Hudson	bowled	103	6927	407	2486	24.13	5	1	67.25
			17.3	4	30	2	KC Wessels	ct AR Border	104	7029	411	2516	24.19	5	1	67.58
			34.2	9	57	3	DJ Richardson	ct AR Border	105	7130	416	2543	24.21	5	1	67.90
			37.3	11	59	4	BM McMillan	bowled	106	7149	418	2545	24.00	5	1	67.44
			44.5	14	86	4			106	7193	421	2572	24.26	5	1	67.86
25	44	Cape Town	26.3	8	42	1	PN Kirsten	lbw	107	7352	429	2614	24.42	5	1	68.71
			40.5	14	69	2	BM McMillan	bowled	108	7438	435	2641	24.45	5	1	68.87
			42.1	15	73	3	PS De Villiers	ct MA Taylor	109	7446	436	2645	24.26	5	1	68.31
			47.0	18	78	3			109	7475	439	2650	24.31	5	1	68.58
	45		0.4	–	0	1	G Kirsten	lbw	110	7479	439	2650	24.10	5	1	67.99
			14.2	8	18	2	PN Kirsten	ct MA Taylor	111	7561	447	2668	24.03	5	1	68.11
			14.5	8	18	3	PS De Villiers	lbw	112	7564	447	2668	23.82	5	1	67.53
			30.0	13	38	3			112	7655	452	2688	24.00	5	1	68.35
26	46	Durban	20.1	8	32	1	WJ Cronje	ct SR Waugh	113	7776	460	2720	24.07	5	1	68.81
			36.0	13	64	2	JN Rhodes	lbw	114	7871	465	2752	24.14	5	1	69.04
			51.1	18	89	3	DJ Richardson	ct PR Reiffel	115	7962	470	2777	24.14	5	1	69.23
			54.5	19	92	4	CR Matthews	lbw	116	7984	471	2780	23.96	5	1	68.82
			55.0	20	92	4			116	7985	472	2780	23.96	5	1	68.84
1994–95 v Pakistan in Pakistan																
27	47	Karachi	2.5	–	14	1	Aamir Sohail	ct MG Bevan	117	8002	472	2794	23.88	5	1	68.39
			16.0	5	46	2	Inzamam-ul-Haq	ct MA Taylor	118	8098	477	2840	24.06	5	1	68.62
			17.0	6	46	3	Rashid Latif	ct MA Taylor	119	8087	478	2840	23.86	5	1	67.95
			27.0	10	61	3			119	8147	482	2841	23.87	5	1	68.46
	48					1	Zahid Fazal	ct DC Boon	120							
						2	Akram Raja	lbw	121							
						3	Wasim Akram	cght & bwld	122							
						4	Waqar Younis	ct IA Healy	123							
			36.1	12	89	5			123	8364	494	2930	23.63	6	1	67.45

Test	Inn	Venue	Ovrs	Md	Rns	Wk	Batsman	How Out	Wkt	Balls	Mdns	Runs	Avrge	5	10	Stk/Rt
1994–95 v Pakistan in Pakistan (cont'd)																
28	49	Rawalpindi	15.0	5	44	1	Inzamam-ul-Haq	lbw	125							
			21.4	8	58	1			125	8494	502	2988	23.90	6	1	67.95
			25.0	6	56	–			125	8644	508	3044	24.35	6	1	69.15
29	50	Lahore	2.3	1	1	–	Saeed Anwar	bowled	126	8653	509	3045	24.16	6	1	68.67
			21.2	5	65	2	Basit Ali	ct ME Waugh	127	8772	513	3109	24.48	6	1	69.07
			28.3	8	102	3	Ijaz Ahmed	ct DC Boon	128	8812	516	3146	24.57	6	1	68.84
			29.0	9	102	4	Akram Raza	bowled	129	8815	517	3146	24.38	6	1	68.33
			40.0	12	126	5	Aaqib Javed	ct ME Waugh	130	8884	520	3170	24.38	7	1	68.33
			41.5	12	136	6	Mohsin Kamal	lbw	131	8895	520	3180	24.27	7	1	67.90
	51		23.1	1	88	1	Aamir Sohail	ct PA Emery	132	9034	521	3268	24.75	7	1	68.43
			27.0	2	95	2	Akram Raza	lbw	133	9057	522	3275	24.62	7	1	68.09
			27.5	2	97	3	Aaqib Javed	bowled	134	9062	522	3277	24.45	7	1	67.62
			30.0	2	104	3			134	9075	522	3284	24.51	7	1	67.72
1994–95 v England in Australia																
30	52	Brisbane	7.3	2	7	1	GP Thorpe	cght & bwld	135	9120	524	3291	24.37	7	1	67.55
			18.2	6	34	2	PAJ DeFreitas	ct IA Healy	136	9185	528	3318	24.39	7	1	67.53
			21.2	7	39	3	PCR Tufnell	ct MA Taylor	137	9203	529	3323	24.26	7	1	67.18
	53		1.5	–	9	1	AJ Stewart	bowled	138	9214	529	3332	24.14	7	1	66.76
			2.3	–	10	2	MA Atherton	lbw	139	9218	529	3333	23.97	7	1	66.31
			30.2	12	49	3	GP Thorpe	bowled	140	9385	541	3372	24.08	7	1	67.03
			31.1	13	49	4	GA Hick	ct IA Healy	141	9390	542	3372	23.91	7	1	66.59
			45.5	19	69	5	GA Gooch	ct IA Healy	142	9478	548	3392	23.88	8	1	66.74
			46.1	20	69	6	PAJ DeFreitas	bowled	143	9480	549	3392	23.72	8	1	66.29
			46.2	20	69	7	MJ McCague	lbw	144	9481	549	3392	23.55	8	2	65.84
			50.2	22	71	8	D Gough	ct ME Waugh	145	9505	551	3394	23.41	8	2	65.55
31	54	Melbourne	10.3	3	21	1	MA Atherton	lbw	146	9568	554	3415	23.39	8	2	65.53
			13.1	5	21	2	GP Thorpe	ct ME Waugh	147	9584	559	3415	23.23	8	2	65.19
			17.0	6	29	3	MW Gatting	ct SR Waugh	148	9607	557	3423	23.12	8	2	64.91
			21.3	8	35	4	SJ Rhodes	ct ME Waugh	149	9634	559	3429	23.01	8	2	64.65
			24.1	8	51	5	AJ Stewart	cght & bwld	150	9650	559	3445	22.96	9	2	64.33
			27.0	8	64	6	PAJ DeFreitas	stp IA Healy	151	9667	559	3458	22.90	9	2	64.01
			27.4	8	64	6			151	9671	559	3458	22.90	9	2	64.05
	55		12.4	6	16	1	PAJ DeFreitas	lbw	152	9747	565	3474	22.85	9	2	64.12
			12.5	6	16	2	D Gough	ct IA Healy	153	9748	565	3474	22.70	9	2	63.71
			13.0	6	16	3	DE Malcolm	ct DC Boon	154	9749	565	3474	22.56	9	2	63.31
32	56	Sydney	33.3	10	83	1	DE Malcolm	bowled	155	9950	575	3557	22.94	9	2	64.19
			36.0	10	88	1			155	9965	575	3562	22.98	9	2	64.29
	57		16.0	2	48	–			155	10061	577	3610	23.29	9	2	64.91
33	58	Adelaide	14.0	3	48	1	GP Thorpe	ct MA Taylor	156	10145	580	3658	23.44	9	2	65.03
			21.3	5	59	2	JP Crawley	bowled	157	10190	582	3669	23.36	9	2	64.90
			31.0	9	72	2			157	10247	586	3682	23.45	9	2	65.27
	59		20.0	7	44	1	SJ Rhodes	ct DW Fleming	158	10367	593	3726	23.58	9	2	65.61
			30.5	9	82	2	PCR Tufnell	lbw	159	10432	595	3764	23.67	9	2	65.61

Test	Inn	Venue	Ovrs	Md	Rns	Wk	Batsman	How Out	Wkt	Balls	Mdns	Runs	Avrge	5	10	Stk/Rt
1994–95 v England in Australia (cont'd)																
34	60	Perth	15.3	4	45	1	GP Thorpe	stp IA Healy	160	10525	599	3809	23.80	9	2	65.78
			19.1	7	47	2	MR Ramprakash	bowled	161	10547	602	3811	23.67	9	2	65.50
			23.0	8	58	2			161	10570	603	3822	23.74	9	2	65.65
	61		7.0	3	11	–			161	10612	606	3833	23.81	9	2	65.91
1994–95 v West Indies in West Indies																
35	62	Bridgetown	9.2	2	48	1	WKM Benjamin	ct MA Taylor	162	10668	608	3881	23.95	9	2	65.85
			11.3	2	56	2	CA Walsh	ct SR Waugh	163	10681	608	3889	23.85	9	2	65.52
			12.0	2	57	2			163	10684	608	3890	23.87	9	2	65.55
	63		5.1	1	7	1	SL Campbell	ct SR Waugh	164	10715	609	3897	23.76	9	2	65.33
			19.3	2	42	2	JR Murray	ct SR Waugh	165	10801	610	3932	23.83	9	2	65.46
			26.3	5	64	3	KCG Benjamin	bowled	166	10843	613	3954	23.82	9	2	65.32
36	64	St John's	7.1	3	10	1	SC Williams	ct DC Boon	167	10886	616	3964	23.73	9	2	65.18
			18.4	8	54	2	JC Adams	lbw	168	10955	621	4008	23.85	9	2	65.20
			26.0	8	82	3	KLT Arthurton	ct MA Taylor	169	10999	621	4036	23.88	9	2	65.08
			28.0	9	83	3			169	11011	622	4037	23.89	9	2	65.15
	65		7.0	–	18	–			169	11053	622	4055	23.99	9	2	65.40
37	66	Port-of-Spain	7.1	4	12	1	WKM Benjamin	ct MJ Slater	170	11096	626	4067	23.92	9	2	65.27
			12.0	5	16	1			170	11125	627	4071	23.95	9	2	65.44
	67		3.5	–	26	–			170	11148	627	4097	24.10	9	2	65.58
38	68	Kingston	5.2	–	26	1	BC Lara	ct IA Healy	171	11180	627	4123	24.11	9	2	65.38
			22.4	5	70	2	CO Browne	ct DC Boon	172	11284	632	4167	24.22	9	2	65.60
			25.0	6	72	2			172	11298	633	4169	24.24	9	2	65.69
	69		15.3	7	40	1	KLT Arthurton	lbw	173	11391	640	4209	24.32	9	2	65.84
			16.3	7	44	2	CEL Ambrose	stp IA Healy	174	11397	640	4213	24.21	9	2	17.80
			22.1	7	63	3	CA Walsh	ct GS Blewett	175	11431	640	4232	24.18	9	2	65.32
			23.4	8	70	4	KCG Benjamin	ct MA Taylor	176	11440	641	4239	24.09	9	2	65.00
1995–96 v Pakistan in Australia																
39	70	Brisbane	3.2	1	7	1	Rameez Raja	ct MA Taylor	177	11460	642	4246	23.98	9	2	64.74
			7.0	3	13	2	Aamir Sohail	stp IA Healy	178	11482	644	4252	23.88	9	2	64.50
			9.2	5	13	3	Inzamam-ul-Haq	ct SR Waugh	179	11496	646	4252	23.75	9	2	64.22
			11.5	7	17	4	Moin Khan	ct CJ McDermott	180	11511	648	4256	23.64	9	2	63.95
			12.3	7	17	5	Basit Ali	ct MA Taylor	181	11515	648	4256	23.51	10	2	63.61
			14.4	8	21	6	Wasim Akram	ct DC Boon	182	11528	649	4260	23.40	10	2	63.34
			16.1	9	23	7	Mohammad Akram	ct GS Blewett	183	11537	650	4262	23.29	10	2	63.04
	71		22.1	6	53	1	Wasim Akram	ct MJ Slater	184	11670	656	4315	23.45	10	2	63.42
			22.5	6	53	2	Salim Malik	ct CJ McDermott	185	11674	656	4315	23.32	10	2	63.10
			27.1	10	54	3	Waqar Younis	lbw	186	11700	660	4316	23.20	10	2	62.90
			27.5	10	54	4	Mohammad Akram	lbw	187	11704	660	4316	23.08	10	3	62.59
40	72	Hobart	–	–	–	–			187	11704	660	4316	23.08	10	3	62.59
	73		–	–	–	–			187	11704	660	4316	23.08	10	3	62.59
41	74	Sydney	5.1	3	6	1	Rameez Raja	ct MJ Slater	188	11735	663	4322	22.98	10	3	62.42
			14.0	8	21	2	Inzamam-ul-Haq	ct IA Healy	189	11788	668	4337	22.94	10	3	62.37
			32.2	18	55	3	Ijaz Ahmed	ct GD McGrath	190	11898	678	4371	23.00	10	3	62.62

Test	Inn	Venue	Ovrs	Md	Rns	Wk	Batsman	How Out	Wkt	Balls	Mdns	Runs	Avrge	5	10	Stk/Rt
1995–96 v Pakistan in Australia (cont'd)																
			33.3	19	55	4	Mushtaq Ahmed	ct CJ McDermott	191	11905	659	4371	22.88	10	3	62.32
			34.0	20	55	4			191	11908	680	4371	22.88	10	3	62.35
	75		5.5	–	10	1	Ijaz Ahmed	lbw	192	11943	680	4381	22.81	10	3	62.20
			10.3	2	24	2	Rameez Raja	ct ME Waugh	193	11971	682	4395	22.77	10	3	62.02
			17.0	6	28	3	Basit Ali	bowled	194	12010	686	4399	22.67	10	3	61.90
			32.4	10	60	4	Rashid Latif	lbw	195	12104	690	4431	22.72	10	3	62.07
			37.0	13	66	4			195	12130	693	4437	22.75	10	3	62.21
1995–96 v Sri Lanka in Australia																
42	76	Perth	2.0	1	4	1	PA De Silva	cght & bwld	196	12142	694	4441	22.65	10	3	61.94
			22.5	5	61	2	RS Kaluwitharana	ct MA Taylor	197	12267	698	4498	22.83	10	3	62.26
			24.1	6	66	3	WPUJC Vaas	ct IA Healy	198	12275	699	4503	22.74	10	3	61.99
			27.0	7	75	3			198	12292	700	4512	22.79	10	3	62.08
	77		7.0	3	13	1	PA De Silva	ct RT Ponting	199	12334	703	4525	22.72	10	3	61.97
			28.0	6	88	2	HP Tillakaratne	ct RT Ponting	200	12460	706	4600	23.00	10	3	62.30
			29.4	6	96	3	WPUCJ Vaas	ct IA Healy	201	12470	706	4608	22.93	10	3	62.04
43	78	Melbourne	13.3	5	35	1	HP Tillakaratne	ct MA Taylor	202	12551	711	4643	22.98	10	3	62.13
			18.0	5	49	1			202	12578	711	4657	23.05	10	3	62.27
	79		7.5	2	13	1	UC Hathurusinghe	lbw	203	12625	713	4670	23.00	10	3	62.19
			16.1	3	36	2	RS Kaluwitharana	stp IA Healy	204	12675	714	4693	23.00	10	3	62.13
			36.1	9	71	3	GP Wickramasinghe	stp IA Healy	205	12795	720	4728	23.06	10	3	62.41
			36.2	9	71	4	M Muralidaran	ct MA Taylor	206	12796	720	4728	22.95	10	3	62.11
			37.0	10	71	4			206	12800	721	4728	22.95	10	3	62.14
44	80	Adelaide	26.0	4	74	–			206	12956	725	4802	23.31	10	3	62.89
	81		25.4	11	60	1	GP Wickramasinghe	bowled	207	13110	736	4862	23.48	10	3	63.33
			27.0	11	68	1			207	13118	736	4870	23.53	10	3	63.37
1996–97 v West Indies in Australia																
45	82	Brisbane	26.0	3	80	1	IR Bishop	lbw	208	13274	739	4950	23.79	10	3	63.81
			27.0	3	88	2	KCG Benjamin	lbw	209	13280	739	4958	23.72	10	3	63.54
	83		4.0	1	19	1	RG Samuels	ct MA Taylor	210	13304	740	4977	23.70	10	3	63.35
			30.2	11	67	2	JC Adams	lbw	211	13462	750	5025	23.81	10	3	63.80
			41.0	16	92	2			211	13526	755	5050	23.93	10	3	64.10
46	84	Sydney	20.3	9	28	1	CL Hooper	lbw	212	13649	764	5078	23.95	10	3	64.38
			26.3	12	40	2	S Chanderpaul	cght & bwld	213	13685	767	5090	23.89	10	3	64.24
			35.2	13	65	3	IR Bishop	ct MTG Elliott	214	13738	768	5115	23.90	10	3	64.20
	85		3.4	2	5	1	RG Samuels	bowled	215	13760	770	5120	23.81	10	3	64.00
			13.5	2	65	2	S Chanderpaul	bowled	216	13821	770	5180	23.98	10	3	63.98
			25.0	5	77	3	KCG Benjamin	ct MA Taylor	217	13888	773	5192	23.92	10	3	64.00
			27.4	5	95	4	CA Walsh	ct GD McGrath	218	13904	773	5210	23.90	10	3	63.78
47	86	Melbourne	5.3	2	7	1	RG Samuels	ct MA Taylor	219	13937	775	5217	23.82	10	3	63.63
			22.2	3	50	2	CEL Ambrose	bowled	220	14038	776	5260	23.90	10	3	63.80
			28.1	3	72	3	CA Walsh	ct ME Waugh	221	14073	776	5282	23.90	10	3	63.68
	87		3.0	–	17	–			221	14091	776	5299	23.98	10	3	63.76

Test	Inn	Venue	Ovrs	Md	Rns	Wk	Batsman	How Out	Wkt	Balls	Mdns	Runs	Avrge	5	10	Stk/Rt
1996–97 v West Indies in Australia (cont'd)																
48	88	Adelaide	0.4	–	1	1	BC Lara	ct GS Blewett	222	14095	776	5300	23.87	10	3	63.49
			2.0	–	7	2	S Chanderpaul	ct MA Taylor	223	14107	776	5206	23.34	10	3	63.26
			12.0	3	30	3	JC Adams	cght & bwld	224	14163	779	5329	23.79	10	3	63.22
			16.0	4	42	3			224	14187	780	5341	23.84	10	3	63.33
	89		10.0	1	40	1	CL Hooper	lbw	225	14247	781	5381	23.91	10	3	63.32
			12.3	2	46	2	IR Bishop	ct MG Bevan	226	14262	782	5387	23.83	10	3	63.10
			16.3	4	52	3	BC Lara	ct IA Healy	227	14286	784	5393	23.75	10	3	62.93
			20.0	4	68	3			227	14307	784	5409	23.83	10	3	63.03
49	90	Perth	11.3	4	43	1	BC Lara	ct IA Healy	228	14376	788	5452	23.91	10	3	63.05
			15.3	6	48	2	RG Samuels	ct ME Waugh	229	14400	790	5457	23.82	10	3	62.88
			19.0	8	55	2			229	14421	792	5464	23.86	10	3	62.97
	91		–	–	–	–			229	14421	792	5464	23.86	10	3	62.97
1996–97 v South Africa in South Africa																
50	92	Johannesburg	20.4	7	46	1	WJ Cronje	ct ME Waugh	230	14545	799	5510	23.95	10	3	63.23
			27.4	9	68	2	PR Adams	lbw	231	14587	801	5532	23.95	10	3	63.15
	93		3.4	2	2	1	G Kirsten	bowled	232	14609	803	5534	23.85	10	3	62.96
			7.4	4	7	2	DJ Cullinan	ct IA Healy	233	14633	805	5539	23.77	10	3	62.80
			22.3	11	35	3	JN Rhodes	lbw	234	14722	811	5567	23.79	10	3	62.91
			28.0	15	43	4	JH Kallis	bowled	235	14755	816	5575	23.72	10	3	62.79
51	94	Pt Elizabeth	18.3	5	49	1	DJ Richardson	ct GD McGrath	236	14866	821	5624	23.83	10	3	62.99
			22.4	5	61	2	BM McMillan	ct SR Waugh	237	14891	821	5636	23.78	10	3	62.83
			23.4	5	62	3	AA Donald	cght & bwld	238	14897	821	5637	23.68	10	3	62.59
	95		13.4	5	18	1	SM Pollock	lbw	239	14979	826	5655	23.66	10	3	62.67
			17.4	7	20	2	PR Adams	ct MA Taylor	240	15003	828	5657	23.57	10	3	62.51
52	96	Centurion	36.0	11	89	–			240	15219	839	5746	23.94	10	3	63.41
	97		–	–	–	–			240	15219	839	5746	23.94	10	3	63.41
1997 v England in England																
53	98	Birmingham	28.0	6	102	1	N Hussain	ct IA Healy	241	15387	845	5848	24.26	10	3	63.84
			35.0	8	110	1			241	15429	847	5856	24.30	10	3	64.02
	99		7.3	–	27	–			241	15474	847	5883	24.41	10	3	64.21
54	100	Lord's	2.0	–	9	–			241	15486	847	5892	24.45	10	3	64.26
	101		11.5	3	22	1	N Hussain	cght & bwld	242	15557	850	5914	24.43	10	3	64.28
			12.2	3	24	2	MA Butcher	bowled	243	15560	850	5916	24.34	10	3	64.03
			19.0	4	47	2			243	15600	851	5939	24.44	10	3	64.20
55	102	Manchester	6.1	3	11	1	AJ Stewart	ct MA Taylor	244	15637	854	5950	24.38	10	3	64.08
			10.2	3	27	2	GP Thorpe	ct MA Taylor	245	15662	854	5966	24.35	10	3	63.92
			12.3	5	27	3	N Hussain	ct IA Healy	246	15675	856	5966	24.25	10	3	63.71
			14.3	6	28	4	JP Crawley	ct IA Healy	247	15689	857	5967	24.15	10	3	63.51
			18.4	8	30	5	D Gough	lbw	248	15712	859	5969	24.06	11	3	63.35
			28.4	12	48	6	AR Caddick	ct ME Waugh	249	15772	863	5987	24.04	11	3	63.34
			30.0	14	48	6			249	15780	865	5987	24.04	11	3	63.37

Test	Inn	Venue	Ovrs	Md	Rns	Wk	Batsman	How Out	Wkt	Balls	Mdns	Runs	Avrge	5	10	Stk/Rt
1997 v England in England (cont'd)																
	103		2.3	1	5	1	AJ Stewart	bowled	250	15789	866	5992	23.96	11	3	63.15
			10.4	4	15	2	GP Thorpe	ct IA Healy	251	15844	869	6002	23.91	11	3	63.12
			30.4	8	63	3	AR Caddick	ct JN Gillespie	252	15964	873	6050	24.01	11	3	63.35
56	104	Leeds	1.0	–	2	–			252	15970	873	6052	24.02	11	3	63.37
	105		15.0	4	31	1	N Hussain	ct JN Gillespie	253	16060	877	6083	24.04	11	3	63.47
			21.0	6	53	1			253	16096	879	6105	24.13	11	3	63.62
57	106	Nottingham	6.3	1	22	1	MA Atherton	ct IA Healy	254	16135	880	6127	24.12	11	3	63.52
			9.2	2	31	2	AJ Stewart	ct IA Healy	255	16152	881	6136	24.06	11	3	63.34
			13.0	4	36	3	N Hussain	bowled	256	16174	883	6141	23.98	11	3	63.17
			29.2	8	69	4	GP Thorpe	ct GS Blewett	257	16272	887	6174	63.31	11	3	63.31
			32.0	8	86	4			257	16288	887	6191	24.09	11	3	63.38
	107		9.0	2	21	1	BC Hollioake	lbw	258	16342	889	6212	24.07	11	3	63.34
			10.0	2	27	2	RDB Croft	ct GD McGrath	259	16348	889	6218	24.00	11	3	63.11
			11.4	3	27	3	AR Caddick	lbw	260	16258	890	6218	23.91	11	3	62.50
			16.0	4	43	3			260	16384	891	6234	23.98	11	3	63.02
58	108	The Oval	10.4	6	16	1	AJ Hollioake	bowled	261	16448	897	6250	23.94	11	3	63.01
			17.0	8	32	2	PCR Tufnell	ct GS Blewett	262	16486	899	6266	23.92	11	3	62.92
	109		7.3	5	29	1	N Hussain	ct MTG Elliott	263	16531	904	6295	23.93	11	3	62.85
			25.1	9	54	2	MR Ramprakash	stp IA Healy	264	16637	908	6320	23.93	11	3	63.01
			26.0	9	57	2			264	16642	908	6323	23.95	11	3	63.04
1997–98 v New Zealand in Australia																
59	110	Brisbane	14.5	6	28	1	BA Pocock	ct MA Taylor	265	16731	914	6351	23.96	11	3	63.13
			29.2	9	77	2	CD McMillan	lbw	266	16818	917	6400	24.06	11	3	63.22
			35.1	10	91	3	AC Parore	ct MA Taylor	267	16853	918	6414	24.02	11	3	63.11
			41.3	12	103	4	CZ Harris	bowled	268	16891	920	6517	24.31	11	3	63.02
			42.0	13	106	4			268	16894	921	6429	23.99	11	3	63.04
	111		20.0	5	42	1	CZ Harris	bowled	269	17014	926	6471	24.05	11	3	63.24
			20.3	5	42	2	DL Vettori	ct MA Taylor	270	17017	926	6471	23.96	11	3	63.02
			25.0	6	54	3	GI Allott	lbw	271	17044	927	6483	23.92	11	3	62.89
60	112	Perth	2.0	–	4	1	SP Fleming	ct GS Blewett	272	17056	927	6487	23.84	11	3	62.70
			18.4	3	64	2	CL Cairns	ct ME Waugh	273	17156	930	6547	23.98	11	3	62.84
			19.4	3	72	3	SB Doull	ct MA Taylor	274	17162	930	6555	23.92	11	3	62.63
			22.4	3	83	4	GI Allott	bowled	275	17180	930	6566	23.88	11	3	62.47
	113		7.5	2	12	1	DL Vettori	ct MA Taylor	276	17227	932	6578	23.83	11	3	62.41
			11.0	2	26	2	SP Fleming	ct GS Blewett	277	17246	932	6592	23.79	11	3	62.25
			26.0	4	64	2			277	17336	934	6630	23.94	11	3	62.58
61	114	Hobart	21.4	2	69	1	RG Twose	lbw	278	17466	936	6699	24.09	11	3	62.82
			27.0	4	81	1			278	17498	938	6711	24.14	11	3	62.94
	115		4.5	–	24	1	CL Cairns	stp IA Healy	279	17527	938	6735	24.13	11	3	62.82
			6.0	1	24	2	SP Fleming	stp IA Healy	280	17534	939	6735	24.05	11	3	62.62
			10.5	2	49	3	BA Young	ct RT Ponting	281	17563	940	6760	24.05	11	3	62.50
			13.1	2	54	4	CD McMillan	ct MA Taylor	282	17577	940	6765	23.98	11	3	62.32
			22.1	2	86	5	AC Parore	ct MTG Elliott	283	17631	940	6797	24.01	12	3	62.30
			28.0	6	88	5			283	17666	944	6799	24.02	12	3	62.42

Test	Inn	Venue	Ovrs	Md	Rns	Wk	Batsman	How Out	Wkt	Balls	Mdns	Runs	Avrge	5	10	Stk/Rt
1997–98 v South Africa in Australia																
62	116	Melbourne	14.5	5	25	1	WJ Cronje	ct GS Blewett	284	17755	949	6824	24.02	12	3	62.51
			34.4	12	53	2	SM Pollock	lbw	285	17874	956	6852	24.04	12	3	62.71
			41.4	14	64	3	L Klusener	lbw	286	17916	958	6863	24.00	12	3	62.64
			42.0	15	64	3			286	17918	959	6863	24.00	12	3	62.65
	117		12.1	1	32	1	AM Bacher	ct MA Taylor	287	17991	960	6895	24.02	12	3	62.68
			13.3	2	32	2	DJ Cullinan	bowled	288	17999	961	6895	23.94	12	3	62.49
			36.0	7	83	3	BM McMillan	ct MA Taylor	289	18134	966	6946	24.03	12	3	62.74
			44.0	11	97	3			289	18182	970	6960	24.08	12	3	62.91
63	118	Sydney	24.0	6	50	1	SM Pollock	ct MA Taylor	290	18326	976	7010	24.17	12	3	63.19
			25.4	6	54	2	DJ Richardson	bowled	291	18327	976	7014	24.10	12	3	62.97
			30.1	7	69	3	WJ Cronje	ct MA Taylor	292	18366	977	7029	24.07	12	3	62.89
			31.4	8	75	4	PL Symcox	ct IA Healy	293	18372	978	7035	24.01	12	3	62.70
			32.1	8	75	5	PR Adams	ct SR Waugh	294	18375	978	7035	23.93	13	3	62.50
	119		2.0	–	2	1	WJ Cronje	ct RT Ponting	295	18387	978	7037	23.85	13	3	62.32
			6.2	3	3	2	HH Gibbs	ct GS Blewett	296	18413	981	7038	23.77	13	3	62.20
			8.0	4	6	3	BM McMillan	bowled	297	18423	982	7041	23.70	13	3	62.03
			9.3	4	13	4	SM Pollock	ct MA Taylor	298	18432	982	7048	23.65	13	3	61.85
			10.0	4	13	5	DJ Richardson	cght & bwld	299	18435	982	7048	23.57	14	4	61.65
			16.4	5	31	6	JH Kallis	bowled	300	18475	983	7066	23.55	14	4	61.58
			21.0	9	34	6			300	18501	987	7069	23.56	14	4	61.67
64	120	Adelaide	16.0	3	44	1	WJ Cronje	bowled	301	18597	990	7113	23.63	14	4	61.78
			22.0	4	61	2	DJ Richardson	ct MA Taylor	302	18633	991	7130	23.60	14	4	61.69
			33.0	6	95	2			302	18699	993	7164	23.72	14	4	61.92
	121		6.3	1	17	1	AM Bacher	ct SCG MacGill	303	18738	994	7181	23.69	14	4	61.84
			15.0	2	52	1			303	18789	995	7216	23.82	14	4	62.01
1997–98 v India in India																
65	122	Chennai	14.5	5	45	1	SR Tendulkar	ct MA Taylor	304	18878	1000	7261	23.88	14	4	62.09
			19.4	7	56	2	M Azharuddin	ct PR Reiffel	305	18907	1002	7272	23.84	14	4	61.99
			31.2	10	80	3	J Srinath	ct MA Taylor	306	18977	1005	7296	23.84	14	4	62.01
			34.4	11	85	4	RS Dravid	ct GR Robertson	307	18997	1006	7301	23.78	14	4	61.87
			35.0	11	85	4			307	18999	1006	7301	23.78	14	4	61.89
	123		20.3	5	84	1	RS Dravid	ct IA Healy	308	19122	1011	7385	23.97	14	4	62.08
			30.7	7	122	1			308	19179	1013	7423	24.10	14	4	62.27
66	124	Calcutta	42.0	4	147	–			308	19431	1017	7570	24.58	14	4	63.09
67	125	Bangalore	11.2	5	14	1	NS Sidhu	bowled	309	19499	1022	7584	24.54	14	4	63.10
			12.5	5	17	2	RS Dravid	bowled	310	19508	1022	7587	24.47	14	4	62.92
			29.5	8	90	3	NR Mongia	ct RT Ponting	311	19610	1025	7660	24.63	14	4	63.05
			35.0	9	106	3			311	19641	1026	7676	24.68	14	4	63.15
	126		4.0	–	22	1	VVS Laxman	ct RT Ponting	312	19665	1026	7698	24.67	14	4	63.02
			7.2	1	24	2	NS Sidhu	ct DS Lehmann	313	19685	1027	7700	24.60	14	4	62.89
			25.6	6	80	2			313	19791	1032	7756	24.78	14	4	63.23

Test	Inn	Venue	Ovrs	Md	Rns	Wk	Batsman	How Out	Wkt	Balls	Mdns	Runs	Avrge	5	10	Stk/Rt
1998–99 v England in Australia																
68	127	Sydney	0.4	–	4	1	MA Butcher	lbw	314	19795	1032	7760	24.71	14	4	63.04
			20.0	4	67	1			314	19911	1036	7823	24.91	14	4	63.41
	128		1.0	–	2	1	MA Butcher	st IA Healy	315	19917	1036	7825	24.84	14	4	63.22
			19.0	3	43	1			315	20025	1039	7866	24.97	14	4	63.57

Batting

Opponents	Debut	M	Inn	NO	Runs	HS	0s	50	100	Avrge	Ct
India	1991–92	5	9	1	133	35	1	–	–	16.63	1
Sri Lanka	1992–93	5	4	–	99	35	—	–	–	24.75	6
New Zealand	1992–93	9	9	3	205	74 *	–	1	–	34.17	5
England	1993	18	27	4	371	53	6	1	–	16.13	13
South Africa	1993–94	12	19	2	126	18	3	–	–	7.41	10
Pakistan	1994–95	6	8	1	108	33	1	–	–	15.43	2
West Indies	1994–95	13	19	-	198	30	4	—	–	10.42	11
Total		**68**	**95**	**11**	**1240**	**74 ***	**15**	**2**	**–**	**14.76**	**48**

Highest score

74* Australia v New Zealand, Brisbane, 1993–94

International Limited-Overs

Debut: 1992–93 Australia v New Zealand, Wellington

Bowling

Season	Series	Cty	M	Balls	Mdns	Runs	Wkts	Avrge	5	Best	Stk/Rt	RPO
1992–93	New Zealand v Australia	NZ	1	60	–	40	2	20.00	–	2/40	30.00	4.00
1993–94	World Series	AUS	10	540	5	301	22	13.68	–	4/19	24.55	3.34
1993–94	Sth Africa v Australia	SAF	8	414	3	285	11	25.91	–	4/36	37.64	4.13
1993–94	Austral-Asia Cup	UAE	3	174	1	103	9	11.44	–	4/34	19.33	3.55
1994–95	Singer World Series	SL	3	168	1	109	7	15.57	–	3/29	24.00	3.89
1994–95	Wills Triangular Series	PAK	6	350	4	238	6	39.67	–	4/40	58.33	4.08
1994–95	World Series	AUS	4	234	1	133	6	22.17	–	2/27	39.00	3.41
1994–95	New Zealand Centenary	NZ	4	240	6	140	5	28.00	–	2/18	48.00	3.50
1994–95	West Indies v Australia	WI	4	235	4	204	4	51.00	–	2/33	58.75	5.21
1995–96	World Series	AUS	9	481	7	317	15	21.13	–	3/20	32.07	3.95
1995–96	World Cup	IPS	7	411	3	263	12	21.92	–	4/34	34.25	3.84
1996–97	CUB Series	AUS	8	454	6	325	19	17.11	1	5/33	23.89	4.30
1996–97	Sth Africa v Australia	SAF	6	325	2	272	10	27.20	–	2/36	32.50	5.02
1997	England v Australia	ENG	3	174	–	129	1	129.00	–	1/39	174.00	4.45
1997–98	CUB Series	AUS	10	561	3	405	12	33.75	–	3/48	46.75	4.33
1997–98	Triangular Cup	IND	5	294	–	219	5	43.80	–	2/45	58.80	4.47
1997–98	Coca-Cola Cup	SHJ	5	282	2	221	4	55.25	–	2/28	70.50	4.70
Total			**96**	**5397**	**48**	**3704**	**150**	**24.69**	**1**	**5/33**	**35.98**	**4.12**

Record against each country

Opponents	Debut	M	Balls	Mdns	Runs	Wkts	Avrge	5	Best	Stk/Rt	RPO
New Zealand	1992–93	15	866	10	512	34	15.06	–	4/19	25.47	3.55
South Africa	1992–93	30	1630	10	1170	42	27.86	–	4/36	38.81	4.31
Sri Lanka	1993–94	9	498	4	338	15	22.53	–	3/20	33.20	4.07
India	1993–94	10	570	2	439	8	54.88	–	2/40	71.25	4.62
Pakistan	1994–95	8	457	9	298	14	21.29	–	4/37	32.64	3.91
Zimbabwe	1994–95	5	291	2	183	10	18.30	–	4/34	29.10	3.77
England	1994–95	5	294	–	212	4	53.00	–	2/37	73.50	4.33
West Indies	1994–95	13	731	11	527	22	23.95	1	5/33	33.23	4.33
Kenya	1995–96	1	60	–	25	1	25.00	–	1/25	60.00	2.50

Innings by innings comparison

	Balls	Mdns	Runs	Wkts	Avrge	5	Best	Stk/Rt	RPO
First innings	2984	22	2053	78	26.32	–	4/19	38.26	4.13
Second innings	2413	26	1651	72	22.93	1	5/33	33.51	4.11

Venues

	Debut	M	Balls	Mdns	Runs	Wkts	Avrge	5	Best	Stk/Rt	RPO
IN NEW ZEALAND											
Wellington	1992–93	2	120	3	58	4	14.50	–	2/18	30.00	2.90
Auckland	1994–95	2	120	3	61	3	20.33	–	2/21	40.00	3.05
Dunedin	1994–95	1	60	–	61	–	–	–	–	–	6.10
IN AUSTRALIA											
Melbourne	1993–94	15	884	11	553	26	21.27	–	4/19	34.00	3.75
Adelaide	1993–94	4	221	3	147	11	13.36	–	4/25	20.09	3.99
Sydney	1993–94	14	713	6	471	27	17.44	1	5/33	26.41	3.96
Perth	1993–94	4	240	2	154	7	22.00	–	2/27	34.29	3.85
Hobart	1994–95	2	98	–	58	3	19.33	–	2/35	32.67	3.55
Brisbane	1994–95	2	114	–	98	–	–	–	–	–	5.16
IN SOUTH AFRICA											
Johannesburg	1993–94	2	120	–	101	1	101.00	–	1/45	120.00	5.05
Verwoerdburg	1993–94	1	48	1	41	1	41.00	–	1/41	48.00	5.13
Port Elizabeth	1993–94	3	114	–	93	5	18.60	–	4/36	22.80	4.89
Durban	1993–94	2	97	3	68	3	22.67	–	2/36	32.33	4.21
East London	1993–94	2	120	–	70	3	23.33	–	2/36	40.00	3.50
Cape Town	1993–94	2	120	–	95	5	19.00	–	3/31	24.00	4.75
Bloemfontein	1993–94	1	60	–	37	1	37.00	–	1/37	60.00	3.70
Centurion	1996–97	1	60	1	52	2	26.00	–	2/52	30.00	5.20
IN UNITED ARAB EMIRATES											
Sharjah	1993–94	8	456	3	324	13	24.92	–	4/34	35.08	4.26
IN SRI LANKA											
Colombo (SSC)	1994–95	1	60	1	29	3	9.67	–	3/29	20.00	2.90
Colombo (PIS)	1994–95	1	60	–	53	2	26.50	–	2/53	30.00	5.30
Colombo (PSS)	1994–95	1	48	–	27	2	13.50	–	2/27	24.00	3.38
IN PAKISTAN											
Lahore	1994–95	3	180	2	129	–	–	–	–	–	4.30
Multan	1994–95	1	60	1	29	1	29.00	–	1/29	60.00	2.90
Faisalabad	1994–95	1	56	–	40	4	10.00	–	4/40	14.00	4.29
Rawalpindi	1994–95	1	54	1	47	–	–	–	–	–	5.22
Peshawar	1994–95	1	60	–	51	1	51.00	–	1/51	60.00	5.10
IN WEST INDIES											
Bridgetown	1994–95	1	60	–	56	1	56.00	–	1/56	60.00	5.60
Port-of-Spain	1994–95	2	120	1	115	1	115.00	–	1/63	120.00	5.75
Kingston	1994–95	1	55	3	33	2	16.50	–	2/33	27.50	3.60

	Debut	M	Balls	Mdns	Runs	Wkts	Avrge	5	Best	Stk/Rt	RPO
IN INDIA											
Visakhapatnam	1995–96	1	60	–	25	1	25.00	–	1/25	60.00	2.50
Mumbai	1995–96	1	60	1	28	1	28.00	–	1/28	60.00	2.80
Nagpur	1995–96	1	57	1	34	4	8.50	–	4/34	14.25	3.58
Jaipur	1995–96	1	60	1	30	–	–	—	–	–	3.00
Chennai	1995–96	1	60	–	52	2	26.00	–	2/52	30.00	5.20
Chandigarh	1995–96	1	54	–	36	4	9.00	–	4/36	13.50	4.00
Kochi	1997–98	1	60	–	42	–	–	–	–	–	4.20
Ahmedabad	1997–98	1	60	–	45	2	22.50	–	2/45	30.00	4.50
Kanpur	1997–98	1	54	–	43	1	43.00	–	1/43	54.00	4.78
Delhi	1997–98	2	120	–	89	2	44.50	–	1/35	60.00	4.45

Record in each country

	Debut	M	Balls	Mdns	Runs	Wkts	Avrge	5	Best	Stk/Rt	RPO
New Zealand	1992–93	5	300	6	180	7	25.71	–	2/18	42.86	3.60
Australia	1993–94	41	2270	22	1481	74	20.01	1	5/33	30.68	3.91
South Africa	1993–94	14	739	5	557	21	26.52	–	4/36	35.19	4.52
Sharjah	1993–94	8	456	3	324	13	24.92	–	4/34	35.08	4.26
Sri Lanka	1994–95	3	168	1	109	7	15.57	–	3/29	24.00	3.89
Pakistan	1994–95	7	410	4	296	6	49.33	–	4/40	68.33	4.33
West Indies	1994–95	4	235	4	204	4	51.00	–	2/33	58.75	5.21
India	1995–96	11	645	3	424	17	24.94	–	4/34	37.94	3.94

Batting

Opponents	Debut	M	Inn	NO	Runs	HS	0s	50	100	Avrge	Stk/Rt	Ct
New Zealand	1992–93	15	5	1	41	24	–	–	–	10.25	100.00	8
South Africa	1992–93	30	20	4	198	55	3	1	–	12.38	76.45	12
Sri Lanka	1993–94	9	2	1	5	3*	–	–	–	5.00	55.56	1
India	1993–94	10	10	3	58	19	2	–	–	8.29	80.56	-
Pakistan	1994–95	8	6	1	69	30	–	–	–	13.80	71.88	3
Zimbabwe	1994–95	5	2	1	16	11*	–	–	–	16.00	106.67	3
England	1994–95	5	4	1	41	21	–	–	–	13.67	68.33	2
West Indies	1994–95	13	6	4	41	12	–	–	–	20.50	105.13	5
Kenya	1995–96	1	1	1	0	0*	–	–	–	–	0.00	–
Total		96	56	17	469	55	5	1	–	12.03	79.09	34

Highest score

55 (58) Australia v South Africa, Port Elizabeth, 1993–94

Sheffield Shield

Debut: 1990–91 Victoria v Western Australia, St Kilda

Season	M	Balls	Mdns	Runs	Wkts	Avrge	5	10	Best	Stk/Rt
1990–91	1	222	13	102	1	102.00	–	–	1/41	222.00
1991–92	6	1341	65	569	12	47.42	–	–	4/75	111.75
1992–93	4	909	24	486	12	40.50	1	–	5/49	75.75
1993–94	4	1486	64	643	27	23.81	2	–	6/42	55.03
1994–95	2	703	39	265	13	20.38	1	–	5/104	54.07
1995–96	3	1021	36	426	11	38.73	1	–	5/122	92.81
1996–97	2	582	31	201	5	40.20	–	–	3/25	116.40
1997–98	3	846	28	488	8	61.00	–	–	3/70	105.75
1998–99	4	835	26	521	8	65.13	–	–	2/80	104.38
Total	29	7945	326	3701	97	38.15	5	–	6/42	81.91

Opponents	Debut	M	Balls	Mdns	Runs	Wkts	Avrge	5	10	Best	Stk/Rt
Western Australia	1990–91	6	1543	73	658	24	27.42	2	–	6/42	64.29
Tasmania	1991–92	4	991	50	413	15	27.53	1	–	5/104	66.07
New South Wales	1991–92	9	2578	94	1286	30	42.87	2	–	5/77	85.93
South Australia	1991–92	5	1393	62	651	15	43.40	–	–	4/119	92.87
Queensland	1992–93	5	1440	47	693	13	53.31	–	–	3/70	110.77

Best bowling

Wkts	Opponent	Venue	Season
5/49	Western Australia	St Kilda	1992–93
6/42	Western Australia	Melbourne	1993–94
5/77	New South Wales	Sydney	1993–94
5/104	Tasmania	Melbourne	1994–95
5/122	New South Wales	Melbourne	1995–96

Batting

Opponents	Debut	M	Inn	NO	Runs	HS	0s	50	100	Avrge	Ct
Western Australia	1990–91	6	8	–	136	69	1	1	–	17.00	5
Tasmania	1991–92	4	6	1	64	34	–	–	–	12.80	1
New South Wales	1991–92	9	12	1	186	52	1	1	–	16.91	7
South Australia	1991–92	5	5	1	64	30*	1	–	—	16.00	2
Queensland	1992–93	5	7	3	95	31*	1	–	–	23.75	6
Total		29	38	6	545	69	4	2	–	17.03	21

Highest score

69 Victoria v Western Australia, St Kilda, 1992–93

Domestic Limited-Overs

Debut: 1992–93 Victoria v Tasmania, Devonport

Bowling

Opponents	Debut	M	Balls	Mdns	Runs	Wkts	Avrge	5	Best	Stk/Rt	RPO
Tasmania	1992–93	2	95	1	66	8	8.25	1	5/35	11.88	4.17
Queensland	1993–94	2	114	1	96	1	96.00	–	1/36	114.00	5.05
South Australia	1993–94	3	180	3	113	4	28.25	–	2/34	45.00	3.77
New South Wales	1995–96	3	114	2	83	4	20.75	–	3/43	28.50	4.37
Western Australia	1995–96	2	120	2	68	2	34.00	–	2/17	60.00	3.40
Total		**12**	**623**	**9**	**426**	**19**	**22.42**	**1**	**5/35**	**32.79**	**4.10**

Best bowling

5/35 Victoria v Tasmania, Carlton, 1996–97

Batting

Opponents	Debut	M	Inn	NO	Runs	HS	0s	50	100	Avrge	Stk/Rt	Ct
Tasmania	1992–93	2	1	–	26	26	–	–	–	26.00	76.47	3
Queensland	1993–94	2	–	–	–	–	–	–	–	–	–	1
South Australia	1993–94	3	2	1	44	32	–	–	–	44.00	115.79	3
New South Wales	1995–96	3	3	–	43	24	–	–	–	14.33	74.14	–
Western Australia	1995–96	2	2	–	15	15	1	–	–	7.50	51.72	–
Total		12	8	1	128	32	1	–	–	18.29	80.50	7

Highest score

32 (26) Victoria v South Australia, Adelaide, 1994–95

Index

T

Y

Z

PHOTO CREDITS

Cover

Front cover: Stuart Milligan/Sporting Pix (Allsport); back cover: The Age; back flap: Dean Golja.

Inside pages

1. Natural leader: The Age (courtesy of Mentone Grammar School); 2. Happy and hirsute: The Age; 3. Bagging the baggy green: The Age; 4. The pay-off: Jason Childs/The Age; 5. May the spinning begin: The Age; 6. Shouldering responsibility: Sport the Library/Michael Rayner; 7. Chapeau magic (3 pics): Jack Atley/The Age; 8. Upper cut: Sport the Library/Tony Nolan; 9. Mirror image: Tony Feder/Sporting Pix (Allsport); 10. That little vice: Sport the Library/Michael Rayner; 11. Spinning Jenner: Ray Kennedy/The Age; 12. When we were mates: Reuters; 13. The Chanderpaul ball: Tim Clayton/The Sydney Morning Herald; 14. The punter rap: Mark Baker/Reuters: 15. Body speak: David Davies/ Professional Sport (Allsport); 16. A Saint at Lord's: Sport the Library/ Sergio Dionisio; 17. Praying or appealing?: Stuart Milligan/Sporting Pix (Allsport); 18. Dance of the *derrière*: Australian Picture Library/Clive Mason/Allsport; 19. The taming of Hussein: AAP Image/Rebecca Naden; 20. I'm no dummy: Pat Scala/The Age; 21. Mark's catch: Australian Picture Library/ Joanne Adams (Allsport); 22. The great slipper skipper: Stuart Milligan/Sporting Pix (Allsport); 23. Wicket fever: Tim Clayton/ The Sydney Morning Herald; 24. Three hundred and climbing: John Daniels/Sporting Pix (Allsport); 25. Meeting his match: Ben Radford/ Allsport; 26. Which delivery?: Tony Feder/Sporting Pix (Allsport); 27. Down pat: Dean Golja; 28. A kiss for the girl in his life: Dean Golja; 29. Birds of a flutter: Simon Alekna/The Sun Herald.

Every effort has been made to identify individual photographers and permission holders, but for some photographs this has not been possible. The publishers would be pleased to hear from any copyright holders who have not been acknowledged.